# LEGAL PERSPECTIVE
## INSTITUTIONS

Due to the continuing expansion of the notion of security, various national, regional and international institutions now find themselves addressing diverse contemporary security issues. While institutions may evolve by adjusting themselves to new challenges, they can also fundamentally alter the intricate balance between security and current legal frameworks.

This volume explores the tensions that occur when institutions address contemporary security threats, in both public and international law contexts. As part of the Connecting International Law with Public Law series, it provides important and valuable insights into the legal issues and perspectives which surround the institutional responses to contemporary security challenges. It is essential reading for scholars, practitioners and policy makers seeking to understand the legal significance of security institutions and the implications of their evolution on the rule of law and legitimacy.

HITOSHI NASU is a Senior Lecturer at the ANU College of Law, The Australian National University. His expertise lies in public international law, particularly international security law and international humanitarian law.

KIM RUBENSTEIN is Professor and Director of the Centre for International and Public Law at the ANU College of Law, The Australian National University. Her work spans constitutional, administrative and citizenship law.

# CONNECTING INTERNATIONAL LAW WITH PUBLIC LAW

This six-volume series flows from workshops bringing public and international lawyers and public and international policy-makers together for interdisciplinary discussion on selected topics and themes.

The aim of the series is to broaden both public law's and international law's understanding of how these two areas intersect. Until now, international law and public law have mainly overlapped in discussions on how international law is implemented domestically.

This series is unique in consciously bringing together public and international lawyers to consider and engage in each other's scholarship.

*Series editors*

Kim Rubenstein is Professor and Director of the Centre for International and Public Law (CIPL) in the ANU College of Law, Australian National University. Her current research projects are at the cutting edge of the intersection between public and international law. Her public law work spans constitutional and administrative law, and also includes her expertise in citizenship law.

Professor Thomas Pogge is Leitner Professor of Philosophy and International Affairs and founding Director of the Global Justice Programme at Yale University, with part-time appointments at King's College London and the Universities of Oslo and Central Lancashire. He writes and teaches on moral and political philosophy and Kant, with a special emphasis on global justice.

# LEGAL PERSPECTIVES ON SECURITY INSTITUTIONS

Edited By

HITOSHI NASU

KIM RUBENSTEIN

CAMBRIDGE
UNIVERSITY PRESS

# CAMBRIDGE
## UNIVERSITY PRESS

University Printing House, Cambridge CB2 8BS, United Kingdom

One Liberty Plaza, 20th Floor, New York, NY 10006, USA

477 Williamstown Road, Port Melbourne, VIC 3207, Australia

314-321, 3rd Floor, Plot 3, Splendor Forum, Jasola District Centre, New Delhi - 110025, India

79 Anson Road, #06-04/06, Singapore 079906

Cambridge University Press is part of the University of Cambridge.

It furthers the University's mission by disseminating knowledge in the pursuit of education, learning and research at the highest international levels of excellence.

www.cambridge.org
Information on this title: www.cambridge.org/9781107501072

© Cambridge University Press 2015

First published 2015
First paperback edition 2018

*A catalogue record for this publication is available from the British Library*

ISBN 978-1-107-10278-1 Hardback
ISBN 978-1-107-50107-2 Paperback

# CONTENTS

# CONTRIBUTORS

## Editors

HITOSHI NASU is a Senior Lecturer at the ANU College of Law, Australian National University, with expertise in public international law, particularly in the fields of international security law and international humanitarian law. He holds Bachelor's and Master's Degrees in Political Science from Aoyama Gakuin University and a Master's Degree and a Ph.D in Law from the University of Sydney. He is the author of *International Law on Peacekeeping: A Study of Article 40 of the UN Charter* (2009); and a co-editor of *Human Rights in the Asia-Pacific Region: Towards Institution Building* (with Ben Saul, 2011); *Asia-Pacific Disaster Management: Comparative and Socio-legal Perspectives* (with Simon Butt and Luke Nottage, 2013); and *New Technologies and the Law of Armed Conflict* (with Robert McLaughlin, 2014).

KIM RUBENSTEIN is Professor and Director of the Centre for International and Public Law with the ANU College of Law, Australian National University. A graduate of the University of Melbourne and Harvard University, her public law work spans constitutional and administrative law, and also includes her expertise in citizenship law. Her international law work focuses on the status of nationality. In 2011 and 2012 she was also inaugural Convenor of the ANU Gender Institute.

## Other contributors

BINA D'COSTA is a peace and conflict specialist at the Australian National University and currently a visiting fellow at the Graduate Institute of Geneva. Her research focuses on the nexus between development, human rights and security in Asia. She has worked in South and Southeast Asia, South Africa and East Africa; and contributed to policy research in the Department of Foreign Affairs and Trade in Australia, the United Nations Research in Social Development, USAID and Department for International Development in the United Kingdom. She is also on the United Nations Development Programme Gender, Crisis Prevention and Recovery expert panel and is an Advisory Council member of its newly formed International Center for Gender, Peace and Security. Her books include *Children, International Politics and Armed Conflict* (co-authored, Cambridge University Press, forthcoming 2015); *Children and Violence: Politics of Conflict in South Asia* (editor, Cambridge University Press, forthcoming 2015); *Nationbuilding, Gender and War Crimes in South Asia* (2011; 2nd edn, 2013); and *Gender and the Global Politics of the Asia-Pacific* (co-editor, 2010).

MICHAEL EWING-CHOW is an Associate Professor at the Faculty of Law, National University of Singapore (NUS) where he teaches corporate law and world trade law. He has a LLB (First Class Hons) from NUS and a LLM from Harvard University. After graduation, he worked in the corporate department of Allen & Gledhill before returning to NUS. He has been a consultant to the Singapore Ministry of Trade and Industry, Ministry of Foreign Affairs and Ministry of Finance, as well as the World Bank and the World Trade Organization. He has also been involved in the building of trade law capacity of government officials in Asia and Latin America. On the corporate side, he has also assisted the Singapore Company Law Reform and Frameworks Committee which was tasked in 2001 with a major overhaul of corporate law in Singapore and in 2008 was appointed to a Working Group of the Steering Committee for the review of the Singapore Companies Act. He also volunteers with various local non-governmental organisations and co-founded Aidha, a non-governmental organisation which provides financial education and microfinance opportunities for domestic migrant workers and for which he was awarded a Social Entrepreneur of the Year Award in 2007. He was also awarded the Teaching Excellence Award in 2007 and the Inspiring Mentor Award in 2009.

LIU GEHUAN currently practices as a registered foreign lawyer at Clifford Chance, Hong Kong. Previously, she worked as a Research Fellow at the Centre for International Law, National University of Singapore.

ANNA HOOD is a Lecturer at Melbourne Law School, the University of Melbourne. Her academic research focuses primarily on public international law. She has a particular interest in international law and security issues, and in the intersection between public international law and domestic public law matters. Anna has a Bachelor of Arts and a Bachelor of Laws (Hons) from the University of Melbourne and a Master of Laws (International Legal Studies) from New York University. She is currently completing her Ph.D, which is entitled 'The Security Council's Legislative Phase and the Rise of Emergency International Law-Making'.

ADAM KAMRADT-SCOTT is a Senior Lecturer at the Department of Government and International Relations, the University of Sydney. He completed his Ph.D in International Politics at the Centre for Health and International Relations, in the Department of International Politics, Aberystwyth University. He also worked as a legislative and political adviser to an Australian Senator before taking up a position in the Australian Public Service where he worked in the Department of the Prime Minister and Cabinet as part of a small team tasked with revising and testing Australia's pandemic preparedness plans. He has published over twenty journal articles and book chapters along these themes and has two co-authored books, *The Transformation of Global Health Governance* (2014) and *Disease Diplomacy* (2015), and is author of *Managing Global Health Security: The World Health Organization and Disease Outbreak Control* (2015).

CHIE KOJIMA is an Associate Professor at the Faculty of Law, Musashino University, Tokyo, Japan. Aside from holding Bachelor's and Master's Degrees in Law, Kojima received a Doctor of Laws from Chuo University, and an LLM and a JSD from Yale Law School. Previously, she served as an Assistant Professor of Maritime Law and Policy at the World Maritime University in Malmö, a Senior Research Fellow at the Max Planck Institute for Comparative Public Law and International Law in Heidelberg, and a judicial clerk to Judges Hisashi Owada and Vladlen S. Vereshchetin at the International Court of Justice in The Hague. Her research interests are in the international law of the sea, in particular contemporary maritime security issues such as piracy and armed robbery at sea, irregular migrants by sea, and illegal, unreported and unregulated fishing. She is an editor of *Piracy at Sea* (together with Maximo Q. Mejia, Jr and Mark Sawyer, 2013); *Solidarity: A Structural Principle of International Law* (together with Rüdiger Wolfrum, 2010); and an assistant editor of *Law of the Sea, Environmental Law and Settlement of Disputes, Liber Amicorum Judge*

*Thomas A. Mensah* (Tafsir Malick Ndiaye and Rüdiger Wolfrum, eds., 2007).

ANNE MCNAUGHTON is a Senior Lecturer at the ANU College of Law, Australian National University. She graduated with a Bachelor of Arts Degree from the University of Newcastle and a Bachelor of Laws Degree from the University of New South Wales. She holds Master of Laws Degrees from Eberhard-Karls-Universität, Tübingen, Germany and from the University of Technology, Sydney.

THOMAS POGGE is Leitner Professor of Philosophy and International Affairs and founding Director of the Global Justice Programme at Yale, Research Director at the Oslo University Centre for the Study of Mind in Nature (CSMN), Professor of Political Philosophy at the University of Central Lancashire and Professor of Philosophy and Global Justice at the Dickson Poon School of Law at King's College London. Focused on Kant and in moral and political philosophy, his publications include: *Politics as Usual* (2010), *World Poverty and Human Rights* (2nd edn, 2008); *John Rawls: His Life and Theory of Justice* (2007); *Freedom from Poverty as a Human Right* (editor, 2007); and *Global Justice / Global Ethics* (co-editor, 2008). Pogge is editor for social and political philosophy for the Stanford Encyclopedia of Philosophy and a member of the Norwegian Academy of Science. With support from the European Research Council, he currently heads a team effort toward developing a complement to the pharmaceutical patent regime that would improve access to advanced medicines for the poor worldwide (see www.healthimpactfund.org).

OTTAVIO QUIRICO is a Senior Lecturer in the School of Law at the University of New England, Australia. He holds an LLM in International Relations and a Ph.D in Law from the University of Social Sciences, Toulouse, France. Prior to joining the University of New England, he was a Visiting Fellow at the Lauterpacht Centre for International Law, Cambridge; Max Weber Fellow at the European University Institute, Florence; Lecturer at University Lille Nord de France; and Marie Curie Fellow at University Panthéon-Assas, Paris. He also delivered undergraduate and postgraduate courses at Washington State University, Pullman, US; Federal University of Paraiba, João Pessoa, Brazil; Federal University of Porto Alegre, Brazil; and at the United Nations Academic Campus, Turin.

KALMAN A. ROBERTSON is a Lecturer in the School of Politics and International Relations at the Australian National University (ANU) where he convenes the Politics of Nuclear Weapons programme. He holds a BSc (Hons), an LLB (Hons) and the University Medal for Physics from the ANU. He recently completed a doctoral dissertation on nuclear safeguards, arms control and non-proliferation policy at the Strategic and Defence Studies Centre of the ANU. He has worked extensively for the ANU Department of Nuclear Physics, specialising in nuclear structure and radiation dosimetry. He has been Australia's official representative to the Nuclear Energy Experts Group of the Council for Security Cooperation in the Asia Pacific since its establishment in 2012.

IMOGEN SAUNDERS is a Lecturer at the ANU College of Law, Australian National University. She completed her Ph.D at the same institution, writing on the General Principles of Law under Article 38(1)(c) of the Statute of the International Court of Justice.

MELANIE VILARASAU SLADE is a Senior Research Fellow at the Centre for International Law, National University of Singapore, where she focuses on international trade and food security issues, particularly in Southeast Asia. She was trained at Allen & Overy LLP in London and practised in their Brussels office dealing with matters of European Union law, competition law and policy, and international trade. Following a move to Bird & Bird LLP her scope of practice widened to include intellectual property and public procurement issues.

SOLON SOLOMON is the former member of the Legal Department in the Knesset (Israeli Parliament) in charge of international and constitutional issues. He received the George Weber Award from the Hebrew University of Jerusalem Faculty of Law and has published and lectured on constitutional as well as public international law issues. His first book, *Justiciability of International Disputes: The Advisory Opinion on Israel* (2009), was cited before the Permanent Court of Arbitration in *Chevron* v. *Ecuador*. He is also a co-editor of *Applying International Humanitarian Law in Judicial and Quasi-Judicial Bodies: International and Domestic Aspects* (with Derek Jinks and Jackson Nyamuya Maogoto, 2014).

SEE SENG TAN is Deputy Director of the Institute of Defence and Strategic Studies, Head of the Centre for Multilateralism Studies and Associate Professor at the S. Rajaratnam School of International Studies, Nanyang Technological University, Singapore. A student of Asian security, he is the author or editor of nine books and has published over forty scholarly papers and book chapters. His latest book is *The Making of the Asia Pacific* (2013). He has been a consultant for international institutions and national governments, including the Singapore government, and has held visiting appointments at various universities and research institutes. He holds BA Hons (First Class) and MA Degrees from the University of Manitoba and a Ph.D from Arizona State University.

DILAN THAMPAPILLAI is a Lecturer at the ANU College of Law, Australian National University. He was previously a Lecturer and a Senior Lecturer at the School of Law, Deakin University. Prior to becoming an academic he was a lawyer with the Attorney-General's Department and the Australian Government Solicitor. He specialises in intellectual property, free speech and public law. He has a Bachelor of Laws Degree from the Australian National University, a Master of Laws from Cornell University and is a Ph.D candidate at the University of Melbourne.

ALEXANDRA WALKER has a Ph.D in International Law from the Australian National University, which was completed with an Australian Postgraduate scholarship (2009–2012). Her thesis explored group consciousness in the global community. In addition to her doctorate, she has a Master's Degree in International Law and International Relations, and two undergraduate Degrees in Law (With Merit) and Arts (Politics and International Relations) from the University of New South Wales.

# ABBREVIATIONS

| | |
|---|---|
| APTERR | ASEAN Plus Three Emergency Rice Reserve |
| ARF | ASEAN Regional Forum |
| ASCM | Agreement on Subsidies and Countervailing Measures |
| ASEAN | Association of Southeast Asian Nations |
| ASLSI | anti-state local security institution |
| AU | African Union |
| AWN | Afghan Women's Network |
| BMP | Best Management Practice |
| CAR | Central African Republic |
| CBD | Convention on Biological Diversity |
| CEDAW | Convention on the Elimination of All Forms of Discrimination Against Women |
| CEMAC | Economic and Monetary Community of Central Africa |
| CERT | Computer Emergency Response Team |
| CJEU | Court of Justice of the European Union |
| CWC | Chemical Weapons Convention |
| DPRK | Democratic People's Republic of Korea |
| DRC | Democratic Republic of the Congo |
| DSB | Dispute Settlement Body (WTO) |
| ECCAS | Economic Community of Central African States |
| ECOWAS | Economic Community of West African States |
| EEAS | European External Action Service |
| EU | European Union |
| EVAW | Elimination of Violence Against Women |
| FAO | Food and Agriculture Organization |
| GATT | General Agreement on Tariffs and Trade |
| GISN | Global Influenza Surveillance Network |
| GPA | Government Purchase Agreement |
| IAEA | International Atomic Energy Agency |
| ICJ | International Court of Justice |
| ICTY | International Criminal Tribunal for the former Yugoslavia |
| IHR | International Health Regulations |

| | |
|---|---|
| IMO | International Maritime Organization |
| ITPGRFA | International Treaty on Plant Genetic Resources for Food and Agriculture |
| NATO | North Atlantic Treaty Organization |
| NPT | Nuclear Non-Proliferation Treaty |
| OAS | Organization of American States |
| OAU | Organization of African Unity |
| OECD | Organisation for Economic Co-operation and Development |
| OPCW | Organisation for the Prohibition of Chemical Weapons |
| OSCE | Organization for Security and Co-operation in Europe |
| PCASP | privately contracted armed security personnel |
| PIPF | Pandemic Influenza Preparedness Framework |
| PRC | People's Republic of China |
| SADC | Southern African Development Community |
| SOLAS | International Convention for the Safety of Life at Sea |
| TAC | Treaty of Amity and Cooperation (ASEAN) |
| TEU | Treaty on European Union |
| TFEU | Treaty on the Functioning of the European Union |
| TRIPS Agreement | Agreement on Trade-Related Aspects of Intellectual Property Rights |
| UN | United Nations |
| UNCLOS | UN Convention on the Law of the Sea |
| UNDP | United Nations Development Programme |
| UPOV Convention | International Convention for the Protection of New Varieties of Plants |
| VCLT | Vienna Convention on the Law of Treaties |
| WHA | World Health Assembly |
| WHO | World Health Organization |
| WIPO | World Intellectual Property Organization |
| WTO | World Trade Organization |

# TABLE OF CASES

## Cases

# WTO decisions

# TABLE OF LEGISLATION

## National legislation

## European legislation

# TABLE OF TREATIES

## Treaties and other international instruments

# SERIES EDITORS' PREFACE

The idea for this series began in June 2005, when Kim Rubenstein applied for the position of Professor and Director of the Centre for International and Public Law at the ANU College of Law. The Centre is recognised as the leading Australian academic centre bringing together public lawyers (constitutional and administrative law broadly, but also specific areas of government regulation) and international lawyers from around the world. Established in 1990 with its inaugural director Professor Philip Alston, the impact of the Centre and its work can be seen further at law.anu.edu.au/cipl.

In discussing with the law faculty ideas for the Centre's direction, Kim raised the concept underpinning this series. Each of the volumes flows from workshops bringing public and international lawyers and public and international policy experts together for interdisciplinary discussion on selected topics and themes. The workshops attract both established scholars and outstanding early scholars. At each of the workshops participants address specific questions and issues developing each other's understandings and knowledge about public and international law and policy and the links between the disciplines as they intersect with the chosen subject. These papers are discussed and reviewed at the workshop collaboratively, then after the workshop the papers are finalised for the final editing phase for the overall manuscript.

The series seeks to broaden understanding of how public law and international law intersect. Until now, international and public law have mainly overlapped in discussions on how international law is implemented domestically. While there is scholarship developing in the area of global administrative law, and some scholars have touched upon the principles relevant to both disciplines, those publications do not concentrate upon the broader mission of this series. This series is unique in consciously bringing together public and international lawyers to consider and engage in each others' scholarship.

Beyond the first topic of sanctions (Volume 1), the other topics draw from the research themes underpinning the International Alliance of Research Universities (IARU) which is made up of ANU, Berkeley, Cambridge, University of Copenhagen, ETH Zurich, National University of Singapore, Oxford, Peking University, University of Tokyo and Yale. The topics include volumes on Health (Volume 2), Environment (Volume 3), Movement of People (Volume 4) and Security (Volume 5). A new volume was added to the planned series in 2012 with a focus on Gender (Volume 6), and this too is one of the IARU areas of interest.

After the first successful workshop was completed, Professor Rubenstein contacted Professor Thomas Pogge to co-host the second workshop and in addition to doing that, he has enthusiastically joined with Professor Rubenstein as a joint series editor. His contributions to each volume are an expression of his cosmopolitan outlook which is a theme engaged with throughout the series.

*Kim Rubenstein and Thomas Pogge*
*September 2014*

# EDITORS' PREFACE

As explained in the Series Editors' Preface, this series is a result of workshops bringing together public and international lawyers with inter-disciplinary scholars relevant to the respective volume's themes, for discussion on selected topics and themes. From the second volume onwards, the topics revolve around the International Association of Research Universities (IARU) thematic research topics.

When Kim Rubenstein began thinking about organising the fifth workshop around the theme of Security, she was enthusiastic about inviting her ANU College of Law colleague Dr Hitoshi Nasu to join her in running it as he had already developed some interesting ideas around this theme.

The fifth workshop 'Security Institutions and International and Public Law' took place on 27–29 June 2011 at the Australian National University. The nineteen paper presenters and a further group of parti-cipants, who had read all the papers, enjoyed vigorous discussion, enga-ging fully with each other and the material.

We thank Commodore Ian Campbell, Giovanni Di Lieto, Tom Faunce, Chris Michaelsen and Natasha Tusikov for presenting stimulat-ing papers at the workshop even though their papers were not developed for the resulting book.

The event was ably organised by the ANU College of Law Outreach and Administrative Support Team and in particular we thank Wendy Mohring and Sarah Hull. ANU law student Zoe Winston-Gregson worked with us reviewing the papers on style matters and we thank her for her assistance in putting this volume together. We also thank the many anonymous reviewers whose critiques of the papers strengthened the chapters in this collection.

The staff at Cambridge University Press, especially Finola O'Sullivan and Elizabeth Spicer, have been enthusiastic in supporting this series and Elizabeth Davison as copy-editor has been excellent.

Finally, we would like to thank our colleagues at the ANU and in the Centre for International and Public Law in the ANU College of Law and our respective families and friends for their support and inspiration in all that we do.

All the online references are correct as at 30 September 2014 unless otherwise indicated.

*Hitoshi Nasu and Kim Rubenstein*
*September 2014*

~

# Introduction: the expanded conception of security and institutions

HITOSHI NASU AND KIM RUBENSTEIN

## 1 Introduction

Security is a dynamic, context-dependent concept that is inevitably shaped by social conditions and practices. The socio-political perception of security threats influences our security policies relevant to political decisions about the design of social institutions specifically addressing those security concerns. Security is traditionally understood to be physical protection of national territory and its population from the destructive effects of warfare through military means.[1] Social institutions including but not limited to national governing institutions, inter-governmental institutions and the military are all devices developed through human history to collectively address traditional security threats.

Security is often considered to be an antithesis of the rule of law and civil liberty, justifying violation of rules and the restriction of freedom.[2] However, the development of international law and the institutionalisation of international public authorities have contributed to the increased normalcy or containment of extra-legal responses to security threats. For example, the Charter of the United Nations ('UN Charter') provides institutionalised mechanisms as the means of regulating the behaviour of sovereign states and conflict among them.[3] The nuclear

---

[1] Hans Kelsen, *Collective Security under International Law* (United States Government Printing Office, Washington, DC, 1957) p. 1 (defining security as 'the protection of men against the use of force by other men').

[2] For discussion, see especially, Jeremy Waldron, 'Security and Liberty: The Image of Balance' (2003) 11 *Journal of Political Philosophy* 191. See also Concluding Remarks by Thomas Pogge.

[3] Charter of the United Nations, opened for signature 26 June 1945, 1 UNTS XVI (entered into force 24 October 1945), Art. 24.

1

non-proliferation regime establishes mechanisms for preventing the proliferation of nuclear weapons and facilitating the development of peaceful nuclear energy technology by institutionalising the asymmetric obligations between designated nuclear-weapon states and other non-nuclear-weapon states.[4]

Yet, towards the end of the Cold War the concept of security began to expand, which subsequently led to the proliferation of contemporary security issues such as economic security, environmental security, energy and resource security, health security and bio-security.[5] The conception of security also took a dramatic turn following the 2001 terrorist attacks on New York and Washington, blurring the traditional boundaries between international security and national security threats.[6] Those changes in the conception of security world-wide have tested the potential of existing institutions, such as the World Trade Organization (WTO), the World Health Organization (WHO), the International Maritime Organization (IMO), the Organization for Security and Co-operation in Europe (OSCE), the European Union (EU) and the Association of Southeast Asian Nations (ASEAN), to assume a new role in the changing security paradigms, both at international and domestic levels.

The greater diversity in the range of security threats and actors in the modern globalised world challenges our traditional understanding of security institutions with the need for re-evaluating the role, value and limits of institutions in their relationship with security and the law. While institutions evolve by finding the need or an opportunity to adjust themselves to meet new challenges, that may well result in changing the intricate balance between security and the law that has been sustained within current legal frameworks. It is this tension, both in public and international law contexts, arising from the institutional development to address contemporary security threats and the existing legal frameworks delimiting the institutional response to security that forms the subject of this volume.

---

[4] Treaty on the Non-Proliferation of Nuclear Weapons, opened for signature 1 July 1968, 729 UNTS 161 (entered into force 5 March 1970). See also Kalman Robertson, Chapter 9.

[5] See generally, Jessica Tuchman Mathews, 'Redefining Security' (1989) 68(2) *Foreign Affairs* 162; Richard H. Ullman, 'Redefining Security' (1983) 8 *International Security* 129.

[6] See e.g., Miriam Gani and Penelope Matthew (eds.), *Fresh Perspectives on the 'War on Terror'* (ANU E-Press, Canberra, 2008); Dora Kostakopoulou, 'How to Do Things with Security Post 9/11' (2008) 28 *Oxford Journal of Legal Studies* 317; Benjamin J. Goold and Liora Lazarus (eds.), *Security and Human Rights* (Hart Publishing, Oxford/Portland, OR, 2007).

This fifth volume in the series connecting public and international law, engages with this tension from legal perspectives linking international law and public law, forming the underlying theme throughout the series. Both international law and public law have been central not only to the normative foundation for the formation, development and exercise of public authority to address security threats by institutionalised mechanisms, but also to the regulation and restriction of the exercise of such public authority. It is these legal perspectives and issues that commonly characterise the chapters in this volume, providing a variety of theoretical inquiries and case studies critically examining sociological, psychological, political and economic factors surrounding institutional evolution in response to contemporary security challenges. It is the intention of this volume to unravel intricate issues at the intersection of the tripartite relationship between public law and international law, security and institutions in light of the expansion of contemporary security threats.

## 2  Defining security institutions

Institutions are not mere instruments of the creators, but are autonomous entities operating, to varying degrees, within an organisational structure and decision-making processes. Institutions seek to act in conformity with the norms that guide their operation, interpret and apply them, and often generate friction due to the inherent indeterminacy of norms. As Ian Johnstone observes, institutions engage, through operational activities, in legal argumentation with other stakeholders and contribute to cause indeterminate norms and soft law to 'harden' with shared understandings about what those norms truly mean in practice.[7]

For the purpose of this book, security institutions are defined broadly, drawing on the definition of institutions proposed by Robert O Keohane, as 'persistent and connected sets of rules, formal and informal, that prescribe behavioral roles, constrain activity, and shape expectations',[8]

---

[7] Ian Johnstone, 'Law-making through the Operational Activities of International Organizations' (2008) 40 *George Washington International Law Review* 87, 122.

[8] Robert O. Keohane, *International Institutions and State Power* (Westview Press, Boulder, CO, 1989) 3. Similarly, Robert Jervis, 'Security Regime' (1982) 36 *International Organization* 357. Compare this definition with the legal definition of international organisations adopted by the International Law Commission in Draft Articles on the Responsibility of International Organizations (2011) *Yearbook of International Law*

which by design or through operational activities, deal with public security issues arising in the global or cross-border environment. This definition is broad and flexible enough to allow for the normative inquiries this volume is designed for, without necessarily restricting the scope of inquiry to the relationship between their constituent members within institutions.[9] Although this broad definition may not be suited for empirical inquiry,[10] it allows us to conceive of institutions in various forms as independent and autonomous entities capable of adaptation and evolution in response to the changing security paradigms as a framework of normative inquiry.

Traditionally, the concept of security was narrowly confined in military terms with the primary focus on state protection from threats to national interests.[11] Therefore, national military forces have long been the dominant focus of security institutions. In comparison, there are only a handful of security institutions at the international level originally designed to address traditional security concerns, including the UN Security Council and the Nuclear Non-Proliferation Treaty (NPT) regime. Celeste Wallander, Helga Haftendorn and Robert Keohane accordingly defined 'security institutions' rather narrowly, with a military-oriented, state-centric view, as those 'designed to protect the territorial integrity of states from the adverse use of military force; to guard states' autonomy against the political effects of the threat of such force; and to prevent the emergence of situations that could endanger states' vital interests as they define them'.[12] However, the expansion of the security concept, particularly after the end of the

*Commission* vol. II, Part 2, Art. 2(a) (defining 'international organization' as 'an organization established by a treaty or other instrument governed by international law and possessing its own international legal personality').

[9] Cf. John J. Mearsheimer, 'The False Promise of International Institutions' (1994–1995) 19(3) *International Security* 5, 8 (defining institutions as 'sets of rules that stipulate the ways in which states should cooperate and compete with each other').

[10] See Beth A. Simmons and Lisa L. Martin, 'International Organizations and Institutions' in Walter Carlsnaes, Thomas Risse and Beth A. Simmons (eds.), *Handbook of International Relations* (SAGE Publications, London, 2002) p. 194.

[11] See e.g., Kelsen, *Collective Security under International Law*, above n. 1, p. 1; Hans Morgenthau, *Politics Among Nations: The Struggle for Power and Peace* (Alfred A. Knopf, New York, 1950); Thomas Shelling, *Arms and Influence* (Yale University Press, New Haven, CT, 1966); Kenneth Waltz, *Theory of International Politics* (Random House, New York, 1979).

[12] Celeste A. Wallander, Helga Haftendorn and Robert O. Keohane, 'Introduction' in Helga Haftendorn, Robert O. Keohane and Celeste A. Wallander (eds.), *Imperfect Unions: Security Institutions over Time and Space* (Oxford University Press, Oxford, 1999) pp. 1, 2.

Cold War and by a variety of institutions contributing to this expansion, indicates a greater scope for considering a wider variety of institutions to be security institutions.

Indeed the departure from the very narrow meaning and usage of security emerged even amidst the Cold War rivalry. For example, the nuclear arms race and in particular United States' President Reagan's new nuclear deterrence policy led to the idea of common security in the 1980s to promote confidence between states and the cause of disarmament.[13] The move towards an expanded notion of security has accelerated since the end of the Cold War, spawning a growth of security literature in the areas of economic security,[14] environmental security,[15] energy and resource security,[16] food security,[17] bio-security[18] and health security.[19] The UN Development Programme (UNDP) introduced the concept of human security into international policy discourse in its 1994 *Human Development Report*,[20] which has since been incorporated into

---

[13] Independent Commission on Disarmament and Security Issues, *Common Security: A Blueprint for Survival* (Simon and Schuster, New York, 1982); Independent Commission on Disarmament and Security Issues, *North-South: A Programme for Survival* (Pan Books, London, 1980). See also R. Väyryen, 'Multilateral Security: Common, Cooperative or Collective?' in M.G. Schechter (ed.), *Future Multilateralism: The Political and Social Framework* (United Nations University Press, Tokyo, 1999) pp. 43, 55–7.

[14] See e.g., V. Cable, 'What is International Economic Security?' (1995) 71 *International Affairs* 305.

[15] See e.g., Simon Dalby, *Security and Environmental Change* (Polity Press, Cambridge, 2009) especially ch. 2; Simon Dalby, *Environmental Security* (University of Minnesota Press, Minneapolis, MN, 2002).

[16] See e.g., Sam Raphael and Doug Stokes, 'Energy Security' in Alan Collins (ed.), *Contemporary Security Studies* (2nd edn, Oxford University Press, Oxford, 2010) p. 379.

[17] See e.g., Wael Allam, 'Food Supply Security, Sovereignty and International Peace and Security: Sovereignty as a Challenge to Food Supply Security' in Ahmed Mahiou and Francis Snyder (eds.), *Food Security and Food Safety* (Martinus Nijhoff, Leiden, 2006) p. 325; Melaku Geboye Desta, 'Food Security and International Trade Law: An Appraisal of the World Trade Organization Approach' (2001) 35 *Journal of World Trade* 449.

[18] See e.g., David P. Fidler and Lawrence O. Gostin, *Biosecurity in the Global Age: Biological Weapons, Public Health, and the Rule of Law* (Stanford University Press, Stanford, CA, 2008); Mark Wheelis and Malcolm Dando, 'Neurobiology: A Case Study of the Imminent Militarization of Biology' (2005) 87 *International Review of the Red Cross* 553; David L. Heymann, 'The Evolving Infectious Disease Threat: Implications for National and Global Security' (2003) 4 *Journal of Human Development* 191.

[19] See e.g., David P. Fidler, 'From International Sanitary Conventions to Global Health Security: The New International Health Regulations' (2005) 4 *Chinese Journal of International Law* 325; Lincoln Chen and Vasant Narasimhan, 'Human Security and Global Health' (2003) 4 *Journal of Human Development* 181.

[20] United Nations Development Programme, *Human Development Report 1994* (United Nations, 1994) p. 22.

key policy documents such as the 2000 UN Millennium Declaration.[21] The UN Secretary-General's High-Level Panel identified economic and social threats and transnational organised crime, as well as inter-state conflict, internal conflict, terrorism and weapons of mass destruction as global security threats.[22] The former UN Secretary-General's 2005 Report, *In Larger Freedom*, adds to the list poverty, deadly infectious disease and environmental degradation, on the grounds that these can have equally catastrophic consequences.[23]

The expansion of the concept of security has been progressively, and yet often variably recognised as new security agendas by traditional security institutions such as the North Atlantic Treaty Organization (NATO).[24] One most notable example is the debate on various human security agendas in the Security Council.[25] It formally acknowledged an expanded notion of security when world leaders gathered in 1992, referring to a range of non-military sources of instability in the economic, social, humanitarian and ecological fields as threats to international peace and

---

[21] GA Res. 55/2 (8 September 2000). See also *Human Security: Report of the Secretary-General*, UN Doc. A/64/701 (8 March 2010).

[22] *A More Secure World: Our Shared Responsibility, Report of the United Nations Secretary-General's High-Level Panel on Threats, Challenges and Change*, UN Doc. A/59/565 (2 December 2004) p. 23. For discussion, see G. Shafir, 'Legal and Institutional Responses to Contemporary Global Threats: An Introduction to the U.N. Secretary-General's High-Level Panel Report on Threats, Challenges and Change' (2007) 38 *California Western International Law Journal* 1, 6–14.

[23] Kofi A. Annan, *In Larger Freedom: Towards Development, Security and Human Rights for All* (United Nations, New York, 2005) para. 78.

[24] For the transformation of NATO's security agendas, see e.g., Mats Berdal and David Ucko, 'Whither NATO' in Bruce D. Jones, Shepard Forman and Richard Gowan (eds.), *Cooperating for Peace and Security: Evolving Institutions and Arrangements in a Context of Changing U.S. Security Policy* (Cambridge University Press, Cambridge, 2010) p. 98; Frank Schimmelfennig, 'Transatlantic Relations, Multilateralism and the Transformation of NATO' in Dimitris Bourantonis, Kostas Ifantis and Panayotis Tsakonas (eds.), *Multilateralism and Security Institutions in an Era of Globalization* (Routledge, Abingdon, 2008) p. 183; James Sperling, 'Eurasian Security Governance: New Threats, Institutional Adaptations' in James Sperling, Sean Kay and S. Victor Papacosma (eds.), *Limiting Institutions? The Challenge of Eurasian Security Governance* (Manchester University Press, Manchester, 2003) pp. 3, 7–10. More generally, Emil J. Kirchner, 'Regional and Global Security: Changing Threats and Institutional Responses' in Emil J. Kirchner and James Sperling (eds.), *Global Security Governance: Competing Perceptions of Security in the 21st Century* (Routledge, London/New York, 2007) pp. 3, 5–16.

[25] For a detailed analysis of different views expressed by states in the Security Council, see Hitoshi Nasu, 'The Place of Human Security in Collective Security' (2013) 18 *Journal of Conflict and Security Law* 95.

security.[26] In 2000, the Security Council discussed the impact of HIV/ AIDS on peace and security in Africa under the Council Presidency of US Vice-President Al-Gore,[27] which set a precedent for Security Council debate on a broader security agenda.[28] Subsequently, the Security Council discussed the issue of Africa's food security,[29] largely in respect of its 'incontrovertible link' to peace and security,[30] and the issue of climate change,[31] which caused a stark division among states as to what can or should be appropriately considered as a security issue.[32]

Other institutions have also been instrumental to this expansion of the concept of security. For example, the Conference on Security and Co-operation in Europe (CSCE; later renamed as the Organization for Security and Co-operation in Europe: OSCE), a unique product of Cold War politics established by the 1975 Helsinki Accords,[33] provided for the first time a formal basis for the human rights agenda in the political discourse with the Soviet Union, building a foundation for its comprehensive security approach across politico-military, economic and ecological, and human dimensions.[34] The IMO has addressed maritime security issues since 1985, following the *Achille Lauro* incident, against unlawful, deliberate acts of violence against ships and persons on board ships.[35] More recently, the WHO has embraced the idea of global public health security by expanding the scope of its activities to

---

[26] UN Doc. S/PV.3046 (31 January 1992), especially the Presidential statement issued at the end of the proceedings at p. 143.

[27] UN Doc. S/PV.4087 (10 January 2000).    [28] *Ibid.* p. 2.

[29] UN Doc. S/PV.4652 (3 December 2002); UN Doc. S/PV.4736 (7 April 2003); UN Doc. S/PV.5220 (30 June 2005).

[30] See especially, UN Doc. S/PV.5220 (30 June 2005), 9 (Romania), 11 (the Philippines), 12 (Japan), 13 (China, Greece), 14 (Benin).

[31] UN S/PV.5663 and S/PV.5663 (Resumption 1) (17 April 2007); UN S/PV.6587 and S/PV.6587 (Resumption 1) (20 July 2011).

[32] For an analysis of the debate, see Nasu, 'The Place of Human Security in Collective Security', above n. 25, 118–20; Shirley V. Scott, 'Securitising Climate Change: International Legal Implications and Obstacles' (2008) 21 *Cambridge Review of International Affairs* 603.

[33] Final Act of the Conference on Security and Co-operation in Europe, adopted 1 August 1975, 14 ILM 1292.

[34] For details, see e.g., Antonio Ortiz, 'Neither Fox nor Hedgehog: NATO's Comprehensive Approach and the OSCE's Concept of Security' (2008) 4 *Security and Human Rights* 284.

[35] See generally e.g., Martmut Hesse and Nicolaos L. Charalambous, 'New Security Measures for the International Shipping Community' (2004) 3(2) *World Maritime University Journal of Maritime Affairs* 123, 124. For further analysis, see Chie Kojima, Chapter 4.

encompass 'illness or medical condition, irrespective of origin or source, that presents or could present significant harm to humans' in the 2005 International Health Regulation.[36]

The form of institutions has also diversified, ranging from formal international organisations established by treaties to expert bodies usually for supervising and monitoring compliance with treaty obligations, such as the International Atomic Energy Agency (IAEA), and even to non-treaty based institutions such as OSCE.[37] Domestic government institutions have been building trans-governmental networks to coordinate policy implementation and respond effectively to challenges posed by transnational security issues, such as terrorism, illicit trafficking of weapons of mass destruction-related materials, human trafficking and piracy.[38] In addition, international non-governmental organisations and private entities have also become increasingly drawn into security policy-making and implementation, as can be found in the counter-piracy and cyber security initiatives.[39]

There are also institutions not originally designed to address security issues, adapting to incorporate them through operational activities. For example, the EU has developed civil and military crisis management operations through institutional evolution of its Common Foreign and Security Policy.[40] The Economic Community of Western African States (ECOWAS), established to facilitate economic development of its member states, has engaged in peacekeeping operations, notably in Liberia in the 1990s.[41] ASEAN was established as the political platform with dual functions to maintain the regional stability and to ensure the internal stability and security of the government in each member state,[42] but has also been playing a greater role to address

---

[36] Revision of the International Health Regulations, WHA Res. 58.3 (23 May 2005) ('2005 IHR'), opened for signature 23 May 2005, 2509 UNTS 79 (entered into force 15 June 2007), Art. 1. For further analysis, see Adam Kamradt-Scott, Chapter 10.

[37] Geir Ulfstein, 'Institutions and Competences' in Jan Klabbers, Anne Peters and Geir Ulfstein (eds.), *The Constitutionalization of International Law* (Oxford University Press, Oxford, 2009) pp. 45, 46–55.

[38] See Anne-Marie Slaughter, *A New World Order* (Princeton University Press, Princeton, NJ, 2004) pp. 36–64.

[39] See Chie Kojima, Chapter 4 and Ottavio Quirico, Chapter 14.

[40] See Anne McNaughton, Chapter 3.    [41] See Hitoshi Nasu, Chapter 7.

[42] Amitav Acharya, *Constructing a Security Community in Southeast Asia: ASEAN and the Problem of Regional Order* (Routledge, London, 2001) p. 57; P. Saipiroon, *ASEAN Governments' Attitudes Towards Regional Security 1975–1979* (Institute of Asian Studies, Bangkok, 1982) pp. 5–7.

'non-traditional security issues', whilst being guided by the norm of comprehensive security.[43]

The expansion of the concept of security, together with institutional evolution in a variety of forms, has arguably led to the expanded role for inter-governmental institutions, international expert bodies, domestic government institutions and even private institutions to address a wide range of contemporary security issues that states are facing. The greater role of security institutions through their institutional evolution may well be considered to be the result of a natural progression of institutional activities in response to changing security paradigms. However, institutional evolution does not take place in a political, legal and historical vacuum, but is an inevitable process of adaptation for survival according to the changes in the surrounding security environment.[44] That process may well involve normative influences, challenging the existing institutional rules, raising issues of legitimacy and accountability, and causing collision with other institutions. Thus, institutional evolution, when it is promoted by the security imperative, requires legal inquiries into its effects within the existing legal frameworks, which is facilitated by drawing from the connections between public and international law.

## 3  Themes and structure of the volume

These institutional developments in response to the changing security environment and the emergence of non-traditional security challenges raise a number of normative and legal questions at the intersection of public and international law, security and institutions. Consequently, this volume is divided into four parts, each examining different aspects of the tension between institutional development and the legal frameworks dealing with contemporary security threats.

---

[43] ASEAN Political-Security Community Blueprint, Section B, available at www.asean.org/archive/5187-18.pdf. See generally, Mely Caballero-Anthony, 'Challenging Change: Nontraditional Security, Democracy and Regionalism' in Donald K. Emmerson (ed.), *Hard Choices: Security, Democracy, and Regionalism in Southeast Asia* (Walter H. Shorenstein Asia-Pacific Research Center, Stanford, CA, 2008) p. 191; Mely Caballero-Anthony, 'Revisioning Human Security in Southeast Asia' (2004) 28(3) *Asian Perspective* 155.

[44] See Cheryl Shanks, Harold K. Jacobson and Jeffrey H. Kaplan, 'Inertia and Change in the Constellation of International Governmental Organizations, 1981–1992' (1995) 50 *International Organization* 593.

### 3.1 Security and institutional evolution

The first theme concerns the theoretical underpinning of institutional evolution in the context of changing security paradigms. Different theories have developed different types of institutional analysis in social sciences.[45] The rational choice theory may explain institutional evolution as a result of states attempting to further their own national interests.[46] According to neoliberal institutionalism, institutionalisation is subject to the degree of shared expectations of participatory behaviour, specificity of codified institutional rules, and differentiated functions and responsibilities among its participants.[47] Historical institutionalism, on the other hand, conceives institutional evolution as being affected by various factors, including personal preferences and rules, which can only be explained in a historical and comparative context.[48] The revolutionary theory, which has more recently emerged in literature, attempts to understand institutional evolution as a more dynamic process due to the interdependence and complex interaction of endogenous and exogenous variables.[49] The relevant inquiry for the purpose of this volume is how the concept of security influences institutional evolution in general or in a specific context.

---

[45] Peter Hall and Rosemary Taylor, 'Political Science and the Three New Institutionalism' (1996) 44 *Political Studies* 936.

[46] See e.g., Barbara Koremenos, Charles Lipson and Duncan Snidal, 'The Rational Design of International Institutions' (2005) 55 *International Organization* 761; David A. Lake, 'Beyond Anarchy: The Importance of Security Institutions' (2001) 26 *International Security* 129, 157. Cf. Richard Gowan and Bruce D. Jones, 'Conclusion: International Institutions and the Problems of Adaptation' in Bruce D. Jones, Shepard Forman and Richard Gowan (eds.), *Cooperating for Peace and Security: Evolving Institutions and Arrangements in a Context of Changing U.S. Security Policy* (Cambridge University Press, Cambridge, 2010) pp. 311, 314 and 319 (observing that 'there is no necessary correlation between balance of power in international politics and the structure, or even the behavior, of international institutions' and that 'real shifts in the balance of power do not necessarily create institutional adaptation').

[47] Celeste A. Wallander and Robert O. Keohane, 'Risk, Threat, and Security Institutions' in Helga Haftendorn, Robert O. Keohane and Celeste A. Wallender (eds.), *Imperfect Unions: Security Institutions over Time and Space* (Oxford University Press, Oxford, 1999) pp. 21, 24.

[48] See e.g., Orfeo Fioretos, 'Historical Institutionalism in International Relations' (2011) 65 *International Organization* 367; Sven Steinmo, Kathleen A. Thelen and Frank Longstreth, *Structuring Politics: Historical Institutionalism in Comparative Analysis* (Cambridge University Press, Cambridge, 1992).

[49] See Mark Blyth, Geoffrey M. Hodgson, Orion Lewis and Sven Steinmo, 'Introduction to the Special Issue on the Evolution of Institutions' (2011) 7 *Journal of Institutional Economics* 299, 305–9.

According to the 'securitisation' theory developed by the Copenhagen School, the discourse of security can be understood as a speech-act in the processes of constructing a shared understanding of what is considered a threat.[50] During these processes of securitisation, institutional evolution may well provide a means to regularise the response to a newly identified security threat, as seen in the development of UN collective security institutions, such as the gradual expansion of peacekeeping operations and, more recently, 'quasi-legislative' resolutions adopted by the Security Council.[51] However, the security imperative is not the only factor influencing the direction of institutional evolution, but rather interacts with other factors, some of which may be desirable or undesirable from a normative perspective. What factors will or should interact with the security imperative in facilitating, or hindering, institutional evolution in response to contemporary security issues? Are there particular factors that should assist regularising collective responses to a security threat in institutional settings, rather than undermining or overriding existing institutional processes? Are there any normative considerations that should guide or restrain existing institutional processes,[52] through which the institutional competence can be expanded to respond to contemporary security issues?

In Chapter 1, Alexandra Walker considers the role of 'conscious' and 'unconscious' security in security institution building, drawing on psychological and sociological studies of 'collective self'. From a sociological perspective, the 'collective consciousness' involves a collective narrative identity, which affects how collectives frame their security relationships, and allows the collective self to reflect on its values and goals and possibly to adapt or transform itself in response to the changing security environment. The 'collective unconsciousness', on the other hand, refers to the distorted sense of vulnerability that consists of all the psychic contents that individuals and collectives deem to be worthless which, when repressed, prompt the collective self to overcompensate the vulnerability by controlling all others and the security environment. Having

---

[50] Barry Buzan, Ole Wæver and Jaap de Wilde, *Security: A New Framework for Analysis* (Lynne Rienner, Boulder, CO, 1998) pp. 23–6.

[51] SC Res. 1373 (28 September 2001); SC Res. 1540 (28 April 2004). For further analysis, see Anna Hood, Chapter 6.

[52] Cf. Ian Johnstone, 'Normative Evaluation at the UN: Impact on Operational Activities' in Bruce D. Jones, Shepard Forman and Richard Gowan (eds.), *Cooperating for Peace and Security: Evolving Institutions and Arrangements in a Context of Changing U.S. Security Policy* (Cambridge University Press, Cambridge, 2010) p. 187.

identified that collective selves exist in a state of constant tension between their consciousness and unconscious security, Walker argues that it is optimal for the pursuit of security to be based upon conscious, rather than unconscious, security. It is her finding that institutionalised self-reflective decision-making processes can facilitate a collective self to habitually process its unconscious material and thus help realising conscious security.

Bina D'Costa turns the focus to gender justice in Chapter 2, which often becomes a politicised issue concerning the roles and rights of women in counterproductive ways in post-conflict security institution building. Drawing on experiences of peace building efforts in Pakistan and Afghanistan, D'Costa considers whether normative considerations such as gender justice ought to steer or constrain existing institutional processes, through which institutional capability is strengthened to address contemporary security issues. In particular, this chapter examines the evolution of 'anti-state local security institutions', which are often labelled as 'terrorist organisations' or 'militant groups' in mainstream political discourse, and the role these institutions play in sustaining and reinforcing gender bias. Thus, D'Costa argues, notwithstanding the gender mainstreaming rhetoric and gender justice norm accepted internationally, women's vulnerability and insecurity increases in times of conflicts not only from the actions of the religious forces but also from 'progressive', 'secular' and 'humanitarian' interventions.

In Chapter 3, Anne McNaughton focuses on the EU as a *sui generis* legal system' and its evolution under the Common Foreign and Security Policy. Because of the way in which the competences of the EU and its Member States are carefully articulated and delineated, any institutional evolution challenges the demarcation of competences in light of the jurisprudence underpinning that process. While this is difficult to conceive from the more traditional public and international law perspectives, McNaughton suggests that the concept of 'de-centred regulation' from the regulation literature can better explain how the rule of law in Europe has transcended the state and 'de-centred' security regulation through institutional evolution. Viewed from this perspective, it becomes clear that the EU's institutional evolution in respect of its Common Foreign and Security Policy has not been guided by any centralised security response by the EU institutions, but has rather been a carefully negotiated response to concerns about centralisation of powers to the EU institutions. As McNaughton observes, the de-centralised security regulation in

Europe is a critical factor that has allowed the EU to respond flexibly to new security threats in ways that do not undermine the carefully delineated and articulated institutional relationship between the EU and its Member States.

Chapter 4 by Chie Kojima broadens the scope of inquiry into the maritime domain, with the focus on the evolving role of the IMO in building international maritime security institutions. The IMO has contributed to the building of maritime security institutions not only by assisting its member states to establish cooperative frameworks, but also by providing forums in which public and private actors can form their shared policies. Kojima demonstrates the institutionalising role of the IMO, with many examples of public and private initiatives taken against piracy and armed robbery at sea off the coast of Somalia and in the Gulf of Aden. In her view, this presents a unique case where the notion of security is linked to private interests, which has necessitated the IMO playing a central role in facilitating multiple processes in which all the interested actors, both public and private, participate in order to achieve the common goal of protecting maritime security.

### 3.2 Security institutions and the rule of law

The second theme looks at the relationship between security and the rule of law in international and domestic institutional settings. It is an established principle of international institutional law that the competence of international institutions is not unlimited but is restricted by the provisions of the constitutive instrument, in terms both of form and substance.[53] On the other hand, international institutions' constitutive instruments are often considered as their constitutional documents requiring a teleological approach to interpretation through subsequent practice of the institutions themselves.[54] Domestic security institutions, which are often governed and directed by the executive arm of the government, may have more liberty in institutional development, but

---

[53] See generally, C. F. Amerasinghe, *Principles of the Institutional Law of International Organizations* (2nd edn, Cambridge University Press, Cambridge, 2005) pp. 194–6; Philippe Sands and Pierre Klein, *Bowett's Law of International Institutions* (5th edn, Sweet and Maxwell, London, 2001) pp. 292–3.

[54] See e.g., Bardo Fassbender, *The United Nations Charter as the Constitution of the International Community* (Martinus Nijhoff, Leiden, 2009) pp. 129–36; Catherine Brölmann, *The Institutional Veil in Public International Law: International Organisations and the Law of Treaties* (Hart Publishing, Oxford/Portland, OR, 2007) pp. 113–23.

the growth of public law in the latter half of the twentieth century has led to greater legal restrictions and judicial oversight of their activities.[55]

In the case of security institutions, however, the security imperative appears to have prompted some commentators to observe that institutions may derogate from certain norms or stretch the interpretation of indeterminate norms through operational activities. Such derogation or expansive interpretation raises questions concerning the legal limits of their activities.[56] For example, the strong assertion of national security, especially after the 9/11 terrorist attacks in New York, led to a larger space devoid of the rule of law control over counter-terrorism and counter-insurgency operations, giving rise to a debate over the role and limits of legal institutions in dealing with security issues.[57] In a similar vein, the Security Council has started exercising 'legislative' or 'judicial' powers under Articles 25 and 103 of the UN Charter in dealing with global terrorism threats even at the expense of human rights protection.[58] It is debatable whether this development is to be seen favourably or as the emergence of hegemonic international law that needs to be constrained.[59] In any event, there is a perceived danger that 'many repressive states might see a Security Council Resolution as an excuse to clamp down on dissidents under the guise that they are terrorists'.[60]

While each institution has its own legal framework within which its authority and institutional competence is defined, there are underlying questions common to security institutions. To what extent and in what way should the law respond to the security imperative facilitating institutional evolution? Should there be an international rule of law restraining institutional responses to contemporary security issues?

---

[55] See generally, Mark Aronson, Bruce D. Dyer and Matthew Groves, *Judicial Review of Administrative Action* (4th edn, Thomson, Sydney, 2008); P. Craig, *Administrative Law* (4th edn, Sweet and Maxwell, London, 1999); S.A. de Smith, H. Woolf and J. Jowell, *Judicial Review of Administrative Action* (5th edn, Sweet and Maxwell, London, 1995); H.W.R. Wade and C. Forsyth, *Administrative Law* (8th edn, Oxford University Press, Oxford, 2000).

[56] See generally, Goold and Lazarus, *Security and Human Rights*, above n. 6.

[57] For discussion, see e.g., David Dyzenhaus, *The Constitution of Law: Legality in a Time of Emergency* (Cambridge University Press, Cambridge, 2006) pp. 42–53.

[58] See e.g., SC Res. 1373 (28 September 2001); SC Res. 1333 (19 December 2000); SC Res. 1267 (15 October 1999).

[59] For discussion, see e.g., José E. Alvarez, *International Organizations as Law-Makers* (Oxford University Press, Oxford, 2005) pp. 199–217.

[60] Nigel D. White, 'The Security Council, the Security Imperative and International Law' in Matthew Happold (ed.), *International Law in a Multipolar World* (Routledge, London/ New York, 2012) pp. 4, 15.

Could domestic public law jurisprudence assist in developing such an international rule of law governing institutions? Conversely, how does the security imperative influence security institutions in shaping their legal response or in revisiting their institutional powers and competence?

The starting point in exploring these questions must be located in the traditional sources of international law, as Imogen Saunders does in Chapter 5 with the focus on the general principles of law provided in Article 38(1)(c) of the Statute of the International Court of Justice.[61] The application of the general principles of law has the potential to extend the idea of the rule of law to the conduct of international security institutions, by virtue of its ability to derive binding norms of international law through analogy from domestic legal principles of a horizontal generality across different legal systems, including public law principles. On that basis, Saunders considers three aspects of public law principles – the principle of formal legality, constitutional interpretive principles, and certain administrative principles such as due process, access to remedies, accountability, transparency and judicial review – as potential candidates of the general principles of law in order to examine their applicability to international security institutions. Saunders concludes by arguing that the use of these public law principles can and will confer legitimacy on the conduct of international security institutions that conform to those requirements – a question which is further elaborated upon in the next part of this volume.

The fact that security institutions such as the UN Security Council essentially deal with security threats may mean that their 'legislative' activity is a form of emergency law-making that is analogous to the law that is produced by domestic executives in times of crisis. This is the proposition that Anna Hood explores in Chapter 6, with the focus on the Security Council's 'legislative' activity. In many respects, the Security Council's 'legislative' resolutions share the same characteristics as domestic emergency legislation,[62] and this provides the basis for the application of Carl Schmitt's theory on the state of exception to explain the nature of the Security Council's 'legislative' activities. However, there are several normative considerations in emergency law theories which, as Hood examines, could find useful application

---

[61] Opened for signature 26 June 1945, 1 UNTS 993 (entered into force 24 October 1945).

[62] The 'legislation' for the purpose of Chapter 6 is widely defined to include those that create or modify international legal obligations.

to enhance the Security Council's compliance with the rule of law. Hood reaches the conclusion that while none of these normative considerations is actionable with respect to the Security Council's legislative practice, the emergency law perspective still provides a useful way of re-examining the underlying assumptions of emergency law-making in different institutional settings.

Security imperatives may prompt other types of institutions to evolve and push their boundaries, posing challenges to existing legal arrangements. Chapter 7 by Hitoshi Nasu examines the evolution of African institutions in the 1990s to the early 2000s as case studies, in which irregularities in the decision-making for deployment of peacekeeping forces arguably meant that the institutions acted *ultra vires*. The fact that the African institutions applied the doctrinal framework of traditional peacekeeping was significant and instrumental to compensatory institutional evolution, which according to Nasu has contributed to facilitating general support of their member states for the out-of-competence regional actions. Nasu concludes that even though institutional evolutions, triggered by security imperatives, often pose challenges to the basic principles of international institutional law, the rhetoric and formula of peacekeeping as an 'institution' has assisted in producing a general agreement within a regional organisation in the form of an 'emergency amendment' to its constitutive instrument, muting the issue of validity. One of the potential ramifications of this finding is that the traditional peacekeeping 'institution' can play a valuable role when an international or regional institution which is not originally mandated to deal with peace and security issues finds the need to expand its institutional competence in dealing with pressing security threats.

In Chapter 8, Solon Solomon brings this issue of institutional evolution to Israel's border security which involves both public (domestic) and international institutions. Solomon examines how public and international institutions have approached Israel's national border security in respect of its border with Egypt, the 1967 armistice lines in the West Bank, and the Gaza boundary after the Israeli disengagement from Gaza Strip in 2005. Through his thorough analysis, it becomes clear that institutional settings, decision-making procedures and political conditions surrounding each institution influence the way in which the relationship between security and the law is viewed within the parameters of international law. This leads to his finding that the relationship between security and law is not pre-determined, and that a security imperative is not a monolithic concern shared by different institutions in the same way. This inevitably creates tension as to what extent security concerns should be taken into account in the application of the law and under what circumstances security concerns can override the pre-existing legal arrangements.

### 3.3 Security institutions and legitimacy

The third theme examines the impact of securitisation on the legitimacy and accountability of institutions. Institutions cannot function without the exercise of their power conferred by the legitimate source of authority, be they a democratically elected government or with state consent. When institutions evolve through their operational activities, however, their exercise of power is inevitably one step away from the source of legitimacy. Thus, the delegation of powers to international institutions has often been suspected to undermine the separation of powers within states,[63] to the extent that institutional decisions bypass domestic procedures (often involving democratic processes) for legitimising the delegation of powers,[64] which has raised an issue of institutional legitimacy. This issue of institutional legitimacy is not unique to international institutions, but has also been studied elsewhere in the domestic context, particularly in relation to the accountability of regulatory agencies as the fourth branch of government.[65]

Legitimacy is a highly contested concept and is variously understood in different contexts of international law. Anthony D'Amato describes it simply as a space between international law and international politics by illuminating the existence of such a space in the de facto recognition of a government and the process of forming customary international law.[66] Similarly, in the context of military action, legitimacy is used for different purposes. The 2004 High-Level Panel Report, *A More Secure*

---

[63] Dan Sarooshi, *International Organizations and Their Exercise of Sovereign Powers* (Oxford University Press, Oxford, 2005) p. 15.

[64] Neils Blokker, 'Beyond "Dili": On the Powers and Practice of International Organizations' in Gerard Kreijen *et al.* (eds.), *State, Sovereignty, and International Governance* (Oxford University Press, Oxford, 2002) pp. 299, 307–8.

[65] See Martin Shapiro, *Who Guards the Guardians?: Judicial Control of Administration* (University of Georgia Press, Athens, GA, 1988).

[66] Anthony D'Amato, 'On the Legitimacy of International Institutions' in Rüdiger Wolfrum and Volker Röben (eds.), *Legitimacy in International Law* (Springer, Heidelberg, 2008) pp. 83, 83–6.

*World*, developed guidelines for enhancing the legitimacy of the Security Council's lawful military enforcement action under the UN Charter.[67] A contrasting, more controversial use of legitimacy was made during NATO's intervention in Kosovo by the supporters, acknowledging that the action was unlawful without Security Council authorisation and yet arguing that it was still legitimate.[68] In the seminal work on legitimacy in international law, Thomas Franck defines it as a 'property of a rule or rule-making institution which itself exerts a pull toward compliance on those addressed normatively because those addressed believe that [it] operates in accordance with generally accepted principles of right process'.[69]

However, when the concept is used in institutional settings, it addresses the normative force (or a 'pull') of institutional activity, which often relates to the notion of accountability. Ian Hurd, for example, understands institutional legitimacy as a subjective quality and relational concept, defined by an actor's normative belief or perception that a rule of law ought to be obeyed.[70] Similarly, Allen Buchanan and Robert Keohane define it by reference to certain 'epistemic virtues' that facilitate the ongoing critical revision of the institutional goals, through interaction with the agents and organisations outside the institution.[71]

General discussion about global administrative law and public law perspectives towards the exercise of public authority by international institutions often involves recommendations for greater public participation in institutional decision-making, strict procedural requirements, substantive judicial review, and a combination thereof, as a way of enhancing institutional legitimacy.[72] The question relevant to the context of security institutions is, however: to what extent those

---

[67] *A More Secure World*, above n. 22, pp. 66–7.

[68] See e.g., Anthea Roberts, 'Legality vs Legitimacy: Can Uses of Force be Illegal but Justified?' in Philip Alston and Euan MacDonald (eds.), *Human Rights, Intervention, and the Use of Force* (Oxford University Press, Oxford, 2008) p. 179.

[69] Thomas M. Franck, *The Power of Legitimacy among Nations* (Oxford University Press, Oxford, 1990) p. 24.

[70] Ian Hurd, *After Anarchy: Legitimacy and Power in the United Nations Security* Council (Princeton University Press, Princeton, NJ, 2007) p. 7. It is close to a sociological understanding of organisational legitimacy. See Mark C. Suchman, 'Managing Legitimacy: Strategic and Institutional Approaches' (1995) 20 *Academy of Management Review* 571.

[71] Allen Buchanan and Robert O. Keohane, 'The Legitimacy of Global Governance Institutions' (2006) 20 *Ethics and International Affairs* 405, 406.

[72] See generally, Armin von Bogdandy *et al.* (eds.), *The Exercise of Public Authority by International Institutions: Advancing International Institutional Law* (Springer,

ideas may or may not help security institutions in enhancing the legitimacy of their institutional evolution through operational activities? Does the security imperative prevailing over many aspects of current international and transnational relations require or allow existing international institutions to take their own path, even though it is not explicitly provided for in the constitutive instrument that governs their activities, to facilitate flexible and prompt response? Is there any role that international law can play in enhancing or undermining institutional legitimacy in the process of institutional evolution in response to the emergence of contemporary security issues?

Chapter 9 by Kalman Robertson examines the thesis that challenges to the legitimacy of the International Atomic Energy Agency (IAEA) have been addressed through the development of its legal authority to administer comprehensive safeguards agreements under the Nuclear Non-Proliferation Treaty at least as far as non-nuclear-weapon states are concerned. Challenges have been posed due to the increased tensions between military and peaceful uses of nuclear technologies as these are relied upon to address increasingly serious energy security concerns around the world, following a series of findings of non-compliance in the last twenty years. Through detailed analysis of the IAEA's institutional evolution, particularly in comparison with other monitoring institutions, Robertson finds that its normative foundation lies with the epistemic virtues exhibited through generating reliable information on state behaviour, operating transparently, and providing information for ongoing deliberation, rather than greater public participation in or substantive judicial review of its activities.

As is the case with the evolution of the IAEA, international law has also been instrumental to the evolution of the WHO as a global public health security institution, as Adam Kamradt-Scott discusses in Chapter 10. In recent years, two international agreements have been adopted with a view to expanding the WHO's legal authority to strengthen global response capacity in combating infectious disease outbreaks and other adverse health events: the 2005 International Health Regulations (IHR) 2005;[73] and the 2011 Pandemic Influenza Preparedness Framework (PIPF).[74] The 2005 IHR has altered the nature of the regulations from one of

---

Heidelberg, 2010); Benedict Kingsbury, Nico Krisch and Richard B. Stewart, 'The Emergence of Global Administrative Law' (2005) 68 *Law and Contemporary Problems* 15.

[73] 2005 IHR, above n. 36.

[74] Pandemic Influenza Preparedness: Sharing of Influenza Viruses and Access to Vaccines and Other Benefits, WHA Res. 64.5 (24 May 2011).

reactive border controls to proactive risk management and disease containment. The 2011 PIPF has served to re-shape an established WHO technical cooperation network into a new public-private partnership. By exploring this institutional evolution of the WHO through the securitisation of public health issues, Kamradt-Scott identifies the central role that international law has played in enhancing its institutional legitimacy; however, at the same time warns that global health security is likely to remain elusive and may result in undermining its institutional legitimacy unless states take necessary action to cooperate with the WHO.

A contrasting observation is made by See Seng Tan in Chapter 11, in which Tan examines Southeast Asia's embryonic efforts to settle disputes with an institutional approach. The adoption of the ASEAN Charter in 2007, and the recourse to legal means for dispute settlement by several Southeast Asian states, can be seen as a slow but gradual shift towards a greater acceptance of institutionalised means of dispute settlement in the region. Tan reviews actual state practice in trade and territorial disputes and demonstrates the persistent ambivalence in Southeast Asian states' attitudes towards an institutionalised approach to dispute settlement. This is, Tan argues, due to the consideration shared by ASEAN states that keeping ASEAN as a consensus-based organisation is as significant as keeping an instrumental and strategic choice for individual member states. Indeed, Tan finds paradoxical institutionalising the 'ASEAN Way' in the ASEAN Charter as it has the potential to undermine the legitimacy of ASEAN by depriving it of the benefits of flexible consensus it once enjoyed.

### 3.4   Security institutions and regime collision

The fourth theme focuses on the impact of securitisation by institutions on their interaction or collision with external factors such as competing institutions and legal frameworks. Institutional evolution necessarily takes place within meta-institutional frameworks in which other institutions and interests are influenced by the changes that one institution makes to its own activities. In international law, such interactions and collisions have been studied as an issue of regime conflict.[75] The UN

---

[75] See especially, Dirk Pulkowski, *The Law and Politics of International Regime Conflict* (Oxford University Press, Oxford, 2014); Margaret A. Young (ed.), *Regime Interaction in International Law: Facing Fragmentation* (Cambridge University Press, Cambridge, 2012); Tomer Broude and Yuval Shany (eds.), *Multi-Sourced Equivalent Norms in International Law* (Hart Publishing, Oxford/Portland, OR, 2011).

International Law Commission's work on fragmentation of international law goes some way to address this issue by identifying technical legal methodologies that resolve a conflict of laws.[76] However, these legal methodologies may not be capable of addressing the underlying tension between different normative foundations as well as legal structures, when these interactions and collisions arise from institutional evolution in response to contemporary security challenges.

As Andreas Fischer-Lescano and Gunther Teubner argue, international legal norm collisions 'educ[e] from the underlying conflicts between the "policies" pursued by different international organisations and regulatory regimes'.[77] These interactions and collisions can also be explained in terms of the specific purposes and the institutional design features that underpin each regime, whether they are embedded in the constitutive instrument or are loosely shared by the major decision-makers, as can be seen in the investment treaty arbitration regime.[78] As a result, institutions, international and domestic alike, are increasingly facing the challenge that they have to internalise conflicting norms, obligations and interests, and account for their implementation to other relevant institutions.[79] How and to what extent can existing legal obligations prevent security institutions from effectively responding to contemporary security issues? Is it possible through the process of institutional evolution to accommodate competing norms or interests in creating an effective regime to address a particular security issue?

These questions are examined in Chapters 12 and 13 with the focus on two different types of food security problems: long-term, chronic food security issues by Dilan Thampapillai, and short-term, acute food security issues by Michael Ewing-Chow, Melanie Vilarasau Slade and Liu Gehuan. Thampapillai identifies the causes of chronic

---

[76] Fragmentation of International Law: Difficulties Arising from the Diversification and Expansion of International Law, Report of the Study Group of the International Law Commission, UN Doc. A/CN.4/L.682 (13 April 2006).

[77] Andreas Fischer-Lescano and Gunther Teubner, 'Regime-Collisions: The Vain Search for Legal Unity in the Fragmentation of Global Law' (2004) 25 *Michigan Journal of International Law* 999, 1003.

[78] See especially, Steven R. Ratner, 'Regulatory Takings in Institutional Context: Beyond the Fear of Fragmented International Law' (2008) 102 *American Journal of International Law* 475, 484–521.

[79] Hilary Charlesworth and Christine Chinkin, 'Regulatory Frameworks in International Law' in Christine Parker *et al.* (eds.), *Regulating Law* (Oxford University Press, Oxford, 2004) pp. 246, 247.

food insecurity as a form of market failure facilitated by the rules of international intellectual property law, as primarily embodied in the Agreement on the Trade-Related Aspects of Intellectual Property Rights (TRIPS).[80] While acknowledging that food insecurity is not a problem solely created by the post-TRIPS legal environment, Thampapillai argues that the legal rules on intellectual property play a significant role in supporting and encouraging those market forces that adversely impact upon access to, and the availability and affordability of food, and in causing significant disruptions to the traditional farming practices of farmers in the Global South. International responses, orchestrated by the Food and Agricultural Organization (FAO), to the food security problem in the context of agriculture, comprising the movement towards farmers' rights and the right to food, have offered some useful solutions to the crisis. After examining the legal frameworks relevant to food security, Thampapillai provides three critiques of the FAO's response to the problem of food security with the finding that the regime conflict deprives the FAO of a useful role in norm creation, effective administration of food security, and reconciliation of 'norm collision' to overcome a property-type policy response.

Chapter 13 by Ewing-Chow, Slade and Gehuan considers short-term, acute food security crises in the context of Asia, with the focus on the ASEAN Plus Three Emergency Rice Reserve (APTERR) and its relationship with international trade law. APTERR is an institutional response to an acute food security crisis in 2008, which has created a mechanism whereby its member states maintain a rice reserve which can be released in times of emergency for the benefit of the populations of regional states. When this short-term food security institution emerged, as Ewing-Chow, Slade and Gehuan examine, several legal issues were identified in relation to international trade law rules, particularly in terms of the restriction on the origin of the rice and the way in which the rice was to be released and distributed. In the end, international trade law rules assisted in shaping APTERR rather than causing a collision and, in the authors' view, even facilitated the institution building to achieve a certain level of detail to avoid a potential collision, which is beneficial in ensuring an effective implementation of the regime.

The final chapter by Ottavio Quirico deals with cyber security institutions with a specific focus on the role of private cyber security

---

[80] Opened for signature 15 April 1994, 1869 UNTS 299 (entered into force 1 January 1995).

providers, and their interactions with the international and domestic rules governing the use of force. Cyber security is at the nascent stage of development and its institution building is primarily led by private cyber security providers. However, unlike state authorities, those private actors do not possess legal authority to use armed force beyond the scope of self-defence, for the purpose of law enforcement or military operations. This legal restriction existing under the relevant rules of international and domestic law poses challenges to the operation of private cyber security institutions, depending on how the notion of 'use of force' or 'lethal force' is interpreted when cyber methods are used. Quirico argues that the existing rules of international and domestic law apply to cyber security operations, which prohibit private actors from engaging in cyber security counter-measures beyond the scope of self-defence or, in the situation of an armed conflict, will make them lawful targets as civilians directly participating in hostilities. In his view, these legal consequences might prevent private cyber security institutions from effectively responding to cyber security threats.

## 4  Conclusion

This volume's four parts, in examining different aspects of the tensions between institutional evolution and the public and international law frameworks dealing with contemporary security threats, provide new and important ways of thinking about these pressing issues. Until this series of books developed, international and public law issues had mainly overlapped in discussions on how international law is implemented domestically.[81] The scholarship emerging in the area of global administrative law has also been developing principles relevant to both public and international law,[82] yet these publications contained only a subset of

---

[81] The first volume of this series, Jeremy Farrall and Kim Rubenstein (eds.), *Sanctions, Accountability and Governance in a Globalised World* appeared in 2009. Before that, see e.g., Hilary Charlesworth *et al.* (eds.), *The Fluid State: International Law and National Legal Systems* (Federation Press, Sydney, 2005); and Yuval Shany, *Regulating Jurisdictional Relations Between National and International Courts* (Oxford University Press, Oxford, 2007).

[82] See e.g., Benedict Kingsbury, 'The Concept of "Law" in Global Administrative Law' (2009) 20 *European Journal of International Law* 23; Alexander Somek, 'The Concept of "Law" in Global Administrative Law: A Reply to Benedict Kingsbury' (2009) 20 *European Journal of International Law* 985; Carol Harlow, 'Global Administrative Law: The Quest for Principles and Values' (2006) 17 *European Journal of International Law*

the concepts underpinning this book. By concentrating on legal perspectives on security institutions, this volume has added to this series' contributions by broadening our understanding of how public and international law intersects in harnessing, regulating, legitimising and shaping institutional responses to contemporary security threats as the notion of security expands.

187; Nico Krisch, 'The Pluralism of Global Administrative Law' (2006) 17 *European Journal of International Law* 247; Benedict Kingsbury, Nico Krisch and Richard B. Stewart, 'The Emergence of Global Administrative Law' (2005) 68(15) *Law and Contemporary Problems* 15; David Dyzenhaus (ed.), *The Unity of Public Law* (Hart Publishing, Oxford/Portland, OR, 2004).

# PART I

Security and institutional evolution

# Conscious and unconscious security responses

ALEXANDRA WALKER

## 1 Introduction

The global community is constituted by a diverse range of socially constructed collective selves: families, organisations, corporations, institutions, nation-states and the global community. All of these collective selves are key referents in the contemporary security debate. In this context, a collective self is defined as a community, however small or large, that shares collective representations, forms of reflectivity and unconscious material.[1] This chapter explores the concept of security in the collective self as a social construct,[2] in the form of conscious and unconscious security responses.

In this chapter, conscious security refers to the individual or collective responses to threats that are derived from stable relationships, constructive internal narratives, and the presence of ontological security. In contrast, unconscious security refers to the distorted sense of vulnerability that occurs when an individual or collective is influenced or dominated by unconscious material: archetypes, destructive narratives, paranoia and compulsions (for example, to control and to acquire power). Unconscious security leads to constant threat anticipation, threat management and the need for external control. The chapter

---

[1] A collective self is defined as '[a] group or population of individuals (or collective agents as members) that possesses or develops collective representations of itself: its values and goals, its structure and modes of operating, its strategies, developments, strengths and weaknesses': Tom Burns and Erik Engdahl, 'The Social Construction of Consciousness: Collective Consciousness and its Socio-Cultural Foundations' (1998) 5 *Journal of Consciousness Studies* 67, 67.

[2] For an overview of the Constructivist approach to security, see Alexander Wendt, 'Anarchy is What States Make of It: The Social Construction of Power Politics' (1992) 46 *International Organization* 391.

argues that it may be useful to treat the pursuit of security as an ongoing, symbiotic interaction between conscious and unconscious influences. In fact, the central argument of the chapter is that the interactive relationship between conscious and unconscious material is primary in the pursuit of security, and as such, the psychology of individuals and collectives are influential in forming their security responses.

In order to make these arguments, the chapter uses a combination of psychological and sociological approaches to show that collectives, like individuals, can be understood as 'selves' or 'agents' with personalities that have conscious and unconscious aspects. Adopting the 'sociology of human consciousness' model developed by Tom Burns and Erik Engdahl,[3] this chapter shows that collective selves operate as autonomous agents and personalities in the global community. The development of collective consciousness (collective awareness) occurs through social and reflective activities, formed through language, collective representations, institutional and cultural arrangements and self-reflectivity. The chapter then draws on the work of Swiss psychiatrist Carl Jung and post-Jungian theorists to suggest that security in the collective self is also shaped by 'unconscious' material such as archetypes and cultural complexes.

The chapter concludes that all individuals and collectives ultimately benefit from a state of conscious security. The first and most important step towards security institution building, therefore, is an awareness of unconscious material, and its effect on security. This chapter attempts to aid this process by providing an analytical framework for understanding the conscious and unconscious material of the collective self.[4]

---

[3] Burns and Engdahl, 'The Social Construction of Consciousness', above n. 1, 67–85; Tom Burns and Erik Engdahl, 'The Social Construction of Consciousness: Individual Selves, Self-Awareness, and Reflectivity' (1998) 5 *Journal of Consciousness Studies* 166.

[4] In relation to the terminology adopted in this chapter, the terms 'collective self', 'collective consciousness' and the 'collective unconscious' must be clarified. The 'collective self' refers to the totality of all conscious and unconscious processes that occur in the collective. The 'collective consciousness' refers to all aspects of the collective that have been named and recognised by the collective (the aspects of which the collective is aware). Finally, the 'collective unconscious' refers to those aspects of collective life of which the collective is unaware or which it is unable to understand. These aspects of the collective self remain unnamed and unrepresented, though they may impact heavily upon collective life, for example, in the form of recurring patterns and archetypes.

## 2   Subjective and objective security

It is commonly acknowledged in security literature that the term 'security' refers to objective and subjective conditions.[5] Objective security is considered a factual reality, which refers to protection from 'real and observed threats'.[6] Arnold Wolfers characterised objective security as 'the absence of threats to acquired values',[7] which David Baldwin rephrased as a 'low probability of damage to acquired values'.[8] From this perspective, security is either materially present or it is not: either there are bombs being dropped in a city or there are not; and either a nation-state is peaceful or it is at war. These are objective, external facts.

However security also has a subjective state, which refers to the particular and unique 'sense we have of our own safety'.[9] Lucia Zedner has identified two aspects of subjective security. The first aspect is 'the absolute condition of feeling safe',[10] whereas the second aspect is more nuanced. It is:

> a qualified condition of freedom from anxiety or apprehension because feelings of insecurity have been allayed. Here, both 'security' and its antonym 'insecurity' refer to an existential state that varies not only according to objective risk but also to extraneous factors such as individual sensitivity to risk and danger.[11]

This means that the subjective security of individuals and collectives, such as institutions or nation-states, is not necessarily based upon the absolute condition of feeling safe. In reality, subjective security is

---

[5] See e.g., Joseph de Rivera, 'Emotional Climate, Human Security and Cultures of Peace' (2007) 63 *Journal of Social Issues* 233; Robert Jervis, 'Cooperation under the Security Dilemma' (1978) 30 *World Politics: A Quarterly Journal of International Relations* 167; Frank Traeger and Frank Simonie, 'An Introduction to the Study of National Security' in Frank Traeger and Philip Kronenberg (eds.), *National Security and American Society: Theory, Process and Policy* (University Press of Kansas, Lawrence, KA, 1973) p. 36; Richard Ullman, 'Redefining Security' (1983) 8 *International Security* 129; Lucia Zedner, 'Too Much Security?' (2003) 31 *International Journal of the Sociology of Law* 155.

[6] J. Peter Burgess, *Security as Ethics*, International Peace Research Institute Policy Brief 6 (Oslo, 2008) 2, available at www.prio.org/Publications/Publication/?x=7336.

[7] Arnold Wolfers, 'National Security as an Ambiguous Symbol' (1952) 67 *Political Science Quarterly* 481, 485.

[8] David Baldwin, 'The Concept of Security' (1997) 23 *Review of International Studies* 5, 13.

[9] Lucia Zedner, *Security* (Routledge, Abingdon/New York, 2009) p. 16.    [10] *Ibid.*

[11] *Ibid.*

influenced and framed by the changing perceptions of reality and consciousness (the pre-interactional awareness of individuals and groups).

While the state of objective security appears to be based on external conditions, and subjective security seems to be a reaction to objective security, it can be argued that in fact, objective and subjective security are symbiotic and synchronised. For example, one nation-state may 'believe' that it needs to eradicate a form of religious or political extremism from a certain region in the world in order to reinforce its security. This belief is subjective. As a result of the belief, this nation-state may act belligerently towards the extremist state (for example, by imposing sanctions). This belligerence may result in unforeseen outcomes that undermine the nation-state's objective security more than the existence of perceived extremism ever did. In this example, the 'beliefs' of the nation-state collective self have directly affected its objective security. As such, it is often difficult to distinguish whether objective security causes subjective security or vice versa.

Furthermore, objective security is never fixed, and hence, inherently variable. Zedner observes that objective security 'implies a condition of being without threat, which, even if it could be achieved today, is always called into question by the emergence of new threats tomorrow'.[12] It is thus inextricably linked to subjective security, because the subjective evaluations of security in the present directly influence the objective conditions of security in the future. Jay Forrester explains a systemic relationship such as this as a feedback loop.[13]

This chapter goes beyond the dichotomy of objective and subjective security to show that there are conscious and unconscious factors at work in the construction of security. Those existing approaches to security focusing on objective and subjective conditions do not recognise or acknowledge the 'collective self' with conscious and unconscious material behind the search for security. Traditional approaches to security consequently leave the following questions in security literature:

(1) how threats or perceived threats are formulated in or experienced by the particular collective self or agent (for example, are they real or imagined threats?); and

[12] *Ibid.* p. 14.
[13] Jay Forrester, *Principles of Systems* (Wright-Allen Press, Cambridge, MA, 1969).

(2) how collective selves or agents can become aware of unconscious material in order to transform real or perceived threats into conscious security.[14]

## 3   Conscious and unconscious security responses

The premise of this chapter is that collectives have personalities with conscious and unconscious material, in a similar way to individual selves. Collectives have cultural values, complexes, archetypes and relationships with other collectives that determine their responses to various security events. A conscious response to security refers to individual or collective reactions to threats that are derived from stable relationships, constructive internal narratives and the presence of 'ontological security', which is a sense of order and continuity in regard to individual or collective experiences.[15] The presence of conscious security does not indicate the absence of threats; rather, it indicates that threats will be received in an environment where they are more easily neutralised, rationalised or confronted with reflective responses that do not destabilise the identity of the collective self. Conscious security responses arise from a collective state of mind whereby the subjective sense of security is accurately reflected in the objective state of security (thus, how safe one feels is accurately reflected in how safe one is).

In contrast, unconscious security responses are based upon a distorted sense of vulnerability that occurs when an individual or collective self is influenced by unconscious material: archetypes, destructive narratives, paranoia and compulsions (for example, to create defences, divisions, borders, adversaries and conflicts). Unconscious security is characterised by constant threat anticipation, threat management and the need for external control. This leads to security measures taken in reaction to subjective fears, possible threats and risk aversion. In the nation-state

---

[14] This point must be distinguished from the securitisation theory of the Copenhagen School, which is concerned with how certain issues or sectors are given primacy in policy-making when they are transformed into 'matters of security'. This is not necessarily a conscious process. Once an issue becomes 'securitised', then certain extraordinary policies can be legitimised in order to solve a perceived problem: Barry Buzan, Ole Wæver and Jaap de Wilde, *Security: A New Framework for Analysis* (Lynne Rienner Publishers, Covent Garden/Colorado, 1998) pp. 25–32.

[15] Anthony Giddens, *Modernity and Self-Identity: Self and Society in the Late Modern Age* (Polity Press, Cambridge, 1991); Jennifer Mitzen, 'Ontological Security in World Politics: State Identity and the Security Dilemma' (2006) 12 *European Journal of International Relations* 341.

context, it is based upon obsessive threat management and the continuous expenditure on weaponry. Unconscious security is based upon
certain assumptions about the nature of security; for example, that
vulnerability must be avoided at all costs; and that defence against
potential threats is the core of security policy.[16]

The difference between conscious and unconscious security responses
in two individuals is demonstrated by the following example. Imagine
two women lying in their beds at night, about to fall asleep. The two
women are next-door neighbours and are around the same age. They
both live alone in houses that are on a safe street, in a safe suburb, that is,
to a great extent crime-free. The first woman feels completely secure
believing that she is free from threats to her safety and wellbeing. This
woman's doors and windows are locked. She sleeps soundly. She is
objectively and subjectively secure. As a result of her congruent relationship between objective and subjective security, this woman experiences
conscious security.

Yet just next door, the other woman is paralysed by fears of intruders,
such that she is unable to sleep. Despite this woman's locked doors and
windows, her unconscious material is creating and sustaining irrational
fears. She is so scared during the night that the following day she invests
in a comprehensive security system for her house, complete with closed-
circuit television (CCTV) technology, security cameras inside and outside the house, and twenty-four hour a day monitoring by a security
company. The next night, while this woman rationally understands that
she is protected from threats to her physical safety, she now feels compelled to constantly watch the CCTV monitor in order to check any
intruders on her property. This frightened woman is objectively secure,
and yet her relationship to security remains unconscious. This is consistent with Zedner's observation that 'subjective security may be corre-
lated with objective security but may equally be quite unrelated to the
level of objective threat faced'.[17] In the example, the 'insecure' woman
has been compelled to reinforce her objective security because of her
unconscious response to subjective security. Yet her investments in
objective security have not been transformed into subjective security,
because the motivation to create objective security was based upon
unconscious compulsions.

---

[16] Karin Fierke, *Critical Approaches to International Security* (Polity Press, Cambridge/
Malden, MA, 2007) pp. 193–204.
[17] Zedner, *Security*, above n. 9, p. 16.

It is arguable that the same experience of conscious or unconscious security can be true for collectives. Imagine that in the above scenario, the two women are not individuals, but two nation-states that are geographically proximate, such as Turkey and Syria, Poland and Germany, or Japan and South Korea. It is self-evident that although these nation-states may be geographically close, each pair of nation-states has as different a conception of objective and subjective security as the two women described above. This is because both individuals and nation-states have different experiences of consciousness, with particular histories, personalities and relationships that shape their subjective sense of security. It is therefore crucial to acknowledge the conscious and unconscious dimensions of subjective security in individuals and collectives in order to understand their relationship to objective security. The next section of the chapter introduces a psycho-social approach to analyse the conscious and unconscious dynamics of the collective self.

## 4    Analysing the collective self

This chapter suggests that the collective self can usefully be analysed using a combination of sociological and psychological approaches. The sociological approach analyses the nature of 'collective consciousness' based on the sociology and social psychology of human consciousness model.[18] The psychological approach, on the other hand, analyses the nature of the 'collective unconscious' using analytical psychology, which was developed by Swiss psychiatrist Carl Jung. The Jungian structure of the psyche provides a multi-faceted treatment of unconscious material, giving language and substance to phenomena such as archetypes, cultural complexes, defence mechanisms and the significance of symbols and mythology. Therefore, this chapter proposes to combine both methods into a psycho-social Collective Self Framework, as shown in Figure 1.1.

### 4.1    Collective consciousness

The sociology of human consciousness model connects the consciousness of individuals with the consciousness possessed by collective

---

[18]    Burns and Engdahl, 'The Social Construction of Consciousness', above n. 1; Walter Buckley, 'Mind, Mead, and Mental Behaviorism' in Kian Kwan (ed.), *Individuality and Social Control: Essays in Honor of Tamotsu Shibutani* (JAI Press, Greenwich, 1996) p. 337; Norbert Wiley, *The Semiotic Self* (Polity Press, Cambridge, 1994).

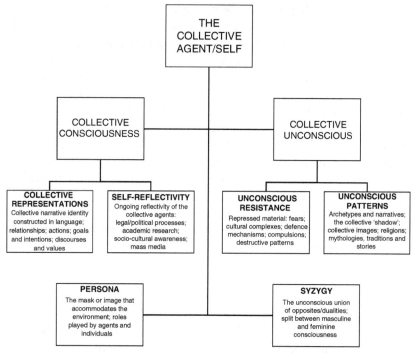

**Figure 1.1**   The Collective Self Framework

institutions and agents, as there is an interplay between the consciousness of individual selves and collective selves. Thus, according to the sociology of consciousness model, all human groups and institutions form a collective self, such as families, corporations, nation-states, international institutions and the global community, and these collective selves demonstrate evidence of consciousness.

In defining collective consciousness, Burns and Engdahl note that while 'consciousness is typically an umbrella term for a variety of different phenomena',[19] in this context it refers to 'socially based cognitions, representations and reflective processes, based on language, collective representations, and the capabilities of discursive reflection'.[20] Accordingly, the term 'collective consciousness' is used to encompass all collective processes

[19] Burns and Engdahl, 'The Social Construction of Consciousness', above n. 1, 68.
[20] *Ibid.* 69.

entailing reflection. This includes meta-awareness (being aware of possessing awareness), which is expressed through language-based processes of communication, representation and reflection. Observing, monitoring and judging 'self', among other things, are encoded in language, and are generated in conversations about collective and individual selves.[21]

In this model, there are two main features of collective consciousness: collective representations and self-reflectivity. Collective representations are 'socially constructed complexes of concepts and symbols that are applied to objects, events and situations, including the collective agent itself, other agents, and their interaction'.[22] These are essentially agreed upon narratives and descriptions for the group, and the medium of collective representations is predominantly language.[23] Examples of collective representations include scientific models, religious dogma or a set of political policies. Such representations ultimately form a 'narrative identity' for the collective because all of the individuals within the collective agree upon the shared discourses, values, norms, expectations and intentions. Even where individuals do not personally agree with particular collective representations, they generally abide by them, for example, laws and policies of a national government. A collective narrative identity is also closely related to the collective's relationship to security, because our view of ourselves 'directly affects how we view and construct reality'.[24] This extends to the way that collectives frame their security relationships. The narrative identity becomes so intrinsic to the collective identity that it is tied into cultural and social patterns, and therefore shapes the collective's subjective sense of its security.

The second feature of collective consciousness is self-reflectivity, which involves a 'collectivity conceptualising and reflecting on its values and goals, its conceptual framework, its organisation and its repertoire of strategies and practices'.[25] The important aspect of reflectivity is that it includes an assessment of the collective, and the capacity to possibly adapt or transform it. In modern societies, this type of reflectivity occurs through social science research, court and justice processes, mass media reporting and commentary, and political and legal discourse. Thus, the collective self is a conscious and dynamic entity in its own right. As Burns and Engdahl observe, '[a] collective monitors its

---

[21] *Ibid.* 68.    [22] *Ibid.* 75.    [23] *Ibid.*
[24] Gail Holland, *A Call for Connection: Solutions for Creating a Whole New Culture* (New World Library, California, 1998) p. 15.
[25] Burns and Engdahl, 'The Social Construction of Consciousness', above n. 1, 70.

activities, achievements and failures, and reflects on itself as a defined and on-going collective being'.[26]

According to the sociological model, collective selves are socially constructed and characterised by social realities, which consist of community, language-based communications, institutional and cultural arrangements, collective representations, self-conceptions and self-referentiality.[27] The collective consciousness is shaped by all of the individuals in the collective community, who in turn, participate in institutions and processes. These institutions include nation-states, international institutions (such as the United Nations), international courts (such as the International Court of Justice or the International Criminal Court), non-governmental organisations and various media outlets.

In sum, collective selves are conscious because they possess powers, make choices and act purposively. They have an identity, a name, particular values, 'defined social relationships, procedures, and the capacity to make collective choices, determine goals or intentions, and to take collective action'.[28] Tamotsu Shibutani refers to collectives as 'social worlds' in which each forms a universe 'where institutional arrangements or particular social organization facilitates anticipating the behaviour of others and in generating regularised responses'.[29] In this way, a collective self adopts consistency in its identity and behaviour.

The sociological model acknowledges that the collective self may have material that is unidentified or unrepresented (referred to as 'unconscious material' in analytical psychology). From a sociological perspective, 'unconscious' collective material is treated as that which is unrepresented and unnamed by the collective.[30] Burns and Engdahl write, '[u]nnamed objects and processes are experienced differently from those that are named and reflected upon within a cultural cognitive system',[31] and are linked to severe limitations or distortions in reflectivity. Therefore, the material that the collective is unable or unwilling to reflect upon becomes unconscious. This may occur for one or more of the following reasons:[32]

(1) there is a failure to 'acquire tools of language essential to learning and developing collective representations';

[26] Ibid.    [27] Ibid. 67.    [28] Ibid. 74.
[29] Tamotsu Shibutani, 'Reference Groups and Social Control' in Arnold Marshall Rose (ed.) *Human Behavior and Social Processes: An Interactionist Approach* (Houghton-Mifflin, Boston, 1961) pp. 128, 136-7.
[30] Burns and Engdahl, 'The Social Construction of Consciousness', above n. 1, 81.
[31] Ibid.    [32] Ibid.

(2) the agent is 'unable or unwilling to engage in reflective processes' as 'its activities are largely habitualised and beyond reflective attention, or its members are totally involved in practical activities and lack time and resources to devote to reflective processes'; or

(3) the 'agent experiences deep anxieties associated with, and a reluctance to engage in, self-reflective activities'.

As a result of being unable or unwilling to reflect on any given events or experiences, the unconscious material is stored by the collective and can manifest itself in unconscious security responses. It is clear that the sociology of human consciousness model is useful for analysing collective consciousness; however, it is limited in its treatment of unconscious collective material. The chapter now turns to Jungian theories in analytical psychology that give language and substance to explaining the role and nature of unconscious material.

## 4.2    The unconscious

As the Collective Self Framework above shows, the collective self is not limited to collective consciousness. If that were the case, there would be no dissonance between collective intentions and collective actions, or between objective and subjective security. The security environment would be transparent, and nation-states with objective security would not invest overwhelmingly in military expenditure or engage in provocative acts of aggression. It is clear that collective selves also possess unconscious material, which represents thoughts, behaviours or actions that are inconsistent with conscious attitudes or intentions.

In the Jungian framework, the first layer of the unconscious is the 'personal' or 'cultural' unconscious, which contains all of the psychic activities and contents that are incongruous with the conscious orientation. In the collective setting, the personal unconscious is best described as a cultural unconscious.[33] Jung explains the nature of the personal/cultural unconscious as consisting 'firstly of all those contents that became unconscious either because they lost their intensity and were forgotten or because consciousness was withdrawn from them (repression), and secondly of contents, some of them sense-impressions, which never had sufficient intensity to reach

---

[33] Joseph Henderson, *Cultural Attitudes in Psychological Perspective* (Inner City Books, Toronto, 1984).

consciousness but have somehow entered the psyche'.[34] According to Jungian theory, the unconscious can be played out in dreams, synchronicity, or recurring, unwanted patterns of drama or conflict. Recurring patterns of drama or conflict, to the extent that these are experienced by the collective through, for example, the public media, are particularly relevant in the global security environment. In Jungian terms, this layer of the unconscious is essentially the repository for repressed material deriving from personal or cultural biographical details.[35]

The unconscious is often mistakenly perceived as a threatening feature of our psyche, because as Edward Whitmont notes, '[w]hat is not consciously developed remains primitive and regressive and may constitute a threat'.[36] However, on this point, Jung notes that the unconscious is only threatening to the extent that it remains repressed:

> The unconscious is not a demoniacal monster, but a natural entity which, as far as moral sense, aesthetic taste, and intellectual judgment go, is completely neutral. It only becomes dangerous when our attitude to it is hopelessly wrong. To the degree that we repress it, its danger increases. But the moment the [psyche] begins to assimilate contents that were previously unconscious, its danger diminishes.[37]

Therefore the unconscious is not necessarily negative; it merely consists of all of the psychic contents that individuals and collectives have deemed to be worthless. As such, unconscious material is extremely potent, because it holds all of the material, whether positive or negative, that is repressed from consciousness. In the security context, vulnerability is often repressed in favour of control. Rather than nation-states exposing their fears and vulnerabilities to one another, there is psychic overcompensation through attempts to control all others and the security environment.

In addition to the personal/cultural unconscious, Jung was the first theorist to identify a second layer of the unconscious: the 'collective unconscious'. In introducing the collective unconscious, Jung wrote:

---

[34] Carl Jung, 'The Structure of the Psyche' in Sir Herbert Read, Michael Fordham and Gerhard Adler (eds.), *The Collected Works of C.G. Jung: 8* (R.F.C. Hull trans., Routledge and Kegan Paul/Princeton University Press, London/New York, 1927) paras. 283–342, 321.

[35] Christopher Hauke, 'The Unconscious: Personal and Collective' in Renos Papadopoulos (ed.) *The Handbook of Jungian Psychology: Theory, Practice and Applications* (Routledge, New York, 2006) pp. 54, 65.

[36] Edward Whitmont, *The Symbolic Quest: Basic Concepts of Analytical Psychology* (Princeton University Press, Princeton, NJ, 1969) p. 17.

[37] Carl Jung, *Dreams* (Routledge, London, [1974] 2001) p. 100.

> In addition to our immediate consciousness, which is of a thoroughly personal nature and which we believe to be the only empirical psyche ... there exists a second psychic system of a collective, universal and impersonal nature which is identical in all individuals ... It consists of pre-existent forms, the archetypes, which can only become conscious secondarily and which give definite form to certain psychic elements.[38]

Jung considered the collective unconscious to be acquired by an individual's participation in collective processes such as culture, society, language and religion. For Jung, the collective unconscious is:

> the part of the psyche that is not a personal acquisition and has not been acquired through personal experience. Its contents have never been in consciousness – they are not repressed or forgotten – and they are not acquired, but owe their existence to a form of heredity.[39]

Christopher Hauke observes:

> the collective unconscious was derived through aeons of repetition of cultural imagery and experience that, despite differences in detail, remains typically human with recognisable common qualities and meanings.[40]

Therefore, Jung argued that each individual contains layers of personal and collective unconscious. Each individual participates in collective selves and collective processes through their access to the collective unconscious. In the collective self, the individual is situated between the collective consciousness and collective unconscious, at 'the midpoint of psychic life'.[41] This chapter adopts the Jungian argument that collectives also possess both layers of the personal/cultural and the collective unconscious.[42] The nature of this unconscious material, for example, cultural complexes and archetypes, will be outlined as follows.

---

[38] Carl Jung, 'The Concept of the Collective Unconscious' in Sir Herbert Read, Michael Fordham and Gerhard Adler (eds.), *The Collected Works of C.G. Jung: 9* (R.F. C. Hull, trans., Routledge and Kegan Paul/Princeton University Press, London/New York, 1936) paras. 87, 90.

[39] Hauke, 'The Unconscious: Personal and Collective', above n. 35, pp. 66–7.

[40] *Ibid.* p. 59.

[41] Warren Colman, 'The Self' in Renos Papadopoulos (ed.) *The Handbook of Jungian Psychology: Theory, Practice and Applications* (Routledge, New York, 2006) pp. 153, 154.

[42] For an overview of this argument, see Nicholas Lewin, *Jung on War, Politics and Nazi Germany: Exploring the Theory of Archetypes and the Collective Unconscious* (Karnac Books, London, 2009).

## 4.2.1    Unconscious resistance

Like individuals, the first unconscious layer of collective selves 'contains information that has been forgotten or repressed but that might be made conscious again, under the right circumstances'.[43] If this material is not made conscious, this unresolved and repressed unconscious material forms complexes. Complexes are 'thoughts, feelings and memories that group themselves into dynamic clusters, which function like sub-personalities',[44] or 'split-off psychic fragments with a semi-autonomous existence'.[45]

In the last two decades, post-Jungian theorists have adapted Jung's theory of personal complexes, and used the theory to analyse the psychological nature of conflicts occurring in groups and cultures. Joseph Henderson carved out a cultural space between the personal and archetypal aspects of psychological experience, which he called 'the cultural level' of the psyche with social, aesthetic, spiritual and philosophical dimensions.[46] Thomas Singer and Samuel Kimbles then integrated these two theories (the complex and the cultural psyche) and formulated the 'cultural complex'.

Cultural complexes operate in a similar way to individual complexes, and are based on 'repetitive, historical group experiences which have taken root in the cultural unconscious of the group'.[47] These experiences are generally associated with 'trauma, discrimination, feelings of oppression and inferiority at the hands of another offending group'.[48] Examples of cultural complexes include the ongoing conflicts between Israel and Palestine, North and South Korea, and Russia and Chechnya. These conflicts are so engrained at the cultural level of the psyche that they become an element of cultural identity, even for children who may never have directly encountered members of the other culture.[49] The

---

[43] John Sommers-Flanagan and Rita Sommers-Flanagan, *Counseling and Psychotherapy Theories in Context and Practice: Skills, Strategies and Techniques* (John Wiley and Sons, Hoboken, NJ, 2004) p. 116.

[44] Jung, *Dreams*, above n. 37, p. 15.

[45] David Tacey, *How to Read Jung* (Granta Books, London, 2006) p. 3.

[46] Henderson, *Cultural Attitudes in Psychological Perspective*, above n. 33.

[47] Thomas Singer and Samuel L. Kimbles, 'Introduction' in Thomas Singer and Samuel Kimbles (eds.), *The Cultural Complex: Contemporary Jungian Perspectives on Psyche and Society* (Brunner-Routledge, New York, 2004) pp. 1, 7.

[48] *Ibid.*

[49] See generally, Daniel Bar-Tal, *Shared Beliefs in a Society: Social Psychological Analysis* (Sage Publications, London, 2000).

presence of cultural complexes leads to unconscious security because the unconscious complex dominates the collective response to security.

### 4.2.2    Unconscious patterns

The next layer of the unconscious – archetypes – includes the 'shadow'. Jung wrote:

> The shadow personifies everything that the subject refuses to acknowledge about himself and yet is always thrusting itself upon him directly or indirectly – for instance, inferior traits of character and other incompatible tendencies.[50]

Ann Casement observes that collective selves have shadows:

> Apart from the personal shadow there is also the collective shadow of which history provides many examples. The most notorious example from the twentieth century was the projection of collective shadow by the Nazis into the Jews, who could then be portrayed as inferior or evil beings to be exterminated ... The phenomenon of shadow also varies from one culture to another so that what is unacceptable in the United States may not be in Japan.[51]

The shadow plays a particularly important role in the unconscious of the collective self because it refers to the aspect of the psyche that directly contradicts the conscious identity.[52] Often collective selves will despise in other collective selves what they refuse to acknowledge in themselves. As such, 'an enemy' may in fact be a guide for the collective because the enemy represents what is unconscious for the collective.

The collective unconscious is also made up of archetypes, symbols and mythologies. Archetypes are a principal feature of the collective unconscious. Inspired by the Platonic concept of Forms, archetypes are primordial categories, common to all humankind, that are expressed through symbolic images. They are linked to innate modes of perception and describe universal symbols that evoke meanings of basic human experiences,[53] including the hero, the warrior and the leader.

---

[50] Jung, 'The Concept of the Collective Unconscious', above n. 38, para. 513.

[51] Ann Casement, 'The Shadow' in Renos Papadopoulos (ed.), *The Handbook of Jungian Psychology: Theory, Practice and Applications* (Routledge, New York, 2006) p. 96.

[52] Sommers-Flanagan and Sommers-Flanagan, *Counseling and Psychotherapy Theories in Context and Practice*, above n. 43, p. 118.

[53] Maggie Hyde and Michael McGuinness, *Introducing Jung* (Icon Books, Duxford, 1999) p. 172.

Jung believed that archetypes formed part of the collective unconscious and were manifested in myth, symbol, art and religion.[54]

Understanding the existence of archetypes can illuminate the global security environment. An example of how archetypes are central to security analysis can be found in the United States of America, which arguably possesses the 'moral leader' as one of its archetypes. This archetype has characterised the nature of security policy of the United States since its creation, and has conscious and unconscious aspects. It is argued that the 'shadow' of this archetype manifests itself as security missions that are couched in the language of moral leadership,[55] but are ultimately based upon self-interest; for example, the 2003 military operation in Iraq,[56] and the United States' support for Nicaraguan rebels in the late 1970s to early 1980s.[57]

From this psycho-social analysis of the collective self, it becomes evident why the global security environment is characterised by such complexity and tension. Each collective self comprises conscious aspects (collective representations and forms of reflectivity) as well as unconscious aspects (complexes, shadow material and archetypes). In addition, each collective self then directly interacts with other collective selves. The next section considers how the Collective Self Framework may be applied in the context of security institution building.

## 5    Creating conscious security

Based on the Collective Self Framework outlined above, it is argued that national security responses are based on socially constructed narratives in the nation-state collective self. As such, nation-state collective selves exist in a constant feedback loop between their cultural narratives (based on conscious and unconscious material) and their external circumstances (such as relationships, agreements, institutional memberships and threats). It is argued that for nation-states, the pursuit of security is linked to dynamic narratives about the nature of safety, risk and predictability.

---

[54] See Clive Hamilton, *The Freedom Paradox: Towards a Post-Secular Ethics* (Allen and Unwin, Sydney, 2008) p. 233.

[55] John Edwards, 'Reengaging with the World: A Return to Moral Leadership' (2007) 86 *Foreign Affairs* 19.

[56] See e.g., Thomas Franck, 'What Happens Now? The United Nations After Iraq' (2003) 97 *American Journal of International Law* 607.

[57] See e.g., James Meernik, 'United States Military Intervention and the Promotion of Democracy' (1996) 33 *Journal of Peace Research* 391.

These narratives are constantly being revised in relation to external circumstances. The Collective Self Framework therefore adequately explains the 'widening' of security beyond 'traditional security thinking',[58] to encompass non-traditional security issues such as human security, food security, economic security and environmental security.[59] This is because all forms of security arise from socially constructed narratives influenced by conscious and unconscious material.

Nation-state collective selves oscillate between conscious and unconscious security responses, which are reflected in their commitment to, and subsequent violation of, relevant rules of international security law such as Article 2(4) of the Charter of the United Nations and the Treaty on the Non-Proliferation of Nuclear Weapons.[60] Any acts that violate these obligations can be considered to constitute examples of unconscious security responses. The question then is how the collective self can create and strengthen conscious security, whilst reducing unconscious security responses.

The creation of conscious security begins by conducting a proactive assessment of how the collective self wants to be positioned in a security context, as opposed to reacting to each new security threat that arises. Interestingly, the nature and meaning of security is often taken as given at the nation-state level, and thus most collective selves only ever articulate and focus on what they are trying to avoid (risks and threats), rather than what they are consciously trying to attract. Creating conscious security involves a consideration of the meaning of security for that collective self.

The principle of territorial integrity offers an example of how nation-states can create conscious security. An unconscious response to a desire for territorial integrity is to fortify borders and invest in weaponry for defence, based on the assumption that other collective selves ('enemies') will want to invade or intervene. This unconscious security inevitably leads to what is commonly known as the security dilemma.[61] A conscious response to a desire for territorial integrity may be to

---

[58] Ken Booth, 'Security and Emancipation' (1991) 17 *Review of International Studies* 313, 318.
[59] See Hitoshi Nasu and Kim Rubenstein, Introduction.
[60] See Kalman Robertson, Chapter 9.
[61] This term was first used by John Herz in *Political Realism and Political Idealism* (University of Chicago Press, Chicago, IL, 1951). It maintains that both strong and weak national security policies can provoke other nations and disturb the balance of power.

establish positive relationships with surrounding nation-states and to create mutual guarantees of territorial integrity. In this scenario, conscious security engages in communication through institutions, rather than investing excessively in the latest weapons technology, because this is inconsistent and does not inspire trust.[62] As Robert Jervis observes, 'most means of self-protection simultaneously menace others'.[63] A communication-based approach is not weak; rather it draws on the honesty and trust of a community of nations to create greater security through openness and exchange. It is, perhaps, a feminine, rather than a masculine approach to collective security.[64] This concept of conscious security is also compatible with Ken Booth's conceptualisation of security, which observes that '[s]table security can only be achieved by people and groups if they do not deprive others of it; this can be achieved if security is conceived as a process of emancipation'.[65]

In a conscious response to security, there is no dissonance between how secure a collective is, and how secure a collective feels. Conscious security is based upon respect for human rights, mutual trust, transparency, reflectivity and communication. It is the by-product of sophisticated reflective processes that allow the collective to talk openly about 'its inner states and processes, and changes in these'.[66] However, this collective state of mind can only be accessed as a by-product of integration, and integration involves the processing of unconscious material in the self. Once unconscious material is brought to consciousness, it ceases to be experienced as a threat, or as something to be feared. Even unexpected traumas or conflicts are identified as opportunities for growth and maturation. It is thus argued that the realisation of conscious security depends upon the integration of unconscious material.

According to the Jungian model, the first step of this therapeutic process is becoming aware of unconscious material.[67] In order to achieve a state of conscious security, it is first necessary to bring consciousness to the unconscious material being contained in the collective

---

[62] Robert Jervis, *Perception and Misperception in International Politics* (Princeton University Press, Princeton, NJ, 1976) p. 63.

[63] *Ibid.*

[64] See generally, Annick T.R. Wibben, *Feminist Security Studies: A Narrative Approach* (Routledge, Abingdon, Oxford, NY, New York, 2011).

[65] Booth, 'Security and Emancipation', above n. 58, 319.

[66] Burns and Engdahl, 'The Social Construction of Consciousness', above n. 1, 70.

[67] This model is usefully outlined in Murray Stein, *The Principle of Individuation: Toward the Development of Human Consciousness* (Chiron Publications, Wilmette, IL, 2006) pp. 5–28.

self. This involves an identification of what material has been repressed (both internal and external to the collective self) which can be facilitated by institutionalised self-reflective decision-making processes. Such processes would require the collective self to explore its conscious orientation in contrast to its internal contradictions, archetypes and cultural complexes that have been consistently played out in the security environment. In this way, security threats are in fact reflected in the attitudes or behaviour of the collective self.

This awareness can arise from within the collective consciousness, or from observers outside the collective. For example, in the case of mass violence or racism in a country, the awareness of such unconscious material may only be identified by external actors such as other states, academics, media outlets, international institutions and non-government organisations. However, if a collective is unable to process and reflect on its unconscious material, it will remain trapped in a pattern of unconscious security responses.

## 6   Conclusion

This chapter has argued that it is optimal for the pursuit of security to be based upon conscious, rather than unconscious responses. In order to work towards conscious security, the chapter has provided a theoretical framework derived from the sociology of human consciousness model and theories from Jungian psychology, showing that collective selves are made up of collective consciousness, and unconscious material such as cultural complexes, shadow material and archetypes. Based on this framework, it was suggested that collective selves exist in a state of constant tension between their consciousness and their unconscious material. This conscious/unconscious dichotomy then manifests itself in conscious and unconscious security responses.

On the one hand, the 'conscious security' is based upon a congruent relationship between the objective and subjective states of security, where collective selves articulate their ideal state of security, and communicate this to their individual members and other collective selves. Conscious security involves the acknowledgement of vulnerability and strengths, and the creation of strong alliances and collective security. On the other hand, the 'unconscious security' is characterised by the compulsion to create defences, divisions, borders, adversaries and conflicts. It is based upon the assumptions that all other collective selves represent potential threats, and that the pursuit of security requires obsessive threat management and the accumulation of weaponry. Unconscious material manifests itself in behaviours, compulsions and attitudes that violate or contradict the conscious orientation, for example, any type of aggression or war, and the continuing oppression and exploitation of the environment, women, children and racial minorities.

This chapter concludes that institutionalised self-reflective decision-making processes can facilitate a collective self to habitually process its unconscious material. In this way, it will be closer to the realisation of conscious security. In forging a conscious path through the complex security environment, awareness of the collective self is paramount, and processing unconscious material must be an ongoing practice. The message of this chapter is that reflective awareness of the conscious and unconscious aspects of the collective self can transform the pursuit of security.

2

# 'You cannot hold two watermelons in one hand': gender justice and anti-state local security institutions in Pakistan and Afghanistan

BINA D'COSTA

## 1 Introduction

Although religion has been discussed through various disciplinary frameworks,[1] we do not know enough to explain security institutions and their negotiations with interest groups that employ specific religious and traditional ideologies. The 'global war on terror' has generated scholarship focusing extensively on extremist groups, the entrenched debates between fundamentalism and Islamism and also between fundamentalism and secularism. However, those discussions have also excluded women, except for their role as mothers of suicide bombers, members of extremist groups themselves and cultural bearers of their religion through clothing choice.[2]

Feminist scholars focusing on human rights have often used gender justice interchangeably with notions of 'gender equality', 'gender equity',

---

A Dari proverb used in Afghanistan. While it implies 'one cannot do too many things at once', during an interview with a senior Afghan security adviser, he noted that women's rights is not a priority at these early times of security sector reform in Afghanistan. D'Costa's interview with a senior Afghan security adviser conducted in Canberra, 2009.

[1] With specific focus on identity politics as the central tenet of theological study, religion and conflict, faith and peace building. See further, Romila Thaper, 'Imagined Religious Communities? Ancient History and the Modern Search for a Hindu Identity' (1989) 23 *Modern Asian Studies* 209; Valentine M. Moghadam, 'Revolution, Religion, and Gender Politics: Iran and Afghanistan Compared' (1999) 10(4) *Journal of Women's History* 172; Jacob Bercovitch and Ayse S. Kadayifci-Orellana, 'Religion and Mediation: The Role of Faith-based Actors in International Conflict Resolution' (2009) 14 *International Negotiation* 175; Tariq Modood, 'Moderate Secularism, Religion as Identity and Respect for Religion' (2010) 81 *Political Quarterly* 4.

[2] See generally, Lila Abu-Lughod (ed.), *Remaking Women: Feminist and Modernity in the Middle East* (Princeton University Press, Princeton, NJ, 1998).

'women's empowerment', 'women's rights' and 'women's security'. Those who have worked on the intersection of rights and development have also often conceptualised gender justice as a process that requires women to ensure that power-holders – whether in the household, the community, the market or the state – can be held to account for actions that limit women's access to resources or capacity to make choices on the grounds of gender.[3] Contemporary concepts of gender justice in women's human rights and critical security discourse encompass: human agency, rights and capabilities in political philosophy;[4] debates within politics, anthropology, sociology and law about democratisation, citizenship, constitutionalism, 'women's rights as human rights' and cosmopolitanism;[5] and in the field of law, judicial reform and practical matters of access to justice.[6] Feminist approaches enable a focus around a common issue (with many recognised variations) and ultimately, with the use of the political tools of lobbying, caucusing and networking.[7] While there have been attempts to create solidarity in feminist spaces, it should also be noted that there are criticisms within feminist circles against these attempts as elitist, imperialist or merely disconnected from the lives of most of the world's women.[8]

[3] Anne Marie Goetz, 'Gender Justice, Citizenship and Entitlements: Core Concepts, Central Debates and New Directions for Research' in Maitrayee Mukhopadhyay and Navsharan Singh (eds.), *Gender Justice, Citizenship and Development* (Zubaan, New Delhi, 2007) pp. 15, 30–1.

[4] Brooke A. Ackerly and Susan Moller Okin, 'Feminist Social Criticism and the International Movement for Women's Rights as Human Rights' in Ian Shapiro and Casiano Hacker-Cordón (eds.), *Democracy's Edges* (Cambridge University Press, Cambridge, 1999) p. 134; Martha C. Nussbaum, *Women and Human Development: The Capabilities Approach* (Cambridge University Press, Cambridge, 2000); Susan M. Okin, 'Equal Citizenship: Gender, Justice and Gender – An Unfinished Debate' (2004) 72 *Fordham Law Review* 1537.

[5] Hilary Charlesworth and Christine Chinkin, *The Boundaries of International Law: A Feminist Analysis* (Manchester University Press, Manchester, 2000); Niamh Reilly, *Women's Human Rights* (Polity Press, Malden, MA, 2009); Bina D'Costa and Katrina Lee Koo, 'The Politics of Voice: Feminist Security Studies and the Asia-Pacific' (2013) 3 *International Studies Perspective* 451.

[6] Rachel Sieder and John Andrew McNeish, *Gender Justice and Legal Pluralities: Latin American and African Perspectives* (Routledge, New York, 2013).

[7] Margaret E. Keck and Kathryn Sikkink, *Activists Beyond Borders: Advocacy Networks in International Politics* (Cornell University Press, Ithaca, NY, 1998); Brooke A. Ackerly and Bina D'Costa, 'Transnational Feminism and Women's Rights: Successes and Challenges of a Political Strategy' in Anne Marie Goetz (ed.), *Governing Women* (Routledge, New York, 2008) pp. 63–85.

[8] Gayatri Chakravorty Spivak, 'Can the Subaltern Speak?' in Cary Nelson and Lawrence Grossberg (eds.), *Marxism and the Interpretation of Culture* (University of Illinois Press, Urbana, IL, 1988) p. 271; Chandra Talpade Mohanty, 'Under Western Eyes: Feminist Scholarship and Colonial Discourses' in Chandra Talpade Mohanty,

Drawing on feminist insights and advocacy on identity politics and security, and peace/state/nation building literature, this chapter considers whether normative considerations ought to steer or constrain existing institutional processes, through which, taking into account contemporary security issues, institutional capability is strengthened. This is done with a particular focus on gender justice issues during the peace building process in Pakistan and Afghanistan. Through this enquiry, this chapter provides two observations. First, the pervasive militarisation of these societies where a mutant identity or identities of Western and religious/traditional forms of securitised behaviour, policies and new structures co-exist, reinforces gender biases. In this context religious minorities have been doubly marginalised and silenced by military intervention. In Pakistan, for example, a balancing and shifting of alliances has evolved into a competitive system of security institutions, which can be identified as anti-state local security institutions (ASLSIs). Second, top level advocacy in international agencies, which is viewed as modern, secular and 'Western', is becoming more distanced from, instead of grounded in, bottom-up gender activism that engages with issues of traditional, religious and 'local' identities. The example of Afghanistan elucidates that simply adding women in security institutions based on a top-down gender mainstreaming agenda,[9] does not necessarily ensure gender justice.

## 2   Gender violence, identity and security

Conflict zones are controlled not only through military force and economic regulation, but also through the reconstruction and management of identities. While multiple layers of identities such as racial, ethnic, religious and territorial co-exist, and gender operates through each of these, in peacetime most citizens of a nation-state identify themselves

---

Ann Russo and Lourdes Torres (eds.), *Third World Women and the Politics of Feminism* (Indiana University Press, Bloomington, IN, 1993) p. 52; Bina D'Costa, 'Marginalized Identity: New Frontiers of Research for IR?' in Brooke A. Ackerly, Maria Stern and Jacqui True (eds.), *Feminist Methodologies for International Relations* (Cambridge University Press, Cambridge, 2006) p. 129.

[9] The United Nations defines gender mainstreaming as 'a strategy for making women's as well as men's concerns and experiences an integral dimension of the design, implementation, monitoring and evaluation of policies and programs in all political, economic and societal spheres so that women and men benefit equally and inequality is not perpetuated': *Report of the Economic and Social Council*, UN Doc. A/52/3 (18 September 1997).

with a dominant political identity.[10] They have a sense of belonging to their nation, and for most, this identification supersedes all other identities that may exist. Although in everyday social practice family, social networks and communities may come first, in times of national crisis and conflicts the national identity often has the power to take precedence over everything else.[11]

Relevant to the discussion in this chapter is religious identity politics. The identity constructed to form a religious community is capable of superseding other identity dissimilarities. In ancient Israel, common religion allowed group survival, whereas in modern history, India was partitioned based on religion. For Hobsbawm, the relationship between religious and national identity is 'extremely opaque'.[12] The Islamic nation (the Ummah) in Iran, as well as Northern Ireland and Lebanon, are some examples of national communities with strong religious identity components. Similarly, Emile Durkheim observed that there was no real distinction between religion and nationality, and that religion maintained the solidarity of the national community. He argued that 'the idea of society is the soul of religion',[13] and saw 'in the Divinity only society transfigured and symbolically expressed'.[14] Religion was understood by Durkheim to stem not only from social life, but also to be a system of ideas that allowed individuals to identify themselves as a group within the society to which they belonged and their relationship to it.[15] In many contemporary conflicts, for example in Kashmir, Sri Lanka, the former Yugoslavia, Pakistan and Afghanistan, it is difficult to separate religious identity and its overlapping connection with political movements.

Both in the Global South and the North, practising religious women and men are deeply committed to the rituals and rites of their religion. For religious communities (and perhaps more for minority communities) in the Global South, participation in religious life through congregational worship, discussion of religious texts and social events

---

[10] Mark Nolan and Kim Rubenstein, 'Citizenship and Identity in Diverse Societies' (2009) XV *Humanities Research* 29.

[11] See Bina D'Costa, *Nationbuilding, Gender and War Crimes in South Asia* (Routledge, London, 2011) ch. 1.

[12] E.J. Hobsbawm, *Nations and Nationalism Since 1780: Programme, Myth and Reality* (Cambridge University Press, Cambridge, 1990) p. 71.

[13] Emile Durkheim, *The Elementary Forms of Religious Life* (Free Press, New York, [1912] 1947) p. 419.

[14] Emile Durkheim, 'The Determination of Moral Facts' in *Sociology and Philosophy* (D.F. Pocock, trans., Free Press, New York, [1906] 1974) p. 52.

[15] D'Costa, *Nationbuilding, Gender and War Crimes in South Asia*, above n. 11, p. 15.

surrounding religious and cultural ceremonies has a special meaning and social significance. Gathering in religious spaces therefore is not only an engagement with God, but rather a confirmation of belonging to a community. If these individuals are made to feel unequal in religious space it casts them as second-class citizens. In Muslim society, while women may be part of the religious majority, they may find themselves equal in the larger national/secular society and unequal in their own communal space.

Through a gender lens, feminist approaches to identity politics explore the nexus of religion, class, race, tradition and caste (in some cases) that are at the core of power struggles. For many gender activists and advocates in the Global South, particularly in South Asia, 'feminist' is a politically problematic label evoking such associations as man hater, home wrecker, colonialist, imperialist, Western influenced, national or cultural traitor, and so on – associations that they do not like or that make their life more difficult. Regardless of how they identify themselves, feminist and women's activists share a conceptual understanding that it is important to put women's interests and experiences of injustice on the political agenda and to treat knowledge from women's experiences as analytically important when addressing important political, economic and social issues and injustices. Consequently, whether or not they are feminist, whether or not they are women, whether or not they use a rights-based approach, feminists and activists for women share a need for an integrated and structural gender analysis of political, economic and social conditions and processes, with a view to political, economic and social fairness.[16] Many activists do not have as developed a critique of these processes (nor do many feminist scholars); others can give experience-based accounts of gendered racism that might help the feminist scholar who is inclined to disaggregate oppression on axes of race, class and gender (for example) to rethink her approach.[17] All of these perspectives are respected informants in this chapter and together they illustrate the use and value of their collective view of rights as indivisible and humans' experiences as interrelated.

Development, rights and security discourses are intimately connected. In Pakistan and Afghanistan, demands for women's rights and justice generate certain anxieties about power relations. While international and local institutions employ gender as an analytical and policy tool to bring

---

[16] Ackerly and D'Costa, 'Transnational Feminism and Women's Rights', above n. 7.
[17] *Ibid.* 64.

both women's and men's rights-based issues into a variety of agendas, the compromises that have had to be made on the ground also have had some negative impacts on women's rights. Home-based critics such as the local media, religious elite and political leaders, have discredited conversations that began with women's rights as Western ideas corrupting and/or breaking down traditional norms and structures.[18] As a response, a new kind of engagement has emerged where gender tools do not necessarily employ feminist insights from feminist tools and methods. This new strategy of both local and international organisations does not necessarily analyse various power struggles, and has remained vague about women's empowerment as a key objective. The strategy uses other socially, culturally and politically acceptable objectives injected into education, health, livelihood programmes for communities and within the legal and political reforms of the states. One detrimental outcome of these compromises and strategies is that many projects claiming to be gender sensitive are not only explicitly un-feminist but are gender-biased. As such, while feminist projects are gender-sensitive, not all gender projects are necessarily feminist.

At the international level, various gender-sensitive legal and technical mechanisms within the United Nations (UN) have endeavoured to respond to the gendered impacts of armed conflicts. Following decades of activism and advocacy by women's lobbies and non-governmental organisations, in October 2000 the UN Security Council adopted Resolution 1325 on women, peace and security, mandating women's direct participation in security matters.[19] Although Barrow argues that it is not 'radical enough to be used as a transformative gender mainstreaming tool',[20] this Resolution is ground-breaking in initiating a process that ensures women's equal representation in security institutions and decision-making bodies. Resolution 1325 and Resolution 1820, subsequently adopted in 2008, both affirm women's roles in the prevention and resolution of conflicts, and also call for special measures to protect women and girls from gender-based violence, especially rape and other forms of sexual abuse.[21] They call for full and equal participation of women at all levels in issues ranging from early conflict

---

[18] The author conducted interviews with Pakistani and Afghan women's rights activists in Pakistan, June 2013.

[19] SC Res. 1325 (31 October 2000).

[20] Amy Barrow, '"[It's] Like a Rubber Band": Assessing UNSCR 1325 as a Gender Mainstreaming Process' (2009) 5 *International Journal of Law in Context* 51.

[21] SC Res. 1325 (31 October 2000) para. 10; SC Res. 1820 (19 June 2008) paras 3 and 10.

prevention to post-conflict reconstruction, peace and security.[22] Resolutions 1325 and 1820 were later followed by five additional Resolutions (1888, 1889, 1960, 2106 and 2122). Together, they frame the women, peace and security agenda. The universal norms of gender equality and gender justice, enshrined in the Convention on the Elimination of All Forms of Discrimination Against Women (CEDAW),[23] Resolution 1325 and subsequent Resolutions, are powerful instruments for advancing women's rights especially when used in combination with each other.

These universal instruments also take into account culturally relevant measures in ensuring peace and security. As such, female peacekeepers have been deployed as role models in the host community to empower local women and improve their access to gender justice. The first example of women's involvement in peace missions was the UN Transition Assistance Group, which operated in Namibia from 1989 to 1990.[24] While there has not yet been any clear recruitment and participation strategy, the presence of blue-helmeted women in conflict zones is a significant gender-mainstreaming measure. A force of 125 female police officers from India's Central Reserve Police Force is currently deployed in Liberia as UN peacekeepers to assist in the nation's recovery from years of civil war.[25] As Liora Sion argues, however, peacekeeping still reproduces the traditional hyper-masculine gender roles in missions,[26] with insufficient attention to gender-sensitive institutional responses. The recruitment of former military personnel for humanitarian and peacekeeping work, including within policy and programme sectors, and the 'cultural inappropriateness' argument of integrating gender on the ground,[27] have arguably contributed to the ineffectiveness of UN institutions that deal with women's security and gender justice.

[22]  SC Res. 1325 (31 October 2000) para. 2; SC Res. 1820 (19 June 2008) para. 12.
[23]  Opened for signature 18 December 1979, 1249 UNTS 13 (entered into force 3 September 1981).
[24]  Janet Beilstein, 'The Expanding Role of Women in United Nations Peacekeeping' in Lois Ann Lorentzen and Jennifer Turpin (eds.), *The Women and War Reader* (New York University Press, New York, 1988) pp. 140, 141.
[25]  D'Costa, *Nationbuilding, Gender and War Crimes in South Asia*, above n. 11, p. 7.
[26]  Liora Sion, 'Peacekeeping and the Gender Regime: Dutch Female Peacekeepers in Bosnia and Kosovo' (2008) 37 *Journal of Contemporary Ethnography* 561, 567.
[27]  Angela Raven-Roberts, 'Gender Mainstreaming in United Nations Peacekeeping Operations: Talking the Talk; Tripping over the Walk' in Dyan Mazurana and Angela Raven-Roberts (eds.), *Gender, Conflict and Peacekeeping* (Rowman and Littlefield, Lanham, MD, 2005) pp. 43–61.

### 3   Building peace, a nation and a state?

The second theoretical view this chapter draws on is the scholarship on state building, nation building and peace building. This is important in the context of the two case studies examined later in this chapter as the international community and local institutions have been involved heavily over the last few decades in various peace building and state building efforts in both Pakistan and Afghanistan. Peace building in the UN discourse originally had a strong post-conflict connotation, fitting at the end of a perceived continuum from conflict prevention to peace building (presumably, if conflict prevention failed and a violent conflict erupted).[28] In this sense it connoted an attempt to 'identify and support structures which will tend to consolidate peace' including 'reforming or strengthening governmental institutions',[29] which was later seen as relating to 'the creation of structures for the institutionalisation of peace'.[30] While Kofi Annan defined peace building as 'actions undertaken at the end of a conflict to consolidate peace and prevent a recurrence of armed confrontation',[31] the use and understanding of the term within the UN system has more recently broadened, with its application to activities across the whole spectrum of situations, not merely post-conflict situations.[32] The UN Peacebuilding Commission's mandate is thus not confined to post-conflict situations, but incorporates a preventative dimension (although it requires a host state's invitation or Security Council authorisation to engage in any country situation).

Scholars and politicians in the United States (US) tend to use nation building to refer to what many other observers would refer to as 'state building' or 'peace building' tasks.[33] Their use of the term has had a distinct connection to the use of armed force in building state capacity, especially

---

[28] For the author's discussion on this point, see Bina D'Costa and Jo Ford, *Terminology Matters: Peacebuilding, Statebuilding and Nationbuilding* (Center for International Governance and Justice, Canberra, 2009), available at http://regnet.anu.edu.au/publications/terminology-matters-statebuilding-nationbuilding-and-peacebuilding.

[29] *An Agenda for Peace*, UN Doc. A/47/277-S/24111 (17 June 1992) para. 55.

[30] *Supplement to an Agenda for Peace*, UN Doc. A/50/60-S/1995/1 (25 January 1995) para. 49. See generally, Paul Diehl, *Peace Operations* (Polity, Cambridge, 2008) pp. 3–11.

[31] *The Causes of Conflict and the Promotion of Durable Peace and Sustainable Development in Africa*, UN Doc. A/52/871-S/1998/318 (13 April 1998) para. 63.

[32] Charles T. Call, 'Ending Wars, Building States' in Charles T. Call with Vanessa Wyeth (eds.), *Building States to Build Peace* (International Peace Institute and Lynne Reinner, Boulder, CO, 2008) pp. 1, 5.

[33] D'Costa and Ford, *Terminology Matters*, above n. 28, p. 31.

state security capacity, so that foreign 'nation building' troops can 'exit'.[34] Nation building in this sense connotes armed intervention (including the pre-emptive pursuit of security interests) to administer and then consolidate regime change and a 'new order'. For instance, the RAND Corporation, the US-based think tank, defines nation building as 'the use of armed force in the aftermath of a conflict to promote a durable peace and representative governance structure'.[35] These references to nation building actually mean state building, which through institutional practices produces a masculine, interventionist process of building the institutions and infrastructure of states after conflict.

In general, contemporary discourses outside the US avoid 'nation building' as a project for the international community, on the assumption that nation building is something for 'locals' to do, in tandem with state building. For example, Simon Chesterman suggests that nation building is a 'broad, vague, and often pejorative' term,[36] which refers to various domestic policies to inspire, unite or stimulate the people towards what Benedict Anderson terms as an 'imagined community'.[37] Nation building, therefore, should be considered an internal organic process where a society contests, considers, reaches consensus on and consolidates a national identity towards which the society is oriented.[38] While it can be stimulated or affected by foreign action, it is inherently an internal process.[39] In this sense, only the political communities can build a nation, and it is they who have exclusive ownership over the nation building process. While the process of national adaptation is ongoing and shaped by various events, the idea of nation building is intrinsically tied with significant historical

---

[34] See e.g., Kate Jenkins and William Plowden, *Governance and Nationbuilding: The Failure of International Intervention* (Edward Elgar, Cheltenham, 2006); James Dobbins *et al.*, *America's Role in Nation-Building: From Germany to Iraq* (RAND Corporation, Santa Monica, CA, 2003).

[35] This usage would not conceive of nation building as distinct from peace building or state building.

[36] Simon Chesterman, *You, the People* (Oxford University Press, Oxford, 2004) p. 4.

[37] Benedict Anderson, *Imagined Communities* (Verso Books, London, 1991).

[38] D'Costa and Ford, *Terminology Matters*, above n. 28, p. 33.

[39] Organization for Economic Cooperation and Development (OECD), 'Concepts and Dilemmas of State Building in Fragile Situations: From Fragility to Resilience' (2008) 9(3) *OECD Journal on Development* 61. State building findings take care to distinguish nation building from state building. While it acknowledges that the two processes may be mutually enforcing, nation building is seen as 'the process of building a sense of common national identity' and is not a process over which state authorities have a monopoly since rebel movements are often engaged in attempted nation building.

'circuit-breaking' moments, whereby a new national group is discernible and, suddenly, discerns itself from the old one.

There is also a need to critically examine international and national interventions and policy-making in relation to the host of post-Cold War 'new wars' – generally intra-state civil conflicts involving regional dynamics, and some Cold War legacies.[40] The general consensus, among policy-makers and scholars themselves building on the legacy of multilateral conflict management experiences post-1945, would appear to be that the likelihood, duration, severity or recurrence of violent conflict can be decreased by deliberate external interventions of some sort.[41]

Another contextual point may be the link that has increasingly been drawn or discerned between the 'development' and 'security' discourses,[42] and in particular the perceived link between state weakness or failure, and insecurity.[43] In the scholarship from the Global North, there is a tendency to focus on tangible interventions (with a visible foreign presence) as 'state building' to the neglect of more pervasive but less obvious channels of power and influence by external actors, for example, through political and economic frameworks. These power relations might have far more influence on the shape and capacity of the state than programmed state building activities. The term 'state builders' calls to mind groups of UN humanitarian actors, peace-keepers or coalition troops undertaking various implementation, advisory or assistance tasks 'in country'. While this is what the literature generally concentrates on, the state building discourse overlooks the fact that the real 'state shapers' might be those in more remote, less visible but hugely influential roles in how the state is built or broken. As will be discussed in the two case studies below, the local power-brokers in Pakistan and Afghanistan are the Pakistani and Afghan Taliban factions and the religious and traditional interest groups who have excessive powers in the absence of strong and stable state institutions in remote areas.

---

[40] Mary Kaldor, *New and Old Wars: Organised Violence in a Global Era* (Polity, Cambridge, 1999).

[41] For a review of literature, see D'Costa and Ford, *Terminology Matters*, above n. 28, p. 33.

[42] See e.g., Mark Duffield, *Global Governance and the New Wars: The Merging of Development and Security* (Zed Books, New York, 2001).

[43] See e.g., Roland Paris, *At War's End: Building Peace After Civil Conflict* (Cambridge University Press, Cambridge, 2004); Simon Chesterman, Michael Ignatieff and Ramesh Thakur (eds.), *Making States Work: State Failure and the Crisis of Governance* (United Nations University Press, New York, 2005).

There is also a suggestion in the scholarship of homogeneity among states,[44] where 'state building' as a concept conveys an approach viewing the state as overwhelmingly the solution, rather than the problem.[45] In many cases, however, the problem is that the state (even if it is manifested in informal or unrecognised 'institutions') is historically too strong, rather than too weak, or is too strong in some areas and too weak in others, or perhaps that there is not enough relative power in local government or in non-state institutions in society. The project of state building and peace building is often premised upon certain institutional forms. Kosovo and East Timor after 1999 might be examples of this quite literal building of a new state, which, as in most cases of external involvement, means institution building: the formation of new institutions or strengthening existing ones within what is otherwise a nominal state.

However, Western conceptions of the state do not take into account the idea that state institutions may not be desirable options for some political communities.[46] The embedded anomalies between Western conceptions of the state and 'other' ideas of how a political entity may form reinforce structural problems in state building, if it is understood as a nation building process. While the term is not so blunt that 'state building' cannot encompass reforming power balances in society, it is possible that the approach conveys a fixed notion about formal state institutions, to the neglect of the other possible forms of governance involving extra-state or sub-state entities or traditions, which are typically seen to be the weakness of the state in tribal and remote regions of Pakistan and Afghanistan.

Through humanitarian intervention and state building policies by the international community, it is possible to contribute to the stability of a particular state in ways that encourage various communities of that state to construct a shared identity. However, this is not a homogeneous construction; nor is it based on one singular identity and common interest, but rather on a plurality of identities that co-exist despite intermittent conflicts. This shared identity assumes that various communities have a responsibility towards each other, binding them within

---

[44] Francis Fukuyama, *State-Building: Governance and World Order in the 21st Century* (Cornell University Press, Ithaca, NY, 2004).
[45] For a summary of definitional aspects of state building, see generally, Call, 'Ending Wars, Building States', above n. 32, pp. 8–16.
[46] The OECD has in the present context acknowledged that state building is 'rooted in the history of a state': OECD, *State Building in Situations of Fragility* (August 2008), available at www.oecd.org/development/incaf/41212290.pdf.

one overarching political community of a state.[47] Political conflicts, which may be violent, also 'harden' identities,[48] and as such nation building could emancipate some identity communities and trap or exclude others, such as gender identities or the identities of various indigenous groups.[49] Nation building therefore needs to be understood as a more complex and long-term sociological and political process than the term 'state building' would suggest. The endogenous, organic, cultural, historically situated and emotive aspects of nation building express the power relations within a society – many of them resistant to external intervention. Therefore, it is imperative to consider nationalism and national movements that further explore the value of shared myths, symbols, anthems and histories in various ways, with an eye to creating the foundations for a common identity formation for political communities.[50]

Nationalism-focused feminist literature from the Global North provides valuable insights and an analytical point of departure for scholars of the South, for whom experiences of colonialism, discrimination, suppression of rights and various kinds of structural violence (such as poverty and patriarchy) have shaped the understanding of gender. On the other hand, the analysis has not paid sufficient attention to women's experiences of peace/nation/state building processes. Despite claims of following democratic principles, cultural norms have often taken precedence over ensuring gender-sensitive security practices on the ground. The following section explores women's experiences of realising their own security in the context of nation building beneath the gaze of the 'global war on terror'.

## 4   Pakistan: buying peace through unholy alliances

The first case study of Pakistan is based on the premise that national identity and nation building are not static processes. Rather, they emerge

---

[47] An overarching political community also exists beyond the state, of course. Indeed, in the globalised era, the nation-state may not even be a desirable outcome for many communities for whom transnational loyalties and interests exist.

[48] Valentine Moghadam, *Globalizing Women: Transnational Feminist Network* (JHU Press, Washington, DC, 2005) p. 63.

[49] John Braithwaite and Bina D'Costa, *Cascades of Violence: The Chittagong Hill Tracts, Kashmir and Pakistan*, Peacebuilding Compared Working Paper (The Australian National University, Canberra, 2012), available at http://regnet.anu.edu.au/sites/default/files/Cascades_of_Violence_in_Bangladesh_13thdecember_0.pdf.

[50] D'Costa, *Nationbuilding, Gender and War Crimes in South Asia*, above n. 11, p. 15.

through naturalised methods cultivated by various state institutions such as schooling, cultural practices, sports, religious ceremonies and state rituals. The persistent militarisation of Pakistan, especially in its north-western regions in Khyber-Pakhtunkwa and Federally Administered Tribal Areas (FATA), have intensified identity conflicts and have reinforced gender biases.

Religious identity is deeply embedded in Pakistan's national identity as the state was carved out of India in 1947 on the basis of its distinct Islamic identity.[51] Religion has a more diffuse presence in Pakistan, as politicians, the military elite and other powerful actors demonstrate their political legitimacy by stressing their personal religiosity. Commentators of Pakistan's security refer to a nexus between 'mullah'[52] and the military that implies a mutually symbiotic relationship between the religious elite and the military elite. Asaf Husain reflected on this as early as in 1979 stating that:

> the military-state relation conceptualises a dialectical relationship between Islam, Pakistan and the military. Without Islam, Pakistan would not have been able to come into existence; without Pakistan the military would not be able to exist; and without the military, Islam and Pakistan would be threatened. In perpetuating such a state, the military was perpetuating Islam.[53]

As will be explained below, the mullah-military nexus has been replaced by an identity war between the Pakistani state still struggling with its nation building and state building policies, and the anti-state actors not concerned with the idea of a unified national state. In Pakistan's north-western regions, following Pakistan's troop deployment as its contribution to the global war on terror, the armed conflict began on 16 March 2004. It is estimated that over 50,000 members of Pakistan's security forces are fighting Taliban militants in Swat valley alone. In the author's interviews human rights activists and journalists from the region stress that this massive militarisation only adds to the community's fear and insecurity generated by Taliban violence.[54]

The Pakistani Taliban is perhaps most infamously known in the Global North for its attack on Malala Yousafzai in October 2012. Maulana Sufi

---

[51] For details on India's Partition, see *ibid.* ch. 3.
[52] Generally referred to as a Muslim man educated in Islamic theology and sacred law. In South Asia, it is commonly used to describe local Islamic clerics or mosque leaders.
[53] Asaf Hussain, *Elite Politics in an Ideological State: The Case of Pakistan* (Dawson, Folkestone, 1979) p. 133.
[54] D'Costa's interviews carried out in Pakistan, 2009 and 2013.

Muhammad founded Tehrik-e-Nifaz-e-Shariat-e-Muhammadi (TNSM; Movement for the Enforcement of Muhammadan Law) in 1992. He was in prison until 2008, during which time Maulana Fazlullah,[55] his son-in-law, became the leader, and later ordered the assassination of Malala Yousafzai. Mufti Munir Shakir founded Lashker-e-Islam (LeI) in 2004,[56] and Baitullah Mehsud united thirteen different groups and formed the Tehrik-i-Taliban Pakistan (TTP), alternatively referred to as Pakistani Taliban in December 2007.[57] Following the death of the current leader, Hakimullah Mehsud,[58] Maulana Fazlullah became the head of the Pakistani Taliban in November 2013. TNSM and TTP have set and enforced their own regulations, which have had a drastic impact on cultural expressions, education, health sectors, and most importantly on women's rights. To buy peace and appease a war weary army, the Pakistani government had to give way to the Pakistani Taliban in the northwest. As a precondition of the peace accord with the Taliban, Pakistan promulgated the Nizam-e-Adal Regulation on 16 April 2009. On 19 April 2009, while addressing a large gathering, Maulana Sufi Muhammad of the TNSM stated that after twenty years of struggle his movement had succeeded in implementing pure Islamic law in Malakand. This controversial Shariah law was promulgated in Swat, including six other districts of Malakand Division, in return for peace.[59] The US reportedly supported the 'Sharia law for peace' deal as an attempt to create a division between the Pakistani Taliban and the Al-Qaeda-linked Taliban.[60]

---

[55] Maulana Fazlullah is known as the radio mullah for starting an illegal local FM radio station in the Swat Valley. In 2006 and 2007, he became very popular with the local women who donated cash and jewellery when he broadcast his intention to establish a madrassa in Mamdheri, where the station was based. While at the beginning his broadcasts were not taken so seriously, after a ban on women visiting markets and girls' education, which were complied with by the local communities either out of fear or of support, mainstream civil society began to pay notice.

[56] LeI is currently headed by Haji Amir Mangal Bhagh. There are unverified reports that the group may have changed its name to Jaish-e-Islami.

[57] Baitullah Mehsud was severely injured by a US drone attack in South Waziristan and later died.

[58] Hakimullah Mehsud, a feared commander of the Pakistani Taliban, became the chief in 2009 and was killed in another drone attack on 1 November 2013.

[59] Malakand Division comprises seven districts: Malakand Protected Area, Swat, Shangla, Buner, Upper Dir, Lower Dir and Chitral. Swat, Buner, Upper Dir and Lower Dir have been worst hit by drone strikes.

[60] 'US privately backs Pakistan's "Sharia Law for Peace" deal with Taliban', *Daily Telegraph*, available at www.telegraph.co.uk/news/worldnews/asia/pakistan/4681480/US-privately-backs-Pakistans-Sharia-law-for-peace-deal-with-Taliban.html.

In Pakistan's northwestern regions, Khyber Pukhtunkhwa and FATA, the mullah-military nexus has seen compromises made to bring 'stability' to the region. Zahid Hussain, a journalist, in his book *Scorpion's Tail*, provides some accounts of the peace accord and the mullah-military nexus, relevant to this chapter.[61] He notes that the accord had been supported especially strongly by the military and that the government did not consider this as a sign of weakness but rather what people of the region wanted.[62]

As a backdrop to the signing of the peace accord with the Pakistani Taliban, the video of Chand Bibi, a seventeen-year-old adolescent mother being flogged in Kala Killay village of the Kabal sub-division, provoked national outrage in Pakistan in March 2009,[63] with critics pointing out the state's failure, unwillingness and inability to regulate or provide security of life and liberty for women. In fact, the Pakistani Taliban relied on these punitive practices against women to enforce their legitimacy by successfully bargaining with the state actors, who become their allies in the name of pragmatism and 'transition to peace'.[64] While Chand Bibi's ordeal was not the only case of public punishment of women in Pakistan, due to the wide social media coverage there was an immediate reaction. President Asif Ali Zardari and Prime Minister Yousuf Raza Gilani ordered an investigation into the case, and Chief Justice Iftikhar Muhammad Chaudhry ordered the settlement of the matter before an eight-member larger bench of the Supreme Court under article 184(3) of the Constitution.[65] Similar to this case, reports of other publicised gender crimes have been perceived by urban media consumers as 'evil deeds' committed by feudal factions and 'crude', 'primitive' patriarchal tribesmen.

---

[61]  Zahid Hussain, *The Scorpion's Tails* (Simon & Schuster Inc., New York, 2010) pp. 145–55.

[62]  *Ibid.* 152. Before the accord was signed there were roughly 3,000 Taliban fighters. However, by March 2009 the number in the valley was believed to be 6,000 to 8,000.

[63]  The National Child Policy, adopted in 2006, recognises the right of the child to protection from corporal punishment but there is no prohibition in law. Provisions against violence and abuse in the Penal Code, the Punjab Destitute and Neglected Children Act, the Sindh Children Act, the Guardians and Wards Act, and the Code of Criminal Procedure are not interpreted as prohibiting corporal punishment for children.

[64]  For a comparative analysis on Afghanistan, see Jonathan Goodhand and Mark Sedra, 'Bribes or Bargains? Peace Conditionalities and "Post-Conflict" Reconstruction in Afghanistan' (2007) 14 *International Peacekeeping* 41.

[65]  'Pak CJ Takes Notice of Swat Girl Flogging', *Free Library*, 4 April 2009, available at www. thefreelibrary.com/Pak+CJ+takes+notice+of+Swat+girl+flogging.-a0199262393.

While honour crimes and anti-women jirga decisions focus on culture, tradition and patriarchal practices, the nature of the punishment in Swat discussed above reveals that the focus of the debate is on religion. It is also about the public nature of the punishment. In reality, all these cases are still about women as identity markers in matters of 'honour' and the regulation of women's sexuality and mobility. When the video went viral, senior politicians denied that such an incident ever occurred. Pakistan People's Party publicly stated that the Malakand Division needed to return to peace at all costs, that non-governmental organisations should refrain from exploiting the 'flogging issue', that they were causing more damage to Pakistan than the perpetrators of the event. Similarly, Awami National Party, leading the North-West Frontier Province (NWFP) coalition government, made an official statement that a 'third party' was trying to derail the 'peace for Sharia' deal.

Scholarship on security, especially on what is now referred to as 'new' security threats since the end of the Cold War, considers the role of security institutions with regard to region specific dynamics, security sector reform and security governance.[66] In the Pakistani security architecture what we see is a balancing and shifting of alliances that have evolved into a competitive system of security institutions. Whereas the formal state security institutions with a variety of support from international security institutions and alliances are serving as the recognised protector of the Pakistani state's security, the militants have also formed their exclusive, anti-state security institutions fighting against 'Western imperialism' and defending Islam, which could be perceived as 'primitive' alliances in Western discourse. These anti-state security institutions are legitimised through interpretations of religious texts, norms and restrictions; forming alliances within and across national borders, which are negotiated and endorsed by other interest groups to promote particular political agendas and also create a competing security system. These institutions are also more organised than loosely defined militant networks, as these govern society by causing and controlling insecurity and succeed in persuading the state in proclaiming new regulations and policies.

As such, the Pakistani Taliban factions could be characterised as ASLSIs. Instead of analysing these interest groups as just 'terrorist organisations', 'militants' and as comprising only small fractions of

---

[66] See Hitoshi Nasu and Kim Rubenstein, Introduction.

the Pakistani political actors, it is useful to recognise these as ASLSIs. In Pakistan they mobilise in the name of religion. These ASLSIs should not be regarded as faith-based security institutions because the binary labelling assumes that state-based and multilateral security institutions exclude policies and practices in accordance with a variety of religious norms and traditions. In addition, categorising these as faith-based ASLSIs inevitably legitimises the position of these groups as protectors of a particular religion, in this case Islam. While the ASLSIs invoke Islam as discussed below, they do so by contributing to gendered political violence in Pakistan. These anti-state security institutions are founded by actors who either construe or misconstrue scriptures, evoke the rhetoric of religious norms and traditions, control their armed forces, enforce or advocate religious laws and succeed in gaining at least some public support and therefore achieving legitimacy in their territories.

These institutions use neither development nor rights discourse to legitimise their actions, but essentially securitise both development and rights-based sectors by bringing every aspect of everyday lives under the scrutiny of security. For example, the ASLSIs have attacked education institutions and girls schools.[67] Maulana Fazlullah discouraged music, dancing and all forms of entertainment through his broadcasts on a pirated radio station.[68] He had also discouraged education for girls, anti-polio drops, and all forms of artistic expressions.[69]

Women are at the centre of this turf war between 'modernised state institutions' and 'traditional/primitive' institutions such as the ASLSIs.

---

[67] According to the Human Rights Commission in Pakistan (HRCP), there were at least 135 attacks on educational institutions across Pakistan in 2011, of these 76 attacks took place in Khyber Pukhtunkhwa, 53 in FATA, two in Balochistan, and four in Gilgil Baltistan. Of these institutions, 60 were girls' private schools and 109 were government run public schools: Human Rights Commission of Pakistan, 'State of Human Rights in 2011', p. 178, available at http://hrcp-web.org/publication/book/annual-report-2011-english/.

[68] Interestingly, while radio and television stations are often criticised as tools of Western propaganda and as Maulana Fazlullah claimed 'sources of loose morality', local 'FM mullahs' are using them consistently to issue warnings to both the government and non-governmental organisations, demanding to stop 'unIslamic' activities. In March 2012, there were also demands made to non-Muslim minorities in Malakand to pay 'jazya' (protection tax) or 'face jihad'.

[69] In his broadcasts, Maulana Fazlullah claimed that the global polio eradication campaign was an anti-Muslim plot by the Christian and Jews to keep Muslims impotent. The promotion of health rights suffered a set-back, when some of the facts of Osama Bin Laden's death were revealed, such as the CIA's strategies to confirm his hideout by covertly aiding a free hepatitis-B vaccination campaign in some neighbourhoods of Abbottabad and using health workers to provide critical information.

This can be explained in several ways. First, the armed conflict and the intense militarisation and 'securitisation' of the region have resulted in growing conservatism. The regulations on cultural activities reveal that Islamic revivalism in Pakistani national identity politics has pushed women back into the private sphere. Bombing, raids, attacks, public abuse and sexual violence constrict the space for women to negotiate with both the state and the ASLSIs. Second, minority groups, especially minority women and children in semi-urban and rural areas, have suffered from the mullah-military nexus and the emergence of the ASLSIs. Leading politicians, including Punjab's Governor Salman Taseer and Minorities Minister Shahbaz Bhatti, were assassinated in 2011 for challenging the blasphemy law and taking up the case of Aasia Bibi, a Christian woman who was sentenced to death in November 2010 for allegedly committing blasphemy against Prophet Muhammad.[70] Riftaa, an eleven-year-old girl with Down's Syndrome, was arrested for allegedly violating the strict blasphemy laws by burning the pages of the Quran on 20 August 2012.[71] Finally, women have actively participated in the conservative politics and militancy in Pakistan. The anti-state security alliances include women activists, as evidenced by the Lal Masjid (Red Mosque) incident in 2007.[72] A government order was issued in late 2006 to demolish eleven unauthorised mosques and madrassas, following which there was a protest campaign. The liberal, Islamic experts and government officials engaged in a public theological debate about whether or not it was permissible in Islam to destroy the mosque.[73]

---

[70] TTP claimed the responsibility for killing Bhatti: 'Shahbaz Bhatti assasinated', *Express Tribune*, 2 March 2011, available at Tribune.com.pk/story/126287/shabaz-bhatti-attacked-in-islamabad. While this is beyond the scope of this chapter, it must be noted that minority rights have been severely affected in Pakistan. Sexual and gender-based violence against minorities has significantly increased since the 1980s. For details, see Iftikhar Malik, *Religious Minorities in Pakistan* (Minority Rights Group International, 2002), available at www.refworld.org/pdfid/469cbfc30.pdf.

[71] In 2000, Pakistan passed the Juvenile Justice System Ordinance offering greater protection to girls and boys who come into conflict with the law. Its implementation is rather slow and, as demonstrated by Riftaa's case, it has not been consistently used across the country.

[72] 'Pakistani soldiers storm mosque', *BBC News*, 10 July 2007, available at http://news.bbc.co.uk/2/hi/6286500.stm.

[73] For an analysis of the crisis, see Farida Shaheed, *Gender, Religion and the Quest for Justice, Final Research Report* (United Nations Research in Social Development, September 2009) pp. 30–5, available at http://r4d.dfid.gov.uk/pdf/outputs/womenempmus/shaheed_genderreligionjusticepakistan.pdf.

The Pakistani state's reluctance and inability to censure the AsLSIs was demonstrated by tactical and strategic alliances developed over the years between the state elite including the military and AsLSIs, for example, in the 1953 Lahore riots against the Ahamadiyaa community, during various Afghan wars and in post-9/11 periods.[74] Indeed, the 'flogging' incident has exposed the long-term disregard of the privatisation of religion and punishment in the name of religion and culture. However, the consequent political expression of privatised religion, promoted and intensified by the presence of AsLSIs, is uncontrollable, splintered and vicious in its backlash. While the women's movement has been at the forefront of the struggle against a state that has institutionalised punitive action against women, the movement (or movements) has not managed to respond to the challenges of growing Talibanisation and institutionalisation of these forces in the northwest since the Pakistani state is complicit in this security arrangement.

## 5   Afghanistan: gender justice as the hostage of geopolitics

The battleground for several intra-state and international conflicts, including the Cold War and the 'global war on terror', has deeply affected the Afghan socio-political infrastructure. While the Afghan public generally welcomed the US-led international military intervention ousting the Taliban regime, the state building and peace building efforts in Afghanistan have not been successful.[75] Following the Bonn Agreement to draw a road map for Afghanistan's state building, adopted in December 2001,[76] several benchmarks were set to establish key institutions of democratic Afghanistan. These include a transitional government, a new constitution, a presidential election by September 2004, and parliamentary and provincial council elections by October

---

[74] For various perspectives on this issue, see Husain Haqqani, *Pakistan: Between Mosque and Military* (Carnegie Endowment of International Peace, Washington, DC, 2005); Ayesha Siddiqa, *Military Inc.: Inside Pakistan's Military Economy* (Pluto Press, London, 2007); Hasan-Askari Rizvi, *Military, State and Society in Pakistan* (Macmillan, Basingstoke, 2000).

[75] Lucy Morgan Edwards, 'Statebuilding in Afghanistan: A Case Showing the Limits?' (2010) 92 *International Review of the Red Cross* 967.

[76] Agreement on Provisional Arrangements in Afghanistan Pending the Re-establishment of Permanent Government Institutions, adopted 5 December 2001, available at www.un.org/news/dh/latest/afghan/afghan-agree.htm.

2005.[77] The Bonn Agreement addressed security sector reform indirectly and not as part of a broader rule of law reform. It emphasised the need for an international security force until such time as an Afghan security force could be developed. The focus, however, was not on building credible institutions, but rather ensuring a minimal security presence in provinces and districts. As a result, the actual progress on reforms of the Afghan National Police (including the border police), the Afghan National Army and the National Security Directorate was compromised during the Bonn process.[78]

The international intervention in Afghanistan has been a gendered process that has been concerned mainly with negotiations and political settlements between the Afghan state and the Taliban. Laura Bush, in a November 2001 radio address, noted that 'the fight against terrorism is also a fight for rights and dignity of women'.[79] The US-led intervention used women's rights and security in Afghanistan as a key rhetoric in Afghan state building and reconstruction efforts. By the end of the decade, the increased interest of the international community in the present form of Afghanistan has generated a rushed transition process, including gendered and inefficient reconstruction efforts. Women leaders have been excluded from consultation processes, not only by the Afghan government but also by the international organisations focusing on security issues.[80]

Despite the efforts of Afghan women's groups and organisations there has not been a systematic effort to ensure the full implementation of Security Council Resolutions 1325 and 1820 through a comprehensive action plan, even after Afghanistan adopted the National Action Plan for the Women of Afghanistan and became a signatory of CEDAW. Afghan women's groups and international organisations lobbied hard to include women in the Afghan state building projects and to ensure their legal protection, resulting in the insertion of a gender equality clause in the 2004 Constitution. Seats were reserved for women in the Wolesi Jirga, the lower house of the Parliament, on a 25 per cent quota, and in the Mesharano Jirga, the upper house of the Parliament, on a 17 per cent quota. Women were also given the right to

---

[77] Fatima Ayub, Sari Kouvo and Rachel Wareham, *Security Sector Reform in Afghanistan* (International Center for Transitional Justice, New York, 2009).

[78] *Ibid.* 11.

[79] 'Radio Address by Mrs. Bush', American Presidency Project, 17 November 2001, available at www.presidency.ucsb.edu/ws/?pid=24992.

[80] D'Costa's interviews carried out with Afghan women activists in 2009 and 2013.

vote in elections and the Ministry of Women's Affairs was established. In a set-back, the Wolesi Jirga approved in July 2013 a revised electoral law that included the reduction of the guaranteed seat allocation for females from 25 per cent to 20 per cent.

Many Afghan women, especially the parliamentarians and human rights activists, have been subjected to threats, attacks and assassinations.[81] In addition, male members of the Parliament often threaten and insult their female colleagues, and government officials remain hostile towards women's activists and advocacy organisations.[82]

The complicity of local communities and state authorities, morally legitimised by patriarchal prescriptions invoked in the name of either tradition or religion, increases women's insecurity. There are approximately 400 women imprisoned for 'moral crimes'; these are women found guilty of running away from home as a result of domestic violence, having extra-marital relationships or being sexually abused.[83] These acts of violence against women are not committed by evil, uneducated feudal men or 'fallen' Muslims but are a tool of control used equally by liberal, educated, urban, 'good' Muslims who call themselves moderate actors. In addition, discussions on women's rights, punishment, citizenship and public and private roles are fixed within what is religiously appropriate. The only manoeuvring space that the religious and traditional moderate factions offer is that women can fight to interpret texts in their favour. Within this limited scope and with the state complicity in violence against women, today the very survival of Afghan women depends on these interpretations rather than any universal guarantee of the protection and security of life, regardless of belief or creed.

On 22 March 2011, the President of Afghanistan, Hamid Karzai, announced that the first phases of the security transition would be completed by the end of 2014.[84] By the end of 2012, the Afghan National Security Forces were meant to have taken over 87 per cent

---

[81] Several women leaders were killed in 2012, including two directors of the Department of Women's Affairs, a branch of the Afghan government, in the eastern province of Laghman. Both women were strong advocates for the equal treatment of women.

[82] For details, see David Cortright and Kristen Wall, *Afghan Women Speak: Enhancing Security and Human Rights in Afghanistan* (University of Notre Dame, South Bend, IN, 2012).

[83] Human Rights Watch, *World Report 2012: Afghanistan*, available at www.hrw.org/world-report-2012/world-report-2012-afghanistan.

[84] Afghan Women's Network (AWN), *Baseline Report: Afghanistan: Monitoring Women's Security in Transition* (Afghan Women's Network, Kabul, 2013).

of Afghanistan's security situation, with twenty-three out of thirty-four provinces completing the transition process.[85] However, by the end of 2013, evidence from the field suggests that overall security conditions have deteriorated in Afghanistan, as a result of increased militant attacks on civilians, greater restrictions on the civil society, and in particular women's rights groups.[86]

The Afghan Women's Network (AWN) serves as the umbrella organisation for 112 non-governmental organisations and 5,000 individual members committed to supporting women's rights in Afghanistan.[87] Women who come forward to speak and pursue opportunities that are available to them are risking their lives and are accused of being anti-Islamic and Western agents. The AWN identifies three security themes for women in Afghanistan to address in this security transition period: overall security and access to justice; access to work and public life; and mobility and access to services.[88] Based on these identified themes, AWN carried out a baseline survey and concluded that with the completion of the security transition of the rural districts, especially those surrounding the provincial capitals, gender justice was increasingly inaccessible, and women's freedom of movement in remote areas was increasingly restricted and they were deprived of opportunities including education, literacy courses and vocational trainings.[89] Their access to both formal and informal justice services has been increasingly restricted.

President Karzai issued the Elimination of Violence Against Women (EVAW) law by Presidential decree in August 2009. EVAW bans twenty-two different harmful practices against women and girls, including rape, physical violence, child marriage, forced marriage and the denial of rights to education or work. The Afghan Parliament held a debate in which some members criticised portions of the EVAW law as 'un-Islamic', specifically its prohibition of child marriage, forced marriage and restrictions on women's access to healthcare and education. EVAW was never ratified by Parliament, and some activists fear the legislative body could amend or overturn it in the future. The EVAW law reinforces the duties of the Afghan police to assist victims, protect individual's rights and freedoms, and detect, combat and investigate crimes.

---

[85] *Ibid.*

[86] *Ibid.* pp. 55–67. There is a strong correlation between the haste of the international forces in withdrawing from rural districts in eastern and southern Afghanistan and the increased activity of the armed opposition groups in these areas.

[87] D'Costa's interview with AWN members in Peshawar, 2013.

[88] AWN, *Baseline Report: Afghanistan*, above n. 84, p. 12.      [89] *Ibid.*

However, a recent UN study noted 'negative attitudes towards the EVAW as well as a reluctance to apply it' among many judicial and law-enforcement officers, which 'discouraged women from reporting violence perpetrated against them'.[90] The report suggests that many 'Afghan women (and their families) still remained reluctant to approach police and prosecutors with their complaints'.[91] In fact, most incidents of violence against women still remain largely unreported, especially in rural areas, due to social norms and cultural restrains.

International organisations have come forward with several training programmes. For example, the European Union Police Mission in Afghanistan has provided training on the EVAW law and on police-prosecutor collaboration.[92] The Mission's gender and human rights unit staff noted that the confusion about different responsibilities of the police and the prosecutors in addressing gender-based violence is a weakness of the programme.[93]

As a means of combating violence against women and girls, the UN report recommended: recruiting more women into the Afghan police force, of which they currently constitute only 1 per cent; establishing a system to track incidents of violence against women; and increasing funding and training for EVAW commissions in each province to enable more follow-up on cases.[94] While there have been some efforts to improve the Afghan National Police roles and responsibilities to protect women's interests and strengthen its ability to respond to gender-based violence, women's rights activists have noted that in Afghanistan, the lack of empowered female police staff is a major challenge. The police force added 1,000 women between 2007 and 2012 and hopes to recruit 5,000 women by June 2014.[95] In 2005, the Afghan National Police employed only 180 women out of 53,400 personnel and in July 2013,

---

[90] United Nations Assistance Mission in Afghanistan (UNAMA), *A Way to Go: An Update on Implementation of Elimination of Violence Against Women in Afghanistan* (United Nations Office of the High Commissioner for Human Rights, Kabul, December 2013) 26, available at http://unama.unmissions.org/Portals/UNAMA/Documents/UNAMA% 20REPORT%20on%20EVAW%20LAW_8%20December%202013.pdf.
[91] *Ibid.*
[92] International Crisis Group (ICG), *Women and Conflict in Afghanistan*, Asia Report No. 252 (14 October 2013).
[93] *Ibid.* 18.   [94] UNAMA, *A Way to Go*, above n. 90, p. 7.
[95] United Nations Development Programme (UNDP), 'Afghan Police Force Recruits Women to Avoid Crime and Stigma', available at www.undp.org/content/undp/en/home/ourwork/womenempowerment/successstories/afghan-women-join-police-force/.

1,551 policewomen were serving out of 157,000.[96] It has established thirty-three 'family-response units' staffed by women trained in crime-scene investigation, handling evidence, taking statements and interviewing witnesses and victims.

The armed opposition groups often target policewomen. Female police officers, especially in more rural areas, are extremely vulnerable. This is partly because there are so few of them they are easily spotted, and also because of an ingrained cultural resistance to women taking public roles. In much of Afghanistan, the idea of a woman working outside the home is only beginning to be accepted, but employment as a policewoman is still viewed as shameful by many people because it often means working side by side with men. In September 2008, the Taliban killed Lt Colonel Malalai Kakar, head of the department of crimes against women in Kandahar. In July 2013, Islam Bibi, a senior female officer in southern Helmand province, was killed; and her successor Nigar was killed in September.[97] In December 2013, Masooma, a fourth policewoman, was killed in Nimruz province.[98]

While both the government and international community's efforts in improving the Afghan National Police, and the drive to recruit women in the police force are worth mentioning, numerous challenges exist and the target of 5,000 policewomen by the end of 2014 is likely to fail. Male police officers believe that women's issues are 'soft issues', not a matter of security, and they see domestic violence as a private matter to be dealt with within families and communities.[99] There is also sexual harassment with allegations of widespread rape and assault by male colleagues, and demands for sexual favours, in exchange for promotions in the police force, which is another serious challenge.[100] In addition, the lack of female-friendly facilities such as bathrooms and separate sleeping areas makes policewomen vulnerable. Despite the rhetoric of gender-sensitivity, neither the Afghan Ministry of the Interior nor the international security institutions working in Afghanistan put any pressure on the police chiefs to recruit more women. Even though the Afghan

---

[96] Oxfam, *Women and the Afghan Police*, Briefing Paper 173 (10 September 2013), available at www.oxfam.org/sites/www.oxfam.org/files/bp-173-afghanistan-women-police-100913-en.pdf.

[97] ICG, *Women and Conflict in Afghanistan*, above n. 92, p. 104.

[98] Alissa J. Rubin, 'Afghan policewoman is killed, fourth in last six months', *New York Times*, 5 December 2013, available at www.nytimes.com/2013/12/06/world/asia/gun men-kill-afghan-policewoman.html.

[99] D'Costa's interviews carried out in Peshawar, 2013.      [100] *Ibid.*

National Police reserve positions for 3,249 female civil servants and police officers, women fill fewer than half of these jobs.[101] Policewomen themselves also lack motivations as opportunities are extremely limited and some of them find themselves performing menial tasks such as making tea, and receive limited or no training. Another significant challenge is the level of literacy in the Afghan National Police, with 70 to 80 per cent of the police being illiterate.[102]

Understanding these challenges and measuring progress is crucial if the Afghan National Police is to be transformed into a gender responsive institution. The UNAMA Police Advisory Unit, the European Union Police Mission and other agencies need to play a role in improving the collection and use of gender disaggregated data, prioritising and strengthening the role of policewomen within overall police reforms and ensuring equal access to professional training and opportunities for women. International police missions could also provide capacity building with special focus on social awareness of cultural, traditional and religious gendered practices for the gender and human rights units within police reform efforts. As discussed above, despite the gender mainstreaming rhetoric, there are inherent tensions between the goals of state building according to international norms and the pragmatic activity on the ground. The involvement of warlords in state administration and international negotiations with militia leaders as high priority solutions to the criminalised narcotics economy and grand scale corruptions has meant that women's security and the gender justice agenda is severely compromised in Afghanistan.

## 6   Conclusion

It is far easier to identify the 'barbaric' Taliban as the inconvenient Muslim, and not acknowledge the emergence of different challenges due to identity politics and a variety of state/nation/peace building approaches as problematic to security institutions. This 'inconvenient Muslim' argument has given an opportunity for liberal factions in Pakistani and Afghan politics to actually pronounce themselves 'secular' by virtue of merely denouncing the Taliban and their traditional leaders for their gender insensitive practices. However, it is crucial to recognise that a sprinkling of vague liberal ideals on essentially 'theocratised' states such as Pakistan and Afghanistan does not give

---

[101] Oxfam, *Women and the Afghan Police*, above n. 96, p. 108.    [102] *Ibid.* 23.

misogynist political systems and institutions the right to claim secular credentials while still accommodating, appeasing and supporting ASLSIs or the traditional patriarchal systems for political expediency. Until such inherent contradictions are resolved and secular alternatives take the form of policies that challenge and remove all forms of institutionalised and gendered discrimination at state, social and domestic levels, the self-acclaimed liberal security institutions cannot be identified as gender sensitive in their politics. Until then, they remain as much a part of the problem as the ASLSIs in Pakistan and Afghanistan.

In Pakistan and Afghanistan the implementation and delivery of gender justice often relies on local elites who are part of the problem. While the international state building agenda necessitates engagement and dialogue with these local elites, these are exactly the individuals who are complicit in various injustices that communities, especially women, experience every day. The nation building processes have always subsumed women's identity for the broader purposes of the nation. As such, the international state building strategies and the local nation building identity politics are a double-edged sword for women's rights, security and development, all of which are critical to the gender justice agenda. Through the nation building agenda, the traditional and religious elites maintain and reinforce control over women and their sexuality, whereas the state building agenda of the international community relies on a democratic and a secular notion of women's freedom and choices. Sandwiched between these two, women become the battleground for ideological warfare.

# 3

# Institutional competence and the Common Foreign and Security Policy of the European Union

ANNE MCNAUGHTON

## 1 Introduction

The European Union (EU) is a unique legal system.[1] This is so notwithstanding the fact that the comment, indeed perhaps a criticism, has been made that lawyers tend to categorise the EU as a *sui generis* legal system 'without further explanation'.[2] In the case of the EU, we see an intriguing model of security regulation positioned, as the title of this series collection states, at the intersection of international and public law. The legislative measures of the EU are embedded directly (in the case of Regulations),[3] or indirectly (in the case of Directives),[4] in the legal

---

[1] There are multiple layers of treaties that form the legal framework of the EU. With the entry into force of the 2007 Lisbon Treaty, the constitutive instruments of the EU were significantly amended: Treaty of Lisbon amending the Treaty on European Union and the Treaty Establishing the European Community, opened for signature 13 December 2007 [2007] OJ C306/1 (entered into force 1 December 2009). The Lisbon Treaty made amendments to the Treaty on European Union, opened for signature 7 February 1992 [1992] OJ C191/1 (entered into force 1 November 1993), as subsequently amended (TEU (Maastricht)); and the Treaty Establishing the European Community, opened for signature 7 February 1992 [1992] OJ C224/6 (entered into force 1 November 1993) (TEC); the latter was renamed as the Treaty on the Functioning of the European Union [2012] OJ C326/01 (TFEU). For the sake of convenience, the EU will be used in this chapter to refer to the European Union and its predecessors.

[2] Karen J. Alter, *Establishing the Supremacy of European Law: The Making of an International Rule of Law in Europe* (Oxford University Press, Oxford, 2001) pp. viii–ix; see also, Wojciech Sadurski, *Constitutionalism and the Enlargement of Europe* (Oxford University Press, Oxford, 2012) p. xviii.

[3] Regulations have general application, are binding in their entirety and directly applicable in all Member States: TFEU, Art. 288; formerly TEC, Art. 249.

[4] Directives are binding upon each Member State to which they are addressed as to the result to be achieved but not as to the choice of form and method for achieving that result: TFEU, Art. 288; formerly TEC, Art. 249.

systems of its Member States. Jurisprudentially, the preliminary ruling mechanism,[5] and the doctrines of supremacy and direct effect,[6] combine to embed the rulings of the Court of Justice of the European Union ('the Court') in the legal systems of the Member States.[7] By virtue of this unique legal structure, therefore, the Member States' national and regional policies are synthesised into a unique form of regulation that, to use a (by now) rather clichéd term, lies 'beyond the state'. In other words, this form of regulation is one developed and administered, not by states exercising unfettered sovereignty either unilaterally or in the context of a multilateral organisation, but rather by states exercising more limited sovereignty, together with the EU institutions to which those states have transferred part of their sovereignty. Acting together, the Member States and the EU jointly exercise a 'blended' sovereignty.

The purpose of this chapter is to map the landscape of security regulation under the Common Foreign and Security Policy and to explore the way in which the competences of the EU and its Member States engage with each other in this policy area. This chapter does not, however, consider this institutional evolution as the 'constitutionalisation' of Europe, upon which voluminous literature exists and continues to grow.[8] The focus of this chapter is rather on explaining the concept of security within the EU;[9] the way in which legislative competence in this policy area is shared between the EU institutions and the Member States; and the way in which the EU and the Member States engage with the rest of the world in this area.

---

[5] As set out originally in the Treaty Establishing the European Economic Community, opened for signature 25 March 1957, 298 UNTS 11 (entered into force 1 January 1958), Art. 177 (Treaty of Rome); currently contained in TFEU, Art. 267. For details, see e.g., Thomas de la Mare and Catherine Donnelly, 'Preliminary Rulings and EU Legal Integration: Evolution and Stasis' in Paul Craig and Gráinne de Búrca (eds.), *The Evolution of EU Law* (2nd edn, Oxford University Press, Oxford, 2011) p. 363.

[6] For details, see e.g., Bruno de Witte, 'Direct Effect, Primacy and the Nature of the Legal Order' in Paul Craig and Gráinne de Búrca (eds.), *The Evolution of EU Law* (2nd edn, Oxford University Press, Oxford, 2011) p. 323.

[7] See, however, section 3 below for an explanation of the relationship of the Court of Justice of the European Union and the Common Foreign and Security Policy.

[8] An indicative, by no means exhaustive list of references can be found in Sadurski, *Constitutionalism and the Enlargement of Europe*, above n. 2, ch. 2. See also generally, J.H.H. Weiler, *The Constitution of Europe* (Cambridge University Press, Cambridge, 1999); and J.H.H. Weiler and Marlene Wind, *European Constitutionalism Beyond the State* (Cambridge University Press, Cambridge, 2003).

[9] In this respect, this chapter is aligned with the themes in Weiler and Wind, *European Constitutionalism Beyond the State*, above n. 8, p. 3.

This chapter first sketches out the original plans for a European Defence Community and traces the development of the current Common Foreign and Security Policy. It then examines the demarcation of competences under the Lisbon Treaty in light of the jurisprudence underpinning this process. The last section seeks to explain the institutional evolution in this 'new' policy area of security by introducing the idea of 'de-centred regulation' from the regulation literature – a field that seems to have more successfully moved beyond 'state-centric' analyses of governance. This regulatory concept, as distinct from the more traditional public and international law perspectives which, understandably, remain 'state-centric', will better explain how the rule of law in Europe has transcended the state and 'de-centred' security regulation through institutional evolution.

## 2   Development of the European Union's Common Foreign and Security Policy

A security dimension to the EU was envisaged from the outset when the three European Communities (the European Economic Community, European Coal and Steel Community, and European Atomic Energy Community) were established; even if this was to be achieved first through economic integration of the coal and steel sectors with the creation of the European Coal and Steel Community and subsequently through the integration of other sectors of the economy. This is clearly acknowledged in the opening paragraphs to the Preamble to the 1951 Treaty Establishing the European Coal and Steel Community, which reads:

> Considering that world peace can be safeguarded only by creative efforts commensurate with the dangers that threaten it,
> Convinced that the contribution which an organized and vital Europe can make to civilization is indispensable to the maintenance of peaceful relations.[10]

From the creation of the European Coal and Steel Community, it was understood that the realisation of the ideal of 'an ever closer union' of the peoples of Europe required some form of cooperation between the Member States in the area of foreign and security policy. An early

---

[10] Opened for signature 18 April 1951, 261 UNTS 140 (entered into force 23 July 1952). For details, see Fraser Cameron, *The Foreign and Security Policy of the European Union: Past, Present and Future* (Sheffield Academic Press, Sheffield, 1999).

manifestation of this attempt was the idea of a European Defence
Community which was to have been created by the founding Member
States of the European Coal and Steel Community. The European
Defence Community Treaty would have established a supranational
defence organisation responsible for a European defence policy and
would have provided for a European army.[11] In the circumstances
at the time, this was an ambitious project and, perhaps unsurprisingly,
it failed.[12]

With the creation of the European Economic Community in 1957,[13]
economic integration instead became the focus of European integration. It was not until 1992, some thirty-five years later, that security
and defence was set down as a distinct EU policy area in the Treaty
on European Union (TEU).[14] Anchored by the central pillar of the
European Communities ('EC pillar'), this treaty introduced two
further, inter-governmental pillars: those of Justice and Home
Affairs; and the Common Foreign and Security Policy. Those two
additional pillars only contained provisions dealing with the development of EU policy in these areas, without separate institutional structures. Both policy areas were initially predicated upon cooperation
between the Member States and were managed by the Member States
according to the traditional rules of international law, whereas the EC
pillar was of a supranational nature with its management through the
EC institutional structure comprising the Commission, Council,
Parliament and the Courts.

In the intervening decades much of the subject matter of the Justice
and Home Affairs pillar has been folded into the EC pillar largely as a
result of the 1997 Treaty of Amsterdam,[15] and is currently dealt with
under the 2007 Treaty on the Functioning of the European Union

---

[11] Martin Trybus and Nigel D. White, 'An Introduction to European Security Law' in
Martin Trybus and Nigel D. White (eds.), *European Security Law* (Oxford University
Press, Oxford, 2007) pp. 1, 5.

[12] For a comprehensive treatment of the idea of European Defence Community, see
E. Fursdon, *The European Defence Community: A History* (Macmillan, London, 1980);
Martin Trybus, 'The Vision of the European Defence Community and a Common
Defence for the European Union' in Martin Trybus and Nigel D. White (eds.),
*European Security Law* (Oxford University Press, Oxford, 2007) pp. 13–42.

[13] Treaty of Rome, see above n. 5, and the Protocols signed on 17 April 1957.

[14] TEU (Maastricht), see above n. 1.

[15] Treaty of Amsterdam amending the Treaty on European Union, the Treaties Establishing
the European Communities and Certain Related Acts, opened for signature 2 October
1997 [1997] OJ C340/1 (entered into force 1 May 1999) (TEU as amended by this Treaty,
TEU (Amsterdam)).

(TFEU).[16] The Common Foreign and Security Policy, by contrast, continues to be a policy area apart. The 2007 Lisbon Treaty abolished the EC and completely amended the constitutive instruments of the EU and the EC.[17] The result is one legal entity – the European Union – anchored in two treaties: the TEU and the TFEU. Whereas the majority of EU policy areas are dealt with under the TFEU, the Common Foreign and Security Policy remains under the TEU. The policy must, nonetheless, be read and understood in the wider context of the provisions of the TFEU as a distinct policy area of the EU, rather than as a coordination solely of the foreign and security policies of the individual Member States.

The Lisbon Treaty, which entered into force in 2009, marked the beginning of a new phase in the evolution of the EU, particularly in respect of its Common Foreign and Security Policy.[18] Building on the previous treaty amendments of Amsterdam and Nice, the Lisbon Treaty introduced a specific legal framework governing the Union in this policy area.[19]

When first introduced, responsibility for the development of the Common Foreign and Security Policy rested primarily with the Member States either acting cooperatively in their own right or acting through the Council of Ministers or the European Council.[20] Under the original TEU the Union and its Member States were to 'define and implement a common foreign and security policy'.[21] The objectives set out in this area were to be pursued 'by establishing systematic cooperation between Member States in the conduct of policy'.[22] The European Council was to 'define the principles of and general guidelines for the common foreign and security policy'.[23] The Council of Ministers was responsible for deciding, on the basis of such guidelines, what matters should be the subject of joint action.[24]

Although this 'pillar' of the Union was described as operating on an inter-governmental basis, EU institutions (the European Council and the Council of Ministers) were central to the work in this area. The

---

[16] TFEU, see above n. 1.   [17] See above n. 1.
[18] Panos Koutrakos, *The EU Common Security and Defence Policy* (Oxford University Press, Oxford, 2013) p. 23.
[19] *Ibid.*
[20] The European Council (an institution separate from the Council of Ministers) consists of the heads of state or government, a President of the Council, the President of the Commission and the High Representative for Foreign Affairs. These three officials do not have voting rights in the Council: TEU (post-Lisbon), Art. 15.
[21] TEU (Maastricht), Art. J.1(1).   [22] *Ibid.* Art. J.1(3).   [23] *Ibid.* Art. J.8(1).
[24] *Ibid.* Art. J.3(1).

distinction with the first 'pillar' (that of the European Communities) was that in relation to Common Foreign and Security Policy the Commission had nothing more than a passive, 'bystander' role.[25] One of the most significant changes introduced by the Lisbon Treaty was the abolition of the three pillar structure, with its attendant mix of inter-governmentalism and supranationalism. A second significant change in this area was the creation of the role of the High Representative for Foreign Affairs and Security Policy; and the third, an autonomous 'diplomatic service' for the EU – the European External Action Service. These three developments will be dealt with in turn.

By subsuming the topics of the three separate pillars into a single, integrated entity (the EU) the Lisbon Treaty makes the roles and activities of the EU institutions responsible for the Common Foreign and Security Policy clearer and stronger. This, in turn, contributes to a greater sense of a single, integrated policy system for external policies.[26] This is not to suggest that the EU institutions have competence (or sovereignty) in this policy system to the exclusion of the Member States, but rather that the EU institutions and the Member States exercise a 'blended sovereignty' in this area. A 'single' system is not necessarily a 'unitary' system; Australia and the Federal Republic of Germany, for example, are single but not unitary polities.[27] Much has already been written about the EU and the concept of federalism.[28] It is not intended

---

[25] *Ibid.* Art. J.9 (stating that '[t]he Commission shall be fully associated with the work carried out in the common foreign and security policy field').

[26] Koutrakos, *The EU Common Security and Defence Policy*, above n. 18, p. 27.

[27] For discussion on unitary and non-unitary actors, see e.g., J.H.H. Weiler, *The Constitution of Europe* (Cambridge University Press, Cambridge, 1999) p. 184.

[28] *Ibid.* pp. 130–87; see also e.g., R. Daniel Kelemen, *The Rules of Federalism: Institutions and Regulatory Politics in the EU and Beyond* (Harvard University Press, Cambridge, MA, 2004); R. Daniel Kelemen, 'The Structure and Dynamics of EU Federalism' (2003) 36 *Comparative Political Studies* 184; Kalypso Nicolaidis and Robert Howse (eds.), *The Federal Vision: Legitimacy and Levels of Governance in the U.S. and EU* (Oxford University Press, Oxford, 2001); David McKay, *Federalism and European Union: A Political Economy Perspective* (Oxford University Press, New York, 1999); Rey Koslowski, 'A Constructivist Approach to Understanding the European Union as a Federal Polity' (1999) 6 *Journal of European Public Policy* 561; Jenna Bednar, John Ferejohn and Geoffrey Garrett, 'The Politics of European Federalism' (1996) 16 *International Review of Law and Economics* 279; Andre Bzdera, 'Comparative Analysis of Federal High Courts: A Political Theory of Judicial Review' (1993) 26 *Canadian Journal of Political Science* 3; Daniel J. Elazar, *Exploring Federalism* (University of Alabama Press, Tuscaloosa, AL, 1987); Mauro Cappelletti, Monica Seccombe and Joseph Weiler (eds.),

to engage further with that literature here. The point here is that just as Member States' courts are also 'European Union' courts, giving effect to 'European Union' law as distinct from purely domestic law; so too are Member States 'European Union' actors, giving effect to 'European Union' policy as distinct from purely domestic policy. When Member States act as constituents of the European Council and the Council of Ministers, they are not engaging with each other as actors under international law in its broadest sense. They are engaging with each other as actors in the European Union legal order. Their conduct is shaped and constrained by the tasks, obligations and procedures of EU law and policy applying to the European Council and the Council of Ministers. Approached in this way, we 'de-centre' the state in the European Union; when acting in the European Council and the Council of Ministers, the Member States are acting as part of a greater whole, they are not acting unilaterally, indifferent to their obligations in these EU institutions.

Restructuring the EU and integrating all policy areas into the TEU and the TFEU, the Lisbon Treaty amendments provide the opportunity to think of the EU as a single entity across all policy areas. Legislative competence may be exercised differently in different policy areas but it is always exercised as part of the EU legal order, not as part of the international legal order more generally. In other words, when Member States exercise their competence in the area of the Common Foreign and Security Policy, even when acting in their own right and not as a member of either of the EU institutions referred to above, they are still exercising that competence as a matter of EU law and within the EU legal order.

The second change introduced by the Lisbon Treaty was the establishment of the role of the High Representative for Foreign Affairs and Security Policy. The function of the High Representative in this policy area had already been created by the Treaty of Amsterdam, although the function was to be carried out by the Secretary-General of the Council of Ministers.[29] The Lisbon Treaty amendments established the separate role

---

*Integration Through Law: Europe and the American Federal Experience* (De Gruyter, New York, 1986).

[29] Treaty of Amsterdam, Art. 10. The provision concerning the role of the High Representative was introduced in TEU (Maastricht), Art. J.16. This provision became TEU (Amsterdam), Art. 26 following the renumbering and consolidation of the EU and EC treaty provisions in accordance with the Table of Equivalences contained in the Treaty of Amsterdam, Art. 85. See also, Koutrakos, *The EU Common Security and Defence Policy*, above n. 18, p. 40, discussing the contribution of the only incumbent of that position, Javier Solana.

of the High Representative of Foreign Affairs and Security Policy, combining the functions of the High Representative introduced by the Amsterdam Treaty amendments, with the Vice President of the European Commission and President of the Foreign Affairs Council.[30] This position is 'unique in the Union's institutional constellation',[31] having a presence on both the Commission and the Council of Ministers meeting as the Foreign Affairs Council.[32] She also has executive powers as she is entrusted with the implementation of the Common Foreign and Security Policy.[33] It must be remembered, however, that this policy is 'defined and implemented by the European Council and . . . shall be put into effect by the High Representative . . . and by the Member States in accordance with the Treaties'.[34] Therefore, while the High Representative provides a focal point for EU foreign and security policy, its development and implementation is much more nuanced than this might suggest; it is ultimately achieved through the exercise of a 'blended sovereignty' referred to earlier.

The third significant development is the creation of the European External Action Service (EEAS).[35] The EEAS was formally launched on 1 January 2011, as a result of a decision of the European Council of 26 July 2010.[36] The existing delegations of the European Commission became EEAS delegations. Significantly, the EEAS is 'a functionally autonomous body of the European Union, separate from the General Secretariat of the Council and from the Commission, with the legal capacity necessary to perform its tasks and attain its objectives'.[37] However, the EEAS must also 'assist the President of the European Council, the President of the Commission, and the Commission in the exercise of their respective functions in the area of external relations'.[38] Further, it must also cooperate with the diplomatic services of the Member States, the General Secretariat of the Council and with the services of the Commission 'in order to ensure consistency between the different areas of the Union's external action and between those

---

[30] TEU (post-Lisbon), Art.18.

[31] Koutrakos, *The EU Common Security and Defence Policy*, above n. 18, p. 40.

[32] The inaugural High Representative was Baroness Catherine Ashton who was appointed in 2009. Her term ended on 31 October 2014, when she was succeeded by Italy's Foreign Minister, HE Federica Mogherini.

[33] Koutrakos, *The EU Common Security and Defence Policy*, above n. 18, p. 41.

[34] TEU (post-Lisbon), Art. 24(1).    [35] TEU (post-Lisbon), Art. 27(3).

[36] Council Decision 2010/427/EU of 26 July 2010 establishing the organisation and functioning of the European External Action Service [2010] OJ L201/30, 3 August 2010.

[37] *Ibid.* Art. 1(2).    [38] *Ibid.* Art. 2(2).

areas and its other policies'.[39] Thus, while the EEAS is a functionally autonomous service, it continues to play an important role in the work of the Commission in the area of external affairs. As a result of the Lisbon Treaty amendments, however, its primary role is to support and assist the High Representative in giving effect to the EU's Common Foreign and Security Policy.

In relation to the other policy areas of the EU, the Commission has primary, if not sole, responsibility for policy development and implementation. The other institutions, such as the Council and the Parliament, are also involved in those areas, not least because the default voting procedure in the EU is the 'co-decision' procedure, now called the 'ordinary voting procedure'.[40] In relation to the Common Foreign and Security Policy, however, responsibility has not been given to the Commission; nor has it been left solely to the Member States to coordinate individual domestic policies. Rather, as already noted, responsibility for policy development and implementation in this area has been given to a different set of EU institutions: the European Council, the Council of Ministers and the High Representative, supported and assisted by the EEAS which, in turn, cooperates with the Commission and the diplomatic services of the Member States. There may have been a shift away from the Commission, Council, Parliament (and the Court) in this policy area, but the shift is not 'back' to the Member States. Rather, it is 'onward' to a different set of EU institutions: the European Council, Council of Ministers and the High Representative.

## 3   Demarcation of the European Union's competences under the Common Foreign and Security Policy

Article 3 of the TFEU sets out the exclusive competences of the EU; but in respect of the Common Foreign and Security Policy, the Union has competence only to develop policy pursuant to Article 2(4) of the TFEU.[41] This competence to develop a common foreign and security policy is to be exercised in accordance with the provisions contained in Chapter 2 of the TEU, which deals with the Union's Common Foreign and Security Policy. It is clear from the text of the EU constitutive treaties that the EU and its Member States are to exercise shared competence in

---

[39] *Ibid.* Art. 3(1).    [40] TFEU, Art. 294.
[41] It reads: 'The Union shall have competence in accordance with the provisions of the Treaty on European Union to define and implement a common foreign and security policy, including the progressive framing of a common defence policy'.

the area of foreign and security policy. Article J.1 of the original TEU (the Maastricht Treaty), for example, provided that the Union and its Member States 'shall define and implement a common foreign and security policy, governed by the provisions of [Title V of the Treaty] and covering all areas of foreign and security policy'. The EU institutions (the Council and the Commission) had respective roles in developing these policy areas jointly with the EU Member States.

This does not mean, however, that the demarcation of competence is settled. Indeed, the Court of Justice of the European Union (formerly the European Court of Justice)[42] has played a leading role through its case law in expanding the EU's legislative competence, often at the expense of Member State competence and, arguably, in a way that went beyond what could have been envisaged by the founders of the EU.[43] There are two legal bases that have contributed to the active role of the Court. First, the Court is given jurisdiction to review binding Union legislative acts on the grounds of 'lack of competence, infringement of an essential procedural requirement, infringement of the Treaties or *any rule of law* relating to their application or misuse of powers' (emphasis added).[44] Second, the power of the 'preliminary ruling',[45] which was originally intended as a means of achieving uniform interpretation of Union law, has allowed the Court in practice to hear challenges by citizens of the Member States to domestic laws that arguably infringed the former's rights under EU law. From these jurisdictional bases, the Court has developed the principle of Union supremacy, initially drawing upon the doctrine of implied powers,[46] with the view that 'the community constitutes a new legal order of international law for the benefit of which the states have limited their sovereign rights, albeit within limited fields'.[47]

---

[42] The Court's name was changed with the entry into force of the Lisbon Treaty in 2009.

[43] See e.g., John Usher, *European Community Law and National Law: Irreversible Transfer* (Unwin & Hyman, London, 1981) pp. 43–82.

[44] TFEU, Art. 263(2).    [45] *Ibid.* Art. 267.

[46] See e.g., Case 8/55 *Fèdèration Charbonnière de Belgique* v. *ECSC High Authority* [1956] ECR 292, 299; Case 22/70 *European Commission* v. *Council of the European Communities* [1971] ECR 263, 274–76, paras. 15–31; Cases 281, 283–5, 287/85, *Germany* v. *European Commission* [1987] ECR 3203, 3245, 3253, para. 28. See also T. Hartley, *The Foundations of European Union Law* (7th edn, Oxford University Press, Oxford, 2010) p. 111.

[47] See e.g., Case 26/62 *NV Algemene Transporten Expeditie Onderneming van Gend en Loos* v. *Nederlandse Administratie der Belastingen* [1963] ECR 1, paras. 12–13; Case 6/64 *Costa* v. *ENEL* [1964] ECR 585, 593. Note that this view has not necessarily been shared by Member States' constitutional courts: see e.g., Bill Davies, *Resisting the European Court of Justice: West Germany's Confrontation with European Law, 1949-1979* (Cambridge University

In the area of the Common Foreign and Security Policy, however, the Court's approach must be different. This is because, as a consequence of the Lisbon Treaty amendments, Article 24 of the TEU expressly stipulates that:

> [t]he Court of Justice of the European Union shall not have jurisdiction with respect to these provisions with the exception of its jurisdiction to monitor compliance with Article 40 of [the TEU] and to review the legality of certain decisions as provided for by the second paragraph of Article 275 of the Treaty on the Functioning of the European Union.

Article 40 of the TEU also seeks to separate out the role and competence of the Union and its institutions in respect of the implementation of the Common Foreign and Security Policy, from those relating to the exercise of Union competence as provided for in the TFEU.[48] This provision expressly provides that implementation of the Common Foreign and Security Policy is not to intrude on the policy areas in which exclusive and shared competences referred to in Articles 3 to 6 of the TFEU are exercised. Conversely, the Common Foreign and Security Policy is not to be subordinated to those policy areas.[49] Unlike the situation in the other EU policy areas (all of which are dealt with in the TFEU, not the TEU) the provisions of the Common Foreign and Security Policy are thus not justiciable.

That does not mean that the Court cannot hear matters that might impact on the Common Foreign and Security Policy.[50] It rather means that the measures adopted under this policy cannot be the subject of arguments relying on doctrines of EU law, such as those of direct effect and supremacy. In other words, due to this jurisdictional limit of the Court, the Member States do not have to rely on the principles of

---

Press, Cambridge, 2012); Paul Craig and Gráinne de Búrca, *EU Law: Text, Cases and Materials* (5th edn, Oxford University Press, Oxford, 2011) pp. 256–301.

[48] It reads: 'The implementation of the common foreign and security policy shall not affect the application of the procedures and the extent of the powers of the institutions laid down by the Treaties for the exercise of the Union competences referred to in Articles 3 to 6 of the Treaty on the Functioning of the European Union. Similarly, the implementation of the policies listed in those Articles shall not affect the application of the procedures and the extent of the powers of the institutions laid down by the Treaties for the exercise of the Union competences under this Chapter'.

[49] Damian Chalmers, Gareth Davies and Giorgio Monti, *European Union Law* (2nd edn, Cambridge University Press, Cambridge, 2010) p. 667.

[50] See e.g., Case C-91/05 *Commission v. Council (ECOWAS)* [2008] ECR I-3651 (concerning a measure adopted under the Common Foreign and Security Policy pillar that was challenged by the European Commission on the basis that the measure should have been adopted under the development cooperation competence of what is currently TFEU, Art. 209).

subsidiarity and proportionality in resisting the centralisation of legislative powers to the Union as they do in other policy areas.[51] Even
so, reading the language of the original TEU, it is clear that once the
Union and the Member States had defined the Common Foreign and
Security Policy, the extent to which the Member States could then act
unilaterally in this area was constrained by their obligations under the
TEU. Article J.1(3) of the original TEU indeed stipulated that the
Union would pursue the objectives set down in the Common Foreign
and Security Policy by 'establishing systematic cooperation between
Member States in the conduct of policy ... [and] by gradually
implementing ... joint action in the areas in which the Member
States have important interests in common'. The Member States are
thus required to 'support the Union's external and security policy
actively and unreservedly in a spirit of loyalty and mutual solidarity'.[52]
Member States are also required to 'refrain from any action which is
contrary to the interests of the Union or likely to impair its effectiveness
as a cohesive force in international relations'.[53]

The changes introduced by the Lisbon Treaty have, it is thus suggested, strengthened the role of the Union.[54] However, unlike the
developments in the competences of the EU and its institutions through
the Court's jurisprudence, the strengthening of the role of the Union
has not been made 'at the expense of' the role of the Member States.
Rather, as the language of the provisions in Title V of the TEU indicates,
the role of both the Union and the Member States has been enhanced by
the complementary structure through which both the Union and the
Member States exercise their respective competences in the form of
'blended sovereignty'.

## 4   European security regulation as 'de-centred' regulation

Writing in 1994, Giandomenico Majone gave the concept of regulation a
narrow justification as '[i]mproving the efficiency of the economy by
correcting specific forms of market failure such as monopoly, imperfect
information, and negative externalities'.[55] In the interim, regulation as a

---

[51] For the principle of subsidiarity, see e.g., Nicholas Tsagourias, 'Security Council
Legislation, Article 2(7) of the U.N. Charter and the Principle of Subsidiarity' (2011) 24
*Leiden Journal of International Law* 539.

[52] TEU (Maastricht), Art. J.1(4); currently, TFEU, Art. 24(3).    [53] *Ibid.*    [54] *Ibid.*

[55] Giandomenico Majone, 'The Rise of the Regulatory State in Europe' (1994) 17(3) *West
European Politics* 77, 79.

concept and as an academic discipline has matured and developed beyond this narrow focus.[56]

Defining regulation as 'a process involving the sustained and focused attempt to alter the behaviour of others according to defined standards or purposes with the intention of producing a broadly defined outcome or outcomes',[57] Julia Black explained the term 'de-centring' as follows:

> to express the observation that governments do not, and the proposition that they should not, have a monopoly on regulation and that regulation is occurring within and between other social actors, for example large organizations, collective associations, technical committees, professions etc., all without the government's involvement or indeed formal approval: there is 'regulation in many rooms' ... Decentring is further used to express the observation (and less so the normative goal) that governments are constrained in their actions, and that they are as much acted upon as they are actors. Decentring is thus part of the globalization debate on one hand, and of the debate on the developments of mezzo-levels of government (regiononalism, devolution, federalism) on the other ... Finally, ... decentring can be used, positively and normatively, to express 'de-apexing': the removal of the state from the conceptual hierarchy of state-society, and the move to a heterarchical relationship in which the roles of governors and governed are both shifting and ill-defined.[58]

It must be understood that this observation is made with a focus on domestic regulation. Regulatory scholars are seeking to understand regulatory changes in the way in which the state intervenes in society; the society on which their analysis focuses is the society in and of a particular state. A better way of expressing this, therefore, is to say that their writing is concerned in the first instance with understanding how government intervenes 'within' a state; to what extent government 'steers' activity in that state through, for example, 'overall strategic management, goal

---

[56] The developments in this field include work on multi-level governance and regulation. The term 'multi-level governance' was coined, most notably, by Liesbet Hooghe and Gary Marks in their seminal monograph, *Multi-level Governance and European Integration* (Rowman and Littlefield Publishers, Maryland, 2001). The nature of multi-level governance is still explained in a context that assumes the 'nation-state' as the dominant, if not the sole, source of regulatory authority and legitimacy. See also Andreas Follesdal, Ramses A. Wessel and Jan Wouters (eds.), *Multilevel Regulation and the EU: The Interplay between Global, European and National Normative Processes* (Martinus Nijhoff Publishers, Leiden, 2008); Paul Craig, 'Integration, Democracy and Legitimacy' in Paul Craig and Grainne de Burca (eds.), *The Evolution of EU Law* (2nd edn, Oxford University Press, Oxford, 2011) pp. 13, 21.

[57] Julia Black, 'Decentring Regulation: Understanding the Role of Regulation and Self-regulation in a "Post-Regulatory" World' (2001) 54 *Current Legal Problems* 103, 142.

[58] *Ibid.*

setting, coordination and control of specific governance arrangements',[59] and to what extent it 'rows' by more direct intervention.[60]

The dominant paradigm in which EU regulation is examined has therefore remained state-centred. This is true also, for the most part, in respect of narratives and discussions of EU law insofar as the perspectives are overwhelmingly drawn from those of public law, constitutional law and international law, including international trade law. Even while acknowledging the 'sui generis' nature of the EU legal system,[61] or observing that the EU 'is not a state but an international organization, albeit a very special one',[62] discussion invariably defaults, for better or worse, to a consideration of the EU from a 'state-centric' perspective. In other words, scholarly debate begins, by and large, from the position that it is the Member States or the EU alone, rather than the Member States 'and' the EU in its own right, that possess an inherent sovereignty, competence and sphere of policy autonomy. This is reinforced by the express demarcation of competences in the Lisbon Treaty as discussed above, according to the principle of conferral.[63]

In the context of the Common Foreign and Security Policy, however, the situation is more nuanced and contested than the foregoing comments suggest. There are three elements that, it is suggested, are still given insufficient attention. First, in establishing the doctrine of direct effect, as discussed above, the Court has described the European (Economic) Community as 'a *new legal order* of international law for the benefit of which the states have limited their sovereign rights, albeit within limited fields, *and the subjects of which comprise not only Member States but also their nationals*' (emphasis added).[64] It is, therefore, not simply a new

---

[59] Stephen Bell and Andrew Hindmoor, *Rethinking Governance: The Centrality of the State in Modern Society* (Cambridge University Press, Cambridge, 2009) p. 47.

[60] This idea of government 'steering' instead of 'rowing' was developed by D. Osborne and T. Gaebler, *Reinventing Government* (Plume, New York, 1992).

[61] See above n. 2 and accompanying text.

[62] Ramses A. Wessel and Bart Van Vooren, 'The EEAS's Diplomatic Dreams and the Reality of European and International Law' (2013) 17 *Journal of European Public Policy* 1, 1.

[63] TEU (post-Lisbon), Art. 5 (providing that '[t]he limits of Union competences are governed by the principle of conferral'). This provision was formerly Art. 5 of the TEC and was worded slightly differently ('[t]he Community shall act within the limits of the powers conferred upon it by this Treaty and of the objectives assigned to it therein'). The principle of conferral is also referred to in Art. 7 of the TFEU (providing that '[t]he Union shall ensure consistency between its policies and activities, taking all of its objectives into account and in accordance with the principle of conferral of powers').

[64] Case 26/62 *NV Algemene Transporten Expeditie Onderneming van Gend en Loos* v. *Nederlandse Administratie der Belastingen* [1963] ECR 1, 12.

international organisation 'albeit a special one' but a new legal order, which is the reason why it is frequently described as a 'supranational' legal order. This term masks the complexity of this order when one considers the EU externally, as an actor on the international plane.

Where the EU exercises exclusive competence (in relation to the Customs Union, or the Common Commercial Policy, for example) supranational is an apt description. However, in respect of international agreements, competence is often exercised by both the EU and the Member States resulting in, among other things, the (in)famous 'mixed agreements' of the EU.[65] This term refers to international agreements, the subject matter of which may fall into policy areas of EU competence (whether exclusive or shared) and Member State competence (again, whether exclusive or shared). The EU and its Member States are signatories to more than a hundred mixed agreements across all EU policy areas having an international aspect, such as aid and development, the environment, international trade, security, agriculture, fisheries and transport. In areas where mixed agreements are concluded, the external manifestation of the EU is not only the exercise by the EU institutions of EU competence in the particular policy area but the exercise by the Member States of their competence in the same area. The EU and the Member States act 'in tandem',[66] not independently of each other. The same idea applies to the competence for the Common Foreign and Security Policy in which the EU as an external actor and the Member States exercise a 'blended sovereignty' – that of the EU institutions and of the Member States.

Second, whether by accident or design, there has been policy 'spillover' from the original eleven fields of activity of the EEC/EU institutions.[67] Since its inception, the areas of EU competence have grown

---

[65] The nature and complexity of mixed agreements has been dealt with extensively elsewhere: see e.g., Christoph Hillion and Panos Koutrakos (eds.), *Mixed Agreements Revisited: The EU and Its Member States in the World* (Hart Publishing, Oxford, 2010); Joni Heliskoski, *Mixed Agreements as a Technique for Organizing the External Relations of the European Community and Its Member States* (Kluwer Law International, The Hague, 2001); Martti Koskenniemi (ed.), *International Law Aspects of the European Union* (Kluwer Law International, The Hague, 1998); D. O'Keefe and H.G. Schermers (eds.), *Mixed Agreements* (Kluwer Law International, The Hague, 1983).

[66] Rikard Bengtsson refers to the 'the institutionalization of the external relations of the EU and the representational function of the Presidency [having] to be conceived of as two interactive dimensions, which have developed in tandem': Rikard Bengtsson, 'The Council Presidency and External Representation' in Ole Elgström (ed.), *European Union Council Presidencies: A Comparative Analysis* (Routledge, London, 2003) p. 55, 55.

[67] As set out in Treaty of Rome, Art. 3.

steadily through successive treaty amendments, extending to policy areas beyond those central to the creation of the common market. If we accept that European integration has developed around a core of the funda-mental freedoms and measures intended to promote economic integra-tion, it should come as no surprise that there will be a policy spill-over into other areas, including those that lie more closely at the heart of traditional notions of state sovereignty, such as security and defence. Notwithstanding how narrow the margin was, the fact remains that, toward the end of the twentieth century, the twelve Member States of the European Communities voted in favour of the Treaty on European Union and its Common Foreign and Security Policy. In the first decade of the twenty-first century, a membership of twenty-seven States assented to the Lisbon Treaty – a Treaty that consolidates and deepens this *sui generis* legal system. As a consequence, we see a governance structure that has evolved from a hierarchy of an international organisation subordinated to its Member State creators; to a heterarchical relationship in which 'the roles of governors and the governed are both shifting and ill-defined'.[68] In a few policy areas, the EU institutions have competence to legislate to the exclusion of the Member States acting in their own right.[69] In most policy areas, legislative competence is shared between the EU institutions and the Member States, each within their own sphere of competence, able to legislate on these policy areas.[70] In the area of the Common Foreign and Security Policy, however, we see a third facet of the relationship between the EU institutions and the EU Member States, in which the EU institutions and the Member States exercise a 'blended sovereignty' even though express legislative competence rests solely with (a different con-figuration of) EU institutions.[71]

Third, since its establishment under the European Coal and Steel Community Treaty in 1952, the Court's task has been to ensure 'that the law is observed'. Notwithstanding the numerous opportunities Member States have had to restrict the general authority and jurisdiction of the Court, it has suited them not to do so. In specific instances, treaty amendments have either limited the scope of the Court's jurisdiction,[72]

---

[68] Black, 'Decentring Regulation', above n. 57, 142.     [69] See TFEU, Art. 3.
[70] *Ibid.* Art. 4.     [71] See the discussion above n. 40 and the following text.
[72] TFEU, Art. 269 stipulates that '[t]he Court shall have jurisdiction to decide on the legality of an act adopted by the European Council or by the Council pursuant to Article 7 of the Treaty on European Union solely at the request of the Member State concerned by a determination of the European Council or of the Council and in respect solely of the procedural stipulations contained in that Article'. TFEU, Art. 271 expressly limits the

or excluded it completely.[73] However, these are few in number and only in relation to traditionally sensitive policy areas (such as monetary and fiscal policy; security and defence policy). This demonstrates that the Member States are willing (if not necessarily always happy) to acquiesce in the scope of the Court's jurisdiction and how it exercises its authority within that jurisdiction. Much has been written about the Court, including about its role in the integration of the European Union.[74] The simple point being made here is that the Court enjoys the powers and competence it has, at the discretion and pleasure of the Member States. While some of its decisions have, from time to time, been controversial, the Member States have seen no reason to curtail its powers.[75]

These three elements are fundamental parts of the foundations from which the present heterarchical structure has evolved. Understanding them goes a long way to explaining why the Common Foreign and Security Policy is located in the TEU rather than in the TFEU; why the institutional structure giving effect to this policy is different to that used to give effect to the other EU policies; and why the TEU expressly sets down that, in effect, the Common Foreign and Security Policy is not subordinate to other policy areas of the EU; nor are those policy areas subordinate to the Common Foreign and Security Policy.[76] There is a growing literature giving a detailed account of the variety of actions and

Court's jurisdiction in relation to disputes concerning Member States' obligations under the Statute of the European Investment Bank; measures adopted by the Bank's Board of Governors or its Board of Directors; and the fulfilment by national central banks of obligations under the Treaties and the Statute of the European System of Central Banks and of the European Central Bank.

[73] TFEU, Art. 275 expressly stipulates that the Court 'shall not have jurisdiction with respect to the provisions relating to the common foreign and security policy nor with respect to acts adopted on the basis of those provisions'.

[74] See especially, G. de Burca and J.H.H. Weiler (eds.), *The European Court of Justice* (Oxford University Press, Oxford, 2001); L. Neville Brown and Tom Kennedy, *The Court of Justice of the European Communities* (5th edn, Sweet & Maxwell Ltd, London, 2000); Karen Alter, *The European Court's Political Power: Selected Essays* (Oxford University Press, Oxford, 2009); Renaud Dehousse, *The European Court of Justice* (Macmillan, London, 1998); Paul Lasok and Timothy Millett, *Judicial Control in the EU: Procedures and Principles* (Richmond Law & Tax Ltd, Richmond, 2004); Miguel P. Maduro, *We the Court: The European Court of Justice and the European Economic Constitution* (Hart Publishing, Oxford, 1998).

[75] In fact, it is the Member States' constitutional courts, particularly those of Germany, France and Italy, that have resisted and challenged the European Court's rulings from time to time on matters involving the supremacy of EU over Member States' constitutional laws: for details, see e.g., Davies, *Resisting the European Court of Justice*, above n. 47.

[76] TEU (post-Lisbon), Art. 40.

initiatives undertaken by the EU institutions and the Member States that comes within the scope of the Common Foreign and Security Policy.[77] Two examples suffice here to illustrate the 'de-centred' nature of security regulation in this area: the first is an operation under the EU's Common Security and Defence Policy;[78] and the second is the EU's response to the hostilities in Ukraine that began in the first half of 2014.

As a result of European Council decisions adopted in June and December 1999, the EU has been developing a Common Security and Defence Policy.[79] As a general rule, the operation of this Policy will be based on 'a UN Security Council mandate, peace agreement, and/or host state consent'.[80] On 1 January 2003, the EU 'launched its first ESDP [European Security and Defence Policy] operation, the EU Police Mission in Bosnia and Herzegovina (EUPM), which succeeded the UN's International Police Task Force (IPTF)'.[81] The objective of the EUPM was 'to establish sustainable policing arrangements under [Bosnia and Herzegovina] ownership in accordance with best European and international practice, and thereby raising current [Bosnia and Herzegovina] police standards'.[82] The EU measure establishing this operation was one concluded under the Common Foreign and Security Policy.[83] The EU Special Representative for Bosnia and Herzegovina was the intermediary between the Head of Mission on the one hand, and the High Representative for the Common Foreign and Security Policy and the Secretary-General of the EU Council of Ministers on the other.[84] It must be remembered that this operation, and the EU legislative framework that brought it into existence, took place at a time when the Common

---

[77] See e.g., Koutrakos, *The EU Common Security and Defence Policy*, above n. 18; Trybus and White, 'An Introduction to European Security Law', above n. 11; Ramses A. Wessel, *The European Union's Foreign and Security Policy: A Legal Institutional Perspective* (Kluwer Law International, The Hague, 1999).

[78] Also referred to as the European Security and Defence Policy. The Common Security and Defence Policy is dealt with in Section 2, Chapter 2 (Specific Provisions on the Common Foreign and Security Policy) of the TEU (post-Lisbon), Arts. 42–46.

[79] Frederik Naert, 'ESDP in Practice: Increasingly Varied and Ambitious EU Security and Defence Operations' in Martin Trybus and Nigel D. White (eds.), *European Security Law* (Oxford University Press, Oxford, 2007) p. 61.

[80] *Ibid.* 64

[81] *Ibid.* 65. This operation was initially intended to run from 2003 to early 2005, however was extended until late 2005.

[82] *Ibid.*

[83] Joint Actions Council, Joint Action 2002/210/CFSP of 11 March 2002 [2002] OJ L70/1, 13 March 2002.

[84] Naert, 'ESDP in Practice', above n. 79, 65.

Foreign and Security Policy was still one of the two inter-governmental pillars of the EU. However, as the constitutive instruments for the operation reveal, the operation was established through the action of the Council of Ministers, the Commission, the High Representatives for the Common Foreign and Security Policy and the Political and Security Committee of the EU.[85] This indicates that even in the 'inter-governmental pillar' there is a complex web of EU institutions and agencies acting with the Member States in tandem (through the Political and Security Committee and the Council).

The second illustration of this de-centred regulation of security is the EU's response to the hostilities in Ukraine that began in December 2013. The action undertaken by the EU in this instance was quite different to that undertaken in the first illustration. In late 2013 civil unrest broke out in Ukraine, continuing into 2014 as pro-Russian citizens sought to break away from Ukraine and have the territory in Eastern Ukraine resumed by Russia.[86] On 10 February 2014, the High Representative convened a meeting of the Foreign Affairs Council which adopted conclusions 'underlining its concern ... over reported abuses of human rights and cases of violence, intimidation and missing persons, expressing its readiness to react quickly to any deterioration on the ground'.[87] The second extraordinary meeting of the Foreign Affairs Council was held on 20 February 2014 at which it was decided to introduce 'targeted sanctions' to be imposed by the EU.[88] Following another Council meeting on 5 March 2014, EU sanctions were adopted, targeting 18 people identified as responsible for the misappropriation of Ukrainian state funds and whose assets within the European Union were to be frozen.[89]

---

[85] A committee responsible for monitoring the international situation in the areas covered by the Common Foreign and Security Policy and contributing to the definition of policies by delivering opinions to the Council at the request of the Council, High Representative for the Common Foreign and Security Policy on its own motion: TEU (post-Lisbon), Art. 38.

[86] One of the contributing factors to this unrest is the negotiations between the Ukrainian Government and the EU concerning Ukraine joining the EU.

[87] EU European External Action Service, *Fact Sheet: EU-Ukraine Relations* (12 September 2014), available at http://eeas.europa.eu/statements/docs/2014/140514_02_en.pdf (referring to Conclusions of the Council of the European Union, Foreign Affairs Council meeting, 10 February 2014).

[88] *Ibid.* (referring to Conclusions of the Council of the European Union, Foreign Affairs Council meeting, 20 February 2014).

[89] Council Regulation (EU) 208/2014 of 5 March 2014 concerning restrictive measures directed against certain persons, entities and bodies in view of the situation in Ukraine [2014] OJ L66/1, 6 March 2014.

The decision of the Council meeting was endorsed by all Member States in a Statement of the Heads of State or Government.[90] The Statement set out a strong message to the Russian Federation calling, among other things, for the 'common objective' of the EU and the Russian Federation 'of a relationship based on mutual interest and international obligations' to be promptly restored.[91] Further measures were adopted by the EU against certain persons 'responsible for actions which undermine or threaten the territorial integrity, sovereignty and independence of Ukraine'.[92] The list of persons to whom the sanctions applied was expanded on 11 July 2014 and on 29 July when the Presidents of the Commission and the European Parliament announced that the EU had agreed 'on a package of significant additional restrictive measures targeting sectoral cooperation and exchanges with the Russian Federation'.[93] These measures limit access to EU capital markets for Russian state-owned financial institutions, impose an embargo on trade in arms, establish an export ban for dual use goods for military end users, and curtail Russian access to sensitive technologies particularly in the oil sector.[94] The EU kept up the pressure on Russia 'to stop the flow of weapons, equipment and militants across the border',[95] as well as continuing to express its support for the Ukrainian government and people. In August, the European Council asked the European Commission and the EEAS to propose further steps that the EU could take in light of the continuing conflict and unrest in Eastern Ukraine. The proposed measures were adopted on 8 September 2014, and came into force on 12 September 2014.[96]

The EU's response to the situation in Ukraine has been strong, coherent and purposeful. The response has involved a variety of EU

---

[90] European Council, Statement of Heads of State or Government on Ukraine, Brussels, 6 March 2014, available at www.consilium.europa.eu/uedocs/cms_data/docs/pressdata/en/ec/141372.pdf.

[91] Ibid. [92] Ibid.

[93] Statement by the President of the European Council Herman Van Rompuy and the President of the European Commission in the name of the European Union on the Agreed Additional Restrictive Measures against Russia, Brussels, 29 July 2014, available at www.consilium.europa.eu/uedocs/cms_data/docs/pressdata/en/ec/144158.pdf.

[94] Council Decision 2014/508/CFSP of 30 July 2014 amending Council Decision 2014/145/CFSP concerning restrictive measures in respect of actions undermining or threatening the territorial integrity, sovereignty and independence of Ukraine [2014] OJ L226/23.

[95] EU European External Action Service, Fact Sheet: EU-Ukraine Relations, above n. 87.

[96] Council Regulation (EU) 960/2014 of 8 September 2014 amending Regulation (EU) 833/2014 concerning restrictive measures in view of Russia's actions destabilizing Ukraine [2014] OJ L271/3, 12 September 2014.

institutions and agencies as well as coordination by the Member States of their own domestic positions. It has been successful because the EU institutions and the Member States have acted 'in tandem'; there has been no attempt to suggest that these responses have been those of the EU to the exclusion of the Member States. There is no suggestion here that the EU has been exercising the sort of exclusive competence it might exercise in relation to the Common Commercial Policy, for example. Similarly, however, the responses are not those of the Member States acting cooperatively. Rather, the response has been a series of instruments created in a de-centred regulatory structure.

In other words, the development and integration of the EU has not occurred 'in spite of' the Member States but 'because of' them. The traditional 'state-centred' or 'state-centric' approach to analysing and explaining the EU no longer best serves us in understanding, preserving and protecting it.

## 5   Conclusion

Beginning with the idea that the EU is a 'sui generis' legal system, this chapter has sought to contribute to a clearer understanding of the concept of security and the regulatory and governance regimes that have developed for security within such a legal system. By first describing the development of the Common Foreign and Security Policy and how the respective competences of the EU and its Member States have been demarcated, this chapter has identified that the EU and its Member States have been acting in tandem, exercising a 'blended sovereignty', which is the hallmark of this sui generis legal system, and the 'new legal order'.

This chapter has then examined this phenomenon of 'blended sovereignty' by applying the notion of 'de-centred' regulation. From this perspective, it becomes clear that the institutional evolution of the EU in respect of its Common Foreign and Security Policy is not guided by a centralised security response by the EU institutions to the exclusion and at the expense of the Member States; rather it has been a carefully negotiated response to concerns about centralisation of power to the EU institutions. This, in turn, has resulted in an entity in which the institutions and the Member States share shifting competencies and exercise blended sovereignty moving beyond implicitly 'statal notions' of security.

The ideas canvassed in this chapter point to a critical factor that facilitates institutional evolution in response to contemporary security challenges. In a de-centred, heterarchical structure, competency and sovereignty are enjoyed and exercised in shifting, ill-defined ways. This can be uncomfortable and challenging for those dealing with the EU. However, it is this very flexibility that ensures the European Union is able to act externally in a way that does not undermine the carefully delineated and articulated institutional relationship between the EU and its Member States.

# 4

# Building international maritime security institutions: public and private initiatives

CHIE KOJIMA

## 1 Introduction

The traditional law enforcement functions of states in the capacity of flag, coastal or port states, according to the ocean zones set forth under the United Nations Convention on the Law of the Sea (UNCLOS),[1] have been found insufficient in addressing maritime security threats today. Maritime security threats concern not only 'peace, good order or security of the coastal State' as provided under Article 19 of UNCLOS, but also piracy, armed robbery against ships, arms or human trafficking by sea, irregular migrants by sea, illegal, unreported and unregulated fishing and marine pollution. This contemporary perception of maritime security reflects human security on a global scale, such as the safety of lives at sea, protection of human rights at sea, protection of the marine environment, and sustainable management of fisheries.[2] Those maritime security threats stem mostly from a mixture of transnational lawful and unlawful activities of individuals at sea resulting in the loss of lives, injuries or serious environmental and economic damage. When tackling these global security issues at the national level, the vast areas of oceans as well as the absence of an effective exercise of jurisdiction due to the lack of incentives and/or capacity of states appear to be major obstacles.

Various efforts have been institutionalised at the international, regional and national levels, along with private initiatives, in order to

---

[1] United Nations Convention on the Law of the Sea, opened for signature 10 December 1982, 1833 UNTS 3 (entered into force 16 November 1994).

[2] For the wider conception of security including human security, see Hitoshi Nasu and Kim Rubenstein, Introduction. In the specific context of maritime security, see also Natalie Klein, *Maritime Security and the Law of the Sea* (Oxford University Press, Oxford/New York, 2011).

complement individual states' enforcement capabilities in addressing maritime security threats. In the context of the present volume, it may not be entirely appropriate to characterise the International Maritime Organization (IMO) as a 'security institution' itself because its primary role is to regulate and facilitate commercial shipping through the member states.[3] However, the IMO has contributed to the building of maritime security institutions by assisting its member states to establish cooperative frameworks and by providing forums where public and private actors can form their shared policies against global maritime security threats such as piracy and armed robbery against ships. A study of international responses against piracy and armed robbery illustrates multiple processes towards institutionalisation, in which all the interested actors participate either formally or informally.

The IMO plays an important role in institutionalising these public and private initiatives against piracy and armed robbery at sea as a maritime security framework. The IMO adopts, as one of its mandates, binding and non-binding instruments concerning 'maritime safety and security' for the purpose of unifying rules within its member states and disseminating recommended practices towards the shipping industry. In order to make widely accepted rules and policies, the IMO invites a number of non-governmental organisations and other inter-governmental organisations to its meetings where those rules and recommended practices are drafted. The IMO also assists individual states to develop regional maritime security institutions by taking initiatives in fund-raising and capacity building. In its efforts to suppress piracy and armed robbery against ships, for example, the IMO assisted the conclusion of a non-binding regional cooperation agreement called the Code of Conduct concerning the Repression of Piracy and Armed Robbery against Ships in the Western Indian Ocean and the Gulf of Aden ('Djibouti Code of Conduct'),[4] and advances its effective implementation through the Djibouti Code of Conduct Trust Fund and the Djibouti Regional Training Centre.

---

[3] See the definition of security institutions in Hitoshi Nasu and Kim Rubenstein, Introduction as 'any institutions (formal, informal, inter-governmental, trans-governmental) that deal with public security issues arising in the global or cross-border environment'.

[4] Code of Conduct concerning the Repression of Piracy and Armed Robbery against Ships in the Western Indian Ocean and the Gulf of Aden, IMO Doc. C102/14 (3 April 2009) ('Djibouti Code of Conduct').

This chapter first explores the contemporary notion of maritime security, and then evaluates the evolving role of the IMO in building international maritime security institutions. Finally, it examines multiple processes of public and private initiatives taken against piracy and armed robbery at sea off the coast of Somalia and in the Gulf of Aden as an illustration of how international maritime security institutions have evolved as a process towards the development of international law.

## 2   Contemporary notion of maritime security

There is no generally accepted definition of the term 'maritime security' under international law. The term is not defined anywhere in treaties. The traditional notion of security under the law of the sea is related to sovereignty, defence and security of coastal states within the territorial waters and the peaceful use of the oceans beyond the territorial waters. According to Article 19 of UNCLOS, passage of a foreign ship is considered to be prejudicial to the peace, good order or security of the coastal state when the ship engages in any act that affects the defence or security of the coastal state,[5] or in any act that infringes sovereign rights of the coastal states or violates their laws and regulations.[6] Article 88 of UNCLOS ensures that the high seas should be used for peaceful purposes, which also applies to the exclusive economic zones.[7]

Before the 9/11 terrorist attacks in New York, issues related to 'maritime security' were generally considered to be political and discussed within the diplomatic arena of the United Nations (UN), while issues related to 'maritime safety' were considered to be technical and discussed within the IMO.[8] After the 9/11 terrorist attacks, this division

---

[5] For example, any threat or use of force against the sovereignty, territorial integrity or political independence of the coastal state, exercise or practice with weapons of any kind, act of collecting information to the prejudice of the defence or security of the coastal state, act of propaganda, the launching, landing or taking on board of any aircraft or any military device. UNCLOS, Art. 19(a), (b), (c), (d), (e) and (f).

[6] For example, any act of wilful and serious pollution, fishing activities, interfering with any systems of communication or any other facilities or installations of coastal states, the loading or unloading of any commodity, currency or person contrary to the customs, fiscal, immigration or sanitary laws and regulations of coastal states. UNCLOS, Art. 19(g), (h) and (k).

[7] UNCLOS, Art. 58(2).

[8] Marie Jacobsson, 'Maritime Security: An Individual or a Collective Responsibility?' in Jarna Petman and Jan Klabbers (eds.), *Nordic Cosmopolitanism: Essays in International Law for Martti Koskenniemi* (Martinus Nijhoff, Leiden, 2003) pp. 391, 393.

of labour between the UN and the IMO became obscure. States have expanded their jurisdiction over increasing maritime security threats,[9] and the IMO initiated its review of measures and procedures to prevent acts of terrorism that threaten the security of passengers and crews and the safety of ships.[10]

As the IMO started its involvement in 'maritime security', some maritime experts tried to distinguish it from 'maritime safety' from a technical perspective. Max Mejia Jr and P.K. Mukherjee define 'maritime security' as 'those measures employed by maritime administrations, vessel owners and operators, port facilities, offshore installations, and other maritime organizations to protect against unlawful acts such as piracy, armed robbery, terrorism, or maritime violence', as opposed to 'maritime safety' defined as 'those measures employed by maritime administrations, vessel owners and operators, port facilities, offshore installations, and other maritime organizations to prevent or minimize the occurrence of accidents at sea that may be caused by substandard ships, unqualified crew, or operator error'.[11] Mejia and Mukherjee exemplify these two notions by referring to the two IMO conventions: the International Convention for the Safety of Life at Sea (SOLAS Convention)[12] for maritime safety, and the Convention for the Suppression of Unlawful Acts against the Safety of Maritime Navigation (SUA Convention)[13] for maritime security.

Some other writers consider criminality as a criterion of the concept of maritime security. Marie Jacobsson includes as acts to be categorised within maritime security: 'piracy, armed robbery against ships, trafficking in migrants, illegal migration, drug trafficking, smuggling of goods, illegal, unregulated or unreported fishing, environmental pollution, terrorism, mutinous acts, and unlawful broadcasting'.[14] This list

---

[9] See generally, Stuart Kaye, 'Freedom of Navigation in a Post 9/11 World: Security and Creeping Jurisdiction' in David Freestone, Richard Barnes and David Ong (eds.), *The Law of the Sea: Progress and Prospects* (Oxford University Press, Oxford/New York, 2006) pp. 347, 351–6.

[10] *Review of Measures and Procedures to Prevent Acts of Terrorism which Threaten the Security of Passengers and Crews and the Safety of Ships*, IMO Doc. A.924(22) (20 November 2001).

[11] Max Mejia Jr and P.K. Mukherjee, 'Selected Issues of Law and Ergonomics in Maritime Security' (2004) 10 *Journal of International Maritime Law* 316, 317.

[12] International Convention for the Safety of Life at Sea, adopted 1 November 1974, 1184 UNTS 2 (entered into force 25 May 1980).

[13] Convention for the Suppression of Unlawful Acts against the Safety of Maritime Navigation, adopted 10 March 1988, 1678 UNTS 221 (entered into force 1 March 1992).

[14] Jacobsson, 'Maritime Security', above n. 8, p. 395.

confirms that what is considered as a criminal offence at sea is transnational and relates not only to the public order of a coastal state but also to the public order of the international community as a whole.

A further complex conception of maritime security is succinctly described in the 2008 Report of the UN Secretary-General on Oceans and the Law of the Sea as follows:

> There is no universally accepted definition of the term 'maritime security'. Much like the concept of 'national security', it may differ in meaning, depending on the context and the users. At its narrowest conception, maritime security involves protection from direct threats to the territorial integrity of a State, such as an armed attack from a military vessel. Most definitions also usually include security from crimes at sea, such as piracy, armed robbery against ships, and terrorist acts. However, international and unlawful damage to the marine environment, including from illegal dumping and the discharge of pollutants from vessels, and depletion of natural resources, such as from IUU fishing, can also threaten the interests of States, particularly coastal States. Various approaches have been taken to maritime security, depending on the State's perspective of the interests that may be threatened, either directly or indirectly, by activities in the oceans and seas.[15]

The Report of the Secretary-General further points out that '[t]oday's threats recognize no national boundaries, are connected, and must be addressed at all levels',[16] and observes that:

> Those threats go well beyond use of force, and extend to poverty, infectious disease and environmental degradation, internal conflicts, the spread and possible use of biological, chemical or nuclear weapons, terrorism, and transnational organized crime ... Many threats to collective security have the potential to undermine human security.[17]

These remarks by the Secretary-General indicate that the widest notion of maritime security concerns the protection of the interests of states, which are linked to the protection of human security issues, such as economic security, health security, food security and environmental security.[18]

---

[15] *Oceans and the Law of the Sea: Report of the Secretary-General*, UN Doc. A/63/63 (10 March 2008) para. 39.

[16] *Ibid.* para. 40. [17] *Ibid.*

[18] The trends in maritime security seem to correspond to the expanding notion of international peace and security today. The maintenance of international peace and security, which is enshrined as one of the purposes of the Charter of the United Nations, refers not only to states' security interests, such as arms control and non-proliferation of nuclear weapons, but also individuals' security interests, such as the protection of the

## 3　Initiatives of the IMO in building international maritime security institutions

The role of the IMO in maritime security has evolved since its establishment. As a specialised agency of the UN, the IMO is given a certain mandate under its constitutive instrument. The IMO was first established as the Inter-Governmental Maritime Consultative Organization (IMCO) in 1948 and changed its name to the International Maritime Organization in 1982.[19] Article 1(a) of the Convention establishing the IMO (then IMCO) provides that the purposes of the organisation are:

> to provide machinery for cooperation among Governments in the field of governmental regulation and practices relating to technical matters of all kinds affecting shipping engaged in international trade; to encourage and facilitate the general adoption of the highest practicable standards in matters concerning *maritime safety, efficiency of navigation and prevention and control of marine pollution from ships* (emphasis added).

As of June 2014, the IMO had 170 member states and three associate members (Hong Kong, China; Macao, China; Faroe Islands, Denmark). Around eighty non-governmental organisations (e.g. shipping associations, seafarers' advocacy organisations) are given consultative status and around sixty inter-governmental organisations (e.g. international and regional organisations) are given observer status. These non-governmental organisations and inter-governmental organisations are invited to subcommittee meetings and working groups where binding and non-binding instruments are mostly drafted.

Since its establishment, the IMO has facilitated the adoption of a number of conventions, associated rules, codes and guidelines mainly related to maritime safety, the facilitation of international maritime traffic, marine pollution, and more recently maritime terrorism. The maritime safety conventions sponsored by the IMO, most importantly the 1974 SOLAS Convention, specify minimum standards for the construction, equipment and operation of ships for safety. Under the SOLAS Convention, flag states are responsible for ensuring that

---

environment and human rights. See Bruno Simma, 'From Bilateralism to Community Interest in International Law' (1994) 250 *Recueil des Cours* 217, 237.

[19] Convention on the International Maritime Organization, adopted 6 March 1948, 289 UNTS 3 (entered into force 17 March 1958), as amended by IMO Doc. A.358(IX) (14 November 1975) and A.371(X) (9 November 1977) ('IMO Convention').

the ships flying their flags meet the safety standards and port states are allowed to inspect ships of other contracting states if there are clear grounds to believe that the ship does not comply with the safety requirements under the SOLAS.

The IMO first adopted a Resolution on piracy and armed robbery against ships in 1983.[20] The *Achille Lauro* incident in 1985 led the IMO to adopt the SUA Convention in 1988. The SUA Convention criminalises unlawful acts associated with terrorist attacks at sea, such as the seizure of merchant ships by force, acts of violence against persons on board ships, and the placing of devices on board a ship which are likely to destroy or damage the ship. The SUA Convention obliges its contracting states to make the offences punishable by appropriate penalties, establish jurisdiction over the offences and extradite or prosecute the offenders.

In 1998, the IMO started a long-term project to enhance the development of regional agreements on counter-piracy measures, by holding regional seminars and workshops, as well as by sending evaluation and assessment missions to regions. As acts of piracy and armed robbery at sea in the Gulf of Aden and off the coast of Somalia dramatically increased, the IMO adopted, in 2005, a Resolution requesting its Secretary-General to urge the UN Secretary-General to bring the matter before the Security Council.[21] The IMO adopted another Resolution in 2007 requesting the Transitional Federal Government of Somalia to advise the Security Council that the Government gives consent to navy vessels and military aircrafts entering the territorial seas of Somalia for the suppression of piracy and armed robbery against ships.[22] The matter was taken up by the Security Council, which led to the adoption of a series of Resolutions under Chapter VII of the UN Charter.[23] In 2009, the IMO adopted a set of recommendations to the IMO member states on possible counter-measures that could be employed in cases of piracy attacks, as well as guidelines to shipowners, ship operators, shipmasters and crews on measures that can be taken on board for

---

[20] Measures to Prevent Acts of Piracy and Armed Robbery against Ships, IMO Res. A.545(13) (17 November 1983).

[21] Piracy and Armed Robbery against Ships in Waters off the Coast of Somalia, IMO Res. A.979(24) (23 November 2005).

[22] Piracy and Armed Robbery against Ships in Waters off the Coast of Somalia, IMO Res. A.1002(25) (29 November 2007).

[23] SC Res. 1816 (2 June 2008); SC Res. 1846 (2 December 2008); SC Res. 1851 (16 December 2008).

the prevention of piracy attacks or the minimisation of the danger to the crew and ship when attacks occur.[24]

In responding to UN Security Council Resolutions 1816, 1846 and 1851, the IMO held a high-level meeting on maritime security, piracy and armed robbery against ships for Western Indian Ocean, Gulf of Aden and Red Sea states in Djibouti from 26 to 29 January 2009, which resulted in the adoption of the Djibouti Code of Conduct by the participants.[25] The observers in the meeting included twelve states from outside the region,[26] four UN bodies and programmes,[27] nine inter-governmental organisations[28] and three non-governmental organisations.[29] The Djibouti Code of Conduct is meant to be non-binding,[30] though the participants are encouraged to develop, with the assistance of the IMO, a binding agreement.[31] The participants are also encouraged to cooperate in arresting, investigating and prosecuting those who committed piracy and armed robbery against ships, seizing their ships or ships under their control, and rescuing ships, persons and property subject to piracy.[32]

The IMO assists in the effective implementation of the Djibouti Code of Conduct by establishing the multinational Project Implementation Unit which undertakes regional training, capacity building, reviewing

---

[24] Recommendations to Governments Preventing and Suppressing Acts of Piracy and Armed Robbery Against Ships, IMO Doc. MSC.1/Circ.1333 (26 June 2009); Guidance to Shipowners and Ship Operators, Shipmasters and Crews on Preventing and Suppressing Acts of Piracy and Armed Robbery Against Ships, IMO Doc. MSC.1/Circ.1334 (23 June 2009).

[25] Djibouti Code of Conduct, above n. 4. The participants in the meeting included governments of Comoros, Djibouti, Egypt, Eritrea, Ethiopia, France, Jordan, Kenya, Madagascar, Maldives, Mauritius, Mozambique, Oman, Saudi Arabia, Seychelles, Somalia, South Africa, Sudan, the United Arab Emirates, the United Republic of Tanzania and Yemen.

[26] Canada, India, Indonesia, Iran, Italy, Japan, Nigeria, Norway, the Philippines, Singapore, the United Kingdom and the United States.

[27] UN Department for Peacekeeping Operations, UN Office on Drugs and Crime, UN Political Office for Somalia, and World Food Programme.

[28] European Commission, International Criminal Police Organizations (INTERPOL), League of Arab States, Regional Co-operation Agreement on Combating Piracy and Robbery against Ships in Asia-Information Sharing Center (ReCAAP-ISC), Regional Organization for the Conservation of the Environment of the Red Sea and Gulf of Aden, African Union, Intergovernmental Authority on Development, North Atlantic Treaty Organization (NATO) and Organization of the Islamic Conference.

[29] Baltic and International Maritime Council (BIMCO), International Association of Independent Tanker Owners and Port Management Association of Eastern and Southern Africa.

[30] Djibouti Code of Conduct, above n. 4, Art. 15(1).    [31] *Ibid.* Art. 13.    [32] *Ibid.* Art. 6.

national legislation and information sharing. Another important form of assistance by the IMO is the establishment of the Djibouti Code of Conduct Trust Fund in September 2009, which funds the work of the Project Implementation Unit. In this way, the IMO not only develops anti-piracy policies across sectors but also helps develop a regional cooperation framework, functioning local maritime administration and an enforcement agency in the long run.

Since the Djibouti Code of Conduct is still a new framework for cooperation, its full effect and outcome are yet to be seen. The Code of Conduct is modelled after the Regional Cooperation Agreement on Combating Piracy and Armed Robbery against Ships in Asia (ReCAAP),[33] which has been observed as a relatively successful anti-piracy cooperation framework in Asia. However, the situation concerning piracy and armed robbery against ships in Asia is different from that in Africa. Taking the statistics of incidents occurring in Asia during January-December 2013 as an example, a majority of moderately significant incidents occurred while ships were anchored or berthed at ports and anchorages (80 per cent), while the rest of the incidents occurred when ships were sailing (20 per cent) as in most Somali piracy incidents.[34] While pirates and armed robbers against ships off the coast of Somalia are highly organised and aim to hold ships and their crews for ransom, most comparable incidents in East and South East Asia – notably piracy attacks against ships that are underway in the South China Sea and the Straits of Malacca and Singapore – involve only robbing the crews and the ships of money and valuables. Furthermore, those Asian states neighbouring the high-risk areas are all industrialised nations capable of enforcing their maritime interests. On the contrary, piracy and armed robbery against ships off the coast of Somalia and the Gulf of Aden occur more frequently in much larger areas without adequate law enforcement capabilities of the nearest coastal state, Somalia, where ships and hostages are kept as security for ransom.

---

[33] Regional Cooperation Agreement on Combating Piracy and Armed Robbery against Ships in Asia, adopted 11 November 2004, 2398 UNTS 199 (entered into force 4 September 2006). See generally, Maximo Mejia, 'Regional Cooperation in Combating Piracy and Armed Robbery against Ships: Learning Lessons from ReCAAP' in Anna Petrig (ed.), *Sea Piracy Law: Selected National Legal Frameworks and Regional Legislative Approaches/Droit de la piraterie maritime: Cadres juridiques nationaux et approches législatives regionals* (Duncker and Humblot, Berlin, 2010) p. 125.

[34] ReCAAP Information Sharing Centre, *Piracy and Armed Robbery against Ships in Asia: Annual Report* (January–December 2013), available at www.recaap.org.

While the challenges against piracy attacks off the coast of Somalia and in the Gulf of Aden continue to exist, the IMO's long-term project described above demonstrates its capability to help build international maritime security institutions. Simultaneously, the role of the IMO in maritime security could be seen as an outcome of the institutional evolution.[35] The IMO's Strategic Plan for the Organization for the six-year period 2010 to 2015 states:

> The mission of the International Maritime Organization (IMO) as a United Nations specialized agency is to promote safe, secure, environmentally sound, efficient and sustainable shipping through cooperation. This will be accomplished by adopting the highest practicable standards of *maritime safety and security*, efficiency of navigation and prevention and control of pollution from ships, as well as through consideration of the related legal matters and effective implementation of IMO's instruments with a view to their universal and uniform application (emphasis added).[36]

The statement uses the phrase 'maritime safety and security', which clearly adds the notion of maritime security to Article 1(a) of the IMO Convention. Although the scope of maritime security covered by the work of the IMO today may not be as wide as the scope of human security, it can be seen as an example of institutional development arising out of common security concerns of the maritime community today.


## 4   Public initiatives against piracy and armed robbery at sea

The questions concerning piracy and armed robbery against ships off the coast of Somalia and in the Gulf of Aden are related to the maintenance and restoration of public order.[37] One of the major challenges

---

[35]  See Hitoshi Nasu and Kim Rubenstein, Introduction.

[36]  Strategic Plan for the Organization (for the six-year period 2010 to 2015), IMO Res. A.1011(26) (26 November 2009).

[37]  Mahnoush H. Arsanjani and W. Michael Reisman, 'East African Piracy and the Defense of World Public Order' in Holgar Hestermeyer *et al.* (eds.), *Law of the Sea in Dialogue* (Springer, Heidelberg, 2011) p. 137. According to Arsanjani and Reisman, there are a set of fundamental sanctioning strategies for the protection, restoration and improvement of public order: preventing imminent discrete public order violations; suspending current public order violations; deterring potential future public order violations; restoring public order after it has been violated; correcting the behaviour that generates public order violations; rehabilitating victims who have suffered the brunt of public order violations; and reconstructing, in a larger social sense, in order to remove conditions that appear likely to generate public order violations: *ibid.* p. 138.

is that while maritime powers demonstrate their active role in the maintenance and restoration of public order, developing states and landlocked states are either reluctant to take action against threats that are not directly linked to their national security or they are simply incapable of taking action due to the lack of financial or human resources. Facing the reality that all states are not always capable of maintaining public order of the oceans, private actors (shipping industry, non-governmental organisations, insurance companies and private military and security companies) have developed self-help measures and safeguards against piracy and armed robbery against ships, including privately contracted armed security personnel (PCASP) on board vessels.

The remainder of this chapter examines these public and private initiatives as a spectrum by categorising measures adopted by both state and non-state actors into the following stages:

(1) measures for the prevention of piracy and armed robbery against ships;
(2) measures for the deterrence of imminent attacks by pirates and armed robbers at sea;
(3) measures for the arrest of suspected pirates and armed robbers at sea (public initiatives only), as well as the release of the ship and hostage; and
(4) measures for the punishment of pirates and armed robbers at sea (public initiatives only).

By placing the public and private initiatives into these stages, this section first examines how states can cooperate to maintain and restore public order of the oceans.

## 4.1   Legislative and administrative measures

In preventing piracy and armed robbery at sea, governments take necessary legislative and administrative measures in accordance with relevant international instruments. Having been faced with increased incidents of piracy and armed robbery against ships off the coast of Somalia, the UN General Assembly urged states to adopt measures including capacity building and to adopt necessary national legislation, with the assistance of the IMO.[38] The UN Security Council

---

[38] GA Res. 64/71 (12 March 2010).

also repeatedly called upon states to criminalise piracy under their domestic law.[39]

One illustration of legislative efforts is the enactment of a special criminal law in Japan: the Law on the Penalization of Acts of Piracy and Measures against Acts of Piracy.[40] Under the Law, acts of piracy are defined as punishable offences committed by any person on board a ship for private ends on the high seas or in the territorial sea or internal water of Japan. The Law also stipulates measures taken by the Japanese Coast Guard and, in emergency situations, by the Japanese Self-Defense Force, against acts of piracy. Since the enactment of the Law to 2013, the Japanese Self-Defense Force escorted 3,166 ships in total in the areas of the Gulf of Aden and off the coast of Somalia, fifteen vessels flying the flag of Japan, 584 vessels flying the flag of foreign states and operated by Japanese companies, and 2,567 vessels flying the flag of foreign states and operated by foreign companies.[41] A few other states amended their legislation, such as the Act of 5 January 2011 in France and Law No. 130 of 2 August 2011 in Italy, both of which concern measures against maritime piracy.[42]

In addition to these legislative efforts, national maritime safety authorities participate in the IMO meetings as national delegates, and disseminate relevant IMO recommendations and guidance to both the public

---

[39] See e.g., SC Res. 1897 (30 November 2009) Preamble; SC Res. 1918 (27 April 2010) para. 2; SC Res. 1950 (23 November 2010) para. 13; SC Res. 1976 (11 April 2011) para. 13; SC Res. 2015 (24 October 2011) para. 9; SC Res. 2020 (22 November 2011) para. 15.

[40] Kaizokukōi no shobatsu oyobi kaizokukōi e no taisho ni kansuru hōritsu [Law on the Penalization of Acts of Piracy and Measures against Acts of Piracy], Law No. 55 of 2009, adopted 19 June 2009, promulgated 24 June 2009, entered into force 24 July 2009 (Japan). 'Law on the Penalization of Acts of Piracy and Measures against Acts of Piracy' is a provisional translation of the title by the Ministry of Foreign Affairs of Japan. See 'Statement by Mr Hirofumi Nakasone', Press Release, 19 June 2009, available at www.mofa.go.jp/announce/announce/2009/6/1193289_1136.html. An unofficial translation of the law is available on the website of the Ocean Policy Research Foundation at www.sof.or.jp/en/topics/pdf/09_01.pdf.

[41] Ministry of Defense, 'Kaizokutaisho no tameni haken sareta suijōbutai no goeijisseki ni tsuite [Record of Ship-Guarding Operations Provided by the Japanese Maritime Self-Defense Force for the Suppression of Piracy]', Press Release, 6 December 2013.

[42] See the database on national legislation concerning piracy on the website of the UN Division for Ocean Affairs and the Law of the Sea, available at www.un.org/Depts/los/piracy/piracy_national_legislation.htm. See also Annex, *Compilation of Information Received from Member States on Measures They have Taken to Criminalize Piracy under their Domestic Law and to Support the Prosecution of Individuals Suspected of Piracy Off the Coast of Somalia and Imprisonment of Convicted Pirates*, UN Doc. S/2012/177 (26 March 2012).

and private sectors for the effective prevention of piracy and armed robbery against ships.

### 4.2   Protection of ships from imminent attacks

It is reported that the number of piracy and armed robbery incidents against ships in the world, both actual and attempted, amounted to 410 in 2009, 445 in 2010, 439 in 2011, 297 in 2012, and 264 in 2013.[43] Among these incidents, the number of attacks that took place in the areas off the coast of Somalia and in the Gulf of Aden were significantly high, though the number has been in decline in recent years: a total of 219 incidents in 2010,[44] 237 in 2011,[45] 75 in 2012,[46] and 15 in 2013.[47] A number of merchant ships were attacked, including oil tankers and even ships chartered by the World Food Program for delivery of food aid and other humanitarian assistance to the people of Somalia.

Piracy and armed robbery against ships off the coast of Somalia raise special problems under UNCLOS. One problem is that the Transitional Federal Government (TFG) of Somalia lacks capacity to control vessels suspected of piracy and armed robbery against ships within its territorial waters.[48] Another problem is related to the applicability of UNCLOS provisions to piracy attacks that take place within the territorial waters of Somalia. Article 101 of UNCLOS defines piracy as acts consisting of: any illegal acts of violence or detention, or any act of depredation,

[43] International Maritime Bureau, *Piracy and Armed Robbery against Ships: Report for the Period 1 January–31 December 2013* (International Chamber of Commerce, 2014), available at www.icc-ccs.org.
[44] International Maritime Bureau, *Piracy and Armed Robbery against Ships, Annual Report for the Period 1 January–31 December 2010* (International Chamber of Commerce, 2014), available at www.icc-ccs.org.
[45] International Maritime Bureau, *Piracy and Armed Robbery against Ships, Annual Report for the Period 1 January–31 December 2011* (International Chamber of Commerce, 2014), available at www.icc-ccs.org.
[46] International Maritime Bureau, *Piracy and Armed Robbery against Ships, Annual Report for the Period 1 January–31 December 2012* (International Chamber of Commerce, 2014), available at www.icc-ccs.org.
[47] International Maritime Bureau, *Report for the Period 1 January–31 December 2013*, above n. 43.
[48] The Reports of the Secretary-General on Somalia continue reporting that the security situation in Sudan remains extremely fragile, unpredictable, fluid and volatile: see e.g., *Report of the Secretary-General on Somalia*, UN Docs. S/2010/675 (30 December 2010); S/2011/759 (9 December 2011); S/2012/74 (31 January 2012).

committed for private ends by the crew or the passengers of a private ship or a private aircraft, and directed: (i) on the high seas, against another ship or aircraft, or against persons or property on board such ship or aircraft; (ii) against a ship, aircraft, persons or property in a place outside the jurisdiction of any state. Similarly, Article 105 of UNCLOS refers only to the seizure and arrest of a pirate ship on the high seas. In order to regulate acts not covered under UNCLOS, the IMO added, in 2002, the term 'armed robbery against ships', which was defined as 'any unlawful act of violence or detention or any act of depredation, threat thereof, other than an act of "piracy", directed against a ship or against persons or property on board such ships, within a State's jurisdiction over such offences'.[49]

This unique situation regarding piracy and armed robbery off the coast of Somalia called upon collective enforcement action by the international community. The UN Security Council adopted, under Chapter VII of the UN Charter, a series of Resolutions that authorised states to use their military forces against piracy within the territorial waters of Somalia. In Resolution 1816, the UN Security Council determined that 'incidents of piracy and armed robbery against vessels in the territorial waters of Somalia and the high seas off the coast of Somalia exacerbate the situation in Somalia which continues to constitute a threat to international peace and security in the region'.[50] It then authorised states, based on the consent of and with cooperation of the TFG, to enter the territorial waters of Somalia and take all necessary measures for the purpose of repressing acts of piracy and armed robbery at sea.[51] Resolution 1846 called upon states and regional organisations to coordinate their efforts to deter acts of piracy and armed robbery at sea off the coast of Somalia in cooperation with each other, the IMO, the international shipping community, flag states and the TFG.[52] Resolution 1851 further urged states and regional organisations to conclude special agreements or arrangements with countries willing to take custody of pirates for law enforcement, provided that the advance consent of the TFG is obtained for the exercise of third state jurisdiction.[53]

---

[49] Draft Code of Practice for the Investigation of Crimes of Piracy and Armed Robbery against Ships, IMO Doc. MSC/Circ. 984 (20 December 2000), Art. 2.2.
[50] SC Res. 1816 (2 June 2008) Preamble.     [51] Ibid. para. 7.
[52] SC Res. 1846 (2 December 2008) para. 7.
[53] SC Res. 1851 (16 December 2008) para. 3. This resolution also extended the area where states and regional organisations can exercise their powers to the land of Somalia.

The Security Council's repeated calls for collective enforcement action resulted in multinational naval operations. These are Operation ATALANTA by the European Union; Combined Task Force 151 (CTF 151), a multinational coalition under US leadership; and Operation Ocean Shield by the North Atlantic Treaty Organization (NATO), as well as navies under national command (e.g. Iran, India, Japan, Malaysia, the People's Republic of China, the Republic of Korea, the Russian Federation, Saudi Arabia and Yemen in 2010; India, Indonesia, Japan, the People's Republic of China, the Republic of Korea, Malaysia, Pakistan and the Russian Federation in 2013).[54] These naval operations undertaken by governments and regional organisations serve as short-term solutions for the deterrence of imminent attacks by pirates and armed robbers against ships.

### 4.3    Seizure and arrest

In a successful scenario, naval vessels and other governmental ships with law enforcement officers on board seize pirate ships as well as hijacked ships, arrest the suspected pirates, seize the property on board for investigation, and release hostages. These law enforcement powers are endorsed under Articles 110 (the right of visit) and 105 (the right to arrest and seize pirate ships) of UNCLOS. The powers were extended to armed robbery against ships within the territorial waters of Somalia by the Security Council Resolutions referred to above. However, this successful scenario envisaged by UNCLOS and the Security Council Resolutions did not easily eventuate, with piracy incidents off the coast of Somalia continuing to occur for a number of reasons, including the large number of piracy attacks; the lack of law enforcement capabilities of the TFG; the 'catch and release' practice;[55] the lack of political will among the international community; and the hindrance of military intervention due to the increasing violence against seafarers as a strategy to deter navy vessels.

One of the legal strategies recommended by the Security Council Resolutions is the conclusion of shiprider agreements. Resolutions 1851

---

[54] SC Res. 1950 (23 November 2010) Preamble; SC Res. 2125 (18 November 2013) Preamble.
[55] Robin Geiss and Anna Petrig, *Piracy and Armed Robbery at Sea: The Legal Framework for Counter-Piracy Operations in Somalia and the Gulf of Aden* (Oxford University Press, Oxford, 2011) pp. 29–30; James Kraska, *Contemporary Maritime Piracy: International Law, Strategy, and Diplomacy at Sea* (Praeger, Santa Barbara, CA, 2010) p. 157.

and 1897 invite states to conclude shiprider agreements with countries willing to take custody of pirates to facilitate the investigation and prosecution of persons detained as a result of counter-piracy operations conducted under Security Council authorisation.[56] While those Resolutions require cooperating states to observe applicable international humanitarian and human rights law in undertaking enforcement measures, there remains a risk that a transfer or extradition of a pirate or armed robber at sea to the shipriders' states may violate the *nonrefoulement* principle.[57]

### 4.4  Punishment

The prosecution of pirates by the capturing state is assumed by the well-established principle of universal jurisdiction for the crime of piracy. Under this principle, all states, wherever the piracy takes place, and even without any link to the crime, are authorised to arrest and prosecute the pirates under their own jurisdiction.[58] This customary international law rule on universal jurisdiction for the crime of piracy is codified in Article 105 of UNCLOS, though its application is limited to the crime of piracy committed on the high seas.

The SUA Convention also requires the prosecution of captured pirates to be conducted by the capturing state, but limits the basis of its jurisdiction to cases where the offence was committed upon a ship or a person or in a place associated with that state.[59] The SUA Convention, however, does not limit the scope of those crimes committed on the high seas but applies also to ships navigating, or scheduled to navigate into, through or from waters beyond the outer limit of the territorial sea of a single state, or the lateral limits of its territorial sea with an adjacent state.[60]

In the case of Somalia, while a number of states cooperated in the prevention and deterrence of piracy and armed robbery against ships, they faced a number of problems in relation to the prosecution of suspected pirates. This is due to the detention cost of a large number of pirates and armed robbers, procedural complications such as calling witnesses and providing translators, and the total imbalance of living

---

[56]  SC Res. 1851 (16 December 2008) para. 3; SC Res. 1897 (30 November 2009) para. 6. This legal strategy has been integrated into the Djibouti Code of Conduct, above n. 4, Art. 7.
[57]  Geiss and Petrig, *Piracy and Armed Robbery at Sea*, above n. 55, p. 93.
[58]  *Ibid.* pp. 143–4.    [59]  SUA Convention, Art. 6.    [60]  SUA Convention, Art. 4(1).

standards between Somalia and the prosecuting state, where those convicted pirates apply for asylum.[61] Therefore, in reality, capturing states prosecute pirates only when doing so serves their own interests. These interests include where a crew member or a passenger who was injured or killed on board by pirates is from the capturing state, or when the capturing state is the flag state of the attacked vessel.

For the rest of the cases, institutional arrangements for the prosecution of Somali pirates have been made, upon the Security Council's call to make special agreements and arrangements for the purpose of investigation and prosecution of captured pirates, between several states providing naval forces in the Gulf of Aden and off the coast of Somalia and regional states. Kenya is one of the regional states that concluded a bilateral agreement with the United Kingdom, the United States, the European Union, Denmark, the People's Republic of China and Canada, respectively, in order to make the transfer of captured pirates for trial before Kenyan courts.[62] Seychelles and Mauritius concluded similar agreements with the European Union in 2009 and 2011, respectively. Further institutional arrangements – the establishment of specialised Somali anti-piracy courts both in Somalia and in the region – are contemplated by the international community with the assistance of the UN Office on Drugs and Crime and the UN Development Programme.[63] By January 2012, it was reported that the number of states prosecuting Somali pirates had reached 20 and the total number of prosecutions was 1,063.[64]

## 5    Private initiatives against piracy and armed robbery at sea

This section looks at the extent to which the maintenance and restoration of public order can be privatised, and how the IMO plays a role in linking the public and private initiatives in building maritime security institutions.

---

[61] Kraska, *Contemporary Maritime Piracy*, above n. 55, p. 169.

[62] James Thuo Gathii, 'Kenya's Piracy Prosecutions' (2010) 104 *American Journal of International Law* 416, 416–17.

[63] SC Res. 1976 (11 April 2011) Preamble; *Report of the Secretary-General on the Modalities for the Establishment of Specialized Somali Anti-Piracy Courts*, UN Doc. S/2011/360 (15 June 2011); *Report of the Secretary-General on Specialized Anti-Piracy Courts in Somalia and Other States in the Region*, UN Doc. S/2012/50 (20 January 2012).

[64] *Report of the Secretary-General on Specialized Anti-Piracy Courts in Somalia and Other States in the Region*, UN Doc. S/2012/50 (20 January 2012) para. 10.

## 5.1   Passive protection measures

Private initiatives in preventing piracy and armed robbery off the coast of Somalia include the adoption of the Best Management Practices for Protection against Somalia-Based Piracy (BMPs) by the shipping industry organisations.[65] The most recent version of the BMPs is signed by a group of shipping associations and non-governmental organisations,[66] with the support of relevant naval forces and law enforcement agencies.[67] The BMPs aim to 'assist ships to avoid, deter or delay piracy attacks in the High Risk Area' by providing shipowners, operators, managers and masters of vessels with operational strategies that prevent a ship from becoming a victim of piracy. The BMPs include situation analyses of successful attacks, common vulnerabilities of ships, and recommendations to masters of vessels, as well as managers of the companies owning the vessels on how they should act prior to their transit, during their transit, and when they are attacked by pirates. The BMPs describe recommendable ship protection measures such as enhanced bridge protection, the control of access to bridge, accommodation and machinery spaces, the use of physical barriers, water spray, foam monitors, alarms, closed circuit television, upper deck lighting, the protection of equipment stored on the upper deck, and the use of citadels. The BMPs advise each ship master to register the entry into the High Risk Area and to report daily its position by e-mail while transiting through the High Risk Area to the UK Maritime Trade Organisation, which works in close contact with the Maritime Security

---

[65] See e.g., Best Management Practices for Protection against Somalia Based Piracy: Suggested Planning and Operational Practices for Ship Operators, and Masters of Ships Transiting the High Risk Area: Version 4, 2011, available at www.mschoa.org/docs/public-documents/bmp4-low-res_sept_5_2011.pdf?sfvrsn=0 ('BMP 4').

[66] The BMP 4 has been signed by the Baltic and International Maritime Council (BIMCO), the Cruise Lines International Association, the International Chamber of Shipping, the International Group of P&I Clubs, the International Maritime Bureau, the International Maritime Employers' Committee Ltd, the International Association of Dry Cargo Ship-Owners, the InterManager, the International Association of Independent Tanker Owners, the International Shipping Federation, the International Transport Workers' Federation, the International Parcel Tankers Association, the Joint Hull Committee, the Joint War Committee, the Oil Companies International Marine Forum, the Society of International Gas Tanker and Terminal Operators, the Mission to Seafarers and the World Shipping Council.

[67] The supporting naval forces and law enforcement agencies include the Combined Maritime Forces, the European Union Naval Force, INTERPOL, the US Navy Maritime Liaison Office, the Maritime Security Centre–Horn of Africa, the NATO Shipping Centre, the Operation Ocean Shield and the UK Maritime Trade Operations.

Centre–Horn of Africa, a coordination centre for EU forces in the region. Although compliance with the BMPs is of voluntary nature, these industry initiatives are highly praised in the Report of the Special Advisor to the Secretary-General on Legal Issues related to Piracy off the Coast of Somalia, which notes:

> The best management practices defined by the maritime community and disseminated in particular by IMO remain the best tool for protection against acts of piracy. They include passive protection measures to discourage attacks, and defensive measures to counter the pirates in the event of an attack.[68]

The International Maritime Bureau (IMB) of the International Chamber of Commerce took early initiatives for enhanced information sharing by creating the IMB Piracy Reporting Centre in Kuala Lumpur in 1992, which urged ship masters and owners to report all incidents of actual and attempted piracy and armed robbery. The IMB Piracy Reporting Centre not only collects data from victim ships and discloses it to governments in order to urge them to take certain action but also advises merchant ships navigating in the oceans to monitor warnings broadcast by the IMB Piracy Reporting Centre in Kuala Lumpur, including the description of the pirate vessels in the navigating area. Early detection of piracy ships allows navigating ships to take preventive measures and request assistance from governments in emergency situations.

### 5.2 Self-defence measures against imminent attacks

If navy vessels and other governmental ships are incapable of suppressing imminent piracy attacks, there are currently no alternatives for merchant ships to protect themselves from attacks other than employing privately contracted armed security personnel (PCASP) on board their ships.

Private military and security companies can provide shipowners with services that cannot be provided by multinational naval forces or governmental agencies. The services of private military and security companies generally include risk assessment and consultation on preventive measures, provision of armed guards on board vessels and vessel escorts, and post-attack services such as investigation and

---

[68] *Report of the Special Advisor to the Secretary-General on Legal Issues Related to Piracy off the Coast of Somalia*, UN Doc. S/2011/30 (25 January 2011).

recovery of hijacked vessels and cargoes, delivery of ransoms, and the rescue of kidnapped crew members.

The use of PCASP for the deterrence of piracy and armed robbery against ships remains controversial among both public and private sectors, though the trends indicate increasing employment of PCASP by the private sector and the introduction of new regulations over PCASP by flag states. Previously, both regulators and the majority of the shipping industry were rather cautious about the use of PCASP due to a number of legal uncertainties. The IMO, for example, initially issued the following guidance to the maritime sector:

> 60. The carrying and use of firearms by seafarers for personal protection or for the protection of a ship is strongly discouraged. Seafarers are civilians and the use of firearms requires special training and aptitudes and the risk of accidents with firearms carried on board ship is great. Carriage of arms on board ship may encourage attackers to carry firearms or even more dangerous weapons, thereby escalating an already dangerous situation. Any firearm on board may itself become an attractive target for an attacker.
>
> 61. It should be borne in mind that shooting at suspected pirates may impose a legal risk for the master, shipowner or company, such as collateral damages. In some jurisdictions, killing a national may have unforeseen consequences even for a person who believes he or she has acted in self defence. Also the differing customs or security requirements for the carriage and importation of firearms should be considered, as taking a small handgun into the territory of some countries may be considered an offence.[69]

The IMO also discouraged its member states from allowing ships flying their flags to have PCASP on board, while admitting that the relevant decision is subject to the flag state's regulation, in the following way:

> The use of privately contracted armed security personnel on board ships may lead to an escalation of violence. The carriage of such personnel and their weapons is subject to flag State legislation and policies and is a matter for flag States to determine in consultation with shipowners, companies, and ship operators, if and under which conditions this will be allowed. Flag States should take into account the possible escalation of violence which could result from carriage of armed personnel on board merchant ships, when deciding on its policy.[70]

---

[69] Guidance to Shipowners and Ship Operators, Shipmasters and Crews on Preventing and Suppressing Acts of Piracy and Armed Robbery Against Ships, above n. 24, paras. 60–1.

[70] Recommendations to Governments for Preventing and Suppressing Piracy and Armed Robbery against Ships, above n. 24, para. 7.

Furthermore, if a flag state decides to allow its ships to use PCASP on board,[71] '[a]ll legal requirements of flag, port and coastal States should be met'.[72] Merchant ships and fishing vessels with firearms on board are, when entering the territorial sea and/or ports of another state, subject to that state's relevant regulations. As of 2013, employing PCASP and carrying weapons on board a vessel is not explicitly prohibited in most flag states. Due to the increased number of modern piracy incidents, some states, such as Italy, Greece and Spain, have even adopted legislation that explicitly allows PCASP on board vessels flying their flags.[73]

This policy change, both in public and private sectors, started in early 2011. Having faced increased violence in the Indian Ocean, together with unwillingness on the part of governments to commit greater military resources in the region, and with growing economic costs of piracy,[74] the shipping industry decided to use PCASP as a necessary alternative to stopping navigating in the Indian Ocean completely.[75] Shortly after this policy change by the shipping industry, the IMO's Maritime Safety Committee, during its 89th session, considered six proposals submitted by both member states and non-governmental organisations representing the shipping industry,[76] recommending that the Committee develop guidelines for shipowners and ship operators regarding the employment

---

[71]  See International Chamber of Shipping (ICS) and the European Community Shipowners Associations (ECSA), *Flag State Rules and Requirements on Arms and Private Armed Guards on Board Vessels* (November 2013).

[72]  Guidance to Shipowners and Ship Operators, Shipmasters and Crews on Preventing and Suppressing Acts of Piracy and Armed Robbery Against Ships, above n. 24, para. 63.

[73]  See ICS and ECSA, above n. 71. SC Res. 2125 (18 November 2013) notes the efforts of flag states in taking measures to permit vessels flying their flags transiting the High Risk Area to embark PCASP and '[e]ncourages flag States and port States to further consider the development of safety and security measures on board vessels, including, where applicable, developing regulations for the use of PCASP on board ships, aimed at preventing and suppressing piracy off the coast of Somalia, through a consultative process, including through the IMO and ISO'.

[74]  The cost of piracy to the international economy was estimated between US$7–12 billion per year in 2010. The direct cost of piracy includes the cost of ransoms, insurance, re-routing, deterrent security equipment, naval operations, piracy prosecutions and piracy-deterrence organisations. Anna Bowden *et al.*, *The Economic Cost of Maritime Piracy*, One Earth Future Working Paper (2010), available at www.oneearthfuture.org/.

[75]  International Chamber of Shipping, 'Shipping Industry Changes Stance on Armed Guards', Press Release, 15 February 2011.

[76]  IMO Docs. MSC 89/18/1 (Cook Islands); MSC 89/18/5 (the Philippines, Singapore, BIMCO and ICS); MSC 89/18/6 (Liberia); MSC 89/18/7 (Bahamas and Marshall Islands); MSC 89/18/10 (BIMCO); and MSC 89/18/11 (IPTA). The IPTA proposal states that 'IPTA recognizes that many Member States have reservations about the use of private armed security providers on board merchant ships and respects their concerns. We are

of PCASP on board their ships. The industry guidelines on the use of PCASP and the International Code of Conduct for Private Security Service Providers developed by the Swiss Government and the International Committee of the Red Cross were submitted for consideration, along with various supplementary materials provided by shipping associations.[77]

Consequently, the IMO's Maritime Safety Committee adopted an interim guidance for shipowners, ship operators and shipmasters on the use of PCASP.[78] In the document, the IMO does not explicitly endorse the use of PCASP, but prescribes a set of recommendations on risk assessment, criteria for selecting maritime security companies, insurance cover for both shipowners and maritime security companies, command and control of PCASP, management and use of weapons and ammunition at all times when on board, the rules for the use of force agreed between the shipowner, the maritime security company and the master of the ship. At the same time, the Maritime Safety Committee adopted interim recommendations for flag states regarding the use of PCASP, which urged flag states to consider whether or not the use of PCASP would be permitted under their domestic laws and to set up minimum criteria or requirements that PCASP should comply with.[79] Although the Maritime Safety Committee emphasises that the interim recommendations are not to endorse or institutionalise the use of PCASP,[80] this serves as an example where private actors pressure governments through an international institution.

Another example of public-private interaction at the IMO can be seen in the work of the sub-committees and working groups. For instance, the Maritime Safety Committee revised the interim guidance to shipowners, ship operators and ship masters on the use of PCASP, drafted by the Intersessional Maritime Security and Piracy Working Group in which

---

nevertheless of the opinion that the time has come for a frank and open discussion of the various issues, be they legal, practical or otherwise, within the IMO'.

[77] IMO Doc. MSC 89/18/10 (22 March 2011) (BIMCO).

[78] Interim Guidance to Shipowners, Ship Operators, and Shipmasters on the Use of Privately Contracted Armed Security Personnel On Board Ships in the High Risk Area, IMO Doc. MSC.1/Circ.1405 (23 May 2011), revised by IMO Docs. MSC.1/Circ.1405/Rev.1 (16 September 2011) and MSC.1/Circ.1405/Rev.2 (25 May 2012).

[79] Interim Recommendations for Flag States regarding the Use of Privately Contracted Armed Security Personnel On Board Ships in the High Risk Area, IMO Doc. MSC.1/Circ.1406 (23 May 2011), revised by IMO Docs. MSC.1/Circ.1406/Rev.1 (16 September 2011) and MSC.1/Circ.1406/Rev.2 (25 May 2012).

[80] *Ibid.* para. 1.

member states, inter-governmental organisations and non-governmental organisations participated.[81] During the meeting of the Working Group, the concerns expressed by the industry regarding the different categorisations of PCASP given by flag states and the liability issues that arise from it were taken into account and resulted in the introduction of a new section in the guidance.[82]

### 5.3    Marine insurance for the release of the ship and hostages

There are a number of instances where Somali pirates have brought captured ships and hostages to the coast of Somalia to wait for ransom negotiations. The number of ransoms demanded for the release of ships and hostages has dramatically increased in recent years. It is reported that the average ransom was around US$150,000 in 2005 and went up to around US$3,400,000 in 2009, and to US$5,400,000 in 2010.[83] In November 2010, US$9,500,000 was paid to Somali pirates for the release of the South Korean oil tanker, Samho Dream.[84] Ransoms are paid by the marine insurance over the ship. The cost of ransoms paid by insurance is, however, considered to be relatively small for the shipping industry, compared to the value of the ship and the lives of crew members.[85]

While the payment of ransoms to pirates is not illegal per se and is integrated into the marine insurance scheme in the domain of private law, there are a number of public policies preventing ransoms from becoming institutionalised internationally. One of the negative effects of ransoms in the public law domain arises when piracy is possibly considered as organised crime or terrorism. In these cases, ransoms could be strictly prohibited under a series of international instruments on anti-terrorism, if they amount to funding terrorist activities. In

---

[81] *Report of the Intersessional Maritime Security and Piracy Working Group: Note by the Secretariat*, IMO Doc. MSC 90/20/1 (22 September 2011).

[82] Revised Interim Guidance to Shipowners, Ship Operators, and Shipmasters on the Use of Privately Contracted Armed Security Personnel On Board Ships in the High Risk Area, IMO Doc. MSC.1/Circ.1405/Rev.1 (16 September 2011) Annex, p. 8.

[83] Bowden *et al.*, *The Economic Cost of Maritime Piracy*, above n. 74.      [84] *Ibid.*

[85] Roger Middleton, *Piracy in Somalia: Threatening Global Trade, Feeding Local Wars*, Chatham House Briefing Paper No. AFP BP 08/02 (October 2008) pp. 5–6, available at www.chathamhouse.org/sites/files/chathamhouse/public/Research/Africa/1008piracyso malia.pdf; Charles Marts, *Piracy Ransoms: Conflicting Perspectives*, One Earth Future Foundation Working Paper (2010), available at https://oneearthfuture.org/research/pub lications/piracy-ransoms-conflicting-perspectives.

particular, Security Council Resolution 1373 requests all UN member states to criminalise the wilful provision or collection of funds by their nationals or in their territories that are to be used for terrorist acts, to freeze funds and other financial assets or economic resources of persons involved in the commission of terrorist acts, and to prohibit their nationals or any persons and entities within their territories from making any funds available for those involved in the commission of terrorist acts.[86] The International Convention for the Suppression of the Financing of Terrorism also explicitly criminalises acts of providing or collecting funds for the commission of terrorist acts.[87] Policies might also conflict with Security Council Resolution 1844 and its implementing instruments, such as EU Council Regulation 356/2010,[88] which prohibits the transfer of any funds or economic resources made available to individuals and entities engaging in acts that threaten the peace, security or stability of Somalia.

## 6  Conclusion

The overview of measures taken by public and private actors against piracy and armed robbery at sea in this chapter indicates the expanding institutionalisation of maritime security at the international and regional level, as well as a high degree of privatisation of maritime security at the domestic level. The privatised measures have been developed out of necessity due to the absence of functioning public institutions in the international arena. These institutional developments are not regime collisions per se but can be seen as interactions of public and private institutions that are both directed towards the common goal of protecting maritime security.

Piracy and armed robbery at sea presents a unique case where the notion of security is linked to private interests. The role of the IMO is significant not only in terms of capacity building of regional states but also in terms of liaising between public and private sectors when adopting relevant recommendations and guidance. The IMO's policy-making, together with its member states, industry stakeholders and

---

[86] SC Res. 1373 (28 September 2001) para. 1(b).

[87] International Convention for the Suppression of the Financing of Terrorism, adopted 9 December 1999, 2178 UNTS 197 (entered into force 10 April 2002).

[88] SC Res. 1844 (20 November 2008); Council Regulation (EU) 356/2010 of 26 April 2010 imposing certain specific restrictive measures directed against certain natural or legal persons, entities or bodies, in view of the situation in Somalia [2010] OJ L105/1.

non-governmental organisations, contributes to the institutionalisation of common security interests of the international community. In other words, the common goal towards the protection against maritime security threats for the international community as a whole can be realised only through these multiple processes in which all the interested actors participate.

Emerging instruments, such as the BMPs developed by the shipping industry organisations, and the IMO documents including the recommendations to governments and the guidance to shipowners, ship operators, ship masters and crews on preventing and suppressing acts of piracy and armed robbery against ships, remain non-binding. These soft law instruments, however, have the potential to go beyond the binding capacity of international law and help form common expectations of the international community linking national security, international security and human security. Public and private initiatives can thus co-exist and form a complementary maritime security institution in which those soft law instruments supplement public law enforcement as a process towards the development of international law for all.

# PART II

Security institutions and the rule of law

# 5

# General principles of law and a source-based approach to the regulation of international security institutions

IMOGEN SAUNDERS

## 1  Introduction

The traditional role of international security institutions as conceptualised post-Second World War was to maintain and restore international peace and security: security relations between sovereign states. However, as the world has become increasingly globalised, many security issues are of a transnational and international nature, requiring international responses beyond that of nation-states. Because of this, the role of international security institutions has necessarily increased in scope and importance. The question then becomes what law applies to these institutions. Attempts have been made to identify the legitimacy of international institutions,[1] including a 'common law' of international institutions[2] and a 'global administrative law'.[3] However, many of these

---

[1] See e.g., Rüdiger Wolfrum, 'Legitimacy of International Law and the Exercise of Administrative Functions: The Example of the International Seabed Authority, the International Maritime Organization (IMO) and the International Fisheries Organizations' in Armin von Bogdandy *et al.* (eds.), *The Exercise of Public Authority by International Institutions* (Springer, Heidelberg, 2010) p. 917; Terrence L. Chapman, 'International Security Institutions, Domestic Politics, and Institutional Legitimacy' (2007) 51 *Journal of Conflict Resolution* 134; Jean-Marc Coicaud and Veijo Heiskanen (eds.), *The Legitimacy of International Organizations* (United Nations University Press, New York, 2001).

[2] Finn Seyersted, *Common Law of International Organisations* (Martinus Nijhoff Publishers, Leiden, 2008).

[3] See e.g., Benedict Kingsbury, 'The Concept of "Law" in Global Administrative Law' (2009) 20 *European Journal of International Law* 23; Alexander Somek, 'The Concept of "Law" in Global Administrative Law: A Reply to Benedict Kingsbury' (2009) 20 *European Journal of International Law* 985; Carol Harlow, 'Global Administrative Law: The Quest for Principles and Values' (2006) 17 *European Journal of International Law* 187;

attempts fail to ground the discussion in the established 'sources' of international law, primarily (as will be argued in this chapter) due to the unnecessarily restricted understanding of this legal concept.

This chapter argues that Article 38(1)(c) of the Statute of the International Court of Justice (ICJ) – the general principles of law ('General Principles') – provides the most relevant norms to assess and regulate international security institutions.[4] The chapter first sets out an understanding of General Principles as a source of international law. Second, it looks to the rule of law issues of international security institutions and explains how the application of General Principles has the potential to extend the idea of the rule of law to the conduct of international security institutions. Third, the chapter looks to three key areas where the General Principles can, and should operate: (1) the formation of international security institutions' responses to international security threats; (2) the interpretation of the normative documents of international security institutions; and (3) the assessment and review of the actions of international security institutions. In doing so, the chapter presents a source-based approach to determining the rule of law governing international security institutions.

## 2 General Principles and Article 38(1)(C) of the ICJ Statute

The general principles of law recognised by civilised nations are, in many respects, the forgotten source of international law. They are often derided as 'antiquated',[5] more trouble in theory than in practice;[6] or as a source of last resort, referred to in dissenting judgments rather than used in judgments of international courts. While it is true that the source has been used mostly in separate or dissenting judgments, no international court has ever indicated that it does not view General Principles as a binding source of international law.[7] Indeed, recent trends in

---

Nico Krisch, 'The Pluralism of Global Administrative Law' (2006) 17 *European Journal of International Law* 247; Benedict Kingsbury, Nico Krisch and Richard B. Stewart, 'The Emergence of Global Administrative Law' (2005) 68(15) *Law and Contemporary Problems* 15.

[4] Opened for signature 26 June 1945, 1 UNTS 993 (entered into force 24 October 1945).

[5] Robert Jennings, 'What Is International Law and How Do We Tell It When We See It?' (1981) 37 *Schweitzerisches Jahrbuch für Internationales Recht* 59, 71.

[6] See e.g., Robert Jennings, 'The Identification of International Law' in Bin Cheng (ed.), *International Law: Teaching and Practice* (Stevens, London, 1982) pp. 3, 4.

[7] See e.g., *Military and Paramilitary Activities in and against Nicaragua (Nicaragua v. United States of America) (Merits)* [1986] ICJ Rep. 14, 98–9.

international criminal law in particular see increasing references to this source of international law.[8]

The potential significance of the general principles of law as a source of international law, both in respect of its application to international security institutions and more generally, becomes clear when we accept five key aspects of the source. First, as alluded to above, General Principles are a formal source of international law; capable of giving rise to binding norms of international law.[9]

Second, the General Principles are fundamentally drawn from domestic laws,[10] and require a horizontal generality between different legal systems.[11] Although there has been some suggestion that the source

---

[8]  See e.g., *Prosecutor* v. *Kupreskić et al.* (Judgment), Case No. IT-95-16-T, International Criminal Tribunal for the former Yugoslavia, Trial Chamber III, 14 January 2000; *Prosecutor* v. *Erdemović* (Judgment), Case No. IT-96-22-A, International Criminal Tribunal for the former Yugoslavia, Appeals Chamber, 7 October 1997 (Joint Separate Opinion of Judge McDonald and Judge Vohrah); *Prosecutor* v. *Kunarac et al.* (Judgment), Case No. IT-96-23-T and IT-96-23/1-T, International Criminal Tribunal for the former Yugoslavia, Trial Chamber II, 22 February 2001; *Prosecutor* v. *Tadić* (Appeal of Vujin), Case No. IT-94-1-A-AR77, International Criminal Tribunal for the former Yugoslavia, Appeals Chamber, 31 January 2000; *Prosecutor* v. *Furundžija* (Judgment), Case No. IT-85-17/1-T, International Criminal Tribunal for the former Yugoslavia, Trial Chamber II, 10 December 1998; *Prosecutor* v. *Thomas Lubanga Dyilo* (Judgment on the Prosecutor's Application for Extraordinary Review of Pre-Trial Chamber I's 31 March 2006 Decision Denying Leave to Appeal), Case No. ICC-01/04-01/06, International Criminal Court, Pre-Trial Chamber I, 13 July 2006; *Prosecutor* v. *Thomas Lubanga Dyilo* (Decision on Witness Familiarisation and Proofing), Case No. ICC-01/04-01/06, International Criminal Court, Pre-Trial Chamber I, 8 November 2006.

[9]  See e.g., Johan G. Lammers, 'General Principles of Law Recognized by Civilised Nations' in Frits Kalshoven, Pieter Jan Kuyper and Johan G. Lammers (eds.), *Essays on the Development of the International Legal Order in Memory of Haro F Van Panhuys* (Sijthoff and Noordhoff, Alphen aan den Rijn, 1980) pp. 53, 65, 69; Herman Mosler, *The International Society as a Legal Community* (Sijthoff and Noordhoff, Alphen aan den Rijn, 1980) p. 135; Bruno Simma, 'International Human Rights and General International Law: A Comparative Analysis' (1993) 4(2) *Collected Courses of the Academy of European Law* 153, 226; Dinah Shelton, 'Normative Hierarchy in International Law' (2006) 100 *American Journal of International Law* 291, 299.

[10]  See e.g., *International Status of South West Africa* (Advisory Opinion) [1950] ICJ Rep. 128, 148 (Separate Opinion of Sir Arnold McNair); *Right of Passage over Indian Territory (Portugal* v. *India) (Merits)* [1960] ICJ Rep. 6, 90 (Separate Opinion of Judge Quintana); *Certain Phosphate Lands in Nauru (Nauru* v. *Australia) (Preliminary Objections)* [1992] ICJ Rep. 240, 287-9 (Separate Opinion of Judge Shahabuddeen).

[11]  See e.g., Michael Akehurst, 'The Application of General Principles of Law by the Court of Justice of the European Communities' (1981) 52 *British Yearbook of International Law* 29; Hanna Bokor-Szegö, 'General Principles of Law' in Mohammaed Bedjaoui (ed.), *International Law: Achievements and Prospects* (Martinus Nijhoff Publishers, Boston, 1991) pp. 213, 215, 217. This includes religious and chthonic legal systems: see e.g., *North*

should additionally draw on international fora,[12] this proposition is not yet well accepted.[13]

Third, General Principles are not limited to principles in the sense of norms of 'low generality',[14] however, can encompass rules of high specificity, provided that the requisite elements of commonality and appropriateness are satisfied, as will be discussed further below.[15]

Fourth, General Principles as a source of international law is, by its nature, built on analogy. We look to domestic rules and principles and, if appropriate, analogise them to the international sphere. This concept of appropriateness and analogy is rooted in Lord McNair's separate opinion in *International Status of South-West Africa*,[16] in which he observed that '[t]he way in which international law borrows from this source is not by means of importing private law institutions "lock, stock and barrel", ready-made and fully equipped with a set of rules'.[17] In his view, municipal laws are seen 'as an indication of policy and principles rather than as directly importing these rules and institutions'.[18] The general nature of the source requires these policies and principles to be applicable 'in municipal, international, transnational and supranational law'.[19]

Fifth, General Principles can encompass both private law and public law rules and principles. Although Hersch Lauterpacht's seminal work

---

Sea Continental Shelf (Federal Republic of Germany v. Denmark; Federal Republic of Germany v. Netherlands (Merits) [1969] ICJ Rep. 3, 136 (Separate Opinion of Judge Ammoun); Gabčikovo-Nagymaros Project (Hungary v. Slovakia) (Merits) [1997] ICJ Rep. 7, 96 (Separate Opinion of Judge Weeramantry).

[12] For discussion, see especially, Bruno Simma and Philip Alston, 'The Sources of Human Rights Law: Custom, Jus Cogens and General Principles' (1988–89) 12 *Australian Yearbook of International Law* 82.

[13] Indeed, Bruno Simma in his later role as a judge of the International Court of Justice, considered a General Principle drawing only from municipal sources: Oil Platforms (Islamic Republic of Iran v. United States of America) (Merits) [2003] ICJ Rep. 161, 354–8 (Separate Opinion of Judge Simma).

[14] Robert Alexy, A Theory of Constitutional Rights (Julian Rivers, trans., Oxford University Press, Oxford, 2002) p. 45.

[15] See e.g., Maurice Mendelson, 'The International Court of Justice and the Sources of International Law' in Vaughan Lowe and Malgosia Fitzmaurice (eds.), Fifty Years of the International Court of Justice: Essays in Honour of Sir Robert Jennings (Cambridge University Press, Cambridge, 1996) pp. 63, 80.

[16] International Status of South-West Africa (Advisory Opinion) [1950] ICJ Rep. 128, 148 (Separate Opinion of Judge McNair).

[17] Ibid.    [18] Ibid.

[19] Vladmir Duro Degan, Sources of International Law (Martinus Nijhoff Publishers, Boston, 1997) p. 103.

on General Principles links the principles to private law,[20] Lauterpacht himself never limited the source to private law only and indeed stated that 'the general principles of law are, in the great majority of cases, in substance coextensive with the general principles of private law ... the general principles of public law are equally applicable'.[21] In any case, any historical justification for limiting General Principles to the sphere of private law has fallen away with the growth of international law. As Wolfgang Friedmann noted in 1964:

> Many kinds of international activities, formerly taken as a matter of course to be in the sphere of private international relations, have become a matter of public international concern through the participation of public entities – either states or public international organisations – as well as through the transfer of that activity in question.[22]

In a similar vein, Sir Robert Jennings noted in 1984 that the 'big change in content' in international law was from the 'actual necessities arising from the juxtaposition of a larger number of States, all of them pushed by modern economic and technological developments into ever-increasing interdependence in even more matters; matters which therefore imperatively required regulation by international law'.[23] In the twenty-first century, this trend has accelerated. More states have been created; technological advances are creating new areas requiring regulation; and importantly for the focus of this chapter, they are creating new areas of security risk. Confirmation of the applicability of general principles of law to public law principles is seen in the embrace of the source by international criminal law.[24]

Taking these five key aspects – that General Principles are binding, built by analogy from common rules and principles of domestic law, encompassing both public and private law – General Principles are able

---

[20] Hersch Lauterpacht, *Private Law Sources and Analogies of International Law* (Archon Books, Hamden, [1927] 1970).

[21] Hersch Lauterpacht, *The Function of Law in the International Community* (Clarendon Press, Oxford, 1933) p. 123.

[22] Wolfgang Friedmann, *The Changing Structure of International Law* (Stevens & Sons, London, 1964) p. 190. See also Wolfgang Friedmann, 'The Uses of "General Principles" in the Development of International Law' (1963) 57 *American Journal of International Law* 279, 281.

[23] Robert Jennings, 'Teachings and Teaching in International Law' in Jerzy Makarczyk (ed.), *Essays in International Law in Honour of Judge Manfred Lachs* (Martinus Nijhoff Publishers, The Hague, 1984) pp. 121, 124.

[24] See the cases cited above n. 8.

to fill in legal lacunae in areas where customary international law cannot, such as the conduct of international security institutions.

## 3   General Principles and the rule of law

One core aspect common to international institutions is that 'an international organisation is established by international law, or by subjects of international law; that is governed by international law, rather than incorporated in a national legal order; and that it has a degree of autonomy'.[25] It is the second element here that is important: international institutions being 'governed' by international law. The decision of the ICJ in the *World Health Organisation* Advisory Opinion,[26] states that 'international organisations are subjects of international law and, as such, are bound by any obligations incumbent on them under general rules of international law'.[27] Keeping in mind the fundamental fact that international institutions are made up of states, we can posit an argument that the shared core values of those states may find reflection in those domestic laws and principles common to them; that is, the applicable General Principles. Thus, if an international institution complies with the relevant General Principles, it can be argued that it is acting in accordance with core values of the rule of law, and this is justified in its position of political primacy. This view is favoured by C.F. Amerasinghe, who argues for judicial functions of international organisations to be governed by General Principles.[28]

Not only can General Principles offer a base of core values relevant to the rule of law over international security institutions, there are further reasons why General Principles in particular should apply to international security institutions in this manner.

First, some of the reasons for reluctance to expand international law to non-state actors are alleviated by the use of General Principles. Indeed, even those who deny the application of international law to non-state actors recognise its applicability to international organisations as 'already

---

[25] Catherine Brölmann, *The Institutional Veil in Public International Law: International Organisations and the Law of Treaties* (Hart Publishing, Oxford, 2007) p. 20.

[26] *Interpretation of the Agreement of 25 March 1951 between the World Health Organisation and Egypt* (Advisory Opinion) [1980] ICJ Rep. 73.

[27] *Ibid.* 89–90.

[28] C.F. Amerasinghe, *Principles of Institutional Law of International Organizations* (2nd edn, Cambridge University Press, Cambridge, 2005) p. 226. Note, however, that Amerasinghe contends that such General Principles are drawn from both national and international law.

constituted subjects of international law'.[29] Cedric Ryngaert argues that world governance through directly elected representatives is 'misconceived' as, in part, 'the tendencies of nation-state democracies to decide by majority may silence minority views that are widely shared across national boundaries (for example the interests of diasporas, religious groups, environmental groups, and so forth)'.[30] By contrast, General Principles are unique in that although they draw from the domestic 'level', they are not necessarily constrained to laws within national borders; they can encompass religious laws, as well as laws of chthonic societies.[31] Given this universal nature, the applicability of such General Principles to international security institutions – undoubtedly the subjects of international law – should not be contentious.

Second, relying on a source that draws laws from the domestic level avoids the trap of the 'international project';[32] where 'anything international is good, as long as it is international'.[33] Jan Klabbers summarises the state/international divide as 'States, we tend to think, are bad; international organizations, on the other hand, are good'.[34] Such black and white analysis inserts a dichotomy between the domestic and international that has the potential to undermine rather than promote the rule of law in international law. Indeed, Klabbers goes on to set out a trend towards informal state-based action rather than formal action by international institutions.[35] Rather than exacerbate tensions between the domestic and the international, General Principles confirm the applicability of the common rules and principles derived from the domestic level to international institutions.

Third, it is argued that the current assessment of international institutions is that 'there are few hard and fast rules'.[36] On most issues, Klabbers observes that 'the question is not simply one of which rule to apply and how to apply it, but rather of how to make an argument based on policy preferences'.[37] In the context of security institutions in particular, this

---

[29] Cedric Ryngaert, 'Imposing International Duties on Non-State Actors and the Legitimacy of International Law' in Math Noortman and Cedric Ryngaert (eds.), *Non-State Actor Dynamics in International Law* (Ashgate, Burlington, 2010) p. 69.

[30] *Ibid.* p. 74.

[31] See above n. 11. See also H. Patrick Glenn, *Legal Traditions of the World* (2nd edn, Oxford University Press, Oxford, 2004) p. 69.

[32] See e.g., David Kennedy, 'A New World Order: Yesterday, Today, Tomorrow' (1994) 4 *Transnational Law and Contemporary Problems* 329.

[33] Jan Klabbers, 'The Changing Nature of International Organizations' in Jean-Marc Coicaud and Veijo Heiskanen (eds.), above n. 1, 221, 225.

[34] *Ibid.*    [35] *Ibid.* 236–8.    [36] *Ibid.* 234.    [37] *Ibid.*

poses a problem as the legitimacy of such institutions should not be decided by shifting policy, but rather by assessment to some standard, derived from a valid norm-creating process. General Principles provide this, while other sources of international law cannot. There is no treaty on assessment, review or construction of international institutions – and those treaties that may assist are often lacking in detail.[38] Customary international law, in its traditional form, regulates behaviour at the same level it is formed at; in other words, the behaviour of states is regulated 'by' the behaviour of states. There is no appropriate mechanism for translating the behaviour of states to the behaviour of international institutions – nor indeed would such a mechanism be helpful. The types of processes in international institutions we seek to regulate and review are most analogous to processes occurring within states, not between them.[39] As such, General Principles is the most appropriate source of law to provide the 'hard and fast rules' needed.

Indeed, some international institutions are already heading down a path of applying General Principles to increase their legitimacy. Veijo Heiskanen refers to the corporatisation of certain international organisations,[40] describing the practice 'of engaging in direct "consultations" with various "stakeholder" groups' as establishing 'a direct and more formalized relationship between the organizations and its stakeholders ... enhancing the perceived legitimacy of its decision-making'.[41] This informal and voluntary adoption of domestic regulatory processes to confer legitimacy indicates the potential success of a more rigorous adoption of domestic regulatory processes through the

---

[38] See, e.g., criticisms of the applicability of the Vienna Convention on the Law of Treaties to international organisations in Jose E. Alvarez, 'Constitutional Interpretation in International Organizations' in Jean-Marc Coicaud and Veijo Heiskanen (eds.), *The Legitimacy of International Organizations* (United Nations University Press, New York, 2001) pp. 104, 115–17.

[39] The applicability of analogy to domestic systems of governance will be discussed further, see below nn. 77, 105 and accompanying text.

[40] In particular, the World Intellectual Property Organization (WIPO) and the Internet Corporation for Assigned Names and Numbers (ICANN). Although ICANN is a private, non-governmental organisation, WIPO fits the criteria for an international organisation discussed above, and arguably has security dimensions through its regulation of the Uniform Domain Name Dispute Resolution Policy.

[41] Veijo Heiskanen, 'Introduction' in Jean-Marc Coicaud and Veijo Heiskanen (eds.), *The Legitimacy of International Organizations* (United Nations University Press, New York, 2001) pp. 1, 10.

use of General Principles in assessing the conduct of international security institutions.

## 4 Regulating responses to international security threats

In this age of rapidly developing technology, as well as shifting boundaries between states and non-state actors, international security institutions must face the reality of having to respond to unprecedented or unforeseen security threats. In situations where there are no pre-existing rules set down in the constitutive documents of an international security institution, how must or must not it respond to these threats? An answer can be found by recourse to General Principles, drawing on domestic responses to emergency situations, and in particular to terrorism post-9/11 terrorist attacks.

### 4.1 Principle of legality

In assessing state responses, it is apparent that states generally revert to and rely on 'formal' legality for actions taken in response to terrorism. This is the case even where the basis for legality is subsequently questioned; the initial response of the state is to rely on 'formal' legality by enacting laws to allow it to act. Reviewing the operation of the rule of law and legality in response to emergencies in the United Kingdom, Canada and Australia, David Dyzenhaus is critical of the 'thin veneer of legality' apparent in some situations.[42] Dyzenhaus identifies two cycles of legality in response to emergency situations: the first cycle devises controls on public actors to ensure their actions confirm with substantive understandings of the rule of law; while the second is a more formalistic adherence to legality, 'resulting in the mere appearance or even ... the pretence of legality'.[43] Leaving criticism of the robustness (or not) of the legality in these cases,[44] the point here is that the response to security threats entails recourse to legality; even, as Dyzenhaus terms it, the 'compulsion of legality'.[45]

---

[42] David Dyzenhaus, 'Cycles of Legality in Emergency Times' (2007) 18 *Public Law Review* 165, 168.

[43] *Ibid.*

[44] Dyzenhaus argues that the judiciary cedes too easily to the will of the executive in interpretation of emergency legislation.

[45] Dyzenhaus, 'Cycles of Legality in Emergency Times', above n. 42, 167.

This phenomenon is also considered in Eric A. Posner and Adrian Vermeule's work on *Terror in the Balance*.[46] Writing in the context of the United States, the authors state:

> When national emergencies strike, the executive acts, Congress acquiesces and courts defer. When emergencies decay, judges become bolder and soul searching begins. In retrospect, many of the executive's actions will seem unjustified, and people will blame Congress for its acquiescence and courts for their deference.[47]

Again, the argument here lies not in the validity of the so-called acquiescence and deferral, but the necessity of legality, even in emergency situations. While courts may stretch the law by 'creatively constru[ing] justifying provisions in the law',[48] this reflects the same underlying need for legality in response to security threats.

This adherence to the principle of legality is seen more broadly in the response to 9/11; while Security Council Resolution 1373 called on states to enact laws to implement various counter-terrorism measures,[49] the actual national legislation enacted went well beyond those authorised by the Security Council.[50] This trend is seen outside of the 9/11 context as well. For example, Indonesia reacted to the 2002 Bali bombing with new legislation that year, despite the fact that it often resorted to extra-legal measures in response to domestic unrest.[51] The People's Republic of China has a long history of responding to terrorist threats with new legislation.[52] Japan has responded to various terrorist attacks with specific laws,[53] including

---

[46] Eric A. Posner and Adrian Vermeule, *Terror in the Balance: Security, Liberty and the Courts* (Oxford University Press, New York, 2007).

[47] *Ibid.* p. 3.

[48] Terry M. Moe and William G. Howell, 'The Presidential Power of Unilateral Action' (1999) 15 *Journal of Law, Economics and Organisation* 132, 174.

[49] SC Res. 1373 (28 September 2001).

[50] Victor V. Ramraj, 'The Impossibility of Global Anti-Terrorism Law' in Victor V. Ramraj *et al.* (eds.), *Global Anti-Terrorism Law and Policy* (2nd edn, Cambridge University Press, New York, 2012) pp. 44, 45.

[51] Hikmahanto Juwana, 'Anti-Terrorism Effects in Indonesia' in Victor V. Ramraj *et al.* (eds.), *Global Anti-Terrorism Law and Policy* (2nd edn, Cambridge University Press, New York, 2012) pp. 290, 291.

[52] Fu Hauling, 'Responses to Terrorism in China' in Victor V. Ramraj *et al.* (eds.), *Global Anti-Terrorism Law and Policy* (2nd edn, Cambridge University Press, New York, 2012) pp. 334, 335–6.

[53] Mark Fenwick, 'Japan's Response to Terrorism Post-9/11' in Victor V. Ramraj *et al.* (eds.), *Global Anti-Terrorism Law and Policy* (2nd edn, Cambridge University Press, New York, 2012) pp. 390, 394–5.

those enacted in the aftermath of the subway sarin gas attacks of 1995, and new laws enacted post 9/11.[54]

Overwhelmingly, states respond to new security threats with formal legality 'before' taking action. A General Principle would then suggest that international security institutions operate the same way; any threat must be met with formal legality, rather than in an ad hoc or unauthorised manner. This requirement explains an underlying concern in the discussions following the bombing campaign by the North Atlantic Treaty Organization (NATO) in Kosovo absent explicit UN Security Council approval.[55] There are various arguments for the justification of the bombing: Bruno Simma, for example, argues that Security Council actions and inactions 'could be seen as an implicit authorization granted ex post',[56] while Jules Lobel and Michael Ratnor abandon formal legality, arguing instead for a violation of formal law 'in the extreme case of a genocide for which the Security Council will not authorize force';[57] and Antonio Cassese expressed the view that NATO's action led to the crystallisation of a 'new' rule of international law 'authorizing armed countermeasures for the exclusive purpose of putting an end to large-scale atrocities'.[58]

Although Cassese, Lobel and Ratnor abandon the principle of legality in favour of arguing an exception to justify NATO's actions, Jose Alvarez observes that they and Simma are all operating from the same desire: to escape the confines of the UN Charter and constitutional order.[59] In doing so, he argues, 'all sought to avoid establishing expansive legal precedents that, given inherent reciprocity, could prove troublesome in the future'.[60] While Alvarez regards this as fealty to 'faithful

---

[54] *Ibid.* p. 391.
[55] See especially, Bruno Simma, 'NATO, the UN and the Use of Force: Legal Aspects' (1999) 43 *European Journal of International Law* 1, 3–5; Jose E. Alvarez, 'Constitutional Interpretation in International Organizations' in Jean-Marc Coicaud and Veijo Heiskanen, (eds.), *The Legitimacy of International Organizations* (United Nations University Press, New York, 2001) pp. 104, 126.
[56] Simma, 'NATO, the UN and the Use of Force', above n. 55, 10.
[57] Jules Lobel and Michael Ratnor, 'By-passing the Security Council: Ambiguous Authorisations to Use Force, Cease-Fires and the Iraqi Inspection Regime' (1999) 93 *American Journal of International Law* 124, 136.
[58] Antonio Cassese, '*Ex iniuria ius oritur*: Are We Moving Towards International Legitimation of Forcible Humanitarian Countermeasures in the World Community?' (1999) 10 *European Journal of International Law* 23, 25.
[59] Alvarez, 'Constitutional Interpretation in International Organizations', above n. 55, p. 136.
[60] *Ibid.*

constitutional interpretation',[61] these views of exceptionalism can also be addressed in the context of the need for international security institutions to act with legality. When NATO arguably did not comply with the legal requirement for the use of force, the response in commentary was either to find such legality (albeit implicitly) or to justify that particular set of circumstances as an 'exception' to the rule, thus rendering the action legitimate. The application of General Principles in this context confirms what underlies justifications for actions; international institutions must act with formal legality in response to security threats.

## 4.2    Interpretive principles

The second area where General Principles are relevant in assessing the operations of international security institutions relates to 'how' the normative documents (often constitutive instruments) of international security institutions should be interpreted. Where these documents are treaties, international law provides guidance by way of the Vienna Convention on the Law of Treaties (VCLT).[62] However, as Alvarez explains, there is a common but false assumption that these 'legal rules of interpretation are more precise or clearer than they actually are'.[63]

The problem then is where to look when the VCLT is silent, or of limited assistance. Georg Ress argues that in the context of the UN Charter 'the appropriate parallelism can only be found in domestic public law, e.g., the constitutional and administrative law of the member states'.[64] This chapter does not seek to outline the various constitutional and administrative approaches to statutory interpretation, but rather to ask whether there is a sound legal basis for adopting constitutional

---

[61]  *Ibid.*

[62]  Vienna Convention on the Law of Treaties, opened for signature 23 May 1969, 1155 UNTS 331 (entered into force 27 January 1980).

[63]  Alvarez, 'Constitutional Interpretation in International Organizations', above n. 55, p. 115.

[64]  Georg Ress, 'The Interpretation of the Charter' in Bruno Simma, Daniel-Erasmus Khan and George Nolte (eds.), *The Charter of the United Nations: A Commentary* (Oxford University Press, Oxford, 1994) pp. 25, 27. Note that the most recent edition of this publication has replaced Ress's chapter on interpretation with one by Stefan Kadelbach. Although Kadelbach moves away from Ress's reliance on domestic systems for Charter interpretation, he nonetheless makes reference to a principle of interpretation that can only be a general principle of law (the principle of effectiveness) and to domestic practice: Stefan Kadelbach, 'Interpretation of the Charter' in Bruno Simma *et al.* (eds.), *The Charter of the United Nations: A Commentary* (3rd edn, Oxford University Press, Oxford, 2012) pp. 71, 80, 85.

interpretative principles for the normative documents of international security organisations. Alvarez argues against such an approach, criticising it as lacking support from 'logic, function, text or history'.[65]

An alternate basis for this approach lies instead in the use of General Principles. Domestic public law principles are the legitimate basis for General Principles, provided appropriate horizontal commonality exists. The use of General Principles can in fact address Alvarez's criticisms. First, Alvarez argues that logically, domestic 'constitutional' analogies cannot work because 'there is nothing in the texts of these charters comparable to the typical national constitution's explicit conferral of "legislative", "executive" or "judicial" authority'.[66] As will be discussed in the next section, however, some of the disparity here can be minimised by the concept of the functional separation of powers. At an even more basic level, the foundational requirement for General Principles of 'analogy where appropriate',[67] keeping in mind McNair's warning not to import principles 'lock, stock and barrel',[68] would counsel against a straight application of domestic constitutional rules and principles to the constitutive instruments of international security institutions. Rather, it is only those principles that are 'appropriate' to be applied in the international setting that will satisfy the threshold test and be considered General Principles under international law.

Further, Alvarez argues against the imposition of arguments premised upon 'democratic principles',[69] as the UN Charter is not 'in any sense, a "democratic" document'.[70] The significance of relying on General Principles to found principles of constitutional interpretation is that the question will not be what the political nature of the normative document is, but rather what the common rules of interpretation within states are. Thus, if a General Principle of constitutional interpretation can be made out, with the requisite horizontal generality, then it must be applied to these normative documents as a matter of international law.[71] Thus by explicitly requiring that principles of constitutional

---

[65] Alvarez, 'Constitutional Interpretation in International Organizations', above n. 55, p. 110.

[66] *Ibid.* p. 106.    [67] See above nn. 17–19 and accompanying text.

[68] *International Status of South-West Africa* (Advisory Opinion) [1950] ICJ Rep. 128, 148 (Separate Opinion of Judge McNair).

[69] Alvarez, 'Constitutional Interpretation in International Organizations', above n. 55, p. 105.

[70] *Ibid.* p. 107.

[71] Erika de Wet, 'The International Constitutional Order' (2006) 55 *International and Comparative Law Quarterly* 51, 55, 60; Amerasinghe, *Principles of Institutional Law of*

interpretation be based on General Principles, we avoid the phenomenon of lawyers 'invent[ing] any theory that may help demonstrate the legality of the conduct of UN organs'.[72]

### 4.3   Administrative law principles

The final way in which General Principles will impact on international security institutions relates to legitimacy through administrative processes: concepts such as due process, access to remedies, accountability, transparency and review of decisions and decision-making processes. The application of these principles to international institutions is not novel; the past decade in particular has seen an influx of writings that consider regulation of international institutions from an administrative law perspective. The field of global administrative law is one example,[73] as is Seyersted's conception of a 'common law' of international institutions.[74] However, discussion has tended to develop a set of regulatory rules without necessarily examining the source of international law upon which these rules can be formed. This is despite a clear parallel between such attempts and the use of General Principles.

Thus, Laurence Boisson de Chazournes and Edouard Fromageau write on due process in the context of the World Bank sanction regime,[75] arguing that '[a]ccess to remedies is a global public good',[76] which should apply equally in international institutions as in other forums, as part of the basic right of access to justice.[77] In doing so, Boisson de Chazournes and Fromageau refer to domestic laws, by reference to which the World Bank sanctions process is to be assessed.[78] Although general principles of law in the sense of Article 38(1)(c) are not explicitly referred to,[79] a commonality across states in access to remedies within domestic governmental financial institutions analogous to the World Bank may arguably be considered a basis for a General Principle that could found an international norm of access to remedies, applicable to international financial

---

*International Organizations*, above n. 28, p. 17; Kadelbach, 'Interpretation of the Charter', above n. 64, pp. 80, 85 (with reference to effectiveness).

[72]  G. Arangio-Ruiz, 'The "Federal Analogy" and UN Charter Interpretation: A Crucial Issue' (1997) 51 *European Journal of International Law* 1, 2.

[73]  See literature cited above n. 3.

[74]  Seyersted, *Common Law of International Organisations*, above n. 2.

[75]  Laurence Boisson de Chazournes and Edouard Fromageau, 'Balancing the Scales: The World Bank Sanctions Process and Access to Remedies' (2012) 23 *European Journal of International Law* 963.

[76]  *Ibid.* 964.    [77]  *Ibid.* 964–5.    [78]  *Ibid.* 972–3.    [79]  *Ibid.* 972.

institutions. Similarly, Ricardo Gosalbo-Bono surveys the existence of the rule of law in domestic systems,[80] concluding on the basis of this survey that a 'universal' rule of law would have three common elements: abuse of power; the supremacy of law; and non-discrimination.[81]

Armin von Bogdandy suggests the use of General Principles relating to international public authorities, albeit in a limited fashion.[82] Ultimately he argues against such an approach,[83] identifying two key problems:

> the comparison of administrative legal systems can easily conclude that there are hardly principles in the sense of art. 38 §I lit. c ICJ-Statute. Comparative research is largely limited to a few legal systems and its findings mostly regard administrative action directly affecting the legal positions of individuals, which is rarely the case with international institutions.[84]

First, as discussed above, the disparity between domestic administrative institutions and international institutions cannot prevent a General Principle from being formed.[85] The task is to 'transform' the principle from the domestic context, by way of analogy, to the international one, not to simply import it 'lock, stock and barrel'.[86] Domestic administrative processes will never be identical to international administrative processes, but are still valuable through analogy by examining the underlying rationale behind domestic processes. Such processes can be transformed so that they are applicable to international institutions.

In any event, the extent of transformation needed could be minimal. Administrative actions that directly affect the legal positions of individuals are a neat corollary to the actions of international institutions that directly affect the position of states (the subjects of international law). In this case, administrative requirements such as review or due process would need to be afforded to states, to the same extent they are afforded to individuals at the domestic level. Moreover, given that international law is increasingly impacting upon and regulating

---

[80] Ricardo Gosalbo-Bono, 'The Significance of the Rule of Law and Its Implications for the European Union and the United States' (2010) 72 *University of Pittsburgh Law Review* 229, 240–87.

[81] *Ibid.* 290.

[82] Armin von Bogdandy, 'General Principles of International Public Authority: Sketching a Research Field' (2009) 9 *German Law Journal* 1909.

[83] *Ibid.* 1926.    [84] *Ibid.* 1924.    [85] See above nn. 17–19 and accompanying text.

[86] *International Status of South-West Africa* (Advisory Opinion) [1950] ICJ Rep. 128, 148 (Separate Opinion of Judge McNair).

the behaviour of individuals, the same requirements should be afforded to those who are directly affected by decisions made by an international institution so that they are protected in international law just as they are protected at domestic law.[87]

The second problem identified by von Bogdandy relates to commonality. It must first be noted that a true lack of commonality between legal systems on administrative law principles would defeat the formation of any General Principles; as such principles must be found with horizontal generality.[88] Carol Harlow criticises global administrative law scholarship as favouring Western administrative law, and perpetuating a 'double-colonization' by firstly absorbing 'background values of the global governance or human rights movement, notably the ideals of democracy, participation, transparency and accountability' and secondly 'cross-fertilising' these values from one administrative law system to another, until other forms of administrative law are replaced.[89] In contrast, by insisting that the methodology of Article 38(1)(c) be followed, rather than some amorphous derivation of 'principles' from the international ether, only those principles truly reflective of all types of legal systems, not just Western ones, become international norms.[90] This does not, of course, entirely prevent the imposition of Western administrative law, because of the already well-established spread of Western law through non-Western legal systems, primarily as a result of the British Empire and French colonisation schemes.[91]

If there is a lack of commonality it may be overcome by approaching the problem with a narrower focus. Rather than attempting to derive foundational and holistic principles of global administrative law, or the 'common law' of international institutions, steps may be taken to ascertain General Principles for certain aspects of administrative law.

---

[87] Such protection may still need be provided via a claim of diplomatic protection, however, depending on avenues open to individuals rather than states, and provided that the criteria for diplomatic protection are met: see e.g., Enrico Milano, 'Diplomatic Protection and Human Rights before the International Court of Justice: Re-Fashioning Tradition?' (2004) 35 *Netherlands Yearbook of International Law* 85.

[88] See above n. 11 and accompanying text.

[89] Harlow, 'Global Administrative Law', above n. 3, 209.

[90] For examples of such practice in the International Court of Justice, see *North Sea Continental Shelf (Federal Republic of Germany v. Denmark; Federal Republic of Germany v. Netherlands) (Merits)* [1969] ICJ Rep. 3, 139–40 (Separate Opinion of Judge Ammoun); *Gabčíkovo-Nagymaros Project (Hungary v. Slovakia) (Merits)* [1997] ICJ Rep. 7, 97 (Separate Opinion of Judge Weeramantry).

[91] Harlow, 'Global Administrative Law', above n. 3, 208–9.

Examples of this approach could include a focus on due process or access to remedies,[92] or various aspects of the rule of law, such as abuse of power, the supremacy of the law and non-discrimination, as identified by Gosalbo-Bono.[93] This way, an international system of institutional law applicable to international security institutions can be built, while still maintaining a firm foundation in an established source of international law.

Further, both the applicability of administrative law principles to international security institutions and the correctness of using General Principles to apply such principles are strengthened by concepts of functional separation of powers. The Appeals Chamber of the International Criminal Tribunal for the former Yugoslavia (ICTY) in *Tadić* confirmed that separation of powers, in the domestic sense, does not apply to international organisations.[94] Nonetheless, the legitimacy of the activities of international organisations can arguably be assessed by classifying whether they are 'acting in an executive, legislative or judicial capacity'.[95] Thus, in the context of the Security Council, Tetsuo Sato argues that:

> when the Security Council steps into the judicial, rather than executive, function, it is possible to use such frames of references as independence from political influences and requirements inherent in judicial function (such as due process, publication of justified reasoning, principle of *nemo judex in sua casua*, equality of the parties).[96]

These principles find a better basis in General Principles rather than as those 'inherent in judicial function' – those principles truly inherent will be found with requisite horizontal generality in any case. In the context of the World Trade Organization, Robert Howse argues that 'fair procedures can play an important role in the legitimation of adjudicative decisions',[97] and further that there are minimum fair procedures;

---

[92]  As seen in the work of Boisson de Chazournes and Fromageau, 'Balancing the Scales', above n. 75.
[93]  See, Gosalbo-Bono, 'The Significance of the Rule of Law', above n. 80.
[94]  *Prosecutor* v. *Dusko Tadić (Jurisdiction)*, Case No. IT-94-1-AR72, International Criminal Tribunal for the former Yugoslavia, Appeals Chamber, 2 October 1995, paras. 46–47.
[95]  Tetsuo Sato, 'The Legitimacy of Security Council Actions under Chapter VII of the UN Charter Since the End of the Cold War' in Jean-Marc Coicaud and Veijo Heiskanen (eds.), *The Legitimacy of International Organizations* (United Nations University Press, New York, 2001) pp. 309, 314.
[96]  *Ibid.* p. 330.
[97]  Robert Howse, 'The Legitimacy of the World Trade Organisation' in Jean-Marc Coicaud and Veijo Heiskanen (eds.), *The Legitimacy of International Organizations* (United Nations University Press, New York, 2001) pp. 355, 376.

'legislators and elected executives, as well as adjudicators are constrained, in most liberal democracies, by rules on conflict of interest, and at a minimum, prohibitions on bribery or the taking of public decisions for purely personal advantage'.[98] For both Sato and Howse's arguments, if the identified principles are in fact General Principles, then use of such norms can and will confer legitimacy on those international security institutions that conform to these requirements.

## 5   Conclusion

The issue of the rule of law governing the conduct of institutions is not a new one. However, the regulation of international security institutions becomes more important, as technological advances and increased inter-dependence necessarily means that security problems once constrained by national borders become international or transnational problems. International problems require international solutions, and international security institutions will, and do, respond. It is imperative then to have some means to assess the legality of these actions: to provide a regulatory framework for setting out how international security institutions can act, and to be able to assess when such rules have been breached.

General Principles as a source of international law fits into this regulatory framework for international security organisations. It provides a framework whereby the common core values of members can provide norms of international law where treaty does not and custom cannot. This chapter has sought to set out three key areas where General Principles can interact with and impact on international security institutions: the principle of legality; constitutional interpretation; and administrative law principles. The aim was not to provide a guide to which General Principles 'may' in fact apply (although various norms were suggested) but rather set up a theoretical conception of how this area of law should be addressed. By using General Principles, we rely on an established source of international law providing a foundation for developing the rule of law and governing the conduct of international security institutions.

---

[98] *Ibid.* p. 377.

# 6

# The United Nations Security Council's legislative phase and the rise of emergency international law-making

ANNA HOOD

## 1 Introduction

In recent decades the United Nations (UN) Security Council has significantly developed the tools it employs to address threats to the peace, breaches of the peace and acts of aggression under Chapter VII of the UN Charter.[1] One of the tools it has developed is Security Council 'legislation';[2] that is, Security Council Resolutions that create or modify

---

[1] Charter of the United Nations, opened for signature 26 June 1945, 1 UNTS xvi (entered into force 24 October 1945), Art. 39, as amended by GA Res. 1991, 557 UNTS 143 (1963); GA Res. 2101, 638 UNTS 308 (1965); GA Res. 2847, 892 UNTS 119 (1971).

[2] The use of the word 'legislation' in relation to any form of international law, let alone Security Council Resolutions, is controversial. A significant number of international lawyers have rejected the idea that any sort of international legislation exists because there is no international legislature that is comparable to domestic legislatures and no form of international legislation that mirrors domestic legislation: see e.g., G.M. Danilenko, *Law-Making in the International Community* (Martinus Nijhoff, Leiden, 1993) pp. 6–7; Lori Fisler Damrosch et al., *International Law Cases and Materials* (4th edn, West Group, St Paul, MN, 2001) p. 16. However, the vast majority of definitions for the word 'legislation' in domestic contexts do not require legislation to be produced by legislatures and in many jurisdictions the executive arm of government has the ability to produce certain forms of legislation. Furthermore, there is a long history of the term 'legislation' being used in international law to refer to different forms of international law-making: see e.g., Martti Koskenniemi, 'International Legislation Today' (2005) 23 *Wisconsin International Law Journal* 61, 66; Manley O. Hudson, *International Legislation: A Collection of the Texts of Multipartite International Instruments of General Interest beginning with the Covenant of the League of Nations* (Carnegie Endowment for International Peace, 1931) p. xviii (employing the term 'international legislation' to refer to treaties); Edward Yemin, *Legislative Powers in the United Nations and Specialized Agencies* (A.W. Sijthoff, 1969) pp. 2–3, 6 (employing the term 'international legislation' to refer to the law-making activities of international organisations). It is in this context that the activities of the Security Council described in this chapter can be understood as a form of 'legislation'.

international legal obligations.[3] The Council has issued a wide array of legislative resolutions including those that create or modify specific legal obligations in relation to a target state;[4] those that create or modify specific legal obligations for all UN member states;[5] and, most controversially, those that create or modify general, abstract legal obligations for all UN member states.[6] The definition of Security Council legislation has been keenly contested, with some scholars asserting that the term should only be used to refer to Security Council Resolutions that create or modify general, abstract obligations.[7] For the purpose of this chapter, however, a broader definition is adopted because in domestic contexts legislation can create specific legal obligations such as private acts, acts of attainder and acts of pains

---

[3] See generally e.g., Keith Harper, 'Does the United Nations Security Council Have the Competence to Act as Court and Legislature?' (1994–1995) 27 *New York University Journal of International Law and Politics* 103, 106, 108; Munir Akram and Syed Haider Shah, 'The Legislative Powers of the United Nations Security Council' in Ronald St John Macdonald and Douglas M. Johnston (eds.), *Towards World Constitutionalism: Issues in the Legal Ordering of the World Community* (Martinus Nijhoff, Leiden, 2005) pp. 431, 436.

[4] SC Res. 687 (3 April 1991) para. 8(a) (requiring Iraq to relinquish its chemical weapons at the conclusion of the 1990–1991 Gulf War); SC Res. 748 (31 March 1992) para. 1 (modifying Libya's international obligations under the Montreal Convention by requiring it to extradite the Lockerbie bombing suspects).

[5] SC Res. 1267 (15 October 1999) paras. 3–4 (requiring member states to impose sanctions against individuals); SC Res. 827 (25 May 1993) and SC Res. 955 (8 November 1994) (establishing the International Criminal Tribunal for the former Yugoslavia and the International Criminal Tribunal for Rwanda, respectively). These Resolutions fit within the definition of legislation because some of the procedural requirements contained within the statutes annexed to the Resolutions imposed legal obligations on states. See e.g., Statute of the International Criminal Tribunal for the former Yugoslavia, SC Res. 827 (25 May 1993) Art. 10(1); Statute of the International Criminal Tribunal for Rwanda, SC Res. 955 (8 November 1994) Art. 9(1).

[6] SC Res. 1373 (28 September 2001) para. 1(b) (requiring member states, *inter alia*, to take steps to criminalise the financing of terrorism); SC Res. 1540 (28 April 2004) paras. 1–3 (requiring member states to implement measures to prevent the spread of weapons of mass destruction to non-state actors); SC Res. 1422 (12 July 2002) SC Res. 1487 (12 June 2003) (requesting the International Criminal Court to refrain from prosecuting persons working on UN operations who came from states not party to the Rome Statute for a period of twelve months, and requiring all UN member states not to take any action that was inconsistent with this request).

[7] Stefan Talmon, 'The Security Council as World Legislature' (2005) 99 *American Journal of International Law* 175, 176; Georges Abi-Saab, 'The Security Council *Legibus Solutus?* On the Legislative Forays of the Council' in Laurence Boisson de Chazournes and Marcelo Kohen (eds.), *International Law and the Quest for Its Implementation* (Brill, Leiden/Boston, MA, 2010) pp. 23, 26–7.

and penalties that common law countries have adopted over the last four centuries.[8]

This chapter seeks to generate insights into the Security Council's legislative activity as an institutional response to the changing nature of international security threats by understanding the phenomenon as a form of emergency law-making that is analogous to the law that is produced by domestic executives in times of crisis. In order to do this section 2 explores the similarities between Security Council legislation and emergency laws that are produced by domestic executives ('domestic emergency legislation').

Section 3 examines the idea that in many respects the Security Council's legislative activity reflects Carl Schmitt's theory on the state of exception which holds that executives' law-making activities in times of crisis cannot be constrained by the rule of law. Section 4 then explores whether emergency law theories that have sought to counter Schmitt's theory on the state of exception and ensure that executives abide by the rule of law during periods of emergency could be applied to the Council's legislative practice. In so doing it endeavours to determine whether there are any normative considerations in emergency law theories that could enhance the Council's compliance with the rule of law when it legislates. The chapter concludes that while emergency law theories provide several normative ideas for controlling the Security Council's legislative activity, all of them have significant limitations and the extent to which any of them could in fact be implemented is questionable.

## 2 Understanding Security Council legislation as emergency law-making

Over the last three to four hundred years, in times of crisis, many states have determined that their standard law-making procedures (such as requiring Bills to pass through legislatures) are too slow and cumbersome to respond effectively to the dangers at hand and that it is therefore necessary for them to transfer law-making powers to the more decisive

---

[8] See generally, Kath Hall, *Butterworths Guides: Legislation* (Butterworths, Chatswood, 2002) p. 25; Ivor Richardson, 'Private Acts of Parliament' (2010) 41 *Victoria University of Wellington Law Review* 653; Duane Ostler, 'Bills of Attainder and the Formation of the American Takings Clause at the Founding of the Republic' (2010) 32 *Campbell Law Review* 227; David Miers and Alan Page, *Legislation* (Sweet and Maxwell, London, 1990) p. 2; Jacob Reynolds, 'The Rule of Law and the Origins of the Bill of Attainder Clause' (2005) 18 *St Thomas Law Review* 177.

and efficient, executive branch of government.[9] At times the transfer of power has been sanctioned by a constitutional or statutory provision. For example, article 48 of the Weimar Constitution provided that law-making powers could be transferred from the German legislature to the President of the Reich 'if security and public order are seriously disturbed or threatened'.[10] During the First World War, the French legislature passed a law empowering the French Cabinet 'to regulate by decree the production and trade of food stuffs'.[11] At other times law-making power has been transferred to the executive branch without the sanction of law. Some of the most well-known examples of this occurring include Abraham Lincoln issuing the Emancipation Declaration during the United States' Civil War,[12] and Franklin Roosevelt closing all banks in the United States and seizing all private gold collections during his first five days in office in 1933.[13]

Regardless of the way in which executives assume law-making powers, most forms of domestic emergency legislation share three characteristics. First, they are generated during a period of national emergency. There is no common understanding of what constitutes an emergency.[14] Traditionally, most definitions have asserted that emergencies are phenomena that pose exceptional, imminent threats to the existence of states (such as war).[15] Over time, however, both of these elements have at times been undermined with executives constructing 'fictitious emergencies' that lack the gravity and imminence that 'real emergencies' possess and executives extending the duration of crises or failing to confine them temporally.[16]

---

[9] Oren Gross and Fionnuala Ní Aoláin, *Law in Times of Crisis: Emergency Powers in Theory and Practice* (Cambridge University Press, Cambridge, 2006) p. 59; Giorgio Agamben, *State of Exception* (University of Chicago Press, Chicago, IL, 2005) pp. 11–22; David Golove, 'Exception and Emergency Powers: Comment on Exception and Emergency Powers' (2000) 21 *Cardozo Law Review* 1895, 1897–8.

[10] Weimar Constitution, art. 48, as cited in Agamben, *State of Exception*, above n. 9, p. 14.

[11] *Ibid.* p. 12.

[12] Louis Fisher, 'Invoking Inherent Powers: A Primer' (2007) 37(1) *Presidential Quarterly Studies* 3. Note that some scholars view the Emancipation Declaration as an exercise of inherent presidential powers not as extra-legal activity. See e.g., Gross and Aoláin, *Law in Times of Crisis*, above n. 9, pp. 47–8.

[13] Proclamation 2039 (1933); Roger I. Roots, 'Government by Permanent Emergency: The Forgotten History of the New Deal Constitution' (1999–2000) 33 *Suffolk University Law Review* 259, 262–3.

[14] Gross and Aoláin, *Law in Times of Crisis*, above n. 9, pp. 5, 40.    [15] *Ibid.* pp. 171–2.

[16] *Ibid.*; Agamben, *State of Exception*, above n. 9, pp. 2–5; Mary Dudziak, 'Law, War and the History of Time' (2009) 98 *California Law Review* 1669, 1670.

The second characteristic of domestic emergency legislation is that it is intended to last for the duration of the crisis only.[17] Theoretically this means that emergency laws are short, temporary measures. However, with the erosion of the temporal limits around emergencies, it has become increasingly common for the life-spans of emergency laws to be extended and in some cases pieces of domestic emergency legislation have become permanent fixtures in legal systems.[18]

The final characteristic that most forms of domestic emergency legislation possess is that they involve a transfer of law-making power from the ordinary law-making branch of government (the legislature) to the executive. The precise part of the executive that is endowed with legislative power varies from state to state and crisis to crisis; in some cases it is the head of state, at other times it is the Cabinet or another entity within a state's executive.

Security Council legislation can be understood as a form of emergency law-making because, to a significant degree, legislative Security Council Resolutions also exhibit these three characteristics. It is possible to understand Security Council legislation as being adopted during a period of emergency because legislative resolutions are passed under Chapter VII of the UN Charter,[19] and in order for Chapter VII powers to be invoked there must be a 'threat to the peace, breach of the peace or act of aggression' pursuant to Article 39 of the Charter. The concepts of threats to the peace, breaches of the peace and acts of aggression encompass many of the situations that are regarded as emergencies in domestic spheres, including wars and other forms of conflict. Further, the most commonly employed component of Article 39 – a threat to the peace – has undergone a transformation comparable to that which has affected domestic emergencies. Originally it referred to imminent international military action, but over time the Council has stretched it into a more nebulous concept

---

[17] Jared Schott, 'Chapter VII as Exception: Security Council Action and the Regulative Ideal of Emergency' (2007) 6 *Northwestern Journal of International Human Rights* 24, 32.

[18] Gross and Aoláin, *Law in Times of Crisis*, above n. 9, pp. 171, 175; Nicola McGarrity, Andrew Lynch and George Williams, *Counter-Terrorism and Beyond: The Culture of Law and Justice after 9/11* (Routledge, London, 2010) p. 4.

[19] Whether legislative resolutions are *intra vires* or *ultra vires* under the UN Charter will be discussed below in section 3. However, it should be appreciated at this point that the legality of legislative resolutions does not affect them being understood as emergency legislation. This is because, as explained above, in domestic spheres executives assume emergency law-making powers both legally and extra-legally.

that encompasses a wide array of situations, including humanitarian crises and unrest within states.[20]

Security Council legislation also reflects the second characteristic of executive-produced emergency law as the vast majority of legislative Security Council Resolutions are intended to endure for the period of the crisis which they have been designed to address and no longer. Some legislative resolutions, such as Resolution 1422 and Resolution 1487, contain explicit temporal constraints,[21] while others, such as Resolution 687, Resolution 748 and Resolution 1054, contain implicit time limits in that they are intended to stay in place only until the state(s) against which they are directed complies with the Council's demands.[22]

Similarly to the situation in the domestic sphere, the life-spans of some legislative resolutions have been extended beyond the time limits that were initially prescribed for them. For example, Resolution 1422 was intended to last for twelve months but was extended for another twelve months by Resolution 1487. Further, with regard to legislative resolutions of a general nature, the Council has identified open-ended threats to the peace (for example, international terrorism in Resolution 1373 and the threat of non-state actors acquiring weapons of mass destruction in Resolution 1540) and issued legislative resolutions in response to them without any temporal limits. The lack of temporal boundaries in Resolutions 1373 and 1540 has led some commentators to conclude that Security Council legislation

---

[20] At the Security Council Heads of State and Government Meeting in 1992 the Council issued a statement stating that '[t]he absence of war and military conflict amongst states does not in itself ensure international peace and security. The non-military sources of instability in the economic, social and humanitarian and ecological fields have become threats to the peace and security': UN Doc. S/23500 (31 January 1992) 3. On the change in the nature of threats to the peace, see generally, Karel Wellens, 'The UN Security Council and New Threats to the Peace: Back to the Future' (2003) 8 *Journal of Conflict and Security Law* 15; Robert Cryer, 'The Security Council and Article 39: A Threat to Coherence?' (1996) 1 *Journal of Armed Conflict Law* 161; Frederic L. Kirgis Jr, 'The Security Council's First Fifty Years' (1995) 89 *American Journal of International Law* 506.

[21] Both SC Res. 1422 (12 July 2002) and SC Res. 1487 (12 June 2003) were designed to last for twelve months only.

[22] SC Res. 687 (3 April 1991) paras. 10, 13; SC Res. 748 (31 March 1992) para. 3; SC Res. 1054 (26 April 1996) para. 3. See also Eric Rosand, 'The Security Council as Global Legislator: Ultra Vires or Ultra Innovative' (2005) 28 *Fordham International Law Journal* 542, 568; Paul C. Szasz, 'The Security Council Starts Legislating' (2002) 96 *American Journal of International Law* 901, 901–2.

cannot be classified as emergency law.[23] However, given the fact that the temporal limits surrounding domestic emergencies and the domestic emergency measures enacted in response to them have also been challenged,[24] the absence of a time limit does not prevent legislative resolutions from being characterised as a form of emergency law.

The final characteristic of emergency law produced by domestic executives is that it involves a transfer of law-making power from the legislative branch to the executive branch. It is possible to understand the production of Security Council legislation as a result of the transfer of legislative power from the legislative branch of the international community to the executive branch of the international community if UN member states are understood as the world's legislature and the Security Council is understood as the world's executive. The analogy is imperfect because there is no clear division of executive, legislative and judicial powers at the international level.[25] However, it is possible to view the UN membership at large as a loose form of international legislature as it is sovereign states that have traditionally had the power to create and modify international obligations through the production of treaties and customary international law. Further, it is widely recognised that the Security Council is a body that is comparable to domestic executives because it exercises many of the powers that characterise domestic executives, such as the powers to implement and enforce laws and the power to respond to security threats.[26]

---

[23]   Andrea Bianchi, 'Assessing the Effectiveness of the UN Security Council's Anti-Terrorism Measures: The Quest for Legitimacy and Cohesion' (2006) 17 *European Journal of International Law* 881, 892.

[24]   Illustrative is the US Presidential Military Order of 13 November 2001 which allowed for the detention of individuals. The perpetual nature of the 'War on Terror' has been discussed by the US Supreme Court in *Hamdi* v. *Rumsfeld*, 542 US 507, 520 (2004) and *Boumediene* v. *Bush*, 553 US 723, 785 (2008). See also Gross and Aoláin, *Law in Times of Crisis*, above n. 9, pp. 179–80; Dudziak, 'Law, War and the History of Time', above n. 16, 1697–9.

[25]   Antonio Tzanakopoulos, *Disobeying the Security Council: Countermeasures Against Wrongful Sanctions* (Oxford University Press, Oxford, 2011) p. 7; Nigel D. White, 'The United Nations System: Conference, Contract or Constitutional Order?' (2000) 4 *Singapore Journal of International and Comparative Law* 281, 293; *Prosecutor* v. *Tadić (Jurisdiction)*, Case No. IT-94-1-AR72, International Criminal Tribunal for the former Yugoslavia, Appeals Chamber, 2 October 1995, para. 43.

[26]   Tzanakopoulos, *Disobeying the Security Council*, above n. 25, p. 8; Dan Sarooshi, 'The Legal Framework Governing United Nations Subsidiary Organs' (1996) 47 *British Yearbook of International Law* 463; Karel Wellens, 'Fragmentation of International Law and Establishing an Accountability Regime for International Organizations: The Role of

It is thus apparent that there are strong parallels between domestic emergency legislation and the Council's production of legislative resolutions.

## 3 Schmittian nature of Security Council legislation

Understanding Security Council legislation as a form of emergency law opens up the possibility of drawing on the wealth of literature that underpins the field of emergency law to better understand and guide the Council's legislative activities. One of the central questions of emergency law scholarship has been whether and how an executive, wielding emergency law-making powers, can be constrained and the rule of law protected.[27] In 1922, the German legal philosopher Carl Schmitt set out his theory on the state of exception which held that it is naïve to believe that emergencies can be constrained by law.[28] According to Schmitt the challenges, uncertainties and dangers that crises create mean that it is impossible for a legal system to prescribe effective rules to address the contingencies of an emergency.[29] Rather, the only way in which a state can hope to navigate the complexities of a crisis is for 'the sovereign' to have the power to decide that an emergency exists and then adopt whatever measures are necessary to resolve the situation, including amending and overriding existing laws and fashioning new ones.[30] In his view, emergencies reveal the limits of the law and any states that seek to fashion rules to constrain executives during such periods are simply creating a thin veneer of legality in a fruitless attempt to obscure what in fact dictates the course of events – pure political discretion.[31]

---

the Judiciary in Closing the Gap' (2003–2004) 25 *Michigan Journal of International Law* 1159, 1179.

[27] See generally e.g., David Dyzenhaus, *The Constitution of Law: Legality in a Time of Emergency* (Cambridge University Press, Cambridge, 2006).

[28] Schmitt's theory on the state of exception is set out in Carl Schmitt, *Politische Theologie: Vier Kapitel zur Lehre von der Souveranitat* (1922), translated in George Schwarb, *Political Theology: Four Chapters on the Concept of Sovereignty* (University of Chicago Press, Chicago, IL, 2005).

[29] *Ibid.* p. 13.

[30] *Ibid.* pp. 6–7; John McCormick, 'The Dilemmas of Dictatorship: Carl Schmitt and Constitutional Emergency Powers' (1997) 10 *Canadian Journal of Law and Jurisprudence* 163, 170; Oren Gross, 'The Normless and the Exceptionless Exception: Carl Schmitt's Theory of Emergency Powers and the "Norm-Exception" Dichotomy' (1999–2000) 21 *Cardozo Law Review* 1825, 1845.

[31] David Dyzenhaus, '*Schmitt v. Dicey*: Are States of Emergency Inside or Outside the Legal Order?' (2006) 27 *Cardozo Law Review* 2005, 2015.

The implications of Schmitt's theory are grave. If an executive wields unlimited power during a crisis and can determine what constitutes a crisis, there is little to stop it invoking its extensive powers whenever it pleases and the prospect of permanent authoritarian rule becoming the norm is very real.[32] As Oren Gross states, 'should the sovereign dictator so decide, his unlimited powers – originally designed to apply to the exceptional case – may come to control the norm, indeed *be* the norm'.[33] Concerned at this prospect, legal scholars have sought to counter Schmitt's theory in a variety of ways. Some have designed mechanisms intended to help bind executives to the rule of law during crises, while others have accepted Schmitt's premise that laws cannot constrain executives in emergencies but sought to develop an array of moral, political and legal measures to ensure that executives' extra-legal activity is limited. The rest of this section explores how, in many respects, the Council's production of legislation appears to fit within Schmitt's theory on the state of exception. Section 4 then considers whether any of the domestic legal theories that have been developed in response to Schmitt's approach to emergencies could be applied to the Council's legislative activity.

*Prima facie*, the idea that Security Council legislation resembles Schmitt's conception of the state of exception seems misplaced as the UN Charter appears to provide a number of legal provisions that the Council must adhere to even when formulating a legislative resolution. Under Article 39, the Council can employ law-making powers only when there is any 'threat to the peace, breach of the peace, or act of aggression' and Article 41 restricts the sorts of law-making activity the Council can engage in to 'measures not involving the use of armed force ... include[ing] complete or partial interruption of economic relations and of rail, sea, air, postal, telegraphic, radio and other means of communication, and the severance of diplomatic relations'. Even though it is widely acknowledged that Article 41 is not limited to the sanctions measures specified in the text of the provision,[34] many commentators assert that enforcement measures under Article 41 are still subject to restraints, including the requirement that they be specific in nature and time-limited.[35] Further, many scholars contend that the

---

[32] Gross, 'The Normless and the Exceptionless Exception', above n. 30, 1845–6.
[33] *Ibid.* 1846 (original emphasis).  [34] *Prosecutor* v.*Tadić*, above n. 25, para. 35.
[35] Abi-Saab, 'The Security Council *Legibus Solutus?* ', above n. 7, pp. 30–1; Arangio Ruiz, 'On the Security Council's Law-Making' (2000) 83 *Rivista di diritto internazionale* 609, 660–82. It should be noted that some commentators suggest that Art. 41 has evolved to

Council's production of legislation is subject to an array of purposes and principles of the UN as required by Article 24 of the Charter, including *jus cogens* principles,[36] the principle of good faith,[37] and human rights standards,[38] as well as provisions in Article 26 of the Charter prohibiting the Council from legislating in relation to armament and disarmament issues.[39]

On examining the Council's legislative practice, however, it is apparent that the extent to which these provisions in fact constrain the Council's legislative activity is open to question. In many respects the legal principles surrounding the Council's production of legislative resolutions act as the 'thin veneer of legality' that lulls those committed to the rule of law into a false sense of security; they purport to restrict and constrain the Council's legislative actions but in reality do little to prevent the Council from operating in a space beyond law.[40] They resemble what David Dyzenhaus has termed 'grey holes'.[41] Drawing on Schmitt's work, Dyzenhaus suggests that emergency law-making is prone to both black and grey holes. Black holes are spaces where law ceases to operate and executives wield unfettered discretion,[42] whereas grey holes are black holes in disguise.[43] They are spaces where there is a façade of law but it is so vague or malleable that it fails, in any meaningful way, to constrain executives in exercising discretion.[44] It is arguable that the provisions of the Charter that are intended to control the Council's legislative activity in fact facilitate the production of grey holes to a significant degree and

---

empower the Council to pass general measures without time constraints. This issue is discussed below.

[36] See e.g., Erika de Wet, *Chapter VII Powers of the Security Council* (Hart Publishing, Oxford/Portland, OR, 2004) pp. 187–91; Axel Marschik, 'Legislative Powers of the Security Council' in Ronald St John Macdonald and Douglas M. Johnston (eds.), *Towards World Constitutionalism: Issues in the Legal Ordering of the World Community* (Martinus Nijhoff, Leiden, 2005) pp. 487.

[37] See e.g., de Wet, *Chapter VII Powers of the Security Council*, above n. 36, pp. 195–200.

[38] *Ibid.* pp. 198–200.

[39] Daniel H. Joyner, *International Law and the Proliferation of Weapons of Mass Destruction* (Oxford University Press, New York, 2009) pp. 188–9.

[40] Cf. Gabriël H. Oosthuizen, 'Playing the Devil's Advocate: The United Nations Security Council is Unbound by Law' (1999) 12 *Leiden Journal of International Law* 549. The argument in this chapter is distinguished in that the author acknowledges that the Council is bound by law and argues that because the Council operates in emergency situations, the law is relatively ineffective in constraining the Council.

[41] Dyzenhaus, '*Schmitt v. Dicey*', above n. 31, 2018.    [42] *Ibid.* 2015.

[43] *Ibid.* 2018; Adrian Vermeule, 'Our Schmittian Administrative Law' (2009) 122 *Harvard Law Review* 1095, 1096.

[44] Dyzenahus, '*Schmitt v. Dicey*', above n. 31, 2018.

that, to the limited extent that they manage to provide some weak parameters for the Council's activities, the Council has exhibited few qualms in overriding them when it deems necessary.

Article 39 can be understood as producing a grey hole because while it appears to restrict the situations which enliven the Council's law-making powers, it has been understood as a political, not legal, provision that is 'entirely within [the Council's] discretion'.[45] This understanding of the term has allowed the Council to mould and expand its scope significantly to encompass situations well beyond what the drafters of the UN Charter ever envisaged and outside what the ordinary meaning of the terms within it cover. As discussed above, the Council has used its discretion to extend the term 'a threat to the peace' to situations outside the military scenarios envisaged by the Charter's drafters.[46] Further, it has dispensed with the imminence requirement which was an integral part of the word 'threat' when the term was created and which is still inherent in defini-tions of the term today.[47] Indeed, in many respects the Council now appears to respond to 'risks' to the peace, not 'threats' to the peace in the sense that threats are imminent and computable dangers whereas risks have broader temporal dimensions and refer to perceptions of future dangers.[48] A prominent example of the Council issuing a legislative resolution in response to a risk, as opposed to a threat, is Resolution 1373. The 'threat' identified in Resolution 1373 was international terror-ism. However, the prospect of international terrorism occurring at the time of Resolution 1373's passage in September 2001 was not a specific, imminent danger. The Council did not identify any specific group that

---

[45] *Questions of Interpretation and Application of the 1971 Montreal Convention arising from the Aerial Incident at Lockerbie (Libyan Arab Jamahiriya v. United Kingdom) (Provisional Measures)* [1992] ICJ Rep. 114, 170 (Judge Weeramantry Dissenting Opinion).

[46] See above n. 20 and accompanying text.

[47] *Legal Consequences for States of the Continued Presence of South Africa in Namibia (South West Africa) notwithstanding Security Council Resolution 276* (Advisory Opinion) [1971] ICJ Rep. 16, 328, para. 34 (Judge Gros Dissenting Opinion; stating that the Council was not empowered to respond to a 'matter [that] may have a distant repercussion on the maintenance of peace'). See also de Wet, *Chapter VII Powers of the Security Council*, above n. 36, p. 139.

[48] This conception of 'risks' and 'threats' is drawn from the sociological field focused on risk and modernity that was generated by Ulrich Beck, *Risk Society: Towards a New Modernity* (Sage, London, 1992). For a discussion of the definitions of the terms 'risks' and 'threats' in this field, see Mikkel Vedby Rasmussen, *The Risk Society at War* (Cambridge University Press, Cambridge, 2006) pp. 1–2; M.J. Williams, '(In)Security Studies, Reflexive Modernization and Security Studies' (2008) 43(1) *Cooperation and Conflict* 57, 65–6.

was planning an imminent terrorist attack; rather, the prospect of international terrorism was a perception of a future danger.

The Council and those supporting its actions have sought to justify the expansion of Article 39 by claiming that the nature of the threats facing the international community is very different to the one confronting the world when the UN Charter first entered into force, and that the term 'a threat to the peace' must be interpreted to recognise this change of circumstances.[49] Article 31(3)(b) of the Vienna Convention on the Law of Treaties indeed allows for treaty terms to evolve.[50] However, the evolution that has occurred with the term 'a threat to the peace' has been so great that it now allows the Council to operate in a 'grey hole'.

In theory, Article 41 is not as malleable as Article 39 because the *travaux préparatoires* of the UN Charter, the structure of the UN Charter and the wording of Article 41 all suggest that the provision limits Council action to measures that are specific and time-limited.[51] This means it can only produce specific decisions that relate to a specific crisis and that are temporally limited. The Council, however, has shown scant regard for the boundaries of Article 41, as evidenced by its production of a number of legislative resolutions that contain general, abstract norms which in some cases last indefinitely.

Two of the most common ways in which the Council's disregard for the limits of Article 41 has been justified, when it produces general legislative resolutions, contain strong Schmittian overtones. First, some

---

[49] See e.g., Harper, 'Does the United Nations Security Council Have the Competence', above n. 3, 149; Rosand, 'The Security Council as Global Legislator', above n. 22, 570–3; Talmon, 'The Security Council as World Legislature', above n. 7, 180–1.

[50] Opened for signature 23 May 1969, 1155 UNTS 331 (entered into force 27 January 1980). For detailed analysis of the scope for 'evolutive interpretation' of treaties through Art. 31(3)(b), see Georg Nolte, *First Report on Subsequent Agreements and Subsequent Practice in relation to Treaty Interpretation*, UN Doc. A/CN.4/660 (International Law Commission, 19 March 2013) pp. 23–7 (finding that 'evolutive interpretation does not seem to be a separate method of interpretation but rather the result of a proper application of the usual means of interpretation': *ibid.* p. 26, para. 62). Further, many commentators hold that it is particularly important for constitutive treaties of international organisations (such as the UN Charter) to be interpreted in a teleological manner to enable them to remain relevant. See e.g., Blaine Sloan, 'The United Nations Charter as a Constitution' (1989) 1 *Pace Yearbook of International Law* 61, 105; Louis Sohn, 'The UN System as Authoritative Interpreter of Its Law' in Oscar Schachter and Christopher Joyner (eds.), *United Nations Legal Order* (Cambridge University Press, Cambridge, 1995) pp. 169, 227. Cf. Jan Klabbers, *An Introduction to International Institutional Law* (2nd edn, Cambridge University Press, Cambridge, 2009) p. 100.

[51] See e.g., Abi-Saab, 'The Security Council *Legibus Solutus?*', above n. 7, pp. 30–1; Ruiz, 'On the Security Council's Law-Making', above n. 35, 660–82.

scholars such as Eric Rosand have argued that the Council's production of legislative resolutions with general, abstract norms does not in fact violate the bounds of Article 41.[52] To do this Rosand has interpreted Article 41 in a way that reduces it to a provision that generates 'grey holes'. He has asserted that it should be interpreted in accordance with the UN Charter's object and purpose. As the purpose of the Charter is the maintenance of international peace and security, he has contended that the Council is empowered to adopt whatever measures it deems necessary under Article 41 to ensure the maintenance of international peace and security.[53] There is much to be said for ensuring that a treaty is interpreted effectively and in accordance with its object and purpose. However, this approach arguably allows a teleological interpretation to be applied at the expense of all other considerations and grants the Council *carte blanche* to respond to crises in any way it pleases (short of resorting to force).[54] It allows the Council to carry out activities with the sanction of a law that is deprived of all meaningful content.

A second Schmittian justification for the Council's production of general legislative resolutions has involved states admitting that these resolutions violate Article 41 but asserting that this should be overlooked because of the need for the Council to respond to extreme situations. An example of this reasoning arose in the debates surrounding the passage of Resolution 1540. During those debates Algeria, Jordan, Liechtenstein, Mexico, New Zealand, the Philippines, the Republic of Korea, Singapore and Switzerland all expressed unease with the Council imposing general legal obligations on states and noted that the normal course of action would have been for states to develop a multilateral treaty.[55] Each of these states, however, determined that in the circumstances it was necessary for the Council to pass the Resolution because general, abstract norms were required to meet the exceptional threat posed by non-state actors seeking

---

[52] Rosand, 'The Security Council as Global Legislator', above n. 22, 552–60.    [53] *Ibid.*

[54] There is strong support for the idea that teleological approaches to treaty interpretation must not be applied exclusively, that is, without regard for other principles of treaty interpretation. See e.g., Alexander Orakhelashvili, *The Interpretation of Acts and Rules in Public International Law* (Oxford University Press, Oxford, 2008) p. 396; David Schweigman, *The Authority of the Security Council under Chapter VII of the UN Charter: Legal Limits and the Role of the International Court of Justice* (Martinus Nijhoff Publishers, Boston, 2001) p. 19.

[55] UN SCOR, 4950th mtg, 59th sess., UN Doc. S/PV.4950 (22 April 2004) pp. 2–3, 5, 20–1, 25, 28; UN SCOR, 4950th mtg, 59th sess., UN Doc. S/PV.4950 (Resumption 1) (22 April 2004) pp. 4–5, 8, 10–11, 12.

weapons of mass destruction.[56] This rationale appears to bear out Schmitt's belief that where laws seek to curtail the methods a sovereign can employ to respond to a crisis, they will inevitably be trampled on as 'one [cannot] spell out what may take place [in an emergency] . . . and of how it is to be eliminated'.[57]

The legal restrictions outside of Articles 39 and 41 that scholars assert bind the Council when it acts under Chapter VII have proved similarly ineffective at tempering the Council's legislative activities. For example, in passing Resolution 1540 the Council arguably violated the process for creating laws concerning the regulation of arms and disarmament as set down in Articles 11(1) and 26 of the UN Charter.[58] These provisions require the involvement of the General Assembly and UN member states in the generation of laws regarding arms and disarmament. Further, in Resolution 1267 (one the most Schmittian legislative resolutions issued to date) the Council breached numerous human rights obligations, such as the right to due process and the right to property, by requiring states to freeze the assets of listed individuals, who were suspected of involvement with the Taliban and Al-Qaeda,[59] without any criminal charge or procedures to inform them of the actions taken against them.[60]

It is thus clear that in several significant ways the Council's legislative activity reflects Schmitt's theory on the state of exception. Many of the key rules and principles that are designed to restrict the Council's actions in fact afford it great discretion and where limits do exist they are vulnerable to being overridden whenever the Council deems it necessary to ensure international peace and security.

## 4   Countering the Schmittian nature of Security Council legislation

In domestic emergency law literature, legal theorists have asserted that while Schmitt's theory may describe common tendencies in emergency

---

[56] *Ibid.*      [57] Schmitt, *Politische Theologie*, above n. 28, pp. 6–7.

[58] Joyner, *International Law and the Proliferation of Weapons of Mass Destruction*, above n. 39, pp. 188–9.

[59] SC Res. 1267 (15 October 1999) para. 4(b).

[60] See e.g., Rosemary Foot, 'The United Nations, Counter Terrorism, and Human Rights: Institutional Adaptation and Embedded Ideas' (2007) 29 *Human Rights Quarterly* 489, 493, 496; Peter Guthrie, 'Security Council Sanctions and the Protection of Individual Rights' (2004) 60 *NYU Annual Survey of American Law* 491, 499.

law-making, it is not a normative theory.[61] It depicts what tends to occur in crises but abandons all hope that reality could be different. These scholars insist that periods of emergency need not be permanently consumed by an all-powerful, authoritarian sovereign and have devised a number of mechanisms to help prevent Schmitt's vision from arising. This section explores the three most common approaches for warding off Schmitt's state of exception and seeks to determine the scope for applying some of the normative considerations within them to the Council's legislative activity.

### 4.1 Division of emergency powers between the legislature and the executive

The first approach accepts Schmitt's belief that substantive rules about what constitutes an emergency and what measures can be taken in response to an emergency are unlikely to control executives' behaviour during times of crisis but asserts that executives' emergency activities may be restricted through procedural limitations.[62] This approach enables executives to assume wide-ranging powers in times of crisis but seeks to limit when and how such powers are employed by devising certain constitutional procedures that must be adhered to.[63]

It draws inspiration from the Romans' idea of a commissarial dictatorship.[64] In times of crisis, the Romans bestowed extensive powers on a dictator but sought to prevent dictatorial rule becoming the norm by ensuring that an entity other than the dictator determined the existence of an emergency and that the dictator could only exercise the powers for a limited period of time.[65] It was believed that by separating the power to make the decision that a crisis exists from the power to take action to resolve the crisis, the dictator's ability to invoke emergency powers without warrant would be diminished. Further, any chance of the dictator abusing its powers would be reduced by the imposition of temporal limits.

There have been several modern manifestations of the Roman commissarial dictatorship. For example, some states have vested the power to decide that a state of emergency exists with the legislative branch of government while granting the executive branch the power to respond

---

[61] Gross, 'The Normless and the Exceptionless Exception', above n. 30, 1828–9.
[62] William Scheuerman, 'Survey Article: Emergency Powers and the Rule of Law After 9/11' (2006) 14 *Journal of Political Philosophy* 61, 75–6.
[63] *Ibid.*   [64] *Ibid.* 74.   [65] Dyzenhaus, '*Schmitt v. Dicey*', above n. 31, 2012–13.

to the emergency.[66] Further, some states have placed specific time limits on states of emergency or vested the legislative branch with the power to terminate states of emergency.[67] Bruce Ackerman has drawn on these ideas to develop what he calls the 'supermajoritarian escalator', which allows a short-term state of emergency to come into existence but only with the approval of the legislature.[68] If the executive wants to extend the state of emergency beyond the temporal limits set down in the constitution it must seek approval from the legislature and each time it seeks to extend the period of emergency, it must attain a greater majority of the legislature than the time before.[69] Underpinning all of these models are the beliefs that legislative oversight of executive emergency powers enhances democratic accountability in a state of emergency, increases the degree of deliberation that occurs in times of crisis, and diminishes the chance that emergency powers will be exercised arbitrarily.[70]

The application of these procedural limits to the Council's legislative activity would involve vesting the power to decide the existence of a threat to the peace, a breach of the peace or an act of aggression with the General Assembly. It would also involve either placing limits on the period for which a threat to the peace, a breach of the peace or an act of aggression could last or endowing the General Assembly with the power to terminate an Article 39 situation. Initiating these changes would likely enhance the deliberation and transparency around the use of the Council's legislative powers as it would require the existence of a threat to the peace to be clearly identified, justified and debated. However, it is highly unlikely that these changes would ever eventuate as they would require significant amendments to the UN Charter. It is nonetheless possible that some of the ideas embedded in the procedural limitations approach could be implemented in a less comprehensive, more ad hoc manner by, for example, the Council vesting the General Assembly with the power to terminate legislative measures on a case-by-case basis. Such a state of affairs is not beyond the realms of possibility as the Council has,

---

[66] See e.g., Constitution of the Republic of South Africa 1996, art. 37; Constitution of Greece 1975, art. 48(1); Basic Law for the Federal Republic of Germany 1949, art. 115(a); Basic Laws of the State of Israel 2001, art. 38(a).

[67] See e.g., Constitution of the Republic of South Africa 1996, art. 37(2); Basic Law for the Federal Republic of Germany 1949, art. 115(l); Basic Laws of the State of Israel 2001, art. 38(b).

[68] Bruce Ackerman, 'The Emergency Constitution' (2004) 113 *Yale Law Journal* 1029, 1047.

[69] *Ibid.*    [70] Scheuerman, 'Survey Article', above n. 62, 75–7.

on occasion, endowed the UN Secretary-General with the ability to terminate Security Council resolutions when the threat to the peace that gave rise to them has ceased to exist.[71]

A different problem with implementing the procedural limits of the Roman commissarial dictatorship in the context of Security Council legislation is that it is questionable whether this approach would resolve the problem of the Council producing legislation in a 'lawless void' without regard for the legal limits imposed on it under the UN Charter. This is because, as Dyzenhaus has explained in the domestic context, the idea of placing procedural controls around the exercise of emergency power fails to ensure that executives adhere to any principles that are central to the rule of law.[72] In fact, procedural limits still leave a black hole by creating the space in which the executive is allowed to do as it pleases.

### 4.2 Judicial review

The second approach to countering Schmitt's theory holds that rather than relying on constitutional procedures to constrain executives in times of crisis, states should look to courts to conduct robust judicial review of executives' actions.[73] Proponents of this approach assert that judges are well placed to hold the executive to account for its activities because they are independent from the political process and can assess the executive's actions on a case-by-case basis after the intensity of the emergency has waned.[74] Further, their judgments create precedents that can help guide executives in future emergencies.[75] In reviewing emergency action, David Dyzenhaus asserts that judges should apply a 'substantive or thick conception of the rule of law',[76] where the executive's activities are assessed not only by the laws set down in statutes but also by principles such as necessity and good faith.

The problems with judicial review of the Council's activities are well known. There is no independent power for the International Court of Justice (ICJ) to review Security Council Resolutions and uncertainty surrounds the extent to which it can review Security Council Resolutions in contentious proceedings.[77] Further, it is unclear what

---

[71] See e.g., SC Res. 1074 (1 October 1996). See also Schott, above n. 17, 51.
[72] Dyzenhaus, 'Schmitt v. Dicey', above n. 31, 2018.   [73] Ibid. 2031–9.
[74] Scheuerman, 'Survey Article', above n. 62, 78.   [75] Ibid.
[76] Dyzenhaus, 'Schmitt v. Dicey', above n. 31, 2031.
[77] De Wet, Chapter VII Powers of the Security Council, above n. 36, p. 69.

the consequences of the ICJ finding that a legislative resolution is *ultra vires* in contentious proceedings would be.[78] While the ICJ can review legislative resolutions in advisory proceedings there has been reluctance from UN bodies to seek advisory opinions on Security Council action.[79]

In recent years regional and domestic courts have begun to hear cases requiring them to engage with, and at times pass judgment on, legislative Security Council Resolutions.[80] However, numerous problems surround relying on these proceedings to keep the Council's actions in check. For example, most regional and domestic courts can only review domestic legislation implementing Security Council Resolutions, not the Resolutions themselves,[81] and have shown a preference for reviewing implementing legislation against regional and domestic laws, not international law, thus preventing any direct assessment of whether the Council itself has acted *ultra vires*.[82]

Despite the limitations of the judicial review processes that have taken place regionally and domestically, some of the human rights cases that have grown out of legislative Security Council Resolutions have had an effect on the Council's legislative activity;[83] for example, compelling the Council to introduce an Ombudsperson to review the cases of all individuals sanctioned by the Resolution 1267 regime.[84] This suggests that if a more formal system of judicial review of the Council's decisions could be established it might have some hope of influencing the Council's legislative activities.[85] It should be noted,

---

[78] José Alvarez, 'Judging the Security Council' (1996) 90 *American Journal of International Law* 1, 5.

[79] De Wet, *Chapter VII Powers of the Security Council*, above n. 36, p. 67.

[80] See e.g., Case T-315/01 *Kadi v. Council and Commission* (2006) 45 ILM 81.

[81] See e.g., Cases C-402/05 P and C-415/05 P *Kadi and Al Barakaat v. Council and Commission* [2008] ECR I-6351; *HM Treasury* v. *Mohammed Jabar Ahmed and others (FC), HM Treasury* v. *Mohammed al-Ghabra (FC), R (on the application of Hani El Sayed Sabaei Youssef)* v. *HM Treasury* [2010] UKSC 2. See also Antonios Tzanakopoulos, 'United Nations Sanctions in Domestic Courts: From Interpretation to Defence in *Abdelrazik v. Canada*' (2010) 81 *Journal of International Criminal Justice* 249, 250.

[82] José Alvarez, 'The Security Council's War on Terrorism: Problems and Policy Options' in Erika de Wet and André Nollkaemper (eds.), *Review of the Security Council by Member States* (Intersentia, Antwerp, 2003) 119, 136–7.

[83] See e.g., *Kadi*, above n. 81; *Abousfian Abdelrazik v. Canada* [2009] FC 580; *Hay v. HM Treasury* [2009] EWHC 1677.

[84] SC Res. 1904 (17 December 2009) para. 20.

[85] Jared Schott has also drawn on emergency law literature to suggest that the Council's Chapter VII actions should be subject to robust judicial review by the ICJ: Schott, 'Chapter VII as Exception', above n. 17, 66.

however, that even if a formal process of judicial review could be initiated, the domestic experience suggests that it is unlikely to offer a perfect antidote to the Council's propensity to issue legislative resolutions that are *ultra vires*. This is because during times of crisis domestic courts have tended to defer to executives and have frequently declined to second guess executives' decisions.[86] There is a risk that such reluctance would also manifest itself in any judicial review process established on the international stage.

## 4.3 Extra-legal approach

The third approach – the extra-legal approach – differs considerably from the first two. Rather than seeking to bring the executive's exercise of emergency powers within legal limits, it adheres to Schmitt's view that the exception cannot be contained by law and that any procedural or substantive limits set will be cast aside in extreme conditions.[87] Unlike Schmitt, however, it holds that the result of this state of affairs need not be an authoritarian dictatorship. Instead, it suggests that states should allow executives to act extra-legally during a crisis, and take whatever measures are necessitated by the exigencies of the situation to then employ an array of moral, political and legal measures to ensure that their extra-legal activity is limited and it does not become permanent.[88] It further provides that by allowing the executive's emergency actions outside the legal system, the system is better protected because it cannot be damaged or eroded.[89]

There have been numerous formulations of the extra-legal approach over the last few centuries. The following sections explore three of the most prominent variations of the extra-legal approach and how some of the normative considerations within them might be applied to the Council's legislative activity.

---

[86] Gross and Aoláin, *Law in Times of Crisis*, above n. 9, p. 63. On the tendency of domestic courts to exercise judicial restraint generally when reviewing executive decisions, see Hitoshi Nasu, 'Who Guards the Guards? Towards Regulation of the UN Security Council's Chapter VII Powers through Dialogue' in Kim Rubenstein and Jeremy Farrall (eds.), *Sanctions, Accountability and Governance in a Globalised World* (Cambridge University Press, 2009) pp. 123, 126-7.

[87] Oren Gross, 'Extra-Legality and the Ethic of Political Responsibility' in Victor Ramraj (ed.) *Emergencies and the Limits of Legality* (Cambridge University Press, Cambridge, 2008) pp. 60, 63.

[88] *Ibid.* pp. 62-3.   [89] *Ibid.*

### 4.3.1 Enlightenment extra-legal approach

John Locke, David Hume, Alexander Hamilton and James Madison propounded the earliest versions of the extra-legal approach.[90] These enlightenment figures believed that executives ought to be able to act outside the law during times of crisis but feared that such a situation would lead to severe abuses of power, with executives employing extra-legal powers to further illegitimate, personal ends.[91] To avoid such eventualities, they determined it was essential to force the executive to channel his or her power for the public good.[92] They held that this could be most effectively achieved not through political or legal mechanisms that might be manipulated and corrupted in times of crisis but rather through appointing executives of high moral virtue.[93] Specifically, they held that executives should exhibit moral qualities such as 'honesty, moderation, frugality, patriotism, self-control, disinterestedness, justice and humanity',[94] and that the greater the evidence of these moral qualities, the greater the power the executive was entitled to wield in emergencies.[95]

Jan Klabbers has put forward ideas for controlling international organisations that in certain respects reflect the enlightenment figures' idea that extra-legal actions can be kept in check by requiring the executive to possess strong moral virtues. Klabbers advocates the application of Aristotelian virtue ethics to international organisations, including the Security Council, arguing that international law is at times ill-equipped to hold international organisations to account for their actions and that organisations may function more effectively and deliver better results if their leaders are assessed against the yardstick of Aristotelian virtue ethics.[96] Specifically, he suggests that the leaders of international organisations should be evaluated against

---

[90] Clement Fatovic, *Outside the Law: Emergency and Executive Power* (Johns Hopkins University Press, Baltimore, MD) pp. 5–6.

[91] *Ibid.*

[92] *Ibid.* In Locke's words '[t]his power to act according to discretion for the public good, without the prescription of law and sometimes even against it, is that which is called prerogative': John Locke, *Two Treatises of Government* (1689) p. 176.

[93] Fatovic, *Outside the Law*, above n. 90, pp. 5–6; Locke, *Two Treatises of Government*, above n. 92, pp. 176–9.

[94] Fatovic, *Outside the Law*, above n. 90, p. 20.

[95] *Ibid.* p. 6; Locke, *Two Treatises of Government*, above n. 92, pp. 177–8.

[96] Jan Klabbers, 'Controlling International Organisations: A Virtue Ethics Approach' (2011) 2(2) *Helsinki Review of Global Governance* 49, 49–51. Note that Klabbers' idea is not developed in the context of extra-legal action.

ethical principles that echo, to a significant extent, those articulated by the enlightenment figures, namely, honesty, modesty, courage, empathy, charity, temperance and justice.[97]

While building a Council with virtuous individuals has much to recommend it, neither the conception of moral virtue put forward by the enlightenment figures nor Aristotle's theory of virtue ethics is unproblematic. To start with, what constitutes a virtue is contentious and arguably varies across different contexts, time periods and cultures.[98] It is questionable whether, at this point in the international community's development, agreement could be reached as to the virtues that individuals sitting on the Security Council should possess.

Further, in the event that such agreement were reached, it is doubtful whether virtue ethics would provide a path for determining what the right course of action in any concrete situation facing the Council would be.[99] This is because these theories focus primarily on the character of the agent wielding power without providing a methodology for guiding the agent's use of power. Some virtue ethicists counter this critique by asserting that under a virtue ethics approach, the right course of action in any given situation is the one that a fully virtuous individual would characteristically take in the circumstances.[100] There are, however, numerous problems with this prescription. First, the concept of 'a fully virtuous individual' is a vague concept and virtue ethicists fail to provide guidance for identifying such a person.[101] Second, there are multiple examples of when the right course of action may not be the action of 'a fully virtuous individual'.[102] For example, if an individual does something wrong, it is problematic for her to ask what a fully virtuous individual would do in the circumstances because a fully virtuous individual would not have found herself in those circumstances in the first

---

[97] *Ibid.* 51.

[98] Paul Woodruff, 'Virtue Ethics and the Appeal to Human Nature' (1991) 17(2) *Social Theory and Practice* 307, 308; Alasdair MacIntyre, *After Virtue* (3rd edn, Duckworth, London, 2007) pp. 181–6.

[99] Frans Svensson, 'Virtue Ethics and the Search for an Account of Right Action' (2010) 13 *Ethical Theory and Moral Practice* 255, 256; Julia Annas, 'Being Virtuous and Doing the Right Thing' (2004) 78(2) *Proceedings and Addresses of the American Philosophical Association* 61.

[100] Svensson, 'Virtue Ethics and the Search for an Account of Right Action', above n. 99, 256; Annas, 'Being Virtuous and Doing the Right Thing', above n. 99, 67.

[101] Annas, 'Being Virtuous and Doing the Right Thing', above n. 99, 67.

[102] *Ibid.*; Svensson, 'Virtue Ethics and the Search for an Account of Right Action', above n. 99, 259–61.

place.[103] To put this in the context of the Council, on discovering that a legislative resolution breaches human rights, it would be problematic for the members of the Council to ask how a virtuous individual would resolve the breaches as a virtuous individual would not have created a resolution that breached fundamental rights in the first place.[104]

In light of the difficulties both in determining what amounts to a virtue and how it should guide the Council's actions in specific situations, it is doubtful whether a virtue-based approach should be relied upon to check the extra-legal activities of the Council.

### 4.3.2   Thomas Jefferson's extra-legal approach

Thomas Jefferson also affirmed the use of extra-legal powers. He believed, however, that rather than relying on the moral virtue of the person wielding the power, extra-legal activity should be constrained by requiring the executive to submit its actions to the legislature for ratification after the fact.[105] In determining whether to ratify the executive's extra-legal activity, the legislature would have to determine whether the activity had been necessary in the circumstances.

Jefferson's idea of requiring the executive to submit its extra-legal actions to the legislature for *ex post facto* ratification could manifest itself in the context of Security Council legislation if the General Assembly were to support or condemn the Council's extra-legal resolutions after their passage. At the moment the Council's extra-legal activity can be remedied through the ad hoc process of state acquiescence.[106] Introducing a standardised process within the General Assembly would formalise this practice and perhaps encourage the Council to craft its legislative resolutions

---

[103]   Annas, 'Being Virtuous and Doing the Right Thing', above n. 99, 67; Svensson, 'Virtue Ethics and the Search for an Account of Right Action', above n. 99, 259–60.

[104]   There are numerous other examples of the problematic nature of the fully virtuous individual formula. See generally, Svensson, 'Virtue Ethics and the Search for an Account of Right Action', above n. 99.

[105]   Jefferson's ideas were set out in a letter he wrote to John C. Breckinridge on 12 August 1803. The relevant parts of the letter are quoted in John Yoo, 'Jefferson and Executive Power' (2008) 88 *Boston University Law Review* 421, 439 and the letter is reproduced in Paul Leicester Ford, *The Works of Thomas Jefferson: Volume 10* (G.P. Putnam's Sons, New York/London, 1905) p. 7. See also, Gross and Aoláin, *Law in Times of Crisis*, above n. 9, p. 126.

[106]   Marschik, 'Legislative Powers of the Security Council', above n. 36, p. 474; Georges Abi-Saab, 'The Security Council as Legislator and Executive in Its Fight Against Terrorism and Against Proliferation of Weapons of Mass Destruction: A Question of Legitimacy' in Rüdiger Wolfrum and Volker Röben (eds.), *Legitimacy in International Law* (Springer, Berlin, 2008) pp. 109, 124–5.

narrowly and in politically palatable terms. There are, however, several issues with this approach. The first is that it is questionable whether the risk of states potentially refusing to approve the Council's actions in the General Assembly would be sufficient to alter the Council's extra-legal behaviour. To date, the Council has rarely been deterred from passing legislative resolutions by the prospect of opposition to them. For example, prior to the passage of Resolutions 1422, 1487 and 1540, the Council held open debates to give states opportunities to voice their views on the Resolutions. Many states expressed hostility towards the contents of the Resolutions at the respective debates.[107] However, only in the case of Resolution 1540 did the Council take any steps to accommodate the concerns expressed by states and the steps it did take ignored many of the issues that states had raised.[108] It is thus debatable whether the prospect of a formal vote in the General Assembly would alter the Council's sensitivity to international opinion.

Even if the introduction of General Assembly oversight might affect the Council's behaviour, another problem would plague the application of Jefferson's theory to the Council's legislative activity. Jefferson's theory requires the legislature to approve the executive's action because it believes that the action was 'necessary' in the circumstances. However, research suggests that when states currently acquiesce to legislative resolutions that are *ultra vires* they are motivated by a range of factors, including international pressure and domestic political agendas.[109] It is likely that such factors would continue to influence states if they were asked to vote on the necessity of Security Council legislation in the General Assembly.

### 4.3.3 Oren Gross's extra-legal approach

In more recent times Oren Gross has developed another version of the extra-legal approach, suggesting that an executive can take extra-legal action provided that the executive's actions are necessary for the

---

[107] See UN SCOR, 4568th mtg, 57th sess., UN Doc. S/PV.4568 (10 July 2002); UN SCOR, 4568th mtg, 57th sess., UN Doc. S/PV.4568 (10 July 2002) (Resumption 1); UN SCOR, 4772nd mtg, 58th sess., UN Doc. S/PV.4772 (12 June 2003); UN SCOR, 4950th mtg, 59th sess., UN Doc. S/PV.4950 (22 April 2004); UN SCOR, 4950th mtg, 59th sess., UN Doc. S/PV.4950 (22 April 2004) (Resumption 1).

[108] For example, multiple states wanted Resolution 1540 to contain binding disarmament provisions but the only reference to disarmament was in the Preamble. See UN SCOR, 4950th mtg, 59th sess., UN Doc. S/PV.4950 (22 April 2004); UN SCOR, 4950th mtg, 59th sess., UN Doc. S/PV.4950 (Resumption 1) (22 April 2004).

[109] See e.g., Abi-Saab, 'The Security Council *Legibus Solutus?*', above n. 7, pp. 33–4.

protection of the nation; the executive publicly declares the nature of its actions; and society provides direct or indirect *ex post facto* ratification of the actions.[110] This may involve formal ratification by a legislature as Jefferson suggested but could also be satisfied more informally, for example, by a prosecutor deciding not to bring criminal charges against the executive; a jury finding the executive 'not guilty' where charges have been brought; individuals declining to seek damages for wrongs done to them; the electorate re-electing the executive or society honouring the executive for its actions by awarding it medals or positions of political importance.[111] Gross believes that if the executive knows it will have to account for its actions and be subject to potential public condemnation, it will only resort to extra-legal measures in the most extreme circumstances and its actions will be limited because of the uncertainty surrounding how they will be received by the population.[112]

There would be numerous problems in seeking to impose Gross' extra-legal model on the Security Council. Gross' extra-legal theory seeks to allow executives to act outside the law but to limit their willingness to engage in extra-legal activity and constrain the sorts of activity they engage in by making the cost of employing extra-legal measures very high. In order to do this it is necessary for executives to face the threat of an array of penalties when they act that could damage their freedom, reputation, position or bank balance.[113] It is difficult to conceive of many penalties that might be imposed on the Council or its members to significantly raise the costs of the Council issuing extra-legal resolutions.

There is, of course, the threat that states will decide not to follow Security Council Resolutions that are *ultra vires*,[114] which will not only lead to the adopted measures being ineffective but might also undermine the credibility of the Council itself. It is questionable, however, whether

---

[110] Gross, 'Extra-Legality and the Ethic of Political Responsibility', above n. 87, p. 60; Gross and Aoláin, *Law in Times of Crisis*, above n. 9, pp. 111–12.

[111] Gross, 'Extra-Legality and the Ethic of Political Responsibility', above n. 87, pp. 65–9.

[112] *Ibid*. pp. 71–81.    [113] *Ibid*. pp. 64–9.

[114] It is widely acknowledged that Art. 25 of the UN Charter does not require states to follow Security Council Resolutions that are *ultra vires*: see e.g., de Wet, *Chapter VII Powers of the Security Council*, above n. 36, p. 376. An alternative rationale for states not following Security Council Resolutions that are *ultra vires* is Tzanakopoulos' controversial idea that state disobedience of the Council can be understood through the paradigm of the law of international responsibility as a counter-measure: Tzanakopoulos, *Disobeying the Security Council*, above n. 25, pp. 191–200.

this alone would satisfy the requirements of Gross's theory. As has already been acknowledged, the extent to which potential disobedience from states gives the Council pause for thought is variable. Further, it is relatively common for UN member states to acquiesce even if a particular legislative resolution is arguably *ultra vires*.[115] If the Council is fairly confident that the measures it enacts *ultra vires* will be remedied or will do little to dent its credibility, then there is little risk to the Council engaging in the extra-legal activity and it falls short of fulfilling the requirement of Gross's model that executives face a high level of uncertainty when they act extra-legally.[116]

Moreover, even if there were cases where the Council feared its activity undertaken *ultra vires* might affect the Council's credibility, Council members and their individual delegates would be relatively immune from any personal loss. This is problematic because an integral part of Gross' theory relies on raising the stakes for the individuals who decide to engage in the extra-legal activity. In the domestic sphere, Gross suggests that this can be achieved by society expressing its approval or disapproval for executives' extra-legal activities through criminal and civil suits, elections and national honours systems.[117] The prospect of the international community employing these sorts of mechanisms in the context of Security Council legislation is negligible. Because of the nature of the Council and international law in general, states are unlikely to have opportunities to legally challenge Council members or their delegates for extra-legal activities. They are similarly unlikely to be able to seek damages for harm caused by the Council's extra-legal actions. Further, the Council cannot look to elections for ratification of its extra-legal activities because the permanent members (P5) do not face election and the Council's non-permanent members are ineligible for immediate re-election when their terms end.

## 5   Conclusion

Emergency law theories provide a number of normative ideas for restraining the Council's legislative practice and binding it more tightly to the rule of law. There are institutional arrangements, such as vesting

---

[115] Marschik, 'Legislative Powers of the Security Council', above n. 36, pp. 473–81 (arguing that SC Res. 1373 and SC Res. 1540 are *ultra vires*, but have simply been acquiesced in by member states).

[116] Gross, 'Extra-Legality and the Ethic of Political Responsibility', above n. 87, p. 72.

[117] *Ibid.* pp. 65–9.

the General Assembly with power over the process of declaring (and possibly terminating) the existence of a threat to the peace, a breach of the peace or an act of aggression, and endowing judicial institutions with the power to review legislative resolutions. There are also a number of normative considerations that arise in the extra-legal literature, such as applying virtue theories to the individual delegates to the Security Council in the hope that this will prevent the Council from exercising its legislative powers too expansively, and seeking to develop methods of allowing states (either collectively in the General Assembly or individually) to pass judgement on the Council's legislative activity. As has been argued in this chapter, however, all of these normative ideas suffer from a number of limitations when applied to the Security Council's legislative practice not least of which is the extent to which they could ever be practically implemented.

The limitations inherent in adapting the normative ideas within emergency law literature to the Council's legislative activity do not mean that emergency law theories should be discarded from analyses of the Council's legislative action. They do suggest, however, that emergency law theories should be employed in a different manner; instead of focusing on the normative prescriptions directly applicable to the Council, future research could turn to examining the elements of emergency law theories that question some of the underlying assumptions of emergency law-making. For example, regard could be had to emergency law scholarship that questions whether there is a need for distinct law-making practices in periods of emergency and whether executive bodies are equipped to engage in emergency law-making.[118] Given the Schmittian nature of the Council's legislative activity, it is perhaps time this scholarship was applied to the Council's actions and greater thought was given to the necessity and utility of the Council engaging in emergency international law-making.

[118] See e.g., Gross and Aolain, *Law in Times of Crisis*, above n. 9, pp. 86–109; Scheuerman, 'Survey Article', above n. 62, 79.

# 7

## Institutional evolution in Africa and the 'peacekeeping institution'

HITOSHI NASU

### 1 Introduction

Peacekeeping has been the primary instrument of the United Nations (UN) in the pursuit of its objective to maintain international peace and security. It has evolved through the practice of UN organs, primarily the UN Security Council but also the UN General Assembly, in response to imperative security concerns of the time. This practice of peacekeeping operations has generated a set of doctrines such as consent, neutrality/impartiality and non-use of force except for self-defence,[1] which, one may argue, has resulted in the emergence of a 'peacekeeping institution'.[2] Indeed, peace-keeping practices have been adopted by regional institutions, including the Organization of African Unity (OAU), the Economic Community of West African States (ECOWAS), South African Development Community (SADC), Economic and Monetary Community of Central Africa (CEMAC), and more recently the African Union (AU).[3] Particularly in Africa, peacekeeping practices can arguably be seen as instrumental to

---

[1] See especially, UN Department of Peacekeeping Operations and Department of Field Support, *United Nations Peacekeeping Operations: Principles and Guidelines* (2008) p. 31, available at http://pbpu.unlb.org/pbps/library/capstone_doctrine_eNg.pdf.

[2] See e.g., Christopher Daase, 'Spontaneous Institutions: Peacekeeping as an International Convention' in Helga Haftendorn, Robert O. Keohane and Celeste A. Wallander (eds.), *Imperfect Unions: Security Institutions over Time and Space* (Oxford University Press, Oxford, 1999) p. 223.

[3] See generally, Thierry Tardy and Marco Wyss (eds.), *Peacekeeping in Africa: The Evolving Security Architecture* (Routledge, London, 2014); Adekeye Adebajo, *UN Peacekeeping in Africa: From the Suez Crisis to the Sudan Conflicts* (Lynne Rienner, Boulder, CO, 2011); Norrie MacQueen, *UN Peacekeeping in Africa Since 1960* (Longman, London, 2002).

compensatory institutional evolution, which has arisen from the lack of institutional competence in situations where security concerns require institutional responses.

However, characterising peacekeeping as an 'institution' rather than a practice does not suggest that an international or regional institution can deploy peacekeeping operations as it sees necessary without having regard to its own institutional competence and procedures. It is an established principle of international institutional law that the competence of international institutions is not unlimited but is restricted by the provisions of the constitutive instrument, in terms both of form and substance.[4] Yet, institutions are not mere instruments of the creators, but are autonomous entities operating, to varying degrees, within an institutional structure and regularised decision-making processes.

This chapter examines the interaction between the development of peacekeeping as an 'institution' and the evolution of institutional competence by international organisations, with a particular focus on how African institutions developed their peacekeeping practices in the 1990s to early 2000s as case studies. To this end, section 2 reviews the early development of peacekeeping practices within the UN, highlighting the controversy over its legality in light of the UN's institutional competence. Section 3 focuses on African peacekeeping practices in the 1990s to the early 2000s, as the legal basis remains controversial to this day.[5] It describes irregularities in the deployment of peacekeeping operations which heralded the emergence of the 'African Peace and Security Architecture' in the 2000s.[6] Section 4 discusses this process of institutional evolution within the context of the traditional law of international institutions. Section 5 then considers the role that peacekeeping, as an 'institutution' among other factors, played in facilitating a general acceptance of the institutional evolution among regional states.

---

[4] See generally, C.F. Amerasinghe, *Principles of the Institutional Law of International Organizations* (2nd edn, Cambridge University Press, Cambridge, 2005) pp. 194–6; Philippe Sands and Pierre Klein, *Bowett's Law of International Institutions* (5th edn, Sweet and Maxwell, London, 2001) pp. 292–3.

[5] Erika de Wet, 'The Evolving Role of ECOWAS and the SADC in Peace Operations: A Challenge to the Primacy of the United Nations Security Council in Matters of Peace and Security?' (2014) 27 *Leiden Journal of International Law* 353.

[6] See generally, Ulf Engel and João Gomes Porto (eds.), *Africa's New Peace and Security Architecture: Promoting Norms, Institutionalizing Solutions* (Ashgate, Farnham, 2010); Ademola Abass, 'African Peace and Security Architecture and the Protection of Human Security' in Ademola Abass (ed.), *Protecting Human Security in Africa* (Oxford University Press, Oxford, 2010) p. 247.

## 2 Peacekeeping as institutional evolution

It is a generally held belief that the UN Charter does not authorise peacekeeping and therefore it emerged as a practical experiment invented out of necessity.[7] Due to this general belief, the institution of peacekeeping required the derivation of legitimacy from the tripartite doctrines – consent, neutrality/impartiality, and the restriction on the use of force – as articulated by former UN Secretary-General Dag Hammerskjöld based on the experience of the UN Emergency Force (UNEF) in the Sinai.[8] These tripartite doctrines ensured a pragmatic evolution of this weak institution, despite it often being dictated to and trifled with by sovereign states.

I have argued elsewhere that a variety of peacekeeping measures was indeed envisaged during the drafting of Article 40 of the UN Charter,[9] and therefore UN peacekeeping operations must meet relevant legal requirements as identified through the application and interpretation of Article 40 within the context of the UN Charter.[10] Similarly, the legal basis of and requirements for peacekeeping operations deployed by other organisations, such as ECOWAS and SADC, must be examined separately in light of their constitutive treaties and other relevant instruments. The extent to which, and the way in which, peacekeeping operations can be authorised may well differ according to the text of the constitutive treaty and the institutional competence.

In this respect, one may regard the classic debate as to whether peacekeeping operations can be authorised without specific legal basis in the UN Charter with renewed interest,[11] particularly in assessing the legality of peacekeeping practices by regional organisations. One perspective proposed by Michael Akehurst, in considering the legal basis of the Inter-American Force authorised by the Organization of American

---

[7] See e.g., Edward C. Luck, *UN Security Council: Practice and Promise* (Routledge, London/ New York, 2006) pp. 36–7; United Nations, *The Blue Helmets: A Review of United Nations Peacekeeping* (3rd edn, United Nations, New York, 1996) pp. 1–15.

[8] *Summary Study of the Experience Derived from the Establishment and Operation of the Force*, UN Doc. A/3943 (9 October 1958).

[9] Charter of the United Nations, opened for signature 26 June 1945, 1 UNTS xvi (entered into force 24 October 1945), Art. 39, as amended by GA Res. 1991, 557 UNTS 143 (1963); GA Res. 2101, 638 UNTS 308 (1965); GA Res. 2847, 892 UNTS 119 (1971).

[10] Hitoshi Nasu, *International Law on Peacekeeping: A Study of Article 40 of the UN Charter* (Martinus Nijhoff Publishers, Leiden, 2009).

[11] See especially, Finn Seyersted, 'Can the United Nations Establish Military Forces and Perform Other Acts without Specific Basis in the Charter?' (1962) 12 *Österreichische Zeitschrift für Öffentliches Recht* 125.

States (OAS) for restoration of normal conditions in the Dominican Republic in 1965,[12] is that 'there is no reason why regional agencies should not possess the same *implied powers* as the United Nations to take peacekeeping action with the consent of the States concerned'.[13] An alternative perspective is that the legal authority may be derived from the international legal personality of an institution, which possesses inherent powers to perform all the acts necessary to attain its aims without requiring the search for a basis of implication as the source of the powers.[14]

As will be discussed below, the question then becomes one of treaty interpretation, specifically involving the constitutive treaty of an international institution. In the absence of a specific legal basis or mandate within the constitutive treaty governing the operation of a regional organisation, the decision to deploy peacekeeping operations in order to respond to immediate security threats will necessarily challenge its institutional authority and competence. The next section reviews the development of peacekeeping practice by African institutions with a particular focus on their institutional authority and competence to deploy peacekeeping forces.

## 3   Evolution of African institutions through peacekeeping

The shift towards regional management of security issues emerged during the 1990s, particularly in Africa.[15] The OAU, the primary region-wide organisation which had led much of the anti-colonial struggles in Africa since the 1960s, remained dysfunctional in dealing with regional security issues within the prevailing international legal order African states inherited from their colonial past.[16] The role of regional and

---

[12] The text of the OAS Resolution of 6 May 1965 is reproduced in UN Doc. S/6333/Rev.1 (7 May 1965).

[13] Michael Akehurst, 'Enforcement Action by Regional Agencies, with special reference to the Organization of American States' (1967) 42 *British Year Book of International Law* 175, 208 (original emphasis). See also Marten Zwarenburg, 'Regional Organisations and the Maintenance of International Peace and Security: Three Recent Regional African Peace Operations' (2006) 11 *Journal of Conflict and Security Law* 483, 487.

[14] For details, see Jan Klabbers, *An Introduction to International Institutional Law* (Cambridge University Press, Cambridge, 2002) pp. 75–8; Finn Seyersted, 'International Personality of Intergovernmental Organizations: Do Their Capacities Really Depend upon Their Constitutions?' (1964) 4 *Indian Journal of International Law* 1, 19–25.

[15] See e.g., *An Agenda for Peace*, UN Doc. A/47/277 (17 June 1992) paras. 60–65.

[16] See especially, Abou Jeng, *Peacebuilding in the African Union: Law, Philosophy and Practice* (Cambridge University Press, Cambridge, 2012) pp. 123–5.

sub-regional organisations, in departing from their original mandate and re-orienting it towards autonomous response to regional conflicts without UN authorisation, must be understood against this background.[17] This re-orientation of institutional mandates has resulted in stretching the institutional competence of regional and sub-regional organisations. This section briefly examines four African regional and sub-regional organisations that deployed peacekeeping forces autonomously outside their institutional mandate or competence.

### 3.1 Organization of African Unity (OAU)

The first regional peacekeeping force was deployed by the OAU in Chad for a short period between November 1981 and June 1982,[18] in response to the request made in the Lagos Peace Accord reached on 21 August 1979 between different factions in Chad.[19] On 15 February 1980, the OAU Council of Ministers reaffirmed the Lagos Accord as the mandating document for the deployment of an OAU peacekeeping force.[20] In early November 1981, Libya, which had been providing assistance for the Front de Libération Nationale du Tchad (FROLINAT),[21] started withdrawing its troops from Chad. Faced with

---

[17] This raises an additional legal question, which is not dealt with in this chapter, as to whether regional peacekeeping operations amount to 'enforcement action' requiring the authorisation of the UN Security Council in accordance with Art. 53 of the UN Charter. On this issue, see especially, Ademola Abass, *Regional Organisations and the Development of Collective Security: Beyond Chapter VIII of the UN Charter* (Hart Publishing, Oxford/ Portland, OR, 2004); de Wet, 'The Evolving Role of ECOWAS and the SADC in Peace Operations', above n. 5; Zwanenburg, 'Regional Organisations and the Maintenance of International Peace and Security', above n. 13.

[18] OAU subsequently dispatched a small group of military observers in Rwanda, Burundi, the Comoros, Democratic Republic of the Congo, and Eritrea and Ethiopia. For an overview, see Eric G. Berman and Katie E. Sams, 'The Peacekeeping Potential of African Regional Organizations' in Jane Boulden (ed.), *Dealing with Conflicts in Africa: The United Nations and Regional Organizations* (Palgrave, New York, 2003) pp. 35, 37–42; Eric G. Berman and Katie E. Sams, *Peacekeeping in Africa: Capabilities and Culpabilities* (UN Institute for Disarmament Research, Geneva, 2000) ch. 3.

[19] For the background and the text of the Lagos Accord, see Terry M. Mays, *Africa's First Peacekeeping Operation: The OAU in Chad, 1981–1982* (Praeger, Westport, CT, 2002) pp. 45–7.

[20] OAU Doc. CM/Res. 769 (15 February 1980) p. 34.

[21] On 6 January 1981, Libya's Colonel Qaddafi and the FROLINAT's leader Weddeye announced the merger of the two countries, which alarmed many African countries: Amadu Sesay, 'The Limits of Peacekeeping by a Regional Organization: The OAU Peacekeeping Force in Chad' (1991) *Conflict Quarterly* 7, 11.

the urgent concern of the resulting security vacuum created,[22] the OAU convened a gathering of Foreign Ministers on 13 November 1981, during which operational details were discussed.[23] The OAU peacekeeping troops operated under a vague mandate of ensuring the defence and security of the country but maintained strict neutrality, contrary to the expectation of the transitional government that they would protect the government from rebel forces.[24] The peacekeeping troops remained on the ground until June 1982 when the transitional government was overthrown by rebel forces.

Despite reference to a Defence Commission and a general obligation to cooperate in the field of defence and security,[25] the OAU Charter lacked a legal basis and institutional mechanism for the deployment of a peace-keeping force.[26] Naldi considers that a call for military action did not exceed the competence of the OAU, arguing that the implied powers doctrine, developed by the International Court of Justice (ICJ) in *Certain Expenses of the United Nations*,[27] could be applicable, *mutatis mutandis*, to the OAU.[28] There are difficulties with this argument, however, given that the principle of non-interference – one of the fundamental tenets of the OAU – would have prevented the OAU from interfering in the Chadian conflict, which was essentially an internal conflict despite the fact that some African states, in particular Libya, were involved in support of the civil strife.[29]

It appears that the OAU member states avoided this legal conundrum, advertently or inadvertently, by resorting and strictly adhering to the doctrines of peacekeeping as developed through UN

---

[22] Roy May and Simon Massey, 'The OAU Interventions in Chad: Mission Impossible or Mission Evaded?' (1998) 5(1) *International Peacekeeping* 46, 51 (observing that 'the general absence of serious objections by the member states, and the temporary unity created by the Qaddafi-factor, might be advanced as motives for the intervention').

[23] For details, see Mays, *Africa's First Peacekeeping Operation*, above n. 19, pp. 80–1.

[24] See May and Massey, 'The OAU Interventions in Chad', above n. 22, 51–5; Mays, *Africa's First Peacekeeping Operation*, above n. 19, pp. 82–100.

[25] Charter of the Organization of African Unity, adopted 25 May 1963, 479 UNTS 39 (entered into force 13 September 1963), Arts. 2(f) and 20.

[26] May and Massey, 'The OAU Interventions in Chad', above n. 22, 51.

[27] *Certain Expenses of the United Nations* (Advisory Opinion) [1962] ICJ Rep. 151, 168 ('*Certain Expenses*').

[28] G.J. Naldi, 'Peacekeeping Attempts by the Organisation of African Unity' (1985) 34 *International and Comparative Law Quarterly* 593.

[29] See e.g., James O.C. Jonah, 'The OAU: Peace Keeping and Conflict Resolution' in Yassin El-Ayouty (ed.), *The Organization of African Unity After Thirty Years* (Praeger, Westport, CT, 1994) pp. 3, 9.

practice.[30] The mandates for peacekeepers were derived from the Lagos Accord, to which all the factional leaders pledged their commitment, even though they frequently violated the terms of the Accord.[31] The OAU peacekeepers also strictly adhered to the principle of neutrality, when faced with pressure from the transitional government to defend it from the rebel offensive in May–June 1982, by not resorting to the use of force to fulfil their mission except for the purpose of defending themselves.[32] The significance of the OAU's adoption of peacekeeping doctrines cannot be fully appreciated without having regard to the fact that the concept of peacekeeping was an anathema to many African states and was considered rather as 'an imperialistic instrument to subvert African independence',[33] in light of the passive involvement of the UN Operation in the Congo (ONUC) in the death of Prime Minister of the Congo, Patrice Lumumba, in 1960.[34] The deployment of traditional, neutral peacekeeping was the last resort that African states reluctantly accepted, essentially in order to defend the regional security from external interference in dealing with the Chadian conflict.

### 3.2 Economic Community of West African States (ECOWAS)

ECOWAS was established by the Treaty of the Economic Community of Western African States with the purpose of accelerating economic growth and development in West Africa.[35] Even though its original mandate was stipulated in purely economic terms, ECOWAS started recalibrating itself by adopting the Protocol relating to Non-Aggression in 1978 and the Protocol relating to Mutual Assistance on Defence Matters ('Mutual Defence Protocol') in 1981.[36] The former sets out

---

[30] There were, of course, practical reasons for doing so, given the fact that there was no clear authority or procedure for peace-keeping decision-making: see Jonah, 'The OAU: Peace Keeping and Conflict Resolution', above n. 29, p. 7.

[31] Mays, *Africa's First Peacekeeping Operation*, above n. 19, pp. 151–2.   [32] *Ibid.* p. 152.

[33] Jonah, 'The OAU: Peace Keeping and Conflict Resolution', above n. 29, p. 4.

[34] For details of the UN's controversial involvement in the Congo's constitutional crisis, see e.g., Georges Abi-Saab, *The United Nations Operation in the Congo 1960–1964* (Oxford University Press, Oxford, 1978) pp. 81–91; Brian Urquhart, *Hammarskjold* (Bodley Head, London, 1972) pp. 479–80; Catherine Hoskyns, *The Congo Since Independence: January 1960–December 1961* (Oxford University Press, London, 1965) pp. 178–96.

[35] Treaty of the Economic Community of Western African States, adopted 28 May 1975, 1010 UNTS 17 (entered into force 20 June 1975).

[36] Protocol on Non-Aggression, adopted 22 April 1978, 1690 UNTS 39 (entered into force 13 May 1982); Protocol relating to Mutual Assistance on Defence Matters, adopted

basic principles, such as the prohibition of the threat or use of force and the prohibition of the use of territory for destabilising other member states, with a view to ensuring regional peace and security which was seen as essential for rapid integration and development. The latter institutionalises military commitments, conferring on the Authority of Heads of State and Government ('ECOWAS Authority') the power to 'decide on the expediency of the military action' and to appoint the Force Commander of the Allied Forces of the Community, and establishes the ECOWAS Defence Council as the supervisory body and the Defence Commission as the technical advisory body.[37] These changes foreshadowed ECOWAS's new role as a peacekeeping institution, which it assumed when it deployed the ECOWAS Ceasefire Monitoring Group (ECOMOG) in Liberia on 24 August 1990 under Nigerian leadership to halt an armed rebellion against Liberia's President Samuel Doe.[38]

The deployment of this peacekeeping mission was fraught with two possible legal challenges to its validity and legality. First, doubt has been cast on the legal basis upon which ECOMOG was deployed under international law. ECOWAS invoked the 1978 Protocol on Non-Aggression, reiterating 'the imperative of securing peace and maintaining stability in the ECOWAS subregion', and considered that the Liberian crisis had given the Protocol 'a fresh validity'.[39] Reference was also made, at a later stage, to the 1981 Mutual Defence Protocol,[40] which called for military support in cases of, *inter alia*, 'internal armed conflict within any Member State engineered and supported actively from outside likely to endanger the security and peace in the entire Community'.[41] However, as Georg Nolte rightly observes, the ambiguous reference to security in the

---

29 May 1981, 1690 UNTS 51 (entered into force 30 September 1986) ('Mutual Defence Protocol').

[37] Mutual Defence Protocol, Art. 6. For details, see Kofi Oteng Kufuor, *The Institutional Transformation of the Economic Community of West African States* (Ashgate, Aldershot, 2006) pp. 24–5; Julius Emeka Okolo, 'Integrative and Cooperative Regionalism: The Economic Community of West African States' (1985) 39 *International Organisation* 121, 147; Julius Emeka Okolo, 'Securing West Africa: The ECOWAS Defence Pact' (1983) 39(5) *World Today* 177.

[38] For details, see Marc Weller (ed.), *Regional Peacekeeping and International Enforcement: The Liberian Crisis* (Cambridge University Press, Cambridge, 1994) pp. 60–1.

[39] ECOWAS, First Extraordinary Session of the Authority of Heads of State and Government, Bamako, 27 and 28 November 1990, Final Communiqué, UN Doc. A/45/894–S/22025 (20 December 1990) Annex, paras. 13–14.

[40] See e.g., *Report of the Secretary-General on the Question of Liberia*, UN Doc. S/25402 (12 March 1993) para. 15.

[41] Mutual Defence Protocol, Art. 4.

Protocol on Non-Aggression would have hardly provided the institutional competence to authorise deployment of troops, and further ECOMOG did not operate under the common command structure envisaged under the Mutual Defence Protocol.[42]

Second, the question arises as to whether ECOMOG was validly deployed in accordance with the procedural rules governing ECOWAS operations. Article 6 of the Mutual Defence Protocol affirms that only the ECOWAS Authority (which is 'the principal governing institution of the Community' created by Article 5.1 of the ECOWAS Treaty and makes decisions by consensus) can decide 'on the expediency of military force'. Due to the fact that Côte d'Ivoire and Burkina Faso supported rebellions against Samuel Doe, it was the Standing Mediation Committee, which had been specially created on Nigeria's initiative, that made the decision to deploy ECOMOG.[43] Thus, Burkina Faso disputed whether an appropriate authorisation had in fact been given.[44]

Katharina Coleman, through interviews with diplomats reflecting upon this decision to deploy ECOMOG, has found that 'ECOMOG's defenders have tended to justify these breaches of both international law and internal ECOWAS rules by highlighting the urgent need to respond to the Liberian crisis'.[45] For Nigeria, ECOWAS was a political platform legitimising the Nigerian-led intervention force against the dominant rebel force led by Charles Taylor on the international stage and, to a lesser extent, at the regional level by emphasising the regional unity behind the operation.[46] While the legality and validity of the deployment of ECOMOG remained precarious, ECOWAS was swift in amending its constitutive treaty to fill the legal gap by expanding the institutional competence 'to establish a regional peace and security observation system and peace-keeping forces',[47] and also by establishing the Mediation and Security Council which was empowered to make

---

[42] Georg Nolte, 'Restoring Peace by Regional Action: International Legal Aspects of the Liberian Conflict' (1993) 53 *Zeitschrift für ausländisches öffentliches Recht und Völkerrecht* 603, 614–5.

[43] For details, see e.g., Katharina P. Coleman, *International Organisations and Peace Enforcement: The Politics of International Legitimacy* (Cambridge University Press, Cambridge, 2007) pp. 77–80.

[44] Nolte, 'Restoring Peace by Regional Action', above n. 42, 616.

[45] Coleman, *International Organisations and Peace Enforcement*, above n. 43, p. 80.

[46] *Ibid.* pp. 86–103.

[47] Treaty of the Economic Community of West African States, adopted 24 July 1993, 2373 UNTS 233 (entered into force 23 August 1995), Art. 58.

decisions on behalf of the ECOWAS Authority, including the decision to authorise 'all forms of intervention'.[48]

### 3.3   Southern African Development Community (SADC)

SADC was formed in 1992 following the decline of the apartheid government of South Africa to enhance the legal framework for cooperation in the areas of development and economic growth, poverty alleviation, enhancement of the standard and quality of life of the peoples of Southern Africa.[49] Despite the primary focus on economic development, the SADC Treaty is also aimed to 'promote and defend peace and security'.[50] In 1996, the Organ on Politics, Defence and Security (OPDS) was established as a key organ that would 'function independently of other SADC structures' with the mandate, *inter alia*, to 'protect the people and safeguard the development of the region, against instability arising from the breakdown of law and order, inter-state conflict and external aggression'.[51] However, the precise authority of the OPDS, as well as its relationship with the heads of state and government summit ('SADC Summit'), which is the SADC's 'supreme policy-making institution',[52] was left indeterminate.[53] The rivalry between the two dominant regional leaders in Zimbabwe and South Africa stalled the adoption of the draft Protocol on Politics, Defence and Security Cooperation,[54] leaving the OPDS dysfunctional.

Despite the ambiguity of its authority and institutional structure, the SADC was relied upon as the political leverage of legitimacy in authorising the deployment of troops in the Democratic Republic of the Congo on 18 August 1998 when the newly installed President Kabila,

---

[48] Protocol relating to the Mechanism for Conflict Prevention, Management, Resolution, Peacekeeping and Security, ECOWAS Doc. A/P10/12/99 (10 December 1999).

[49] Treaty of the Southern African Development Community, adopted 17 August 1992, 32 ILM 116 (entered into force 30 September 1993), Art. 5(1)(a) ('SADC Treaty'). For background to its establishment, see e.g., C. Ng'ong'ola, 'Regional Integration and Trade Liberalisation in Southern Africa Development Community' (2000) 3 *Journal of International Economic Law* 485.

[50] SADC Treaty, Art. 5(1)(c).

[51] SADC Summit Heads of State or Government, Communiqué, Gaborone, Botswana, 28 June 1996, available at www.sadc.int/files/3913/5292/8384/SADC_SUMMIT_COM MUNIQUES_1980–2006.pdf.

[52] SADC Treaty, Art. 10(1).

[53] See Coleman, *International Organisations and Peace Enforcement*, above n. 43, pp. 117–19.

[54] Ibid. p. 119.

following the 1997 Kinshasa cease-fire agreement, appealed for assistance to SADC leaders. In response to this call, three states party to SADC, namely Zimbabwe, Namibia and Angola, decided to intervene by launching Operation Restore Sovereign Legitimacy, allegedly in order to repel invasion by Burundi, Rwanda and Uganda. Critical for the purpose of this chapter is the fact that the decision for military intervention was made, not by the SADC Summit or the OPDS, but at the meeting between Defence Ministers under the auspices of the Inter-State Defence and Security Committee, which could only make recommendations to the SADC Summit.[55] Nevertheless, recourse to the SADC framework contributed to the setting that 'was conducive to generating at least a façade of consensus behind the initiative',[56] despite there being strong opposition, as will be discussed below, concerning the legality of the deployment.

Likewise, the institutional basis for military intervention in the midst of the constitutional crisis in Lesotho on 22 September 1999 was called into question. South African-led Operation Boleas, which was deployed reportedly with the mandate to prevent any further anarchy and to create a stable environment for the restoration of law and order,[57] may have found its legal basis in the OPDS mandate of protecting the region 'against instability arising from the breakdown of law and order'. However, the OPDS was dysfunctional at that time,[58] and the SADC Summit, the alternative authority empowered to authorise military intervention, did not go further than 'welcom[ing] the mediation led by the South African government'.[59] Given that the dispute concerned

---

[55] Berman and Sams, *Peacekeeping in Africa: Capabilities and Culpabilities*, above n. 18, pp. 177–8. In the meeting, only nine out of fourteen members were in attendance. For details, see Coleman, *International Organisations and Peace Enforcement*, above n. 43, pp. 124–5.

[56] Coleman, *International Organisations and Peace Enforcement*, above n. 43, p. 145. See also SC Res. 1234 (9 April 1999) para. 11.

[57] South African National Defence Force, 'Southern African Development Community Combined Task Force Boleas: Operation Boleas and Campaign Charon as presented to the Joint Standing Committee of Parliament on Defence and the Portfolio Committee on Foreign Affairs on 2 November 1998', as cited in Coleman, *International Organisations and Peace Enforcement*, above n. 43, p. 163. See also Laurie Nathan, *Community of Insecurity: SADC's Struggle for Peace and Security in Southern Africa* (Ashgate, Farnham, 2012) pp. 83–4.

[58] Fako Johnson Likoti, 'The 1998 Military Intervention in Lesotho: SADC Peace Mission or Resource War?' (2007) 14 *International Peacekeeping* 251, 255.

[59] SADC Summit Heads of State or Government, Communiqué, Grand Baie, Mauritius, 13–14 September 1998, available at www.sadc.int/files/3913/5292/8384/SADC_SUM MIT_COMMUNIQUES_1980-2006.pdf.

the question of governmental authority following allegedly fraudulent elections, the operation could not have been sufficiently justified on the basis of consent by the incumbent government without authorisation by SADC.[60] Nevertheless, Operation Boleas did not provoke any international criticism.[61]

These two institutional crises highlighted the significance of SADC as the political leverage for legitimacy of military operations within the region, forcing South Africa and Zimbabwe to recognise the lack of a functioning security organ as a serious issue. As a result, in August 1999, the SADC Summit tasked the Council of the Ministers 'to review the operations of all SADC institutions, including the Organ on Defence, Politics and Security', which led on 31 March 2001 to the integration of the OPDS into the SADC structures accountable to the SADC Summit.[62] The Protocol on Politics, Defence and Security Co-operation was also adopted on 14 August 2001 to provide a legal framework for the operation of the OPDS.[63] Furthermore, the Mutual Defence Pact adopted in 2003 re-affirmed the renewed relationship between the SADC Summit and the OPDS by stating that '[c]ollective action shall be mandated by [the] Summit on the recommendation of the Organ [OPDS]'.[64] Although no military operation has since been authorised under the more institutionalised collective security arrangements,[65] SADC has thus developed as a security institution through challenges to its institutional authority and competence in dealing with immediate security threats.

---

[60] See Coleman, *International Organisations and Peace Enforcement*, above n. 43, pp. 164–9; Rocky Williams, 'From Peacekeeping to Peacebuilding? South African Policy and Practice in Peace Missions' (2000) 7(3) *International Peacekeeping* 84, 100–1; R.J. Southall, 'SADC's Intervention into Lesotho: An Illegal Defence of Democracy?' in O. Furley and R. May (eds.), *African Interventionist States* (Ashgate Publishing, Abingdon, 2001) p. 29.

[61] Mark Malan, 'Leaner and Meaner? The Future of Peacekeeping in Africa' (1999) 8(4) *African Security Review* 45, 53.

[62] SADC Extra-Ordinary Summit of Heads of State and Government, Communiqué, Windhoek, Namibia, 9 March 2001, para. 11, available at www.sadc.int/files/3913/5292/8384/SADC_SUMMIT_COMMUNIQUES_1980–2006.pdf.

[63] Protocol on Politics, Defence and Security Co-operation, signed 14 August 2001 (entered into force 2 March 2004), available at www.sadc.int/files/3613/5292/8367/Protocol_on_Politics_Defence_and_Security20001.pdf.

[64] SADC Mutual Defence Pact, signed 26 August 2003 (entered into force 17 August 2008), Art. 6(2), available at www.sadc.int/files/2913/5333/8281/SADC_Mutual_Defence_Pact2003.pdf.

[65] International Crisis Group, *Implementing Peace and Security Architecture (II): Southern Africa*, Africa Report No. 191 (15 October 2012) p. 6.

### 3.4 Economic and Monetary Community
### of Central Africa (CEMAC)

CEMAC was established in 1999 with the aim of promoting harmonious development across its member states.[66] Despite its strictly economic mandate, CEMAC decided to deploy a multinational force following Libyan troops' intervention in the Central African Republic (CAR) in May and November 2001 to repel the coup against President Ange-Félix Patassé. Initially, the peacekeeping force was deployed under the authority of the Community of Sahel-Saharan States (CEN-SAD). CEMAC established its own peacekeeping operation (FOMUC) on 2 October 2002, which officially replaced the CEN-SAD mission on 19 December 2002 and successfully removed the Libyan troops from the CAR under international and regional pressure.[67]

FOMUC was mandated to ensure the safety of President Patassé, observe security on the border between the CAR and Chad, and participate in the restructuring of the CAR armed forces.[68] When troops supportive of former CAR general Francois Bozize succeeded in overthrowing the Patassé government in March 2003 while the President was out of the country, the FOMUC peacekeepers decided not to intervene since the President's life was not in danger.[69] FOMUC continued to remain in the country after the coup at the request of the newly installed leader Bozize.[70]

At the time when FOMUC was deployed, peacekeeping was not part of CEMAC's strictly economic mandate.[71] The Peace and Security Council for Central Africa was established within a separate and larger institution, the Economic Community of Central African States

---

[66] Traité instituant la Communauté Economique et Monétaire de l'Afrique Centrale, adopted 16 March 1994 (entered into force 25 June 1999), available at www.cemac.int/ TextesOfficiels/Traite_CEMAC.pdf. CEMAC is composed of six states, namely, Gabon, Cameroon, CAR, Chad, Democratic Republic of the Congo and Equatorial Guinea.

[67] Terry M. Mays, *Historical Dictionary of Multinational Peacekeeping* (3rd edn, Scarecrow Press, Plymouth, 2011) pp. 93–4.

[68] Annex to the letter dated 4 October 2002 from the Permanent Representative of Gabon to the United Nations addressed to the President of the Security Council, UN Doc. S/2002/ 1113 (4 October 2002) p. 3.

[69] Mays, *Historical Dictionary of Multinational Peacekeeping*, above n. 67, p. 94.

[70] *Ibid.* Since then CEMAC has renewed the mandate several times and on 12 July 2008 the FOMUC was transitioned to the Mission for the Consolidation of Peace in Central Africa.

[71] International Crisis Group, *Implementing Peace and Security Architecture (I): Central Africa*, Africa Report No. 181 (7 November 2011) p. 6.

(ECCAS),[72] and was not ready to assume this role either.[73] It is not clear on what legal basis, even with the doctrine of implied powers, the deployment of FOMUC was authorised. Notwithstanding the fact that there was no clear legal basis for and limitation of the deployment, FOMUC strictly followed the traditional peacekeeping doctrines – consent, neutrality and non-use of force – with no serious attempt to prevent the successful coup led by Bozize.[74] This stands in sharp contrast with the earlier deployment of the Inter-African Mission to Monitor Implementation of the Bangui Accords (Mission interafricaine de surveillance des accords de Bangui: MISAB) in 1997–1998, which engaged in heavy bombardment resulting in the death of civilians.[75]

## 4   Institutional competence

Constitutive instruments of international institutions arguably allow for a liberal interpretation of their provisions, informed through 'the subsequent practice in the application of the treaty which establishes the agreement of the parties regarding its interpretation',[76] so that the institution can adapt itself to changing socio-political environments within the limit of its competence. The four African case studies above demonstrate the idea that regional security imperatives may prompt institutional evolution so as to enable appropriate regional action, whilst challenging the basic legal premise that 'collective security action has to fit within the consensual limits of delegation'.[77] The development of

---

[72] Treaty Establishing the Economic Community of Central African States, adopted 18 October 1983 (entered into force 18 December 1984), available at www.wipo.int/wipo lex/en/other_treaties/details.jsp?treaty_id=297. ECCAS is composed of eleven member states, namely Angola, Burundi, Cameroon, CAR, Chad, Congo (Brazzaville), Democratic Republic of the Congo, Equatorial Guinea, Gabon, Rwanda, and São Tomé and Príncipe. For details of its peace and security mandate, see e.g., Jakkie Cilliers and Johann Pottgieter, 'The African Standby Force' in Ulf Engel and João Gomes Porto (eds.), Africa's New Peace and Security Architecture: Promoting Norms, Institutionalizing Solutions (Ashgate, Farhham, 2010) pp. 111, 135–6.

[73] International Crisis Group, Implementing Peace and Security Architecture (I): Central Africa, above n. 71, p. 6.

[74] Ibid.

[75] For details, see e.g., MacQueen, UN Peacekeeping in Africa Since 1960, above n. 3, pp. 96–104.

[76] Vienna Convention on the Law of Treaties, adopted 23 May 1969, 1155 UNTS 331 (entered into force 27 January 1980), Art. 31(3)(b). See also Anna Hood, Chapter 6 (section 3 in particular).

[77] Alexander Orakhelashvili, Collective Security (Oxford University Press, Oxford, 2011) p. 2. Cf. Marco Sassòli, 'The Concept of Security in International Law relating to Armed

African institutions through peacekeeping practices has uniquely resulted in the stretch of their competence beyond their original mandate, blurring the line that delineates the validity of their activities.

The basic premise of the law of international institutions is that international institutions have competence to act on the international plane to the extent authorised by the states parties, as derived from the constitutive instrument. Thus, the Permanent Court of International Justice, in its Advisory Opinion on *Jurisdiction of the European Commission of the Danube*, observed that '[a]s the European Commission is not a State, but an international institution with a special purpose, it only has the functions bestowed upon it by the Definitive Statute with a view to the fulfilment of that purpose'.[78] Likewise, the ICJ, in its Advisory Opinion on *Legality of the Use by a State of Nuclear Weapons in Armed Conflict*, held that '[i]nternational organizations are governed by the "principle of speciality", that is to say, they are invested by the States which create them with powers, the limits of which are a function of the common interests whose promotion those States entrust to them'.[79] Thus, an international institution is required to exercise powers that are expressly authorised by the constitutive instrument, or those 'conferred upon it by necessary implications as being essential to the performance of its duties'.[80] Although the scope of implied powers has been subject to various interpretations among commentators,[81] this doctrine in essence imposes functional limitations upon the autonomous growth of an institution by restricting the exercise of its powers to the extent necessary and essential to the performance of its duties.[82]

---

Conflicts' in Cecilia M. Bailliet (ed.), *Security: A Multidisciplinary Normative Approach* (Martinus Nijhoff Publishers, Leiden, 2009) pp. 7, 14–15.

[78] *Jurisdiction of the European Commission of the Danube between Galatz and Braila* (Advisory Opinion) [1927] PCIJ (ser. B) No. 14, 64, para. 179.

[79] *Legality of the Use by a State of Nuclear Weapons in Armed Conflict* (Advisory Opinion) [1996] ICJ Rep. 66, 78, para. 25.

[80] *Reparation for Injuries Suffered in the Service of the United Nations* (Advisory Opinion) [1949] ICJ Rep. 174, 182–3.

[81] See e.g., Henry G. Schermers and Niels M. Blokker, *International Institutional Law* (5th rev. edn, Martinus Nijhoff Publishers, Leiden, 2011) pp. 180–9; Nigel D. White, *The Law of International Organisations* (2nd edn, Manchester University Press, Manchester, 2005) pp. 128–31; P.H.F. Bekker, *The Legal Position of Inter-Governmental Organizations: A Functional Necessity Analysis of Their Legal Status and Immunities* (Martinus Nijhoff, Dordrecht, 1994) pp. 82–3.

[82] Manuel Rama-Montaldo, 'International Legal Personality and Implied Powers of International Organizations' (1970) 44 *British Year Book of International Law* 111, 148.

At the same time, however, international instruments that establish those institutions have often been regarded as 'constitutional' in that, once established, they take on a life of their own through institutional practice, interpretation, and by formal amendment.[83] In the case of a treaty constituting an international institution, the interpretive exercise through institutional practice, some argue, plays a central role in setting a 'precedent', for the sake of consistency and stability, which fills the legal gap within the framework of the institution.[84] Finn Seyersted has theorised such institutional evolution by developing the doctrine of inherent powers derived from the objective legal personality of international institutions, separate from the intentions of the authors of the constitutive instrument.[85] According to Seyersted, inter-governmental '[o]rganizations are, like States, in principle free to perform any sovereign act, or any act under international law, which they are in a factual position to perform to attain these aims, provided that their constitutions do not preclude such acts'.[86] Thus, this doctrine allows international institutions to satisfy a functionalist agenda in fulfilling their aims and duties, as long as the action in question aims to achieve one of their purposes and it is not expressly prohibited by their constitutive provisions.[87]

---

[83] See e.g., Heidrun Abromeit and Tanja Hitzel-Cassagnes, 'Constitutional Change and Contractual Revision: Principles and Procedures' (1999) 5 *European Law Journal* 23, 32; Bruno Simma, 'From Bilateralism to Community Interest in International Law' (1994–VI) 250 *Recueil des Cours* 217, 258–62; R.St.J. Macdonald, 'The United Nations Charter: Constitution or Contract?' in R.St.J. Macdonald and Douglas M. Johnston (eds.), *The Structure and Process of International Law: Essays in Legal Philosophy, Doctrine, and Theory* (Martinus Nijhoff Publishers, The Hague, 1983) p. 889.

[84] See e.g., José E. Alvarez, *International Organizations as Law-Makers* (Oxford University Press, Oxford, 2005) pp. 87–90; José E. Alvarez, 'Constitutional Interpretation in International Organizations' in Jean-Marc Coicaud and Veijo Heiskanen (eds.), *The Legitimacy of International Organizations* (UN University Press, Tokyo, 2001) pp. 104, 136–7. This leads to the discussion of customary powers where the relevant institutional practice has been repeated and consistent: see Amerasinghe, *Principles of the Institutional Law of International Organizations*, above n. 4, pp. 50–1. This point will not be elaborated in this chapter, as the institutional practices at issue here are instantaneous.

[85] His seminal work in this respect includes Finn Seyersted, *United Nations Force in the Law of Peace and War* (A.W. Sijthoff, Leiden, 1966); Finn Seyersted, 'Jurisdiction over Organs and Officials of States, the Holy See and Intergovernmental Organizations' (1965) *International and Comparative Law Quarterly* 493; Finn Seyersted, 'International Personality of Intergovernmental Organizations' (1964) 4 *Indian Journal of International Law* 1, 233. For his most recent publication on the topic, see Finn Seyersted, *Common Law of International Organizations* (Martinus Nijhoff Publishers, Leiden, 2008) pp. 29–33, 65–70.

[86] Seyersted, *United Nations Force in the Law of Peace and War* 1966, above n. 85, pp. 154–5.

[87] Nigel D. White, 'The UN Charter and Peacekeeping Forces: Constitutional Issues' (1996) 3(4) *International Peacekeeping* 43, 46–9.

Those two approaches start from diametrically opposing premises: the strict approach to the scope of institutional competence is premised upon the intention of the sovereign states that created the institution; whereas the liberal approach assumes international institutions to be separate entities exercising their powers independently from the will of the member states. The distinction becomes blurred when the implied power is applied in a liberal fashion by reference to the two-pronged test: the purposes of the institution and the absence of express provisions prohibiting the exercise of the power at issue.[88]

There is an obvious risk involved in a liberal application of the implied powers doctrine or the reliance on the inherent powers doctrine, which envisages institutional evolution beyond the scope of the original mandates of the institution. Judge Fitzmaurice, in his Dissenting Opinion in the ICJ's Advisory Opinion on *Namibia*, cautioned against such a wide interpretation, stating that:

> Without in any absolute sense denying that, through a sufficiently steady and long-continued course of conduct, a new tacit agreement may arise having a modificatory effect, the presumption is against it – especially in the case of an organization whose constituent instrument provides for its own amendment, and prescribes with some particularity what the means of effecting this are to be.[89]

Indeed, the ICJ held in its Advisory Opinion on *Conditions of Admission of a State to Membership in the United Nations* that '[t]he political character of an organ cannot release it from the observance of the treaty provisions established by the Charter when they constitute limitations on its powers or criteria for its judgment'.[90] Likewise, the Appeals Chamber of the International Criminal Tribunal for the former Yugoslavia (ICTY) observed in *Tadić (Jurisdiction)* that '[t]hose powers cannot, in any case, go beyond the limits of the jurisdiction of the Organization at large, not to mention other specific limitations or those which may derive from the internal division of power within the Organization'.[91] It is thus established that institutional action

---

[88] *Ibid.*

[89] *Legal Consequences for States of the Continued Presence of South Africa in Namibia (South West Africa) Notwithstanding Security Council Resolution 276 (1970)* (Advisory Opinion) [1971] ICJ Rep. 16, 282 (Judge Fitzmaurice Dissenting Opinion).

[90] *Conditions of Admission of a State to Membership in the United Nations (Article 4 of the Charter)* (Advisory Opinion) [1948] ICJ Rep. 57, 64.

[91] *Prosecutor v. Tadić (Jurisdiction)*, Case No. IT-94-1-AR72, International Criminal Tribunal for the former Yugoslavia, Appeals Chamber, 2 October 1995, para. 28. See

cannot be unbound by the legal restrictions imposed upon the particular institution by its own constitutive instrument. The question remaining, however, is: whether and to what extent security imperatives may seek to expand the institutional legal boundaries through the doctrine of implied powers or inherent powers, as has been seen in the African institutional evolution through peacekeeping practices?

## 5  Role of peacekeeping as a security institution

During the early phase of the Cold War, it was generally considered that the Security Council had no power to undertake military action in the absence of special agreements under Article 43 of the UN Charter.[92] However, this view eventually gave way to a more flexible reference to Chapter VII in general to authorise member states to take military action, which has widely been accepted since the adoption of Resolution 678 during the 1990–1991 Gulf Crisis.[93] In this respect, the ICJ made a pertinent observation in its Advisory Opinion on *Certain Expenses*, stating that 'it cannot be said that the Charter has left the Security Council impotent in the face of *an emergency situation* when agreements under Article 43 have not been concluded'.[94] Derived from this is a hypothesis that an institutional action not envisaged in the constitutive instrument can be justified in the face of a security imperative.

One may argue that ultimately it is each organ that has the inherent power to determine its own competence ('*la compétence de la compétence*').[95] C.F. Amerasinghe has observed that the organ must pursue

  also *Certain Expenses*, above n. 27, 196 (Judge Spender Separate Opinion observing that '[i]f, however, the authority purported to be exercised against the objection of any Member State is beyond power it remains so').
[92]  See e.g., Leland M. Goodrich, Edvard Hambro and Anne Patricia Simons, *Charter of the United Nations: Commentary and Documents* (3rd rev. edn, Columbia University Press, New York, 1969) pp. 315–17, 629–32; Hans Kelsen, *The Law of the United Nations: A Critical Analysis of Its Fundamental Problems* (Stevens and Sons, London, 1951) p. 756.
[93]  Roland Rich, 'Crafting Security Council Mandates' in Edward Newman and Roland Rich (eds.), *The UN Role in Promoting Democracy: Between Ideals and Reality* (UN University Press, Tokyo, 2004) p. 62.
[94]  *Certain Expenses*, above n. 27, 167 (emphasis added). See also G. Kirk, 'The Enforcement of Security' (1946) 55 *Yale Law Journal* 1081, 1088 (observing that 'the Council should have the greatest possible flexibility in handling a situation which menaced the peace of the world').
[95]  For the concept of *la compétence de la compétence*, see Bin Cheng, *General Principles of Law as Applied by International Courts and Tribunals* (Stevens & Sons, London, 1953) pp. 275–8. Cf. *Certain Expenses*, above n. 27, 223–4 (Judge Morelli Separate Opinion disputing the application of this doctrine to UN organs).

the conduct in the belief that it was acting lawfully under the constitutive instrument.[96] While acknowledging that each organ must, in the first place at least, determine its own jurisdiction, the ICJ has repeatedly confirmed that the organ's determination enjoys *prima facie* validity and is only 'presumed' not to be *ultra vires*.[97] This leaves scope for member states to protest against the organisation's decisions and challenge their validity.[98]

Decisions made initially in breach of the constitutive instrument may well be retrospectively validated.[99] Often under international law, as Gerard Kreijen observes, 'a lack of institutional and executive machinery to guarantee the enforcement of legal rules necessarily creates a tendency to regard established facts as decisive for the determination of legal titles'.[100] The same can be applied to the expansion of institutional competence. Indeed, despite the clear legal limitations and the legal presumption against tacit modification, the practices of African institutions to deploy peacekeeping forces without the relevant institutional mandate or authority under their respective constitutive instrument did not invite much criticism from the international community. Rather, those practices often received subsequent support and endorsement by the UN Security Council.[101] However, justifying an action that is otherwise *ultra vires* with the expectation of subsequent rectification does not appear to be particularly convincing, and at least is not widely accepted by states, as regional organisations would otherwise be tempted to initiate invalid action in the hope that it would be rectified afterwards.[102]

---

[96] Amerasinghe, *Principles of the Institutional Law of International Organizations*, above n. 4, p. 51.

[97] See e.g., *Interpretation and Application of the 1971 Montreal Convention Arising from the Aerial Incident at Lockerbie (Libyan Arab Jamahiriya v. United Kingdom) (Provisional Measures)* [1992] ICJ Rep. 3, 15, paras. 39–41; *Namibia*, above n. 89, 22, para. 20; *Certain Expenses*, above n. 27, 168.

[98] See e.g., Orakhelashvili, *Collective Security*, above n. 77, pp. 343–6; Nasu, *International Law on Peacekeeping: A Study of Article 40 of the UN Charter*, above n. 10, pp. 127, 246–9.

[99] Cf. Felice Morgenstern, 'Legality in International Organisations' (1976–1977) 48 *British Yearbook of International Law* 241, 255–6.

[100] Gerard Kreijen, *State Failure, Sovereignty and Effectiveness* (Martinus Nijhoff, Leiden, 2004) p. 175

[101] See Statements by the President of the Security Council, UN Doc. S/22133 (22 January 1991), UN Doc. S/23886 (7 May 1992) (commending the efforts of ECOWAS); UN Doc. S/PRST/2005/35 (22 July 2005) (commending FOMUC).

[102] See Akehurst's argument in the context of retrospective authorisation under Art. 53 of the UN Charter: Akehurst, 'Enforcement Action by Regional Agencies', above n. 13, 241.

When an institution operates outside its competence, recourse can be had to an amendment of the constitutive instrument. In fact, the expanded role of ECOWAS for the purpose of maintaining regional peace and security was formally incorporated into the constitutive instrument in the aftermath of its first peacekeeping operation in Liberia.[103] Also, the recognition by regional rival states within SADC of the lack of a functioning security organ as a serious issue subsequently led to the adoption of the 2001 Protocol on Politics, Defence and Security Co-operation and the 2003 Mutual Defence Pact as a legal framework for the operation of the new regional security mechanism.[104] Yet, when an expanded application of the institutional competence meets disagreement, the autonomous course of action may still result without having recourse to an amendment. The decisions made *ultra vires* by ECOWAS Standing Mediation Committee,[105] and also by SADC Inter-State Defence and Security Committee on military intervention in the Democratic Republic of the Congo (DRC),[106] were illustrative of this possibility.

It is thus difficult to find legal justification for actions taken *ultra vires* by regional organisations in the traditional law of international institutions. It is arguable that the regional authorisation made *ultra vires* is simply aimed to generate international and regional legitimacy of military intervention that serves the political interest of a powerful regional state.[107] Whilst seeking legitimacy may help explain the motivation for out-of-competence action, it does not necessarily explain why these actions have received general acceptance by other member states as well as by the international community. There is no denying that there is a varying degree of regional politics involved behind what appears to be regional unity, and international

Cf. Christian Walter, 'Security Council Control over Regional Action' (1997) 1 *Max Planck Yearbook of United Nations Law* 129, 178–9.

[103] See above nn. 47–48 and accompanying text.

[104] See above nn. 63–64 and accompanying text.

[105] See above nn. 43–44 and accompanying text.

[106] See above nn. 55–56 and accompanying text.

[107] See Coleman, *International Organisations and Peace Enforcement*, above n. 43, pp. 91–3 (observing that Nigerian-led ECOMOG offered Nigeria a chance to bolster its regional and international profile); pp. 134–7 (observing that Zimbabwe's leadership in the SADC operation in the Congo was linked to its desire to demonstrate regional leadership); pp. 174–7 (noting South Africa's interest in projecting itself as a force for regional peace and security without stirring up memories of apartheid aggression and fears of dominance).

endorsement, in support of those out-of-competence regional actions.[108] However, it is also arguable that recourse and adherence to peacekeeping doctrines that have developed through UN peacekeeping practices appears to have contributed to facilitating general support of member states for these regional operations.

In fact, peacekeeping troops deployed by the OAU in Chad and by CEMAC in the CAR both adopted and strictly adhered to the requirements of consent, neutrality and non-use of force except for purposes of defending themselves.[109] Even though ECOMOG and the SADC operation in Lesotho were in reality intervention forces to fight against rebels to defend the governments in power,[110] their official purpose was described in neutral tones as being 'to stop the senseless killing of innocent civilian nationals and foreigners, and to help Liberian people to restore their democratic institutions',[111] and 'to prevent any further anarchy and to create a stable environment for the restoration of law and order'.[112] The Zimbabwe-led Operation Sovereign Legitimacy deployed within SADC's framework, on the other hand, did not enjoy the general agreement of its member states, with South Africa in particular reportedly disputing the nature of the operation described as a peacekeeping exercise.[113]

---

[108] This is particularly the case with ECOWAS, where the consensus rule muted formal opposition: see Coleman, *International Organisations and Peace Enforcement*, above n. 43, p. 95.

[109] See above nn. 30–32, 74 and accompanying text.

[110] For details, see e.g., D. Elwood Dunn, 'Liberia's Internal Responses to ECOMOG's Interventionist Efforts' in Karl P. Magyar and Earl Conteh-Morgan (eds.), *Peacekeeping in Africa: ECOMOG in Liberia* (Macmillan Press, Hampshire, 1998) pp. 76, 87–92.

[111] Statement dated 9 August 1990 by His Excellency Dr Rilwanu Lukman, Honourable Minister of External Affairs of the Federal Republic of Nigeria, on the conclusion of the first session of the Economic Community of West African States (ECOWAS) Standing Committee on the conflict in the Republic of Liberia, UN Doc. S/21485 (10 August 1990) p. 3. It also states that 'ECOWAS intervention is in no way designed to save one part or another': *ibid.*

[112] South African National Defence Force, 'Southern African Development Community Combined Task Force Boleas: Operation Boleas and Campaign Charon as presented to the Joint Standing Committee of Parliament on Defence and the Portfolio Committee on Foreign Affairs on 2 November 1998', as cited in Coleman, *International Organisations and Peace Enforcement*, above n. 43, p. 163.

[113] See Coleman, *International Organisations and Peace Enforcement*, above n. 43, pp. 152–3. It should be noted, however, that South Africa later abandoned its public opposition in order to maximise the legitimacy of Operation Boleas: *ibid.* pp. 189–90.

In cases where no specific provision confers upon the institution the authority to deal with peace and security matters, it would be difficult to argue that the institutional competence has been expanded through interpretation of a treaty provision by reference to the subsequent practice. Nevertheless, the general acceptance by member states carries weight in maintaining the presumed validity of out-of-competence decisions, which neither the implied powers doctrine nor the inherent powers doctrine sufficiently appreciates. The application of and adherence to the established formula of peacekeeping, and arguably even the rhetoric of peacekeeping, appears to assist in producing a general agreement between the member states of a regional organisation, which in effect results in an 'emergency amendment' to its constitutive instrument for the purpose of immediately and effectively responding to security imperatives facing the region.

## 6   Conclusion

It is an undeniable fact that institutions are capable of development in response to new security issues not perceived at the time of their establishment. However, such institutional evolution often poses challenges to the basic principle of international institutional law, which requires each institution to operate within its competence as derived from its constitutive instrument. The doctrines of inherent powers and, to a lesser extent, implied powers, may go some way in providing a legal basis for expansive institutional activities, yet potentially conflict with the established rule of international institutional law that institutional action cannot be unbound by the legal restrictions imposed upon the particular institution by its own constitutive instrument.

The African institutional developments through peacekeeping practices examined in this chapter demonstrate that the rhetoric and the formula of peacekeeping have assisted in producing a general agreement of regional states, muting the issue of validity. Such practices arguably constitute an 'emergency amendment' to their constitutive instruments for the purpose of immediate and effective response to security imperatives facing the region. This observation may have wider ramifications for institutional evolution in responding to contemporary security challenges. International and regional institutions that are not originally mandated to deal with peace and security issues may well find the need to expand their institutional competence.[114] In such an event, the traditional peacekeeping 'institution' can play a valuable role in securing a general acceptance of their member states as an effective response to a particular regional security threat.

---

[114] See e.g., Fuadi Pitsuwan, 'Time for ASEAN Peacekeeping Force', *The Diplomat* (online), 2 May 2011, available at http://thediplomat.com/2011/05/02/time-for-asean-peacekeep ing-force/.

# 8

## Security and the law in international and domestic institutions: lessons from Israel's border security

SOLON SOLOMON

## 1 Introduction

Security and the law are inextricably interrelated, particularly in the international field.[1] While the law justifies security measures,[2] security nurtures a sense of stability, so that both notions become indispensable. Domestic as well as international institutions often find themselves struggling to maintain a precarious balance between security and the law.[3] This chapter sketches this balance in public and international institutions with the understanding that the relationship between security and the law is neither static nor monolithic, but rather dynamic, like a pendulum swinging from one end to another. In fact, neither excessive security measures at the expense of legal protection nor excessively legalistic positions endangering security can enjoy triumph over the other for long. It may take place even unconsciously by international and domestic players, thus strengthening international law's unconscious facet that Alexandra Walker developed in Chapter 1 of this volume.

---

[1] Martti Koskenniemi, 'The Place of Law in Collective Security' (1996) 17 *Michigan Journal of International Law* 456.

[2] *Ibid.* 478.

[3] Tal Becker, 'Address to the American International Law Association' (2004) 10 *ILSA Journal of International and Comparative Law* 481. For such balancing in domestic contexts, see e.g., the position expressed by the Israeli Supreme Court, as examined by Baruch Bracha, 'Judicial Review of Security Powers in Israel: A New Policy of the Courts' (1991) 28 *Stanford Journal of International Law* 61. For criticisms on the Court's position, see Solon Solomon, *The Justiciability of International Disputes: The Advisory Opinion on Israel's Security Fence as a Case Study* (Wolf Legal Publishers, Nijmegen, 2009) pp. 168–71.

This chapter examines this precarious relationship between security and the law with the focus on how public and international institutions have approached Israel's national border security issues: namely, Israel's border with Egypt, the 1967 armistice lines, and the Gaza boundary after the Israeli disengagement in 2005. To that end, it first reviews the historical context in which Israel's borders with Egypt and the 1967 armistice lines in the West Bank and Gaza have been institutionalised in response to border security concerns. The chapter then examines how different institutions have dealt with Israel's national security claim in justifying its naval blockade and Operation Cast Lead in the 2009 Gaza conflict.

## 2   Israeli-Egyptian border

After the occupation by Israel during the 1967 Six Day War, Sinai was returned to Egypt following the signing of the Camp David Peace Accord between the two countries, on the condition that the Peninsula would remain partially demilitarised, and that any different arrangement would constitute an amendment to the Peace Accord requiring Israel's consent.[4] Thus, when riots erupted in January 2011,[5] Egypt's decision to impose law and order in Sinai was legally subject to Israel's consent.[6] The question ultimately became whether the consent should be obtained in advance of any Egyptian Sinai military activity. In 2007 when Egypt filed several requests for policing measures on the grounds of combating arms smuggling to Gaza, Israel refused to give consent.[7] Yet, in 2011, the Israeli

---

[4] Arie Kacowicz, *Peaceful Territorial Change* (South Carolina University Press, Columbia, SC, 1994) p. 139.

[5] 'Mubarak plays last card, the Army; police vanish', *World Tribune* (online), 31 January 2011, available at www.worldtribune.com/worldtribune/WTARC/2011/me_egypt0078_01_31.asp.

[6] Jonathan Lis and Jack Khoury, 'Netanyahu warns Egypt losing control of growing terror groups in Sinai', *Haaretz* (online), 30 May 2011, available at www.haaretz.com/news/int ernational/netanyahu-warns-egypt-losing-control-of-growing-terror-groups-in-sinai-1. 364949; Amos Harel and Barak Ravid, 'PM warns Islamists could take control in Egypt; Israel approves Sinai troops', *Haaretz* (online), 1 February 2011, available at www.haar etz.com/print-edition/news/pm-warns-islamists-could-take-control-in-egypt-israel-app roves-sinai-troops-1.340452.

[7] Ghassan Bannoura, 'Egypt asks for national troop deployment in Sinai, Israeli refuse', *IMEMC News* (online), 26 December 2007, available at www.imemc.org/article/52103; Marian Houk, 'Israel agrees to exceptional but limited deployment of Egyptian Army personnel in Sinai', *American Chronicle* (online), 30 January 2011, available at www.ame ricanchronicle.com/articles/view/215366.

government ultimately decided to grant its consent.[8] In the summer of 2012, this consent was again granted after Egypt launched helicopter air strikes in pursuit of those who had orchestrated an attack leading to the death of sixteen Egyptian soldiers in Sinai.[9] Thus, the relationship between security and the law at the Israeli-Egyptian border since the conclusion of the Camp David Accords has gradually shifted towards the security end of the spectrum, substantially diminishing the significance of the legal requirement agreed upon in the Peace Accords in the name of security.

This evolution of practice is even more problematic under Israel's domestic law. Reacting to this development, the Speaker of the Knesset (Israel's Parliament) twice instructed the Knesset Legal Advisor to examine whether the government's consent constituted in essence an amendment of the Camp David Accords, requiring parliamentary approval.[10] Although Israeli law does not expressly require parliamentary approval for the signature of or an amendment to a major political agreement,[11] constitutional custom compels such approval.[12]

---

[8] 'Israel agrees to some Egyptian troops in Sinai', *Yediot Aharonot* (online), 31 January 2011, available at www.ynetnews.com/articles/0,7340,L-4021890,00.html; Oren Kessler, 'Egyptian Army deploys additional soldiers in Sinai', *Jerusalem Post* (online), 18 February 2011, available at www.jpost.com/MiddleEast/Article.aspx?id=208762; 'Barak: we'll allow helicopters, more troops in Sinai', *Yediot Aharonot* (online), 26 August 2011, available at www.ynetnews.com/articles/0,7340,L-4114141,00.html.

[9] 'Israel OKs Egypt attack helicopters in Sinai', *Jerusalem Post* (online), 9 August 2012, available at www.jpost.com/MiddleEast/Article.aspx?id=280732.

[10] 'Knesset Speaker Rivlin instructed to explore whether permission for the deployment of Egyptian troops in Sinai is subject to Knesset approval' (in Hebrew), *Haaretz* (online), 31 January 2011, available at www.haaretz.co.il/news/politics/1.1470101; Pinchas Wolf, 'Rivlin: deployment of troops in Sinai? Only after Knesset approval' (in Hebrew), *Walla News Network* (online), 26 August 2011, available at http://news.walla.co.il/?w=/9/1854429.

[11] *Kamiar v. State of Israel*, Crim. A. 131/67 (1967) 22(2) P.D. 88.

[12] Yaffa Zilbershats, 'The Adoption of International Law into Israeli Law: The Real is Ideal' (1995) 25 *Israel Yearbook on Human Rights* 243; Asher Maoz, 'The Application of Israeli Law to the Golan Heights is Annexation' (1994) 20 *Brooklyn Journal of International Law* 391; Jeffrey Weiss, 'Terminating the Israel-PLO Declaration of Principles: Is It Legal under International Law?' (1995) 18 *Loyola International and Comparative Law Journal* 114, 118. See also the position of the Knesset Foreign Affairs and Defence Committee Legal Advisor, Miri Frenkel-Shor, that in 2005, Israeli withdrawal from a narrow corridor between Egypt and Gaza was subject to parliamentary approval as an amendment to the Camp David Peace Accords: Gideon Alon, 'Mazuz has yet to decide on Philadelphi deal, MKs told', *Haaretz* (online), 5 July 2005, available at www.haaretz.com/news/mazuz-has-yet-to-decide-on-philadelphi-deal-mks-told-1.163009.

It is generally considered that security measures are to be exercised *infra* and *secundum legem*. Yet, at the same time, the law itself acknowledges that in cases where a state emergency has been declared, security concerns can serve as a ground for temporary derogation from legal restrictions.[13] In fact, most constitutions acknowledge the executive's emergency power with discretionary decision-making.[14] What is peculiar to the Egyptian requests for law and order in Sinai is that security concerns, which were potentially used as a ground by the Israeli government for bypassing the Parliament, stemmed not from the situation inside Israel but from disputed border areas.

Facing this legal challenge, the Israeli government and the Knesset chose to take diametrically opposed positions regarding the desired balance between security and the law. While the Knesset Speaker preferred to deal with the issue on the basis that existing legal arrangements should always be followed even at the cost of security in the border areas, the government chose to advocate a more pragmatic position, arguing that under certain circumstances, security can temporarily override the law, without annulling it.

The temporal parameter is critical. Preponderance of security over the law should not be perceived as a permanent arrangement. From the outset, Israel's Defence Minister made clear that the arrangement was meant to be exceptional and time-limited, advocating for a more permanent solution through an amendment to the military appendix of the Camp David Accords.[15]

Security concerns are not meant to replace law *in abstracto* but justify derogation *in concreto*. In the absence of clear legal authorisation, such as an emergency power provision in the Constitution or a derogation clause

---

[13] See e.g., International Covenant on Civil and Political Rights, opened for signature 16 December 1966, 999 UNTS 171 (entered into force 23 March 1976), Art. 4; European Convention on Human Rights, opened for signature 4 November 1950, ETS 5 (entered into force 3 September 1953), Art. 15.

[14] See e.g., Constitution of Former Yugoslav Republic of Macedonia 1991, art. 126; Constitution of the Republic of Croatia 1990, art. 101; Constitution of Greece 1975, art. 44; Spanish Constitution 1978, art. 86. See also Anna Hood, Chapter 6.

[15] See the statement of Israel's Defense Minister that the deployment of the Egyptian troops in Sinai constituted a 'temporary situation', cited in Dan Williams, 'Israel approves more Egyptian troops in Sinai', *Reuters* (online), 16 February 2011, available at http://in.reuters.com/article/2011/02/16/idINIndia-54932520110216. See also the statement of Israeli Brigadier-General Tzvika Foghel, cited in Houk, 'Israel agrees to exceptional but limited deployment of Egyptian Army personnel in Sinai', above n. 7; Yaakov Katz, 'Israel may amend Military Appendix of Egypt Peace Treaty', *Jerusalem Post* (online), 1 September 2011, available at www.jpost.com/Defense/Article.aspx?id=236235.

in human rights legislation, Israel's domestic institutions have thus been required to flexibly respond to the evolving security challenges along the borders with Egypt.

## 3   The 1967 armistice line

In June 1967, the armistice signed between Israel and the Arab states terminating the Six Day War resulted in considerable military gains for Israel, which retained, *inter alia*, the West Bank from Jordan and the Gaza Strip from Egypt.[16] The 1967 lines became the lines distinguishing these occupied – or according to Israel, disputed – territories from Israeli territories, but were never treated as borders.[17] In November 1967, in the aftermath of the Six Day War, the United Nations (UN) Security Council adopted Resolution 242.[18] The Resolution was heralded as the 'most significant international pronouncement on the Arab-Israeli dispute',[19] and came to be regarded as the cornerstone of any future settlement.

More importantly, the Resolution took a pragmatic approach to bridging the gap between security and the law.[20] The 1967 armistice lines have always been considered by Israel as not able to meet its security concerns. Thus, Israel has appeared reluctant to acquiesce in a complete return to these armistice lines.[21] The Resolution takes this concern into

[16] For details, see Sydney Dawson Bailey, *The Making of Resolution 242* (Martinus Nijhoff Publishers, Dordrecht, 1985) p. 90.

[17] Meir Shamgar, 'Legal Concepts and Problems of the Israeli Military Government: The Initial Stage' in Meir Shamgar (ed.), *Military Government in the Territories Administered by Israel 1967–1980: The Legal Aspects* (Harry Sacher Institute for Legislature Research and Comparative Law, Jerusalem, 1982) p. 13; Kenneth Anderson, 'Israel's Views of the Application of IHL to the West Bank and Gaza Strip' in Roy Gutman, David Rieff and Anthony Dworkin (eds.), *Crimes of War: What the Public Should Know* (W.W. Norton & Company, New York, 2007) p. 54; Robbie Sabel, 'The Status of the Territories: The International Court of Justice Decision on the Separation Barrier and the Green Line' (2005) *38 Israel Law Review* 316.

[18] SC Res. 242 (22 November 1967); Bailey, *The Making of Resolution 242*, above n. 16, p. 5.

[19] Avi Shlaim, *The Iron Wall: Israel and the Arab World* (Oxford University Press, Oxford, 2000) pp. 259–60.

[20] SC Res. 242 (22 November 1967) para. 1; Omar Dajani, '"No Security Without Law": Prospects for Implementing a Rights-Based Approach in Palestinian-Israeli Security Negotiations' in Susan Akram *et al.* (eds.), *International Law and the Israeli-Palestinian Conflict* (Routledge, London, 2011) p. 191; Bailey, *The Making of Resolution 242*, above n. 16, p. 146.

[21] Natasha Mosgovaya, 'Netanyahu to AIPAC: Israel can not return to "indefensible" 1967 lines', *Haaretz* (online), 24 May 2011, available at www.haaretz.com/news/diplo macy-defense/netanyahu-to-aipac-israel-cannot-return-to-indefensible-1967-lines-1. 363705; Yaakov Amidror, *Israel's Requirement for Defensible Borders* (Jerusalem

account, in an effort to bridge the gap between law and the security concerns of the involved parties, especially those of Israel.[22] In its Preamble, the Resolution incorporates the law of occupation by prohibiting territorial acquisition by force, whereas in its text, the Resolution omits the definitive article before the word 'territories'. Israel was called to withdraw from 'territories', not necessarily from all 'the territories', captured during the Six Day War. Although this omission of the definitive article is only relevant to the English version of the Resolution, English was the language used in the negotiations during the drafting of the Resolution and, as such, it is this particular version that depicts the drafters' original intent.[23] Relevant statements made by those who drafted the Resolution support this interpretation,[24] which has been shared by Israel as well as by scholars.[25]

While the Resolution left conspicuous scope for further negotiations and discussions between Israel and Arab states as well as the Palestinians,[26] gradually it became subject to adjustments through

Center for Public Affairs, 2005), available at www.defensibleborders.org/amidror.htm. But see 'Today's borders are the "indefensible" ones', *Haaretz* (online), 22 May 2011, available at www.haaretz.com/print-edition/opinion/today-s-borders-are-the-indefen sible-ones-1.363224; Gil Maguire, 'Defensible Borders for Israel: The 1967 Lines are Just Fine' (21 May 2011), available at http://savingisrael.wordpress.com/2011/05/21/ defensible-borders-for-israel-the-1967-lines-are-just-fine/; Reuven Pedatzur, 'What is a defendable border' (in Hebrew), *Haaretz* (online), 6 June 2011, available at www.haar etz.co.il/hasite/spages/1230373.html.

[22] SC Res. 242 (22 November 1967) para. 1; Bailey, *The Making of Resolution 242*, above n. 16, p. 146; Dajani, '"No Security Without Law"', above n. 20, p. 191.

[23] Ruth Lapidoth, 'Security Council Resolution 242 at Twenty-Five' (1992) 26 *Israel Law Review* 306, 306–7.

[24] See e.g., the opinion of Eugene Rostow, who actively contributed to the wording of the Resolution, in Eugene Rostow, 'Legal Aspects in the Search for Peace in the Middle East' (1970) 64 *American Society of International Law Proceedings* 68, 68–9. See also Lord Caradon's similar view as the representative of the United Kingdom to the Security Council and sponsor of the Resolution, as cited in Julius Stone, *Conflict Through Consensus: United Nations Approaches to Aggression* (John Hopkins University Press, Baltimore, MD, 1977) pp. 57–60, 63.

[25] Lapidoth, 'Security Council Resolution 242 at Twenty-Five', above n. 23.

[26] Charles Enderlin, *Shattered Dreams: The Failure of the Peace Process in the Middle East, 1995–2002* (Other Press LLC, New York, 2003) p. 185 (citing Mohammed Dahlan stating that once the Israeli side recognises the 4 June 1967 armistice line as the basis for the negotiations, the Palestinians can talk of modifications of the border). See also Russell Korobkin and Jonathan Zasloff, 'Roadblocks to the Road Map: A Negotiation Theory Perspective on the Israeli-Palestinian Conflict After Yasser Arafat' (2005) 30 *Yale Journal of International Law* 50; Dennis Ross, *The Missing Peace: The Inside Story of the Fight for Middle East Peace* (Farrar, Straus and Giroux, New York, 2004) p. 614.

doctrinal interpretations, and the 1967 armistice lines came to be treated as a de facto border.[27] In 2004, the International Court of Justice held that the territories captured in 1967 were under occupation.[28] Accordingly, many UN General Assembly Resolutions and Security Council Resolutions refer to the 1967 armistice lines as the base point for dispute resolution by calling for an Israeli withdrawal to those lines.[29]

The practice of UN organs has not been consistent in relation to the claim that a new norm has emerged regarding the 1967 armistice lines, contrary to the wording adopted in Resolution 242.[30] The various General Assembly Resolutions, which refer to the 1967 borders, also underlined that these borders had to be secure.[31] Nevertheless, those General Assembly Resolutions added an authoritative value to the view that any Israeli withdrawal should take place from all the territories captured during the Six Day War.[32]

In November 2012, and following the recognition of Palestinian statehood by a number of states,[33] the UN General Assembly acknowledged

---

[27] See e.g., the Saudi peace initiative, endorsed by the Arab League, available at www.mide astweb.org/saudipeace.htm. See also Roi Maor, 'Preeminent Israelis to support Palestinian State, 1967 borders', +972 Magazine, 20 April 2011, available at http://972m ag.com/group-of-preeminent-israelis-to-support-palestinian-state-along-1967-borders/; Ari Shavit, '1967', Haaretz (online), 12 May 2011, available at www.haaretz.com/print-edition/opinion/1967–1.361194.

[28] Legal Consequences of the Construction of a Wall in the Occupied Palestinian Territory (Advisory Opinion) [2004] ICJ Rep. 136, 167, para. 78.

[29] Goran Lysen, 'Some Reflections on International Claims to Territory' in Jerzy Sztucki, Ove Bring and Said Mahmoudi (eds.), Current International Law Issues: Nordic Perspectives (Martinus Nijhoff Press, Dordrecht, 1994) p. 127. See e.g., GA Res. 44/42 (6 December 1989); GA Res. 54/42 (21 January 2000) para. 5; GA Res. 59/123 (10 December 2004); GA Res. 58/292 (6 May 2004); GA Res. 64/19 (2 December 2009); GA Res. 64/21 (2 December 2009) (calling for a withdrawal to the 1967 lines regarding the Golan Heights); SC Res. 1397 (12 March 2002).

[30] See e.g., GA Res. ES-10/14 (12 December 2003) (referring specifically to the 1949 armistice lines).

[31] Tim Hillier, Sourcebook on Public International Law (Cavendish Publishing, London, 1998) p. 214.

[32] 'Quartet may support Palestinian State along 1967 borders', Jerusalem Post (online), 19 April 2011, available at www.jpost.com/DiplomacyAndPolitics/Article.aspx?I D=217136&R=R1; 'Erekat: if '67 Lines are an Illusion, peace is an illusion', Jerusalem Post (online), 23 May 2011, available at www.jpost.com/DiplomacyAndPolitics/Article. aspx?id=221788; 'G-8 leaders omit mention of 1967 borders in Middle East statement', Haaretz (online), 27 May 2011, available at www.haaretz.com/news/diplomacy-defense/ g8-leaders-omit-mention-of-1967-borders-in-middle-east-statement-1.364459.

[33] 'Israel ire as Argentina and Brazil recognize Palestine', BBC News (online), 7 December 2010, available at www.bbc.co.uk/news/world-middle-east-11941172; Jordana Horn, Hilary Leila Krieger and Herb Keinon, 'South American countries recognize Palestinian

Palestine as a 'non-member observer state'.[34] The Assembly adopted Resolution 67/19, which in several points made reference to the Israel-captured territory as the territory of a future Palestinian state and to the 1967 armistice lines as this state's borders with Israel.[35] The tentative arrangements made for the purpose of maintaining international peace and security in 1967 have thus become the quasi-legal foundation of a possible border delineation between the two sides.

## 4 Israel-Gaza border

In acknowledging the temporary character of the occupation regime,[36] Israel commenced withdrawal of its troops from Gaza and dismantled its settlements, terminating occupation of the Strip in 2005.[37] In light of the continuous Hamas rocket attacks towards south of Israel,[38] however, in

State', *Jerusalem Post* (online), 6 December 2010, available at www.jpost.com/Internatio nal/Article.aspx?id=198288; Harriet Sherwood, 'Dmitry Medvedev restates Russian support for Palestinian State', *Guardian* (online), 18 January 2011, available at www.guar dian.co.uk/world/2011/jan/18/dmitry-medvedev-russia-palestinian-state; Khaled Abu Toameh, 'Spain will recognize Palestinian State on 1967 borders', *Jerusalem Post* (online), 30 May 2011, available at www.jpost.com/MiddleEast/Article.aspx?id=222873.

[34] *General Assembly Votes Overwhelmingly to Accord Palestine 'Non Member Observer State' Status in United Nations*, UN Doc. GA/11317 (29 November 2012).

[35] GA Res. 67/19 (29 November 2012).

[36] Adam Roberts, 'Prolonged Military Occupation: The Israeli-Occupied Territories 1967–1988' in Emma Playfair (ed.), *International Law and the Administration of Occupied Territories* (Oxford University Press, Oxford, 2003) p. 28; Christopher Greenwood, 'The Administration of Occupied Territory' in Emma Playfair (ed.), *International Law and the Administration of Occupied Territories* (Oxford University Press, Oxford, 2003) pp. 241, 244; *Beit Sourik Village Council v. Israel*, HCJ 2056/04 (2004) 58(5) P.D. 807, para. 27.

[37] Revised Disengagement Plan, 6 June 2005, section 1, para. 6, available at www.strategi cassessments.org/library/Disengagement/Revised_Disengagement_Plan_-_Cabinet_A pproval_June_2004.pdf; Harvard Program on Humanitarian Policy and Conflict Research, *Legal Aspects of Israel's Disengagement Plan under International Humanitarian Law* (12 April 2005) p. 5, available at www.reliefweb.int/library/docu ments/2004/hvu-opt-20oct.pdf. For the debate on the question of Gaza's status after the Israeli disengagement and all the different opinions as to whether it is still considered occupied, see Solon Solomon, 'Occupied or Not: The Question of Gaza's Legal Status After the Israeli Disengagement' (2011) 19 *Cardozo Journal of International and Comparative Law* 76 (arguing that Gaza cannot be deemed to be under Israeli occupation any longer).

[38] The severity of these rocket attacks led Israel to declare 'a special situation', permitting the army to take emergency decisions for the civilian population near the border with Gaza. See Rebecca Anna Stoil, '"Special situation" declared for Sderot', *Jerusalem Post* (online), 14 December 2007, available at www.jpost.com/servlet/Satellite?cid= 1196847330565&pagename=JPost%2FJPArticle%2FShowFull.

September 2007 the Israeli government declared Gaza a 'hostile territory'.[39] Accordingly, Israel decided to restrict entry of persons and goods to and from Gaza as well as the electricity and gas supply to the Strip, in the hope that such measures would exert pressure on the Palestinians to halt the rocket attacks, ultimately reassuring Israel's security.[40]

This particular policy reflects Israel's general security viewpoint that pervaded the granting of free movement to people and goods to and from the West Bank and Gaza under the Oslo Accords as well,[41] where such freedoms were granted subject to security considerations.[42] The Israeli judiciary accorded weight to the Israeli government's security concerns in justifying the reduction of fuel and electricity supplies in Gaza.[43]

Against this background, activists attempted to break Israel's naval blockade in Gaza by sailing on board *Flotilla*, which in May 2010 led to clashes with Israeli marines, resulting in the death of nine Turkish nationals.[44] Amidst global outcry, the UN responded by establishing two committees to investigate the matter – one by the Human Rights Council,[45]

---

[39]  Israeli Ministry of Foreign Affairs, 'Security Cabinet Declares Gaza Hostile Territory' (19 September 2007), available at www.mfa.gov.il/MFA/Government/Communiques/ 2007/Security+Cabinet+declares+Gaza+hostile+territory+19-Sep-2007.htm.

[40]  See the relevant statements made by senior Israeli defence officials that 'we need to show the residents of Gaza that life does not carry on freely when Kassam rockets fall in Israel. If rockets are fired, then the Palestinians will pay a price', quoted by Yaakov Katz, 'Barak set to approve list of sanctions against Gaza', *Jerusalem Post*, 23 October 2007. See also the statement made in the plaintiff's writ to the Israeli Supreme Court in *Jaber Al-Bassiouni et al. v. Prime Minister of Israel* (Plaintiff's Writ), HCJ 9132/07, 28 October 2007, 14, 46, available at www.gisha.org/UserFiles/File/Legal%20Documents%20/fuel%20and%20elec tricity_oct_07/petition-fuel%20and%20electricity%20-%20final-no%20details.pdf.

[41]  Protocol concerning Redeployment and Security Arrangements, Annex I of the Israeli-Palestinian Interim Agreement on the West Bank and the Gaza Strip (signed and entered into force 28 September 1995), Art. IX (1)(d) and (2)(a).

[42]  Dajani, '"No Security Without Law"', above n. 20, p. 186.

[43]  *Jaber Al-Bassiouni et al. v. Prime Minister of Israel* (Judgment), HCJ 9132/07, 30 January 2008, para. 4, available at http://elyon1.court.gov.il/Files_ENG/07/320/091/n25/07091320. n25.pdf.

[44]  'Turkey FM: we can't stop upcoming aid flotilla to Gaza', *Haaretz* (online), 30 May 2011, available at www.haaretz.com/news/diplomacy-defense/turkey-fm-we-can-t-stop-upco ming-aid-flotilla-to-gaza-1.364980.

[45]  *Report of the International Fact-Finding Mission to Investigate Violations of International Law, including International Humanitarian and Human Rights Law, resulting from the Israeli Attacks on the Flotilla of Ships Carrying Humanitarian Assistance*, UN Doc. A/HRC/15/21 (21 September 2010) ('Human Rights Council Report').

and the other at the initiative of the UN Secretary-General.[46] In parallel, both Israel and Turkey formed committees to investigate the incident.[47]

Besides procedural differences stemming from Israel's cooperation and a lack thereof,[48] those four reports differed primarily on the extent to which Israel's security concerns were to be taken into account. The Human Rights Council Report did not take into account any security concerns within the parameters of its consideration and focused solely on a doctrinal application of human rights and humanitarian law obligations without placing them in the context of Israel's complex security concerns,[49] including all the scenarios under which the particular Israeli policy had been developed as a response to the increased threats to Israel's national security in Gaza, especially after Hamas' rising to power. Similarly, the Turkish Report gave little weight to the security concerns as a reason for the imposition of the blockade, referring to the Hamas rocket attacks towards south of Israel as a pretext for the blockade and Israel's military response to these attacks as 'punitive measures'.[50]

On the other hand, the UN Panel Report, known also as the Palmer Report, took notice that it was security needs that prompted Israel's imposition of a naval blockade,[51] relevantly observing that 'it is evident that the stated primary objective of the naval blockade was for security'.[52] Along the same lines, the Israeli Committee Report also examined the blockade by incorporating security concerns in its legal analysis.[53] The Committee had at its disposal the testimonies of major actors in the Israeli political and military echelon, who stressed the importance of security considerations in the decision-making

---

[46] Sir Geoffrey Palmer et al., Report of the Secretary-General's Panel of Inquiry on the 31 May 2010 Flotilla Incident (July 2011), available at www.un.org/News/dh/infocus/middle_east/Gaza_Flotilla_Panel_Report.pdf ('UN Panel Report').

[47] Turkel Committee, Report of the Public Commission to Examine the Maritime Incident of 31 May 2010 (2011), available at www.turkel-committee.gov.il/files/wordocs/8808report-eng.pdf; Turkish National Commission of Inquiry, Report on the Israeli Attack on the Humanitarian Aid Convoy to Gaza on 31 May 2010 (2011), available at www.mfa.gov.tr/data/Turkish%20Report%20Final%20-%20UN%20Copy.pdf.

[48] 'Israel rejects UN Council flotilla investigation', Voice of America News (online), 24 August 2010, available at www.voanews.com/english/news/Israel-Rejects-UN-Council-Flotilla-Investigation-101379189.html. The Turkish Report also lacked any feedback from Israel, as noted in the UN Panel Report, above n. 46, p. 81.

[49] Human Rights Council Report, above n. 45, pp. 51, 53, 59–60.

[50] Turkish National Commission of Inquiry, above n. 47, pp. 12–13, 66.

[51] UN Panel Report, above n. 46, pp. 70–2.     [52] Ibid. pp. 77, 82.

[53] Turkel Committee, above n. 47, p. 51.

process, and there is no doubt that these testimonies played a role. For example, Amos Gilad, the head of the Political, Military and Policy Affairs Bureau at the Ministry of Defense, clearly stated that:

> In summary, the need to impose a naval blockade on the Gaza Strip arises from security and military considerations of great weight, which are mainly the need to prevent a military strengthening of terrorists in the Gaza Strip, the entry of terrorists and the smuggling of weapons into the Gaza Strip by sea.[54]

The security concerns thus understood ultimately led the Committee to the conclusion that the aim of the blockade was 'to restrict the military resources available to the Hamas for carrying out hostilities against Israel',[55] and that it was imposed 'for military-security reasons, which focused on preventing weapons, ammunition, military supplies, terrorists and money from entering the Gaza Strip, and the need to prevent the departure of terrorists, vessels filled with explosives and other maritime borne threats from Gaza'.[56]

A similar disagreement is observed in relation to the legality of Operation Cast Lead during the 2009 Gaza conflict.[57] The UN Human Rights Council instituted a fact-finding mission, headed by Justice Goldstone, which found that the operation was 'a deliberately disproportionate attack designed to punish, humiliate and terrorize a civilian population'.[58] In contrast, the Israel Ministry of Foreign Affairs placed a greater emphasis on the national security threat necessitating the military action against Hamas in Gaza.[59]

These differences in approach to the significance of security concerns in examining the legality of Israel's naval blockade and military operations in Gaza suggest that institutional settings, decision-making procedures and political conditions influence the way in which the relationship between security and the law is viewed within the parameters of international law. Ultimately, various institutional frameworks provide the ground upon which the relationship between security and the law is tested, contested and occasionally adjusted.

---

[54]  *Ibid.* p. 50.     [55]  *Ibid.* p. 48.     [56]  *Ibid.*

[57]  For details, see Michael Schmitt, 'Investigating Violations of International Law in Armed Conflict' (2011) 2 *Harvard National Security Journal* 31.

[58]  *Report of the UN Fact Finding Mission on the Gaza Conflict*, UN Doc. A/HRC/12/48 (15 September 2009) para. 1894.

[59]  Israel Ministry of Foreign Affairs, *The Operation in Gaza: Factual and Legal Aspects* (29 July 2009), available at www.mfa.gov.il/MFA/Terrorism-+Obstacle+to+Peace/Terrorism+and +Islamic+Fundamentalism-/Operation_in_Gaza-Factual_and_Legal_Aspects.htm.

## 5 Conclusion

The relationship between security and the law has been studied widely, yet exactly how the two elements interact with each other is not pre-determined and must be observed in specific contexts. This chapter has attempted to tease out this relationship between security and the law by examining the views of domestic and international institutions in responding to security concerns and claims with the focus on Israel's national border security.

Along Israel's borders, the notion of security has played diverse roles. In the case of the Israeli-Egyptian border, through controversial doctrinal manoeuvres, security needs have institutionalised tentative arrangements into more established practice. With regard to the 1967 armistice line, the need for security has recoiled as the lines have become a quasi-legal foundation of possible border delineation between Israel and a Palestine state. Finally, the security challenges from Gaza and subsequent Israeli military operations in the Strip only highlighted disagreement among various international and domestic quasi-judicial bodies over the balance that has to be struck between security and law.

It is arguable that the disagreement stems from various factors, such as institutional settings, decision-making procedures and political conditions in which the institutions operate. In all cases, these contrasting illustrations of the relationship between security and law further demonstrate that the security imperative is not a monolithic concern shared by different institutions in the same way. Thus, the questions as to what extent security concerns should be taken into account in the application of the law, or under what circumstances security concerns can override the pre-existing legal arrangements, necessarily invite tension in the process of institutional evolution.

# PART III

Security institutions and legitimacy

# 9

# The evolution of the nuclear non-proliferation regime: the International Atomic Energy Agency and its legitimacy

KALMAN A. ROBERTSON

## 1 Introduction

The international nuclear non-proliferation regime, established by the Nuclear Non-Proliferation Treaty (NPT),[1] endeavours to address the challenges posed by the expansion of nuclear energy world-wide and the dual use of nuclear technology.[2] Nuclear safeguards are an essential element of the non-proliferation regime, in which the International Atomic Energy Agency (IAEA) is responsible for verifying state compliance with international legal obligations and detecting the misuse of nuclear material.[3] Nuclear technologies, whilst posing a threat of nuclear weapons proliferation, are also relied upon to address increasingly serious energy security concerns around the world.[4] The resulting tensions between military and peaceful uses have been highlighted by a series of findings of non-compliance in the last twenty years.

---

[1] Treaty on the Non-Proliferation of Nuclear Weapons (NPT), opened for signature 1 July 1968, 729 UNTS 161 (entered into force 5 March 1970).

[2] The NPT has three central objectives: (1) preventing the proliferation of nuclear weapons to non-nuclear-weapon states (Arts. I, II, III); (2) facilitating the development of peaceful nuclear energy (Arts. IV, V); and (3) promoting disarmament (Art. VI).

[3] Statute of the International Atomic Energy Agency, opened for signature 23 October 1956, 276 UNTS 3 (entered into force 29 July 1957) (as amended on 4 October 1961, 471 UNTS 334) ('IAEA Statute'). Under Art. III(A)(5), the IAEA is empowered to apply safeguards at the request of members of a multilateral agreement, such as the NPT. See generally, Lawrence Scheinman, 'Nuclear Safeguards and Non-Proliferation in a Changing World Order' (1992) 23(4) *Security Dialogue* 37.

[4] Energy security exists when adequate energy sources are available to meet the needs of the community in a reliable manner for the foreseeable future: see Sam Raphael and Doug Stokes, 'Energy Security' in Alan Collins (ed.), *Contemporary Security Studies* (2nd edn, Oxford University Press, Oxford, 2010) p. 379.

The conventional wisdom is that global governance of the nuclear industry has become increasingly inadequate in the last twenty years.[5] The collapse of Cold War bipolarity has strengthened perceptions of the utility of nuclear weapons for regional security and has highlighted the entrenched discrimination between the states permitted to possess nuclear weapons and the states prohibited from acquiring them.[6] This has created new incentives for non-compliance,[7] challenging the legitimacy of the IAEA as the world nuclear 'watchdog'.[8] This chapter critically examines how the IAEA has maintained its legitimacy by reference to the development of its legal authority to administer comprehensive safeguards agreements in NPT non-nuclear-weapon states, focusing on on-site inspections, which are the Agency's primary mechanism for the independent verification of state declarations.

This chapter shows that the institution possesses (at least to a moderate degree) epistemic virtues: generating reliable information on state behaviour; operating transparently as necessary to allow evaluation of safeguards effectiveness and efficiency; and providing information

---

[5] Henry D. Sokolski, 'Assessing the IAEA's Ability to Verify the NPT' in Henry D. Sokolski (ed.), *Falling Behind: International Scrutiny of the Peaceful Atom* (Strategic Studies Institute, Carlisle, 2008) pp. 3–51; Canadian Centre for Treaty Compliance and Centre for International Governance Innovation, *Nuclear Energy and Global Governance to 2030: An Action Plan* (2010), available at http://acuns.org/wp-content/uploads/2012/06/Nucle arEnergyandGlobalGovernance.pdf; Orde F. Kittrie, 'Averting Catastrophe: Why the Nuclear Nonproliferation Treaty is Losing Its Deterrence Capacity and How to Restore It' (2006–2007) 28 *Michigan Journal of International Law* 337, 345, 346, 429; Michael Wesley, 'It's Time to Scrap the NPT' (2005) 59 *Australian Journal of International Affairs* 283.

[6] Nuclear-weapon states are permitted to possess nuclear weapons with only an obligation 'to pursue negotiations in good faith on effective measures relating to . . . nuclear disarmament': NPT, Art. VI. Although disarmament could provide a disincentive to horizontal proliferation, the obligation has proven illusory, see Australian Government Department of Foreign Affairs and Trade, *Report of the Canberra Commission on the Elimination of Nuclear Weapons* (14 August 1996) p. 1, available at www.dfat.gov.au/publications/secur ity/canberra-commission-report/. In contrast, any state with chemical weapons may be considered a pariah due to the total prohibition of chemical weapons, as will be explained below.

[7] Dong-Joon Jo and E. Gartzke, 'Determinates of Nuclear Weapons Proliferation' (2007) 51 *Journal of Conflict Resolution* 167, 186; William C. Potter and Gaukhar Mukhatzhanova, 'Divining Nuclear Intentions: A Review Essay' (2008) 33 *International Security* 139.

[8] As discussed by Hitoshi Nasu and Kim Rubenstein in the Introduction, legitimacy is a highly contested concept and is variously understood in different contexts. For a debate on the legitimacy of international institutions in general, see Rüdiger Wolfrum and Volker Röben (eds.), *Legitimacy in International Law* (Springer, Berlin, 2008).

for ongoing deliberation about the requirements of global justice and the scope of institutional responsibilities. To that end, section 2 reviews the legal framework for the IAEA's public authority and the conditions for effective verification. Section 3 examines the role of nuclear safe-guards in the nuclear non-proliferation regime and how it has evolved. Section 4 assesses the legal authority of the IAEA to conduct on-site inspections. Section 5 considers the findings from the previous sections in light of the relationship between the investigative authority of the IAEA and the enforcement authority of the Security Council in order to ascertain the normative foundation of the IAEA's institutional legiti-macy. The role of the IAEA in nuclear-weapon states is comparatively limited and will not be a focus of this chapter.[9]

## 2   IAEA and the nuclear non-proliferation regime

The IAEA is an inter-governmental organisation established in 1957 to promote peaceful nuclear cooperation and to administer safeguards over nuclear material placed under its supervision by states.[10] The IAEA Board of Governors consists of thirty-five states. Decisions about imple-menting safeguards and findings of non-compliance are made by a simple majority vote, ensuring that individual states on the Board cannot veto a non-compliance finding to suit their political interests.[11]

---

[9] The NPT defines a nuclear-weapon state as a state that tested nuclear weapons before 1967: NPT, Art. IX(3). These states (France, the People's Republic of China, Russia, the United Kingdom and the United States) each have a safeguards agreement, known as a 'voluntary offer agreement' with the IAEA covering some of their peaceful nuclear facilities: see e.g., Agreement of 18 November 1977 between the United States of America and the Agency for the Application of Safeguards in the United States of America (entered into force 9 December 1980), IAEA Doc. INFCIRC/288 (December 1981). Similarly, India, Israel and Pakistan have non-NPT 'item-specific' safeguards over some of their peaceful facilities: see *The Agency's Safeguards System*, IAEA Doc. INFCIRC/66/Rev.2 (16 September 1968). For an example of this type of agreement, see e.g., Agreement of 24 February 1993 between the IAEA and the Government of the Islamic Republic of Pakistan for the Application of Safeguards in Connection with the Supply of a Nuclear Power Station from the People's Republic of China, INFCIRC/418 (March 1993).

[10] IAEA Statute, Arts. III(A) and XXII; Charles Parker, *Controlling Weapons of Mass Destruction: An Evaluation of International Security Regime Significance* (Coronet Books, Uppsala, 2001) p. 67. 'Nuclear material' to be supervised includes thorium, uranium and plutonium, refined and converted from sources such as ore and capable of being used in reactors, specialised facilities or weapons: see definitions in IAEA Statute, Art. XX.

[11] IAEA Statute, Art. VI. The June 2011 finding of non-compliance by Syria passed with seventeen states in favour and six (including Russia and the People's Republic of China) against. See IAEA Board of Governors Resolution, Implementation of the NPT

The IAEA is a traditional security institution in the sense that it is designed to reduce the risk to states of the use of nuclear weapons and to protect their autonomy against the political effects of the threat of such force by restricting access to nuclear weapons.[12] The public authority of the IAEA is threefold: (1) investigative authority to review state reports on nuclear activities and to inspect nuclear facilities according to the relevant safeguards agreement; (2) quasi-judicial authority to identify non-compliance; and (3) a very limited enforcement authority.[13] If the Board of Governors determines that non-compliance has occurred, it must inform the United Nations (UN) General Assembly and the Security Council and call upon the state to remedy the non-compliance.[14] The IAEA has the power to 'direct' other member states to suspend nuclear cooperation with a non-compliant state and call for return of materials.[15] It is unclear (and untested) whether such a direction of the IAEA would be legally binding in the absence of a decision of the Security Council.[16]

Verification reinforces the norms of the non-proliferation regime by providing an objective (or at least a technocratic) mechanism for identifying non-compliance.[17] It builds trust and helps to address 'the temptations of unilateralism and militarism',[18] which encourage countries to take up nuclear arms. If the IAEA and its safeguards conclusions are seen

Safeguards Agreement in the Syrian Arab Republic, IAEA Doc. GOV/2011/41 (9 June 2011); James Blitz, 'IAEA refers Syria to UN over "reactor"', *Financial Times* (online), 9 June 2011, available at www.ft.com/cms/s/0/bf2e5d3c-92b3-11e0-bd88-00144feab49a. html#axzz3AtPU8KBh.

[12] See Hitoshi Nasu and Kim Rubenstein, Introduction.

[13] IAEA Statute, Arts. III(B)(4), V, XII(A), (C), XIX. On the distinguishing features of enforcement authority generally, see Volker Röben, 'The Enforcement Authority of International Institutions' (2008) 9 *German Law Journal* 1965.

[14] IAEA Statute, Art. XII(C). This provision is ambiguous as to whether the inspectors, the Director General or the Board makes the determination of non-compliance but, in practice, the Board makes the final determination.

[15] *Ibid.* Arts. XII(C), XIX.

[16] See generally, Paul Szasz, 'Sanctions' in Jozef Goldblat (ed.), *Safeguarding the Atom: A Critical Appraisal* (Taylor and Francis, Philadelphia, PA, 1985) pp. 135, 143.

[17] In this sense, the IAEA Department of Safeguards, and its inspectors and analysts, may embody the 'epistemic virtues'. Compare this with the community responsible for implementing nuclear arms control agreements between the United States and the Soviet Union discussed in Emanuel Adler, 'The Emergence of Cooperation: National Epistemic Communities and the International Evolution of the Idea of Nuclear Arms Control' (1992) 46 *International Organization* 101.

[18] Richard Tanter, *The Re-emergence of an Australian Nuclear Weapons Option?*, Austral Policy Forum (Nautilus Institute) 07-20A (29 October 2007) p. 1, available at http://nauti lus.org/apsnet/the-re-emergence-of-an-australian-nuclear-weapons-option/.

as legitimate and effective, then states will have confidence that their neighbours are abiding by their commitments, and therefore do not present a nuclear threat, unless the Agency has made a finding of non-compliance. By constraining the use of declared nuclear materials and increasing the chance of detection, verification also creates barriers to the acquisition of nuclear weapons.[19] Iran, Iraq and Libya each managed to conceal nuclear programmes for over a decade but none have successfully overcome the barriers to obtaining nuclear weapons.[20] By contrast, the absence of a verification mechanism under the Biological and Toxin Weapons Convention[21] contributed to suspicion regarding biological weapons programmes in the former Soviet Union and Iraq.[22] IAEA verification mechanisms have also facilitated international dispute resolution in cases where the verified dismantling of nuclear weapons programmes has been sought, for example, in the Democratic People's Republic of Korea (DPRK), Iraq, Libya and South Africa.[23]

The effective deterrence of violations relies on: (1) an on-site inspection power capable of detecting evidence of non-compliance; (2) a nuclear safeguards evaluation process capable of making a judgement on compliance; and (3) the threat of international enforcement action when violations occur. The extent to which compliance can be verified is 'a function of the precision of treaty language, the sophistication of monitoring techniques, and the quality of the decision-making process'.[24] The quality of monitoring and decision-making depends on the adequacy of legal authority (the focus of this chapter), as well as political considerations and the availability of resources.

The difficulties for IAEA verification arise from the tension between promoting peaceful applications of nuclear science and preventing the

---

[19] John Carlson, 'Experience and Challenges in WMD Treaty Verification: A Comparative View' in R. Avenhaus et al. (eds.), Verifying Treaty Compliance (Springer, Berlin, 2006) pp. 211, 212.

[20] See generally, Michael Spies, 'Iran and the Limits of the Nuclear Non-Proliferation Regime' (2006–2007) 22 American University International Law Review 401.

[21] Convention on the Prohibition of the Development, Production and Stockpiling of Bacteriological (Biological) and Toxin Weapons and on Their Destruction, opened for signature 10 April 1972, 1015 UNTS 163 (entered into force 26 March 1975).

[22] Carlson, 'Experience and Challenges in WMD Treaty Verification', above n. 19, pp. 213–14.

[23] See Etel Solingen, Nuclear Logics: Contrasting Paths in East Asia and the Middle East (Princeton University Press, Princeton, NJ, 2007).

[24] Thomas Bernauer, The Chemistry of Regime Formation: Explaining International Cooperation for a Comprehensive Ban on Chemical Weapons (Dartmouth Publishing, Brookfield, 1993) p. 221.

proliferation of nuclear weapons.[25] The IAEA does not have the technological, legal or political capacity to directly prevent every single violation.[26] Because legitimate, peaceful uses exist for nuclear material and
technology, measures to ensure security against military use during
production, processing, storage and transfer of nuclear material must
be implemented with respect for the sovereign right of states to pursue
peaceful technological development.[27] Yet, in 2003 the IAEA called upon
Iran to suspend uranium enrichment pending implementation of safeguards over material and experiments it had failed to disclose.[28] This
demonstrated that the authority of the IAEA to administer safeguards
was not compromised to accommodate Iran's right to peaceful nuclear
energy enshrined in Article IV of the NPT.[29]

## 3   IAEA and comprehensive safeguards

The first three provisions of the NPT focus on the prevention of
horizontal proliferation. Nuclear-weapon states agree not to transfer
control of nuclear weapons to other states or to assist their development,[30] and non-nuclear-weapon states undertake not to receive or
manufacture nuclear weapons.[31] Under Article III(1), each non-
nuclear-weapon state must also conclude an agreement, referred to as
a 'comprehensive safeguards agreement', with the IAEA for the purpose
of verifying compliance with its obligations not to divert 'nuclear energy
from peaceful uses to nuclear weapons'.[32] Parties also undertake not to

[25] See Sokolski, 'Assessing the IAEA's Ability to Verify the NPT', above n. 5, pp. 34–41;
Russell Leslie, 'The Good Faith Assumption: Different Paradigmatic Approaches to
Nonproliferation Issues' (2008) 15 Nonproliferation Review 479.

[26] Parker, Controlling Weapons of Mass Destruction, above n. 10, p. 70. Prevention is
secondary to detection: see Frank Barnaby, How Nuclear Weapons Spread: Nuclear-
Weapon Proliferation in the 1990s (Routledge, New York, 1993) p. 125.

[27] See NPT, Art. III(3); IAEA Statute, Art. III(D).

[28] IAEA Board of Governors Resolution, Implementation of the NPT Safeguards
Agreement in the Islamic Republic of Iran, IAEA Doc. GOV/2003/81 (26 November
2003) pp. 1, 3. Later endorsed by SC Res. 1737 (23 December 2006).

[29] Sokolski, 'Assessing the IAEA's Ability to Verify the NPT', above n. 5, p. 6. Most nuclear-
weapon states view nuclear cooperation as a secondary objective to the prevention of
proliferation: see Harald Müller, 'Export Controls: Review of Article III' in John Simpson
and Darryl Howlett (eds.), The Future of the Non-Proliferation Treaty (St Martin's Press,
New York, 1995) pp. 129, 133.

[30] NPT, Art. I. On the definition of 'nuclear-weapon state', see above n. 9.

[31] NPT, Art. II.

[32] References to 'diversion of nuclear energy' and 'diversion of nuclear material' mean
substantively the same thing – removal of nuclear material from safeguards and failure

supply non-nuclear-weapon states with any nuclear material or associated equipment unless the material is subject to safeguards.[33]
The text of the NPT is general and the 'negotiating history indicates
that the parties intended to defer debate about the scope of the IAEA's
legal authority until after the Treaty was signed'.[34] The comprehensive
safeguards agreements,[35] which detail the authority of the IAEA and the
obligations of non-nuclear-weapon states, are based on a uniform
verification standard.[36] Safeguards agreements require each state to
maintain inventories of nuclear material, facilitate IAEA inspections,
notify the IAEA of any inter-state or inter-facility transfers, and finance
the IAEA.[37] Nuclear safeguards entail traditional treaty monitoring,
including collection of evidence of concealment or non-compliance
by states.[38] This involves reviewing compulsory state declarations on

to declare: John Carlson, 'Defining Non-Compliance: NPT Safeguards' (2009) 39(4) *Arms Control Today* 21, 22; P.A. Buttar, 'Contextual Syntax of International Instruments Safeguarding against Nuclear Proliferation' (1984–1987) 11 *Australian Year Book of International Law* 141. As of 6 August 2014, safeguards agreements have not come into force in twelve non-nuclear-weapon states (none of these are believed to have significant nuclear industries): IAEA, Status List: Conclusion of Safeguards Agreements, Additional Protocols and Small Quantities Protocols as of 6 August 2014, available at www.iaea.org/OurWork/SV/Safeguards/documents/sir_table.pdf.

[33] NPT, Art. III(2).

[34] David Sloss, 'It's Not Broken, So Don't Fix It: The International Atomic Energy Agency Safeguards System and the Nuclear Nonproliferation Treaty' (1994–1995) 35 *Virginia Journal of International Law* 841, 851. On the role of ambiguity in overcoming controversial issues in negotiation, see also Bernauer, *The Chemistry of Regime Formation*, above n. 24, p. 221.

[35] Comprehensive safeguards agreements are usually bilateral, between the Agency and the state: see e.g., Agreement between Australia and the International Atomic Energy Agency for the Application of Safeguards in connection with the Treaty on the Non-Proliferation of Nuclear Weapons, adopted 10 July 1974 [1974] ATS 16 (entered into force 10 July 1974).

[36] See *The Structure and Content of Agreements between the Agency and States Required in connection with the Treaty on the Non-Proliferation of Nuclear Weapons*, IAEA Doc. INFCIRC/153 (Corrected) (June 1972).

[37] *Ibid.* para. 3; IAEA Statute, Art. XII; Carlton Stoiber *et al.*, *Handbook of Nuclear Law* (International Atomic Energy Agency, Vienna, 2003) pp. 126–8; Carlton Stoiber *et al.*, *Handbook on Nuclear Law: Implementing Legislation* (International Atomic Energy Agency, Vienna, 2010) pp. 113–25.

[38] Morten Bremer Maerli and Roger G. Johnston, 'Safeguarding This and Verifying That: Fuzzy Concepts, Confusing Terminology, and Their Detrimental Effects on Nuclear Husbandry' (2002) 9 *Nonproliferation Review* 54, 58. Although this chapter is primarily concerned with the somewhat adversarial task of identifying state-based proliferation, it is important to keep in mind that many national authorities also closely cooperate with the IAEA to prevent unauthorised access by non-state actors and promote nuclear transparency. See also SC Res. 1540 (28 April 2004).

nuclear activities and verifying compliance by independent accounting, measurement, surveillance and on-site inspections.[39] Each state must establish its own safeguards regulatory authority to report to the IAEA and facilitate IAEA inspections.

The IAEA has the right and obligation 'to ensure that safeguards will be applied . . . on all source or special fissionable material in all peaceful nuclear activities within the territory of the State' and thus to determine what activities are required by the state to fulfil its obligations.[40] The primary objective of comprehensive safeguards is:

> [the] timely detection of diversion of significant quantities of nuclear material from peaceful nuclear activities to the manufacture of nuclear weapons or of other nuclear explosive device or for purposes unknown, and deterrence of such diversion by risk of early detection.[41]

The reference to 'purposes unknown' indicates that proof of a non-peaceful purpose is unnecessary. Once a breach with potential proliferation significance is established, the onus is on the state to prove that its programmes are peaceful.[42] This approach, coupled with the fact that refusing access to IAEA inspectors is itself a violation, means that a state cannot subvert the safeguards system simply by being uncooperative.

The IAEA was criticised for the failure of safeguards to identify the nuclear weapons programme in Iraq prior to the 1991 Gulf War.[43] The situation in Iraq demonstrated the fallacy in the assumption that most states lacked the resources necessary to develop a clandestine fuel cycle

---

[39] Stoiber *et al.*, *Handbook of Nuclear Law*, above n. 37, p. 121; Raymond L. Murray, *Nuclear Energy: An Introduction to the Concepts, Systems, and Applications of Nuclear Processes* (5th edn, Butterworth-Heinemann, Boston, 2001) p. 377.

[40] *The Structure and Content of Agreements between the Agency and States*, above n. 36, para. 2. 'Comprehensive' means covering all nuclear material.

[41] *Ibid.* para. 28. The IAEA aims for 95 per cent confidence of detection, see 'The Technical Objective of Safeguards' (1975) 17(2) *International Atomic Energy Agency Bulletin* 13, 14. 'Other nuclear explosive device' extends to non-military nuclear explosives, for example, in mining: Buttar, 'Contextual Syntax of International Instruments Safeguarding against Nuclear Proliferation', above n. 32, 148; Djali Ahimsa, 'Peaceful Uses: Review of Articles IV and V' in John Simpson and Darryl Howlett (eds.), *The Future of the Non-Proliferation Treaty* (St Martin's Press, New York, 1995) p. 113.

[42] Carlson, 'Defining Non-Compliance', above n. 32. This approach appears to be in use in relation to under-reporting of uranium by Iran: see 'Iran uranium haul enough to make a bomb', *Weekend Australian* (Sydney), 21 February 2009, p. 12.

[43] See e.g., Jennifer Scarlott, 'Nuclear Proliferation After the Cold War' (1991) 8 *World Policy Journal* 687.

that could be both completely independent of their declared facilities for regular inspection and capable of yielding material for a small, strategically useful nuclear arsenal.[44] Since many of the smaller-scale enrichment and reprocessing technologies did not exist at the time of drafting the comprehensive safeguards framework, IAEA Legal and Safeguards Officer Paul Szasz concluded in 1975 that 'even in the most repressed societies rumors and news of the construction of large secret facilities would reach the Agency long before these became operations' as long as inspectors were in regular contact with the state's declared facilities.[45]

The crisis in Iraq and the end of the Cold War catalysed increased interest in special inspections, which would allow the IAEA to search suspected, undeclared nuclear facilities.[46] The IAEA also established an Additional Protocol to the comprehensive safeguards agreements, which strengthens inspection powers and reporting requirements.[47] The majority of non-nuclear-weapon states with significant nuclear activities now have an Additional Protocol in force.[48]

The Additional Protocol increases inspector access to declared facilities and allows for verification of reactor design information, making it difficult to conceal activities at declared sites. The Additional Protocol also increases access away from declared sites, particularly for environmental sampling to detect nuclear activities. These reforms signalled a shift in focus from verifying the correctness of declarations (checking for unexplained losses of safeguarded materials from the declared

---

[44] See Carlson, 'Experience and Challenges in WMD Treaty Verification', above n. 19, p. 223.

[45] Paul C. Szasz, 'The Adequacy of International Nuclear Safeguards' (1975) 10 *Journal of International Law and Economics* 423, 435. Szasz believes that the provision of intelligence from other states to the Agency would be adequate to fill any gaps in the Agency's knowledge of undeclared sites: *ibid.* 433.

[46] Jayantha Dhanapala and Randy Rydell, *Multilateral Diplomacy and the NPT: An Insider's Account* (United Nations, Geneva, 2005) p. 125; Scheinman, 'Nuclear Safeguards and Non-Proliferation in a Changing World Order', above n. 3.

[47] See Model Protocol Additional to the Agreements between State(s) and the International Atomic Energy Agency for the Application of Nuclear Safeguards, IAEA Doc. INFCIRC/540 (Corrected) (1 September 1997). For example, Australia's Additional Protocol is Protocol with the International Atomic Energy Agency, Additional to the Agreement of 10 July 1974 between Australia and the International Atomic Energy Agency for the Application of Safeguards in connection with the Treaty on the Non-Proliferation of Nuclear Weapons of 1 July 1968, adopted 23 September 1997 [1997] ATS 28 (entered into force 12 December 1997).

[48] IAEA, Status List, above n. 32.

nuclear fuel cycle) to verifying their completeness (verifying the absence of clandestine materials or activities in the state as a whole).[49]

The Iranian, Libyan and Syrian cases demonstrate the Agency's reliance on national (liaison) intelligence and satellite imagery for identifying locations to seek access.[50] A recurring theme in the cases of non-compliance is small-scale, covert centrifuge enrichment at undeclared locations.[51] For states that have implemented the Additional Protocol, this challenge to the Agency's detection capabilities is being tackled through increased reporting requirements on the manufacture and transfer of centrifuge components.[52] The Additional Protocol makes state regulatory authorities responsible for reporting to the IAEA on the activities of a wider range of industries, including research, manufacture and export involving sensitive technologies.

## 4   Legal authority of the IAEA to conduct on-site inspections

### 4.1   Evolution of the on-site inspection power

As the Agency develops to meet the challenges posed by clandestine nuclear activities in the post-Cold War period, it has had to balance the increasing emphasis on searching for undeclared sites against normative considerations, including non-discrimination and respect for state sovereignty, which require the Agency to restrain the exercise of its institutional authority. In some cases the evolution of the Agency has meant additional burdens on the state and on the nuclear industry. In other cases this has meant the Agency uses third party intelligence, usually from Western governments, to decide where to focus its attention, despite the potential for bias. Because verification relies on the cooperation of individual states and the preparedness of the UN Security Council to enforce obligations, the Agency can only effectively exercise its authority to investigate more broadly for as long as it maintains its legitimacy in the eyes of the states subject to safeguards.

---

[49] See generally, Mohamed El-Baradei, 'Putting Teeth in the Nuclear Non-Proliferation and Disarmament Regime', speech delivered at Karlsruhe, Germany, 25 March 2006, available at www.iaea.org/NewsCenter/Statements/2006/ebsp2006n004.html.

[50] See, Sokolski, 'Assessing the IAEA's Ability to Verify the NPT', above n. 5, p. 20.

[51] Carlson, 'Experience and Challenges in WMD Treaty Verification', above n. 19, p. 224.

[52] Model Protocol, above n. 47, Art. 2(a), Annex 1. See also Mikael Shirazi and Andreas Persbo, 'Centrifuge Production and the Additional Protocol' (2011) 133 *Trust and Verify* 7.

Each comprehensive safeguards agreement empowers the IAEA to conduct on-site inspections at declared facilities for the purpose of verifying state reports on nuclear activities.[53] Routine inspections may be performed unannounced but the IAEA must not interfere with the operation of any facility.[54] Inspectors may examine records held by the state or facility and make independent measurements of nuclear materials.[55]

Consistent with the basic purposes of the NPT, comprehensive safeguards agreements also permit the IAEA to access information as necessary to verify the absence of undeclared nuclear materials anywhere in the territory of the state. This 'special inspection' power extends to the on-site inspection of suspected undeclared nuclear facilities.[56] In order to protect the state from politically motivated requests that could compromise sensitive industries and information, procedural and evidentiary requirements must be met. In order to commence a special inspection, the IAEA Director General must conclude that information provided by the state and obtained from routine inspections is 'not adequate for the Agency to fulfil its [verification] responsibilities'.[57] The Director General must then provide advance notice to the state indicating the particular inspection site and information sought.[58]

Special inspections outside of declared facilities have been formally invoked twice. In 1992, the post-revolution government of Romania invited the IAEA to conduct special inspections in order to build confidence within the international community that the covert nuclear weapons research carried out under Nicolae Ceaușescu was being dismantled.[59] In the same year, based on routine inspections and US national intelligence, the IAEA determined that the DPRK was not providing consistent accounting of its plutonium. The Agency developed a suspicion that significant quantities had been synthesised

---

[53] *The Structure and Content of Agreements between the Agency and States*, above n. 36, paras. 70–72.

[54] *Ibid.* paras. 83, 84.

[55] *Ibid.* paras. 6, 74, 75; Stoiber *et al.*, *Handbook of Nuclear Law*, above n. 37, p. 121; Stoiber *et al.*, *Handbook on Nuclear Law: Implementing Legislation*, above n. 37, pp. 113–25.

[56] *The Structure and Content of Agreements between the Agency and States*, above n. 36, para. 73.

[57] *Ibid.* para. 73.   [58] *Ibid.* paras. 9, 85; IAEA Statute, Art. XII(A)(6).

[59] Wendy Mbekelu, 'Tracking Nuclear Proliferation: Romania', *Public Broadcasting Service News Hour* (online), 2 May 2005, available at http://archive.today/ZBSZ.

at a declared site and were being diverted to undeclared facilities.[60] The IAEA Director General requested special inspections but the DPRK rejected the request, responding that inspections were unnecessary.[61] The IAEA has also informally requested access to locations outside of declared nuclear sites on a number of occasions, including in Myanmar in December 2010 amid claims of clandestine nuclear activities assisted by the DPRK.[62]

The IAEA's authority to conduct special inspections is related to verifying the non-diversion of nuclear material and the completeness of declarations. It is doubtful whether an inspection of a suspected design facility for nuclear weapons (weaponisation activities) could take place without sufficient evidence to indicate the possibility that it contained nuclear material or equipment especially designed for using nuclear material.[63] The Additional Protocol improves upon special inspections by creating 'complementary access' with specific provisions to facilitate access to any location specified by the IAEA.[64] The IAEA's physical access to industrial sites, particularly privately held sites that are not directly involved in the nuclear fuel cycle (i.e. facilities that do not contain any actual nuclear material), might seem to be a significant imposition on private industry. However, this aspect of complementary

---

[60] *Report of the International Atomic Energy Agency: Compliance with Arms Limitation and Disarmament Agreements: Note by the Secretary-General*, UN Doc. A/48/133-S/25556 (16 April 1993) p. 5 ('Compliance Note').

[61] *Ibid.* p. 3.

[62] For an example of an accusatorial request, see Ashish Kumar Sen, 'IAEA seeks permission from Myanmar for Nuke Inspectors to visit', *Washington Times* (online), 13 January 2011, available at www.washingtontimes.com/news/2011/jan/13/iaea-seeks-permission-from-myanmar-for-nuke-inspec/. Myanmar has since indicated that it has abandoned its ambiguous nuclear plans and will conclude an Additional Protocol but it remains to be seen whether the Agency will press Myanmar to open up suspected hidden mines and research sites: Daryl G. Kimball, 'Myanmar Vows to Upgrade IAEA Safeguards' (2012) 42(10) *Arms Control Today* 16.

[63] See *Implementation of the NPT Safeguards Agreement in the Islamic Republic of Iran: Report by the Director General*, IAEA Doc. GOV/2006/15 (27 February 2006) para. 52. On weaponisation activities not directly involving nuclear material, see Robert Williamson Jr, 'Law and the H-Bomb: Strengthening the Nonproliferation Regime to Impede Advanced Proliferation' (1995) 28 *Cornell International Law Journal* 71, 146; Sloss, 'It's Not Broken, So Don't Fix It', above n. 34, 850. For a more expansive reading of the IAEA's access rights, see George Bunn, 'Nuclear Safeguards: How Far Can Inspectors Go?' (2007) 48(2) *International Atomic Energy Agency Bulletin* 49.

[64] Model Protocol, above n. 47, Arts. 4, 5, 7, 15. Complementary access is intended to remove the accusatory and political overtones from requests for access to additional locations: see Laura Rockwood, 'The IAEA's Strengthened Safeguards System' (2002) 7 *Journal of Conflict and Security Law* 123.

access does not appear to have raised many issues because of the procedural constraints on its employment and practical limitations on the Agency's budget for inspecting additional locations.[65] The Agency can only call for physical access after consulting with the state about a specific question pertaining to the site.[66] The IAEA's physical access is primarily for the purposes of taking environmental samples. Where the state 'is unable to provide such access',[67] for example because the private owner refuses to allow inspectors onto the property and a warrant is impractical, the state may be able to satisfy Agency requirements by facilitating access to neighbouring locations.

Recent developments in Iran, Syria and Myanmar, which have not yet ratified the Additional Protocol, demonstrate the continued relevance of efforts to give the greatest possible legal effect to the provisions of the original comprehensive safeguards agreements.[68] According to the text of each comprehensive safeguards agreement, the terms of reference for the special inspection are subject to consultation with the state.[69] Where a state refuses an inspection request, it may discuss its reasons with the Board of Governors, which may resolve the Agency's questions. However, the Board may call upon the state to take immediate action (in this case, permit an inspection) if the Board decides that it is 'essential and urgent' to verify compliance with the agreement.[70] Continued refusal amounts to non-compliance with the safeguards agreement and the NPT.[71] The 'essential and urgent' finding signals that the IAEA is close to drawing a conclusion, gives the state a final opportunity to rectify the situation, and underlines international suspicions surrounding the requested site.

The 'essential and urgent' provision is designed to ensure that a state cannot delay and obstruct essential verification measures through obstinate refusal or by taking legal action.[72] Although the Agency cannot

---

[65] See Theodore Hirsch, 'The IAEA Additional Protocol: What It Is and Why It Matters' (2004) 11(3) *Nonproliferation Review* 140, 144.

[66] See Model Protocol, above n. 47, Art. 4(a)(ii), (d).     [67] *Ibid.* Art. 5(c).

[68] See David Albright, Paul Brannan and Andrea Stricker, 'IAEA Safeguards Report on Syria: Cooperation from Syria Worsens, Special Inspection Needed', Media Release, Institute for Science and International Security, 23 November 2010, available at http://isis-online.org/uploads/isis-reports/documents/Syria_IAEA_Report_ISISAnalysis_23 Nov2010.pdf.

[69] *The Structure and Content of Agreements between the Agency and States*, above n. 36, para. 77.

[70] *Ibid.* para. 18.     [71] *Ibid.* paras. 18–19.

[72] The 'essential and urgent' provision overrides the arbitration clause in comprehensive safeguards agreements: *ibid.* paras. 21–2.

compel access to be granted, it can draw adverse conclusions from refusal that may be as compelling as an actual inspection for the purposes of international enforcement action. Indeed in May 2011, based on one successful on-site inspection and several refusals from Syria for follow-up access at related sites, the IAEA Director General concluded that Syria's Dair Alzour site was 'very likely' to have been a covert nuclear reactor prior to the September 2007 bombing by Israel.[73] The standard of proof, 'unable to verify', illustrates how the investigative and enforcement authorities of the IAEA can be effectively decoupled.

Despite a determination by the Board in 1993 that access to sites in the DPRK was essential and urgent,[74] the DPRK continued to deny access to inspectors, rendering the IAEA unable to complete its verification responsibilities. The DPRK claimed that the undeclared sites the IAEA sought to inspect were military installations and accused the United States of using the IAEA to conduct espionage.[75] However, the IAEA's authority extends to inspecting locations characterised as military sites; state security concerns are not a legal basis for immunising them from inspection.[76] Consequently, the Board found that the DPRK was in non-compliance with the NPT.[77] This conclusion was supported by the subsequent DPRK-United States Agreed Framework, which recognised the IAEA's authority, under its comprehensive safeguards agreement with the DPRK, to inspect the military installations.[78]

---

[73] *Implementation of the NPT Safeguards Agreement in the Syrian Arab Republic: Report of the Director General*, IAEA Doc. GOV/2011/30 (24 May 2011) p. 7, para. 24. See also IAEA Board of Governors Resolution, Implementation of the NPT Safeguards Agreement in the Syrian Arab Republic, IAEA Doc. GOV/2011/41 (9 June 2011); Peter Crail, 'IAEA Sends Syria Nuclear Case to UN' (2011) 41(6) *Arms Control Today* 1, 3.

[74] *Report on the Implementation of the Agreement between the Agency and the Democratic People's Republic of Korea for the Application of Safeguards in connection with the Treaty on the Non-Proliferation of Nuclear Weapons*, IAEA Doc. Gov/2636 (25 February 1993).

[75] See Letter dated 12 March 1993 from the Permanent Representative of the Democratic People's Republic of Korea to the United Nations Addressed to the President of the Security Council, UN Doc. S/25407 (12 March 1993) Annex 2-3, reprinted in Compliance Note, above n. 60, 58-9.

[76] Compliance Note, above n. 60, p. 9. Since then, the IAEA has been afforded access to military sites in several other states, especially states with the Additional Protocol: see Mark Hibbs, *The Unspectacular Future of the IAEA Additional Protocol*: Carnegie Proliferation Analysis (26 April 2012), available at http://carnegieendowment.org/2012/04/26/unspectacular-future-of-iaea-additional-protocol.

[77] Compliance Note, above n. 60, p. 10.

[78] Agreed Framework between the United States of America and the Democratic People's Republic of Korea, signed 21 October 1994 (1995) 34 ILM 603, reprinted in (1995) 26 *Security Dialogue* 121, para. IV(2) ('Agreed Framework'). The broad investigative

It is notable that the IAEA 'shall be able to call upon the State to take' any action required to ensure adequate verification under standard comprehensive safeguards agreements.[79] The international community has increasingly recognised the IAEA's legitimacy in the exercise of its legal authority beyond the traditional core safeguards (surveillance, containment, accountancy and inspections) and the punitive provisions under the IAEA Statute.[80] For example, the DPRK-United States Agreed Framework suggests that full compliance with a comprehensive safeguards agreement requires the state to take 'all steps that may be deemed necessary by the IAEA ... with regard to verifying the accuracy and completeness' of declarations.[81] Similarly, in 2003 the Board of Governors adopted a resolution, later endorsed by the Security Council, calling on Iran to suspend uranium enrichment, pending full implementation of safeguards.[82]

### 4.2   Comparison with inspections under the Chemical Weapons Convention

The Organisation for the Prohibition of Chemical Weapons (OPCW), an international verification organisation established by the Chemical Weapons Convention (CWC),[83] has the authority to inspect facilities that produce and use toxic chemicals for industrial applications. OPCW routine inspections are analogous to IAEA routine inspections. The authority of the OPCW attaches to a 'wide range of chemicals, many in large-scale industrial use', making material accountancy impractical.[84]

---

authority of the IAEA assisted the United States in negotiating the Agreed Framework: see Parker, *Controlling Weapons of Mass Destruction*, above n. 10, p. 60; Sloss, 'It's Not Broken, So Don't Fix It', above n. 34, 874–5.

[79]  *The Structure and Content of Agreements between the Agency and States*, above n. 36, para. 18.

[80]  See above n. 13 and accompanying text. See also Sloss, 'It's Not Broken, So Don't Fix It', above n. 34, 859, 873.

[81]  Agreed Framework, above n. 78, para. IV(3).      [82]  See above n. 28.

[83]  Convention on the Prohibition of the Development, Production, Stockpiling and Use of Chemical Weapons and on their Destruction, opened for signature 13 January 1993, 1974 UNTS 45 (entered into force 29 April 1997), Art. IX. As at 14 October 2013, six states have not ratified or acceded to the CWC, see *Status of Participation in the Chemical Weapons Convention as at 14 October 2013*, OPCW Doc. S/1131/2013 (14 October 2013), available at www.opcw.org/index.php?eID=dam_frontend_push&docID=16815. It is notable that Syria acceded to the CWC under pressure from the international community for its alleged use of chemical weapons in the Syrian conflict.

[84]  Carlson, 'Experience and Challenges in WMD Treaty Verification', above n. 19, pp. 224, 225.

In contrast with the NPT, which presumptively allows access to any weapons-usable materials that could have peaceful applications,[85] the CWC exhaustively defines lawful uses and acceptable quantities of restricted chemicals.[86]

Many commentators have argued that the legal authority of the OPCW to conduct 'challenge inspections' is stronger than the authority of the IAEA to conduct special inspections.[87] The OPCW is under a duty to perform challenge inspections of (alleged) undeclared facilities if a party to the CWC reasonably asserts that another party is violating its obligations.[88] The accusing party must identify the location of the undeclared facility through national means and/or OPCW reports. The challenge inspection mechanism has not yet been invoked and the OPCW has never requested an inspection outside of a declared facility.[89]

Challenge inspections under the CWC and special inspections under the NPT differ in three important ways. First, the OPCW may carry out challenge inspections at short notice,[90] whereas IAEA special inspections can only be conducted after consultation with the state.[91] However, short notice inspections are more important for chemical weapons. Chemical weapons can be constructed more quickly than nuclear weapons and may be removed from suspect facilities without leaving a detectable radiation signature, creating the risk that the state could allow the inspection and successfully deceive inspectors.[92]

Second, the OPCW must conduct the challenge inspections of the suspected weapons facilities unless 'it considers the inspection request to be frivolous, abusive or clearly beyond the scope of the Convention'.[93] This represents a lower evidentiary burden than the 'necessary to fulfil its responsibilities' and 'essential and urgent' tests described above.[94]

---

[85] Sokolski, 'Assessing the IAEA's Ability to Verify the NPT', above n. 5, p. 3.

[86] Thomas Bernauer, 'The End of Chemical Warfare' (1993) 24 *Security Dialogue* 97, 103.

[87] See Jessica Eve Stern, 'Cooperative Security and the CWC: A Comparison of the Chemical and Nuclear Weapons Non-Proliferation Regimes' (1994) 15(3) *Contemporary Security Policy* 30, 32; Williamson, 'Law and the H-Bomb', above n. 63, 145.

[88] CWC, Art. IX(3) and (19), Annex on Implementation and Verification Pt. X.

[89] Carlson, 'Experience and Challenges in WMD Treaty Verification', above n. 19, p. 214; Paul F. Walker, 'Abolishing Chemical Weapons: Progress, Challenges, and Opportunities' (2010) 40(9) *Arms Control Today* 20.

[90] CWC, Art. IX and Annex on Implementation and Verification Pt. X.

[91] *The Structure and Content of Agreements between the Agency and States*, above n. 36, paras. 9, 77.

[92] See Richard Garwin and Georges Charpak, *Megawatts and Megatons: A Turning Point in the Nuclear Age?* (Alfred A. Knopf, New York, 2001) pp. 336–7.

[93] CWC, Art. IX(17).    [94] See Sloss, 'It's Not Broken, So Don't Fix It', above n. 34, 881.

Third, the state party being inspected has the right to limit access for several reasons such as to 'protect sensitive installations and prevent disclosure of confidential information'.[95] Consequently, a finding of non-compliance does not immediately follow from refusal to grant full access to inspectors. A dispute about rights of access could stymie inspection efforts. In contrast, the NPT provides no right to limit access to IAEA inspectors and refusing an inspection is itself a violation.[96] Compared with the nuclear non-proliferation regime, a recalcitrant state would find it easier to avoid timely inspections and deflect the repercussions by arguing that the challenging state was abusing its powers for political reasons or (military or industrial) espionage.[97] Evidently, the challenge inspection mechanism is too politically confrontational. Even after accusing China, Iran, Russia and Sudan of violating the CWC, the United States has not pursued the allegations through challenge inspections.[98] Presumably, overwhelming evidence of serious violations at a specific site would be required for a state to take the risk of activating challenge inspections. This weakness of the CWC could in practice negate the provision for short notice challenge inspections.

Although the NPT has procedural hurdles to initiate special inspections, the legal authority of the IAEA to investigate suspicious activities at undeclared sites is at least as robust as the authority of the OPCW under the CWC. Given that states are reluctant to consent to short notice inspections outside of designated facilities with no right of refusal, IAEA special inspections provide a sound compromise to maintain its legitimacy.

## 5   Relationship with the UN Security Council

Commentators tend to be critical of the fact that the IAEA is 'equipped with teeth that are certainly weaker than the corresponding eyes and ears'.[99] However, the IAEA is meant to rely upon the enforcement

---

[95] CWC, Annex on Implementation and Verification Pt. X, para. 48.

[96] See Sloss, 'It's Not Broken, So Don't Fix It', above n. 34, 882.

[97] Cf. in a bilateral context, Sidney N. Graybeal and Michael Krepon, 'On-Site Inspections' in Michael Krepon and Mary Umberger (eds.), *Verification and Compliance: A Problem-Solving Approach* (Macmillan Press, Cambridge, 1988) pp. 92, 106.

[98] Jonathan B. Tucker, 'Verifying the Chemical Weapons Ban: Missing Elements' (2007) 37(1) *Arms Control Today* 6, 12.

[99] Szasz, 'Sanctions', above n. 16, p. 149.

authority of the Security Council.[100] The task of the IAEA is to maximise the likelihood that clandestine nuclear activity is uncovered,
while the Security Council must weigh the political considerations of
taking enforcement action. As former IAEA Director General Hans
Blix put it, '[w]e happen to live in a world of sovereign states ... We
cannot parachute in or shoot our way in'.[101] Consequently, compliance
ultimately depends on the readiness of the international community to
impose sanctions on new candidates for the nuclear club. The IAEA is
in a unique position, with the power to demand inspections and pub-
licise non-compliance but without the responsibility to undertake all of
the diplomatic efforts to arrive at a resolution. The IAEA should not be
reluctant 'to escalate the significance of unresolved discrepancies to the
level of violations'.[102]

In 1983, Julie Dahlitz claimed that 'use of the veto to block sanctions
against a State that had violated clear-cut treaty obligations would be a
very serious step to take, which could damage the whole international
legal system'.[103] The Security Council has taken enforcement action
against each state that the IAEA has found to be in non-compliance
with safeguards,[104] except Romania and Libya,[105] which cooperated
with the IAEA in resolving their non-compliance. The Security
Council has declared through a presidential statement that the proliferation of nuclear weapons amounts to a 'threat to international peace
and security' for the purposes of Chapter VII of the UN Charter and
that UN members 'will take appropriate measures in the case of any
violations of safeguards notified to them' by the IAEA.[106] Enforcement

---

[100] See generally, *The Text of the Agency Agreement with the United Nations*, IAEA Doc.
INFCIRC/11 (30 October 1959) Arts. III, IX; Sloss, 'It's Not Broken, So Don't Fix It',
above n. 34, 890.

[101] Quoted in Christopher Wren, 'Making it easier to uncover nuclear arms', *New York
Times* (online), 16 June 1995, available at www.nytimes.com/1995/06/16/world/making-
it-easier-to-uncover-nuclear-arms.html.

[102] Edwin S. Lyman, 'Can Nuclear Fuel Production in Iran and Elsewhere be Safeguarded
against Diversion?' in Henry D. Sokolski (ed.), *Falling Behind: International Scrutiny of
the Peaceful Atom* (Strategic Studies Institute, Carlisle, 2008) pp. 101, 102.

[103] Julie Dahlitz, *Nuclear Arms Control with Effective International Agreements* (McPhee
Gribble, Melbourne, 1983) pp. 185–6.

[104] See e.g., SC Res. 687 (3 April 1991) para. 12 and SC Res. 1441 (8 November 2002) on Iraq;
SC Res. 1737 (23 December 2006) on Iran; SC Res. 825 (11 May 1993) on the DPRK.

[105] On Libya's cooperation in dismantling its nuclear weapons programme, see 'Security
Council Welcomes Libya's Decision to Abandon Weapons of Mass Destruction
Programs', Press Release, UN Doc. SC/8069 (22 April 2004).

[106] Note by President of the Security Council, UN Doc. S/23500 (31 January 1992) p. 4. See
also SC Res. 1887 (24 September 2009).

action has followed despite controversies over evidence of intention and fears that states might simply withdraw from the NPT, effectively abrogating the international rule of law.[107] The June 2011 resolution of the Board of Governors that found Syria non-compliant is an unprecedented one. The destruction of the reactor by force in 2007 appears to have removed the threat and the nuclear issue has been overshadowed by the ongoing violence in Syria since 2011.[108] As long as verification remains legitimate in the eyes of the international community, the IAEA can expect assistance from the Security Council with the removal of nuclear threats to international security.

## 6   Conclusion

Every arms control treaty must balance the rigorous detection of treaty violations with the risk of compromising sensitive information or impinging upon peaceful industrial development.[109] Notwithstanding criticism of the practical and legal limitations on its enforcement authority, the investigative authority of the IAEA is broad enough to allow necessary expansion of the institutional role to tackle clandestine proliferation. Despite difficulties with detecting non-compliant states, the IAEA's investigative authority in non-nuclear-weapon states is far-reaching, even compared with verification bodies under newer arms control agreements such as the CWC. Within states that have implemented the Additional Protocol, the strengthening of safeguards is at least catching up with improvements in technological weaponisation capabilities. The effective management of the political and resource constraints on the Agency is more important than legal reform for nuclear governance today.

The institutional evolution of the IAEA is ensuring that nuclear safeguards remain sufficiently rigorous to advance the objectives of the non-proliferation regime. Furthermore, because of its long-standing and central presence in multilateral arms control, the IAEA, relying on its

---

[107] Cf. Kittrie, 'Averting Catastrophe', above n. 5, 370; Henry D. Sokolski, 'What Strategic Weapons Proliferation will Demand of Us' in Henry Sokolski and James Ludes (eds.), *Twenty-First Century Weapons Proliferation: Are We Ready?* (Frank Cass Publishers, Portland, OR, 2001) pp. 55, 62.

[108] See SC Res. 2043 (21 April 2012).

[109] See generally, Sloss, 'It's Not Broken, So Don't Fix It', above n. 34, 882; Gregory G. Govan, 'On-Site Inspection as a Verification Tool' in James Brown (ed.), *Old Issues and New Strategies in Arms Control and Verification* (VU University Press, Amsterdam, 1995) p. 385.

technical expertise, provides a model for managing other international security concerns. Its institutional legitimacy is thus defined by epistemic virtues, as argued by Allen Buchanan and Robert Keohane,[110] that have facilitated the ongoing critical revision of the institutional capacity, rather than merely by the normative belief of sovereign states that the NPT obligations must be obeyed.

---

[110] Allen Buchanan and Robert O. Keohane, 'The Legitimacy of Global Governance Institutions' (2006) 20 *Ethics and International Affairs* 405.

# 10

# The World Health Organization, global health security and international law

ADAM KAMRADT-SCOTT

## 1 Introduction

When contemplating the global architecture of contemporary security institutions, the World Health Organization (WHO) does not, perhaps understandably, readily spring to mind. The WHO was founded in 1948 to pursue the 'attainment by all peoples of the highest possible level of health',[1] which was defined then as 'a state of complete physical, mental and social well-being and not merely the absence of disease or infirmity'.[2] When the WHO was established as a specialised agency within the United Nations system, it was originally envisaged that the institution would serve as the world's chief public health agency providing impartial, technical medical advice and direction to governments as, and when, requested; and for more than sixty years the WHO has retained a strong public health profile performing this function. In more recent years, however, it has also adopted a much more explicit security agenda. Indeed, particularly since 2001 the WHO has been actively engaged in re-branding many of its traditional public health roles and functions as 'global health security', in addition to assuming a variety of new duties and responsibilities designed to counter well-established and newly emerging 'threats' to human health.[3]

Importantly, the WHO's global health security agenda has been driven as much by its member states and real-world events as by its own institutional bureaucracy. Although legitimate questions remain

---

[1] Constitution of the World Health Organization, opened for signature 22 July 1946, 14 UNTS 185 (entered into force 7 April 1948), Art. 1.
[2] *Ibid.* Preamble.
[3] Sara Davies, 'Securitizing Infectious Disease' (2008) 84 *International Affairs* 295.

as to who is benefitting most from this agenda,[4] as this chapter reveals, several incidents in the early to mid-1990s generated new impetus amongst governments to develop more effective solutions to global health hazards. The WHO Secretariat, which was at that time confronting accusations of mismanagement, responded to this new demand by launching an extensive review of its disease outbreak policies and procedures. The need for enhanced response mechanisms was then further compounded by a series of naturally occurring and human-induced disease events towards the end of the twentieth century and first few years of the new century, notably including: the 1994 outbreak of plague in Surat, India; the 1995 outbreak of Ebola Haemorrhagic Fever in the former Zaire; the 2001 anthrax letter attacks in the United States; the 2003 Severe Acute Respiratory Syndrome (SARS) outbreak; and the progressive international spread of the H5N1 avian influenza virus from late 2003 onwards.

In response to these events, WHO member states adopted two international legal agreements: the 2005 International Health Regulations (IHR);[5] and the 2011 Pandemic Influenza Preparedness Framework (PIPF).[6] As this chapter explores, the acknowledged purpose of these agreements has been to strengthen global response capacity in combating infectious disease outbreaks and other adverse health events. In this regard, international law has become intrinsic to the WHO's global health security efforts. Both the WHO Secretariat and its member states have expended considerable political capital in developing new norms and expectations surrounding disease-related events, and then enshrining those principles within new legal frameworks, policies and procedures to guide inter-state behaviour. Importantly, however, the creation of these two agreements reflects a shift in the way in which the WHO, and the broader international community, views certain hazards to human health as security threats. This chapter explores this institutional evolution of the WHO through the securitisation of global health issues, with a particular focus on the 2005 IHR and 2011 PIPF, and considers the benefits, drawbacks and potential

---

[4] Simon Rushton, 'Global Health Security: Security for Whom? Security from What?' (2011) 59 *Political Studies* 779.

[5] Revision of the International Health Regulations, WHA Res. 58.3 (23 May 2005), opened for signature 23 May 2005, 2509 UNTS 79 (entered into force 15 June 2007) (2005 IHR).

[6] Pandemic Influenza Preparedness: Sharing of Influenza Viruses and Access to Vaccines and Other Benefits, WHA Res. 64.5 (24 May 2011) (2011 PIPF).

impact of those two new frameworks on the WHO's normative authority and legitimacy in enhancing global health security.

## 2   WHO and global health security

Since its creation in 1948, the WHO has played a central role in the prevention, control and eradication of human disease.[7] Indeed this objective is pursued by the WHO Secretariat as a fundamental obligation. This is perhaps nowhere more clearly articulated than in Article 2 of the WHO Constitution, which requires it 'to stimulate and advance work to eradicate epidemic, endemic and other diseases'.[8] Its duty to pursue the eradication of disease has also been repeatedly stressed by member states through a series of World Health Assembly (WHA) resolutions,[9] several other references and provisions contained within its constitution,[10] and through the adoption of various international legal instruments such as the 2005 IHR (including previous versions),[11] the Framework Convention on Tobacco Control,[12] and the 2011 PIPF. When viewed collectively, these documents (and the stipulations and provisions they contain therein) form the basis of an embedded 'contract' whereby member states have conferred upon the WHO the authority to take measures for disease outbreak alert and control. Its institutional authority has thus developed to include: using non-governmental sources of information to identify and verify disease outbreaks; the ability to 'name and shame' recalcitrant member states not adhering to WHO recommendations; allowing the WHO to assess and critique the public health capabilities of governments to respond to disease outbreaks; as well as leading and coordinating numerous programmes and initiatives designed to reduce disease-related human morbidity and mortality.

As it currently exists, however, this 'contract' is a very fluid, and in some ways discrete pact. Even following the entry into force of the 2005 IHR (an agreement which, like its earlier predecessor agreements,

---

[7] See generally, Theodore Brown, Marcos Cueto and Elizabeth Fee, 'The World Health Organization and the Transition from "International" to "Global" Public Health' (2006) 96 *American Journal of Public Health* 67.

[8] WHO Constitution, Art. 2(g).

[9] See Global Health Security: Epidemic Alert and Response, WHA Res. 54.14 (21 May 2001).

[10] WHO Constitution, Preamble, Arts. 2(s) and 21.

[11] The history of IHR amendments will be reviewed in section 3.1.

[12] World Health Organization Framework Convention on Tobacco Control, adopted 23 May 2003, 2302 UNTS 166 (entered into force 27 February 2005).

explicitly addresses the international spread of disease) it is still not possible to point to one specific document that comprehensively outlines the parameters of the WHO's disease eradication responsibilities, obligations or powers. Rather, as indicated above, the 'contract' is comprised of a series of provisions and stipulations that are contained within multiple documents. Each of these documents serves to establish, expand and/or further nuance the WHO's delegated, contractual obligations in assisting its member states to respond to infectious disease outbreaks. Moreover, the 'contract' itself may generally be perceived to have evolved and expanded over time, as WHA resolutions, new legal instruments and new operational practices have altered the nature of the original contract.

At times, the institutional efforts to fulfil this duty have taken on mammoth proportions, with the launch of several major global disease eradication campaigns such as the highly successful Smallpox Eradication Program, and the ongoing global campaign to eradicate polio. For decades, the WHO Secretariat has been responsible for providing broad oversight and technical assistance to member states on a variety of disease-specific programmes ranging from infectious diseases such as dengue, malaria and cholera, to chronic diseases such as cancer, asthma and cardiovascular disease. Due to budgetary limitations and the reality that member states' health systems remain the responsibility and domain of individual governments, much of the WHO's activity in this field has involved developing best practice guidelines,[13] issuing recommendations,[14] and providing technical advice,[15] as opposed to operationalising disease prevention and control programmes.

For over fifty years the WHO Secretariat has largely pursued its disease control and eradication objectives by emphasising the public health imperative and need for such work. Admittedly, it has utilised several tools to achieve its goal, including periodically drawing on various economic and rights-based arguments to encourage its member states to allocate more resources to combatting disease.[16] By and large,

---

[13] WHO, *Guideline: Neonatal Vitamin A Supplementation* (2011), available at whqlibdoc. who.int/publications/2011/9789241501798_eng.pdf.

[14] See Health Workforce Strengthening, WHA Res. 64.6 (24 May 2011).

[15] See e.g., WHO, *Best Practice for Developing Standards for Infectious Disease Laboratories in Europe* (2010), available at www.euro.who.int/document/e94772.pdf.

[16] Colin McInnes and Simon Rushton, 'HIV, AIDS and Security: Where Are We Now?' (2010) 86 *International Affairs* 225.

however, the fundamental reasoning that the WHO and indeed the majority of the international community has advanced, until recently, has remained unapologetically public health-focused.

In the past decade, a change has occurred to the type of arguments that the WHO utilises. Since the beginning of the twenty-first century the WHO Secretariat has been actively engaging in a re-branding exercise, recasting much of its traditional public health work in reducing the risk of disease in light of global health security. The first public announcement of this shift occurred in May 2001, following the passage of Resolution WHA54.14 on 'Global Health Security: Epidemic Alert and Response'.[17] The focus of this resolution was to formally endorse the creation of the Global Outbreak Alert and Response Network, which signalled a more proactive approach by the WHO Secretariat in responding to acute public health emergencies.

Significantly, the trend towards viewing certain health hazards as security threats can be traced back much earlier. A series of events in the early to mid-1990s marked a distinct turning point in the international community's approach to acute public health hazards. First, there were several serious outbreaks of infectious disease. These notably included: the reappearance of cholera in 1991 in Latin America a decade after it had been eradicated; an outbreak of plague in the Indian city of Surat in 1994 that caused over US$2 billion damage to the national economy; and an outbreak in 1995 of Ebola Haemorrhagic Fever in the former Zaire. Adding to these concerns was also the discovery in 1991 during the first Gulf War of substantial stockpiles of biological and chemical weapons – a discovery that raised the prospect that adverse disease events may not always be accidental.[18] This discovery was then followed in 1992 by the Russian government's admission that the former Soviet Union had maintained an offensive biological and chemical weapons programme throughout the duration of the Cold War.[19] Aside from the concern that the weapons themselves might fall into the hands of unsavoury groups, there were also fears that the scientists who

---

[17] Global Health Security: Epidemic Alert and Response, WHA Res. 54.14 (21 May 2001).

[18] Jonathan B. Tucker, 'From Arms Race to Abolition: The Evolving Norm Against Biological and Chemical Warfare' in Sidney D. Drell, Abraham D. Sofaer and George D. Wilson (eds.) *The New Terror: Facing the Threat of Biological and Chemical Weapons* (Hoover Institution Press, Stanford, CA, 1999) pp. 159, 205–6.

[19] David P. Fidler, 'From International Sanitary Conventions to Global Health Security: The New International Health Regulations' (2005) 4 *Chinese Journal of International Law* 325, 341.

had worked on developing these weapons might be recruited to work for terrorist organisations. The subsequent terrorist attack on a Tokyo subway in March 1995 by a Japanese doomsday cult appeared to confirm that such fears might in fact be well founded.[20]

By May 1995, the culmination of these events had generated a new incentive amongst WHO member states that the international community needed to be better prepared to meet such challenges. For many years, even though the IHR had only pertained to a limited number of diseases (namely, cholera, plague and yellow fever), these incentives nevertheless existed as the WHO was the only international agreement designed to 'ensure maximum security against the international spread of diseases with a minimum interference with world traffic'.[21] Adopted in 1951, the IHR underwent a series of revisions in 1969 and 1981, yet member states had increasingly begun to view the IHR framework as out-dated and dysfunctional.[22] In part this was due to the fact that the international community confronted several new and resurgent diseases that the IHR did not address – diseases which notably included HIV/AIDS, Ebola, West Nile virus, variant Creutzfeld Jacob Disease, polio and tuberculosis, to name a few.[23] However, governments had also become reluctant to report outbreaks of those diseases subject to the IHR, using creative means to avoid notifying the WHO Secretariat due to the risk of trade and travel-related restrictions imposed by other countries.[24]

A strong incentive for developing more robust response mechanisms to disease outbreaks existed within the WHO Secretariat as well. Indeed, by mid-1995 the WHO had become embroiled in a number of controversies, so much so that the reputation and value of the institution was being openly questioned.[25] The 1994 decision to establish the Joint

---

[20] Ibid.; Adam Kamradt-Scott, 'The WHO Secretariat, Norm Entrepreneurship, and Global Disease Outbreak Control' (2010) 1 Journal of International Organizations Studies 72, 77.

[21] International Health Regulations, WHA Res. 22.46 (25 July 1969).

[22] For details, see e.g., Fidler, 'From International Sanitary Conventions to Global Health Security', above n. 19, 337–8; Kamradt-Scott, 'The WHO Secretariat, Norm Entrepreneurship, and Global Disease Outbreak Control', above n. 20, 78; P.J. Delon, The International Health Regulations: A Practical Guide (WHO, Geneva, 1975).

[23] WHO, World Health Report, 1996: Fighting Disease, Fostering Development (WHO, Geneva, 1996) pp. 15, 16.

[24] E.D. Minze, R.V. Tauxe and M.M. Levine, 'The Global Resurgence of Cholera' in Norman Noah and Mary O'Mahony (eds.) Communicable Disease: Epidemiology and Control (Wiley, New York, 1998) pp. 63, 73.

[25] Fiona Godlee, 'WHO in Retreat: Is It Losing Its Influence?' (1994) 309 British Medical Journal 1491.

United Nations Program for HIV/AIDS (UNAIDS) was directly attributed to the WHO's mishandling of the disease, and although never proven, to the accusations of nepotism and corruption that had been levelled against the then WHO Director-General, Dr Hiroshi Nakajima. As a result, by the mid-1990s any opportunity that would afford the WHO Secretariat the ability to reinvigorate its reputation and demonstrate its relevance to member states was readily welcomed.[26]

Accordingly, at the Forty-eighth WHA in May 1995, member states passed two resolutions requesting the Director-General to update the IHR and to review the WHO's disease outbreak control policies and procedures.[27] It was believed that a radical overhaul of the IHR framework was required to address the various shortfalls that had emerged, such as the limited number of diseases that the IHR covered and the extensive non-compliance in reporting disease outbreaks. To inform this process, the Secretariat was also charged with developing and testing a range of new disease eradication policies and procedures. These methods, if proven successful, were to be used as a basis to revise the IHR and improve the WHO's ability to protect and assist its member states.

By 2000, the WHO had successfully developed and tested a range of new mechanisms and procedures to improve disease outbreak detection and reporting, and to assist member states to better respond to adverse health events. Attempts to redevelop the IHR legal framework continued to stagnate, but the success witnessed by the new disease outbreak policies and procedures led the WHO Secretariat to establish the Global Outbreak Alert and Response Network in April 2000.[28] Formal endorsement of the network and its operational procedures was then obtained the following year with the passage of Resolution WHA54.14 in May 2001.[29] Significantly, the resolution, which was widely seen as sanctioning the WHO's new strategy towards responding to naturally occurring infectious disease outbreaks and epidemics, as well as the risks posed by biological agents and antimicrobial

---

[26] Kamradt-Scott, 'The WHO Secretariat, Norm Entrepreneurship, and Global Disease Outbreak Control', above n. 20, 78.

[27] Revision and Updating of the International Health Regulations, WHA Res. 48.7 (12 May 1995); Communicable Diseases Prevention and Control: New, Emerging, and Re-emerging Infectious Diseases, WHA Res. 48.13 (12 May 1995).

[28] *Global Outbreak Alert and Response, Report of a WHO Meeting*, WHO/CDS/CSR/2000.3 (26–28 April 2000).

[29] WHA Res. 54.14 (21 May 2001), above n. 9.

resistance, openly described this activity – for the first time – as 'global health security'.

Since the mid-1990s a number of prominent health experts had been actively engaged in re-framing certain public health issues as security 'threats' – arguments that had, importantly, found support amongst various legitimate government security organisations such as the United States National Intelligence Council.[30] As a result, by the turn of the century a small sub-set of health issues had been successfully 'securitised' in that they were openly described and referred to as national and/or international security threats. While thereby reflective of a broader trend, the passage of Resolution WHA54.14 nonetheless marked an important milestone in that it represented the WHO Secretariat's first official use of security terminology to describe public health incidents. It also established a new paradigm for the institution to function within – that of international security.[31]

Over the next few years the concept of health security gained considerable traction within international public policy circles. In part, this can be attributed to several notable real-world events. The anthrax letter attacks that coincided with the 9/11 terrorist attacks in New York and Washington in 2001, for example, elevated concerns about intentional disease events and prompted considerable new investment in biosecurity research and defence.[32] Likewise, the threat from naturally-occurring disease events was manifested, first by the 2003 SARS outbreak, and soon thereafter again by the progressive cross-border spread of the highly-lethal H5N1 avian influenza virus from late 2003 onwards.

Equally, the WHO Secretariat was fully complicit in promoting the concept of global (public) health security, not only in various WHA reports and guidance documents,[33] but also by WHO staff (including,

---

[30] National Intelligence Council, *National Intelligence Estimate: The Global Infectious Disease Threat and Its Implications for the United States* (January 2000), available at www.wilsoncenter.org/sites/default/files/Report6-3.pdf.

[31] Jiyong Jin and Joe T. Karackattu, 'Infectious Diseases and Securitization: WHO's Dilemma' (2011) 9 *Biosecurity and Bioterrorism* 182.

[32] Ari Schuler, 'Billions for Biodefense: Federal Agency Biodefense Funding, FY2001–FY2005' (2004) 2 *Biosecurity and Bioterrorism* 86.

[33] See e.g., WHO, 'Global Health Security' (2001) 76 *Weekly Epidemiological Record* 166; *Preparedness for the Deliberate Use of Biological Agents: A Rational Approach to the Unthinkable*, WHO/CDS/CSR/EPH/2002.16 (May 2002); *Antimicrobial Resistance: A Threat to Global Health Security: Rational Use of Medicines by Prescribers and Patients, Report by the Secretariat*, WHO Doc. A58/14 (7 April 2005).

notably, the Director-General herself) generating a series of publications in peer-reviewed journals, newspapers and magazines.[34] The 2007 World Health Report was entirely dedicated to the subject of global public health security and defined the concept as 'the activities required, both proactive and reactive, to minimise vulnerability to acute public health events that endanger the collective health of populations living across geographical regions and international boundaries',[35] which proved the Secretariat's definitive endorsement of the security paradigm.

Indeed, health security has subsequently become an important public policy tool that governments and the WHO Secretariat have periodically deployed to great effect, usually in order to advance particular policy goals and objectives, or highlight specific issues. Individual governments have, for instance, used the concept of health security to help pass new domestic (usually biosecurity) legislation,[36] justify the purchase of large quantities of pharmaceutical products,[37] and even criticise the action (or inaction) of other governments.[38] Similarly, the WHO Secretariat has successfully used the concept of health security to argue for new funding to support disease eradication programmes, push for the completion of the IHR revision process, and under that agreement establish new disease outbreak investigation and verification powers, such as the ability to use non-government sources of information to identify disease outbreaks.[39] The concept has thereby become firmly embedded in both domestic and international public policy contexts, arguably as the dominant paradigm in contemporary global public health.

## 3   WHO's institutional evolution

This section explores the introduction and implications of two recent international legal agreements ostensibly seeking to enhance global health security. The first agreement is the 2005 IHR. Although, as Rushton has

---

[34] See e.g., Gro Brundtland, 'Global Health and International Security' (2003) 9 *Global Governance* 417; David L. Heymann, 'SARS: A Global Response to an International Threat' (2004) 10 *Brown Journal of World Affairs* 185.

[35] WHO, *World Health Report 2007, A Safer Future: Global Public Health Security in the 21st Century* (WHO, Geneva, 2007) p. ix.

[36] National Health Security Act 2007 (Cth).

[37] HHS Pandemic Influenza Plan 2005 (US).

[38] Lai-Ha Chan, Lucy Chen and Jin Xu, 'China's Engagement with Global Health Diplomacy: Was SARS a Watershed?' (2010) 7 *Public Library of Science Medicine* 1.

[39] Adam Kamradt-Scott, 'The Evolving WHO: Implications for Global Health Security' (2011) 6 *Global Public Health* 801.

observed, 'the global health security terminology does not appear in the IHR, it has become inextricably linked with them' due to the nature and type of adverse health events the agreement addresses.[40] The second covenant is the 2011 PIPF, which is the latest international agreement negotiated under the auspices of the WHO and seeks to establish a more equitable system for low-income countries to access antiviral medications and H5N1 influenza vaccines, as well as a more equitable distribution of benefits from H5N1-related research and development. Although qualitatively different in terms of their legal status and respective scope, both agreements represent the latest developments in the WHO's efforts to ensure global health security.

### 3.1    2005 International Health Regulations

On 23 May 2005, the Fifty-eighth WHA unanimously passed Resolution WHA58.3 thereby formally endorsing the revised International Health Regulations (2005 IHR) agreement. The passage of this resolution marked the end of a decade-long revision process, and paved the way for the agreement's official entry into force on 15 June 2007. The 2005 IHR, which is automatically binding on all WHO member states, exists only as the inter-governmental agreement designed to limit the international spread of adverse public health events (such as disease outbreaks) while minimising the disruption they may cause to international traffic and trade. While the previous 1969 version of the IHR pertained to only three diseases (cholera, plague and yellow fever),[41] the scope of the revised IHR has been expanded considerably to address any 'illness or medical condition, irrespective of origin or source, that presents or could present significant harm to humans'.[42] Accordingly, the scope of the Regulations has been expanded to include not only naturally-occurring disease outbreaks, but also adverse health events that are initiated either through intentional or accidental release of any biological, chemical, radiological or other toxic substances.

The focus of the 1969 IHR, as of its 1951 predecessor, was to encourage member states to implement public health measures to prevent the importation of diseases from other affected territories. In this regard, the former framework was a reactive system that relied on both the affected governments' honesty and willingness to report

---

[40] Rushton, 'Global Health Security: Security for Whom?', above n. 4, 787.
[41] WHA Res. 22.46 (25 July 1969).     [42] 2005 IHR, Art. 1.

disease outbreaks, as well as the capacity of any unaffected member state to prevent the introduction of disease at various border crossings and ports of entry (i.e. sea, air, land) through stringent public health surveillance and, if required, the quarantine, isolation and treatment of affected individuals or cargo. As noted earlier, however, the arrangement was hamstrung by the fact that member states frequently declined to report disease outbreaks, usually in an attempt to avoid the imposition of international trade and travel barriers by other countries. As a result, diseases would often spread internationally before countries were alerted to an outbreak. The second, associated weakness was the assumption that member states possessed the technical, logistical and financial means to prevent the importation of disease – quite contrary to the reality that confronted many, particularly low-income, countries.

Under the terms of the 2005 IHR, however, the onus of responsibility has been somewhat reversed. Whereas the former system emphasised the need for countries to prevent the importation of disease, under the new IHR governments are obliged to develop certain public health 'core' capacities to prevent diseases from spreading.[43] The 2005 IHR framework thereby adopts a much more proactive approach to adverse disease events by situating responsibility with the country affected by an outbreak to ensure it does not allow the disease to spread to other countries. Governments are expected to first identify an outbreak underway, and then conduct a risk assessment on whether the disease will likely spread to other countries.[44] Where such risk exists, governments are expected to notify the WHO of the presence of an outbreak occurring within their respective territory within twenty-four hours, and accept any offer of technical assistance to help control the event.[45] To facilitate this, governments are obligated to establish a National Focal Point to serve as the central liaison with the WHO,[46] as well as to undertake necessary legislative changes to ensure prompt notification and, where required, appropriate disease control measures.

Equally significant are the new powers that have been granted to the WHO Secretariat under the revised IHR agreement. For example, under the terms of the IHR 2005 the Secretariat is now empowered to identify new disease outbreaks using non-government (otherwise termed as

---

[43] *Ibid.* Annex A.    [44] *Ibid.* Art. 5.    [45] *Ibid.* Arts. 10 and 13.    [46] *Ibid.* Art. 4.

'unofficial') sources of information.[47] This new provision, which was originally introduced by the Global Outbreak Alert and Response Network in April 2000 but has now been formally enshrined within the revised IHR, aims to circumvent the risk of countries not reporting outbreaks. The WHO can use any information it obtains under this new provision to pressurise countries into reporting, and member states are given twenty-four hours in which to verify whether an outbreak is in fact underway. In cases where such an event is occurring that may present a risk to the wider international community, the WHO is required to offer technical assistance. Notably, however, if the government refuses the offer of assistance, and the WHO Director-General is not satisfied that the country has the means or willingness to control the outbreak, the Secretariat is then permitted to publicly notify all member states of the outbreak and the affected country's refusal to accept WHO assistance.[48] This new authority effectively permits the WHO to 'name and shame' any country that appears to be placing its own interests above those of the international community, and reinforces the need for all member states to play by the rules of the new regime.

In an attempt to counter the second core weakness of the former IHR system, namely the capacity for governments to impose unwarranted trade and travel restrictions against countries experiencing an outbreak with impunity, the WHO Secretariat has also been granted new authority with regard to temporary and standing recommendations. The authority of the WHO to issue recommendations pertaining to health-related matters is set down in its founding constitution.[49] Under the terms of the 2005 IHR this authority has been reaffirmed, but with the added proviso that if governments decide to impose measures that either exceed or do not meet the WHO Secretariat's recommendations, the WHO is authorised to request that the member state(s) provide their scientific rationale and justification for their actions. In cases where such information is not provided, or the justification is assessed as insufficient, the Secretariat is authorised to request that the member state(s) adjust their behaviour. In order to encourage member state compliance, the WHO Director-General is further empowered to publicly 'name and shame' those member states that contravene the object and purpose of the IHR with unjustified additional health measures.[50]

[47] *Ibid.* Art. 9.    [48] *Ibid.* Arts. 10 and 11.    [49] WHO Constitution, Art. 2.
[50] 2005 IHR, Art. 43.

## 3.2   2011 Pandemic Influenza Preparedness Framework

The impetus for the creation of the 2011 PIPF was Indonesia's controversial decision in 2007 to cease sharing samples of the highly virulent H5N1 avian influenza ('Bird Flu') virus with the WHO's Global Influenza Surveillance Network (GISN). In announcing her country's withdrawal from the voluntary programme, Indonesia's Health Minister, Siti Fadilah Supari, claimed that the WHO had, on several occasions, breached the terms of its agreement by sharing virus samples with pharmaceutical companies without express permission of the government that provided the original sample.[51] Moreover, Indonesia argued that the entire cooperation system was in dire need of reform to ensure more equitable distribution of, and improved access to, the benefits arising from participating in GISN, such as influenza vaccines.[52] Indonesia's announcement, which came at the height of international concern that an H5N1-related influenza pandemic was imminent, prompted widespread condemnation by commentators in high-income countries that relied on the WHO's virus sharing system to develop influenza vaccines for domestic consumption.[53] In an attempt to resolve the situation, the WHO Secretariat announced the creation of an inter-governmental working group to develop a new cooperation agreement. Four years later, the diplomatic impasse was finally resolved in May 2011 when the Sixty-fourth WHA endorsed the 2011 PIPF.

Importantly, the scope of the PIPF agreement is limited to facilitating the rapid sharing of H5N1 and other influenza viruses with human pandemic potential, and enhancing access to influenza vaccines and other benefits such as new technologies and intellectual property.[54] To achieve these stated objectives, the PIPF agreement identifies a range of principles, norms, mechanisms and oversight procedures that all members of the WHO's (now re-named) Global Influenza Surveillance and Response System (GISRS) and associated institutions are expected to abide by. The framework agreement outlines, for example, a series of recommendations regarding the sharing of influenza viruses; laboratory and disease surveillance capacity building; diagnostic equipment;

---

[51] Engdang Sedyaningsih, Siti Isfandari, Triono Soendoro and Siti Fadilah Supari, 'Towards Mutual Trust, Transparency and Equity in Virus Sharing Mechanism: Avian Influenza Case of Indonesia' (2008) 37 *Annals Academy of Medicine Singapore* 482, 485–6.
[52] *Ibid.* 482–3.
[53] Laurie Garrett and David P. Fidler, 'Sharing H5N1 Viruses to Stop a Global Influenza Pandemic' (2007) 4 *Public Library of Science Medicine* 1712.
[54] 2011 PIPF, s. 3.1.

medication stockpiling; technology transfer arrangements; and tiered pricing, amongst others.[55] It had initially been proposed that the agreement should relate to all influenza samples shared by countries; but by 2008, the scope of the agreement had been scaled back to only the sharing of H5N1 and other viruses with human pandemic potential. This significant caveat has meant that seasonal influenza virus samples have been excluded, with the corresponding outcome that any benefits derived from participation in this network have been reduced to a much smaller proportion of virus sharing activities, namely, only those novel viruses that achieve effective human-to-human transmission.[56]

Arguably, one of the key benefits of the new framework is that it places new obligations on pharmaceutical companies that utilise GISRS data and virus samples. For instance, under the terms of the PIPF, pharmaceutical manufacturers that are members of the GISRS must make financial 'partnership contributions', which member states have currently determined equate to 50 per cent of the network's costs to be used to strengthen global pandemic preparedness.[57] Although the framework document fails to stipulate how costs are to be distributed between companies (for example, based on market share, percentage of overall profits or some other calculation), this new arrangement effectively transforms what was previously a publicly financed network supported by the Australian, Japanese, United Kingdom and United States governments into a new public–private arrangement. Those companies that are not officially members of GISRS (but which still utilise the network's information and samples) are required to agree to a package of measures designed to enable improved access for low-income countries to vaccines, technology and diagnostics in exchange for access to GISRS services.[58] In this regard, the 2011 PIPF agreement has been an important development in further strengthening global pandemic preparedness by creating new opportunities for low-income countries to access potentially life-saving treatments and technologies once a virus with human pandemic potential has been identified.

[55] *Ibid.* s. 6, in particular ss. 6.4, 6.6, 6.8 and 6.12.

[56] Adam Kamradt-Scott and Kelley Lee, 'The 2011 Pandemic Influenza Preparedness Framework: Global Health Secured or a Missed Opportunity?' (2011) 59 *Political Studies* 831.

[57] 2011 PIPF, s. 6.14.3; *Pandemic Influenza Preparedness Framework for the Sharing of Influenza Viruses and Access to Vaccines and Other Benefits, Report by the Director-General*, WHO Doc. EB131/4 (5 April 2012).

[58] 2011 PIPF, Annex 2.

However, aside from some additional requirements on the WHO Director-General to facilitate access for low-income countries to vaccines and antivirals, and maintain general oversight of the network, the remainder of the agreement remains non-binding. Indeed, as evidenced by the repeated use of the term 'should' throughout the text of the agreement (as opposed to 'shall' or 'must'), member states and pharmaceutical companies are only urged to adhere to certain practices and norms. Governments are not obliged, for example, to compel pharmaceutical manufacturers to ensure that a certain percentage of vaccine stock is available for purchase by low-income countries, to transfer vaccine technology, or even to implement tiered pricing arrangements. This is despite the fact that many of these companies are either fully or partially government-owned and/or operated.[59] Nor, importantly, is there any legal requirement for members of the network to assist low-income countries to enhance their laboratory, surveillance or regulatory capacity. Rather, the arrangement is largely predicated upon an assumption of goodwill – that governments and pharmaceutical companies will 'do the right thing' whenever a new pandemic emerges.[60]

To some extent this lack of obligation on governments is understandable, as it reflects the long-standing principle of the inviolability of state sovereignty whereby countries are autonomous and free from external interference. Nevertheless, unlike trade negotiations for the international protection of intellectual property rights,[61] the agreement did not result in the creation of a protectionist regime benefiting influential businesses and industries. In this regard, the negotiators of the PIPF agreement were no doubt conscious that if the barriers for pharmaceutical companies participating in the reformed network were placed too high, the existing

---

[59] Kamradt-Scott and Lee, 'The 2011 Pandemic Influenza Preparedness Framework', above n. 56.

[60] Lawrence O. Gostin and David P. Fidler, 'WHO's Pandemic Influenza Preparedness Framework: A Milestone in Global Governance for Health' (2011) 306 *Journal of the American Medical Association* 200.

[61] See e.g., Thomas Pogge, Matthew Rimmer and Kim Rubenstein, 'Access to Essential Medicines: Public Health and International Law' in Thomas Pogge, Matthew Rimmer and Kim Rubenstein (eds.), *Incentives for Global Public Health: Patent Law and Access to Essential Medicines* (Cambridge University Press, Cambridge, 2010) pp. 1, 8–14; Susan K. Sell, 'Industry Strategies for Intellectual Property and Trade: The Quest for TRIPS, and Post-TRIPS Strategies' (2002) 10 *Cardozo Journal of International and Comparative Law* 79; Peter Drahos, 'Negotiating Intellectual Property Rights: Between Coercion and Dialogue' in Peter Drahos and Ruth Mayne (eds.), *Global Intellectual Property Rights: Knowledge, Access and Development* (Palgrave Macmillan, Hampshire/New York, 2002) pp. 161, 172–4.

influenza vaccine manufacturers might choose to exit what had historically been a low-profit industry.[62] The agreement, as it currently stands,
thereby reflects a compromise deal – one in which low-income countries
have been able to obtain a small number of concessions from pharmaceutical manufacturers that access the samples and data they provide in
order to secure commitments to provide 10 per cent of medicines and
diagnostics at more affordable prices.[63]

## 4    Global health security: the mission accomplished?

So what does the endorsement and subsequent entry into force of these
two agreements mean for global health security? Will these two agreements strengthen global efforts to enhance the health and well-being of
the world's population, thereby ensuring greater health security? Or,
due to the various caveats and qualifications inserted into the agreements, is it more a case that little has really changed? In the remainder
of this chapter, the broader implications of the 2005 IHR and 2011 PIPF
are critiqued and examined with a view to identifying: (1) the benefits
and drawbacks of the two frameworks; and (2) the potential impact that
the passage of these two frameworks will have on the WHO's global
health security duties.

### 4.1    Benefits and drawbacks of the new global health
security frameworks

In assessing the benefits of these two agreements, it must be said that they
generally represent a positive step forward. The 2005 IHR, for example,
outlines a comprehensive strategy for ensuring that the world is better
prepared to respond to those adverse health events that have the potential
to spread internationally. It places new obligations on member states to
build, strengthen and maintain certain 'core capacities' in disease surveillance, detection, verification and response,[64] while simultaneously
granting several new and improved powers to the WHO Secretariat to
better coordinate and direct international response efforts. Likewise, the
2011 PIPF provides some benefits in encouraging greater cooperation

---

[62] Cormac Sheridan, 'The Business of Making Vaccines' (2005) 23 *Nature Biotechnology*
1359.

[63] Kamradt-Scott and Lee, 'The 2011 Pandemic Influenza Preparedness Framework', above
n. 56, 839.

[64] 2005 IHR, Arts. 5 and 13.

between countries in sharing highly lethal influenza virus samples, as well as providing low-income countries with new possibilities to access life-saving influenza vaccines. More broadly, the influenza framework also outlines new principles and norms to encourage the sharing of technology and intellectual property that may enable low-income countries to build and enhance local manufacturing capacity.

Several commentators have welcomed the passage of these two agreements. Although acknowledging several drawbacks, Lawrence Gostin and David Fidler have observed, for instance, that the 2011 PIPF was a 'landmark' agreement in global health governance.[65] Brazilian Ambassador to the WHO, Maria Azevedo, commended it as 'a break-through agreement' and 'historic' in setting 'a very important precedent for WHO'.[66] Similarly, in late 2005 following the WHA's endorsement of the revised IHR, David Fidler observed:

> The revised IHR perceive a new world forming, in which global health security is a fundamental governance challenge for all humanity from the local to the global level. The world of global health security is one in which governments, intergovernmental organizations and non-State actors collaborate in a 'new way of working' by contributing toward a common goal through science, technology and law rather than through anarchical competition for power.[67]

Kumanan Wilson, Barbara von Tigerstrom and Christopher McDougall also noted that the revised IHR 'represent a major step forward in protecting global public health security'.[68]

Much of this acclaim relates to the fact that elements of the two agreements grant the WHO Secretariat new authority to pursue health security objectives. As David Fidler has observed, '[i]n bringing all possible sources of public health emergencies of international concern under the revised IHR, WHO further underscored its effort to develop a comprehensive governance strategy for global health security'.[69] Key

---

[65] Gostin and Fidler, 'WHO's Pandemic Influenza Preparedness Framework', above n. 60, 201.

[66] John Zaracostas, 'Key Players Agree to Share Viruses and Vaccines to Expedite Response to Future Pandemic Influenza' (2011) 342 *British Medical Journal* 2620.

[67] Fidler, 'From International Sanitary Conventions to Global Health Security', above n. 19, 392.

[68] Kumanan Wilson, Barbara von Tigerstrom and Christopher McDougall, 'Protecting Global Health Security through the International Health Regulations: Requirements and Challenges' (2008) 179 *Canadian Medical Association Journal* 44, 44.

[69] Fidler, 'From International Sanitary Conventions to Global Health Security', above n. 19, 363.

amongst the IHR powers is the WHO's ability to draw upon non-government sources of information to identify potential public health emergencies of international concern,[70] the Director-General's authority to declare such emergencies even if an affected country objects,[71] and the institution's licence to 'name and shame' those countries that contravene the IHR framework.[72] In the context of the 2011 PIPF, the WHO Secretariat has been awarded new authority to advocate for the creation of a global stockpile of influenza vaccines and antiviral medications to support low-income countries in the event of a pandemic,[73] as well as campaigning for the implementation of new tiered pricing mechanisms and technology transfers to promote innovation and increased vaccine manufacturing capacity.[74] The 2011 PIPF is also significant in that it amends what was previously an entirely publicly-funded network to a new public-private partnership with pharmaceutical manufacturers making financial contributions to be used to strengthen global preparedness.[75]

Despite such outcomes it is also clear that the 2005 IHR and the 2011 PIPF suffer from several serious limitations and drawbacks that will arguably impinge upon the WHO's global health security efforts. For example, in order for the revised IHR to be effective all member states are required to develop the 'core capacities' – capacities that currently remain beyond the financial, technical and human resource means of many countries. Without considerable (and targeted) financial investment from their high-income country counterparts, it is unlikely that these capacities will be developed, with the corresponding outcome that the 2005 IHR framework may only prove useful for those countries already possessing advanced healthcare infrastructures. In addition, the revised IHR (and by default the WHO) lack enforcement mechanisms which, for example, prevent member states from applying unnecessary and unwarranted travel and trade restrictions against disease-affected countries. As observed in the context of the 2009 H1N1 influenza pandemic, this is a serious shortfall that the IHR revision process was intended to overcome.[76] The inability to compel member states, either

---

[70] 2005 IHR, Art. 9.    [71] *Ibid.* Art. 12.    [72] *Ibid.* Art. 10.

[73] Pandemic Influenza Preparedness: Framework for the Sharing of Influenza Viruses and Access to Vaccines and Other Benefits, WHA Res. 64.8 (5 May 2011) ss. 6.8–6.9.

[74] *Ibid.* ss. 6.12–6.13.    [75] See above n. 58 and accompanying text.

[76] Adam Kamradt-Scott and Simon Rushton, 'The Revised International Health Regulations: Socialization, Compliance and Changing Norms of Global Health Security' (2010) 24 *Global Change, Peace and Security* 57.

in allocating sufficient resources for building the core capacities or even preventing unjustified trade and travel restrictions, is a serious weakness of the 2005 IHR.

Likewise, the non-binding nature of the PIPF may mean that low-income countries have gained very little in the way of improved access to vital, life-saving therapies such as pandemic influenza vaccines and antiviral medications. The structural, market-based inequalities whereby a number of high-income countries have already entered into advance purchase agreements to gain priority access to any new pandemic-specific vaccines have not been sufficiently addressed by the 2011 PIPF.[77] Given that pharmaceutical companies are only 'urged' to consider the income level of a country in determining the price of particular medications, the agreement similarly fails in ensuring that adequate supplies of antiviral medications will be made readily available to low-income countries in their time of need. This effectively means that unless low-income countries build their own local manufacturing capacity (thereby guaranteeing their own supply) they will continue to remain wholly reliant on the goodwill of pharmaceutical companies and high-income countries to donate these drugs at the time of a pandemic, or they will be forced to compete with each other to gain access to the limited supplies that the WHO is able to procure on their behalf. This is an unenviable position for any government to confront, and were another influenza pandemic akin to the 1918 Spanish Flu to emerge it is quite possible that low-income countries would once again suffer the highest morbidity and mortality.

### 4.2    Global health security and WHO's institutional legitimacy

It is also important to highlight that the passage of the 2005 IHR and the 2011 PIPF has additionally placed the WHO in a somewhat precarious position. This is principally because its global health security function, and by default the WHO's reputation, is inherently linked to the success of these two frameworks. The WHO's successful management of the 2003 SARS outbreak has been largely credited with reinvigorating its institutional legitimacy amongst member states; and many of the powers that the WHO exercised in the context of SARS were subsequently incorporated into the 2005 IHR framework. The

---

[77] Kamradt-Scott and Lee, 'The 2011 Pandemic Influenza Preparedness Framework', above n. 56, 840.

operational success of the revised IHR is, however, predicated upon a number of factors such as whether governments actually develop the requisite core capacities for outbreak surveillance and response, as well as their willingness to comply with WHO recommendations when public health emergencies of international concern arise. Wherever member states fail to meet their obligations, either through an inability or unwillingness to develop and maintain the core capacities (thereby inhibiting international disease surveillance networks) or the wilful disregard of WHO recommendations, then the framework, and by extension the WHO's normative authority to lead and coordinate international health matters, will be compromised. Given the behaviour of a small but notable number of member states throughout the 2009 H1N1 influenza pandemic in imposing unwarranted trade barriers, and the indication given by the majority of its member states at the Sixty-fifth WHA in May 2012 that they were applying for extensions to develop the IHR core capacities, it must be concluded that the prospects for the WHO to fulfil its global health security duties do not currently appear favourable.

A similar risk to the WHO's normative authority and institutional legitimacy arises from compliance (or lack thereof) with the 2011 PIPF. As noted above, the 2011 PIPF is a comparatively weak regulatory instrument effectively relying on governments and pharmaceutical companies to 'do the right thing'.[78] The incentive for pharmaceutical manufacturers to comply with the framework is that they obtain access to biological materials and data in return for agreeing to make their products more accessible to low-income countries. Under the terms of the 2011 PIPF, biological materials can only be transferred to pharmaceutical manufacturers once they have signed a Standard Material Transfer Agreement 2 (SMTA2) that specifies how the company can use the material and prevents any unauthorised transfer to third parties.[79] Immediately following the PIPF's entry into force, however, the WHO Secretariat was compelled to reach a compromise deal with pharmaceutical manufacturers whereby they continued to share biological materials even though no SMTA2s had been finalised.[80] While this action was taken ostensibly to ensure that influenza-related research and development continued,[81] it nevertheless reduced the imperative

---

[78] See above n. 60 and accompanying text.    [79] 2011 PIPF, Annex 2.

[80] *Pandemic Influenza Preparedness: Sharing of Influenza Viruses and Access to Vaccines and Other Benefits, Report of the Advisory Group*, WHO Doc. A65/19 (22 March 2012).

[81] WHA Res. 64.8 (5 May 2011).

for pharmaceutical manufacturers to sign transfer agreements. In response, at the Sixty-fifth WHA in May 2012 a large number of low-income countries expressed their frustration and dissatisfaction with the overall lack of progress the WHO Secretariat had made in implementing the 2011 PIPF and finalising the SMTA2 agreements in particular.[82] The WHO Director-General was subsequently pressed to accelerate efforts and agree to demands for increased transparency despite an acknowledged lack of administrative capacity.[83]

Other risks, unrelated to compliance, also exist. As described above, the entire premise of the 2011 PIPF is to facilitate the rapid and equitable distribution of vaccines and other benefits (for example, diagnostic equipment and technology transfers) to low-income countries whenever another pandemic emerges. During the 2009 H1N1 influenza pandemic a number of problems surrounding donated vaccines arose because 'they came from many different sources, at different times, and included a variety of different products'.[84] For example, both donor and recipient governments raised concerns over which countries would be the first to receive supplies, the criteria used to determine allocation, the need to guarantee vaccine quality and safety and, in the event that donated supplies were contaminated or inferior, what liability and compensation arrangements would be available.[85] Importantly, these issues, which caused significant delays to the distribution of donated vaccines in 2009 and impeded the WHO's ability to protect human health, are likely to emerge again in the future. Even though the 2011 PIPF was not specifically designed to address such matters as liability and compensation, the very existence of the agreement understandably raises expectations amongst low-income countries that they will be able to access life-saving treatments equitably and rapidly in the event of another pandemic. If lives are then lost as a result of procedural or administrative delays, it can be anticipated that the WHO will be heavily criticised for failing to ensure that the objectives of the 2011 PIPF are met, no matter how legitimate those delays may be.

---

[82] Adam Kamradt-Scott, 'Global Health Security under Threat? Progress in Implementing IHR 2005' (2012) 3 *Health Diplomacy Monitor* 4, 13–14.

[83] *Ibid.*

[84] WHO, *Main Operational Lessons Learnt from the WHO Pandemic Influenza A(H1N1) Vaccine Deployment Initiative, Report of a WHO Meeting* (Geneva, Switzerland, 13–15 December 2010) p. 10.

[85] WHA Res. 64.8 (5 May 2011).

## 5 Conclusion

The endorsement and subsequent entry into force of the 2005 IHR and the 2011 PIPF have reinforced the WHO's institutional legitimacy in dealing with global health security in a number of important ways. Collectively, these two agreements have bestowed several new powers upon the WHO and have further embedded the WHO Secretariat's authority to serve as the primary authority in directing and coordinating international public health issues. The 2005 IHR has, for example, strengthened its ability to use unofficial sources of information to detect adverse public health events, assess any of these events and, where it offers a clear and present danger, mobilise the international community to contain that event. The revised IHR has also been instrumental in granting the WHO new authority to 'name and shame' countries that breach their international obligations in reporting and responding to disease outbreaks. Through the 2011 PIPF, the WHO's normative powers have been further strengthened to campaign for a more equitable distribution of pandemic influenza vaccines and other associated benefits, while generating new sources of revenue to strengthen global pandemic preparedness from private industry partners. In this context, the office of the WHO Director-General has been particularly strengthened to take a more proactive role, not only in overseeing the global pandemic influenza technical cooperation system, but also in directly assessing global public health events and, if required, confronting those member states that appear to place their own interests above those of the international community.

Most significantly, these changes have been accomplished under the rubric of global health security, effectively transforming the WHO from a conventional public health organisation to a security institution of the twenty-first century. While there appears to be dissatisfaction amongst some quarters with this shift in focus,[86] the majority of governments have welcomed the WHO's recent efforts. Indeed, its attempts to enhance cooperative security mechanisms against adverse public health events that have the potential to spread internationally have been widely supported, and have even been encouraged, by the majority of member states in the wake of several disease-related incidents in the 1990s and beyond. The WHO Secretariat, which had also been suffering from a crisis of confidence in the wake of several scandals of mismanagement and

[86] Rushton, 'Global Health Security', above n. 4.

nepotism, welcomed this new focus and undertook an extensive examination of its disease outbreak alert and control functions. Further incidents, including notably the 2001 anthrax letter attacks in the United States, the 2003 SARS outbreak and the progressive international spread of the H5N1 avian influenza virus, reinforced the need for a comprehensive governance system to respond to such events.

It is in this context that international law has become central to the WHO's strategy to enhance global health security. Weaknesses in this approach obviously remain because its effectiveness is largely dependent upon the willingness of member states to comply with the principles and behavioural norms contained in the agreements. The passage of the two global health security agreements has been a defining moment for the WHO, one in which the institutional mandate has been adjusted to meet the challenges of a highly inter-connected world. The two agreements have bolstered the WHO's institutional legitimacy, granting it new tools, concepts and language to pursue its public health mandate of achieving the highest possible level of health and well-being for all the world's human inhabitants. At the same time, however, the arguably larger challenge of implementing and giving effect to the respective agreements still remains. Without necessary action by all the member states, even for the wealthiest nations, global health security is likely to remain elusive and may result in undermining the institutional legitimacy that the WHO has acquired through its new credential as a global health security institution.

# 11

# The institutionalisation of dispute settlements in Southeast Asia: the legitimacy of the Association of Southeast Asian Nations in de-securitising trade and territorial disputes

SEE SENG TAN

## 1 Introduction

On 20 November 2007, the Association of Southeast Asian Nations (ASEAN) formally adopted the ASEAN Charter, entering into force on 15 December 2008.[1] This development led some observers to speculate on the changing nature of regional security in Southeast Asia from a longstanding preference for informality and consensus-based interactions, to a rule-based and potentially compliance-oriented approach. Regionalism in Southeast Asia has traditionally been averse to institutionalisation. The institutional design of ASEAN has long privileged consensus, consultation, informality and inter-governmental approaches – the so-called 'ASEAN Way'[2] – over obligation, precision, subsidiarity and other ancillary principles typically associated with highly legalised institutions such as the European Union.[3] Furthermore, relative to other regions, ASEAN states have only occasionally relied on legal means to manage and, to the extent possible, settle their disputes with other states. Southeast Asian states

---

[1] Charter of the Association of Southeast Asian Nations, signed 20 November 2007 (entered into force 15 December 2008), available at www.asean.org/asean/asean-charter/asean-charter.

[2] Amitav Acharya, 'Ideas, Identity, and Institution-Building: From the "ASEAN Way" to the "Asia-Pacific Way"' (1997) 10 *Pacific Review* 319; Gillian Goh, 'The "ASEAN Way": Non-Intervention and ASEAN's Role in Conflict Management' (2003) 3 *Stanford Journal of East Asian Affairs* 113; Michael Haas, *The Asian Way to Peace: A Story of Regional Cooperation* (Praeger, New York, 1989).

[3] See Anne McNaughton, Chapter 3.

have ostensibly preferred to manage their relations in a largely consultative fashion, rather than settling their disputes with each other through legal means. Accordingly, the adoption of the ASEAN Charter heralded a new, challenging journey towards a rule-oriented diplomatic convention and security practice among Southeast Asian states.

Against this backdrop, this chapter examines Southeast Asia's embryonic efforts with an institutional approach to dispute settlement and conflict management in intra-regional and extra-regional relations, to assess the implications for regional order and security. To this end, this chapter reviews ASEAN's development and implementation of its Charter in section 2 and the trade and territorial disputes where several Southeast Asian states resorted to legal means for dispute settlement in section 3. Although Southeast Asia continues to lag behind other regions in terms of its willingness to embrace deeper institutionalisation, a growing number of ASEAN states, as the following discussion suggests, are not necessarily loath to rely on third party adjudication. Recent efforts by ASEAN member states to settle disputes between themselves and external parties, on one hand, and among themselves on an intramural basis on the other, may be seen as indicating a slow but gradual shift towards a greater acceptance of institutionalised means of dispute settlement. This is so even in relation to territorial and maritime disputes, a fair number of which have arisen since the entry into force of the United Nations Convention on the Law of the Sea (UNCLOS) in November 1994.[4] Finally, section 4 considers the lack of reliance by regional states on ASEAN-based dispute settlement mechanisms in settling intramural disputes, including the ones discussed below, and its implications for ASEAN's institutional legitimacy.

## 2   ASEAN institutionalisation and dispute settlement

The region's relative ambivalence to institutionalisation – weak at the regional level on one hand, with selective reliance for bilateral disputes on the other – raises interesting questions about the implications, intended or otherwise, of ASEAN's efforts in regional security integration. How, for example, might a predominantly utilitarian approach to institutionalisation, which Southeast Asian states seem to prefer, affect the ASEAN Community (comprising economic, political-security and

---

[4] Opened for signature 10 December 1982, 1833 UNTS 3 (entered into force 16 November 1994).

socio-cultural pillars) that ASEAN members are seeking to establish by 2015? And if ASEAN's vision of regional community presupposes the need for institutional innovations and reforms, what is the prospect of achieving them?

Liberal analysts tend to assume that institutionalisation is designed to achieve a more robust regionalism, and those who are critical of the ASEAN Charter for its purported flaws seem to presuppose that institutionalising ASEAN further necessarily requires innovation and transformation of that less-institutionalised regional organisation and the weak regionalism that has hitherto defined the region.[5] But the instrumentality and strategy with which Southeast Asian states approach their selective recourse to institutionalised means of dispute settlement suggest that their actions are more likely to result in the pursuit of institutional continuity or stasis. Indeed, their relatively conservative approach to institutionalisation at the ASEAN level is designed to ensure maintenance of the regional status quo (or continuity, in short).

This is neither to imply that prospects for institutional and regional transformation are therefore slim, nor that Southeast Asian states are fundamentally opposed to change. If anything, an enhanced regional organisation armed with viable rule-oriented regimes undergirding inter-state relations in Southeast Asia would be integral, and even essential, to the region's future peace and prosperity. This is so, not least, in order to ensure a sustained commitment by ASEAN members (and, conceivably, by external powers as well, including co-signatories to the 1976 ASEAN Treaty of Amity and Cooperation)[6] to peaceful settlement and management of disputes. Ultimately, a region-wide reliance on institutionalisation could lead to an increasing de-securitisation of trade and territorial disputes between Southeast Asian states, whereby legal recourse becomes the regional norm in managing, if not resolving, conflicts.

However, Southeast Asia is still at a nascent stage of institutionalisation. As noted, the apparent ambivalence with which regional states have approached institutionalisation suggests that despite adopting the ASEAN Charter, Southeast Asia still has a long way to go to emulate

---

[5] In fairness, the language of the ASEAN Concord II of 2003 and the Charter itself alludes to the aspirations of its architects. See Declaration of ASEAN Concord II (Bali Concord II), adopted 7 October 2003, available at www.asean.org/news/item/declaration-of-asean-con cord-ii-bali-concord-ii.

[6] Treaty of Amity and Cooperation in Southeast Asia, opened for signature 24 February 1976, 1025 UNTS 317 (entered into force 15 July 1976) (TAC).

the legal character of more advanced international organisations, if indeed that is what Southeast Asian states aim to achieve.[7] Historical institutionalism may provide a compelling theory based on 'path dependence' to argue that more advanced, legalised institution-building is the path that ASEAN will follow.[8] Rodolfo Severino, a former Secretary-General of ASEAN, once lamented that comparisons between ASEAN and the EU are neither fair nor judicious.[9] For Severino, what is especially troubling is the assumption underlying such comparisons that Southeast Asian regionalists not only aspire to attain the institutional standards and practices achieved by their European counterparts, but that they should therefore be held accountable to those expectations. Indeed, as Chapter 3 by Anne McNaughton on the European Union (EU) suggests, European institutions today appear to retreat from the single-minded pursuit of legal institutionalisation which has hitherto characterised their regional institutionalism, in favour of a more flexible approach.

What does ASEAN's historical and contemporary practice suggest about Southeast Asia's efforts in achieving deeper institutionalisation? Two broad observations are noteworthy. First, the adoption and implementation of the ASEAN Charter has caused intense debate over whether this step towards institutionalisation constitutes an institutional and normative progress in regional affairs, or a mere entrenchment of existing norms and principles long held by ASEAN. On the one hand, the Charter's arrival has been heralded as a watershed moment in

[7] In this regard, there is a conceptual distinction between mimicry and emulation. To the extent that ASEAN now has the Charter and promotes a vision for building an ASEAN Community with economic, political-security and socio-cultural pillars (the language is reminiscent of the EU) one can say ASEAN is mimicking the EU in terms of the superficial transplantation of lexicon and institutional conventions. On the other hand, emulation involves greater efforts and deeper internalisation of the principles, norms and practices of the organisation that the emulating actor seeks to emulate. In this sense, ASEAN is a mimicker of more advanced institutions, but whether it successfully evolves into an emulator of such institutions remains to be seen. See Alastair Iain Johnston, *Social States: China in International Institutions, 1980–2000* (Princeton University Press, Princeton, NJ, 2008) pp. 45–73.

[8] Orfeo Fioretos, 'Historical Institutionalism in International Relations' (2011) 65 *International Organization* 367.

[9] Severino has observed: 'Will ASEAN be like the EU? Most likely not. At least not exactly. As the EU itself acknowledges, it is unique as a regional organisation and will probably remain so. But we can expect domestic and external forces, the logic of globalisation, and the imperatives of regionalism to move ASEAN to resemble the EU more closely than it does today, and as ASEAN evolves, more closely than we can foresee today': Rodolfo C. Severino, *Will ASEAN be Like the EU?* (ASEAN, 23 March 2001), available at www.aseansec.org/3112.htm.

Southeast Asian regionalism embracing institutionalisation facilitating the evolution of regionalism from a soft or minimalist approach to a rule-based one. On the other hand, sceptics of ASEAN dismiss the Charter as yet another flight of fancy which, as with most visions and aspirations of ASEAN, will in due course be revealed to be long in word but woefully short in deed.[10] Others welcome the Charter but lament ASEAN's inability to achieve its own targets, not least in driving regionalism and regional economic integration.[11] For still others, the quibble is not over ASEAN's intent to institutionalise itself further but the particular principles enshrined in the Charter, principally legal norms such as sovereignty and non-interference, and social conventions such as the ASEAN Way.

There is much to be said for progressive interpretations of the Charter, not least as far as its liberal implications for regional peace and security are concerned, should the move towards further institutionalisation become accepted among ASEAN states as a common approach in managing and hopefully resolving their intramural disputes in an orderly, non-violent fashion.[12] This is, of course, dependent upon the extent to which the shared commitments of Southeast Asian governments to a legal institution and their refusal to undermine the institution can be sustained, even at risk of incurring relative losses in the short term for the sake of perceived absolute gains over the long term.[13] In the language of neo-institutionalism, a legal institution is robust only if state actors adhere to it on the basis of 'appropriateness' (commitment based on the belief that institutionalisation per se is an essential and inherent good for the region) rather than of 'expected consequences' (commitment based on the view that institutionalisation is a matter of instrumental choice purely in the

---

[10] David Martin Jones and Michael L. R. Smith, 'ASEAN's Imitation Community' (2002) 46 *Orbis* 93.

[11] Rodolfo Severino, 'ASEAN Beyond Forty: Towards Political and Economic Integration' (2007) 29 *Contemporary Southeast Asia* 406.

[12] As Benjamin Schiff has put it: 'Neoliberal institutionalists explain law as a tool to reduce the realm of disorder in international relations, making it a pragmatic step for states concerned not only with relative power, but even more with absolute well being. Legal institutions arise as states seek to stabilise their relations by replacing political power conflict with orderly legal processes – labeled by some observers the process of "institutionalisation"': Benjamin N. Schiff, *Building the International Criminal Court* (Cambridge University Press, Cambridge, 2008) p. 41.

[13] Russell Hardin, *Collective Action* (Johns Hopkins University Press, Baltimore, MD, 1982); Mancur Olson Jr, *The Logic of Collective Action* (Harvard University Press, Cambridge, MA, 1965).

pursuit of self-interest).[14] Given the relative nascence of Southeast Asia's legal institution it is understandable that no robust logic or norm of 'appropriateness' regarding institutionalisation exists in Southeast Asia as yet. On the other hand, it could be argued, as some indeed have done, that the ASEAN Way, which continues to enjoy legitimacy in regional relations, retains the norm of 'appropriateness' and suitability in the eyes of ASEAN states.[15]

Second, at the regional level, there is little doubt that Southeast Asian regionalism has historically eschewed institutionalisation. ASEAN's institutional design has long emphasised an inter-governmental structure, an informal decision-making process based on flexible consensus and consultation, and minimal delegation to quasi-juridical mechanisms (including a relatively weak secretariat).[16] Its founding and ancillary documents are best conceived as multilateral declarations rather than legally binding agreements, even though ASEAN has at times preferred 'hard law' nomenclature. ASEAN has certainly been nothing of the sort that would commit itself to some form of political integration.[17]

ASEAN regionalism has emphasised dispute management rather than resolution; member states essentially agree to shelve rather than settle their disputes. Although ASEAN's 1976 Treaty of Amity and Cooperation established a High Council with the task to recommend ways of resolving disputes,[18] it has never actually been activated. Further, it provides no mechanism through which to enforce any recommendation. This much was clear when the Singapore chair of ASEAN in 2007, confronting the forceful suppression of dissidents by the Burmese military regime in Yangon, conceded that ASEAN has 'little leverage over the internal development' in Myanmar and that '[w]hat we have is moral influence as members of the ASEAN family'.[19] In 2004, ASEAN member

---

[14]  Kjell Goldman, 'Appropriateness and Consequences: The Logic of Neo-Institutionalism' (2005) 18 *Governance: An International Journal of Policy, Administration, and Institutions* 35.

[15]  Amitav Acharya, *Constructing a Security Community in Southeast Asia: ASEAN and the Problem of Regional Order* (Routledge, London, 2001) pp. 54–98.

[16]  Acharya, 'Ideas, Identity, and Institution-Building', above n. 2.

[17]  Michael Leifer, *ASEAN and the Security of South-East Asia* (Routledge, London, 1989) p. 25.

[18]  TAC, Arts. 14 and 15.

[19]  Ministry of Foreign Affairs of Singapore, '*Straits Times* Interview with Singapore Foreign Minister George Yeo', 2–3 October 2007, available at http://app.mfa.gov.sg/pr/read_con tent.asp?View,8389.

states signed the ASEAN Protocol on Enhanced Dispute Settlement Mechanism,[20] which is aimed at dealing with disputes arising from the implementation of ASEAN economic agreements. But as with the 1996 Protocol on Dispute Settlement Mechanism that it replaced, the 2004 Protocol, notwithstanding its 'enhanced' features, lacks effective mechanisms for dealing with non-compliance.

In 2010, ASEAN Foreign Ministers signed the Protocol to the ASEAN Charter on Dispute Settlement Mechanisms,[21] a move that ostensibly signalled ASEAN's evolution from a consensus-based institution to a rule-based one. But concerns over the lack of institutional mechanisms for managing non-compliance continue to haunt ASEAN. As an Indonesian Foreign Affairs Ministry official reportedly noted, any discussion regarding the prospect for imposing sanctions against non-compliant member states would only be conducted after, not before, the Protocol was signed.[22] If anything, the ASEAN Charter underscores the regional organisation's obvious preference for norms and principles embraced by its member states and embedded in every ASEAN declaration and treaty: namely 'respect for the independence, sovereignty and territorial integrity of member states'; 'peaceful settlement of disputes'; 'non-interference in member states' internal affairs'; and the 'right to live without external interference'. For some, this development is arguably regressive since it amounts essentially to a mere reiteration of established regional norms. In the words of one observer:

> Disappointment comes not so much from things that are found in the charter, but from things that are not but should be. The charter is by all accounts as good a lowest common denominator as could have been expected, given the disparate interests, histories and sensitivities of Southeast Asian countries. Taking in not many important recommendations from the EPG [Eminent Persons Group], the document reaffirms a state-centric ASEAN and institutionalises age-old values of consensus and non-interference. It lacks clear mechanisms for dispute settlement, accountability and redress.[23]

[20] Adopted 29 November 2004, available at www.asean.org/news/item/asean-protocol-on-enhanced-dispute-settlement-mechanism.

[21] Adopted 8 April 2010, available at www.asean.org/news/item/asean-bulletin-april-2010 #Article-5.

[22] Lina A. Alexander, 'ASEAN Dispute Settlement Mechanism: Anything New?', *Jakarta Post*, 9 April 2010, available at www.thejakartapost.com/news/2010/04/09/asean-dispute-settlement-mechanism-anything-new.html.

[23] Thi Thu Huong Dang, *Examining the Engagement Between Civil Society and ASEAN in the ASEAN Charter Process* (GRIN Verlag, Santa Cruz, 2008) p. 24.

To the extent that Southeast Asia has yet to move 'beyond the ASEAN Way',[24] but has in fact extended or reaffirmed its longstanding *modus operandi*, the institutionalisation of principles such as national sovereignty and non-interference could conceivably indicate the entrenched logic of 'appropriateness', as much as that of 'expected consequences', concerning the region's apparent preference for the traditional diplomatic-security convention.[25] In other words, the enshrinement of what is in fact established as principles under international law in the ASEAN Charter reflects the normative as well as strategic intent of the Southeast Asian states, according to which challenges to political independence and territorial sovereignty remain a source of shared concerns.

On the other hand, the Charter's architects, while acknowledging the political horse-trading that invariably comes with compromised agreements of this sort, have nonetheless argued that the Charter constitutes an important achievement upon which further institutional developments and embellishments could and would be made. A year after the Charter's adoption, Ambassador Tommy Koh, a member of the High Level Task Force drafting the Charter, provided the following assessment before the ASEAN Secretariat:

> [W]hat remains to be done? Negotiation on a protocol to implement the chapter in the Charter on dispute settlement is the most important unfinished business. One of ASEAN's past failings was a culture of not taking its commitments seriously. The Charter seeks to change that by giving the Secretary-General the responsibility to monitor the compliance of member-states with their commitments. In the event of a dispute between two states over their commitments, the Charter sets out an ASEAN dispute settlement mechanism. Such an arrangement will give assurance to partners entering into agreements with ASEAN.[26]

Seen from this perspective, the Charter represents a work in progress, and the first step in what could be a long process towards building a culture of compliance to commitments. In October 2010, ASEAN's Foreign Ministers, in anticipation of the Seventeenth ASEAN Summit, agreed to adopt two legal instruments – the Rules for Reference of Unresolved Disputes to the ASEAN Summit, and the Rules of

---

[24] Mely Caballero-Anthony, *Regional Security in Southeast Asia: Beyond the ASEAN Way* (Institute of Southeast Asian Studies, Singapore, 2005).

[25] Goldman, 'Appropriateness and Consequences', above n. 14.

[26] Tommy Koh, 'ASEAN Charter at One: A Thriving Tiger Cub', Second ASEAN Secretariat Policy Forum, 16 December 2009, available at www.asean.org/archive/documents/0912 16-ASEC-Policy-Forum.pdf.

Authorisation for Legal Transactions under Domestic Laws – both of which are critical to the implementation of the ASEAN Charter's dispute settlement mechanism.[27] At the same time, there are worrying signs that ASEAN continues to be hampered by 'problems in implementation', not least those that affect the planned realisation of the ASEAN Economic Community by 2015 as a consequence of the failure by all ASEAN member states to act upon agreements on economic integration.[28] The failure to implement multilateral agreements (in other words, the failure to follow through on institutional commitments) has long been the major constraint on ASEAN's pursuit of intramural cooperation and still remains a concern that could derail its quest to be a functioning security institution.

## 3   Dispute settlement between ASEAN states

Without exception, Southeast Asian countries have avoided the use of ASEAN-based dispute settlement mechanisms. Indeed, Southeast Asians have historically looked to international institutions rather than to their own regional institution, ASEAN, for third party mediation and adjudication.[29] The ambivalent attitude towards institutionalisation at the regional level has not precluded some Southeast Asian states from relying on third party adjudication to settle their trade or territorial disputes. Their resort to institutionalised dispute settlement mechanisms has been extremely selective. In the area of trade-related disputes, the World Trade Organization's (WTO) Dispute Settlement Understanding

---

[27] Instrument of Incorporation of the Rules for Reference of Unresolved Disputes to the ASEAN Summit to the Protocol to the ASEAN Charter on Dispute Settlement Mechanisms, adopted 27 October 2010, available at http://agreement.asean.org/media/download/20131229164511.pdf; Rules of Authorisation for Legal Transactions under Domestic Laws, adopted 27 October 2010, available at http://cil.nus.edu.sg/rp/pdf/2010%20Rules%20of%20Authorisation%20for%20Legal%20Transactions%20under%20Domestic%20Laws-pdf.pdf.

[28] Yang Razali Kassim, *ASEAN Community: Losing Grip over Vision 2015?*, Commentary No. 87/2011, S. Rajaratnam School of International Studies (2 June 2011), available at www.rsis.edu.sg/publications/Perspective/RSIS0872011.pdf.

[29] This is supported by a recent survey of Asian, including Southeast Asian, security and economic policy-makers and analysts conducted by the Washington-based Center for International and Strategic Studies. Survey respondents were asked how significant regional organisations are to their national and regional security. Unsurprisingly, the majority of respondents prized national security strategies and international bodies over and above regional organisations. Bates Gill *et al.* (eds.), *Strategic Views on Asian Regionalism: Survey Results and Analysis* (Center for Strategic and International Studies, Washington, DC, 2009).

has been under-utilised by Southeast Asian countries and indeed by Asian states by and large. The following brief account demonstrates selectivity in the recourse to the WTO dispute settlement mechanism by Southeast Asian states:

- Interestingly (and ironically) the first complaint lodged under the WTO dispute settlement mechanism when it was established involved Singapore and Malaysia over an import ban on polyethylene and polypropylene, which was eventually resolved without WTO adjudication.[30] In other words, the first countries ever to use the WTO dispute settlement mechanism were Southeast Asian states – against one another – both being members of a regional organisation which had long rejected institutionalised dispute settlement.
- The dispute involving the restriction of shrimp imports into the United States (US) was registered with the WTO jointly by Malaysia and Thailand (along with India and Pakistan) against the United States in October 1996. In February 1997, following multiple requests by the complainants, the WTO Dispute Settlement Body (DSB) finally convened a panel. In May 1998, the panel upheld Malaysia's and Thailand's claims;[31] two months later the US appealed against that decision. Although the Appellate Body set aside the panel's finding, the body nonetheless concluded that the US measure failed to meet the requirements under the chapeau of Article XX of the General Agreement on Tariffs and Trade (GATT).[32]
- The Philippines raised a series of complaints against its trading partners regarding what it perceived were unfair import restrictions on its agricultural exports: Brazil's prohibition on desiccated coconut in November 1995; the US' restriction on certain shrimp and shrimp products in October 1996; and Australia's restriction on fresh fruit and vegetables in October 2002. In the case with Brazil, the DSB established a panel in March 1996 after two requests by the Philippines.

---

[30] See *Malaysia: Prohibition of Imports of Polyethylene and Polypropylene*, WTO Doc. DS1 (complaint by Singapore withdrawn on 19 July 1995). For a detailed analysis, see Dukgeun Ahn, *WTO Settlements in East Asia*, National Bureau of Economic Research Working Paper 10178 (December 2003) p. 3, available at www.nber.org/papers/w10 178.pdf.

[31] *United States – Import Prohibition of Certain Shrimp and Shrimp Products*, WTO Doc. WT/DS58/R, Panel Report (15 May 1998).

[32] *United States – Import Prohibition of Certain Shrimp and Shrimp Products*, WTO Doc. WT/DS58/AB/R, Appellate Body Report (12 October 1998), paras. 161–84.

However, after an initial dismissal by the panel,[33] the Philippines'
appeal was also rejected the following year.[34] The consultation request
with the US is still unresolved.[35] In relation to the dispute with
Australia, following multiple requests from the Philippines, the DSB
finally established a panel in August 2003.[36]

- Among the ASEAN countries, Thailand has proved the most litigious
in terms of trade disputes.[37] Before the establishment of the WTO in
1994, Thailand brought a dispute with the US on tobacco-related
issues before the GATT for arbitration. More recently in April 2006,
Thailand, not unlike its ASEAN members, brought a complaint
against the US concerning anti-dumping measures on imports of
frozen warm water shrimp; subsequently, Japan, Brazil and the
People's Republic of China (PRC) followed suit in joining the consultations. In February 2008, the panel convened by the DSB upheld
Thailand's claim that the US had acted inconsistently with Article
2.4.2 of the Anti-Dumping Agreement,[38] which in turn prompted the
US to appeal the panel's decision. In July 2008, the Appellate Body
upheld the panel's conclusion.[39] In April 2009, the US reported to the
DSB that it had taken steps to implement the latter's recommendations and rulings.[40]

- Indonesia has not been directly involved in WTO-related disputes with
any ASEAN member state, although it was a third party in the case

---

[33] *Brazil – Measures affecting Desiccated Coconut,* WTO Doc. WT/DS22/R, Panel Report (17 October 1996).

[34] *Brazil – Measures Affecting Desiccated Coconut,* WTO Doc. WT/DS22/AB/R, Appellate Body Report (21 February 1997).

[35] For details, see WTO, 'Dispute Settlement: Dispute DS61, *United States – Import Prohibition of Certain Shrimp and Shrimp Products*', updated 24 February 2010, available at www.wto.org/english/tratop_e/dispu_e/cases_e/ds61_e.htm.

[36] For details, see WTO, 'Dispute Settlement: Dispute DS270, *Australia – Certain Measures affecting the Importation of Fruit and Vegetables*', updated 24 February 2010, available at www.wto.org/english/tratop_e/dispu_e/cases_e/ds270_e.htm.

[37] Thailand has appeared in 13 cases as a complainant, 3 cases as a respondent, and 69 cases as a third party as at 30 September 2014. See WTO, 'Member Information: Thailand and the WTO', available at www.wto.org/english/thewto_e/countries_e/thailand_e.htm.

[38] *United States – Measures relating to Shrimp from Thailand,* WTO Doc. WT/DS343/R, Panel Report (28 February 2008).

[39] *United States – Measures relating to Shrimp from Thailand,* WTO Docs. WT/DS343/AB/R and WT/DS345/AB/R, Appellate Body Report (16 July 2008).

[40] WTO, 'Dispute Settlement: Dispute DS343 *United States – Measures relating to Shrimp from Thailand*', available at www.wto.org/english/tratop_e/dispu_e/cases_e/ds343_e.htm.

brought by the Philippines against Brazil involving desiccated coconut. It has brought complaints against Argentina, South Africa, the Republic of Korea and the US over issues involving clove cigarettes (a major Indonesian product), footwear and paper.[41]

A few Southeast Asian states also decided to bring their bilateral territorial disputes before the International Court of Justice (ICJ). Two oft-cited cases concern the Ligitan and Sipadan islands disputed by Indonesia and Malaysia, which Malaysia eventually won,[42] and the Pedra Branca/Pulau Batu Puteh island disputed by Malaysia and Singapore, which Singapore eventually won.[43] In *Ligitan/Sipadan*, the ICJ ruled in Malaysia's favour by virtue of the 'effective occupation' and 'effective administration' that Malaysia historically exercised over the islands.[44] Critically, Indonesia (or the Netherlands before it) never registered its disagreement or protest with Malaysia (or Britain before it) when those activities were carried out, including the construction of lighthouses on the islands.[45]

---

[41] WTO, 'Dispute Settlement: Dispute DS123, *Argentina - Safeguard Measures on Imports of Footwear*', available at www.wto.org/english/tratop_e/dispu_e/cases_e/ds123_e.htm; WTO, 'Dispute Settlement: Dispute DS217, *United States - Continued Dumping and Subsidy Offset Act of 2000*', available at www.wto.org/english/tratop_e/dispu_e/cases_e/ds217_e.htm; WTO, 'Dispute Settlement: Dispute DS312, *Korea - Anti-Dumping Duties on Imports of Certain Paper from Indonesia*', available at www.wto.org/english/tratop_e/dispu_e/cases_e/ds312_e.htm; World Trade Organization, 'Dispute Settlement: Dispute DS374, *South Africa - Anti-Dumping Measures on Uncoated Woodfree Paper*', available at www.wto.org/english/tratop_e/dispu_e/cases_e/ds374_e.htm; WTO, 'Dispute Settlement: Dispute DS406, *United States - Measures affecting the Production and Sale of Clove Cigarettes*', available at www.wto.org/english/tratop_e/dispu_e/cases_e/ds406_e.htm.

[42] *Sovereignty over Pulau Ligitan and Pulau Sipadan (Indonesia v. Malaysia)* (Judgment) [2002] ICJ Rep. 625. For detailed analysis, see e.g., J.G. Merrill, 'Sovereignty over Pulau Ligitan and Pulau Sipadan (Indonesia v. Malaysia), Merits, Judgment of 17 December 2002' (2003) 52 *International and Comparative Law Quarterly* 797; David A. Colson, 'Sovereignty over Pulau Ligitan and Pulau Sipadan (Indonesia/Malaysia)' (2003) 97 *American Journal of International Law* 398.

[43] *Sovereignty over Pedra Branca/Pulau Batu Puteh, Middle Rocks and South Ledge (Malaysia v. Singapore)* (Judgment) [2002] ICJ Rep. 12. See generally, S. Jayakumar and Tommy Koh, *Pedra Branca: The Road to the World Court* (NUS Press, Singapore, 2009).

[44] 'The Court notes that the activities relied upon by Malaysia, both in its own name and as successor State of Great Britain, are modest in number but that they are diverse in character and include legislative, administrative and quasi-judicial acts. They cover a considerable period of time and show a pattern revealing an intention to exercise State functions in respect of the two islands in the context of the administration of a wider range of islands': *Ligitan/Sipadan*, above n. 42, 685, para. 148.

[45] *Ibid.*

In *Pedra Branca/Pulau Batu Puteh*, which included Middle Rocks and South Ledge, the analysis of the pre-modern history led the Court to the view that 'the Sultanate of Johor [now part of Malaysia] had original title to Pedra Branca'.[46] However, the Court ultimately ruled in favour of Singapore on the basis of Malaysia's historical failure to respond to Singapore's conduct à *titre de souverain*, that is, its concrete manifestations of the display of territorial sovereignty over the disputed islands.[47]

The preceding two cases can be seen as signalling an embryonic willingness by some Southeast Asian states to accept recourse to judicial settlement of politically sensitive bilateral disputes over territorial title. Questions of sovereignty and territorial title have been the chief reason behind most bilateral tensions between ASEAN states. This is true of Asia in general as well.[48] The settlement of these disputes, to the extent it is possible, has often taken a long time to realise. For example, Hassan Wirajuda, Indonesia's then Foreign Minister, noted in 2009 that it took his country and Vietnam thirty-two years to arrive at an agreement over their adjacent exclusive economic zones in the South China Sea.[49] With respect to a dispute between Indonesia and Singapore over a relatively short stretch of maritime border on their respective western boundaries, it took five years to settle their dispute.[50] Whether by the ICJ or other bodies, however, the readiness of states to adopt third-party dispute settlement – and, crucially, accept and adhere to decisions unfavourable to them – remains the key challenge.

The 2011 Thai-Cambodian border dispute surrounding the Preah Vihear temple has led Phnom Penh, in April 2011, to seek clarification from the ICJ concerning its 1962 decision that awarded the temple to Cambodia.[51] The 1962 decision paved the way to a successful effort by Cambodia to include the temple in the United Nations Educational, Scientific and Cultural Organization (UNESCO) World Heritage List in July 2008. On its part, Thailand claimed ownership of 4.6 kilometres of land adjacent to the temple. Fighting between Cambodian and Thai forces

---

[46] *Pedra Branca/Pulau Batu Puteh*, above n. 43, 28, para. 36.
[47] *Ibid.* 95–6, paras. 274–7.
[48] Ralf Emmers, *Geopolitics and Maritime Territorial Disputes in East Asia* (Routledge, London, 2009).
[49] Nurfika Osman, 'Talks With Malaysia on Ambalat Border Dispute to Resume in July', *Jakarta Globe*, 16 June 2009, available at www.thejakartaglobe.com/national/talks-with-malaysia-on-ambalat-border-dispute-to-resume-in-july/312607.
[50] *Ibid.*
[51] *Case concerning the Temple of Preah Vihear (Cambodia v. Thailand) (Merits)* [1962] ICJ Rep. 6.

broke out in February 2011, following which the Foreign Ministers of both countries appeared before the United Nations Security Council.[52] Mediation efforts by Indonesia at the side-lines of the ASEAN Summit in May, pursued at Jakarta's discretion in its role as chair of ASEAN, initially proved unsuccessful, as neither of the disputing parties were prepared to compromise. In July, the ICJ ruled that both countries were to withdraw their troops from a newly defined provisional demilitarised zone around the temple area and to allow ASEAN-appointed observers to enter the zone.[53] Both Foreign Ministers indicated their willingness to comply with the ICJ's decision.[54] Cambodian-Thai relations improved when the new Thai Prime Minister visited Phnom Penh in September 2011, following the victory by Yingluck Shinawatra, sibling of the ousted Thai Prime Minister Thaksin Shinawatra, at the 2011 national election in Thailand.

Not all the bilateral territorial disputes in Southeast Asia have ended amicably. The Ambalat region, a sea block in the Celebes Sea off the coast of Indonesian East Kalimantan and southeast of Sabah in East Malaysia, reportedly rich in oil and natural gas, has been a source of contention between Indonesia and Malaysia since the 1980s. The dispute erupted following the decision by Petronas, the Malaysian state-owned oil company, to grant a concession for oil and gas exploration to its subsidiary, Petronas Caligari, and to the Anglo-Dutch oil giant, Shell, in a part of the Sulawesi Sea which Indonesia claims is within its exclusive economic zone.[55] Indonesia strongly reacted to Petronas' action, rousing nationalist sentiments and scrambling military aircrafts and warships, which led the two countries to the brink of armed conflict. In 2009, the Indonesian armed forces accused Malaysia of having 'breached the law' by entering the disputed zone on no less than nine occasions during that year alone.[56] Further, a map produced

[52] William M. Reilly, 'UN Security Council hears Cambodia, Thailand on border dispute', *Xinhua Net* (online), 15 February 2011, available at http://news.xinhuanet.com/eng lish2010/world/2011-02/15/c_13732477.htm.

[53] *Request for Interpretation of the Judgement of 15 June 1962 in the Case concerning the Temple of Prear Vihear (Cambodia v. Thailand)* (Request for the Indication of Provisional Measures) [2011] ICJ Rep. 537, 552–4, paras. 61–4.

[54] 'RI [Republic of Indonesia] welcomes Int'l Court's decision on Thai-Cambodian conflict', *AntaraNews.com* (online), 19 July 2011, available at www.antaranews.com/en/news/739 14/ri-welcomes-intl-courts-decision-on-thai-cambodian-conflict.

[55] Yang Razali Kassim, *ASEAN Cohesion: Making Sense of Indonesian Reactions to Bilateral Disputes*, Commentary No. 15/2005, Institute of Defence and Strategic Studies (6 April 2005), available at www.rsis.edu.sg/publications/Perspective/IDSS152005.pdf.

[56] 'TNI moves to secure Ambalat', *Jakarta Post*, 31 May 2009, available at www.thejakarta post.com/news/2009/05/31/tni-moves-secure-ambalat.html.

by Malaysia in 1979, depicting Ambalat, or at least a large portion of it as under Malaysian sovereignty, met with objections not only from Indonesia but other Southeast Asian neighbours (the Philippines, Thailand and Vietnam) as well as the PRC. This dispute raises the question as to whether Indonesia, having lost its claim over Ligitan and Sipadan islands to Malaysia, would subsequently prove twice as shy to bring the Ambalat dispute and/or other territorial disputes it has with Malaysia to the ICJ or other third party dispute settlement bodies.

Another unresolved territorial dispute exists in the South China Sea. Among the six countries involved in territorial and maritime disputes in the South China Sea, four are ASEAN members: Vietnam, the Philippines, Malaysia and Brunei. Their disputes involve two sets of interrelated issues: sovereignty over the islands and their adjacent territorial waters; and sovereign rights over the exclusive economic zone and continental shelf generated from the eligible islands according to the relevant provisions of UNCLOS.[57] Since 2009, the four ASEAN claimants have sought to clarify their claims and bring them into conformity with UNCLOS; specifically, they acknowledge that 'claims to the natural resources in and under the waters in the South China Sea can only be derived from claims to land features'.[58] On the other hand, the PRC has clarified its claims to a limited extent only, leaving others confused as to whether its claims are based on land features alone or cover all the maritime areas within the 'nine-dash line' displayed on the Chinese version of the South China Sea map that ostensibly represents its historic claims.[59] Non-claimant states such as Singapore have called on the PRC to clarify its claims and urged all parties to act with restraint.[60]

---

[57] For detailed analysis, see e.g., Hitoshi Nasu and Donald R. Rothwell, 'Re-Evaluating the Role of International Law in Territorial and Maritime Disputes in East Asia' (2014) 4 *Asian Journal of International Law* 55.

[58] Robert Beckman, 'China, UNCLOS and the South China Sea', paper presented at the Asian Society of International Law, Third Biennial Conference, Beijing, 27–28 August 2011, p. 2, available at http://cil.nus.edu.sg/wp/wp-content/uploads/2009/09/AsianSIL-Beckman-China-UNCLOS-and-the-South-China-Sea-26-July-2011.pdf.

[59] Florian Dupuy and Pierre-Marie Dupuy, 'A Legal Analysis of China's Historic Rights Claim in the South China Sea' (2013) 107 *American Journal of International Law* 124, 131; Zou Keyuan, 'China's U-Shaped Line in the South China Sea Revisited' (2012) 43 *Ocean Development and International Law* 18. Cf. Zhiguo Gao and Bing Bing Jia, 'The Nine-Dash Line in the South China Sea: History, Status, and Implications' (2013) 107 *American Journal of International Law* 98.

[60] 'Singapore asks China to clarify claims on S. China Sea', *Reuters*, 20 June 2011, available at www.reuters.com/article/2011/06/20/idUSL3E7HK1H520110620.

By clarifying its claims, the PRC could ostensibly pave the way for serious discussions with the other claimants on the joint development of natural resources in the South China Sea – assuming, of course, that all are prepared to shelve their sovereignty claims. If the PRC chooses not to clarify its claims, it could drive Southeast Asian claimants to seek resolution through an international court or tribunal.[61] Significantly, the PRC, which has been a party to UNCLOS since 1996, has excluded from the system of compulsory dispute settlement any dispute relating to maritime boundary delimitation.[62] Hence, barring any change in Beijing's abhorrence for 'internationalising' its disputes and relying on institutional bodies to resolve them, the only viable option to manage the disputes is for ASEAN and the PRC to agree to a code of conduct that, legally or otherwise, guides the states involved to the mutual exercise of self-restraint in their conduct within the South China Sea, without which joint development of resources would not be possible. Indeed, some commentators have argued that even the Declaration of the Conduct of Parties in the South China Sea, which ASEAN and the PRC signed in 2002, already provides a requisite framework for mutual restraint and non-provocation.[63] However, what the claimants did not share was the collective will to accept and adhere to the Declaration.

## 4    No institutional imperative in Southeast Asia?

The illustrations above underscore the persistent ambivalence in Southeast Asian states' attitudes towards an institutional approach to dispute settlement. Assurances given by regional states that they will abide by decisions of a judicial or quasi-judicial body do not necessarily imply that they would continue to seek recourse to institutionalised

---

[61] Indeed, on 22 January 2014 the Philippines instituted arbitration proceedings against the PRC under Annex VII to UNCLOS 'with respect to the dispute with China over the maritime jurisdiction of the Philippines in the West Philippines Sea': *Republic of the Philippines* v. *People's Republic of China*, Permanent Court of Arbitration, available at www.pca-cpa.org/showpage.asp?pag_id=1529.

[62] Article 298(1) of UNCLOS provides that when signing, ratifying and/or acceding to UNCLOS or any time thereafter, states may opt to exclude certain disputes from compulsory dispute settlement. See also Junwu Pan, *Towards a New Framework for Peaceful Settlement of China's Territorial and Boundary Disputes* (Martinus Nijhoff, Leiden, 2009) p. 122.

[63] Carlyle A. Thayer, 'South China Sea Tensions: What Role for ASEAN, the United States and the United Nations?' (24 August 2012), available at www.scribd.com/doc/103934560/Thayer-South-China-Sea-ASEAN-and-the-Latest-Tensions.

dispute settlement in the future. The commitment to institutionalised dispute settlement among Southeast Asian states remains weak and selective. This may lead one to conclude that institutionalisation in Southeast Asia is neither an imperative nor an inexorable process. In other words, there is no general acceptance of and strong inclination towards institutionalisation as a normative standard for dispute settlement. Institutionalised dispute settlement remains an instrumental and strategic choice which regional states employ selectively vis-à-vis their ASEAN neighbours as well as extra-regional states.[64]

ASEAN's resistance to institutionalisation, at least until the adoption of its Charter in 2007, cannot be adequately explained by the diplomatic and security culture within the region alone. The preceding analysis in this chapter suggests that ASEAN member states, or at least the founding members which helped define ASEAN's governing conventions, have considered that keeping ASEAN as a consensus-based organisation is as significant as keeping an instrumental and/or strategic choice for individual member states. Indeed, the fact that Vietnam has so far failed in its attempts to obtain agreement from its fellow ASEAN states to legalise a code of conduct for the South China Sea indicates that reluctant member states have chosen not to adopt such a course of action out of concern as to how the PRC might react to it.[65]

Paradoxically, institutionalising the 'ASEAN Way' in the ASEAN Charter could prove problematic for the regional organisation and its member states in that it has the potential to undermine the legitimacy of the organisation by depriving it of the benefits of flexible consensus it once enjoyed. The ASEAN Regional Forum (ARF) has suffered through an inadvertent process of formalisation – operating practically by unanimity instead of flexible consensus – that arguably has hampered attempts towards progress in security cooperation.[66] ASEAN could face a similar

---

[64] Miles Kahler, 'Institutionalisation as Strategy: The Asia-Pacific Case' (2000) 54 *International Organization* 549.

[65] As the Malaysian Minister of Defence noted in October 2010: 'ASEAN has been too divided and fragmented over the [South China Sea] issue and hesitant to negotiate with Beijing from a position of strength': cited in James Chow, 'ASEAN unity crucial to resolve South China Sea disputes: Malaysia Defense Minister', *Epoch Times*, 19 October 2011, available at www.theepochtimes.com/n2/world/asean-unity-crucial-to-resolve-south-china-sea-disputes-malaysia-defense-minister-63126.html.

[66] The incessant failure of the ARF to move from confidence building to preventive diplomacy (in accordance with the road map set out in its 1995 Concept Paper) has been attributed variously to its size (27 participants), institutional design, ASEAN

predicament as a consequence of its codification of pre-existing norms and principles that have governed intramural relations to date but in a sufficiently flexible way that permitted the occasional departure from the 'ASEAN Way', as when ASEAN members intervened in one another's domestic affairs (an infringement of ASEAN's non-interference norm) in order to preserve the regional order.[67]

A serious concern, therefore, may be raised with a potential loss of institutional flexibility. For example, past practice among ASEAN Economic Ministers allowed for member states to agree on economic liberalisation agreements on the basis of '10 minus $x$' and/or '2 plus $x$' principles. This ensured that member states wishing to embark on cooperative initiatives at a pace faster than the rest could still proceed. However, the ASEAN Charter allows for arrangements to be made on the 'ASEAN minus $x$' and other ancillary formulae for flexible participation only if there is consensus to do so.[68] As such, what has so far been regional practice based on flexible consensus has now, by virtue of the institutionalisation of the norm in the Charter, transformed into an inflexible principle based on unanimity. The irony here should not be overlooked; just as highly institutionalised organisations such as the EU are today seeking to develop more flexible modes of operation that would give them greater leeway to advance security agendas, ASEAN appears to be moving in the opposite direction.

## 5   Conclusion

In 2003, ASEAN officially embarked on its vision to become a regional community. Arguably, Southeast Asia's best hope for a lasting peace is for

Way-styled convention, and the highly divergent security perspectives of its participants. Yet it is also clear that the ARF, notwithstanding its express penchant for decision-making by flexible consensus, has acted on the basis of decision-by-unanimity. This has allowed its security agenda to be held hostage by the veto-like actions of states disinclined to participate in more advanced cooperative initiatives out of concern that their sovereignty could be undermined. See Ralf Emmers and See Seng Tan, 'The ASEAN Regional Forum and Preventive Diplomacy: Built to Fail?' (2011) 7 *Asian Security* 44.

[67] See Lee Jones, *ASEAN, Sovereignty and Intervention in Southeast Asia* (Palgrave Macmillan, New York, 2012).

[68] Barry Desker, *Is the ASEAN Charter Necessary?*, S. Rajaratnam School of International Studies (17 July 2008), available at www.rsis.edu.sg/publications/Perspective/RSIS0772008.pdf.

the region to be transformed into a security community.[69] Security communities are enterprises to de-securitise *qua* demilitarisation. The level of institutionalisation in a region is arguably tied to its propensity for development as a security community. Southeast Asia has yet to become a community, much less a security community. So long as institutionalisation is treated as a strategic option by Southeast Asian states to pursue their own national self-interests, regional security ideas that emphasise inclusivity and the collective interest will remain unlikely to be shared among them. This is notably seen in the continued reluctance of some regional governments to discuss the provision of enforcement for dealing with non-compliance in regional economic and security cooperation, despite the growing number of dispute settlement mechanisms (the 1976 Treaty of Amity and Cooperation High Council, the 2010 Protocol to the ASEAN Charter on Dispute Settlement Mechanisms, and the like).

However, as their experiences at the WTO and the ICJ suggest, Southeast Asian states are not fundamentally opposed to the idea of institutionalised dispute settlement. Their ambivalence regarding their own regional instruments can be attributed to the lack of mutual trust and confidence in each other. This raises serious concerns about not only the value of compliance and enforcement provisions in ASEAN dispute settlement mechanisms but, crucially, the legitimacy of the regional dispute settlement bodies entrusted with the responsibility of dealing with regional disputes.

---

[69] Acharya, *Constructing a Security Community in Southeast Asia*, above n. 15; Donald K. Emmerson, 'Security, Community, and Democracy in Southeast Asia: Analyzing ASEAN' (2005) 6 *Japanese Journal of Political Science* 165; Timo Kivimäki, 'The Long Peace of ASEAN' (2001) 38 *Journal of Peace Research* 5.

# PART IV

Security institutions and regime collision

# 12

## The Food and Agriculture Organization and food security in the context of international intellectual property rights protection

DILAN THAMPAPILLAI

## 1 Introduction

The impact of intellectual property rights upon the issue of food security in the Global South exemplifies the fragmentation problem Martti Koskenniemi identified as emerging from the proliferation of different self-contained legal regimes within public international law.[1] Whereas these legal regimes are coherent within themselves, their combined interaction creates incoherency within international law, which in some cases endangers the protection of human rights, as evident in the conflict emerging between the right to food and intellectual property law.[2] Indeed, from inside the confines of the World Trade Organization (WTO) project, the rules of international trade law do not adequately account for the needs of rural smallholders and the rural poor in the Global South.[3] Similarly, the rules of international intellectual property law, which are now largely covered within the Agreement

---

[1] Martti Koskenniemi and Paivi Leino, 'Fragmentation of International Law: Postmodern Anxieties?' (2002) 15 *Leiden Journal of International Law* 553. See also *Fragmentation of International Law: Difficulties Arising from the Diversification and Expansion of International Law, Report of the Study Group of the International Law Commission*, UN Doc. A/CN.4/L.682 (13 April 2006).

[2] See e.g., Chidi Oguamanam, 'Agro-Biodiversity and Food Security: Biotechnology and Traditional Agricultural Practices at the Periphery of the International Intellectual Property Regime Complex' (2007) *Michigan State Law Review* 215; Kojo Yelpaala, 'Quo Vadis WTO? The Threat of TRIPS and the Biodiversity Convention to Human Health and Food Security' (2012) 30 *Boston University International Law Journal* 55.

[3] Peter Straub, 'Farmers in the IP Wrench: How Patents on Gene-Modified Crops Violate the Right to Food in Developing Countries' (2006) 29 *Hastings International and Comparative Law Review* 187. This chapter uses the term 'Global South' to refer to developing countries.

on the Trade-Related Aspects of Intellectual Property Rights (TRIPS),[4] provide states parties with little scope to deny protection to intellectual property rights holders even where those rights imperil the attainment of vital social needs such as food security.[5] The expansion of intellectual property rights into agriculture and the subsequent emergence of intellectual property rights within the WTO regime has aided large transnational agricultural companies and seed patenting companies as they move into agriculture business in the Global South.[6] The effect of this shift has been to displace rural smallholders, to disrupt traditional agricultural practices and to change the whole structure of food production,[7] all cumulatively exacerbating food insecurity.

Increasingly, the Food and Agriculture Organization (FAO) has assumed the role of monitoring the food security problem, championing an approach encompassing both the right to food under international law and the notion of farmers' rights to develop solutions to the crisis.[8] There is certainly some measure of support at an international level for both the right to food and the concept of farmers' rights. Indeed, the right to food appears to be well accepted within the international community.[9] However, both the right to food and farmers' rights exist within a broader international law framework that does not have the ability to interact in a meaningful way with those rules of international trade law that are contained in the TRIPS Agreement.[10]

---

[4] Opened for signature 15 April 1994, 1869 UNTS 299 (entered into force 1 January 1995).

[5] See Straub, 'Farmers in the IP Wrench', above n. 3. See also Michael Blakeney, *Intellectual Property Rights and Food Security* (Cabi, Cambridge, MA, 2009). See also Olivier De Schutter, *Seed Policies and the Right to Food: Enhancing Agrobiodiversity and Encouraging Innovation, Report of the Special Rapporteur on the Right to Food*, UN Doc. A/64/170 (23 July 2009); Conny Almekinders and Niels Louwaars, *Farmers' Seed Production: New Approaches and Practices* (Intermediate Technology Publications, London, 1999).

[6] Chidi Oguamanam, 'Intellectual Property Rights in Plant Genetic Resources: Farmers' Rights and Food Security in Indigenous and Local Communities' (2006) 11 *Drake Journal of Agricultural Law* 273.

[7] Lauren Winter, 'Cultivating Farmers' Rights: Reconciling Food Security, Indigenous Agriculture, and TRIPS' (2010) 43 *Vanderbilt Journal of Transnational Law* 233, 240.

[8] Olivier De Schutter, *International Trade in Agriculture and the Right to Food*, Dialogue on Globalization Occasional Paper No. 46 (Friedrich Ebert Siftung, Geneva, 2009), available at http://library.fes.de/pdf-files/bueros/genf/06819.pdf.

[9] See Smita Narula, 'The Right to Food: Holding International Actors Accountable under International Law' (2006) 44 *Columbia Journal of Transnational Law* 691.

[10] For a critical discussion of the limitations surrounding the right to food, see e.g., Jacqueline Mowbray, 'The Right to Food and the International Economic System: An Assessment of the Rights-based Approach to the Problem of World Hunger' (2007) 20 *Leiden Journal of International Law* 545.

This chapter explores the impact of intellectual property rights upon the problem of food security and canvasses the ways in which a rights-based approach to food security might achieve a higher degree of food security in the Global South. With this perspective the chapter critiques the institutional response of the FAO to the problem of food security. It argues that in tackling a security problem a security institution can only be as effective as the global legal architecture allows.

## 2 Food and Agriculture Organization as a food security institution

In June 2009, in the wake of the global food crisis, the FAO estimated there were 1.02 billion people who were food insecure.[11] This represented an increase of 150 million in two years.[12] The most substantial cause for the rise in the number was the increase in food prices.[13] In part this reflected the aftermath of the global food crisis of 2008.[14] The impact of the price shock on the poor and landless was particularly severe.[15] It is estimated that at present, 70 per cent of those who can be described as food insecure are engaged in agriculture.[16] In 2012, the Committee on World Food Security estimated there were approximately 925 million people facing chronic hunger.[17] The number of people facing severe hunger subsequent to the 2008 food crisis, compared to the slightly lower figure recorded in 2012, highlights the existence of two different forms of food insecurity: (i) chronic food insecurity; and (ii) short-term food insecurity.

---

[11] FAO, *The State of Food Insecurity in the World 2009* (2009) p. 11, available at ftp://ftp.fao.org/docrep/fao/012/i0876e/i0876e.pdf. See also World Food Program, '1.02 Billion People Hungry' (19 June 2009), available at www.wfp.org/news/news-release/102-billion-people-hungry. Of the 1.02 billion people who are food insecure, 15 million reside in the Global North while the remainder reside in the Global South. See also Carmen Gonzalez, 'The Global Food Crisis: Law, Policy, and the Elusive Quest for Justice' (2010) 13 *Yale Human Rights and Development Law Journal* 462.

[12] FAO, *The State of Food Insecurity in the World 2009*, above n. 11, p. 11.     [13] *Ibid.*

[14] See FAO, *The State of Agricultural Commodity Markets 2009* (2009), available at www.fao.org/docrep/012/i0854e00.htm. It was estimated that rising food prices between 2006 and 2008 resulted in a further 115 million people becoming food insecure: *ibid.* pp. 6–9.

[15] *Ibid.* See also *The 2008 Food Price Crisis: Rethinking Food Security Policies*, UN Doc. UNCTAD/GDS/MDP/g24/2009/3 (1 October 2009).

[16] See De Schutter, *Seed Policies and the Right to Food: Enhancing Agrobiodiversity and Encouraging Innovation*, above n. 5, para. 24.

[17] FAO Committee on World Food Security, *Global Strategic Framework for Food Security and Nutrition*, CFS 2012/39/5 Add.1 (15–20 October 2012) para. 1, available at www.fao.org/docrep/meeting/026/ME498E.pdf.

This chapter examines chronic food insecurity.[18] This particular type of food insecurity is long term and is caused by structural problems within the domestic economy.[19] In contrast, short-term food insecurity may be caused by external shocks such as international and civil wars, droughts, famines and other environmental catastrophes and price movements in global commodity markets. This form of food insecurity is likely to be transitory as opposed to chronic.[20] There is some overlap between the two categories as the causes of short-term food insecurity can exacerbate the suffering of those communities and individuals who are experiencing long-term food insecurity.

This chapter is also specifically concerned with those who are food insecure in the rural areas of the Global South who are in that state of insecurity because they are vulnerable to rising food prices or who are smallholder farmers influenced by commercial seed systems due to the price of inputs impairing their ability to produce food.[21] The problem of food security threatens the health and lives of millions of people in the Global South. The causes of food insecurity are complex and inter-related, but in general terms the problem may be characterised as one of access, availability and affordability.[22] Where one or more of these three factors is affected, the food security of vulnerable communities is imperilled.[23] Ironically, within the Global South many of the food insecure are people who work in agriculture or who are part of communities that depend upon small-scale rural farming.[24] The Special Rapporteur on the Right to Food has described rural smallholders as 'the single most important group of those who are food insecure in the world today'.[25]

---

[18] For discussion of an institutional response to the acute, short-term food crisis, see Michael Ewing-Chow, Melanie Vilarasau Slade and Liu Gehuan, Chapter 13.

[19] FAO Committee on World Food Security, *Global Strategic Framework for Food Security and Nutrition*, above n. 17, para. 15.

[20] Vulnerability to price volatility is also a feature of the problem of chronic food insecurity: see World Bank, *Poverty and Hunger: Issues and Options for Food Security in Developing Countries* (World Bank, Washington, DC, 1986).

[21] See Action Group on Erosion, Technology and Concentration (ETC Group), *Who Owns Nature? Corporate Power and the Final Frontier in the Commodification of Life* (November 2008), available at www.etcgroup.org/en/node/707.

[22] FAO, *Trade Reforms and Food Security: Conceptualizing the Linkages* (2003) p. 29, available at ftp://ftp.fao.org/docrep/fao/005/y4671e/y4671e00.pdf.

[23] *Ibid.*

[24] See De Schutter, *Seed Policies and the Right to Food: Enhancing Agrobiodiversity and Encouraging Innovation*, above n. 5, para. 24.

[25] De Schutter, *Agribusiness and the Right to Food, Report of the Special Rapporteur on the Right to Food*, UN Doc. A/HRC/13/33 (22 December 2009) para. 28.

It is this group that is most vulnerable to displacement as a result of the structural changes in the global economy created by the rules of international trade law.

The definitions of food security at an international level have varied as the concept has been debated and refined. The concept of food security first came to international prominence in the 1970s at the time of the global food crisis.[26] The initial discussion of food security focused upon problems of supply. The supply side solution was a response to the global food crisis of the 1970s and attempted to reconfigure the global food economy to avoid a recurrence of the causes of that crisis.[27] Accordingly, the 1974 World Food Security Summit defined food security as 'the availability at all times of adequate world food supplies of basic foodstuffs to sustain a steady expansion of food consumption and to offset fluctuations in production and prices'.[28] The definition offered by the 1974 World Food Security Summit effectively presupposed that the poor in the Global South would have been able to afford food once it was available for purchase. This was a crucial oversight and in 1983 the FAO brought attention to the need to consider both the demand and supply sides of the food security problem.[29] The FAO accordingly redefined food security as requiring 'that all people at all times have both physical and economic access to the basic food that they need'.[30]

In the 1990s the debate on food security broadened the concept of access to include the notion of sufficient food, food safety, nutritional balance and cultural appropriateness.[31] The 1996 World Food Summit thus expanded the concept of food security by stating that:

> Food security, at the individual, household, national, regional and global levels [is achieved] when all people, at all times, have physical, social and economic access to sufficient, safe and nutritious food to meet their dietary needs and food preferences for an active and healthy life.[32]

---

[26] FAO, *The State of Food Insecurity in the World 2009*, above n. 11, p. 26.   [27] *Ibid.*

[28] United Nations, *Report of the World Food Conference, Rome, 5–16 November 1974* (United Nations, New York, 1975).

[29] FAO Committee on World Food Security, *Director-General's Report on World Food Security: A Reappraisal of the Concepts and Approaches* (FAO, Rome, 1983).

[30] *Ibid.*   [31] FAO, *The State of Food Insecurity in the World 2009*, above n. 11, p. 27.

[32] Rome Declaration on World Food Security and World Food Summit Plan of Action, adopted at the World Food Summit, Rome, 13–17 November 1996, available at www.fao.org/docrep/003/w3613e/w3613e00.HTM.

This understanding was largely followed by the 2001 State of Food Insecurity Summit which added the concept of social access to food.[33] The FAO currently defines food security and insecurity in the following manner:

> *Food security* exists when all people, at all times, have physical, social and economic access to sufficient, safe and nutritious food which meets their dietary needs and food preferences for an active and healthy life. Household food security is the application of this concept to the family level, with individuals within households as the focus of concern.
>
> *Food insecurity* exists when people do not have adequate physical, social or economic access to food as defined above.[34]

These definitions offered by the FAO build upon the definitions developed through the World Food Security Summit process and by other commentators and institutions. It is evident that food security is a multifaceted problem and that factors such as availability and affordability, which are most likely to be affected by the operation of intellectual property rights in agriculture in the global food market, form only one aspect of the food security problem. Other concepts such as social access and cultural appropriateness are also important considerations in the overall food security problem.

The FAO has thus been actively involved in monitoring and reporting on the food security problem. Similarly, at a WTO level the 2001 Ministerial Declaration of the Doha Round made a specific reference to food security as a policy problem, acknowledging the need to make effective concessions 'so as to enable developing countries to effectively take account of their development needs, including food security'.[35]

## 3   Legal responses to food insecurity

There are both legal and political responses to food insecurity internationally. At a political level there have been widespread calls within the international community for an end to hunger. At a legal level the right to food and the notion of farmers' rights have emerged.

---

[33] FAO, *The State of Food Insecurity in the World 2001* (2002), available at www.fao.org/docrep/003/y1500e/y1500e00.htm.

[34] FAO, *Trade Reforms and Food Security*, above n. 22, p. 29; Olivier De Schutter, *Agribusiness and the Right to Food, Report of the Special Rapporteur on the Right to Food* , above n. 25.

[35] UN Doc. WT/MIN(01)/DEC/1 (20 November 2001) para. 13.

## 3.1   Right to adequate food

Article 25 of the Universal Declaration of Human Rights states:
'[e]veryone has the right to a standard of living adequate for the health
and well-being of himself and his family, including food'.[36] Principle 4 of
the United Nations Declaration on the Rights of the Child also recognises
that 'the child shall have the right to adequate nutrition'.[37] Article 24(2)
of the Convention on the Rights of the Child and Article 12(2) of the
Convention on the Elimination of All Forms of Discrimination Against
Women make reference to the right to adequate food.[38] Article 11(1) of
the International Covenant on Economic, Social and Cultural Rights
provides for a right to food,[39] as follows:

> The States Parties to the present Covenant recognize the right of every-
> one to an adequate standard of living for himself and his family,
> including adequate food, clothing and housing, and to the continuous
> improvement of living conditions. The States Parties will take appro-
> priate steps to ensure the realization of this right, recognizing to this
> effect the essential importance of international co-operation based on
> free consent.

The existence of the right to food as an obligation set out in a treaty
such as the International Covenant on Economic, Social and Cultural
Rights is highly significant as the status of the treaty, and the
widespread acceptance of the right, indicates that states are under a
clear legal obligation to protect the right to food.[40] There has also
been a proliferation of political agreements and guidelines such as the
UN Millennium Development Goals, the FAO Voluntary
Guidelines,[41] and the Five Rome Principles for Sustainable Global

---

[36] UN GAOR, 3rd sess., 1st plen. mtg., UN Doc. A/810 (9 December 1948).
[37] GA Res. 1386 (XIV) (20 November 1959) para. 4.
[38] Convention on the Elimination of All Forms of Discrimination Against Women, opened
for signature 18 December 1979, 1249 UNTS 13 (entered into force 3 September 1981);
Convention on the Rights of the Child, opened for signature 20 November 1989, 1577
UNTS 3 (entered into force 2 September 1990).
[39] International Covenant on Economic, Social and Cultural Rights, opened for signature
16 December 1966, 993 UNTS 3 (entered into force 3 January 1976), Art. 11.
[40] See Sarah Joseph, *Blame It on the WTO: A Human Rights Critique* (Oxford University
Press, Oxford, 2012) p. 182.
[41] Voluntary Guidelines to Support the Progressive Realization of the Right to
Adequate Food in the Context of National Food Security, adopted by the FAO
Council, 127th sess., November 2004, available at www.fao.org/docrep/meeting/009/
y9825e/y9825e00.htm.

Food Security.[42] However, these instruments are aspirational and do not impose any specific legal obligation.

The Committee on Economic, Social and Cultural Rights has in General Comment 12 sought to address the right to food as a matter of international law involving extra-territorial obligations.[43] The Committee has stated:

> States parties should recognize the essential role of international cooperation and comply with their commitment to take joint and separate action to achieve the full realization of the right to adequate food. In implementing this commitment, States parties should take steps to respect the enjoyment of the right to food in other countries, to protect that right, to facilitate access to food and to provide the necessary aid when required. States parties should, in international agreements whenever relevant, ensure that the right to adequate food is given due attention and consider the development of further international legal instruments to that end.[44]

The Special Rapporteur on the Right to Food further elaborated on the concept of a right to food as a response to the food security problem in his 2009 report to the UN General Assembly. He identified three levels of obligations on the part of states under Article 11 of the International Covenant on Social, Economic and Cultural Rights:[45] first, an obligation to preserve existing access to food and not to engage in measures that would jeopardise such access;[46] second, an obligation to protect the access to food;[47] and third, an obligation to 'fulfil the right to food'.[48]

However, as discussed below, these elaborations do not address the countervailing obligations under international trade law, much less define a clear relationship between the right to adequate food and

---

[42] Declaration of the World Summit on Food Security: Five Principles for Sustainable Global Food Security, adopted 16–18 November 2009, available at www.fao.org/filead min/templates/wsfs/Summit/Docs/Final_Declaration/WSFS09_Declaration.pdf.

[43] General Comment No. 12: The Right to Adequate Food, UN Doc. E/C.12/1999/11 (12 May 1999).

[44] Ibid. para. 36.

[45] See De Schutter, Seed Policies and the Right to Food: Enhancing Agrobiodiversity and Encouraging Innovation, Report of the Special Rapporteur on the Right to Food, above n. 5, para. 4.

[46] Ibid.

[47] Ibid. para. 5. In the context of seed policies the Special Rapporteur has suggested that this obligation is violated where states allow patent holders to exercise their rights in ways that detrimentally affects farmers' rights to food.

[48] Ibid. para. 6.

WTO treaties such as TRIPS and the Agreement on Agriculture.[49] The difficulty with the right to food in public international law is that it must situate itself within the wider framework of international law including international economic law. Moreover, the text of Article 11 of the International Covenant on Economic, Social and Cultural Rights does not create a series of specific obligations relating to food security. The view expressed by the Special Rapporteur on this particular point is merely aspirational rather than determinative, stating that the 'obligation to move towards the realization of the right to food must be facilitated, not impeded, by the organization of the multilateral trade regime'.[50] The Special Rapporteur has recognised the existence of the fragmentation problem, but has not advocated a solution to address it.[51]

### 3.2  Farmers' rights

The concept of farmers' rights has been advanced to counter-balance the TRIPS obligations. It has long been recognised that the impact of intellectual property rights in agriculture has conferred rights on Northern actors while the contribution of Southern farmers has been uncompensated.[52] Similarly, the impact of international trade on domestic farming has disrupted traditional farming practices and jeopardised food security.[53] Accordingly, farmers' rights have been advanced to recognise the contributions of farmers to plant genetic resources and to enhance food security.[54]

The first international instrument to effectively allude to farmers' rights is the non-binding International Undertaking on Plant Genetic Resources,[55] developed at the FAO's conference.[56] The International

---

[49] See Straub, 'Farmers in the IP Wrench', above n. 3. See also De Schutter, *International Trade in Agriculture and the Right to Food*, above n. 8; Mark Ritchie and Kristin Dawkins, 'WTO Food and Agricultural Rules: Sustainable Agriculture and the Human Right to Food' (2000) 9 *Minnesota Journal of Global Trade* 9.

[50] De Schutter, *International Trade in Agriculture and the Right to Food*, above n. 8, p. 8.

[51] *Ibid.* p. 37.   [52] Winter, 'Cultivating Farmers' Rights', above n. 7, 240.

[53] Oguamanam, 'Intellectual Property Rights in Plant Genetic Resources', above n. 6.

[54] *Revision of the International Undertaking: Issues for Consideration in Stage II: Access to Plant Genetic Resources and Farmers' Rights*, FAO Working Document No. CPGR-Ex 1/94/5 (September 1994).

[55] International Undertaking on Plant Genetic Resources for Food and Agriculture, FAO Res. 8/83 (23 November 1983).

[56] Susan Bragdon, Kathryn Garforth and John Harpalaa, 'Safeguarding Biodiversity: The Convention on Biological Diversity (CBD)' in Geoff Tansey and Tamsin Rajotte (eds.), *The Future Control of Food: A Guide to International Negotiations and Rules on*

Undertaking declares that plant genetic resources are a 'heritage of mankind', pursuing an access-based approach to plant genetic resources.[57] The Global South sought an open access approach to plant genetic resources to combat the plant breeder's rights created by the International Convention for the Protection of New Varieties of Plants (UPOV Convention).[58] The FAO subsequently adopted Resolution 5/89 in 1989,[59] that brought farmers' rights within the framework of the International Undertaking.

FAO Resolution 5/89 and the original text of the International Undertaking on Plant Genetic Resources embody two separate approaches to farmers' rights. The first is the common heritage of humankind contained in Article 1 of the International Undertaking. This benefits farmers by preserving access and diversity.[60] The second is a privilege or property-based approach linking farmers' rights to emerging intellectual property concepts such as traditional knowledge.[61] This second method provides a basis for farmers either to receive compensation for their contributions or to be afforded a concession with regard to traditional farming practices. It may also broadly be characterised as a property-based response to the imbalance between Northern intellectual property rights and rights of Southern farmers which aims to vest quasi-intellectual property rights in the latter.

FAO Resolution 5/89 itself refers to the 'purpose of ensuring full benefits to farmers, and supporting the continuation of their contributions, as well as the attainment of the overall purposes of the International Undertaking'.[62] While farmers' rights were recognised within Resolution 5/89 the instrument did not provide an explicit definition of the rights.[63] The absence of any specific definition of farmers' rights in turn impacts upon the content of the rights. Furthermore, the

*Intellectual Property, Biodiversity and Food Security* (International Development Research Centre, Ottawa, 2008) pp. 82, 83.

[57] International Undertaking, above n. 55, Art. 1.

[58] International Convention for the Protection of New Varieties of Plants, adopted 2 December 1961, 815 UNTS 89 (entered into force 10 August 1968). See Blakeney, *Intellectual Property Rights and Food Security*, above n. 5, p. 123.

[59] Farmers' Rights, FAO Res. 5/89 (11–29 November 1989).

[60] See Oguamanam, 'Agro-Biodiversity and Food Security', above n. 2.

[61] See Kirit Patel, 'Farmers' Rights over Plant Genetic Resources in the South: Challenges and Opportunities' in Frederic Erbisch and Karim Maredia (eds.), *Intellectual Property Rights in Agricultural Biotechnology* (CABI Publishers, Cambridge, MA, 2004) pp. 95, 97–8.

[62] FAO Res. 5/89, above n. 59, para. 108.      [63] *Ibid.*

non-binding nature of the International Undertaking and its lack of clarity proved an ineffective tool for achieving farmers' rights. Nevertheless, the International Undertaking did influence the drafting of the Convention on Biological Diversity (CBD),[64] and the access and benefit-sharing scheme in the International Treaty on Plant Genetic Resources for Food and Agriculture (ITPGRFA).[65]

Article 9 of ITPGRFA provides a legal recognition of the concept of farmers' rights, more effective than the International Undertaking or FAO Resolution 5/89. Broadly speaking, farmers' rights are the right to save, replant and share seeds.[66] These rights are fundamental to traditional smallholder and subsistence farming.[67] However, while there is some clarity in ITPGRFA as to the nature of farmers' rights there remains the problem of how those rights are to be given effect within international economic law treaties such as TRIPS and the Agreement on Agriculture.[68]

The Special Rapporteur on the Right to Food has demonstrated support for farmers' rights by championing this concept in his various reports. Further, the Special Rapporteur has investigated means by which the efficacy and strength of farmers' seed systems can be bolstered.[69] Similarly, the FAO has maintained strong support for the notion of farmers' rights. Indeed, as the institution within which the concept of farmers' rights was developed the FAO can be credited as the driving force behind the idea.

The intended operations of the legal responses to food security must contend with the countervailing set of obligations under the international intellectual property regime. The clear difference between the two is the former lacks the level of enforceability within intellectual property rights. This inadequacy provides security institutions such as the FAO with a

---

[64] Opened for signature 5 June 1992, 1760 UNTS 79 (entered into force 29 December 1993).
[65] Adopted 3 November 2001, 2400 UNTS 303 (entered into force 29 June 2004).
[66] *Ibid.* Art. 9.3.
[67] See Bongo Adi, 'Intellectual Property Rights in Biotechnology and the Fate of Poor Farmers' Agriculture' (2006) 9 *Journal of World Intellectual Property* 91.
[68] See Dora Schaffrin, Benjamin Gorlach and Christiane Gerstetter, *The International Treaty on Plant Genetic Resources for Food and Agriculture: Implications for Developing Countries and Interdependence with International Biodiversity and Intellectual Property Law*, Final Report IPDEV Work Package (November 2006) p. 5, available at www.ecolo gic.eu/download/projekte/1800–1849/1802/wp5_final_report.pdf.
[69] De Schutter, *Seed Policies and the Right to Food: Enhancing Agrobiodiversity and Encouraging Innovation*, above n. 5, paras. 26–41.

limited range of policy options that they can feasibly pursue. These constraints, and the impact of intellectual property rights, are mapped out next.

## 4   Legal frameworks relevant to food security

The impact that intellectual property laws have upon agriculture in the Global South is complex and multi-layered. Some of the consequences, including the correlation between intellectual property rights and rising seed prices, are quite predictable given the way markets work.[70] Other effects, such as the prevalence of bio-piracy and the loss of biodiversity, are in part facilitated by gaps in the treaty framework and the deficiencies in domestic legal regimes.[71] The following five elements illustrate the impacts of intellectual property rights on the Global South: displacement of traditional communal farming practices by corporate farming;[72] disruption of established farming practices and food systems;[73] appropriation of the genetic resources of the South by corporate interests in the North;[74] the loss of genetic diversity and diminution of genetic variety;[75] and discrimination against traditional knowledge developed within a communal setting and shared heterogeneously.[76]

The treaty framework supporting international intellectual property law underpins these five negative impacts of international intellectual

---

[70] *Ibid.* para. 24.

[71] For a discussion of bio-piracy generally, see Blakeney, *Intellectual Property Rights and Food Security*, above n. 5, pp. 97–102. See also Muriel Lightbourne, 'Of Rice and Men: An Attempt to Assess the Basmati Affair' (2005) 6 *Journal of World Intellectual Property* 875.

[72] Carmen Gonzalez, 'Institutionalizing Inequality: The WTO Agreement on Agriculture, Food Security and Developing Countries' (2002) 27 *Columbia Journal of Environmental Law* 433.

[73] Keith Aoki, *Seed Wars* (Carolina Academic Press, Durham, NC, 2008). Because of the existence of intellectual property rights, farmers in the South are unable to save and share seeds, which has been central to Southern agriculture for centuries. See Oguamanam, 'Agro-Biodiversity and Food Security', above n. 2; Winter, 'Cultivating Farmers' Rights', above n. 7.

[74] See Paul Heald, 'The Rhetoric of Biopiracy' (2003) 11 *Cardozo Journal of International and Comparative Law* 519.

[75] See Geoff Tansey, 'Global Rules, Local Needs' in Geoff Tansey and Tamsin Rajotte (eds.), *The Future Control of Food: A Guide to International Negotiations and Rules on Intellectual Property, Biodiversity and Food Security* (International Development Research Centre, Ottawa, 2008) pp. 235–44.

[76] For a discussion of traditional knowledge, see David Downes, 'How Intellectual Property Could Be a Tool to Protect Traditional Knowledge' (2000) 25 *Columbia Journal of Environmental Law* 253.

property law on global food security. Four key agreements dealing with intellectual property rights in agriculture are: (1) TRIPS; (2) UPOV; (3) ITPGRFA; and (4) CBD. The TRIPS Agreement and the UPOV provide protection for patents and plant breeders rights, respectively. In contrast, the ITPGRFA and the CBD are concerned with access, preservation and benefit sharing. The inter-relationship between these agreements is at times rather complex, involving the web of obligations facing developing countries where seed patenting and food security are serious issues. For example, the long-term consequence of the obligations created by both the TRIPS Agreement and the UPOV may well be to decrease biological diversity, contradicting the stated aims of the CBD.

### 4.1   Agreement on the Trade Related Aspects of Intellectual Property Rights

The TRIPS Agreement establishes universal minimum standards for the protection of intellectual property rights.[77] Fundamentally, TRIPS creates a dual system for protecting intellectual property rights in agriculture by requiring either patent protection or a *sui generis* system for plant genetic resources.[78] Pursuant to Article 27(1) of TRIPS, member states are required to provide a minimum standard for patent protection. Article 27 does allow for plant genetic resources to be excluded from the patent system. This is given effect in the text of Article 27(3)(b) which covers:

> plants and animals other than micro-organisms, and essentially biological processes for the production of plants or animals other than non-biological and microbiological processes. However, Members shall provide for the protection of plant varieties either by patents or by an effective *sui generis* system or by any combination thereof. The provisions of this subparagraph shall be reviewed four years after the date of entry into force of the WTO Agreement.

Arguably, Article 27(3)(b) enjoys priority over other provisions within the TRIPS Agreement that could function as a restraint on intellectual property rights. For example, Article 8 provides that member states may

---

[77] For a general discussion of the TRIPS Agreement, see e.g., Daniel Gervais, *The TRIPS Agreement: Drafting History and Analysis* (4th edn, Sweet and Maxwell, London, 2012).

[78] See TRIPS, Art. 27. See also Laurence Helfer, *Intellectual Property Rights in Plant Varieties: An Overview with Options for National Governments*, FAO Legal Papers Online No. 31 (2002), available at www.fao.org/fileadmin/user_upload/legal/docs/lpo31-2.pdf.

implement 'measures necessary to protect public health and nutrition'. However, such measures must be 'consistent with the provisions of the Agreement', which would confine Article 8 to those circumstances that are not covered by the rest of the TRIPS Agreement. This qualification within Article 8 would give Article 27(3)(b) priority in the event that a member state seeks to implement a measure under Article 27(3)(b) that would prejudice rights created under Article 8.

Similarly, Article 30 of TRIPS incorporates a modified version of the three-step test established in copyright law under the Berne Convention for the Protection of Literary and Artistic Works,[79] and applies it to patent law. As such, Article 30 sets out a cumulative test that a member state must satisfy before it can restrict the rights of patent holders or plant breeders, stating that:

> Members may provide limited exceptions to the exclusive rights conferred by a patent, provided that such exceptions do not unreasonably conflict with a normal exploitation of the patent and do not unreasonably prejudice the legitimate interests of the patent owner, taking account of the legitimate interests of third parties.

In the context of food security a situation requiring an exception to patent or *sui generis* rights might well exist. However, the restraint on commercial exploitation might be an unreasonable restraint if the right were completely denied, as would be the case if farmers' rights triumphed over patent rights. To establish an arguable case that Article 30 was satisfied a member state might need to compensate the intellectual property rights holder. This requirement might be well beyond the capabilities of most states in the Global South. Similarly, such states might lack the resources to fight the legal battle likely to ensue in the event of a challenge by another member state to any measures that a state might seek to implement under Article 30.

As the TRIPS Agreement requires member states to adopt an effective *sui generis* system it has effectively obligated states in the Global South to adopt the provisions of the 1991 version of the UPOV Convention.[80] A strict reading of Article 27(3)(b) suggests that member states to the

---

[79] Adopted 9 September 1886, as last revised 24 July 1971, 828 UNTS 221 (entered into force 15 December 1972). For a discussion of the three-step test, see Sam Ricketson, 'WIPO Study on Limitations and Exceptions of Copyright and Related Rights in the Digital Era', WIPO, Standing Committee on Copyright and Related Rights, 9th sess., Geneva, 23–27 June 2003, available at www.wipo.int/edocs/mdocs/copyright/en/sccr_9/sccr_9_7.pdf.

[80] The UPOV Convention was amended in 1991, as will be discussed below.

TRIPS Agreement could adopt a *sui generis* system of protection for plant varieties that is customised to suit to their domestic needs.[81] However, the growing number of UPOV accessions is driven by the fact that it is widely regarded by states as being TRIPS compatible and also by the use of TRIPS-plus free trade agreements concluded at the initiative of the United States requiring UPOV accession.[82] The increasing rate of UPOV accession in the Global South has the potential to have a significant impact on the food security concerns of the rural poor and other economically vulnerable members of Southern societies.[83]

### 4.2 International Convention for the Protection of New Varieties of Plants

The UPOV Convention requires member states to establish national laws to protect plant breeders' rights in plant varieties. In effect, this has delivered significant benefits to the owners of intellectual property rights in plant varieties at the cost of smallholder farmers.[84] The UPOV Convention mandates protection where the plant genetic material is new, distinct, uniform and stable.[85] A criticism made of these criteria is that it precludes farmers' varieties and is detrimental to biodiversity as it encourages uniformity within plant varieties.[86]

The 1991 version of UPOV was less amenable to farmers' rights. The 1961 UPOV provided farmers with the right to save, exchange and replant seeds.[87] Under the 1961 UPOV Convention, a farmers' rights in

---

[81] United Nations Development Program (UNDP), *Towards a Balanced 'Sui Generis' Plant Variety Regime: Guidelines to Establish a National PVP Law and an Understanding of TRIPS-plus Aspects of Plant Rights* (2008), available at www.beta.undp.org/undp/en/home/librarypage/poverty-reduction/toward-a-balanced-sui-generis-plant-variety-regime.html.

[82] See Sisule Musungu and Graham Dutfield, *Multilateral Agreements and a TRIPS-plus World: The World Intellectual Property Organization*, Quaker International Affairs Program, TRIPS Issues Papers No. 3 (2003), available at www.geneva.quno.info/pdf/WIPO(A4)final0304.pdf.

[83] UNDP, *Towards a Balanced 'Sui Generis' Plant Variety Regime*, above n. 81, pp. 9–10.

[84] Hans Haugen, Manuel Muller and Savita Narasimhan, 'Food Security and Intellectual Property Rights' in Tzen Wong and Graham Dutfield (eds.), *Intellectual Property and Human Development* (Cambridge University Press, Cambridge, 2011) pp. 103, 117. See also UNDP, *Towards a Balanced 'Sui Generis' Plant Variety Regime*, above n. 81.

[85] UPOV Convention, Art. 5.

[86] Vandana Shiva, 'The Seeds of Our Future' (1996) 4 *Development Journal* 14.

[87] See UPOV Convention, Art. 5.

plant varieties only extended to protection against commercial marketing of plant reproductive materials.[88] As such, traditional farmers' rights were protected. These crucial farmers' rights allowed smallholder farmers to provide seeds for themselves and their local communities thereby avoiding problems of food insecurity.[89] The 1991 iteration of UPOV effectively removed these rights.[90]

Given the threshold for protection under the UPOV Convention, and its clear inconsistency with the well-established practices of rural smallholders, the treaty will arguably advantage commercial agribusinesses. If this particular effect of the UPOV Convention is considered within the context of multinational agribusinesses, displacing rural smallholders and orienting production towards export markets and away from domestic food consumption, it can be argued that the treaty contributes to the overall problem of food insecurity.[91]

### 4.3 International Treaty on Plant Genetic Resources for Food and Agriculture

The ITPGRFA stands somewhat in contradistinction to the UPOV Convention. As discussed above, the ITPGRFA is concerned with preservation, conservation, access and benefit-sharing.[92] Under the ITPGRFA the FAO has sought to give effect to two separate schemes advancing the social and economic needs of the Global South. First, the ITPGRFA identifies sixty-four important crop species where an access and benefit-sharing scheme exists for research, breeding and conservation.[93] The crop species identified under Annex 1 of ITPGRFA form part of a global commons. There are eleven agricultural research centres utilising the crop species identified under the treaty and holding collections of their plant genetic resources. The access and benefit-sharing

---

[88] Ibid.

[89] Shelley Edwardson, 'Reconciling TRIPS and the Right to Food' in Thomas Cottier, Joost Pauwelyn and Elisabeth Bonanomi (eds.), Human Rights and International Trade (Oxford University Press, Oxford, 2005) pp. 382, 386–7.

[90] See UPOV Convention, Art. 15.

[91] See UNDP, Towards a Balanced 'Sui Generis' Plant Variety Regime, above n. 81, pp. 9–10.

[92] For a discussion of ITPGRFA and its interaction with TRIPS, see Charles Lawson, 'Patents and Plant Breeder's Rights over Plant Genetic Resources for Food and Agriculture' (2004) 32 Federal Law Review 107.

[93] See Christiane Gerstetter et al., 'The International Treaty on Plant Genetic Resources for Food and Agriculture within the Current Legal Regime Complex on Plant Genetic Resources' (2007) 10(3–4) Journal of World Intellectual Property 259, 263.

scheme is predicated on the existence of plant genetic resources as sovereign resources which member states share as part of a wider global commons.[94]

Second, Article 9 of ITPGRFA explicitly recognises the responsibility of governments to protect 'farmers' rights'. This provision is highly significant in that it is the first recognition of farmers' rights in a major multilateral treaty.[95] However, this development has been quite controversial and it is not at all clear how states might be able to give effect to the rights recognised in Article 9 and the rights created under the TRIPS Agreement, particularly in circumstances where the two sets of rights might conflict.

### 4.4 Convention on Biological Diversity

The CBD is also relevant to food security as the Convention seeks to protect the diversity of plant genetic resources.[96] The CBD states that one of its primary purposes is 'the conservation of biological diversity, the sustainable use of its components and the fair and equitable sharing of benefits arising out of the utilization of genetic resources'. This goal of protecting biodiversity is closely related to traditional farming practices where seeds are shared, saved and crossbred freely by farmers. In this context, the CBD presents a challenge to the 'propertisation' of plant genetic resources under the TRIPS and UPOV Agreements. However, the interaction between the CBD and the TRIPS and UPOV Agreements remains obscure.[97] Further, as with the ITPGRFA, it is still possible for a commercial actor as an intellectual property rights holder to appropriate from the commons, and by creating something new, to gain some form of intellectual property rights protection.

The multilateral benefit-sharing scheme that the ITPGRFA and the CBD sets up excludes intellectual property rights from their limited

---

[94] Michael Halewood and Kent Nnadozie, 'Giving Priority to the Commons: The International Treaty on Plant Genetic Resources for Food and Agriculture' in Geoff Tansey and Tamsin Rajotte (eds.), *The Future Control of Food: A Guide to International Negotiations and Rules on Intellectual Property, Biodiversity and Food Security* (International Development Research Centre, Ottawa, 2008) pp. 115–40.

[95] Gerstetter *et al.*, 'The International Treaty on Plant Genetic Resources for Food and Agriculture', above n. 93.

[96] See Claudio Chiarolla, 'Commodifying Agricultural Biodiversity and Development-related Issues' (2006) 9 *Journal of World Intellectual Property* 25.

[97] See Lawson, 'Patents and Plant Breeder's Rights over Plant Genetic Resources for Food and Agriculture', above n. 92.

commons. However, where a new variety or invention is created from commons material, then either patent or plant variety protection might apply. Accordingly, criticisms have been made that the TRIPS, UPOV, CBD and ITPGRFA operates as a 'double whammy' for developing countries in that the former two treaties require intellectual property protections, whereas the latter two compel the sharing of genetic resources which Northern industrialists are better placed to transform and exploit through either patents or plant variety protections.[98]

## 5   Critiquing the institutional response to the problem

Having regard to the impact of intellectual property rights on agriculture and the overall treaty framework, it is tempting to characterise the problem as one of displacement of rural smallholders and communities in the Global South as a product of the global economic system, which is in turn sustained by legal rules supporting that system. If this analysis is accepted as an adequate explanation of the problem of intellectual property rights and food security, then the solution lies in part in reforming international trade law.

This section offers three critiques of the FAO's response to the problem of food security. While the FAO is the primary focus of critique, reference is also made in this section to the Special Rapporteur as the policy responses offered by the latter are closely aligned to those of the former. These critiques are confined to the responses the FAO promulgated with respect to the legal aspects of food security. Both the FAO and the UN Special Rapporteur have canvassed non-law solutions in response to the problem of food security, but an analysis of those measures is beyond the scope of this chapter.

The first critique concerns the advantage, viewed from the perspective of enforceability, that the TRIPS Agreement enjoys over all other treaties in its place within the WTO treaty regime. The WTO agreements, including TRIPS, are enforced via the Dispute Settlement Understanding, which is in turn administered by the WTO's Dispute Settlement Body, whereas other treaties such as the ITPGRFA and the CBD are not.[99] Those agreements that are more sensitive to the needs of rural smallholders and communities in the Global South have less scope

---

[98] See Haugen et al., 'Food Security and Intellectual Property Rights', above n. 84.
[99] Though the ITPGRFA does mandate access and benefit-sharing schemes which should benefit rural communities.

for enforcement than the TRIPS Agreement and the UPOV Convention. The entire treaty framework supports a system that increasingly privileges private and sovereign rights over communal rights. In this sense, the 'constitutionalisation' of international trade law has the effect of relegating other sources of law to 'soft law'.[100] In the absence of an enforcement mechanism, and in the face of potentially inconsistent legal obligations to be reconciled within the more powerful WTO regime, these 'soft law' rules must yield to 'hard law'.

This conflict deprives the FAO of a useful role in norm creation. In substance the problem is that of a 'rule gap' within the TRIPS/WTO framework. Indeed, if the TRIPS Agreement is placed squarely within the overall policy context of food security, then it should be apparent that one of the fundamental problems is the lack of flexibility for states around intellectual property law. There is no rule within the TRIPS Agreement that prescribes any type of proportionality test between the obligation to protect intellectual property rights and the right to food or farmers' rights. Yet, it is clear there must be circumstances under which intellectual property rights protection may be suspended or limited in order to protect some other vital social good. Article XX of the GATT Agreement provides a mechanism wherein the free trade in goods can be suspended to protect human rights, safety, the environment and other public concerns.[101] Article 30 of TRIPS also provides a narrow framework for exception. However, as discussed above, Article 30 is too narrow in its scope to accommodate the concerns of food security and there has been little, if any, state practice with respect to the application of Article 30.

It is unclear whether the FAO has conceded the difficulty in amending the TRIPS Agreement and is instead pursuing those policy solutions falling short of any amendment. Many of the policy responses articulated by the FAO seek to work 'within' the established legal architecture and economic system. In this sense, it is apparent that the responses of the FAO signal an acceptance of the status quo. With the TRIPS Agreement having primacy within the international legal architecture, it is pertinent to explore reforms within the context of the TRIPS Agreement and the WTO rather than to seek redress in other forums, even though this approach faces considerable difficulty

---

[100] See Koskenniemi and Leimo, 'Fragmentation of International Law', above n. 1, 571.

[101] See e.g., *United States – Import Prohibition of Certain Shrimp and Shrimp Products*, WT/DSB/AB/R (1998), Appellate Body Report, paras. 156–7.

involving protracted negotiations and debates between the Global North and South within the WTO.

The second critique is that the FAO has not articulated a convincing response to the problem of fragmentation. Just as fragmentation poses a threat to the legitimacy of international law, this problem undermines the effectiveness of the FAO as a security institution. In this context the continued advocacy of the right to food, by both the Special Rapporteur and the FAO, adds to the incoherency stemming from the fragmentation problem. Where the existence of fragmentation creates a conflict between two separate legal regimes, which cannot be solved by legal interpretation, then the best resolution is the creation of a type of 'bridging' rule between the two regimes such as proportionality, as discussed above.

Articulating the case for the existence of a legal right, however compelling that right may be given the genuine needs of the Global South, is a fruitless endeavour if the right does not have a proper legal framework within which it can be realised. Similarly, creating a further series of obligations for states in international law, which would in its realisation bring those states into conflict with their obligations under TRIPS and TRIPS-plus free trade agreements, is a task doomed to failure unless some rule of proportionality is adopted to bridge the two legal regimes, allowing one to be favoured over the other as circumstances demand. The Special Rapporteur has attempted to argue that the right to food is a peremptory norm to be given precedence over the WTO.[102] While it is beyond the scope of this chapter to explore this particular argument it does appear to face significant hurdles in terms of acceptance by states.

The FAO is most certainly aware of the legal problems presented by the TRIPS Agreement. In a study commissioned by the FAO, potential revisions to intellectual property rights agreements affecting agriculture were canvassed.[103] Of particular relevance was the discussion of how the treaties could be amended to allow for flexible government decision-making where intellectual property rights and other societal objectives conflict.[104] The notion of 'policy balancing' is sensible,[105] but as noted above it must have an enforceable legal effect if it is to have any meaningful role in tackling the food security problem.

---

[102] See De Schutter, *International Trade in Agriculture and the Right to Food*, above n. 8, p. 35.
[103] See Helfer, *Intellectual Property Rights in Plant Varieties*, above n. 78.
[104] *Ibid.* p. 86.   [105] *Ibid.*

Similarly, the Special Rapporteur appears to support treaty interpretation as one solution to the fragmentation problem. In a recent briefing note the Special Rapporteur called for a review of the compatibility between WTO rules and the global and national food security initiatives.[106] The Special Rapporteur paid specific attention to the Agreement on Agriculture and explored options for promoting food security within that Agreement. However, the Special Rapporteur noted that the text of the Agreement on Agriculture did not explicitly mention food security whilst the Preamble did.[107] Recasting the rules in light of an established legal obligation will have little effect if the meaning of those rules is already settled. In effect, the fragmentation problem here plays to the legitimacy of the FAO in that the legalisation of the WTO, and the movement of intellectual property rights protection into that framework, has somewhat marginalised the FAO in its role as a security institution charged with administering food security. What then emerges is a problem of institutional legitimacy spurred on by competing legal regimes. The existence of competing, enforceable rules that undermine the right to food stymies the development of the FAO as an effective security institution.

The third critique is that the advocacy of farmers' rights as a form of quasi-intellectual property is a type of 'norm collision'.[108] It represents a move by the FAO to fit the interests of its constituents into the legal paradigm created by the WTO and by Northern intellectual property regimes. Farmers' rights are an emerging norm based upon a long, historical tradition of shared Southern agricultural practices. However, the established intellectual property rules are countervailing norms. The need to resolve this conflict reflects the challenge faced by many security institutions, as alluded to in the Introduction to this volume.

Yet, this resolution is problematic. Recasting farmers' rights as traditional knowledge and then promoting the latter as Southern intellectual property rights represents a property-type response to a policy

---

[106] De Schutter, *International Trade in Agriculture and the Right to Food*, above n. 8, p. 5.
[107] *Ibid.* p. 15.
[108] For a discussion of norm collision in the context of fragmentation, see Bruno Simma and Dirk Pulkowski, 'Of the Planets and the Universe: Self-Contained Regimes in International Law' (2006) 17 *European Journal of International Law* 483; Andreas Fischer-Lescano and Gunther Teubner, 'Regime-Collisions: The Vain Search for Legal Unity in the Fragmentation of Global Law' (2004) 25 *Michigan Journal of International Law* 999.

problem that is broader than intellectual property rights. Simply creating new property rights for one set of stakeholders does not adequately address the problem if the fundamental cause of the problem is that the existence of one set of intellectual property rights is crowding out one of the key stakeholders in the agricultural market. In other words, the essence of the problem is that intellectual property rights in seeds effectively threatens the long-term viability of rural smallholders. This occurs not simply because the farmers cannot replant and save seeds, but also because in order to finance their purchase of seeds they must enter the debt cycle.

Giving those rural smallholders intellectual property rights may well protect those innovations that they themselves have created or which are derived from communal traditional knowledge. This solution might well be an effective counter-measure against bio-piracy notwithstanding the fact that a scheme must be in place to assist largely illiterate and poorly educated Southern farmers to access the registration and enforcement systems for intellectual property rights. However, this solution does not account for the manner in which intellectual property rights in seeds disrupts traditional farming practices. It does not account for the fact that subsidised agriculture in the Global North, primarily the United States and Europe, can from time to time depress staple food prices in the Global South, thereby damaging the livelihoods of vulnerable farmers in the Global South. It does not account for the incentives that are currently in place for transnational agricultural companies to take over farmland in the Global South and to re-orient food production there towards global food markets and away from local needs.[109]

It is for these reasons that the property-type response is quite flawed. The correct response to the dislocation created by intellectual property rights in agriculture is not necessarily to create more intellectual property. Though it is beyond the scope of this chapter to outline a solution to the entire problem, it is imperative that the FAO attempts to establish a rational relationship between the right to food and the obligations created by Article 27 of the TRIPS Agreement at a treaty level.

---

[109] See Olivier De Schutter, *The World Trade Organization and the Post-Global Food Crisis Agenda*, Briefing Note 05, UN Special Rapporteur on the Right to Food (November 2011), available at www.srfood.org/images/stories/pdf/otherdocuments/20111116_brief ing_note_05_en.pdf.

## 6   Conclusion

The developed states of the North brought intellectual property rights into international trade law largely by promising the states in the Global South that trade in agriculture would be liberalised. However, in the Agreement on Agriculture, inadequate measures were put in place to prevent subsidies to Northern farmers. Consequently, over-production of staple crops in the Global North has led to surpluses, further depressing world food prices and adversely affecting the trade balances of the states in the Global South. The North-South divide over agriculture mirrored the divide over intellectual property rights. Indeed, the North's impetus for moving intellectual property rights out of the World Intellectual Property Organization and into the WTO stemmed from the deadlock created by the North-South divide. Regrettably, the Doha Round of the WTO demonstrated that, despite changing the forum, all the same players from the North and South have done little to resolve the fundamental impasse between them. This means that any amendment to the text of the TRIPS Agreement is barely achievable at present. The prospect that the situation may improve seems quite remote. However, unless the legal framework changes, the FAO is forced to function with a restricted set of options. This clearly limits the role that this body can play as a security institution.

# 13

# Rice is life: regional food security, trade rules and the ASEAN Plus Three Emergency Rice Reserve

MICHAEL EWING-CHOW, MELANIE VILARASAU SLADE
AND LIU GEHUAN

## 1 Introduction

In an Asian context, food security is in practice synonymous with 'rice security', and precisely for this reason rice is a highly sensitive and politicised product in the region. In April 2008, the price of rice doubled within a month. Some Asian countries responded to this rice price spike by restricting the export of rice. Public distress at the high prices and anxiety about the rice supply led to riots and protests. Then in May 2008, Cyclone Nargis caused one of the worst natural disasters in Myanmar's history, creating a food emergency. This chapter focuses on acute regional food security crises and considers the legal challenges to the initiatives in Asia when creating an institutional response to address them.

The Association of Southeast Asian Nations (ASEAN)'s institutional response to this food security crisis was the ASEAN Plus Three Emergency Rice Reserve (APTERR).[1] In order to place this initiative in its appropriate security context, sections 2 and 3 explore the background leading to the creation of the APTERR, which lies firmly in the 2008 food crisis, and its effect on the availability of rice in particular. Section 4 then examines the extent to which the international trade law framework in place within the World Trade Organization (WTO) helped or hindered its development. In doing so, this chapter unravels the interaction between a regional stockpile initiative as an institutional

---

[1] ASEAN Plus Three Emergency Rice Reserve Agreement, adopted 7 October 2011, available at www.scribd.com/doc/97411992/APTERR-Agreement.

response to a security challenge, and the 'competing' institutional framework of the WTO centred on trade liberalisation.

## 2 Food security as a security challenge in Southeast Asia

As Dilan Thampapillai's preceding chapter in this volume observes, there are two different forms of food insecurity: (1) chronic food insecurity; and (2) more acute, short-term food insecurity. The APTERR aims to deal with chronic food insecurity by way of collective action, as well as providing a rapid response mechanism to address acute short-term food insecurity.[2] This chapter focuses on the APTERR's primary role in addressing the latter form of food insecurity by providing, as its name indicates, an 'emergency' rice reserve.

In the Asian context, as indicated in the title of this chapter, rice is synonymous with life. Over 90 per cent of the world's rice is produced and consumed in the Asian region by six countries: the People's Republic of China (PRC), India, Indonesia, Bangladesh, Vietnam and Japan.[3] In the ASEAN Plus Three region, referring to ASEAN plus the PRC, Japan and the Republic of Korea, which is the particular focus of this chapter, rice is the main staple and the ASEAN Plus Three region is also the main producer and exporter of rice. Food security for most of the Asian states depends on the safe and uninterrupted supply and distribution of rice.

In 2008, an unexpected and dramatic surge in the price of rice occurred. According to the Food and Agricultural Organization (FAO) Rice Price Update in January 2010, there was an increase of 9 per cent from 2005 to 2006, 17.5 per cent from 2006 to 2007, and 83 per cent from 2007 to 2008.[4]

On 24 February 2011, the *Economist* issued a Special Report on Food. The lead article of this Special Report specifically addressed the issue of food crises and observed that:

---

[2] See ASEAN, 'Integrated Food Security (AIFS) Framework and the Strategic Plan of Action on ASEAN Food Security (SPA-FS): 2009–2013', 14th ASEAN Summit, Cha-am, Thailand, 1 March 2009, available at www.gafspfund.org/sites/gafspfund.org/files/Docu ments/Cambodia_11_of_16_REGIONAL_STRATEGY_ASEAN_Integrated_Food_Secu rity_Framework.pdf (in particular APTERR's dual role under 'Component 1: Food Security and Emergency Shortage/Relief' and 'Component 2: Sustainable Food Trade Development', pp. 10–11).

[3] Alias Bin Abdullah, Shoichi Ito and Kelali Adhana, *Estimate of Rice Consumption in Asian Countries and the World Towards 2050* (Tottori University, Japan, 2005), available at http://worldfood.apionet.or.jp/alias.pdf.

[4] See FAO, 'Rice Price Update' (January 2010), available at www.scribd.com/doc/82308953/The-FAO-Rice-Price-Update-January-2010.

[t]he main reasons for high prices are temporary: drought in Russia and Argentina; floods in Canada and Pakistan; export bans by countries determined to maintain their own supplies, whatever the cost to others; panic buying by importers spooked into restocking their grain reserves.[5]

Whilst unfavourable climatic conditions may generally be considered to be the immediate cause of the 2008 food price spike and the subsequent incidents of high prices, the underlying causes of the dramatic spike in rice price are quite distinct from those behind price rises in other commodities over the same period. Indeed, David Dawe and Tom Slayton argued that government policies and panic were the only plausible explanation for why rice prices increased so much faster than maize and wheat prices.[6] As they pointed out, the rice market did not need to contend with new policy challenges, such as biofuel policies, and was not as affected by climatic irregularities as the maize and wheat markets were. Also, rice is barely traded on futures markets, which arguably influenced the maize and wheat markets. They concluded that '[t]he thin nature of the world rice market, and the large role that governments play in it, make the world rice market more vulnerable to such occurrences'.[7]

Outright export bans had the most detrimental impact during the 2008 crisis. India's decision in October 2007 to ban rice exports, except for basmati, was quickly followed by Vietnam and other major players, with an immediate impact on prices. This then led to panic purchases of rice, especially by large rice importers such as the Philippines, which further aggravated the situation. Speculators, sensing a crisis, sought to gain from the situation by accumulating and holding stocks, which led to even higher prices.[8] As Alexander Sarris identified, uncoordinated individualistic policies by each government resulted in destabilising the global markets, which in turn provided further justifications for national food security concerns and overreactions.[9]

---

[5] 'The future of food: crisis prevention: what is causing food prices to soar and what can be done about it?', *The Economist*, 24 February 2011, available at www.economist.com/node/18229412.

[6] David Dawe and Tom Slayton, 'The World Rice Market Crisis of 2007–2008' in David Dawe (ed.), *The Rice Crisis: Markets, Policies and Food Security* (FAO and Earthscan, London and Washington, DC, 2010) p. 15.

[7] *Ibid.* p. 18.

[8] Hamid R. Alavi *et al., Trusting Trade and the Private Sector for Food Security in Southeast Asia* (World Bank, Washington, DC, 2012) p. 73.

[9] Alexander Sarris, 'Trade-related Policies to Ensure Food (Rice) Security in Asia' in David Dawe (ed.), *The Rice Crisis: Markets, Policies and Food Security* (FAO and Earthscan, London and Washington, DC, 2010) p. 82.

## 3   Evolving regional food security institutions

As examined above, the cause of the dramatic price volatility experienced in 2008 lies firmly with national governments and their choice of policy response. These policies, and the way in which the APTERR institution has sought to address them in the event of acute rice shortage, are explored below.

### 3.1   ASEAN response to the 2008 food security crisis

In response to the 2008 crisis, the immediate priority of ASEAN countries was to mitigate the rise in price. Decisions were made quickly to put in place the most expedient methods of alleviating the effects of food price spike on domestic consumers.[10] ASEAN governments responded to the 2008 crisis by: (1) market interventions to limit the rise of food prices (for example, export bans);[11] (2) market interventions to control inflation (for example, price fixing); and (3) assistance to consumers through safety nets and support to producers (for example, agricultural subsidies).[12] In most cases, those short-term policy responses, whilst adapted to deal with the food price spike, were incorporated into longer-term policy frameworks and were driven by long-term policy objectives, such as national food security and stabilisation of farm revenues.[13]

These measures, when assessed on a regional level, aggravated the rice price spike. In fact, the International Food Policy Research Institute

---

[10] See Dawe and Slayton, 'The World Rice Market Crisis of 2007–2008', above n. 6, p. 4.

[11] Article XI of GATT prohibits import bans and restrictions. However, as affirmed in *China – Exportation of Raw Materials*, Article XI:2(a) permits the application of restrictions or prohibitions for a limited period of time to address 'critical shortage' of 'essential products' when considered in light of 'the particular circumstances faced by that Member at the time when a Member applies a restriction or prohibition': *China – Measures related to the Exportation of Various Raw Materials (China – Exportation of Raw Materials)*, WTO Doc. WT/DS394/R, WT/DS395/R, WT/DS398/R (2011) paras. 7.275–7.276. The Panel decision was upheld by the Appellate Body Report of 30 January 2012. It is understood that this exemption would apply to short-term export bans during a food security crisis: see Siddhartha Mitra and Tim Josling, *Agricultural Export Restrictions: Welfare Implications and Trade Disciplines*, IPC Position Paper, Agricultural and Rural Development Policy Series (International Food and Agricultural Trade Policy Council, 2009) p. 13, available at http://agritrade.org/documents/ExportRestrictions_final.pdf.

[12] Darryl Jones and Andrzej Kwiecinski, *Policy Responses in Emerging Economies to International Agricultural Commodity Price Surges*, OECD Food, Agriculture and Fisheries Papers No. 34 (2010) p. 5, available at http://dx.doi.org/10.1787/5km6c61f v40w-en.

[13] *Ibid.*

observed that 'three-quarters of the increase in the price of rice occurred in 2008 – almost certainly because of adverse policy responses, such as export bans, from some major exporters'.[14] Export restrictions by individual countries, aimed to prevent the transmission of rising international prices onto their domestic markets, inevitably reduced the world supply in cases where those countries were also food producers, pushing food prices to rise even higher.[15] Price fixing also distorted the market, suppressing incentives for domestic food producers to increase production or for consumers to reduce their consumption.[16] Agricultural subsidies in the form of trade distorting market price support or payments linked to production were not only inefficient in terms of bolstering farm incomes,[17] but also severely affected the ability of developing country farmers to sell their products at fair prices.[18] This caused structural problems, as international food security relies on the continued ability of subsidised farming regions to produce sufficient amounts of food. Nevertheless, the discussion at the Organisation for Economic Co-operation and Development (OECD) Global Forum on Agriculture in 2009 suggested that in the absence of new longer-term policies to manage price crisis, similar short-term policy responses could be expected in the future.[19]

---

[14] Derek Headey and Shenggen Fan, *Reflections on the Global Food Crisis* (International Food Policy Research Institute, Washington, DC, 2010) p. 32, available at www.ifpri.org/sites/default/files/publications/rr165.pdf.

[15] See generally, Dawe and Slayton, 'The World Rice Market Crisis of 2007–2008', above n. 6; Mitra and Josling, *Agricultural Export Restrictions*, above n. 11.

[16] An Organisation for Economic Co-operation and Development (OECD) study on the potential market effects of price fixing found that the world food price spike was some 2–3 per cent higher than it would have been without this policy. See Wyatt Thompson and Grégoire Tallard, *Potential Market Effects of Selected Policy Options in Emerging Economies to Address Future Commodity Price Surges*, OECD Food, Agriculture and Fisheries Papers No. 35 (2010) p. 17, available at http://dx.doi.org/10.1787/5km658j3r85b-en.

[17] According to OECD figures, '[o]f every $1 in price support, only $0.25 ends up in the farmer's pocket as extra income. The rest is absorbed by higher land prices, fertiliser and feed costs and other factors': OECD, 'The Doha Development Round of Trade Negotiations: Understanding the Issues', available at www.oecd.org/general/thedohadevelopmentroundoftradenegotiationsunderstandingtheissues.htm.

[18] See especially, Xinshen Diao, Eugenio Diaz-Bonilla and Sherman Robinson, *How Much Does It Hurt? The Impact of Agricultural Trade Policies on Developing Countries* (International Food Policy Research Institute, Washington, DC, 2003), available at www.ifpri.org/sites/default/files/pubs/media/trade/trade.pdf.

[19] See OECD, *Global Forum on Agriculture 2009* (29–30 June 2009), available at www.oecd.org/tad/events/global-forum-agriculture-2009.htm.

## 3.2   ASEAN Plus Three Emergency Rice Reserve

Prior to the 2008 crisis, ASEAN had already been collaborating with the ASEAN Plus Three states on emergency rice reserve systems in the region. The collaboration took the form of a project called the East Asia Emergency Rice Reserve (EAERR), which the Japanese government funded for four years until March 2010.[20] Unfortunately, however, as the processes and triggers of the EAERR were limited and vague, neither the 2007–2008 spike in rice price nor the Cyclone Nargis food emergency triggered the EAERR. As a result, regional states decided to improve food security in the region by developing the APTERR as a permanent institution for the purpose of maintaining and distributing rice in times of emergency for the benefit of the populations of regional states.

The APTERR institution is at its heart (as its name indicates) a rice reserve. The institution was proposed as part of a wider ASEAN Integrated Food Security Framework (AIFS) agreed upon by the ASEAN leaders in 2009.[21] A basic agreement exists in the form of the APTERR Agreement,[22] the terms of which are set out below, however many of the details of the APTERR's operation remain to be settled.

Currently, it is proposed that APTERR members pledge specific volumes of rice per year for the regional stockpile by way of 'earmarked emergency rice reserves' for a virtual stockpile to provide a capital fund. It will also convert the APTERR into a working body coordinating the implementation of the rice reserve system.[23] Each member will then have the responsibility to maintain that earmarked reserve and, upon a request from another APTERR member experiencing a trigger event, will provide that requesting member with rice from the earmarked reserve in accordance with the terms of the APTERR Agreement.[24] The APTERR will also maintain a small physical stockpile of rice contributed by donor nations and international food aid programs.[25]

---

[20] For details, see e.g., Elenita Daño and Elpidio Peria, *Emergency or Expediency? A Study of Emergency Rice Reserve Schemes in Asia* (Asian Partnership for the Development of Human Resources in Rural Asia, 2007), available at http://asiadhrra.org/wordpress/200 7/12/16/emergency-or-expediency-a-study-of-emergency-rice-reserve-schemes-in-asia/.

[21] ASEAN, 14th ASEAN Summit, above n. 2.

[22] Above n. 1. See also APTERR website, www.apterr.org/.

[23] Roehlano M. Briones *et al.*, *Climate Change and Price Volatility: Can We Count on the ASEAN Plus Three Emergency Rice Reserve?*, Asian Development Bank Sustainable Development Working Paper Series No. 24 (2012) pp. 3–4, available at www10.iadb.or g/intal/intalcdi/PE/2012/12264.pdf.

[24] *Ibid.*   [25] *Ibid.*

This regional food security model embodied in the APTERR has the advantage of ensuring that at least 800,000 tons of regional rice will not be subject to export restrictions amongst the APTERR members. This will also help reduce the rice price spikes as it limits the opportunity for speculators to take advantage of a panic by ensuring that there will be enough rice to meet short-term needs.

The Secretariat will manage the rice reserve on behalf of the APTERR states. If a stockpiled rice reserve is to be maintained, a legal mechanism will have to be created for APTERR states to transfer the title of the rice to the Secretariat. Otherwise, even if the trigger for the rice aid as stipulated in the Agreement takes place and the APTERR country in need of rice submits the request to the Secretariat, the Secretariat would not be able to authorise the transfer or sale of the rice. However, there were critical questions to be considered by the participating countries at the very initial stage of planning, which included, among others: where would the rice originate and how should it be released and distributed? The answer to each of these questions is crucial to the APTERR's effectiveness and also to the assessment of the APTERR's compatibility with WTO law.[26] The creation of a regional rice reserve, operating to coordinate rice supply in the case of food emergency in the ASEAN Plus Three region, could, without careful structuring, collide with WTO rules.

## 4   WTO rules: guiding framework or regime collision?

The application of WTO rules to food security initiatives is seen as a controversy between trade law and human rights.[27] However, as will be examined in detail below, in certain circumstances compliance with WTO rules could be seen more as a virtuous discipline than as an undue restriction. By establishing an internationally recognised and agreed framework within which to operate, requiring transparent reporting at the WTO level, the WTO framework allows for wide discretion in the implementation of food security policies whilst curbing excessive ones that could lead to 'beggar thy neighbour' policies. It also curtails

---

[26] At the time when APTERR was agreed, all the APTERR members were WTO members with the exception of Lao PDR, which became a WTO member by accession on 2 February 2013.

[27] See especially, Oliver De Schutter, *The World Trade Organization and the Post-Global Food Crisis Agenda: Putting Food Security in the International Trade System, Activity Report,* UN Special Rapporteur on the Right to Food (November 2011), available at www. wto.org/english/news_e/news11_e/deschutter_2011_e.pdf.

the ability of states to defer important decisions on the details of the proposed scheme, potentially leaving scope for disagreements, disputes and even rent-seeking behaviour. The remainder of this chapter assesses whether the WTO rules are indeed an obstacle to the establishment and implementation of the APTERR.

### 4.1    Origin of the rice

During the negotiations that the principal author of this chapter was privy to, there was considerable debate as to where the rice for stockpiling (whether virtual or physical) should originate. Some APTERR members proposed that the rice for the emergency reserve originate only from APTERR member states, whereas others envisaged imports exclusively from non-APTERR member states. While there may have been different policy considerations supporting these two proposals, any restriction imposed on the origin of rice for the emergency rice reserve would violate the non-discrimination principle under WTO rules.

Article I of the General Agreement on Tariffs and Trade (GATT) requires that 'with respect to all rules and formalities in connection with importation and exportation', all advantages granted to products originating from any other country shall be accorded immediately and unconditionally to the like product originating from all the other WTO members.[28] The principle of non-discrimination, as reflected in the most favoured nation and national treatment obligations, may well be regarded as the most fundamental principle of the WTO trade regime.[29] As the WTO Appellate Body emphasised in *Canada –Auto*,[30] 'the words of Article I:1 refer not to some advantages granted "with respect to" the subjects that fall within the defined scope of the Article, but to "any

---

[28] General Agreement on Tariffs and Trade, opened for signature 15 April 1994, 1867 UNTS 190 (entered into force 1 January 1995), Art. 1. For the original version of the GATT, see General Agreement on Tariffs and Trade, opened for signature 30 October 1947, 55 UNTS 187 (entered into force 29 July 1948). Note that the 1947 GATT has been subsumed into the 1994 GATT.

[29] The Preamble to the Marrakesh Agreement Establishing the World Trade Organization proclaims 'the elimination of discriminatory treatment in international trade relations' as one of the chief objectives of the WTO. See Marrakesh Agreement Establishing the World Trade Organization, opened for signature 15 April 1994, 1867 UNTS 3 (entered into force 1 January 1995), Preamble cl. 3.

[30] *Canada – Certain Measures affecting the Automotive Industry*, WTO Doc. WT/DS139/ AB/R WT/DS142/AB/R (2000), Appellate Body Report, para. 78.

advantage"; not to some products, but to "any product"; and not to like products from some other Members, but to like products originating in or destined for "all other" Members'.[31]

If the APTERR were to specify the origin of rice for stockpiling, this would result in discrimination in favour of rice produced in either APTERR member states or non-APTERR states. This is because, in order to fulfil the obligations to contribute to the rice reserve, member states would have to purchase on a discriminatory basis a certain amount of rice as stipulated in the APTERR Agreement from either member states or non-member states. It not only imposes certain obligations on the APTERR members to discriminate, but also gives certain benefits or advantages to the rice exporting countries, as a set amount of rice export is almost guaranteed.

Relevantly, Article XX(j) of GATT allows WTO members to adopt measures which deviate from their WTO obligations when the measures are 'essential to the acquisition or distribution of products in general or local short supply' provided that such deviation be temporary and that 'all contracting parties are entitled to an equitable share of the international supply of such products'. Article XX(j) could be relied upon for rice in general or local short supply. If the origin of rice for the rice reserve is restricted only to APTERR member states, in the situations where the APTERR is triggered because of local short supply, for example, during natural disasters, the member countries may argue that by giving preference to rice from APTERR members, it may reduce the time of transportation in emergencies. In the event of an emergency, time is of essential importance and regional supply chains would be the most effective way of providing such a supply, especially since Thailand and Vietnam, both APTERR members, are the biggest rice exporters in the world and in 2008, 91 per cent of the rice imports in ASEAN were sourced from the region.[32]

It is less clear how the other condition of Article XX(j) – 'all contracting parties are entitled to an equitable share of the international supply of such products' – should be interpreted. It has been suggested that this requirement should be understood with three elements: first, it applies to WTO members only; second, if a country is 'entitled to' a product, it has a just claim to that product; and third, each individual

[31] *Ibid.* para. 79.

[32] Riza Bernabe, 'The Need for a Rice Reserve Mechanism in Southeast Asia', paper presented at the Asian Farmers' Association, 31 May 2010, available at www.iatp.org/files/451_2_107542.pdf.

member may not be entitled to a strictly equal share of a product.[33] The text of Article XX suggests that the requirement under Article XX(j) is not to guarantee each individual to have an actual equal share of the international supply, but rather to prevent member states from implementing certain measures justified by a shortage of supply which would prevent specific WTO members from having access to the particular product. Indeed, Padideh Ala'i observes that the drafting history of Article XX more generally indicates that 'participants in the multilateral trading system have always recognized that there are equally legitimate interests and policies other than "free trade" that governments often must pursue'.[34] Given the small size of the APTERR which initially will have an earmarked quantity of rice of less than 800,000 tons,[35] it would be hard to argue that, relative to total rice production and consumption figures,[36] the APTERR would impact on other members' right to an equitable share of trade in rice.

However, as clarified in *United States – Gasoline*,[37] all exceptions under Article XX of GATT must meet a two-tiered test: first, the measure at issue must come under one or another of the particular exceptions (paragraphs (a) to (j)) listed under Article XX; second, it must satisfy the requirements imposed by the opening clauses of Article XX *(chapeau)*,[38] which provides that 'such measures are not applied in a manner which would constitute a means of arbitrary or unjustifiable discrimination between states where the same conditions prevail or a disguised restriction on international trade'. The next question is therefore whether the APTERR measure would meet the *chapeau* requirements.

The *chapeau* prohibits arbitrary or unjustifiable discrimination between countries where the same conditions prevail. APTERR members may argue that the conditions in APTERR members and non-APTERR members are not the same, in terms of distance, the rice that

---

[33] Ben Sharp, 'Responding Internationally to a Resource Crisis Interpreting the GATT Article XX(j) Short Supply Exception' (2010) 15 *Drake Journal of Agricultural Law* 259.

[34] See Padideh Ala'i, 'Free Trade or Sustainable Development? An Analysis of the WTO Appellate Body's Shift to a More Balanced Approach to Trade Liberalization' (1999) 14 *American University International Law Review* 1129, 1136.

[35] Briones *et al.*, *Climate Change and Price Volatility*, above n. 23.

[36] See statistics in Abdullah, Ito and Adhana, *Estimate of Rice Consumption in Asian Countries and the World Towards 2050*, above n. 3.

[37] *United States – Standards for Reformulated and Conventional Gasoline*, WTO Doc. WT/DS2/AB/R (1996), Appellate Body Report (*US – Gasoline*).

[38] *Ibid.* 22.

they grow, and the variety of rice that the people usually consume. It may still be difficult to argue that discrimination would be indispensible for general or local short supply, as in most cases food security and emergency crises would not necessitate policies requiring choices about the origin of foodstuff. However, the WTO jurisprudence on Article XX has recognised the right to regulate so long as that regulation does not arbitrarily discriminate.[39] Indeed, it has even been suggested that these exceptions have become dominant over time so that not many 'pure' non-discrimination rules remain in the global trading system.[40] This means that the APTERR is required to ensure that any potential discrimination is reasoned in accordance with Article XX and that in all cases it is not arbitrary.

In addition to GATT, the restriction on the origin of rice may violate the Government Purchase Agreement (GPA).[41] The GPA is to date the only legally binding agreement in the WTO focusing on the subject of government procurement. It is a plurilateral treaty, which is not mandatory for all WTO members. It applies to government procurement by contracting parties and is based on the principles of openness, transparency and non-discrimination. Japan, the Republic of Korea and Singapore are members of the GPA, whereas the People's Republic of China is in the process of acceding to the GPA.

GPA members are required to publish the procurement notice and treat the bidders on a non-discriminatory basis. Article III of the GPA requires that any favourable treatment accorded to the products, services and suppliers of any contracting party of the GPA shall be 'immediately and unconditionally' accorded to the other contracting parties. Therefore, if Japan, the Republic of Korea and Singapore are required to purchase physical stocks of rice pursuant to the APTERR, the non-discrimination rule in the GPA would require them to purchase those stocks on an origin neutral basis.[42] As the GPA is a plurilateral agreement among contracting parties it only binds parties to the GPA to the

---

[39] See especially, *ibid.* 22–9; *United States – Import Prohibition of Certain Shrimp and Shrimp Products*, WTO Doc. WT/DS58/AB/R (1998), Appellate Body Report, paras. 177–86.

[40] T. N. Srinivasan, 'Non-Discrimination in GATT/WTO: Was There Anything to Begin with and Is There Anything Left?' (2005) 4 *World Trade Review* 69.

[41] Agreement on Government Procurement, 1915 UNTS 103, Annex 4(b) of the Marrakesh Agreement Establishing the World Trade Organization, above n. 29.

[42] Article VIII of the GPA also provides that '[i]n the process of qualifying suppliers, entities shall not discriminate among suppliers of other Parties or between domestic suppliers and suppliers of other Parties'.

extent that they have obligations owed to other parties of the GPA. If the APTERR favours rice produced in APTERR states only, it would be discriminatory against other states outside of the APTERR where they are a party to the GPA. Conversely, if the discrimination is against rice produced in the APTERR states then the APTERR members party to the GPA, namely Japan, the Republic of Korea and Singapore, would be entitled to complain against such purchases.

Article XV of the GPA provides an exception for limited tendering if the discrimination is 'strictly necessary ... for reasons of extreme urgency brought about by events unforeseeable', provided that 'such measures are not applied in a manner which would constitute a means of arbitrary or unjustifiable discrimination between states where the same conditions prevail or a disguised restriction on international trade'. However, it is hard to envisage a situation in which this form of origin non-neutral discriminatory measure could be justified as 'strictly necessary' due to 'extreme urgency brought about by events unforeseeable'.

Article XXIII of the GPA, which is similar to Article XX of GATT, allows for discriminatory measures for the purpose of protecting human, animal or plant life or health, as long as 'such measures are not applied in a manner which would constitute a means of arbitrary or unjustifiable discrimination between states where the same conditions prevail or a disguised restriction on international trade'. To the extent that the APTERR mechanism is designed to protect human life, it is arguable that discriminatory rice purchases are necessary to ensure a quick response to an emergency or disaster, although proving that the measure is not arbitrary or unjustifiable discrimination may be more difficult.

### 4.2 Release and distribution of the rice

The pricing scheme in the rice reserve mechanism was not integrated into the previous EAERR, with its implementation left to bilateral negotiations. With regard to the APTERR, it has been proposed that there should be three types of triggers:

(a) Tier 1: a release from earmarked rice reserves under commercial terms;
(b) Tier 2: a release from earmarked rice reserves under long-term loan or grant; and
(c) Tier 3: a release from stockpiled rice reserves (in the case of acute and urgent emergency; or under the circumstance where stockpiled rice

is not utilised within at least twelve months, as food aid for poverty alleviation or the malnourishment eradication programme).

The purpose of Tier 1 and 2 triggers is to provide greater stability of supply. If Tier 1 or Tier 2 is triggered, and the distribution is not carefully managed, APTERR members may be found to be in breach of their existing trade obligations. On the other hand, if Tier 3 is defined in too restrictive terms, such that the rice reserve may only be relied upon in extreme emergency situations, the whole rice reserve mechanism may never be put into actual use. This is because a government may never publicly admit that it is experiencing an emergency so as to avoid exacerbating the crisis situation already developing by causing domestic panic buying or undermining its standing in the region.

If the rice is to be provided on a commercial basis, that mechanism will have to determine the price for the rice. However, if the price is set at a non-market price, this could result in violation of the Agreement on Subsidies and Countervailing Measures (ASCM), which prohibits subsidies if they cause an adverse effect on other WTO members' industry. The ASCM prohibits 'subsidies contingent, in law or fact, whether solely or as one of several conditions, upon export performance'.[43] This comprehensive prohibition on export subsidies is stricter than the regulation of domestic subsidies (subsidies that are not contingent on export performance).[44]

According to Article 1.1 of the ASCM, a subsidy is deemed to exist if there is a financial contribution by a government or any public body, or if there is any form of income or price support and a benefit is thereby conferred. An important point to note is that there has to be both a financial contribution from government and the conferral of a benefit in order for a practice to be treated as a subsidy. If the rice price is set lower than the prevailing market price, this could cause an adverse effect on rice producers in other WTO member states. This could occur if an APTERR member bought rice from its rice producers at the market rate so as to add to the stockpile but was then required to sell the rice below the market rate under the APTERR. Such a measure could have the effect of subsidising their rice producers by facilitating the sale of their rice to

---

[43] Agreement on Subsidies and Countervailing Measures (ASCM), 1867 UNTS 14, Annex 1A of the Marrakesh Agreement Establishing the World Trade Organization, above n. 29, Art. 3.1(a).

[44] Andrew Green and Michael Trebilcock, 'Enforcing WTO Obligations: What Can We Learn from Export Subsidies?' (2007) 10 *Journal of International Economic Law* 653.

other APTERR members and therefore posing serious prejudice to other WTO members' rice producers in their sale of rice to those APTERR states in violation of Article 6.3(d) of the ASCM.[45] Given that the ASCM does not have an exception clause comparable to Article XX of GATT, food security measures under the APTERR will be considered a prohibited subsidy, as long as it causes serious prejudice or a threat thereof to the interests of another WTO member.

Some of the APTERR member states, such as Thailand and Vietnam, are traditionally major rice exporters. Therefore, they may be able to demonstrate with statistics that no increased world market share will result from the APTERR arrangement. As explained above,[46] nonetheless, subsidies should be avoided as they have adverse effects on the long-term global supply of food. The current APTERR proposal avoids such subsidies by introducing a price mechanism in the form of a forward contract based on an average price over a pre-agreed period. As such, the mechanism does not discriminate between APTERR producers and non-APTERR producers. Further, this avoids affecting the market prices for rice, thus allowing for prices to gradually rise whilst preventing rice price spikes.

Legal issues concerning subsidies also arise when stockpiled rice is released as food aid for poverty alleviation or malnourishment eradication programme under Tier 3. Article 10.4 of the Agreement on Agriculture provides that:

> Members donors of international food aid shall ensure: (a) that the provision of international food aid is not tied directly or indirectly to commercial exports of agricultural products to recipient countries; (b) that international food aid transactions, including bilateral food aid which is monetized, shall be carried out in accordance with the FAO 'Principles of Surplus Disposal and Consultative Obligations', including, where appropriate, the system of Usual Marketing Requirements (UMRs); and (c) that such aid shall be provided to the extent possible in fully grant form or on terms no less concessional than those provided for in Article IV of the Food Aid Convention 1986.[47]

---

[45] Article 6.3(d) of the ASCM provides that serious prejudice may arise when the effect of the subsidy is an increase in the world market share of the subsidising member in a particular subsidised primary product or commodity as compared to the average share it had during the previous period of three years and this increase follows a consistent trend over a period when subsidies have been granted.

[46] See above nn. 18 and 19 and accompanying text.

[47] Agreement on Agriculture, 1867 UNTS 410, Annex 1A of the Marrakesh Agreement Establishing the World Trade Organization, above n. 29.

While Article 16 of the Agreement on Agriculture does provide for some flexibility with regard to the implementation of the Marrakesh Decision on Measures concerning the Possible Negative Effects of the Reform Programme on Least-Developed and Net Food-Importing Developing Countries,[48] the specific rules and procedures for implementation are yet to be agreed upon. Further, among APTERR states, only Cambodia, Lao PDR and Myanmar are listed as least developed countries and none currently qualifies as a net food-importing developing country.[49] Therefore, when considering the release of stockpiled rice as food aid, the obligation to comply with the prohibition on subsidies under the WTO agreements must be taken into account and food aid in the form of grant would be the preferred method of distribution.

Further, the ASCM prohibits internal transport and freight charges on export shipments on terms more favourable than for domestic shipments.[50] Therefore, when the APTERR states arrange shipments of rice to the importing states, the internal transport and freight charges should still remain to avoid possible violation of the ASCM. However, an argument may be made that in a Tier 3 situation, since it is an emergency situation requiring an immediate response, no long-term adverse effect could be caused by waiving internal transport and freight charges on domestic industry of other WTO members.

## 5   Conclusion

Amartya Sen suggests that famine is not just a consequence of nature, but also an avoidable economic and political catastrophe.[51] If this is the case, then the solutions to current and future food security challenges will have to be institutionalised. The difficulty lies with the process of balancing

---

[48] WTO, 'Decision on Measures concerning the Possible Negative Effects of the Reform Programme on Least-Developed and Net Food-Importing Developing Countries', available at www.wto.org/english/docs_e/legal_e/35-dag_e.htm.

[49] 'Least developed countries' are defined as 'least developed countries as recognised by the Economic and Social Council of the United Nations'. Under the first criterion, forty-eight least developed countries defined as such by the United Nations are automatically contained in the list. 'Net food-importing developing countries' are defined as 'any developing country Member of the WTO which was a net importer of basic foodstuffs in any three years of the most recent five-year period for which data are available and which notifies the Committee of its decision to be listed as a Net Food-Importing Developing Country for the purpose of the decision'.

[50] ASCM, Annex I(c).

[51] Amartya Sen, *Poverty and Famines: An Essay on Entitlement and Deprivation* (Oxford University Press, Oxford, 1981).

between food security measures to protect domestic populations from severe food shortages and price spikes, and the international trade law rules discouraging protectionism that endangers global or 'collective' food security.

WTO rules are intended to discourage protectionist trade measures and policies. At present, however, numerous distortions of free trade exist in the global food system, which together with the threat of export bans leaves countries with little choice but to use every policy option available to them in order to protect the food security of their own population, regardless of the consequences on a global scale. While the *Economist* article above suggested that '[a]n agreement to limit trade bans might make exporters think twice before disrupting world markets',[52] considering the political sensitivities, it is unlikely that a multilateral agreement against export bans will be forthcoming. Instead, regional arrangements, as this chapter has explored, with the development of a regional emergency rice reserve, may be a viable solution, particularly for price sensitive staples such as rice.

Food security institutions such as the APTERR can devise mechanisms to deal with sudden shortages and price spikes without disrupting global trade. As demonstrated in this chapter, while WTO rules necessarily restrain the shape of the APTERR, this does not automatically make APTERR less effective as a result. Far from constituting a 'collision' between institutional frameworks, the WTO framework simply requires the APTERR to achieve a certain level of detail. This will hopefully avoid the pitfalls of the previous EAERR, the terms of which were too vague to ensure that it was triggered when an emergency occurred. Building confidence in the international trade system through regional institutions such as the APTERR, which enhance security of food supply, may be the most effective method of ensuring long-term collective food security at the global level.

---

[52] See above n. 5.

# 14

# Legal challenges to cyber security institutions

OTTAVIO QUIRICO

## 1 Introduction

The past decade may be portrayed as a period of growing cyber threats and a time of increasing cyber insecurity. In fact, given that societies increasingly rely on information systems and the Internet, cyberspace – a virtual and interactive, non-physical environment created through computer networks accessible regardless of geographic location – has become a vulnerable landscape.[1] Thus, governmental authorities around the world have launched cyber security programmes. For example, the Australian Cyber Security Strategy defines the roles, responsibilities and policies of Australian intelligence, cyber and policing agencies to protect Australian Internet users.[2] The United States (US) funded the Trustworthy Cyber Infrastructure for the Power Grid through its Departments of Energy and Homeland Security, which aims to secure new 'smart meters' against hackers' attacks.[3] Similarly, the Infocomm Security Masterplan in Singapore seeks to defend national critical infrastructures, such as finance, energy, water and telecommunications, against cyber attacks.[4] The European Union considers cyber terrorist threats the highest priority for the security of critical energy infrastructure.[5]

---

[1] See e.g., Bruce Averill and Eric A. M. Luiijf, 'Canvassing the Cyber Security Landscape: Why Energy Companies Need to Pay Attention' (2010) *Journal of Energy Security* (online) paras. 2–5.

[2] See Australian Government Attorney General's Department, 'Australian Cyber Security Strategy', available at www.ag.gov.au/Cybersecurity/Pages/default.aspx.

[3] See www.tcipg.org.

[4] See Infocomm Development Authority of Singapore, 'Infocomm Security Masterplan', available at www.ida.gov.sg.

[5] Council Directive (EC) 2008/114 of 8 December 2008 on the identification and designation of European critical infrastructures and the assessment of the need to improve their protection [2008] OJ L345/75 (23 December 2008) Preamble, para. 3.

In cyber space, the private sector plays a crucial role.[6] For example, the American Gas Association formulated specific recommendations in order to encourage the gas industry to protect its cyber infrastructure from possible attacks.[7] Potentially, any technician working with cyber technology may become a security agent, which seems a necessity rather than an option, given that cyber attacks are likely to target both private and public civil infrastructures.[8] Thus, enterprises specialising in cyber security already operate globally.[9] For instance, in the US, 70 per cent of the intelligence budget is spent with private cyber security providers,[10] and the 2003 National Strategy to Secure Cyberspace notably highlighted that 'the private sector is best equipped and structured to respond to an evolving cyber threat'.[11] The People's Republic of China has reportedly been developing its cyber military capabilities in close relationship with private industry.[12]

This chapter examines the development of cyber security institutions, by focusing on the role of private cyber security providers. The analysis concentrates on rules governing resort to force under domestic law enforcement regulation and the international law of armed conflict, and their application to cyber defence operations within and across national borders. To that end, this chapter first examines different conceptions of cyber security, concentrating on the notion of the use of force and its relevance to the understanding of cyber security. It then outlines the current stage of institutional development for cyber

[6] See Gregory J. Rattray, *Strategic Warfare in Cyberspace* (MIT, Cambridge, MA, 2001) pp. 363–4.

[7] See American Gas Association, *Cryptographic Protection of SCADA Communications*, AGA Report No. 12 (2006), available at www.scadahacker.com/library/Documents/Stan dards/AGA%20-%20Cryptographic%20Protection%20of%20SCADA%20Communicati ons%20-%2012%20Part1.pdf.

[8] Cf. Susan W. Brenner and Donald C. Clarke, 'Civilians in Cyberwarfare: Conscripts' (2010) 43 *Vanderbilt Journal of Transnational Law* 1011; Tim Shorrock, *Spies for Hire: The Secret World of Intelligence Outsourcing* (Simon and Schuster, New York, 2009) p. 174. For a critique of the privatisation of cyber warfare as a necessity rather than an option, see Lucas Lixinski, *Legal Implications of the Privatization of Cyber Warfare* (European University Institute, Florence, 2010) pp. 11–15.

[9] See e.g., Lofty Perch, 'A Global Leader in SCADA and Industrial Control Systems Cyber Security', available at www.loftyperch.com/index.php/use_lang/EN/page/1.html?path= use_lang/EN/page/1.

[10] See, Shorrock, *Spies for Hire*, above n. 8, pp. 18–19.

[11] White House, *The National Strategy to Secure Cyberspace* (2003) p. ix, available at www. us-cert.gov/reading_room/cyberspace_strategy.pdf.

[12] Cf. Daniel Ventre, 'China's Strategy for Information Warfare: A Focus on Energy' (2010) *Journal of Energy Security* (online) para. 5.

security in both public and private realms. Finally, the chapter discusses the major challenges posed to cyber operations by private cyber security institutions through the application of relevant rules on law enforcement and the law of armed conflict.

## 2   The notion of cyber security

The expansion and world-wide utilisation of computers and informatics translated the notion of the use of force from the physical world into cyberspace. Hostile cyber conduct may take place either through remote access, when a computer or network is compromised at distance, or through close access, when a computer or network is compromised via local installation of malicious hardware or software.[13] Depending on how the use of force is defined, some types of hostile cyber conduct may amount to the use of force making it subject to legal regulation under domestic or international law.

### 2.1   Cyber attacks: a typology

Hostile cyber action against a computer system or network can take two different forms, according to its direct effects. The first type is cyber attack, which has destructive direct effects and consists of deliberate actions altering or destroying computer systems and networks or information and programmes transiting them. The aim of a cyber attack is to make the adversary's computer systems and networks unavailable or untrustworthy. This can be achieved, for instance, through the deletion of data by means of computer viruses. The second type is cyber espionage, which has non-destructive direct effects and involves operations aiming to map the web by obtaining confidential information transiting an adversary's computer system or network. Cyber espionage permits the accumulation of information, which is not only a form of hostility in itself, but might also be exploited to enhance further kinetic or cyber attacks.[14] For example, a computer virus may be launched to search the hard disk of any infected computer and collect files containing relevant information.[15]

---

[13] Herbert S. Lin, 'Offensive Cyber Operations and the Use of Force' (2010) 4 *Journal of National Security Law and Policy* 63, 66.

[14] Cf. Dhanashree Nagre and Priyanka Warade, *Cyber Terrorism: Vulnerabilities and Policy Issues* (2011) p. 37, available at www.scribd.com/doc/54213935/Final-Report-Dnagre-Pwarade.

[15] See Lin, 'Offensive Cyber Operations and the Use of Force', above n. 13, 63–4.

Compromises caused by hostile cyber conduct are not limited to cyberspace but may also have indirect effects on connected physical entities, which are usually the ultimate aim of hostile action.[16] A chief example is critical infrastructure that ensures the distribution of electricity from generation to consumption, given that electrical grids are controlled via tools (generators, valves, compressors and pumps) connected to computer systems and networks. Vulnerability mainly stems from the supervisory control and data acquisition (SCADA) systems that command dispersed devices, as well as the fact that most companies rely upon the same computers and networks for internal operations and external business.[17] Further vulnerability derives from the fact that energy industries are developing wireless modems and direct Internet access to core control systems.[18] Finally, a crucial component of energy systems in the twenty-first century is smart grid technology, including digital mechanisms useful for energy saving, emission reduction and system reliability; improving the digital connectivity of grids increases their vulnerability to cyber attacks.[19] The accrued dependence of critical energy infrastructure on cyber technology also enables attacks on installations that were traditionally considered inaccessible, in particular pipelines located in deep water.[20]

## 2.2   Cyber attacks and the use of force

Scholars have elaborated on distinct analytical models of unconventional use of force, including cyber action.[21] Herbert Lin, for example, argues that in order to establish if hostile cyber conduct is tantamount to physical use of force, an assessment should be made as to whether the damage caused by cyber action could have been achieved by way of kinetic action, based on a teleological approach.[22] According to this view, a cyber

---

[16] Cf. Arie J. Schaap, 'Cyberwarfare Operations: Development and Use under International Law' (2009) 64 *Air Force Law Review* 121, 133.

[17] Averill and Luiijf, 'Canvassing the Cyber Security Landscape', above n. 1, para. 2.

[18] *Ibid.* para. 3.    [19] *Ibid.* para. 4.

[20] Cf. Bruce Averill, 'Oil, Gas and Maritime Security' (2010) 6 *Journal of International Peace Operations* 14.

[21] See e.g., Russell Buchan, 'Cyber Attacks: Unlawful Uses of Force or Prohibited Interventions?' (2012) 17 *Journal of Conflict and Security Law* 212; David E. Graham, 'Cyber Threats and the Law of War' (2010) *Journal of National Security Law and Policy* 87, 91.

[22] Lin, 'Offensive Cyber Operations and the Use of Force', above n. 13, 73.

attack conducted for the purpose of disabling a power grid, for example, would be tantamount to the use of force, given that the destruction of the power grid could be achieved by bombing a power station or using some other forms of kinetic action. Therefore, as a general principle, it has to be acknowledged that the criteria may well differ depending on the legal context in which the question is raised. It may be argued that the equivalence between cyber action and physical use of force can be established by reference to the relationship with the physical world. If the indirect effects resulting from a cyber attack involve physical damage as can be produced by kinetic means, the cyber attack is likely to be considered use of force. From this perspective, cyber action amounts to physical force whenever it results in destruction of property, loss of life and loss of well-being in the physical world.[23]

In contrast, the comparison is more problematic when hostile cyber conduct only produces non-physical adverse effects in cyberspace. However, among other possibilities cyber attacks may be comprehensively defined as 'attacks that destroy computerized nodes for critical infrastructures, such as the Internet, telecommunications, or the electric power grid'.[24] Thus, since virtual space is part of the 'critical infrastructure' of a state, any purely virtual cyber attack could be considered an attack on national security.[25] Furthermore, even if cyber conduct does not interfere with the operation of physical infrastructure, it might nonetheless have a negative psychological impact on society. For instance, when Russian hackers allegedly penetrated the computer system of a nuclear power plant near St Petersburg in May 2008, the website was taken offline and rumours of 'radioactive emissions' were spread.[26] Although the cyber attack did not affect the operation of the plant, it caused considerable anxiety among nearby residents.

The wider notion of cyber security encompasses not only cyber attacks, but also cyber espionage. Even though collecting information through hostile cyber action does not necessarily entail adverse effects, it might provide essential support for further cyber and kinetic attacks. Thus, for instance, cyber espionage identifying the vulnerability

---

[23] Cf. Lixinski, *Legal Implications of the Privatization of Cyber Warfare*, above n. 8, p. 6.
[24] See Nagre and Warade, *Cyber Terrorism: Vulnerabilities and Policy Issues*, above n. 14, p. 6.
[25] Critical Infrastructures Protection Act 2001, 42 USC s. 5195c(e) (2006).
[26] Cf. Averill and Luiijf, 'Canvassing the Cyber Security Landscape', above n. 1, para. 1.

of a nuclear power plant may constitute a preliminary step to the perpetration of a cyber or kinetic attack. The causal link seems therefore sufficiently strong in order to consider cyber espionage part of the use of force. Within cyberspace, the link is sometimes so strong that it is almost impossible to separate cyber espionage from cyber attacks. Such is the case when an offensive cyber operation introduces a two-tier software agent into the targeted system, the first one being used for cyber espionage (i.e. monitoring data traffic through the system and transmitting information to a collection point), and the second one for cyber attack, awaiting instructions to operate.[27]

### 3   Institutional design for cyber security

There is currently no international public institution comprehensively governing cyberspace. However, activities, whether hostile or peaceful, are regulated by domestic institutions in each state, with increased attempts among concerned states to coordinate their action. In particular, Article 5A of the International Telecommunications Regulation adopted in Dubai in December 2012 provides that member states endeavour to ensure the 'security', 'robustness', 'avoidance of technical harm' and 'harmonious development' of international telecommunication services.[28] More specifically, the 2001 Budapest Convention on Cybercrime,[29] which has been drafted by the Council of Europe in partnership with the US and Japan among other states, obliges states parties to adopt measures necessary to criminalise under domestic law offences against the confidentiality, integrity and availability of computer data and systems.[30] Such offences include 'access to the whole or any part of a computer system without right' when committed 'by infringing security measures';[31] 'interception without right ... of non-public transmissions of computer data';[32] 'damaging, deletion, deterioration, alteration or suppression of computer data without right';[33] and 'serious hindering without right of the functioning of a computer

---

[27] Cf. Lin, 'Offensive Cyber Operations and the Use of Force', above n. 13, 78.
[28] International Telecommunication Union, Final Acts of the World Conference on International Telecommunications, Dubai, 3–14 December 2012, available at www.itu.int/en/wcit-12/Documents/final-acts-wcit-12.pdf.
[29] Opened for signature 23 November 2001, CETS No. 185 (entered into force 1 July 2004).
[30] *Ibid.* Preamble and Title 1.   [31] *Ibid.* Art. 2   [32] *Ibid.* Art. 3.   [33] *Ibid.* Art. 4.

system by inputting, transmitting, damaging, deleting, deteriorating, altering or suppressing computer data'.[34]

However, individual hostile cyber conduct may take place not only domestically, but also across national borders. With regard to cross-border hostilities, cyberspace is particularly resistant to regulation, leaving much room for interpretation of what constitutes the use of force in the context of public international law, involving the action of both individuals and states.[35] In cases where large-scale hostile attacks against a state's cyber infrastructures originate from an unidentifiable source, significant challenges are posed to the application of traditional rules of international law on the use of force. In fact, it is difficult to ascertain whether attacks are attributable to another state and sufficiently grave to trigger the right of self-defence.[36]

Finally, cyber attacks may take place within the context of international or non-international armed conflicts, where a conflict may be sparked by large-scale cyber attacks,[37] or simply by kinetic armed attacks coordinated with cyber attacks.[38] Since there is no public institution regulating the use of cyberspace during warfare, the use of cyber operations as a method or means of warfare should be subject to applicable rules of the law of armed conflict.[39]

Currently, there are approximately 200 national and regional Computer Emergency Response Teams (CERTs), including the Asia Pacific Computer Emergency Response Team and the European Collaboration of Security Incident Response Teams, which promote the legitimate use of information technology and organise responses to cyber security emergencies.[40] CERTs focus on identifying vulnerabilities and fostering communication between security vendors, users and

---

[34] *Ibid.* Art. 5.

[35] Antonio Segura-Serrano, 'Internet Regulation and the Role of International Law' (2006) 10 *Max Planck Yearbook of United Nations Law* 191, 193.

[36] For discussion, see Mary E. O'Connell, 'Cyber Security without Cyber War' (2012) 2 *Journal of Conflict and Security Law* 187, 191–4.

[37] Michael Schmitt, *Tallinn Manual on the International Law Applicable to Cyber Warfare* (Cambridge University Press, Cambridge, 2013) Pt A, rr. 9 and 13.

[38] For a detailed analysis, see Michael Schmitt, 'Classification of Cyber Conflict' (2012) 17 *Journal of Conflict and Security Law* 245.

[39] See Schmitt, *Tallinn Manual on the International Law Applicable to Cyber Warfare*, above n. 37, Pt B.

[40] See e.g., the website of the CERT Division of the Software Engineering Institute, Carnegie Mellon University, www.cert.org/meet_cert.

private organisations. In particular, they seek to prevent and respond to cyber threats, especially through communication between security teams. Although the majority of CERTs are non-governmental in nature, they tend to provide information to and collaborate with governmental agencies, for instance, via incident reporting, thus facilitating public action and investigation.

The most specialised global cyber security institution is the International Multilateral Partnership Against Cyber Threats (IMPACT), which is a public-private partnership operating as the cyber security executing arm of the International Telecommunication Union.[41] This organisation recognises that responses to dispersed cyber threats must largely rely on the private sector. At the global level, IMPACT offers a real-time warning network to 191 member states and software allowing security organisations to pool resources and coordinate their defence, whilst a clear divide of functions is still maintained between public and private actors.

Overall, although a coherent institutional framework is absent, cooperation is envisaged between private cyber security institutions and public institutions. For instance, internationally the Group of Eight (G8) and INTERPOL established a network of contacts to 'help national governments identify the source of terrorist communications, investigate threats and prevent future attacks'.[42] Domestically, for example, Australian Internet service providers have adopted an Industry Code of Practice on Cyber Security, aiming to improve cyber security throughout Australia,[43] and public-private partnerships are being established for mitigating cyber threats.[44]

With regard to cyber warfare contexts, the US Air Force created the Fifty-seventh Information Aggression Squadron, based in Nevada, while the US Army established the Network Warfare Battalion.[45] The North

---

[41] For details, see the website of the International Multilateral Partnership Against Cyber Threats (IMPACT), www.impact-alliance.org/home/index.html.

[42] 'G8 24/7 High Tech Contact Point', available at www.cybersecuritycooperation.org/mor edocuments/24%20Hour%20Network/24%207%20invitation.pdf.

[43] See Internet Industry Association, *Internet Industry Code of Practice* (1 June 2010), available at http://iia.net.au/userfiles/iiacybersecuritycode_implementation_dec2010.pdf.

[44] Cf. David M. Cook, *Mitigating Cyber-Threats through Public-Private Partnerships: Low Cost Governance with High Impact Returns*, Edith Cowan University Research Online (2010), available at http://ro.ecu.edu.au/cgi/viewcontent.cgi?article=1002&context=icr.

[45] See Corey Kilgannon and Noam Cohen, 'Cadets trade the trenches for firewalls', *New York Times*, 11 May 2009, p. A1.

Atlantic Treaty Organization (NATO) set up a technical response arm in the aftermath of the coordinated cyber attacks which in 2007, targeted websites of Estonian organisations, including the Estonian Parliament, banks, ministries, newspapers and broadcasters, in the midst of the country's dispute with Russia over the relocation of the Bronze Soldier and war graves in Tallinn. The Cooperative Cyber Defence Centre of Excellence (CCDCOE) programme is responsible for training NATO member states through cyber attack exercises, and supports NATO in the event of an international cyber attack.[46] However, not all NATO states joined the CCDCOE programme, since several countries preferred to rely on their own military cyber defence capabilities and their own strategies for cyber warfare. In the People's Republic of China, private units comprising both military and civilian personnel from the industry have reportedly been established in different provinces, with knowledge of information, electronic, psychological and network warfare.[47]

## 4  Legal challenges to cyber security institutions: role of private cyber security providers

In the last two decades, states have developed the tendency to rely increasingly on private providers in the performance of physical security and military operations involving the use of force that once fell exclusively within the public domain. Resort to private security providers is widespread chiefly in the US, but is rapidly extending to other countries, such as Canada and the United Kingdom.[48] This phenomenon has prompted national and international regulation in both public and private domains; for instance, the Draft Convention on the Regulation, Oversight and Monitoring of Private Military and Security Companies,[49] Voluntary

---

[46] See the website of the NATO's Cooperative Cyber Defence Centre of Excellence, www.ccdcoe.org/11.html.

[47] Ventre, 'China's Strategy for Information Warfare', above n. 12, para. 4.

[48] See generally, James Cockayne and Emily S. Mears, *Private Military and Security Companies: A Framework for Regulation* (International Peace Institute, New York, 2009); Kyle M. Ballard, 'The Privatisation of Military Affairs: A Historical Look into the Evolution of the Private Military Industry' in Thomas Jäger and Gerhard Kümmel (eds.), *Private Military and Security Companies* (VS Verlag, Wiesbaden, 2007) p. 37.

[49] *Report of the Working Group on the Use of Mercenaries as a Means of Violating Human Rights and Impeding the Exercise of the Right of Peoples to Self-Determination*, UN Doc. A/HRC/15/25 (2 July 2010) Annex.

Principles on Security and Human Rights,[50] and the International Code of Conduct for Private Security Service Providers.[51]

By shifting the debate to virtual reality, whether and to what extent private security providers can undertake hostile cyber action is a question involving significant legal issues because, owning most cyber infrastructure, civilians and private companies are naturally involved in critical cyber security operations.[52] The legality of forcible operations by private cyber security providers must be assessed according to relevant rules of domestic law enforcement and the international law of armed conflict.[53]

### 4.1   Law enforcement

The United Nations (UN) Principles on the Use of Force and Firearms by Law Enforcement Officials provide that law enforcement officials may resort to force only in self-defence, for preventive purposes or to avert serious crimes involving grave threats to life.[54] In times of peace, private security providers are allowed to use armed force in self-defence, according to the relevant rules of domestic criminal law of the state concerned. Adapting the UN Principles *mutatis mutandis*, the

---

[50] The Voluntary Principles are the main self-regulatory initiative targeting private security companies active in the energy sector and have been commonly followed by states, non-governmental organisations and private companies. The text of the Principles is available at www.voluntaryprinciples.org/files/voluntary_principles_english.pdf.

[51] This is the paramount overarching private initiative in the field of private security services in general, established under the auspices of the Swiss Confederation and adopted by numerous private security companies. The text of the Code is available at www.icoc-psp.org.

[52] Stewart Baker *et al.*, *In the Crossfire: Critical Infrastructure in the Age of Cyber War* (McAfee, Santa Clara, CA, 2009) p. 31.

[53] Cf. Gregory D. Grove, 'Cyber-Attacks and International Law' (2000) 42 *Survival* 89.

[54] Basic Principles on the Use of Force and Firearms by Law Enforcement Officials, adopted at the Eighth UN Congress on the Prevention of Crime and the Treatment of Offenders, Havana, Cuba, 27 August to 7 September 1990, available at www.unrol.org/doc.aspx?d=2246. Principle 9 provides: 'Law enforcement officials shall not use firearms against persons except in *self-defence* or *defence of others* against the imminent threat of death or serious injury, to *prevent the perpetration of a particularly serious crime involving grave threat to life*, to arrest a person presenting such a danger and resisting their authority, or to prevent his or her escape, and only when less extreme means are insufficient to achieve these objectives. In any event, intentional lethal use of firearms may only be made when strictly unavoidable in order to protect life' (emphasis added).

Voluntary Principles on Security and Human Rights provide that private security providers may act exclusively for defensive and preventive purposes.[55] The International Code of Conduct for Private Security Service Providers adopts the same approach by using the language of the UN Principles.[56] In particular, reference to 'crime prevention' in these documents appears to broaden the strict limits of self-defence, since 'crime prevention' is not encompassed by self-defence, but is regarded as alternative conduct, as distinct from 'self-defence'. This approach permits offensive use of force to prevent a potentially wide range of conduct, including terrorist attacks.[57]

While private regulatory initiatives within the field of security usually tend to complement public regulation,[58] in this case private regulation exceeds a purely coordinating function and, by adapting public law enforcement rules, entails the extension to private providers of legal authority exclusively entrusted to public officials. However, given that private regulation is not fully consistent with public law enforcement rules, it is doubtful whether private regulation may alone justify resort to force beyond the scope of self-defence.

Private cyber security providers should nonetheless be allowed to act at least in self-defence to counter cyber attacks aimed at destabilising computer systems controlling physical infrastructure.[59] In this respect,

---

[55] Voluntary Principles on Security and Human Rights, above n. 50. Principle 6 provides that: 'Consistent with their function, private security should provide only *preventative* and *defensive services* and should not engage in activities exclusively the responsibility of state military or law enforcement authorities. Companies should designate services, technology and equipment capable of offensive and defensive purposes as being for defensive use only' (emphasis added).

[56] International Code of Conduct for Private Security Service Providers, above n. 51. Principle 31 states that: 'Signatory Companies will require that their Personnel not use firearms against persons except in *self-defence* or *defence of others* against the imminent threat of death or serious injury, or to *prevent the perpetration of a particularly serious crime involving grave threat to life*' (emphasis added).

[57] See Michael J. Glennon and Serge Sur, *Terrorism and International Law* (Martinus Nijhoff, The Hague, 2006) p. 13; Maura Conway, 'What Is Cyberterrorism?' (2002) 101 *Current History* 436; Mark M. Pollitt, *Cyber Terrorism: Fact or Fancy?* (FBI Laboratory, Washington, DC, 2000); Rosalin Higgins, 'The General International Law of Terrorism' in Rosalin Higgins and Maurice Flory (eds.), *International Law and Terrorism* (Routledge, London/New York, 1997) pp. 13, 28.

[58] See Carsten Hoppe and Ottavio Quirico, 'Codes of Conduct for Private Military and Security Companies: The State of Self-Regulation in the Industry' in Francesco Francioni and Natalino Ronzitti (eds.), *War by Contract* (Oxford University Press, Oxford, 2011) p. 362. See also Chie Kojima, Chapter 4.

[59] See Susan W. Brenner, *Cyber Threats: The Emerging Fault Lines of the Nation State* (Oxford University Press, Oxford, 2009) pp. 3–5.

it is arguable that an imminent threat may be conceived of with respect to the life and integrity of the society benefiting from cyber infrastructure rather than the life of private cyber security providers themselves,[60] at least in those legal systems where self-defence encompasses the defence not only of themselves, but also of others and property from threats posed by means of force, though the use of lethal force is often restricted.[61] Thus, in some countries, private cyber security providers should, as a minimum, be able to lawfully respond by forcible means to cyber attacks seeking, for example, to disrupt the operation of a nuclear power plant.[62] On the other hand, special pre-emptive powers, such as investigation, seizure and arrest,[63] seem unlikely to be justified in cyberspace, in light of existing general rules on the use of force, unless otherwise provided.[64] Furthermore, cyber counter-attacks are problematic if hostile cyber conduct is not deemed to amount to the use of force according to the afore-mentioned effect-based approach to cyber security, as discussed above in section 2.

Thus, specifically in accordance with the effect-based approach to cyber security, the better view would be that private cyber security institutions can effectively react to hostile cyber attacks only in self-defence as applied in the domestic criminal law of the state where they are operating from. Those cyber security 'counter-measures', such as alteration or suppression of targeted computer data or serious hindering of the functioning of a hostile computer system, should not be deemed lawful unless they are covered by self-defence. This is so especially if counter-measures are ultimately intended or expected to result in physical damage, such as loss of life or destruction of property.

---

[60] Cf. Brenner and Clarke, 'Civilians in Cyberwarfare: Conscripts', above n. 8, 1032.

[61] See Criminal Code Act 1995 (Cth), s. 10.4 (providing that '(2) A person carries out conduct in self-defence if and only if he or she believes the conduct is necessary: (a) to defend himself or herself or another person; or ... (c) to protect property from unlawful appropriation, destruction, damage or interference ... and the conduct is a reasonable response in the circumstances as he or she perceives them'). However, under s. 10.3, force that involves death or serious injury cannot be justified as self-defence to protect property in Australia. See also Code pénal [Criminal Code] (France) arts. 122–7.

[62] Within this context, the difficult question of the attribution of an attack taking place in cyberspace (Lixinski, *Legal Implications of the Privatization of Cyber Warfare*, above n. 8, pp. 7–8) is irrelevant for the purpose of justifying a response in self-defence, which remains lawful regardless of the legal qualification of the perpetrator of the attack.

[63] See e.g., Terrorism (Police Powers) Act 2002 (NSW), Pt 2 (Special Powers), s. 14; Police Powers and Responsibilities Act 2000 (QLD), Ch. 2, Pt 1.

[64] But see Jay P. Kesan and Carol M. Hayes, *Self Defense in Cyberspace: Law and Policy* (University of Illinois, Urbana, IL, 2011), arguing in favour of 'active self-defence'.

## 4.2 Military operations in armed conflict

Cyber security measures are not limited to the law enforcement type of operations, but also extend to military operations in the context of international and non-international armed conflicts, in which conventional rules of the law of armed conflict apply.[65] Within the context of cyber warfare, it is likely that the military would seize control of cyber operations and coordinate civilian operators within cyber network systems, thus providing an institutionalised framework for originally non-institutionalised cyber networks.[66] Such assimilation of civilian cyber capabilities for the purpose of cyber warfare necessarily involves a risk of blurring the distinction between combatants and civilians, raising the issue of whether such civilian operators are to be considered directly participating in hostilities.[67]

In other words, private cyber security providers can easily find themselves within a realm of direct participation in hostilities even if they limit their operation to non-physical means.[68] Therefore, whether in an international or non-international armed conflict, private cyber security providers will be placed at risk of becoming legitimate targets of attacks deprived of legal protection under the law of armed conflict.[69]

Because of this concern, Davis Brown proposes a total ban on participation by private security providers in cyber warfare, requiring states to launch cyber attacks only from information systems operated by combatants.[70] In the same vein, the Draft International Convention

---

[65] In favour of the application of the law of armed conflict to cyber conflicts, see Schmitt, *Tallinn Manual on the International Law Applicable to Cyber Warfare*, above n. 37, Pt B. For possible alternative regulation of cyber warfare, see Davis Brown, 'A Proposal for an International Convention to Regulate the Use of Information Systems in Armed Conflict' (2006) 47 *Harvard International Law Journal* 179, 215–21; and the proposal for comprehensive regulation of cyber warfare by Prof. Merezhko, available at www.pol itik.org.ua/vid/publcontent.php3?y=7&p=57, translated into English in Lixinski, *Legal Implications of the Privatization of Cyber Warfare*, above n. 8, p. 18.

[66] See Brenner and Clarke, 'Civilians in Cyberwarfare: Conscripts', above n. 8, 1037; Timothy Shimeall *et al.*, 'Countering Cyber-War' (2001) 49 *NATO Review* 16, 17.

[67] See David Turns, 'Cyber Warfare and the Notion of Direct Participation in Hostilities' (2012) 17 *Journal of Conflict and Security Law* 279.

[68] On the notion of 'direct participation in hostilities' see e.g., Nils Melzer, 'Interpretive Guidance on the Notion of Direct Participation in Hostilities under International Humanitarian Law' (2008) 90 *International Review of the Red Cross* 991, 1017–18.

[69] Cf. Schmitt, *Tallinn Manual on the International Law Applicable to Cyber Warfare*, above n. 37, Pt B, rr. 25, 29, 32, 34 and 35.

[70] Brown, 'A Proposal for an International Convention', above n. 65, 217 (Art. 10).

on the Regulation, Oversight and Monitoring of Private Military and Security Companies limits the scope of activities of private military and security companies and prohibits them from performing 'intrinsically governmental' functions, such as 'waging war and/or combat operations'.[71] Even more explicitly, the Draft Convention prohibits 'private military and security companies and their personnel from directly participating in armed conflicts, military actions or terrorist acts, whether international or non-international in character, in the territory of any State'.[72]

Alternatively, the problem could be resolved by nationalising the entire cyber infrastructure owned by private companies or by conscripting all private cyber security providers.[73] In that context private cyber security providers would no longer qualify as private agents, but would rather be acting as combatants.

## 5  Conclusion

Owing to the open nature of computer networks, the protection of cyberspace from hostile attacks is hardly achievable without the involvement of private cyber security institutions. This is particularly so in the absence of a comprehensive international public institution governing and regulating activities in cyberspace. There is evidence suggesting a movement towards greater cooperation and coordination between national, regional and international public authorities and private cyber security institutions for the purpose of preventing and responding to cyber attacks. However, this public-private partnership challenges relevant rules of domestic law enforcement and the international law of armed conflict.

This chapter has identified two fundamental legal issues arising from cyber operations carried out by private cyber security providers against cyber attacks. First, it is doubtful whether the legality of cyber security 'counter-measures' undertaken by private cyber security providers extends beyond the scope of self-defence. Second, the involvement of private cyber security providers in cyber warfare during an international or non-international armed conflict beyond the limits of

---

[71] *Report of the Working Group on the Use of Mercenaries*, above n. 49, Annex, Art. 8.
[72] *Ibid.* Annex, Art. 10.
[73] Brenner and Clarke, 'Civilians in Cyberwarfare: Conscripts', above n. 8, 1039.

self-defence may constitute direct participation in hostilities and therefore places them at risk of becoming lawful targets of armed attacks deprived of legal protection under the law of armed conflict. Those existing legal restrictions might prevent private cyber security institutions from effectively responding to cyber security issues.

~

# Concluding remarks

THOMAS POGGE

## 1 Institutional responses to security threats and civil liberties

The rationale often given for the modern state understands it as a polity whose members take responsibility, through their collective maintenance of a governmental apparatus, for respecting, protecting and promoting the fulfilment of one another's rights, needs and interests. This responsibility requires citizens to maintain an effective government that avoids oppression, curbs crime and underwrites the law-based freedom of all citizens to lead a life of their own choosing, as well as their access to education, healthcare and an adequate standard of living. In addition to these internal challenges, that same responsibility requires citizens to deal also with external challenges that may likewise endanger the rights, needs or interests of the state's members.

Such external challenges have traditionally been classified under the label of security. Here the most obvious threats involve war: an invasion by foreign military forces that would endanger the lives and well-being of citizens as well as the proper functioning of the governmental apparatus. Another class of threats involve civil war: a group of citizens setting themselves against the polity, perhaps with the intent of taking over some or all of the state or of forcibly altering the state's governmental apparatus. A third kind of threat is terrorism: a group of citizens or foreigners committed to inflicting violent harm on citizens or to disrupting their governmental apparatus. A fourth class of threats is environmental: threats of natural catastrophes including epidemics and human-made ecological disasters. A fifth class of threats is economic, including, for example, threats to the country's trade routes, to its domestic infrastructure, currency or financial system.

In order to protect and promote the fulfilment of their members' rights, needs and interests, states must defend them against these and other external threats when they arise and must also try to anticipate such threats, with the idea of perhaps deterring or preventing their emergence or of pre-empting them or of being well prepared for their occurrence. States can do this individually, but often they can also do it, and often much more effectively, together – for instance, through concerted military action organised under the auspices of an international agency such as the United Nations Security Council or a military alliance such as the North Atlantic Treaty Organization (NATO); through international collaboration in the fight against terrorism; through concerted international action against climate change, epidemics or natural calamities coordinated by international organisations such as the UN Framework Convention on Climate Change (FCCC), the World Health Organization (WHO) or the Food and Agriculture Organization (FAO); and through the World Trade Organization (WTO), designed to safeguard strong, open, stable and rule-governed commercial relations around the world.

The essays collected in this volume discuss threats of all five kinds, and more, under the label of security threats; and they also discuss the institutional responses that states, individually and collectively, have made to such threats. I will here highlight one normative strand of this discussion, which has come in for much public scrutiny in the aftermath of the terror attacks in the early years of the new millennium: the cost of state security efforts to the basic rights and liberties of citizens.

It is obvious that institutional arrangements, policies and governmental actions that can effectively protect the security of citizens against external threats may also themselves pose a threat to the rights, needs or interests of citizens or foreigners. Examples abound. To defend a state against foreign invasion or internal insurrection, it may be important to coercively conscript some of its citizens into its armed forces. To fight or pre-empt a rebellion, it may be useful to prohibit the publication of texts or images that might elicit sympathy or support for the rebels. To combat terrorism, it may be useful to torture suspected terrorists to extract information or to put suspects in indefinite detention even when there is insufficient evidence to charge them with a crime. To battle an epidemic, it may be advantageous to coercively quarantine those suspected of carrying the disease in order to reduce the rate of infection. To safeguard the country's oil supply, it may be beneficial to collaborate in the violent overthrow of the government of an oil exporting country. In all these cases, the security measures taken by the state not merely protect and promote the rights, needs and interests of its citizens but also threaten the rights, needs and interests of citizens and foreigners. How should we think about such trade-offs?

## 2 Rawls's guidance on how to respond to security threats

One important answer to this question is developed by the famous political philosopher John Rawls in his classic work *A Theory of Justice*.[1] His thinking is well illustrated by a pertinent example he offers concerning a potential civil war situation:

> Suppose that, aroused by sharp religious antagonisms, members of rival sects are collecting weapons and forming armed bands in preparation for civil strife. Confronted with this situation the government may enact a statute forbidding the possession of firearms (assuming that possession is not already an offense). And the law may hold that sufficient evidence for conviction is that the weapons are found in the defendant's house or property, unless he can establish that they were put there by another. Except for this proviso, the absence of intent and knowledge of possession, and conformity to reasonable standards of care, are declared irrelevant. It is contended that these normal defenses would make the law ineffective and impossible to enforce. Now although this statute trespasses upon the precept ought implies can it might be accepted by the representative citizen as a lesser loss of liberty, at least if the penalties imposed are not too severe ... Viewing the situation from the legislative stage, one may decide that the formation of paramilitary groups, which the passing of the statute may forestall, is a much greater danger to the freedom of the average citizen than being held strictly liable for the possession of weapons. Citizens may affirm the law as the lesser of two evils, resigning themselves to the fact that while they may be held guilty for things they have not done, the risks to their liberty on any other course would be worse.[2]

The precept 'ought implies can' is an established moral precept that goes back at least to Immanuel Kant.[3] It stipulates that an agent can be held

---

[1] John Rawls, *A Theory of Justice* (Harvard University Press, Cambridge, MA, 1971, revised edn 1999). Subsequent references are to the section and page number of the revised edition.

[2] *Ibid.* pp. 212–13.

[3] 'The action to which the "ought" applies must indeed be possible under natural conditions': Immanuel Kant, *The Critique of Pure Reason* (Norman Kemp Smith ed., trans., Palgrave Macmillan, New York, [1929] 2003) p. 473 (A548/B576). 'For when the moral law commands that we ought now to be better men, it follows inevitably that we must be able to be better men': Immanuel Kant, *Religion within the Limits of Reason Alone* (Theodore M. Greene and Hoyt H. Hudson Harper eds., Torchbooks, New York, 1960) p. 46 (Ak 6:50).

responsible only for what is in her or his power. Rawls extends this precept to the legal domain by explicitly recognising it as a basic liberty,[4] and thus putting it under the protection of his first principle of justice which, in its final formulation, reads as follows: '[e]ach person has the same indefeasible claim to a fully adequate scheme of equal basic liberties, which scheme is compatible with the same scheme of liberties for all'.[5] It is then, according to Rawls, an infringement of a person's basic liberties to hold her criminally liable for some outcome without a showing that it was within her power to avert this outcome.[6]

Yet, this is exactly what is done by the criminal statute Rawls discusses in the quoted passage. Under it, a person may be held strictly liable for weapons found on her property, even without a showing that she was in any way at fault (*mens rea*), for example by having been involved in storing the weapons there or by knowing about these weapons and not notifying the authorities or by failing to take all reasonable precautions to keep her property weapons-free. Rawls writes that such a strict liability criminal statute may permissibly be enacted when doing so decreases the overall danger to the basic liberties of the representative or average citizen. According to him, the government, or more specifically the legislature, should be guided by the goal of reducing the sum of two dangers to the basic rights and liberties of the average citizen: the danger posed by external threats plus the danger posed by the government's own agencies and officials. When the government is organised according to this guidance, then, Rawls holds, citizens can find the resulting infringe-ments of their basic liberties by their own government acceptable on the ground that their basic liberties would be even more imperilled if their government had followed any other course.

Rawls endorses the strict liability statute, but only if its implementa-tion really diminishes the net danger to the representative citizen's basic liberties. It would do so by impeding the spread of weapons. Without the statute, a property owner might be ready to allow illegal weapons to be stored in his barn or basement or on his property, confident in the belief that, should these weapons be found, it would still be very hard for the prosecution to prove beyond a reasonable doubt that he knew about

---

[4] Rawls, *A Theory of Justice*, above n. 1, p. 208.

[5] John Rawls, *Justice as Fairness: A Restatement* (Erin Kelly ed., Harvard University Press, Cambridge, MA, 2001) p. 42.

[6] Following a terminological convention inaugurated by Judith Jarvis Thomson, I distin-guish infringements from violations of rights as follows: 'infringement' leaves open the question of permissibility, and violations are defined as impermissible infringements.

them or was in some way remiss. But once the statute becomes law, the prosecution's case becomes much easier to make; all it must prove is that the weapons were there. The great value of the statute lies then in its contribution to deterrence, which helps reduce the number of weapons in circulation and thereby makes civil war less likely and (should it break out anyway) less bloody. Given these benefits, it is, as Rawls suggests, entirely possible that enacting the statute in question is, on balance, a gain for the security of the representative citizen's basic liberties.

To determine whether it really is a net gain or not, the benefits need to be weighed against the costs which, in Rawls' theory, are estimated in the same currency, namely the degree to which citizens' basic rights and liberties are fulfilled. These costs are false criminal convictions. All people convicted under the statute suffer an infringement of their rights by being so convicted without a showing of fault. And some of these people suffer an even graver rights infringement by being so convicted even though they are completely innocent; they took all reasonable precautions to keep their property weapons-free and really had no knowledge that the weapons were there. According to Rawls' account, the legislature should pass the statute only if it is convinced that this statute brings a net gain in citizens' basic liberties; that the infringements of basic liberties suffered by those convicted under the statute are outweighed by the infringements of basic liberties averted by the statute's reduction of the dangers of civil war.

We have discussed one of Rawls's examples in detail, but he means his broadly consequentialist reasoning to be applied much more widely of course; to all government restrictions of citizens' basic liberties.[7] Rawls discusses a number of examples, including conscription,[8] but it is worth

---

[7] 'Consequentialism' is a technical term in philosophy. It refers to moral theories that base their assessments on some metric for how well the world is going. Utilitarianism is a paradigm example of a consequentialist theory. It bases its moral assessments of the conduct or character of persons or of social rules and procedures on their effects on human happiness or desire fulfillment. Rawls' theory is also broadly consequentialist. Through his thought experiment of the original position, he assesses alternative candidate designs of society's basic institutions by how well each design would fulfil citizens' higher-order interests. And his public criterion of social justice (the two principles of justice) permits official restrictions of basic rights and liberties if and insofar as such restrictions optimise the overall security of these same basic rights and liberties.

[8] He writes: 'I shall assume that since conscription is a drastic interference with the basic liberties of equal citizenship, it cannot be justified by any needs less compelling than those of national security. In a well-ordered society (or in one nearly just) these needs are determined by the end of preserving just institutions. Conscription is permissible only if it

adding some realistic examples of laws and policies that governments might be tempted to adopt specifically in response to security threats. The government may want to monitor communications and to restrict citizens' freedoms of expression, association and assembly; it may be eager to censor the media; it may be keen to reduce or eliminate constraints on unreasonable searches and seizures; it may want the authority to detain people more easily and to keep them in custody for longer periods without charge or trial; it may seek the freedom to use harsh interrogation techniques on suspects; it may favour disproportionately harsh punishments to strengthen deterrence; it may seek greater latitude in regard to what evidence is admissible in court; it may prefer greater freedom to withhold in court cases evidence it deems sensitive; it may want the authority to try certain cases in secret; and it may favour lower thresholds for conviction (e.g. preponderance of evidence rather than beyond a reasonable doubt, a majority vote by the jury rather than unanimity). All these adjustments infringe citizens' basic rights and liberties, but Rawls' theory can justify any of these infringements if it averts even graver encroachments upon citizens' basic rights and liberties.

### 3   Who is to decide about how to respond to security threats?

Although Rawls' position sounds plausible and is widely held, it involves two serious mistakes, which have allowed it to contribute to the horrendous response to terrorism under the governments of George W. Bush and Tony Blair. The first mistake is not to pay enough attention to the question of 'who' will do the balancing of costs and benefits. *Quis judicabit*? Rawls simply assumes that this balancing falls to the legislature, that is, to the party or parties in power. But instructing those in power to make the decision so as to optimise the fulfilment of citizens' basic liberties by no means guarantees that such fulfilment will indeed be optimised. In fact, it almost guarantees the opposite. The reason is that the government is not an unbiased party in regard to the question of whether its powers should be expanded by restricting the basic rights and liberties of citizens. On the contrary, the politicians and officials in power have several obvious strong motives to favour expansion of their powers

is demanded for the defense of liberty itself, including here not only the liberties of the citizens of the society in question, but also those of persons in other societies as well': Rawls, *A Theory of Justice*, above n. 1, pp. 333–4.

and authority at the expense of the basic rights and liberties of citizens. They are therefore prone, at least in their public pronouncements, to exaggerate the security benefits of giving themselves greater powers and to underestimate the dangers their own expanded powers will pose to the basic rights and liberties of citizens. In fact, politicians will often be tempted to invoke security concerns in order to seek expanded powers even when there is no serious security threat at all – as when they are disturbed by harshly critical media coverage or unnerved by the rapidly rising popularity of an opposition party.

Rawls' stated goal is that the security of citizens' basic liberties should be optimised by minimising the sum of (i) the danger to their basic rights and liberties posed by external security threats, plus (ii) the dangers posed to their basic rights and liberties by the government's own agencies and officials. This goal should inform not merely the instructions given to the decision-maker but also the choice of who will make the decision, through what procedure and within what guidelines and constraints. Once this question of who decides is explicitly raised, the answer that the government should be judge in its own case comes to seem far from obvious.

Who else might decide? Among presently existing institutional agents, a far more qualified candidate is a country's highest court. This court would not, of course, be able to act on its own but only pursuant to a suitable application that would have to be submitted by the executive or the legislature or both in concert. This application would ask for, and comprehensively justify, one or more restrictions of the basic rights and liberties of citizens; and the court would then expeditiously decide on each of these restrictions, either granting it, perhaps with certain modifications, or else denying it. Additional safe-guards might be built in, for example requiring a super-majority (e.g. two-thirds) of the court's judges and/or requiring an automatic sunset provision that lets any restriction on citizens' basic rights and liberties expire after some period (determined by the judges and not to exceed twelve months), unless it is expressly re-submitted and re-authorised by the highest court.[9]

My answer to the *quis judicabit* question can probably be improved upon, and some of the essays in this volume provide interesting discussions about how various existing national and supra-national agencies do or could decide proper responses to security threats. My main objective

---

[9] See discussion by Anna Hood, Chapter 6.

here was merely to discredit the most popular answer to the question by showing that there is at least one alternative that is clearly superior to it.

## 4   Should we really seek to optimise the security of citizens' basic rights and liberties?

The second serious mistake in Rawls' position involves the goal itself; the idea that security threats should be handled so as to minimise the aggregate danger to the basic rights and liberties of citizens. This idea is closely related to the very centerpiece of Rawls' theory of justice – his overarching claim that we should morally endorse that public criterion of social justice which rational representatives of prospective citizens would agree upon on purely prudential grounds. This idea is beautifully expressed in Rawls' thought experiment of an original position in which representatives of citizens, mutually disinterested and rational,[10] must agree on a public criterion of social justice while being situated under a veil of ignorance that prevents them from knowing anything specific about the particular citizen each of them is to represent. In such an artificial choice situation, every representative is forced to take equal account of the needs and interest of all citizens, and so these representatives will naturally agree that society should be organised in whatever way is best for its participants. The structure of Rawls' thought experiment ensures that it will result in a purely recipient-oriented theory of justice.

The purely recipient-oriented approach advocates that moral choices should be made so as to achieve the best distribution of relevant goods and ills among those affected (the 'recipients' of the choice). Rawls applies this approach to the choice of a public criterion of social justice, a criterion that citizens are to agree to use for the comparative moral assessment of alternative ways of organising their national society. His response to the problem of security threats is just a specific application of this general idea. So what is wrong with this approach to moral theorising?

What's wrong with it is that, by focusing all attention on citizens as 'affected by' the rules and procedures (social institutions) of their society, Rawls gives no play to the perspective of citizens as 'the authors of' those same rules and procedures. From the standpoint of citizens as recipients there is indeed no reason to care about how and by whom one is harmed

---

[10]   Rawls, *A Theory of Justice*, above n. 1, p. 125.

or endangered; about whether one is, for instance, for no good reason imprisoned by terrorists or by an anti-terrorist state agency. Arguably, this difference is morally highly significant, however, when viewed from the standpoint of those who bear responsibility for the harm. As citizens, we bear a far heavier responsibility for the fate of any innocent persons who are detained and harshly interrogated by an anti-terrorism agency that acts under our authorisation than for the fate of other innocent persons who are detained and similarly abused by terrorists whose crimes, by harsher state tactics, might be averted. This point is familiar to basic ethics classes which introduce the moral significance of the distinction between doing and allowing: it is a greater wrong to kill an innocent person than to fail to rescue another innocent person from being killed by someone else. And it is forbidden to kill a group of innocent people even when doing so is necessary to save a slightly larger group of innocent people from being killed by others. What matters about our conduct decisions are not merely the effects they produce but also the ways in which they produce these effects – the causal pathways. This is so in regard to our day-to-day conduct decisions as individuals, and it is also true of what we collectively decide to do through how we organise and regulate the agencies and officials of our state.

We can find this sentiment expressed, for instance, in the famous adage (which goes back to Sir William Gladstone) that it is better that ten guilty persons escape than that one innocent person be convicted. The background to this adage is that, in organising a criminal justice system, miscarriages of justice cannot be completely avoided. These miscarriages are of two kinds: innocent persons falsely convicted; and guilty persons falsely acquitted. The relative frequency of these two kinds of miscarriages depends on how we design criminal procedures and standards of evidence. The easier we make it to achieve convictions, the more innocents will be convicted and the fewer guilty people will be acquitted. The adage guides us in the opposite direction, favouring a system that makes convictions difficult to achieve with the result that there will be far more miscarriages of the second than of the first kind. This preference cannot be justified by the concern to avert harm from innocents. This is so because the acquittal of guilty persons will also result in a great deal of harm to innocents, namely to those who are endangered by the guilty persons who remain free to offend again or by the crimes of those who would have been deterred if the system had been designed to make convictions easier to achieve. What the adage conveys is then a difference in our responsibility for the harm that innocent people suffer as a consequence of our decision; harms that we directly bring about by organising our criminal justice system so that some innocent persons suffer through false convictions weigh far more heavily than harms that we fail to prevent by organising our criminal justice system so that some guilty parties go free.[11]

The fact that acceptance of the sentiment expressed in the adage is widespread, though not especially deep,[12] in the West shows that Rawls is out of sync with the dominant sentiments of his time and culture. But why should this mean that his view is mistaken? Why cannot ordinary sentiments be mistaken in rejecting the broadly consequentialist reasoning enshrined in Rawls' original position, which makes the perspective of prospective participants paramount and thus leads to a purely recipient-oriented theory?

### 5   Why Rawls' recommended response to security threats defeats his own ambitions

There are two reasons for describing as a mistake Rawls' broadly consequentialist approach to security threats; his suggestion that we should try to minimise the aggregate danger to the basic rights and liberties of citizens. First, it does not fit core values that Rawls himself meant to articulate through his theory of justice. These values are concisely expressed in his most prominent and most frequently quoted sentence, which occurs repeatedly in the book and also opens its back cover synopsis: '[e]ach person possesses an inviolability founded on justice that even the welfare of society as a whole cannot override'.[13] Rawls intended for his theory to be a deontological alternative to the consequentialist thinking epitomised by utilitarianism.[14]

Second, Rawls also wanted to compose a theory of social justice that fits the considered convictions of his compatriot contemporaries after due reflection, in what he calls wide reflective equilibrium.[15] This

---

[11] Insofar as citizens have especially weighty reasons to avoid harms inflicted by the agencies and officials of their state, these reasons further reinforce the conservative conclusion I argued for earlier; that there should be serious checks on the government's ability to obtain authorisation for restricting the basic rights and liberties of citizens. It is far more important to ensure that such authorisations are withheld when they are unwarranted than to ensure that such authorisations are granted when they are warranted.

[12] It was quite amazing how easily citizens, especially in the United States, accepted horrendous government abuses in the aftermath of the 2001 terrorist attacks.

[13] Rawls, *A Theory of Justice*, above n. 1, p. 3, and p. 513; see also pp. 24–5.

[14] *Ibid.*, p. 26; see also p. 220.   [15] *Ibid.*, p. 43.

ambition, too, is ruined by the simple trade-off that his theory licenses between basic rights deficits prevented and basic rights infringements inflicted by governmental agencies. Rawls' readers do not accept that there is moral parity between these two types of basic rights deficits; we do not accept that our governmental apparatus should be organised to infringe basic rights whenever this is necessary to prevent just slightly larger basic rights deficits arising from elsewhere. Although such trade-offs would produce an overall gain for basic rights fulfilment, they are nonetheless widely and strongly condemned.

To see this point clearly, we should illustrate it with cases in which the costs and benefits of institutionalised government action can easily be compared because they affect the same basic right of citizens in similar ways. One especially suitable example concerns the right to life, which is engaged on both sides when we contemplate systematic use of the death penalty for the sake of improving citizens' overall security against violent death. If we follow the logic of Rawls' reasoning, we will conclude that justice permits (and perhaps even requires) us to institute and apply the death penalty for certain offences if the reduction in the frequency of the offence thereby achieved diminishes citizens' premature death risk overall. When this is the case, then citizens may affirm the law as the lesser of two evils, resigning themselves to the fact that while they may be executed for a crime that does not merit the death penalty, the risks of premature death on any other course would be worse.[16]

One rather pedestrian security threat that could be substantially reduced through use of the death penalty is the crime of drunk driving, which kills more people each year than all terrorist attacks combined have killed in the last fifty years. In the United States alone, alcohol-impaired driving crashes reportedly killed 10,322 people in 2012 (31 per cent of all motor vehicle traffic fatalities).[17] It is likely that the United States could reduce this security threat dramatically by introducing the death penalty for the worst repeat offenders. Suppose the law were designed to produce annually about forty executions for drunk driving

---

[16] Paraphrasing the passage quoted earlier from Rawls, A Theory of Justice, above n. 1, p. 213.

[17] United States Department of Transportation, National Highway Traffic Safety Administration, Traffic Safety Facts, 2012 Data: Alcohol Impaired Driving (December 2013), available at www-nrd.nhtsa.dot.gov/Pubs/811870.pdf. Only about 35 per cent of these fatalities are people other than the drunk driver.

nationwide.[18] This would roughly double the number of executions in the United States and garner substantial attention for the statute. Even if the statute reduced drunk driving by only 10 per cent (quite a conservative estimate, in my view) it would on balance save about 1,000 people per year from a premature death and would thus be a substantial gain for Rawls' representative citizen. Nonetheless, I would think that the vast majority of Rawls' readers would strongly reject the proposal. They would not be prepared to impose a clearly disproportional punishment on forty drunk drivers for the sake of saving the lives of 1,000 people.[19] This shows that we do attach moral significance to the distinction between basic rights infringements that we, through the way we organise and regulate our government and its agencies, 'commit' and similar basic rights deficits that we merely 'fail to prevent'. It also shows that the moral significance we attach to this distinction is quite substantial; in excess of 25:1 in the example just discussed.

Clearly, our concern to ensure that our governmental apparatus not infringe basic rights and liberties is not absolute. If it were, we could not operate a criminal justice system at all, knowing what is obvious, namely that any such system will produce some false convictions of innocent persons. But our concern is definitely not captured by Rawls' conclusion when he writes that a criminal justice system involves at least two kinds of disadvantage:

> one kind is the cost of maintaining the agency covered say by taxation; the other is the danger to the liberty of the representative citizen measured by the likelihood that these sanctions will wrongly interfere with his freedom. The establishment of a coercive agency is rational only if these disadvantages are less than the loss of liberty from instability. Assuming this to be so, the best arrangement is one that minimizes these hazards.[20]

## 6    Towards a more adequate account of how to respond to security threats

I conclude that we need systematically to rethink our institutional responses to security threats – not merely the question of 'who decides'

[18] Death Penalty Information Center, 'Executions by Year Since 1976' (2014), available at www.deathpenaltyinfo.org/executions-year.

[19] I discuss this example far more elaborately in my essay 'Equal Liberty for All' (2004) 28 *Midwest Studies in Philosophy* 266, reprinted in David Reidy (ed.), *John Rawls* (Aldershot, Ashgate, 2008) pp. 219–34.

[20] Rawls, *A Theory of Justice*, above n. 1, p. 211.

but also the principles on which such decisions are to be based. To develop such principles within a broadly liberal, individualistic framework, we need to reflect on the following seven issues.

The first issue concerns the distinction between diverse types of causal pathways that may connect institutionalised government action with basic rights deficits. A preliminary list might contain these six types of causal pathways:

(1) There are basic rights infringements that are directly 'mandated' by law or executive order; for example, the death penalty for especially egregious cases of drunk driving or the detention without charge or trial of Japanese-Americans in the Second World War and of many Arab-Americans in the aftermath of the 9/11 terrorist attacks.

(2) There are other such infringements that are 'authorised' by law or executive order; for example, the enslavement of black people in the ante-bellum South.

(3) There are basic rights deficits that are avoidably 'engendered' by laws or executive orders; for example, people dying prematurely through environmental disasters that better regulation of polluting production and consumption would have averted or people being hurt in traffic accidents that would have been averted by better design of the traffic infrastructure or by better traffic regulations.

(4) There are basic rights infringements that a tougher criminal justice system would have averted; for example, crimes that would have been deterred or prevented through more permissive rules of policing, lower standards of evidence or more draconian punishments of offenders.

(5) There are basic rights deficits that more generous state support for citizens' health, education or income would have averted; for example, premature deaths in an epidemic that better public health services would have prevented or contained.

(6) And there are, finally, self-caused basic rights deficits that more generous state support could have averted; for example, premature deaths of recreational sailors or mountaineers who would have been saved if there had been more effective public rescue services.

Needless to say, this list is meant to be indicative, neither final nor exhaustive.

The second issue concerns the relative weights to be assigned to equivalent rights deficits across these types of causal pathways. Such weights are needed to resolve both conflicts and competitions. Conflicts arise when we, for instance, contemplate institutions that directly infringe basic rights (type 1) for the sake of reducing basic rights violations committed by criminals (type 4). Competitions occur when scarcity of resources forces us to choose between reducing rights deficits of different types, for instance, between funding better pollution or traffic control (type 3) and funding better public healthcare (type 5).

The third issue concerns the relative importance of deficits in different rights. I have thus far mostly used the right to life in my illustrations, but there are, of course, many other basic rights to be considered, and most of these rights might be underfulfilled to a greater or lesser extent. A decision about whether and how to respond institutionally to some specific security threat requires a proper balancing of the diverse basic rights deficits that different responses would entail and hence an assignment of weights to such deficits.

The fourth issue concerns the persons whose rights are at stake. Of course, we like to say that, from a suitably universalistic point of view, all human lives are of equal value. But it may nonetheless be permissible for a national society's response to security threats to be biased in some ways toward its own. Such a society would then have to decide what categories of persons need to be distinguished in any balancing of rights for the sake of determining the appropriate response to security threats. Here, one will presumably have to distinguish at least the categories of citizens, residents and foreigners living abroad. But more fine-grained distinctions are likely to be required as well because some basic rights may be waived or forfeited or at least be weakened in some way through conduct on the part of the right holder.

The fifth issue concerns the relative importance to be assigned to the various categories of persons distinguished in the preceding paragraph. This weighting dimension interacts multiplicatively with the other two (first and third issues). The overall importance of a basic right infringement suffered by some particular person depends then on the kind of right at stake (third issue), on the causal pathway on which the governmental apparatus affects the fulfilment of this right (first issue) and on the category of person to which the right holder belongs (fifth issue).

The sixth issue concerns intra-personal aggregation needed in cases where one person is suffering multiple basic rights deficits, either concurrently or sequentially. Of course, one might simply add these together, as it were, thus treating multiple deficits of the same person as on a par with equivalent deficits affecting several persons in the same category.

But this simple addition might be disputed on prioritarian grounds.[21] One might argue that multiple burdens are worse when they are concentrated on one very heavily burdened individual rather than more widely dispersed. On this view, multiple basic rights deficits borne by the same person would be assigned superproportional weight or importance.

The seventh issue, finally, concerns inter-personal aggregation. Again, simple addition is an option. And again this option could be disputed; for instance, on the ground that burdens are of greater moral importance when, rather than being more or less randomly distributed, they predominantly fall upon members of certain groups, identified perhaps by race, ethnicity, gender, religion, sexual preference or linguistic or geographical community.[22] On this view, any correlation of basic rights deficits with relevant group identities would increase the moral importance of these deficits.

A great deal of valuable thinking and writing has been done, in an empirical and normative vein, on the question as to how societies do, may and should organise themselves in response to the security threats they face. In fact, the essays in this volume are an admirable and up-to-date sample of such rich and instructive reflection. But we do not yet have for this challenging problem anything approaching a morally sound unified theory. Rawls does offer a principled normative account of the problem but, as we have seen, his account is defective in various important ways. I have tried to lay out the main complexities of the task, as well as the principal building blocks for accomplishing it. I believe that the task is of great importance because security threats can arise suddenly and are then, in the heat of the moment and in the absence of solid intellectual preparation, often addressed with ad hoc institutional fixes, policies and initiatives that are gravely unjust as well as seriously imprudent. The West's responses to the terrorist attacks provide sobering examples of this. We would do much better if we were intellectually prepared, if we had a principled account that does justice to the above-sketched complexities and can then guide the decision-making, allowing us to cope with the threat while staying true to our values.

---

[21] Prioritarianism is an approach in philosophy according to which hardships are to be given more weight when they affect persons who are worse off. For the classic statement of this approach, see Derek Parfit, *Equality or Priority?* (Lindley Lecture, University of Kansas, 1991).

[22] As discussed by Bina D'Costa, Chapter 2.

# BIBLIOGRAPHY

## Articles, books, reports and papers

Abass, Ademola, *Regional Organisations and the Development of Collective Security: Beyond Chapter VIII of the UN Charter* (Hart Publishing, Oxford/ Portland, OR, 2004)

'African Peace and Security Architecture and the Protection of Human Security' in Ademola Abass (ed.), *Protecting Human Security in Africa* (Oxford University Press, Oxford, 2010)

Abdullah, Alias Bin, Ito, Shoichi and Adhana, Kelali, *Estimate of Rice Consumption in Asian Countries and the World Towards 2050* (Tottori University, Japan, 2005), available at http://worldfood.apionet.or.jp/alias.pdf

Abi-Saab, Georges, *The United Nations Operation in the Congo 1960–1964* (Oxford University Press, Oxford, 1978)

'The Security Council as Legislator and Executive in Its Fight Against Terrorism and Against Proliferation of Weapons of Mass Destruction: A Question of Legitimacy' in Rüdiger Wolfrum and Volker Röben (eds.), *Legitimacy in International Law* (Springer, Berlin, 2008)

'The Security Council *Legibus Solutus?* On the Legislative Forays of the Council' in Laurence Boisson de Chazournes and Marcelo Kohen (eds.), *International Law and the Quest for its Implementation* (Brill, Leiden/ Boston, MA, 2010)

Abromeit, Heidrun, and Hitzel-Cassagnes, Tanja, 'Constitutional Change and Contractual Revision: Principles and Procedures' (1999) 5 *European Law Journal* 23

Abu-Lughod, Lila (ed.), *Remaking Women: Feminist and Modernity in the Middle East* (Princeton University Press, Princeton, NJ, 1998)

Acharya, Amitav, 'Ideas, Identity, and Institution-Building: From the "ASEAN Way" to the "Asia-Pacific Way"' (1997) 10 *Pacific Review* 319

*Constructing a Security Community in Southeast Asia: ASEAN and the Problem of Regional Order* (Routledge, London, 2001)

Ackerly, Brooke A. and D'Costa, Bina, 'Transnational Feminism and Women's Rights: Successes and Challenges of a Political Strategy' in Anne Marie Goetz (ed.), *Governing Women* (Routledge, New York, 2008)

338

Ackerly, Brooke A. and Okin, Susan Moller, 'Feminist Social Criticism and the International Movement for Women's Rights as Human Rights' in Ian Shapiro and Casiano Hacker-Cordòn (eds.), *Democracy's Edges* (Cambridge University Press, Cambridge, 1999)

Ackerman, Bruce, 'The Emergency Constitution' (2004) 113 *Yale Law Journal* 1029

Action Group on Erosion, Technology and Concentration (ETC Group), *Who Owns Nature? Corporate Power and the Final Frontier in the Commodification of Life* (November 2008), available at www.etcgroup.org/en/node/707

Adi, Bongo, 'Intellectual Property Rights in Biotechnology and the Fate of Poor Farmers' Agriculture' (2006) 9 *Journal of World Intellectual Property* 91

Adler, Emmanuel, 'The Emergence of Cooperation: National Epistemic Communities and the International Evolution of the Idea of Nuclear Arms Control' (1992) 46 *International Organization* 101

Afghan Women's Network, *Baseline Report: Afghanistan: Monitoring Women's Security in Transition* (Afghan Women's Network, Kabul, 2013)

Agamben, Giogio, *State of Exception* (University of Chicago Press, Chicago, IL, 2005)

Ahimsa, Djali, 'Peaceful Uses: Review of Articles IV and V' in John Simpson and Darryl Howlett (eds.), *The Future of the Nuclear Non-Proliferation Treaty* (St Martin's Press, New York, 1995)

Ahn, Dukgeun, *WTO Settlements in East Asia* (National Bureau of Economic Research, Cambridge, MA, 2003)

Akehurst, Michael, 'Enforcement Action by Regional Agencies, with Special Reference to the Organization of American States' (1967) 42 *British Year Book of International Law* 175

'Equity and General Principles of Law' (1976) 25 *International and Comparative Law Quarterly* 801

'The Application of General Principles of Law by the Court of Justice of the European Communities' (1981) 52 *British Yearbook of International Law* 29

Akram, Munir and Haider Shah, Syed, 'The Legislative Powers of the United Nations Security Council' in Ronald St John Macdonald and Douglas M Johnston (eds.), *Towards World Constitutionalism: Issues in the Legal Ordering of the World Community* (Martinus Nijhoff Publishers, Leiden, 2005)

Ala'i, Padideh, 'Free Trade or Sustainable Development? An Analysis of the WTO Appellate Body's Shift to a More Balanced Approach to Trade Liberalization' (1999) 14 *American University International Law Review* 1129

Alavi, Hamid R. *et al.*, *Trusting Trade and the Private Sector for Food Security in Southeast Asia* (World Bank, Washington, DC, 2012)

Alexy, Robert, *A Theory of Constitutional Rights* (Julian Rivers, trans., Oxford University Press, Oxford, 2002)

Allam, Weil, 'Food Supply Security, Sovereignty and International Peace and Security: Sovereignty as a Challenge to Food Supply Security' in

Ahmed Mahiou and Francis Snyder (eds.), *Food Security and Food Safety* (Martinus Nijhoff Publishers, Leiden, 2006)

Almekinders, Conny and Louwaars, Niels, *Farmers' Seed Production: New Approaches and Practices* (Intermediate Technology Publications, London, 1999)

Alter, Karen J., *Establishing the Supremacy of European Law: The Making of an International Rule of Law in Europe* (Oxford University Press, Oxford, 2001)

Alter, Karen J. (ed.), *The European Court's Political Power: Selected Essays* (Oxford University Press, Oxford, 2009)

Alvarez, José E., 'Judging the Security Council' (1996) 90 *American Journal of International Law* 1

  'Constitutional Interpretation in International Organizations' in Jean-Marc Coicaud and Veijo Heiskanen (eds.), *The Legitimacy of International Organizations* (UN University Press, Tokyo, 2001)

  'The Security Council's War on Terrorism: Problems and Policy Options' in Erika de Wet and André Nollkaemper (eds.), *Review of the Security Council by Member States* (Intersentia, Antwerp, 2003)

  *International Organizations as Lawmakers* (Oxford University Press, Oxford, 2005)

Amerasinghe, C. F., *Principles of the Institutional Law of International Organizations* (2nd edn, Cambridge University Press, Cambridge, 2005)

American Gas Association, *Cryptographic Protection of SCADA Communications*, AGA Report No. 12 (2006), available at www.scadahacker.com/library/ Documents/Standards/AGA%20-%20Cryptographic%20Protection%20of%20 SCADA%20Communications%20-%2012%20Part1.pdf

Amidror, Yaakov, 'Israel's Requirement for Defensible Borders', *Jerusalem Center for Public Affairs*, available at www.defensibleborders.org/amidror.htm

Anderson, Benedict, *Imagined Communities* (Verso Books, London, 1991)

Anderson, Kenneth, 'Israel's Views of the Application of IHL to the West Bank and Gaza Strip' in Roy Gutman, David Rieff and Anthony Dworkin (eds.), *Crimes of War: What the Public Should Know* (W.W. Norton and Company, New York, 2007)

Annan, Kofi A., *In Larger Freedom: Towards Development, Security and Human Rights for All* (United Nations, New York, 2005)

Annas, Julia, 'Being Virtuous and Doing the Right Thing' (2004) 78(2) *Proceedings and Addresses of the American Philosophical Association* 61

Aoki, Keith, *Seed Wars* (Carolina Academic Press, Durham, NC, 2008)

Arangio-Ruiz, Gaetano, 'The "Federal Analogy" and UN Charter Interpretation: A Crucial Issue' (1997) 51 *European Journal of International Law* 1

  'On the Security Council's Law-Making' (2000) 83 *Rivista di diritto internazionale* 609

Aronson, Mark, Dyer, Bruce D. and Groves, Matthew, *Judicial Review of Administrative Action* (4th edn, Thomson, Sydney, 2008)

Arsanjani, Mahnoush H. and Reisman, W. Michael, 'East African Piracy and the Defense of World Public Order' in Holgar Hestermeyer *et al.* (eds.), *Law of the Sea in Dialogue* (Springer, Heidelberg, 2011)

Averill, Bruce, 'Oil, Gas and Maritime Security' (2010) 6 *Journal of International Peace Operations* 14

Averill, Bruce and Luiijf, Eric A.M., 'Canvassing the Cyber Security Landscape: Why Energy Companies Need to Pay Attention' (2010) *Journal of Energy Security* (online), available at www.ensec.org

Ayub, Fatima, Kouvo, Sari and Wareham, Rachel, *Security Sector Reform in Afghanistan* (International Center for Transitional Justice, New York, 2009)

Bailey, Sydney Dawson, *The Making of Resolution 242* (Martinus Nijhoff Publishers, Dordrecht, 1985)

Baker, Stewart *et al.*, *In the Crossfire: Critical Infrastructure in the Age of Cyber War* (McAfee, Santa Clara, CA, 2009)

Baldwin, David, 'The Concept of Security' (1997) 23 *Review of International Studies* 5

Ballard, Kyle M., 'The Privatisation of Military Affairs: A Historical Look into the Evolution of the Private Military Industry' in Thomas Jäger and Gerhard Kümmel (eds.), *Private Military and Security Companies* (VS Verlag, Wiesbaden, 2007)

Bar-Tal, Daniel, *Shared Beliefs in a Society: Social Psychological Analysis* (Sage Publications, London, 2000)

Barnaby, Frank, *How Nuclear Weapons Spread: Nuclear-Weapon Proliferation in the 1990s* (Routledge, New York, 1993)

Barrow, Amy, '"[It's] Like a Rubber Band": Assessing UNSCR 1325 as a Gender Mainstreaming Process' (2009) 5 *International Journal of Law in Context* 51

Beck, Ulrich, *Risk Society: Towards a New Modernity* (Sage, London, 1992)

Becker, Tal, 'Address to the American International Law Association' (2004) 10 *ILSA Journal of International and Comparative Law* 481

Beckman, Robert, 'China, UNCLOS and the South China Sea', paper presented at the Asian Society of International Law, Third Biennial Conference, Beijing, 27–28 August 2011, available at http://cil.nus.edu.sg/wp/wp-content/uploads/2009/09/AsianSIL-Beckman-China-UNCLOS-and-the-South-China-Sea-26-July-2011.pdf

Bederman, David J., *The Spirit of International Law* (University of Georgia Press, Athens, GA, 2002)

Bednar, Jenna, Ferejohn, John and Garrett, Geoffrey, 'The Politics of European Federalism' (1996) 16 *International Review of Law and Economics* 279

Beilstein, Janet, 'The Expanding Role of Women in United Nations Peacekeeping' in Lois Ann Lorentzen and Jennifer Turpin (eds.), *The Women and War Reader* (New York University Press, New York, 1988)

Bekker, P.H.F., *The Legal Position of Inter-Governmental Organizations: A Functional Necessity Analysis of Their Legal Status and Immunities* (Martinus Nijhoff, Dordrecht, 1994)

Bell, Stephen and Hindmoor, Andrew, *Rethinking Governance: The Centrality of the State in Modern Society* (Cambridge University Press, Cambridge, 2009)

Bengtsson, Rikard, 'The Council Presidency and External Representation' in Ole Elgström (ed.), *European Union Council Presidencies: A Comparative Analysis* (Routledge, London, 2003)

Bercovitch, Jacob and Kadayifci-Orellana, Ayse S., 'Religion and Mediation: The Role of Faith-Based Actors in International Conflict Resolution' (2009) 14 *International Negotiation* 175

Berdal, Mats and Ucko, David, 'Whither NATO' in Bruce D. Jones, Shepard Forman and Richard Gowan (eds.), *Cooperating for Peace and Security: Evolving Institutions and Arrangements in a Context of Changing U.S. Security Policy* (Cambridge University Press, Cambridge, 2010)

Berman, Eric G. and Sams, Katie E., *Peacekeeping in Africa: Capabilities and Culpabilities* (UN Institute for Disarmament Research, Geneva, 2000)

'The Peacekeeping Potential of African Regional Organizations' in Jane Boulden (ed.), *Dealing with Conflicts in Africa: The United Nations and Regional Organizations* (Palgrave, New York, 2003)

Bernabe, Riza, 'The Need for a Rice Reserve Mechanism in Southeast Asia', paper presented at the Asian Farmers' Association, 31 May 2010, available at www.iatp.org/files/451_2_107542.pdf

Bernauer, Thomas, *The Chemistry of Regime Formation: Explaining International Cooperation for a Comprehensive Ban on Chemical Weapons* (Dartmouth Publishing, Brookfield, 1993)

'The End of Chemical Warfare' (1993) 24 *Security Dialogue* 97

Bianchi, Andrea, 'Assessing the Effectiveness of the UN Security Council's Anti-Terrorism Measures: The Quest for Legitimacy and Cohesion' (2006) 17 *European Journal of International Law* 881

Black, Julia, 'Decentring Regulation: Understanding the Role of Regulation and Self-regulation in a "Post-Regulatory" World' (2001) 54 *Current Legal Problems* 103

Blakeney, Michael, *Intellectual Property Rights and Food Security* (Cabi, Cambridge, MA, 2009)

Blokker, Neils, 'Beyond "Dili": On the Powers and Practice of International Organizations' in Gerard Kreijen *et al.* (eds.), *State, Sovereignty, and International Governance* (Oxford University Press, Oxford, 2002)

Blyth, Mark, Hodgson, Geoffrey M., Lewis, Orion and Steinmo, Sven, 'Introduction to the Special Issue on the Evolution of Institutions' (2011) 7 *Journal of Institutional Economics* 299

Bogdan, Michael, 'General Principles of Law and the Problem of Lacunae in the Law of Nations' (1977) 46(1) *Nordisk Tidsskrift for International Ret* 37

Boisson de Chazournes, Laurence and Fromageau, Edouard, 'Balancing the Scales: The World Bank Sanctions Process and Access to Remedies' (2012) 23 *European Journal of International Law* 963

Bokor-Szegö, Hanna, 'General Principles of Law' in Mohammaed Bedjaoui (ed.), *International Law: Achievements and Prospects* (Martinus Nijhoff Publishers, Boston, MA, 1991)

Booth, Ken, 'Security and Emancipation' (1991) 17 *Review of International Studies* 313

Bowden, Anna *et al.*, *The Economic Cost of Maritime Piracy*, One Earth Future Foundation Working Paper (2010), available at www.oneearthfuture.org

Bracha, Baruch, 'Judicial Review of Security Powers in Israel: A New Policy of the Courts' (1991) 28 *Stanford Journal of International Law* 61

Bragdon, Susan, Garforth, Kathryn and Harpalaa, John, 'Safeguarding Biodiversity: The Convention on Biological Diversity (CBD)' in Geoff Tansey and Tamsin Rajotte (eds.), *The Future Control of Food: A Guide to International Negotiations and Rules on Intellectual Property, Biodiversity and Food Security* (International Development Research Centre, Ottawa, 2008)

Braithwaite, John and D'Costa, Bina, *Cascades of Violence: The Chittagong Hill Tracts, Kashmir and Pakistan*, Peacebuilding Compared Working Paper (Australian National University, Canberra, 2012), available at http://regnet.anu.edu.au/sites/default/files/Cascades_of_Violence_in_Bangladesh_13thdecember_0.pdf

Brenner, Susan W., *Cyber Threats: The Emerging Fault Lines of the Nation State* (Oxford University Press, Oxford, 2009)

Brenner, Susan W. and Clarke, Donald C., 'Civilians in Cyberwarfare: Conscripts' (2010) 43 *Vanderbilt Journal of Transnational Law* 1011

Briones, Roehlano M. *et al.*, *Climate Change and Price Volatility: Can We Count on the ASEAN Plus Three Emergency Rice Reserve?*, Asian Development Bank Sustainable Development Working Paper Series No. 24 (2012), available at www10.iadb.org/intal/intalcdi/PE/2012/12264.pdf

Brölmann, Catherine, *The Institutional Veil in Public International Law: International Organisations and the Law of Treaties* (Hart Publishing, Oxford, 2007)

Broude, Tomer and Shany, Yuval (eds.), *Multi-Sourced Equivalent Norms in International Law* (Hart Publishing, Oxford/Portland, OR, 2011)

Brown, Davis, 'A Proposal for an International Convention to Regulate the Use of Information Systems in Armed Conflict' (2006) 47 *Harvard International Law Journal* 179

Brown, N. and Kennedy T., *The Court of Justice of the European Communities* (5th edn, Sweet & Maxwell Ltd, London, 2000)

Brown, Theodore, Cueto, Marcos and Fee, Elizabeth, 'The World Health Organization and the Transition From "International" to "Global" Public Health' (2006) 96 *American Journal of Public Health* 67

Brundtland, Gro, 'Global Health and International Security' (2003) 9 *Global Governance* 417

Buchan, Russell, 'Cyber Attacks: Unlawful Uses of Force or Prohibited Interventions?' (2012) 17 *Journal of Conflict and Security Law* 212

Buchanan, Allen and Keohane, Robert O., 'The Legitimacy of Global Governance Institutions' (2006) 20 *Ethics and International Affairs* 405

Buckley, Walter, 'Mind, Mead, and Mental Behaviorism' in Kian Kwan (ed.), *Individuality and Social Control: Essays in Honor of Tamotsu Shibutani* (JAI Press, Greenwich, 1996)

Bunn, George, 'Nuclear Safeguards: How Far Can Inspectors Go?' (2007) 48(2) *International Atomic Energy Agency Bulletin* 49

Burgess, J. Peter, *Security as Ethics*, International Peace Research Institute Policy Brief 6 (Oslo, 2008), available at www.prio.org/Publications/Publication/? x=7336

Burns, Tom and Engdahl, Erik, 'The Social Construction of Consciousness: Collective Consciousness and its Socio-Cultural Foundations' (1998) 5 *Journal of Consciousness Studies* 67

'The Social Construction of Consciousness: Individual Selves, Self-Awareness, and Reflectivity' (1998) 5 *Journal of Consciousness Studies* 166

Buttar, P.A., 'Contextual Syntax of International Instruments Safeguarding Against Nuclear Proliferation' (1984–1987) 11 *Australian Year Book of International Law* 141

Buzan, Barry, Wæver, Ole and de Wilde, Jaap, *Security: A New Framework for Analysis* (Lynne Rienner Publishers, Boulder, CO, 1998)

Bzdera, Andre, 'Comparative Analysis of Federal High Courts: A Political Theory of Judicial Review' (1993) 26 *Canadian Journal of Political Science* 3

Caballero-Anthony, Mely, 'Revisioning Human Security in Southeast Asia' (2004) 28(3) *Asian Perspective* 155

*Regional Security in Southeast Asia: Beyond the ASEAN Way* (Institute of Southeast Asian Studies, Singapore, 2005)

'Challenging Change: Nontraditional Security, Democracy and Regionalism' in Donald K. Emmerson (ed.), *Hard Choices: Security, Democracy, and Regionalism in Southeast Asia* (Walter H. Shorenstein Asia-Pacific Research Center, Stanford, 2008)

Cable, V., 'What is International Economic Security?' (1995) 71 *International Affairs* 305

Call, Charles T. and Wyeth, Vanessa, *Building States to Build Peace* (International Peace Institute and Lynne Reinner, Boulder, CO, 2008)

Cameron, Fraser, *The Foreign and Security Policy of the European Union: Past, Present and Future* (Sheffield Academic Press, Sheffield, 1999)

Cappelletti, Mauro, Seccombe, Monica and Weiler, Joseph (eds.), *Integration Through Law: Europe and the American Federal Experience* (De Gruyter, New York, 1986)

Carlson, John, 'Experience and Challenges in WMD Treaty Verification: A Comparative View' in R. Avenhaus *et al.* (eds.), *Verifying Treaty Compliance* (Springer, Berlin, 2006)

'Defining Non-Compliance: NPT Safeguards' (2009) 39(4) *Arms Control Today* 21

Casement, Anne, 'The Shadow' in Renos Papadopoulos (ed.), *The Handbook of Jungian Psychology: Theory, Practice and Applications* (Routledge, New York, 2006)

Cassese, Antonio, 'Ex iniuria ius oritur: Are We Moving Towards International Legitimation of Forcible Humanitarian Countermeasures in the World Community?' (1999) 10 *European Journal of International Law* 23

Chalmers, Damian, Davies, Gareth and Monti, Giorgio, *European Union Law* (2nd edn, Cambridge University Press, Cambridge, 2010)

Chan, Lai-Ha, Chen, Lucy and Xu, Jin, 'China's Engagement with Global Health Diplomacy: Was SARS a Watershed?' (2010) 7 *Public Library of Science Medicine* 1

Chapman, Terence L., 'International Security Institutions, Domestic Politics, and Institutional Legitimacy' (2007) 51 *Journal of Conflict Resolution* 134

Charlesworth, Hilary and Chinkin, Christine, *The Boundaries of International Law: A Feminist Analysis* (Manchester University Press, Manchester, 2000)

'Regulatory Frameworks in International Law' in Christine Parker *et al.* (eds.), *Regulating Law* (Oxford University Press, Oxford, 2004)

Charlesworth, Hilary, *et al.* (eds.), *The Fluid State: International Law and National Legal Systems* (Federation Press, Sydney, 2005)

Charney, Jonathon I., 'Universal International Law' (1993) 87 *American Journal of International Law* 529

Chen, Lincoln and Narasimhan, Vasant, 'Human Security and Global Health' (2003) 4 *Journal of Human Development* 181

Cheng, Bin, *General Principles of Law as Applied by International Courts and Tribunals* (Stevens and Sons, London, 1953)

Chesterman, Simon, *You, the People* (Cambridge University Press, Cambridge, 2004)

Chesterman, Simon, Ignatieff, Michael and Thakur, Ramesh (eds.), *Making States Work: State Failure and the Crisis of Governance* (United Nations University Press, New York, 2005)

Chiarolla, Claudio, 'Commodifying Agricultural Biodiversity and Development-related Issues' (2006) 9 *Journal of World Intellectual Property* 25

Cilliers, Jakkie and Pottgieter, Johann, 'The African Standby Force' in Ulf Engel and João Gomes Porto (eds.), *Africa's New Peace and Security Architecture: Promoting Norms, Institutionalizing Solutions* (Ashgate, Farnham, 2010)

Cockayne, James and Mears, Emily S., *Private Military and Security Companies: A Framework for Regulation* (International Peace Institute, New York, 2009)

Coicaud, Jean-Marc and Heiskanen, Veijo (eds.), *The Legitimacy of International Organizations* (United Nations University Press, New York, 2001)

Coleman, Katharina P., *International Organisations and Peace Enforcement: The Politics of International Legitimacy* (Cambridge University Press, Cambridge, 2007)

Colman, Warren, 'The Self' in Renos Papadopoulos (ed.), *The Handbook of Jungian Psychology: Theory, Practice and Applications* (Routledge, New York, 2006)

Colson, David A., 'Sovereignty over Pulau Ligitan and Pulau Sipadan (Indonesia/ Malaysia)' (2003) 97 *American Journal of International Law* 398

Conway, Maura, 'What is Cyberterrorism?' (2002) 101 *Current History* 436

Cook, David M., *Mitigating Cyber-Threats through Public-Private Partnerships: Low Cost Governance with High Impact Returns* (Edith Cowan University, Perth, 2010)

Cortright, David and Wall, Kristen, *Afghan Women Speak: Enhancing Security and Human Rights in Afghanistan* (University of Notre Dame, South Bend, IN, 2012)

Craig, Paul, *Administrative Law* (4th edn, Sweet and Maxwell, London, 1999)
  'Integration, Democracy and Legitimacy' in Paul Craig and Grainne de Burca (eds.), *The Evolution of EU Law* (2nd edn, Oxford University Press, Oxford, 2011)

Craig, Paul and de Burca, Grainne, *EU Law: Text, Cases and Materials* (5th edn, Oxford University Press, Oxford, 2011)
  *The Evolution of EU Law* (2nd edn, Oxford University Press, Oxford, 2011)

Crail, Peter, 'IAEA Sends Syria Nuclear Case to UN' (2011) 41(6) *Arms Control Today* 1

Cryer, Robert, 'The Security Council and Article 39: A Threat to Coherence?' (1996) 1 *Journal of Armed Conflict Law* 161

D'Amato, Anthony, 'On the Legitimacy of International Institutions' in Rüdiger Wolfrum and Volker Röben (eds.), *Legitimacy in International Law* (Springer, Heidelberg, 2008)

D'Costa, Bina, 'Marginalized Identity: New Frontiers of Research for IR?' in Brooke A. Ackerly, Maria Stern and Jacqui True (eds.), *Feminist*

*Methodologies for International Relations* (Cambridge University Press, Cambridge, 2006)

*Nationbuilding, Gender and War Crimes in South Asia* (Routledge, London, 2011)

D'Costa, Bina and Ford, Jo, *Terminology Matters: Peacebuilding, Statebuilding and Nationbuilding* (Center for International Governance and Justice, Canberra, 2009), available at http://regnet.anu.edu.au/publications/termi nology-matters-statebuilding-nationbuilding-and-peacebuilding

D'Costa, Bina and Lee Koo, Katrina, 'The Politics of Voice: Feminist Security Studies and the Asia-Pacific' (2013) 3 *International Studies Perspective* 451

Daase, Christopher, 'Spontaneous Institutions: Peacekeeping as an International Convention' in Helga Haftendorn, Robert O. Keohane and Celeste A. Wallander (eds.), *Imperfect Unions: Security Institutions over Time and Space* (Oxford University Press, Oxford, 1999)

Dahlitz, Julie, *Nuclear Arms Control with Effective International Agreements* (McPhee Gribble, Melbourne, 1983)

Dajani, Omar, '"No Security Without Law": Prospects for Implementing a Rights-Based Approach in Palestinian-Israeli Security Negotiations' in Susan Akram, Michael Dumper, Michael Lynk and Iain Scobbie (eds.), *International Law and the Israeli-Palestinian Conflict* (Routledge, London, 2011)

Dalby, Simon, *Environmental Security* (University of Minnesota Press, Minneapolis, MN, 2002)

*Security and Environmental Change* (Polity Press, Cambridge, 2009)

Dang, Thi Thu Huong, *Examining the Engagement Between Civil Society and ASEAN in the ASEAN Charter Process* (GRIN Verlag, Santa Cruz, CA, 2008)

Danilenko, G.M., *Law-Making in the International Community* (Martinus Nijhoff Publishers, The Netherlands, 1993)

Daño, Elenita and Peria, Elpidio, *Emergency or Expediency? A Study of Emergency Rise Reserve Schemes in Asia* (Asian Partnership for the Development of Human Resources in Rural Asia, 2007), available at http://asiadhrra.org/wordpress/2007/12/16/emergency-or-expediency-a-study-of-emergency-rice-reserve-schemes-in-asia

Davies, Bill, *Resisting the European Court of Justice: West Germany's Confrontation with European Law, 1949–1979* (Cambridge University Press, Cambridge, 2012)

Davies, Sara, 'Securitizing Infectious Disease' (2008) 84 *International Affairs* 295

Dawe, David and Slayton, Tom, 'The World Rice Market Crisis of 2007-2008' in David Dawe (ed.), *The Rice Crisis: Markets, Policies and Food Security* (FAO and Earthscan, London/Washington, DC, 2010)

de Burca, G. and Weiler, J.H.H. (eds.), *The European Court of Justice* (Oxford University Press, Oxford, 2001)

de la Mare, Thomas and Donnelly, Catherine, 'Preliminary Rulings and EU Legal Integration: Evolution and Stasis' in Paul Craig and Gráinne de Búrca (eds.), *The Evolution of EU Law* (2nd edn, Oxford University Press, Oxford, 2011)

de Riviera, Joseph, 'Emotional Climate, Human Security and Cultures of Peace' (2007) 63(2) *Journal of Social Issues* 233

De Schutter, Oliver, *International Trade in Agriculture and the Right to Food*, Dialogue on Globalization Occasional Paper No. 46 (Friedrich Ebert Siftung, Geneva, 2009), available at http://library.fes.de/pdf-files/bueros/genf/06819.pdf

   *The World Trade Organization and the Post-Global Food Crisis Agenda*, Briefing Note 05, UN Special Rapporteur on the Right to Food (November 2011), available at www.srfood.org/images/stories/pdf/otherdocuments/20111116_briefing_note_05_en.pdf

   *The World Trade Organization and the Post-Global Food Crisis Agenda: Putting Food Security in the International Trade System*, Activity Report, UN Special Rapporteur on the Right to Food (November 2011), available at www.wto.org/english/news_e/news11_e/deschutter_2011_e.pdf

de Smith, S. A., Woolf, H. and Jowell, J., *Judicial Review of Administrative Action* (5th edn, Sweet and Maxwell, London, 1995)

de Wet, Erika, *Chapter VII Powers of the Security Council* (Hart Publishing, Oxford/Portland, OR, 2004)

   'The International Constitutional Order' (2006) 55 *International and Comparative Law Quarterly* 51

   'The Evolving Role of ECOWAS and the SADC in Peace Operations: A Challenge to the Primacy of the United Nations Security Council in Matters of Peace and Security?' (2014) 27 *Leiden Journal of International Law* 353

de Witte, Bruno, 'Direct Effect, Primacy and the Nature of the Legal Order' in Paul Craig and Gráinne de Búrca (eds.), *The Evolution of EU Law* (2nd edn, Oxford University Press, Oxford, 2011)

Death Penalty Information Center, 'Executions by Year Since 1976' (2014), available at www.deathpenaltyinfo.org/executions-year

Degan, Vladimir Duro, *Sources of International Law* (Martinus Nijhoff Publishers, Boston, 1997)

Dehousse, R., *The European Court of Justice* (Macmillan, London, 1998)

Delon, P.J., *The International Health Regulations: A Practical Guide* (World Health Organization, Geneva, 1975)

Desker, Barry, *Is the ASEAN Charter Necessary?*, Commentary (S. Rajaratnam School of International Studies, 17 July 2008), available at www.rsis.edu.sg/publications/Perspective/RSIS0772008.pdf

Desta, Melaku Geboye, 'Food Security and International Trade Law: An Appraisal of the World Trade Organization Approach' (2001) 35 *Journal of World Trade* 449

Dhanapala, Jayantha and Rydell, Randy, *Multilateral Diplomacy and the NPT: An Insider's Account* (United Nations, Geneva, 2005)

Diao, Xinshen, Diaz-Bonilla, Eugenio and Robinson, Sherman, *How Much Does It Hurt? The Impact of Agricultural Trade Policies on Developing Countries* (International Food Policy Research Institute, Washington, DC, 2003), available at www.ifpri.org/sites/default/files/pubs/media/trade/trade.pdf

Diehl, Paul, *Peace Operations* (Polity Press, Cambridge, 2008)

Dobbins, James *et al.*, *America's Role in Nation-Building: From Germany to Iraq* (RAND Corporation, Santa Monica, CA, 2003)

Downes, David, 'How Intellectual Property Could Be a Tool to Protect Traditional Knowledge' (2000) 25 *Columbia Journal of Environmental Law* 253

Drahos, Peter, 'Negotiating Intellectual Property Rights: Between Coercion and Dialogue' in Peter Drahos and Ruth Mayne (eds.), *Global Intellectual Property Rights: Knowledge, Access and Development* (Palgrave Macmillan, Hampshire/New York, 2002)

Dudziak, Mary, 'Law, War and the History of Time' (2009) 98 *California Law Review* 1669

Duffield, Mark, *Global Governance and the New Wars: The Merging of Development and Security* (Zed Books, New York, 2001)

Dunn, D. Elwood, 'Liberia's Internal Responses to ECOMOG's Interventionist Efforts' in Karl P. Magyar and Earl Conteh-Morgan (eds.), *Peacekeeping in Africa: ECOMOG in Liberia* (Macmillan Press, Hampshire, 1998)

Dupuy, Florian and Dupuy, Pierre-Marie, 'A Legal Analysis of China's Historic Rights Claim in the South China Sea' (2013) 107 *American Journal of International Law* 124

Durkheim, E., 'The Determination of Moral Facts' in *Sociology and Philosophy* (D F. Pocock, trans., Free Press, New York, [1906] 1974)

*The Elementary Forms of Religious Life* (Free Press, New York, [1912] 1947)

Dyzenhaus, David, *The Constitution of Law: Legality in a Time of Emergency* (Cambridge University Press, Cambridge, 2006)

'*Schmitt v Dicey*: Are States of Emergency Inside or Outside the Legal Order?' (2006) 27 *Cardozo Law Review* 2005

'Cycles of Legality in Emergency Times' (2007) 18 *Public Law Review* 165

Dyzenhaus, David (ed.), *The Unity of Public Law* (Hart Publishing, Oxford/Portland, OR, 2004)

Edwards, John, 'Reengaging with the World: A Return to Moral Leadership' (2007) 86 *Foreign Affairs* 19

Edwards, Lucy Morgan, 'Statebuilding in Afghanistan: A Case Showing the Limits?' (2010) 92 *International Review of the Red Cross* 967

Edwardson, Shelley, 'Reconciling TRIPS and the Right to Food' in Thomas Cottier, Joost Pauwelyn and Elisabeth Bonanomi (eds.), *Human Rights and International Trade* (Oxford University Press, Oxford, 2005)

Elazar, Daniel J., *Exploring Federalism* (University of Alabama Press, Tuscaloosa, AL, 1987)

Emmers, Ralf, *Geopolitics and Maritime Territorial Disputes in East Asia* (Routledge, London, 2009)

Emmers, Ralf and Tan, See Seng, 'The ASEAN Regional Forum and Preventive Diplomacy: Built to Fail?' (2011) 7 *Asian Security* 44

Emmerson, Donald K., 'Security, Community, and Democracy in Southeast Asia: Analyzing ASEAN' (2005) 6 *Japanese Journal of Political Science* 165

Enderlin, Charles, *Shattered Dreams: The Failure of the Peace Process in the Middle East, 1995–2002* (Other Press LLC, New York, 2003)

Engel, Ulf and Gomes Porto, João (eds.), *Africa's New Peace and Security Architecture: Promoting Norms, Institutionalizing Solutions* (Ashgate, Farnham, 2010)

Farrall, Jeremy and Rubenstein, Kim (eds.), *Sanctions, Accountability and Governance in a Globalised World* (Cambridge University Press, Cambridge, 2009)

Fatovic, Clement, *Outside the Law: Emergency and Executive Power* (Johns Hopkins University Press, Baltimore, MD, 2009)

Fidler, David P., 'From International Sanitary Conventions to Global Health Security: The New International Health Regulations' (2005) 4 *Chinese Journal of International Law* 325

Fidler, David P. and Gostin, Lawrence O., *Biosecurity in the Global Age: Biological Weapons, Public Health, and the Rule of Law* (Stanford University Press, Stanford, CA, 2008)

Fierke, Karin, *Critical Approaches to International Security* (Polity Press, Cambridge/Malden, MA, 2007)

Finch, George, *The Sources of Modern International Law* (Carnegie Endowment for International Peace, Washington, DC, [1937] 1971)

Fioretos, Orfeo, 'Historical Institutionalism in International Relations' (2011) 65 *International Organization* 367

Fischer-Lescano, Andreas and Teubner, Gunther, 'Regime-Collisions: The Vain Search for Legal Unity in the Fragmentation of Global Law' (2004) 25 *Michigan Journal of International Law* 999

Fisher, Louis, 'Invoking Inherent Powers: A Primer' (2007) 37(1) *Presidential Quarterly Studies* 3

Fisler Damrosch, Lori *et al.*, *International Law Cases and Materials* (4th edn, West Group Publishing, St Paul, MN, 2001)

Follesdal, Andreas, Wessel, Ramses A. and Wouters, Jan (eds.), *Multilevel Regulation and the EU: The Interplay between Global, European and National Normative Processes* (Martinus Nijhoff Publishers, Leiden, 2008)

Foot, Rosemary, 'The United Nations, Counter Terrorism, and Human Rights: Institutional Adaptation and Embedded Ideas' (2007) 29 *Human Rights Quarterly* 489

Ford, Paul Leicester, *The Works of Thomas Jefferson: Volume 10* (G.P. Putnam's Sons, New York/London, 1905)

Forrester, Jay, *Principles of Systems* (Wright-Allen Press, Cambridge, MA, 1969)

Franck, Thomas M., *The Power of Legitimacy among Nations* (Oxford University Press, Oxford, 1990)

'What Happens Now? The United Nations After Iraq' (2003) 97 *American Journal of International Law* 607

Friedmann, Wolfgang, 'The Uses of "General Principles" in the Development of International Law' (1963) 57 *American Journal of International Law* 279

*The Changing Structure of International Law* (Stevens and Sons, London, 1964)

Fukuyama, Francis, *State-Building: Governance and World Order in the 21st Century* (Cornell University Press, Ithaca, NY, 2004)

Fursdon, E., *The European Defence Community: A History* (Macmillan, London, 1980)

Gani, Miriam and Matthew, Penelope (eds.), *Fresh Perspectives on the 'War on Terror'* (ANU E-Press, Canberra, 2008)

Gao, Zhiguo and Jia, Bing Bing, 'The Nine-Dash Line in the South China Sea: History, Status, and Implications' (2013) 107 *American Journal of International Law* 98

Garrett, Laurie and Fidler, David P., 'Sharing H5N1 Viruses to Stop a Global Influenza Pandemic' (2007) 4 *Public Library of Science Medicine* 1712

Garwin, Richard and Charpak, Georges, *Megawatts and Megatons: A Turning Point in the Nuclear Age?* (Alfred A. Knopf, New York, 2001)

Gathii, James Thuo, 'Kenya's Piracy Prosecutions' (2010) 104 *American Journal of International Law* 416

Geiss, Robin and Petrig, Anna, *Piracy and Armed Robbery at Sea: The Legal Framework for Counter-Piracy Operations in Somalia and the Gulf of Aden* (Oxford University Press, Oxford, 2011)

Gerstetter, Christiane, Gorlach, Benjamin, Neumann, Kirsten and Schaffrin, Dora, 'The International Treaty on Plant Genetic Resources for Food and Agriculture within the Current Legal Regime Complex on Plant Genetic Resources' (2007) 10(3–4) *Journal of World Intellectual Property* 259

Gervais, Daniel, *The TRIPS Agreement: Drafting History and Analysis* (4th edn, Sweet and Maxwell, London, 2012)

Giddens, Anthony, *Modernity and Self-Identity: Self and Society in the Late Modern Age* (Polity Press, Cambridge, 1991)

Gill, Bates, Green, Michael, Tsuji, Kiyoto and Watts, William (eds.), *Strategic Views on Asian Regionalism: Survey Results and Analysis* (Center for Strategic and International Studies, Washington, DC, 2009)

Glenn, H. Patrick, *Legal Traditions of the World* (2nd edn, Oxford University Press, Oxford, 2004)

Glennon, Michael J. and Sur, Serge, *Terrorism and International Law* (Martinus Nijhoff, The Hague, 2006)

Godlee, Fiona, 'WHO in Retreat: Is It Losing Its Influence?' (1994) 309 *British Medical Journal* 1491

Goetz, Anne Marie, 'Gender Justice, Citizenship and Entitlements: Core Concepts, Central Debates and New Directions for Research' in Maitrayee Mukhopadhyay and Navsharan Singh (eds.), *Gender Justice, Citizenship and Development* (Zubaan, New Delhi, 2007)

Goh, Gillian, 'The "ASEAN Way": Non-Intervention and ASEAN's Role in Conflict Management' (2003) 3 *Stanford Journal of East Asian Affairs* 113

Goldman, Kjell, 'Appropriateness and Consequences: The Logic of Neo-Institutionalism' (2005) 18 *Governance: An International Journal of Policy, Administration, and Institutions* 35

Goldsmith, Jack L. and Posner, Eric A., *The Limits of International Law* (Oxford University Press, New York, 2005)

Golove, David, 'Exception and Emergency Powers: Comment on Exception and Emergency Powers' (2000) 21 *Cardozo Law Review* 1895

Gonzalez, Carmen, 'Institutionalizing Inequality: The WTO Agreement on Agriculture, Food Security and Developing Countries' (2002) 27 *Columbia Journal of Environmental Law* 433

'The Global Food Crisis: Law, Policy, and the Elusive Quest for Justice' (2010) 13 *Yale Human Rights and Development Law Journal* 462

Goodhand, Jonathan and Sedra, Mark, 'Bribes or Bargains? Peace Conditionalities and "Post-Conflict" Reconstruction in Afghanistan' (2007) 14 *International Peacekeeping* 41

Goodrich, Leland M., Hambro, Edvard and Simons, Anne Patricia, *Charter of the United Nations: Commentary and Documents* (3rd rev edn, Columbia University Press, New York, 1969)

Goold, Benjamin J. and Lazarus, Liora (eds.), *Security and Human Rights* (Hart Publishing, Oxford/Portland, OR, 2007)

Gosalbo-Bono, Ricardo, 'The Significance of the Rule of Law and its Implications for the European Union and the United States' (2010) 72 *University of Pittsburgh Law Review* 229

Gostin, Lawrence O. and Fidler, David P., 'WHO's Pandemic Influenza Preparedness Framework: A Milestone in Global Governance for Health' (2011) 306 *Journal of the American Medical Association* 200

Govan, Gregory G., 'On-Site Inspection as a Verification Tool' in James Brown (ed.), *Old Issues and New Strategies in Arms Control and Verification* (VU University Press, Amsterdam, 1995)

Gowan, Richard and Jones, Bruce D., 'Conclusion: International Institutions and the Problems of Adaptation' in Bruce D. Jones, Shepard Forman and Richard Gowan (eds.), *Cooperating for Peace and Security: Evolving*

*Institutions and Arrangements in a Context of Changing US Security Policy* (Cambridge University Press, Cambridge, 2010)

Graham, David E., 'Cyber Threats and the Law of War' (2010) *Journal of National Security Law and Policy* 87

Graybeal, Sidney N. and Krepon, Michael, 'On-Site Inspections' in Michael Krepon and Mary Umberger (eds.), *Verification and Compliance: A Problem-Solving Approach* (Macmillan Press, Cambridge, 1988)

Green, A. and Trebilcock, M., 'Enforcing WTO Obligations: What Can We Learn from Export Subsidies?' (2007) 10 *Journal of International Economic Law* 653

Greenwood, Christopher, 'The Administration of Occupied Territory' in Emma Playfair (ed.), *International Law and the Administration of Occupied Territories* (Oxford University Press, Oxford, 2003)

Gross, Oren, 'The Normless and the Exceptionless Exception: Carl Schmitt's Theory of Emergency Powers and the "Norm-Exception" Dichotomy' (1999–2000) 21 *Cardozo Law Review* 1825

'Extra-Legality and the Ethic of Political Responsibility' in Victor Ramraj (ed.), *Emergencies and the Limits of Legality* (Cambridge University Press, Cambridge, 2008)

Gross, Oren and Aoláin, Fionnuala Ní, *Law in Times of Crisis: Emergency Powers in Theory and Practice* (Cambridge University Press, Cambridge, 2006)

Grove, Gregory D., 'Cyber-Attacks and International Law' (2000) 42 *Survival* 89

Guthrie, Peter, 'Security Council Sanctions and the Protection of Individual Rights' (2004) 60 *NYU Annual Survey of American Law* 491

Guzman, Andrew T., *How International Law Works: A Rational Choice Theory* (Oxford University Press, Oxford, 2008)

Haas, Michael, *The Asian Way to Peace: A Story of Regional Cooperation* (Praeger, New York, 1989)

Haftendorn, Helga, Keohane, Robert O. and Wallander, Celeste A. (eds.), *Imperfect Unions: Security Institutions over Time and Space* (Oxford University Press, Oxford, 1999)

Halewood, Michael and Nnadozie, Kent, 'Giving Priority to the Commons: The International Treaty on Plant Genetic Resources for Food and Agriculture' in Geoff Tansey and Tamsin Rajotte (eds.), *The Future Control of Food: A Guide to International Negotiations and Rules on Intellectual Property, Biodiversity and Food Security* (International Development Research Centre, Ottawa, 2008)

Hall, Kath, *Butterworths Guides: Legislation* (Butterworths, Chatswood, 2002)

Hall, Peter and Taylor, Rosemary, 'Political Science and the Three New Institutionalism' (1996) 44 *Political Studies* 936

Hamilton, Clive, *The Freedom Paradox: Towards a Post-Secular Ethics* (Allen & Unwin, Sydney, 2008)

Haqqani, Husain, *Pakistan: Between Mosque and Military* (Carnegie Endowment for International Peace, Washington, DC, 2005)

Hardin, Russell, *Collective Action* (Johns Hopkins University Press, Baltimore, MD, 1982)

Harlow, Carol, 'Global Administrative Law: The Quest for Principles and Values' (2006) 17 *European Journal of International Law* 187

Harper, Keith, 'Does the United Nations Security Council Have the Competence to Act as Court and Legislature?' (1994–1995) 27 *New York University Journal of International Law and Politics* 103

Hartley, T., *The Foundations of European Union Law* (7th edn, Oxford University Press, Oxford, 2010)

Haugen, Hans, Muller, Manuel and Narasimhan, Savita, 'Food Security and Intellectual Property Rights' in Tzen Wong and Graham Dutfield (eds.), *Intellectual Property and Human Development* (Cambridge University Press, Cambridge, 2011)

Hauke, Christopher, 'The Unconscious: Personal and Collective' in Renos Papadopoulos (ed.), *The Handbook of Jungian Psychology: Theory, Practice and Applications* (Routledge, New York, 2006)

Hauling, Fu, 'Responses to Terrorism in China' in Victor V. Ramraj *et al.* (eds.), *Global Anti-Terrorism Law and Policy* (2nd edn, Cambridge University Press, New York, 2012)

Headey, Derek and Fan, Shenggen, *Reflections on the Global Food Crisis* (International Food Policy Research Institute, Washington, DC, 2010), available at www.ifpri.org/sites/default/files/publications/rr165.pdf

Heald, Paul, 'The Rhetoric of Biopiracy' (2003) 11 *Cardozo Journal of International and Comparative Law* 519

Heiskanan, Veijo, 'Introduction' in Jean-Marc Coicaud and Veijo Heiskanen (eds.), *The Legitimacy of International Organizations* (United Nations University Press, New York, 2001)

Helfer, Laurence, *Intellectual Property Rights in Plant Varieties: An Overview with Options for National Governments*, FAO Legal Papers Online No. 31 (2002), available at www.fao.org/fileadmin/user_upload/legal/docs/lpo31-2.pdf

Heliskoski, Joni, *Mixed Agreements as a Technique for Organizing the External Relations of the European Community and Its Member States* (Kluwer Law International, The Hague, 2001)

Henderson, Joseph, *Cultural Attitudes in Psychological Perspective* (Inner City Books, Toronto, 1984)

Herz, John, *Political Realism and Political Idealism* (University of Chicago Press, Chicago, IL, 1951)

Hesse, Martmut and Charalambous, Nicolaos L., 'New Security Measures for the International Shipping Community' (2004) 3(2) *World Maritime University Journal of Maritime Affairs* 123

Heymann, David L., 'The Evolving Infectious Disease Threat: Implications for National and Global Security' (2003) 4 *Journal of Human Development* 191
'SARS: A Global Response to an International Threat' (2004) 10 *Brown Journal of World Affairs* 185
Hibbs, Mark, 'Reporting to the Board of Governors' in Jeffrey Lewis *et al.*, *Arms Control Wonk* (13 September 2011), available at http://hibbs.armscontrolwonk.com/
'The Unspectacular Future of the IAEA Additional Protocol', *Carnegie Proliferation Analysis* (26 April 2012), available at http://carnegieendow ment.org/2012/04/26/unspectacular-future-of-iaea-additional-protocol
Higgins, Rosalin, 'The General International Law of Terrorism' in Rosalin Higgins and Maurice Flory (eds.), *International Law and Terrorism* (Routledge, London/New York, 1997)
Hillier, Tim, *Sourcebook on Public International Law* (Cavendish Publishing, London, 1998)
Hillion, Christoph and Koutrakos, Panos (eds.), *Mixed Agreements Revisited: The EU and its Member States in the World* (Hart Publishing, Oxford, 2010)
Hirsch, Theodore, 'The IAEA Additional Protocol: What it Is and Why it Matters' (2004) 11(3) *Nonproliferation Review* 140
Hobsbawm, E., *Nations and Nationalism Since 1780: Programme, Myth and Reality* (Cambridge University Press, Cambridge, 1990)
Holland, Gail, *A Call for Connection: Solutions for Creating a Whole New Culture* (New World Library, Novato, CA, 1998)
Hooghe, Liesbet and Marks, Gary, *Multi-Level Governance and European Integration* (Rowman and Littlefield Publishers, Lanham, MA, 2001)
Hoppe, Carsten and Quirico, Ottavio, 'Codes of Conduct for Private Military and Security Companies: The State of Self-Regulation in the Industry' in Francesco Francioni and Natalino Ronzitti (eds.), *War by Contract* (Oxford University Press, Oxford, 2011)
Hoskyns, Catherine, *The Congo Since Independence: January 1960–December 1961* (Oxford University Press, London, 1965)
Howse, Robert, 'The Legitimacy of the World Trade Organisation' in Jean-Marc Coicaud and Veijo Heiskanen (eds.), *The Legitimacy of International Organizations* (United Nations University Press, New York, 2001)
Hudson, Manley O., *International Legislation: A Collection of the Texts of Multipartite International Instruments of General Interest beginning with the Covenant of the League of Nations* (Carnegie Endowment for International Peace, 1931)
Human Rights Watch, *World Report 2012: Afghanistan* (2012), available at www.hrw.org/world-report-2012/world-report-2012-afghanistan
Hurd, Ian, *After Anarchy: Legitimacy and Power in the United Nations Security Council* (Princeton University Press, Princeton, NJ, 2007)
Hussain, Asaf, *Elite Politics in an Ideological State: The Case of Pakistan* (Dawson, Folkestone, 1979)

Hussain, Zayid, *The Scorpion's Tails* (Simon and Schuster Inc., New York, 2010)

Hyde, Maggie and McGuinness, Michael, *Introducing Jung* (Icon Books, Duxford, 1999)

Independent Commission on Disarmament and Security Issues, *North-South: A Programme for Survival* (Pan Books, London, 1980)

  *Common Security: A Blueprint for Survival* (Simon and Schuster, New York, 1982)

Infocomm Development Authority of Singapore, *Infocomm Security Masterplan*, available at www.ida.gov.sg

International Crisis Group, *Implementing Peace and Security Architecture (I): Central Africa*, Africa Report No. 181 (7 November 2011), available at www. crisisgroup.org/en/regions/africa/central-africa/181-implementing-peace-and-security-architecture-l-central-africa.aspx

  *Implementing Peace and Security Architecture (II): Southern Africa*, Africa Report No. 191 (15 October 2012), available at www.crisisgroup.org/en/reg ions/africa/southern-africa/191-implementing-peace-and-security-architec ture-ii-southern-africa.aspx

  *Women and Conflict in Afghanistan*, Asia Report No. 252 (14 October 2013), available at www.crisisgroup.org/en/regions/asia/southern-asia/afghani stan/252-women-and-conflict-in-afghanistan.aspx

Jacobsson, Marie, 'Maritime Security: An Individual or a Collective Responsibility?' in Jarna Petman and Jan Klabbers (eds.), *Nordic Cosmopolitanism: Essays in International Law for Martti Koskenniemi* (Martinus Nijhoff Publishers, Leiden, 2003)

Jayakumar, S. and Koh, Tommy, *Pedra Branca: The Road to the World Court* (NUS Press, Singapore, 2009)

Jeng, Abou, *Peacebuilding in the African Union: Law, Philosophy and Practice* (Cambridge University Press, Cambridge, 2012)

Jenkins, K. and Plowden, W., *Governance and Nationbuilding: The Failure of International Intervention* (Edward Elgar, Cheltenham, 2006)

Jennings, Robert, 'What is International Law and How Do We Tell It When We See It?' (1981) 37 *Schweitzerisches Jahrbuch für Internationales Recht* 59

  'The Identification of International Law' in Bin Cheng (ed.), *International Law: Teaching and Practice* (Stevens, London, 1982)

  'Teachings and Teaching in International Law' in Jerzy Makarczyk (ed.), *Essays in International Law in Honour of Judge Manfred Lachs* (Martinus Nijhoff Publishers, The Hague, 1984)

Jervis, Robert, *Perception and Misperception in International Politics* (Princeton University Press, Princeton, NJ, 1976)

  'Cooperation under the Security Dilemma' (1978) 30(2) *World Politics: A Quarterly Journal of International Relations* 167

  'Security Regime' (1982) 36 *International Organization* 357

Jin, Jiyong and Karackattu, Joe T., 'Infectious Diseases and Securitization: WHO's Dilemma' (2011) 9 *Biosecurity and Bioterrorism* 182

Jo, Dong-Joon and Gartzke, E., 'Determinates of Nuclear Weapons Proliferation' (2007) 51 *Journal of Conflict Resolution* 167

Johnston, Alastair Iain, *Social States: China in International Institutions, 1980–2000* (Princeton University Press, Princeton, NJ, 2008)

Johnstone, Ian, 'Law-Making through the Operational Activities of International Organizations' (2008) 40 *George Washington International Law Review* 87

  'Normative Evaluation at the UN: Impact on Operational Activities' in Bruce D. Jones, Shepard Forman and Richard Gowan (eds.), *Cooperating for Peace and Security: Evolving Institutions and Arrangements in a Context of Changing US Security Policy* (Cambridge University Press, Cambridge, 2010)

Jonah, James O.C., 'The OAU: Peace Keeping and Conflict Resolution' in Yassin El-Ayouty (ed.), *The Organization of African Unity After Thirty Years* (Praeger, Westport, CT, 1994)

Jones, D. and Kwiecinski, A., *Policy Responses in Emerging Economies to International Agricultural Commodity Price Surges*, OECD Food, Agriculture and Fisheries Working Papers No. 34 (2010), available at http://dx.doi.org/10.1787/5km6 c61fv40w-en

Jones, David Martin and Smith, Michael L.R., 'ASEAN's Imitation Community' (2002) 46 *Orbis* 93

Jones, Lee, *ASEAN, Sovereignty and Intervention in Southeast Asia* (Palgrave Macmillan, New York, 2012)

Joseph, Sarah, *Blame It on the WTO: A Human Rights Critique* (Oxford University Press, Oxford, 2012)

Joyner, Daniel H., *International Law and the Proliferation of Weapons of Mass Destruction* (Oxford University Press, Oxford, 2009)

Jung, Carl, 'The Structure of the Psyche' in Sir Herbert Read, Michael Fordham and Gerhard Adler (eds.), *The Collected Works of C.G. Jung: 8* (R.F.C. Hull, trans., Routledge and Kegan Paul/Princeton University Press, London/New York, 1927)

  'The Concept of the Collective Unconscious' in Sir Herbert Read, Michael Fordham and Gerhard Adler (eds.), *The Collected Works of C.G. Jung: 9* (R.F.C. Hull, trans., Routledge and Kegan Paul/Princeton University Press, London/New York, 1936)

  *Dreams* (Routledge, London, [1974] 2001)

Juwana, Hikmahanto, 'Anti-Terrorism Effects in Indonesia' in Victor V. Ramraj et al. (eds.), *Global Anti-Terrorism Law and Policy* (2nd edn, Cambridge University Press, New York, 2012)

Kacowicz, Arie, *Peaceful Territorial Change* (South Carolina University Press, Columbia, SC, 1994)

Kadelbach, Stefan, 'Interpretation of the Charter' in Bruno Simma et al. (eds.), *The Charter of the United Nations: A Commentary* (3rd edn, Oxford University Press, Oxford, 2012)

Kahler, Miles, 'Institutionalisation as Strategy: The Asia-Pacific Case' (2000) 54 *International Organization* 549

Kaldor, Mary, *New and Old Wars: Organised Violence in a Global Era* (Polity, Cambridge, 1999)

Kamradt-Scott, Adam, 'The WHO Secretariat, Norm Entrepreneurship, and Global Disease Outbreak Control' (2010) 1 *Journal of International Organizations Studies* 72

    'The Evolving WHO: Implications for Global Health Security' (2011) 6 *Global Public Health* 801

    'Global Health Security under Threat? Progress in Implementing in IHR 2005' (2012) 3 *Health Diplomacy Monitor* 4

Kamradt-Scott, Adam and Lee, Kelley, 'The 2011 Pandemic Influenza Preparedness Framework: Global Health Secured or a Missed Opportunity?' (2011) 59 *Political Studies* 831

Kamradt-Scott, Adam and Rushton, Simon, 'The Revised International Health Regulations: Socialization, Compliance and Changing Norms of Global Health Security' (2010) 24 *Global Change, Peace and Security* 57

Kant, Immanuel, *The Critique of Pure Reason* (Norman Kemp Smith, ed., trans., Palgrave Macmillan, New York, [1929] 2003)

    *Religion within the Limits of Reason Alone* (Theodore M. Greene and Hoyt H. Hudson Harper, eds., Torchbooks, New York, 1960)

Kassim, Yang Razali, *ASEAN Cohesion: Making Sense of Indonesian Reactions to Bilateral Disputes*, Commentary No. 15/2005 (Institute of Defence and Strategic Studies, 6 April 2005), available at www.rsis.edu.sg/publications/Perspective/IDSS152005.pdf

    *ASEAN Community: Losing Grip over Vision 2015?*, Commentary No. 87/2011 (S. Rajaratnam School of International Studies, 2 June 2011), available at www.rsis.edu.sg/publications/Perspective/RSIS0872011.pdf

Kaye, Stuart, 'Freedom of Navigation in a Post 9/11 World: Security and Creeping Jurisdiction' in David Freestone, Richard Barnes and David Ong (eds.), *The Law of the Sea: Progress and Prospects* (Oxford University Press, Oxford, 2006)

Keck, M. and Sikkink, K., *Activists Beyond Borders: Advocacy Networks in International Politics* (Cornell University Press, Ithaca, NY, 1998)

Kelemen, R. Daniel, 'The Structure and Dynamics of EU Federalism' (2003) 36 (1–2) *Comparative Political Studies* 184

    *The Rules of Federalism: Institutions and Regulatory Politics in the EU and Beyond* (Harvard University Press, Cambridge, MA, 2004)

Kelsen, Hans, *The Law of the United Nations: A Critical Analysis of its Fundamental Problems* (Stevens and Sons, London, 1951)

    *Collective Security under International Law* (US Government Printing Office, Washington, DC, 1957)

Kennedy, David, 'A New World Order: Yesterday, Today, Tomorrow' (1994) 4 *Transnational Law and Contemporary Problems* 329

Keohane, Robert O., *International Institutions and State Power* (Westview Press, Boulder, CO, 1989)

Kesan, Jay P. and Hayes, Carol M., *Self Defense in Cyberspace: Law and Policy* (University of Illinois, Urbana, IL, 2011)

Keyuan, Zou, 'China's U-Shaped Line in the South China Sea Revisited' (2012) 43 *Ocean Development and International Law* 18

Kimball, Daryl G., 'Myanmar Vows to Upgrade IAEA Safeguards' (2012) 42(10) *Arms Control Today* 16

Kingsbury, Benedict, 'The Concept of "Law" in Global Administrative Law' (2009) 20 *European Journal of International Law* 23

Kingsbury, Benedict, Krisch, Nico and Stewart, Richard B., 'The Emergence of Global Administrative Law' (2005) 68 *Law and Contemporary Problems* 15

Kirchner, Emil J., 'Regional and Global Security: Changing Threats and Institutional Responses' in Emil J. Kirchner and James Sperling (eds.), *Global Security Governance: Competing Perceptions of Security in the 21st Century* (Routledge, London/New York, 2007)

Kirgis, Frederic L. Jr, 'The Security Council's First Fifty Years' (1995) 89 *American Journal of International Law* 506

Kirk, G., 'The Enforcement of Security' (1946) 55 *Yale Law Journal* 1081

Kittrie, Orde F., 'Averting Catastrophe: Why the Nuclear Nonproliferation Treaty is Losing Its Deterrence Capacity and How to Restore It' (2006–2007) 28 *Michigan Journal of International Law* 337

Kivimäki, Timo, 'The Long Peace of ASEAN' (2001) 38 *Journal of Peace Research* 5

Klabbers, Jan, 'The Changing Nature of International Organizations' in Jean-Marc Coicaud and Veijo Heiskanen (eds.), *The Legitimacy of International Organizations* (United Nations University Press, Tokyo, 2001)

An Introduction to International Institutional Law (2nd edn, Cambridge University Press, Cambridge, 2009)

'Controlling International Organisations: A Virtue Ethics Approach' (2011) 2(2) *Helsinki Review of Global Governance* 49

Klein, Natalie, *Maritime Security and the Law of the Sea* (Oxford University Press, Oxford, 2011)

Koh, Tommy, 'ASEAN Charter at One: A Thriving Tiger Cub', paper presented at the Second ASEAN Secretariat Policy Forum, 16 December 2009, available at www.asean.org/archive/documents/091216-ASEC-Policy-Forum.pdf

Koremenos, Barbara, Lipson, Charles and Snidal, Duncan, 'The Rational Design of International Institutions' (2005) 55 *International Organization* 761

Korobkin, Russell and Zasloff, Jonathan, 'Roadblocks to the Road Map: A Negotiation Theory Perspective on the Israeli-Palestinian Conflict after Yasser Arafat' (2005) 30 *Yale Journal of International Law* 50

Koskenniemi, Martii, 'The Place of Law in Collective Security' (1996) 17 *Michigan Journal of International Law* 456

'International Legislation Today' (2005) 23 *Wisconsin International Law Journal* 61

Koskenniemi, Martii (ed.), *International Law Aspects of the European Union* (Kluwer Law International, The Hague, 1998)

Koskenniemi, Martii and Leino, Paivi, 'Fragmentation of International Law: Postmodern Anxieties?' (2002) 15 *Leiden Journal of International Law* 553

Koslowski, Rey, 'A Constructivist Approach to Understanding the European Union as a Federal Polity' (1999) 6 *Journal of European Public Policy* 561

Kostakopoulou, Dora, 'How to Do Things with Security Post 9/11' (2008) 28 *Oxford Journal of Legal Studies* 317

Koutrakos, Panos, *The EU Common Security and Defence Policy* (Oxford University Press, Oxford, 2013)

Kraska, James, *Contemporary Maritime Piracy: International Law, Strategy, and Diplomacy at Sea* (Praeger, Westport, CT, 2010)

Krasner, Stephen (ed.), *International Regimes* (Cornell University Press, New York, 1983)

Kreijen, Gerard, *State Failure, Sovereignty and Effectiveness* (Martinus Nijhoff Publishers, Leiden, 2004)

Krisch, Nico, 'The Pluralism of Global Administrative Law' (2006) 17(1) *European Journal of International Law* 247

Kufuor, Kofi Oteng, 'The Legality of the Intervention in the Liberian Civil War by the Economic Community of West African States' (1993) 5 *African Journal of International and Comparative Law* 525

*The Institutional Transformation of the Economic Community of West African States* (Ashgate, Aldershot, 2006)

Lake, David A., 'Beyond Anarchy: The Importance of Security Institutions' (2001) 26 *International Security* 129

Lammers, Johan G., 'General Principles of Law Recognized by Civilised Nations' in Frits Kalshoven, Pieter Jan Kuyper and Johan G. Lammers (eds.), *Essays on the Development of the International Legal Order in Memory of Haro F. Van Panhuys* (Sijthoff and Noordhoff, Alphen aan den Rijn, 1980)

Lapidoth, Ruth, 'Security Council Resolution 242 at Twenty-Five' (1992) 26 *Israel Law Review* 306

Lasok, K.P.E., and Millett, T., *Judicial Control in the EU: Procedures and Principles* (Richmond Law and Tax Ltd, Richmond, 2004)

Lauterpacht, Hersch, *Private Law Sources and Analogies of International Law* (Archon Books, Hamden, [1927] 1970)

*The Function of Law in the International Community* (Clarendon Press, Oxford, 1933)

Lawson, Charles, 'Patents and Plant Breeder's Rights over Plant Genetic Resources for Food and Agriculture' (2004) 32 *Federal Law Review* 107

Leifer, Michael, *ASEAN and the Security of South-East Asia* (Routledge, London, 1989)

Leslie, Russell, 'The Good Faith Assumption: Different Paradigmatic Approaches to Nonproliferation Issues' (2008) 15 *Nonproliferation Review* 479

Lewin, Nicholas, *Jung on War, Politics and Nazi Germany: Exploring the Theory of Archetypes and the Collective Unconscious* (Karnac Books, London, 2009)

Lightbourne, Miriam, 'Of Rice and Men: An Attempt to Assess the Basmati Affair' (2005) 6 *Journal of World Intellectual Property* 875

Likoti, Fako Johnson, 'The 1998 Military Intervention in Lesotho: SADC Peace Mission or Resource War?' (2007) 14 *International Peacekeeping* 251

Lin, Herbert S., 'Offensive Cyber Operations and the Use of Force' (2010) 4 *Journal of National Security Law and Policy* 63

Lixinski, Lucas, *Legal Implications of the Privatization of Cyber Warfare* (European University Institute, Florence, 2010)

Lobel, Jules, and Ratnor, Michael, 'By-passing the Security Council: Ambiguous Authorisations to Use Force, Cease-fires and the Iraqi Inspection Regime' (1999) 93 *American Journal of International Law* 124

Locke, John, *Two Treatises of Government* (1689)

Luck, Edward C., *UN Security Council: Practice and Promise* (Routledge, London/ New York, 2006)

Lyman, Edwin S., 'Can Nuclear Fuel Production in Iran and Elsewhere be Safeguarded Against Diversion?' in Henry Sokolski (ed.), *Falling Behind: International Scrutiny of the Peaceful Atom* (Strategic Studies Institute, Carlisle, 2008)

Lysen, Goran, 'Some Reflections on International Claims to Territory' in Jerzy Sztucki, Ove Bring and Said Mahmoudi (eds.), *Current International Law Issues: Nordic Perspectives* (Martinus Nijhoff Press, Dordrecht, 1994)

Macdonald, Ronald St John, 'The United Nations Charter: Constitution or Contract?' in Ronald St John Macdonald and Douglas M. Johnston (eds.), *The Structure and Process of International Law: Essays in Legal Philosophy, Doctrine, and Theory* (Martinus Nijhoff, The Hague, 1983)

MacIntyre, Alasdair, *After Virtue* (3rd edn, Duckworth, London, 2007)

Maduro, M.P., *We the Court: The European Court of Justice and the European Economic Constitution* (Hart Publishing, Oxford, 1998)

Maerli, Morten Bremer and Johnston, Roger G., 'Safeguarding This and Verifying That: Fuzzy Concepts, Confusing Terminology, and Their Detrimental Effects on Nuclear Husbandry' (2002) 9 *Nonproliferation Review* 54

Maguire, Gil, 'Defensible Borders for Israel: The 1967 Lines are Just Fine' (21 May 2011), available at http://savingisrael.wordpress.com/2011/05/21/defensible-borders-for-israel-the-1967-lines-are-just-fine

Majone, Giandomenico, 'The Rise of the Regulatory State in Europe' (1994) 17(3) *West European Politics* 77

Malan, Mark, 'Leaner and Meaner? The Future of Peacekeeping in Africa' (1999) 8(4) *African Security Review* 45

Malik, Iftikhar, *Religious Minorities in Pakistan* (Minority Rights Group International, 2002), available at www.refworld.org/pdfid/469cbfc30.pdf

Maoz, Asher, 'The Application of Israeli Law to the Golan Heights is Annexation' (1994) 20 *Brooklyn Journal of International Law* 391

Marschik, Axel, 'Legislative Powers of the Security Council' in Ronald St John Macdonald and Douglas M. Johnston (eds.), *Towards World Constitutionalism: Issues in the Legal Ordering of the World Community* (Martinus Nijhoff Publishers, The Hague, 2005)

Marts, Charles, *Piracy Ransoms: Conflicting Perspectives*, One Earth Future Foundation Working Paper (2010), available at https://oneearthfuture.org/research/publications/piracy-ransoms-conflicting-perspectives

Mathews, Jessica Tuchman, 'Redefining Security' (1989) 68(2) *Foreign Affairs* 162

May, Roy and Massey, Simon, 'The OAU Interventions in Chad: Mission Impossible or Mission Evaded?' (1998) 5(1) *International Peacekeeping* 46

Mays, Terry M., *Africa's First Peacekeeping Operation: The OAU in Chad, 1981–1982* (Praeger, Westport, CT, 2002)

　*Historical Dictionary of Multinational Peacekeeping* (3rd edn, Scarecrow Press, Plymouth, 2011)

McCormick, John, 'The Dilemmas of Dictatorship: Carl Schmitt and Constitutional Emergency Powers' (1997) 10 *Canadian Journal of Law and Jurisprudence* 163

McGarrity, Nicola, Lynch, Andrew and Williams, George, *Counter-Terrorism and Beyond: The Culture of Law and Justice After 9/11* (Routledge, London, 2010)

McInnes, Colin and Rushton, Simon, 'HIV, AIDS and Security: Where Are We Now?' (2010) 86 *International Affairs* 225

McKay, David, *Federalism and European Union: A Political Economy Perspective* (Oxford University Press, New York, 1999)

Mearsheimer, John J., 'The False Promise of International Institutions' (1994–1995) 19(3) *International Security* 5

Meernik, James, 'United States Military Intervention and the Promotion of Democracy' (1996) 33(4) *Journal of Peace Research* 391

Mejia, Maximo, 'Regional Cooperation in Combating Piracy and Armed Robbery against Ships: Learning Lessons from ReCAAP' in Anna Petrig (ed.), *Sea Piracy Law: Selected National Legal Frameworks and Regional Legislative Approaches/Droit de la piraterie maritime: Cadres juridiques nationaux et approches législatives regionals* (Duncker and Humblot, Berlin, 2010)

Mejia, Maximo and Mukherjee, P.K., 'Selected Issues of Law and Ergonomics in Maritime Security' (2004) 10 *Journal of International Maritime Law* 316

Melzer, Nils, 'Interpretive Guidance on the Notion of Direct Participation in Hostilities under International Humanitarian Law' (2008) 90 *International Review of the Red Cross* 991

Mendelson, Maurice, 'The International Court of Justice and the Sources of International Law' in Vaughan Lower and Malgosia Fitzmaurice (eds.), *Fifty Years of the International Court of Justice: Essays in Honour of Sir Robert Jennings* (Cambridge University Press, Cambridge, 1996)

Meron, Theodore, *Human Rights and Humanitarian Norms as Customary Law* (Oxford University Press, Oxford, 1989)

Merrill, J.G., 'Sovereignty over Pulau Ligitan and Pulau Sipadan (Indonesia v Malaysia), Merits, Judgment of 17 December 2002' (2003) 52 *International and Comparative Law Quarterly* 797

Middleton, Roger, *Piracy in Somalia: Threatening Global Trade, Feeding Local Wars*, Chatham House Briefing Paper No. AFP BP 08/02 (October 2008), available at www.chathamhouse.org/sites/files/chathamhouse/public/Research/Africa/1008piracysomalia.pdf

Miers, David and Page, Alan, *Legislation* (Sweet and Maxwell, London, 1990)

Milano, Enrico, 'Diplomatic Protection and Human Rights Before the International Court of Justice: Re-Fashioning Tradition?' (2004) 35 *Netherlands Yearbook of International Law* 85

Minze, E.D., Tauxe, R.V. and Levine, M.M., 'The Global Resurgence of Cholera' in Norman Noah and Mary O'Mahony (eds.), *Communicable Disease: Epidemiology and Control* (Wiley, New York, 1998)

Mitra, Siddhartha and Josling, Tim, *Agricultural Export Restrictions: Welfare Implications and Trade Disciplines*, IPC Position Paper, Agricultural and Rural Development Policy Series (International Food and Agricultural Trade Policy Council, 2009), available at http://agritrade.org/documents/ExportRestrictions_final.pdf

Mitzen, Jennifer, 'Ontological Security in World Politics: State Identity and the Security Dilemma' (2006) 12 *European Journal of International Relations* 341

Modood, Tariq, 'Moderate Secularism, Religion as Identity and Respect for Religion' (2010) 81 *Political Quarterly* 4

Moe, Terry M. and Howell, William G., *The Presidential Power of Unilateral Action* (1999) 15 *Journal of Law, Economics and Organisation* 132

Moghadam, Valentine M., 'Revolution, Religion, and Gender Politics: Iran and Afghanistan Compared' (1999) 10(4) *Journal of Women's History* 172

*Globalizing Women: Transnational Feminist Network* (JHU Press, Washington, DC, 2005)

Mohanty, Chandra Talpade, 'Under Western Eyes: Feminist Scholarship and Colonial Discourses' in C.T. Mohanty, A. Russo and L. Lourdes Torres (eds.), *Third World Women and the Politics of Feminism* (Indiana University Press, Bloomington, IN, 1993)

Morgenstern, Felice, 'Legality in International Organisations' (1976–1977) 48 *British Yearbook of International Law* 241

Morgenthau, Hans, *Politics Among Nations: The Struggle for Power and Peace* (Alfred A. Knopf, New York, 1950)

Mosler, Herman, *The International Society as a Legal Community* (Sijthoff and Noordhoff, Alphen aan den Rijn, 1980)

Mowbray, Jacqueline, 'The Right to Food and the International Economic System: An Assessment of the Rights-based Approach to the Problem of World Hunger' (2007) 20 *Leiden Journal of International Law* 545

Müller, Harald, 'Export Controls: Review of Article III' in John Simpson and Darryl Howlett (eds.), *The Future of the Non-Proliferation Treaty* (St Martin's Press, New York, 1995)

Murray, Raymond L., *Nuclear Energy: An Introduction to the Concepts, Systems, and Applications of Nuclear Processes* (5th edn, Butterworth-Heinemann, Boston, MA, 2001)

Musungu, Sisule, and Dutfield, Graham, *Multilateral Agreements and a TRIPS-plus World: The World Intellectual Property Organization*, Quaker International Affairs Program, TRIPS Issues Papers No.3 (2003), available at www.geneva. quno.info/pdf/WIPO(A4)final0304.pdf

Naert, Frederik, 'ESDP in Practice: Increasingly Varied and Ambitious EU Security and Defence Operations' in Martin Trybus and Nigel D. White (eds.), *European Security Law* (Oxford University Press, Oxford, 2007)

Nagre, Dhanashree and Warade, Priyanka, *Cyber Terrorism: Vulnerabilities and Policy Issues* (2011), available at www.scribd.com/doc/54213935/Final-Report-Dnagre-Pwarade

Naldi, G.J., 'Peacekeeping Attempts by the Organisation of African Unity' (1985) 34 *International and Comparative Law Quarterly* 593

Narula, Smita, 'The Right to Food: Holding International Actors Accountable under International Law' (2006) 44 *Columbia Journal of Transnational Law* 691

Nasu, Hitoshi, *International Law on Peacekeeping: A Study of Article 40 of the UN Charter* (Martinus Nijhoff Publishers, Leiden, 2009)

'Who Guards the Guards? Towards Regulation of the UN Security Council's Chapter VII Powers through Dialogue' in Kim Rubenstein and Jeremy Farrall (eds.), *Sanctions, Accountability and Governance in a Globalised World* (Cambridge University Press, Cambridge, 2009)

'The Place of Human Security in Collective Security' (2013) 18 *Journal of Conflict and Security Law* 95

Nasu, Hitoshi and Rothwell, Donald R., 'Re-evaluating the Role of International Law in Territorial and Maritime Disputes in East Asia' (2014) 4 *Asian Journal of International Law* 55

Nathan, Laurie, *Community of Insecurity: SADC's Struggle for Peace and Security in Southern Africa* (Ashgate, Farnham, 2012)

Ng'ong'ola, C.,'Regional Integration and Trade Liberalisation in Southern Africa Development Community' (2000) 3 *Journal of International Economic Law* 485

Nicolaidis, Kalypso and Howse, Robert (eds.), *The Federal Vision: Legitimacy and Levels of Governance in the US and EU* (Oxford University Press, Oxford, 2001)

Nolan, Mark and Rubenstein, Kim, 'Citizenship and Identity in Diverse Societies' (2009) XV *Humanities Research* 29

Nolte, Georg, 'Restoring Peace by Regional Action: International Legal Aspects of the Liberian Conflict' (1993) 53 *Zeitschrift für ausländisches öffentliches Recht und Völkerrecht* 603

Nussbaum, M.C., *Women and Human Development: The Capabilities Approach* (Cambridge University Press, Cambridge, 2000)

O'Connell, Mary E., 'Cyber Security Without Cyber War' (2012) 2 *Journal of Conflict and Security Law* 187

O'Keefe, D. and Schermers, H.G. (eds.), *Mixed Agreements* (Kluwer Law International, The Hague, 1983)

Oguamanam, Chidi, 'Intellectual Property Rights in Plant Genetic Resources: Farmers' Rights and Food Security in Indigenous and Local Communities' (2006) 11 *Drake Journal of Agricultural Law* 273

'Agro-Biodiversity and Food Security: Biotechnology and Traditional Agricultural Practices at the Periphery of the International Intellectual Property Regime Complex' (2007) *Michigan State Law Review* 215

Okin, Susan M., 'Equal Citizenship: Gender, Justice and Gender: An Unfinished Debate' (2004) 72 *Fordham Law Review* 1537

Okolo, Julius Emeka, 'Securing West Africa: The ECOWAS Defence Pact' (1983) 39(5) *World Today* 177

'Integrative and Cooperative Regionalism: The Economic Community of West African States' (1985) 39(1) *International Organisation* 121

Olonisakin, Funmi, *Reinventing Peacekeeping in Africa: Conceptual and Legal Issues in ECOMOG Operations* (Kluwer Law International, The Hague, 2000)

Olson, Mancur Jr, *The Logic of Collective Action* (Harvard University Press, Cambridge, MA, 1965)

Oosthuizen, Gabriël H., 'Playing the Devil's Advocate: The United Nations Security Council is Unbound by Law' (1999) 12 *Leiden Journal of International Law* 549

Orakhelashvili, Alexander, *The Interpretation of Acts and Rules in Public International Law* (Oxford University Press, Oxford, 2008)

*Collective Security* (Oxford University Press, Oxford, 2011)

Organization for Economic Cooperation and Development, 'Concepts and Dilemmas of State Building in Fragile Situations: From Fragility to Resilience' (2008) 9(3) *OECD Journal on Development* 61

Ortiz, Antonio, 'Neither Fox Nor Hedgehog: NATO's Comprehensive Approach and the OSCE's Concept of Security' (2008) 4 *Security and Human Rights* 284

Osborne, D. and Gaebler, T., *Reinventing Government* (Plume, New York, 1992)

Ostler, Duane, 'Bills of Attainder and the Formation of the American Takings Clause at the Founding of the Republic' (2010) 32 *Campbell Law Review* 227

Oxfam, *Women and the Afghan Police*, Briefing Paper 173 (10 September 2013), available at www.oxfam.org/sites/www.oxfam.org/files/bp-173-afghanistan-women-police-100913-en.pdf

Pan, Junwu, *Towards a New Framework for Peaceful Settlement of China's Territorial and Boundary Disputes* (Martinus Nijhoff, Leiden, 2009)

Parfit, Derek, *Equality or Priority?* (Lindley Lecture, University of Kansas, 1991)

Paris, Roland, *At War's End: Building Peace After Civil Conflict* (Cambridge University Press, Cambridge, 2004)

Parker, Charles, *Controlling Weapons of Mass Destruction: An Evaluation of International Security Regime Significance* (Coronet Books, Uppsala, 2001)

Patel, Kirel, 'Farmers' Rights over Plant Genetic Resources in the South: Challenges and Opportunities' in Frederic Erbisch and Karim Maredia (eds.), *Intellectual Property Rights in Agricultural Biotechnology* (CABI Publishers, Cambridge, MA, 2004)

Pellet, Allain, 'The Normative Dilemma: Will and Consent in International Law-making' (1988–1989) 12 *Australian Yearbook of International Law* 22

Pogge, Thomas, 'Equal Liberty for All' (2004) 28 *Midwest Studies in Philosophy* 266–81, reprinted in David Reidy (ed.), *John Rawls* (Aldershot, Ashgate, 2008) pp. 219–34

Pollitt, Mark M., *Cyber Terrorism: Fact or Fancy?* (FBI Laboratory, Washington, DC, 2000)

Posner, Eric and Vermeule, Adrian, *Terror in the Balance: Security, Liberty and the Courts* (Oxford University Press, New York, 2007)

Potter, William C. and Mukhatzhanova, Gaukhar, 'Divining Nuclear Intentions: A Review Essay' (2008) 33 *International Security* 139

Pulkowski, Dirk, *The Law and Politics of International Regime Conflict* (Oxford University Press, Oxford, 2014)

Rama-Montaldo, Manuel, 'International Legal Personality and Implied Powers of International Organizations' (1970) 44 *British Year Book of International Law* 111

Ramraj, Victor V., 'The Impossibility of Global Anti-Terrorism Law' in Victor V. Ramraj *et al.* (eds.), *Global Anti-Terrorism Law and Policy* (2nd edn, Cambridge University Press, New York, 2012)

Raphael, Sam and Stokes, Doug, 'Energy Security' in Alan Collins (ed.), *Contemporary Security Studies* (2nd edn, Oxford University Press, Oxford, 2010)

Ratner, Steven R., 'Regulatory Takings in Institutional Context: Beyond the Fear of Fragmented International Law' (2008) 102 *American Journal of International Law* 475

Rattray, Gregory J., *Strategic Warfare in Cyberspace* (MIT, Cambridge, MA, 2001)

Raven-Roberts, Angela, 'Gender Mainstreaming in United Nations Peacekeeping Operations: Talking the Talk: Tripping over the Walk' in Dyan Muzurana and Angela Raven-Roberts (eds.), *Gender, Conflict and Peacekeeping* (Rowman and Littlefield, Lanham, MD, 2005)

Rawls, John, *A Theory of Justice* (Harvard University Press, Cambridge, MA, 1971, revised edn 1999)

*Justice as Fairness: A Restatement* (Erin Kelly, ed., Harvard University Press, Cambridge, MA, 2001)

Reilly, N., *Women's Human Rights* (Polity Press, Malden, MA, 2009)

Ress, Georg, 'The Interpretation of the Charter' in Bruno Simma *et al.* (eds.), *The Charter of the United Nations: A Commentary* (Oxford University Press, Oxford, 1994)

Reynolds, Jacob, 'The Rule of Law and the Origins of the Bill of Attainder Clause' (2005) 18 *St Thomas Law Review* 177

Rich, Roland, 'Crafting Security Council Mandates' in Edward Newman and Roland Rich (eds.), *The UN Role in Promoting Democracy: Between Ideals and Reality* (United Nations University Press, Tokyo, 2004)

Richardson, Ivor, 'Private Acts of Parliament' (2010) 41 *Victoria University of Wellington Law Review* 653

Ricketson, Sam, 'WIPO Study on Limitations and Exceptions of Copyright and Related Rights in the Digital Era', WIPO Standing Committee on Copyright and Related Rights, 9th sess., Geneva, 23–27 June 2003, available atwww.wipo.int/edocs/mdocs/copyright/en/sccr_9/sccr_9_7.pdf

Rimmer, Matthew and Rubenstein, Kim, 'Access to Essential Medicines: Public Health and International Law' in Thomas Pogge, Matthew Rimmer and Kim Rubenstein (eds.), *Incentives for Global Public Health: Patent Law and Access to Essential Medicines* (Cambridge University Press, Cambridge, 2010)

Ritchie, Mark and Dawkins, Kristin, 'WTO Food and Agricultural Rules: Sustainable Agriculture and the Human Right to Food' (2000) 9 *Minnesota Journal of Global Trade* 9

Rizvi, Hasan-Askari, *Military, State and Society in Pakistan* (Macmillan, Basingstoke, 2000)

Röben, Volker, 'The Enforcement Authority of International Institutions' (2008) 9 *German Law Journal* 1965

Roberts, Adam, 'Prolonged Military Occupation: The Israeli-Occupied Territories 1967–1988' in Emma Playfair (ed.), *International Law and the Administration of Occupied Territories* (Oxford University Press, Oxford, 2003)

Roberts, Anthea, 'Legality vs Legitimacy: Can Uses of Force be Illegal but Justified?' in Philip Alston and Euan MacDonald (eds.), *Human Rights, Intervention, and the Use of Force* (Oxford University Press, Oxford, 2008)

Rockwood, Laura, 'The IAEA's Strengthened Safeguards System' (2002) 7 *Journal of Conflict and Security Law* 123

Roots, Roger I., 'Government by Permanent Emergency: The Forgotten History of the New Deal Constitution' (1999–2000) 33 *Suffolk University Law Review* 259

Rosand, Eric, 'The Security Council as Global Legislator: Ultra Vires or Ultra Innovative' (2005) 28 *Fordham International Law Journal* 542

Ross, Dennis, *The Missing Peace: The Inside Story of the Fight for Middle East Peace* (Farrar, Straus and Giroux, New York, 2004)

Rostow, Eugene, 'Legal Aspects in the Search for Peace in the Middle East' (1970) 64 *American Society of International Law Proceedings* 68

Rushton, Simon, 'Global Health Security: Security for Whom? Security from What?' (2011) 59 *Political Studies* 779

Ryngaert, Cedric, 'Imposing International Duties on Non-State Actors and the Legitimacy of International Law' in Math Noortman and Cedric Ryngaert (eds.), *Non-State Actor Dynamics in International Law* (Ashgate, Burlington, 2010)

Sabel, Robbie, 'The Status of the Territories: The International Court of Justice Decision on the Separation Barrier and the Green Line' (2005) 38 *Israel Law Review* 316

Sadurski, Wojciech, *Constitutionalism and the Enlargement of Europe* (Oxford University Press, Oxford, 2012)

Saipiroon, P., *ASEAN Governments' Attitudes Towards Regional Security 1975–1979* (Institute of Asian Studies, Bangkok, 1982)

San Roque, Craig, Dowd, Amanda and Tacey, David (eds.), *Placing Psyche: Exploring Cultural Complexes in Australia* (Spring Journal Books, New Orleans, LA, 2011)

Sands, Philippe and Klein, Pierre, *Bowett's Law of International Institutions* (5th edn, Sweet and Maxwell, London, 2001)

Sarooshi, Dan, 'The Legal Framework Governing United Nations Subsidiary Organs' (1996) 47 *British Yearbook of International Law* 463
  *International Organizations and Their Exercise of Sovereign Powers* (Oxford Press, Oxford, 2005)

Sarris, Alexander, 'Trade-related Policies to Ensure Food (Rice) Security in Asia' in David Dawe (ed.), *The Rice Crisis: Markets, Policies and Food Security* (Food and Agricultural Organization and Earthscan, London/Washington, DC, 2010)

Sassòli, Marco, 'The Concept of Security in International Law relating to Armed Conflicts' in Cecilia M. Bailliet (ed.), *Security: A Multidisciplinary Normative Approach* (Martinus Nijhoff Publishers, Leiden, 2009)

Sato, Tetsuo, 'The Legitimacy of Security Council Actions under Chapter VII of the UN Charter since the End of the Cold War' in Jean-Marc Coicaud and Veijo Heiskanen (eds.), *The Legitimacy of International Organizations* (United Nations University Press, New York, 2001)

Scarlott, Jennifer, 'Nuclear Proliferation After the Cold War' (1991) 8 *World Policy Journal* 687

Schaap, Arie J., 'Cyberwarfare Operations: Development and Use under International Law' (2009) 64 *Air Force Law Review* 121

Schaffrin, Dora, Gorlach, Benjamin and Gerstetter, Christiane, *The International Treaty on Plant Genetic Resources for Food and Agriculture: Implications for Developing Countries and Interdependence with International Biodiversity and Intellectual Property Law*, Final Report, IPDEV Work Package (November 2006), available at www.ecologic.eu/download/projekte/1800-1849/1802/wp5_final_report.pdf

Scheinman, Lawrence, 'Nuclear Safeguards and Non-Proliferation in a Changing World Order' (1992) 23(4) *Security Dialogue* 37

Schermers, Henry G. and Blokker, Niels M., *International Institutional Law* (5th rev edn, Martinus Nijhoff Publishers, Leiden, 2011)

Scheuerman, William, 'Survey Article: Emergency Powers and the Rule of Law After 9/11' (2006) 14 *Journal of Political Philosophy* 61

Schiff, Benjamin N., *Building the International Criminal Court* (Cambridge University Press, Cambridge, 2008)

Schimmelfennig, Frank, 'Transatlantic Relations, Multilateralism and the Transformation of NATO' in Dimitris Bourantonis, Kostas Ifantis and Panayotis Tsakonas (eds.), *Multilateralism and Security Institutions in an Era of Globalization* (Routledge, Abingdon, 2008)

Schmitt, Carl, *Politische Theologie: Vier Kapitel zur Lehre von der Souveranitat* (1922) translated in George Schwarb, *Political Theology: Four Chapters on the Concept of Sovereignty* (University of Chicago Press, Chicago, IL, 2005)

Schmitt, Michael, 'Investigating Violations of International Law in Armed Conflict' (2011) 2 *Harvard National Security Journal* 31

'Classification of Cyber Conflict' (2012) 17 *Journal of Conflict and Security Law* 245

*Tallinn Manual on the International Law Applicable to Cyber Warfare* (Cambridge University Press, Cambridge, 2013)

Schott, Jared, 'Chapter VII as Exception: Security Council Action and the Regulative Ideal of Emergency' (2007) 6 *Northwestern Journal of International Human Rights* 24

Schuler, Ari, 'Billions for Biodefense: Federal Agency Biodefense Funding, FY2001-FY2005' (2004) 2 *Biosecurity and Bioterrorism* 86

Schwarzenberger, Georg and Brown, E.D., *A Manual of International Law* (6th edn, Professional Books, Milton, 1976)

Schweigman, David, *The Authority of the Security Council Under Chapter VII of the UN Charter: Legal Limits and the Role of the International Court of Justice* (Martinus Nijhoff Publishers, Leiden, 2001)

Scott, Shirley V., 'Securitising Climate Change: International Legal Implications and Obstacles' (2008) 21 *Cambridge Review of International Affairs* 603

Sedyaningsih, Engdang *et al.*, 'Towards Mutual Trust, Transparency and Equity in Virus Sharing Mechanism: Avian Influenza Case of Indonesia' (2008) 37 *Annals Academy of Medicine Singapore* 482

Segura-Serrano, Antonio, 'Internet Regulation and the Role of International Law' (2006) 10 *Max Planck Yearbook of United Nations Law* 191

Sell, Susan K., 'Industry Strategies for Intellectual Property and Trade: The Quest for TRIPS, and Post-TRIPS Strategies' (2002) 10 *Cardozo Journal of International and Comparative Law* 79

Sen, Amartya, *Poverty and Famines: An Essay on Entitlement and Deprivation* (Oxford University Press, Oxford, 1981)

Sesay, Amadu, 'The Limits of Peacekeeping by a Regional Organization: The OAU Peacekeeping Force in Chad' (1991) *Conflict Quarterly* 7

Severino, Rodolfo C., *Will ASEAN be Like the EU?* (ASEAN, 23 March 2001), available at www.aseansec.org/3112.htm

'ASEAN Beyond Forty: Towards Political and Economic Integration' (2007) 29 *Contemporary Southeast Asia* 406

Seyersted, Finn, 'Can the United Nations Establish Military Forces and Perform Other Acts Without Specific Basis in the Charter?' (1962) 12 *Österreichische Zeitschrift fur Öffentliches Recht* 125

'International Personality of Intergovernmental Organizations: Do Their Capacities Really Depend upon Their Constitutions?' (1964) 4 *Indian Journal of International Law* 1

'Jurisdiction over Organs and Officials of States, the Holy See and Intergovernmental Organizations' (1965) *International and Comparative Law Quarterly* 493

*United Nations Force in the Law of Peace and War* (A.W. Sijthoff, Leiden, 1966)

*Common Law of International Organizations* (Martinus Nijhoff Publishers, Leiden, 2008)

Shafir, G., 'Legal and Institutional Responses to Contemporary Global Threats: An Introduction to the UN Secretary-General's High-Level Panel Report on Threats, Challenges and Change' (2007) 38 *California Western International Law Journal* 1

Shaheed, Fareeda, *Gender, Religion and the Quest for Justice, United Nations Research in Social Development Final Research Report* (September 2009), available at http://r4d.dfid.gov.uk/pdf/outputs/womenempmus/shaheed_genderreligionjusticepakistan.pdf

Shamgar, Meir, 'Legal Concepts and Problems of the Israeli Military Government: The Initial Stage' in Meir Shamgar (ed.), *Military Government in the Territories Administered by Israel 1967–1980: The Legal Aspects* (Harry Sacher Institute for Legislature Research and Comparative Law, Jerusalem, 1982)

Shanks, Cheryl, Jacobson, Harold K. and Kaplan, Jeffrey H., 'Inertia and Change in the Constellation of International Governmental Organizations, 1981–1992' (1995) 50 *International Organization* 593

Shany, Yuval, *Regulating Jurisdictional Relations Between National and International Courts* (Oxford University Press, Oxford, 2007)

Shapiro, Martin, *Who Guards the Guardians?: Judicial Control of Administration* (University of Georgia Press, Athens, NY, 1988)

Sharp, Ben, 'Responding Internationally to a Resource Crisis: Interpreting the GATT Article XX(j) Short Supply Exception' (2010) 15 *Drake Journal of Agricultural Law* 259

Shaw, Malcolm N., *International Law* (6th edn, Cambridge University Press, Cambridge, 2008)

Shelling, Thomas, *Arms and Influence* (Yale University Press, New Haven, CT, 1966)

Shelton, Dinah, 'Normative Hierarchy in International Law' (2006) 100 *American Journal of International Law* 291

Sheridan, Cormac, 'The Business of Making Vaccines' (2005) 23 *Nature Biotechnology* 1359

Shibutani, Tamotsu, 'Reference Groups and Social Control' in Arnold Marshall Rose (ed.), *Human Behavior and Social Processes: An Interactionist Approach* (Houghton-Mifflin, Boston, NJ, 1961)

Shimeall, Timothy *et al.*, 'Countering Cyber-War' (2001) 49 *NATO Review* 16

Shirazi, Mikael and Persbo, Andreas, 'Centrifuge Production and the Additional Protocol' (2011) 133 *Trust and Verify* 7

Shiva, Vandana, 'The Seeds of Our Future' (1996) 4 *Development Journal* 14

Shlaim, Avi, *The Iron Wall: Israel and the Arab World* (Oxford University Press, Oxford, 2000)

Shorrock, Tim, *Spies for Hire: The Secret World of Intelligence Outsourcing* (Simon and Schuster, New York, 2009)

Siddiqa, Ayesha, *Military Inc.: Inside Pakistan's Military Economy* (Pluto Press, London, 2007)

Sieder, R. and McNeish, J.A., *Gender Justice and Legal Pluralities: Latin American and African Perspectives* (Routledge, New York, 2013)

Simma, Bruno, 'International Human Rights and General International Law: A Comparative Analysis' (1993) 4(2) *Collected Courses of the Academy of European Law* 153

'From Bilateralism to Community Interest in International Law' (1994-VI) 250 *Recueil des Cours* 217

'NATO, the UN and the Use of Force: Legal Aspects' (1999) 43 *European Journal of International Law* 1

Simma, Bruno and Alston, Philip, 'The Sources of Human Rights Law: Custom, Jus Cogens and General Principles' (1988–89) 12 *Australian Yearbook of International Law* 82

Simma, Bruno, Khan, Daniel-Erasmus and Nolte, George (eds.), *The Charter of the United Nations: A Commentary* (3rd edn, Oxford University Press, Oxford, 2012)

Simma, Bruno and Pulkowski, Dirk, 'Of the Planets and the Universe: Self-contained Regimes in International Law' (2006) 17 *European Journal of International Law* 483

Simmons, Beth A. and Martin, Lisa L., 'International Organizations and Institutions' in Walter Carlsnaes, Thomas Risse and Beth A. Simmons (eds.), *Handbook of International Relations* (SAGE Publications, London, 2002)

Singer, Thomas and Kimbles, Samuel (eds.), *The Cultural Complex: Contemporary Jungian Perspectives on Psyche and Society* (Brunner-Routledge, New York, 2004)

Sion, Liora, 'Peacekeeping and the Gender Regime: Dutch Female Peacekeepers in Bosnia and Kosovo' (2008) 37 *Journal of Contemporary Ethnography* 561

Slaughter, Anne-Marie, *A New World Order* (Princeton University Press, Princeton, NJ, 2004) p. 36

Sloan, Blaine, 'The United Nations Charter as a Constitution' (1989) 1 *Pace Yearbook of International Law* 61

Sloss, David, 'It's Not Broken, So Don't Fix It: The International Atomic Energy Agency Safeguards System and the Nuclear Nonproliferation Treaty' (1994–1995) 35 *Virginia Journal of International Law* 841

Sohn, Louis, 'The UN System as Authoritative Interpreter of its Law' in Oscar Schachter and Christopher Joyner (eds.), *United Nations Legal Order* (Cambridge University Press, Cambridge, 1995)

Sokolski, Henry D., 'What Strategic Weapons Proliferation Will Demand of Us' in Henry Sokolski and James Ludes (eds.), *Twenty-First Century Weapons Proliferation: Are We Ready?* (Frank Cass Publishers, Portland, OR, 2001)

'Assessing the IAEA's Ability to Verify the NPT' in Henry D. Sokolski (ed.), *Falling Behind: International Scrutiny of the Peaceful Atom* (Strategic Studies Institute, Carlisle, 2008)

Solingen, Etel, *Nuclear Logics: Contrasting Paths in East Asia and the Middle East* (Princeton University Press, Princeton, NJ, 2007)

Solomon, Solon, *The Justiciability of International Disputes: The Advisory Opinion on Israel's Security Fence as a Case Study* (Wolf Legal Publishers, Nijmegen, 2009)

'Occupied or Not: The Question of Gaza's Legal Status After the Israeli Disengagement' (2011) 19 *Cardozo Journal of International and Comparative Law* 76

Somek, Alexander, 'The Concept of "Law" in Global Administrative Law: A Reply to Benedict Kingsbury' (2009) 20 *European Journal of International Law* 985

Sommers-Flanagan, John and Sommers-Flanagan, Rita, *Counseling and Psychotherapy Theories in Context and Practice: Skills, Strategies and Techniques* (John Wiley and Sons, Hoboken, NJ, 2004)

Southall, R.J., 'SADC's Intervention into Lesotho: An Illegal Defence of Democracy?' in O. Furley and R. May (eds.), *African Interventionist States* (Ashgate Publishing, Abingdon, 2001)

Sperling, James, 'Eurasian Security Governance: New Threats, Institutional Adaptations' in James Sperling, Sean Kay and S. Victor Papacosma (eds.), *Limiting Institutions? The Challenge of Eurasian Security Governance* (Manchester University Press, Manchester, 2003)

Spies, Michael, 'Iran and the Limits of the Nuclear Non-Proliferation Regime' (2006–2007) 22 *American University International Law Review* 401

Spivak, Gayatri Chakravorty, 'Can the Subaltern Speak?' in Cary Nelson and Lawrence Grossberg (eds.), *Marxism and the Interpretation of Culture* (University of Illinois Press, Urbana, IL, 1988)

Srinivasan, T.N., 'Non-Discrimination in GATT/WTO: Was There Anything to Begin with and Is There Anything Left?' (2005) 4 *World Trade Review* 69

Stein, Murray, *The Principle of Individuation: Toward the Development of Human Consciousness* (Chiron Publications, Wilmette, IL, 2006)

Steinmo, Sven, Thelen, Kathleen A. and Longstreth, Frank, *Structuring Politics: Historical Institutionalism in Comparative Analysis* (Cambridge University Press, Cambridge, 1992)

Stern, Jessica Eve, 'Cooperative Security and the CWC: A Comparison of the Chemical and Nuclear Weapons Non-Proliferation Regimes' (1994) 15(3) *Contemporary Security Policy* 30

Stoiber, Carlton *et al.*, *Handbook on Nuclear Law* (International Atomic Energy Agency, Vienna, 2003)

*Handbook on Nuclear Law: Implementing Legislation* (International Atomic Energy Agency, Vienna, 2010)

Stone, Julius, *Conflict Through Consensus: United Nations Approaches to Aggression* (John Hopkins University Press, Baltimore, MD, 1977)

Straub, Peter, 'Farmers in the IP Wrench: How Patents on Gene-Modified Crops Violate the Right to Food in Developing Countries' (2006) 29 *Hastings International and Comparative Law Review* 187

Suchman, Mark C., 'Managing Legitimacy: Strategic and Institutional Approaches' (1995) 20 *Academy of Management Review* 571

Sukma, Rizal, 'Democracy Building in South East Asia: The ASEAN Security Community and Options for the European Union', available at www.idea. int/resources/analysis/upload/Sukma_paper14.pdf

Svensson, Frans, 'Virtue Ethics and the Search for an Account of Right Action' (2010) 13 *Ethical Theory and Moral Practice* 255

Szasz, Paul C., 'The Adequacy of International Nuclear Safeguards' (1975) 10 *Journal of International Law and Economics* 423

'Sanctions' in Jozef Goldblat (ed.), *Safeguarding the Atom: A Critical Appraisal* (Taylor and Francis, Philadelphia, PA, 1985)

'The Security Council Starts Legislating' (2002) 96 *American Journal of International Law* 901

Tacey, David, *How to Read Jung* (Granta Books, London, 2006)

Talmon, Stefan, 'The Security Council as World Legislature' (2005) 99 *American Journal of International Law* 175

Tansey, Geoff, 'Global Rules, Local Needs' in Geoff Tansey and Tamsin Rajotte (eds.), *The Future Control of Food: A Guide to International Negotiations and Rules on Intellectual Property, Biodiversity and Food Security* (International Development Research Centre, Ottawa, 2008)

Tanter, Richard, *The Re-Emergence of an Australian Nuclear Weapons Option?*, Austral Policy Forum (Nautilus Institute) 07-20A (29 October 2007)

Thaper, Romila, 'Imagined Religious Communities? Ancient History and the Modern Search for a Hindu Identity' (1989) 23 *Modern Asian Studies* 209

Thayer, Carlyle A., *South China Sea Tensions: What Role for ASEAN, the United States and the United Nations?* (24 August 2012), available at www.scribd. com/doc/103934560/Thayer-South-China-Sea-ASEAN-and-the-Latest-Tensions

Thompson, Wyatt and Tallard, Grégoire, *Potential Market Effects of Selected Policy Options in Emerging Economies to Address Future Commodity Price Surges*, OECD Food, Agriculture and Fisheries Papers No. 35 (2010), available at http://dx.doi.org/10.1787/5km658j3r85b-en

Traeger, Frank and Kronenberg, Philip, *National Security and American Society: Theory, Process and Policy* (University Press of Kansas, Lawrence, KA, 1973)

Traeger, Frank and Simonie, Frank, 'An Introduction to the Study of National Security' in Frank Traeger and Philip Kronenberg (eds.), *National Security and American Society: Theory, Process and Policy* (University Press of Kansas, Lawrence, KA, 1973)

Trybus, Martin, 'The Vision of the European Defence Community and a Common Defence for the European Union' in Martin Trybus and Nigel D. White (eds.), *European Security Law* (Oxford University Press, Oxford, 2007)

Trybus, Martin and White, Nigel D., 'An Introduction to European Security Law' in Martin Trybus and Nigel D. White (eds.), *European Security Law* (Oxford University Press, Oxford, 2007)

Trybus, Martin and White, Nigel D. (eds.), *European Security Law* (Oxford University Press, Oxford, 2007)

Tsagourias, Nicholas, 'Security Council Legislation, Article 2(7) of the UN Charter and the Principle of Subsidiarity' (2011) 24 *Leiden Journal of International Law* 539

Tucker, Jonathan B., 'From Arms Race to Abolition: The Evolving Norm Against Biological and Chemical Warfare' in Sydney Drell, Abraham Sofaer and George Wilson (eds.), *The New Terror: Facing the Threat of Biological and Chemical Weapons* (Hoover Institution Press, Stanford, CA, 1999)

'Verifying the Chemical Weapons Ban: Missing Elements' (2007) 37(1) *Arms Control Today* 6

Turns, David, 'Cyber Warfare and the Notion of Direct Participation in Hostilities' (2012) 17 *Journal of Conflict and Security Law* 279

Tzanakopoulos, Antonio, 'United Nations Sanctions in Domestic Courts: From Interpretation to Defence in *Abdelrazik v Canada*' (2010) 81 *Journal of International Criminal Justice* 249

*Disobeying the Security Council: Countermeasures Against Wrongful Sanctions* (Oxford University Press, Oxford, 2011)

Ulfstein, Geir, 'Institutions and Competences' in Jan Klabbers, Anne Peters and Geir Ulfstein (eds.), *The Constitutionalization of International Law* (Oxford University Press, Oxford, 2009)

Ullman, Richard H., 'Redefining Security' (1983) 8(1) *International Security* 129

Urquhart, Brian, *Hammarskjold* (Bodley Head, London, 1972)

Usher, J., *European Community Law and National Law: Irreversible Transfer* (Allen & Unwin, London, 1981)

van Hoof, Godefridus J.H., *Rethinking the Sources of International Law* (Kluwer Law and Taxation Publishers, Boston, NJ, 1983)

Väyryen, R., 'Multilateral Security: Common, Cooperative or Collective?' in M.G. Schechter (ed.), *Future Multilateralism: The Political and Social Framework* (United Nations University Press, Tokyo, 1999)

Vedby Rasmussen, Mikkel, *The Risk Society At War* (Cambridge University Press, Cambridge, 2006)

Ventre, Daniel, 'China's Strategy for Information Warfare: A Focus on Energy' (2010) *Journal of Energy Security* (online), available at www.ensec.org

Vermeule, Adrian, 'Our Schmittian Administrative Law' (2009) 122 *Harvard Law Review* 1095

Virally, Michael, 'The Sources of International Law' in Max Sørenson (ed.), *Manual of Public International Law* (St Martin's Press, New York, 1968)

von Bogdandy, Armin, 'General Principles of International Public Authority: Sketching a Research Field' (2009) 9 *German Law Journal* 1909

von Bogdandy, Armin *et al.* (eds.), *The Exercise of Public Authority by International Institutions: Advancing International Institutional Law* (Springer, Heidelberg, 2010)

Wade, H.W.R. and Forsyth, C., *Administrative Law* (8th edn, Oxford University Press, Oxford, 2000)

Waldron, Jeremy, 'Security and Liberty: The Image of Balance' (2003) 11 *Journal of Political Philosophy* 191

Walker, Paul F., 'Abolishing Chemical Weapons: Progress, Challenges, and Opportunities' (2010) 40(9) *Arms Control Today* 20

Wallander, Celeste A., Haftendorn, Helga and Keohane, Robert O., 'Introduction' in Helga Haftendorn, Robert O. Keohane and Celeste A. Wallander (eds.), *Imperfect Unions: Security Institutions over Time and Space* (Oxford University Press, Oxford, 1999)

Wallander, Celeste A. and Keohane, Robert O., 'Risk, Threat, and Security Institutions' in Helga Haftendorn, Robert O. Keohane and Celeste A. Wallender (eds.), *Imperfect Unions: Security Institutions over Time and Space* (Oxford University Press, Oxford, 1999)

Walter, Christian, 'Security Council Control over Regional Action' (1997) 1 *Max Planck Yearbook of United Nations Law* 129

Waltz, Kenneth, *Theory of International Politics* (Random House, New York, 1979)

Weiler, J.H.H., *The Constitution of Europe* (Cambridge University Press, Cambridge, 1999)

Weiler, J.H.H. and Wind, Marlene, *European Constitutionalism Beyond the State* (Cambridge University Press, Cambridge, 2003)

Weiss, Jeffrey, 'Terminating the Israel-PLO Declaration of Principles: Is It Legal under International Law?' (1995) 18 *Loyola International and Comparative Law Journal* 114

Wellens, Karen, 'The UN Security Council and New Threats to the Peace Back to the Future' (2003) 8 *Journal of Conflict and Security Law* 15

'Fragmentation of International Law and Establishing an Accountability Regime for International Organizations: The Role of the Judiciary in Closing the Gap' (2003–2004) 25 *Michigan Journal of International Law* 1159

Weller, Marc (ed.), *Regional Peacekeeping and International Enforcement: The Liberian Crisis* (Cambridge University Press, Cambridge, 1994)

Wendt, Alexander, 'Anarchy is What States Make of It: The Social Construction of Power Politics' (1992) 46 *International Organization* 2

Wesley, Michael, 'It's Time to Scrap the NPT' (2005) 59 *Australian Journal of International Affairs* 283

Wessel, Ramses A., *The European Union's Foreign and Security Policy: A Legal Institutional Perspective* (Kluwer Law International, The Hague, 1999)

Wessel, Ramses A. and Van Vooren, Bart, 'The EEAS's Diplomatic Dreams and the Reality of European and International Law' (2013) 17 *Journal of European Public Policy* 1

Wheelis, Mark and Dando, Malcolm, 'Neurobiology: A Case Study of the Imminent Militarization of Biology' (2005) 87 *International Review of the Red Cross* 553

White, Nigel D., 'The UN Charter and Peacekeeping Forces: Constitutional Issues' (1996) 3(4) *International Peacekeeping* 43

'The United Nations System: Conference, Contract or Constitutional Order?' (2000) 4 *Singapore Journal of International and Comparative Law* 281

*The Law of International Organisations* (2nd edn, Manchester University Press, Manchester, 2005)

'The Security Council, the Security Imperative and International Law' in Matthew Happold (ed.), *International Law in a Multipolar World* (Routledge, London/New York, 2012)

Whitmont, Edward, *The Symbolic Quest: Basic Concepts of Analytical Psychology* (Princeton University Press, Princeton, NJ, 1969)

Wibben, Annick T.R., *Feminist Security Studies: A Narrative Approach* (Routledge, Abingdon/Oxford/New York, 2011)

Wiley, Norman, *The Semiotic Self* (Polity Press, Cambridge, 1994)

Williams, George, *Counter-Terrorism and Beyond: The Culture of Law and Justice After 9/11* (Routledge, London, 2010)

Williams, M.J., '(In)Security Studies, Reflexive Modernization and Security Studies' (2008) 43(1) *Cooperation and Conflict* 57

Williams, Rocky, 'From Peacekeeping to Peacebuilding? South African Policy and Practice in Peace Missions' (2000) 7(3) *International Peacekeeping* 84

Williamson, Robert Jr, 'Law and the H-Bomb: Strengthening the Nonproliferation Regime to Impede Advanced Proliferation' (1995) 28 *Cornell International Law Journal* 71

Wilson, Kumanan, von Tigerstrom, Barbara and McDougall, Christopher, 'Protecting Global Health Security through the International Health Regulations: Requirements and Challenges' (2008) 179 *Canadian Medical Association Journal* 44

Winter, Lauren, 'Cultivating Farmers' Rights: Reconciling Food Security, Indigenous Agriculture, and TRIPS' (2010) 43 *Vanderbilt Journal of Transnational Law* 233

Wolfers, Arnold, 'National Security as an Ambiguous Symbol' (1952) 67(4) *Political Science Quarterly* 481

Wolfrum, Rüdiger, 'Der Beitrag regionaler Abmachungen zur Friedenssicherung: Möglichkeiten und Grenzen' (1990) 53 *Zeitschrift für ausländisches öffentliches Recht und Völkerrecht* 576

'Legitimacy of International Law and the Exercise of Administrative Functions: The Example of the International Seabed Authority, the International Maritime Organization and the International Fisheries Organizations' in Armin von Bogdandy *et al.* (eds.), *The Exercise of Public Authority by International Institutions* (Springer, Heidelberg, 2010)

Wolfrum, Rüdiger and Röben, Volker (eds.), *Legitimacy in International Law* (Springer, Berlin, 2008)

Woodruff, Paul, 'Virtue Ethics and the Appeal to Human Nature' (1991) 17(2) *Social Theory and Practice* 307

World Health Organization, 'Global Health Security' (2001) 76 *Weekly Epidemiological Record* 166

Yelpaala, Kojo, 'Quo Vadis WTO? The Threat of TRIPS and the Biodiversity Convention to Human Health and Food Security' (2012) 30 *Boston University International Law Journal* 55

Yemin, Edward, *Legislative Powers in the United Nations and Specialized Agencies* (A.W. Sijthoff, Leiden, 1969)

Yoo, John, 'Jefferson and Executive Power' (2008) 88 *Boston University Law Review* 421

Young, Margaret A. (ed.), *Regime Interaction in International Law: Facing Fragmentation* (Cambridge University Press, Cambridge, 2012)

Zaracostas, John, 'Key Players Agree to Share Viruses and Vaccines to Expedite Response to Future Pandemic Influenza' (2011) 342 *British Medical Journal* 2620

Zedner, Lucia, 'Too Much Security?' (2003) 31 *International Journal of the Sociology of Law* 155

*Security* (Routledge, Abingdon/New York, 2009)

Zilbershats, Yaffa, 'The Adoption of International Law into Israeli Law: The Real is Ideal' (1995) 25 *Israel Yearbook on Human Rights* 243

Zwarenburg, Marten, 'Regional Organisations and the Maintenance of International Peace and Security: Three Recent Regional African Peace Operations' (2006) 11 *Journal of Conflict and Security Law* 48

## International materials and official documents

Annan, Kofi A., *The Causes of Conflict and the Promotion of Durable Peace and Sustainable Development in Africa*, UN Doc. A/52/871-S/1998/318 (13 April 1998)

Association of Southeast Asian Nations, Integrated Food Security (AIFS) Framework and the Strategic Plan of Action on ASEAN Food Security

(SPA-FS): 2009–2013, 14th ASEAN Summit, Cha-am, Thailand, 1 March 2009, available at www.gafspfund.org/sites/gafspfund.org/files/Documents/ Cambodia_11_of_16_REGIONAL_STRATEGY_ASEAN_Integrated_Food_ Security_Framework.pdf

Australian Government Department of Foreign Affairs and Trade, *Report of the Canberra Commission on the Elimination of Nuclear Weapons* (14 August 1996), available at www.dfat.gov.au/cc/index.html

De Schutter, Olivier, *Seed Policies and the Right to Food: Enhancing Agrobiodiversity and Encouraging Innovation, Report of the Special Rapporteur on the Right to Food*, UN Doc. A/64/170 (23 July 2009)

*Agribusiness and the Right to Food, Report of the Special Rapporteur on the Right to Food*, UN Doc. A/HRC/13/33 (Human Rights Council, 22 December 2009)

EU European External Action Service, *Fact Sheet: EU-Ukraine Relations* (Brussels, 12 September 2014), available at http://eeas.europa.eu/statements/docs/2014/ 140514_02_en.pdf

Food and Agriculture Organization, *Director-General's Report on World Food Security: A Reappraisal of the Concepts and Approaches* (FAO, Rome, 1983)

*Revision of the International Undertaking: Issues for Consideration in Stage II: Access to Plant Genetic Resources and Farmers' Rights*, CPGR-Ex 1/94/5 (September 1994)

Rome Declaration on World Food Security and World Food Summit Plan of Action, adopted at the World Food Summit, Rome, 13–17 November 1996, available at www.fao.org/docrep/003/w3613e/w3613e00.HTM

*The State of Food Insecurity in the World 2001* (2002), available at www.fao.org/ docrep/003/y1500e/y1500e00.htm

*Trade Reforms and Food Security: Conceptualizing the Linkages* (2003), available at ftp://ftp.fao.org/docrep/fao/005/y4671e/y4671e00.pdf

Voluntary Guidelines to Support the Progressive Realization of the Right to Adequate Food in the Context of National Food Security, adopted by the FAO Council, 127th sess., November 2004, available at www.fao.org/docrep/ meeting/009/y9825e/y9825e00.htm

Declaration of the World Summit on Food Security: Five Principles for Sustainable Global Food Security, adopted 16–18 November 2009, available at www.fao.org/fileadmin/templates/wsfs/Summit/Docs/Final_Declaration/ WSFS09_Declaration.pdf

*The State of Agricultural Commodity Markets 2009* (2009), available at www.fao. org/docrep/012/i0854e00.htm

*The State of Food Insecurity in the World 2009* (2009), available at ftp://ftp.fao. org/docrep/fao/012/i0876e/i0876e.pdf

*Global Strategic Framework for Food Security and Nutrition*, CFS 2012/39/5 Add.1 (15–20 October 2012), available at www.fao.org/docrep/meeting/026/ ME498E.pdf

Harvard Program on Humanitarian Policy and Conflict Research, *Policy Brief: Legal Aspects of Israel's Disengagement Plan under International Humanitarian Law*, International Humanitarian Law Research Initiative (12 April 2005), available at www.reliefweb.int/library/documents/2004/hvu-opt-20oct.pdf

International Atomic Energy Agency, *The Agency's Safeguards System*, IAEA Doc. INFCIRC/66/Rev.2 (16 September 1968)

*The Structure and Content of Agreements between the Agency and States Required in connection with the Treaty on the Non-Proliferation of Nuclear Weapons*, IAEA Doc. INFCIRC/153 (Corrected) (June 1972)

'The Technical Objective of Safeguards' (1975) 17(2) *IAEA Bulletin* 13

*Report on the Implementation of the Agreement between the Agency and the Democratic People's Republic of Korea for the Application of Safeguards in connection with the Treaty on the Non-Proliferation of Nuclear Weapons*, IAEA Doc. Gov/2636 (25 February 1993)

*Model Protocol Additional to the Agreements between State(s) and the International Atomic Energy Agency for the Application of Nuclear Safeguards*, IAEA Doc. INFCIRC/540 (Corrected) (1 September 1997)

*Implementation of the NPT Safeguards Agreement in the Islamic Republic of Iran*, IAEA Board of Governors Resolution, IAEA Doc. GOV/2003/81 (26 November 2003)

*Implementation of the NPT Safeguards Agreement in the Islamic Republic of Iran: Report by the Director General*, IAEA Doc. GOV/2006/15 (27 February 2006)

*Implementation of the NPT Safeguards Agreement in the Syrian Arab Republic, Report of the Director General*, IAEA Doc. GOV/2011/30 (24 May 2011)

*Implementation of the NPT Safeguards Agreement in the Syrian Arab Republic, IAEA Board of Governors Resolution*, IAEA Doc. GOV/2011/41 (9 June 2011)

International Chamber of Shipping and the European Community Shipowners Associations, *International, Flag State Rules and Requirements on Arms and Private Armed Guards on Board Vessels* (December 2011)

International Maritime Organization, *Draft Code of Practice for the Investigation of Crimes of Piracy and Armed Robbery against Ships*, IMO Doc. MSC/Circ. 984 (20 December 2000)

*Code of Conduct concerning the Repression of Piracy and Armed Robbery against Ships in the Western Indian Ocean and the Gulf of Aden*, IMO Doc. C102/14 (3 April 2009)

*Guidance to Shipowners and Ship Operators, Shipmasters and Crews on Preventing and Suppressing Acts of Piracy and Armed Robbery Against Ships*, IMO Doc. MSC.1/Circ.1334 (23 June 2009)

*Recommendations to Governments Preventing and Suppressing Acts of Piracy and Armed Robbery Against Ships*, IMO Doc. MSC.1/Circ.1333 (26 June 2009)

*Revised Interim Guidance to Shipowners, Ship Operators, and Shipmasters on the Use of Privately Contracted Armed Security Personnel on Board Ships in the High Risk Area*, IMO Doc. MSC.1/Circ.1405/Rev.1 (16 September 2011)

International Telecommunication Union, Final Acts of the World Conference on International Telecommunications, Dubai, 3–14 December 2012, available *at* www.itu.int/en/wcit-12/Documents/final-acts-wcit-12.pdf

Internet Industry Association, *Internet Industry Code of Practice* (1 June 2010), available at http://iia.net.au/userfiles/iiacybersecuritycode_implementa tion_dec2010.pdf

Israeli Government, *Revised Disengagement Plan* (6 June 2005), available at www.strategicassessments.org/library/Disengagement/Revised_Disengag ement_Plan_-_Cabinet_Approval_June_2004.pdf

Israeli Ministry of Foreign Affairs, 'Security Cabinet Declares Gaza Hostile Territory', 19 September 2007, available at www.mfa.gov.il/MFA/Govern ment/Communiques/2007/Security+Cabinet+declares+Gaza+hostile+ territory+19-Sep-2007.htm

*The Operation in Gaza: Factual and Legal Aspects* (29 July 2009), available at www.mfa.gov.il/MFA/Terrorism+Obstacle+to+Peace/Terrorism+and+ Islamic+Fundamentalism/Operation_in_Gaza-Factual_and_Legal_Aspe cts.htm

Japanese Ministry of Defence, *Kaizokutaisho no tameni haken sareta suijōbutai no goeijisseki nitsuite [Record of Escort Services Provided by the Japanese Maritime Self-Defence Force for the Suppression of Piracy]*, Press Release, 6 December 2013

Nolte, Georg, *First Report on Subsequent Agreements and Subsequent Practice in relation to Treaty Interpretation*, UN Doc. A/CN.4/660 (International Law Commission, 19 March 2013)

Organization for Economic Cooperation and Development, *State Building in Situations of Fragility* (August 2008), available at www.oecd.org/develop ment/incaf/41212290.pdf

*Global Forum on Agriculture 2009* (June 2009), available at www.oecd.org/docu ment/24/0,3746,en_2649_33797_42303192_1_1_1_37401,00.html

'The Doha Development Round of Trade Negotiations: Understanding the Issues', available at www.oecd.org/general/thedohadevelopmentroundoftra denegotiationsunderstandingtheissues.htm

Palmer, Sir Geoffrey *et al.*, *Report of the Secretary-General's Panel of Inquiry on the 31 May 2010 Flotilla Incident* (July 2011), available at http://blog.unwatch. org/wp-content/uploads/Palmer-Committee-Final-report.pdf

Singapore Ministry of Foreign Affairs, 'Straits Times Interview with Singapore Foreign Minister George Yeo', 2–3 October 2007, available at http://app. mfa.gov.sg/pr/read_content.asp?View,8389

Turkel Committee, *Report of the Public Commission to Examine the Maritime Incident of 31 May 2010* (2011), available at www.turkel-committee.gov.il/files/wordocs/8808report-eng.pdf

Turkish National Commission of Inquiry, *Report on the Israeli Attack on the Humanitarian Aid Convoy to Gaza on 31 May 2010* (2011), available at www.mfa.gov.tr/data/Turkish%20Report%20Final%20-%20UN%20Copy.pdf

United Nations, *Report of the World Food Conference, Rome 5–16 November 1974* (United Nations, New York, 1975)

Basic Principles on the Use of Force and Firearms by Law Enforcement Officials, adopted at the Eighth UN Congress on the Prevention of Crime and the Treatment of Offenders, Havana, Cuba, 27 August–7 September 1990, available at www.unrol.org/doc.aspx?d=2246

*Report of the International Atomic Energy Agency: Compliance with Arms Limitation and Disarmament Agreements: Note by the Secretary-General*, UN GAOR, 48th Sess., UN Doc. A/48/133 (S/25556) (16 April 1993)

*Human Development Report 1994* (United Nations, New York, 1994)

*The Blue Helmets: A Review of United Nations Peacekeeping* (3rd edn, United Nations, New York, 1996)

*General Comment No. 12: The Right to Adequate Food*, UN Doc E/C.12/1999/11 (Committee on Economic, Social and Cultural Rights, 1999)

*Security Council Welcomes Libya's Decision to Abandon Weapons of Mass Destruction Programs*, Press Release, UN Doc. SC/8069 (22 April 2004)

*A More Secure World: Our Shared Responsibility, Report of the United Nations Secretary-General's High-Level Panel on Threats, Challenges and Change*, UN Doc. A/59/565 (2 December 2004)

*Fragmentation of International Law: Difficulties Arising from the Diversification and Expansion of International Law, Report of the Study Group of the International Law Commission*, UN Doc. A/CN.4/L.682 (13 April 2006)

*United Nations Peacekeeping Operations: Principles and Guidelines* (Department of Peacekeeping Operations and Department of Field Support, 2008), available at http://pbpu.unlb.org/pbps/library/capstone_doctrine_eNg.pdf

*Report of the UN Fact Finding Mission on the Gaza Conflict*, UN Doc. A/HRC/12/48 (Human Rights Council, 15 September 2009)

*Human Security: Report of the Secretary-General*, UN Doc. A/64/701 (8 March 2010)

*Report of the Working Group on the Use of Mercenaries as a Means of Violating Human Rights and Impeding the Exercise of the Right of Peoples to Self-Determination*, UN Doc. A/HRC/15/25 (2 July 2010) Annex

*Report of the International Fact-Finding Mission to Investigate Violations of International Law, including International Humanitarian and Human Rights Law, resulting from the Israeli Attacks on the Flotilla of Ships*

*Carrying Humanitarian Assistance,* UN Doc. A/HRC/15/21 (Human Rights Council, 21 September 2010)

United Nations Assistance Mission in Afghanistan (UNAMA), *A Way to Go: An Update on Implementation of the Law on Elimination Violence against Women in Afghanistan, Report of the United Nations Assistance Mission in Afghanistan* (United Nations Office of the High Commissioner for Human Rights, Kabul, December 2013), available at http://unama.unmissions.org/Portals/UNAMA/Documents/UNAMA%20REPORT%20on%20EVAW%20LAW_8%20December%202013.pdf

United Nations Conference on Trade and Development (UNCTAD), *The 2008 Food Price Crisis: Rethinking Food Security Policies,* UN Doc. UNCTAD/GDS/MDP/g24/2009/3 (1 October 2009)

United Nations Department of Public Information, 'General Assembly votes overwhelmingly to accord Palestine 'Non Member Observer State' status in United Nations', *United Nations News* (New York), UN Doc. GA/11317 (29 November 2012), available at www.un.org/News/Press/docs//2012/ga11317.doc.htm

United Nations Development Programme, *Towards a Balanced 'Sui Generis' Plant Variety Regime: Guidelines to Establish a National PVP Law and an Understanding of TRIPS-plus Aspects of Plant Rights* (2008), available at www.beta.undp.org/undp/en/home/librarypage/poverty-reduction/toward-a-balanced-sui-generis-plant-variety-regime.html

'Afghan Police Force Recruits Women to Avoid Crime and Stigma', available at www.undp.org/content/undp/en/home/ourwork/stories/afghan-women-join-police-force.html

US National Intelligence Council, *National Intelligence Estimate: The Global Infectious Disease Threat and Its Implications for the United States* (January 2000)

White House, *The National Strategy to Secure Cyberspace* (2003), available at www.us-cert.gov/reading_room/cyberspace_strategy.pdf

World Bank, *Poverty and Hunger: Issues and Options for Food Security in Developing Countries* (World Bank, Washington, DC, 1986)

World Food Program, '1.02 Billion people hungry', 19 June 2009, available at www.wfp.org/news/news-release/102-billion-people-hungry

World Health Organization, *Global Outbreak Alert and Response, Report of a WHO Meeting,* WHO/CDS/CSR/2000.3 (26–28 April 2000)

*Preparedness for the Deliberate Use of Biological Agents: A Rational Approach to the Unthinkable,* WHO/CDS/CSR/EPH/2002.16 (May 2002)

*Antimicrobial Resistance: A Threat to Global Health Security: Rational Use of Medicines by Prescribers and Patients, Report by the Secretariat,* WHO Doc. A58/14 (7 April 2005)

*World Health Report 2007, A Safer Future: Global Public Health Security in the 21st Century* (WHO, Geneva, 2007)

*Best Practice for Developing Standards for Infectious Disease Laboratories in Europe* (2010), available at www.euro.who.int/document/e94772.pdf

*Main Operational Lessons Learnt from the WHO Pandemic Influenza A(H1N1) Vaccine Deployment Initiative, Report of a WHO Meeting* (Geneva, 13–15 December 2010)

*Guideline: Neonatal Vitamin A Supplementation* (2011), available at whqlibdoc. who.int/publications/2011/9789241501798_eng.pdf

*Pandemic Influenza Preparedness: Sharing of Influenza Viruses and Access to Vaccines and Other Benefits, Report of the Advisory Group*, WHO Doc. A65/19 (22 March 2012)

*Pandemic Influenza Preparedness: Framework for the Sharing of Influenza Viruses and Access to Vaccines and Other Benefits, Report by the Director-General*, WHO Doc. EB131/4 (5 April 2012)

## Newspaper articles and media releases

Albright, David, Brannan, Paul and Stricker, Andrea, 'IAEA Safeguards Report on Syria: cooperation from Syria worsens, special inspection needed', Media Release, Institute for Science and International Security, 23 November 2010, available at http://isis-online.org/uploads/isis-reports/documents/Syria_ IAEA_Report_ISISAnalysis_23Nov2010.pdf

Alexander, Lisa A., 'ASEAN Dispute Settlement Mechanism: anything new?', *Jakarta Post*, 9 April 2010, available at www.thejakartapost.com/news/2010/ 04/09/asean-dispute-settlement-mechanism-anything-new.html

Alon, Gideon, 'Mazuz has yet to decide on Philadelphi deal, MKs told', *Haaretz* (online), 5 July 2005, available at www.haaretz.com/news/mazuz-has-yet-to-decide-on-philadelphi-deal-mks-told-1.163009

Arsana, I. Made Andi, 'Singapore gets Pedra Branca: what's next?', *Jakarta Post*, 24 June 2008, available at www.thejakartapost.com/news/2008/06/24/singapore-gets-pedra-branca-what039s-next.html

Bannoura, Ghassan, 'Egypt asks for national troop deployment in Sinai, Israelis refuse', *IMEMC News* (online), 26 December 2007, available at www.imemc. org/article/52103

Blitz, James, 'IAEA refers Syria to UN over "reactor"', *Financial Times* (online), 9 June 2011, available at www.ft.com/intl/cms

Bronner, Ethan, 'Israel speeds withdrawal from Gaza', *New York Times* (online), 19 January 2010, available at www.nytimes.com/2009/01/20/world/middleeast/ 20mideast.html

Chow, James, 'ASEAN unity crucial to resolve South China Sea disputes: Malaysia Defense Minister', *Epoch Times*, 19 October 2011, available at www.theepochtimes.com/n2/world/asean-unity-crucial-to-resolve-south-china-sea-disputes-malaysia-defense-minister-63126.html

Harel, Amos and Ravid, Barak, 'PM warns Islamists could take control in Egypt; Israel approves Sinai troops', *Haaretz* (online), 1 February 2011, available at www.haaretz.com/print-edition/news/pm-warns-islamists-could-take-control-in-egypt-israel-approves-sinai-troops-1.340452

Horn, Jordana, Krieger, Hilary Leila and Keinon, Herb, 'South American countries recognize Palestinian State', *Jerusalem Post* (online), 6 December 2010, available at www.jpost.com/International/Article.aspx?id=198288

Houk, Marian, 'Israel agrees to exceptional but limited deployment of Egyptian Army personnel in Sinai', *American Chronicle* (online), 30 January 2011, available at www.americanchronicle.com/articles/view/215366

Katz, Yaakov, 'Barak set to approve list of sanctions against Gaza', *Jerusalem Post*, 23 October 2007, reproduced at www.unitedjerusalem.org/index2.asp?id=983133&Date=10/25/2007

Kessler, Oren, 'Egyptian Army deploys additional soldiers in Sinai', *Jerusalem Post* (online), 18 February 2011, available at www.jpost.com/MiddleEast/Article.aspx?id=208762

Kilgannon, Corey and Cohen, Noam, 'Cadets trade the trenches for firewalls', *New York Times*, 11 May 2009, p. A1

Lis, Jonathan and Khoury, Jack, 'Netanyahu warns Egypt losing control of growing terror groups in Sinai', *Haaretz* (online), 30 May 2011, available at www.haaretz.com/news/international/netanyahu-warns-egypt-losing-control-of-growing-terror-groups-in-sinai-1.364949

Maor, Roi, 'Preeminent Israelis to support Palestinian State, 1967 borders', *+972 Magazine*, 20 April 2011, available at http://972mag.com/group-of-preeminent-israelis-to-support-palestinian-state-along-1967-borders

Mbekelu, Wendy, 'Tracking nuclear proliferation: Romania', *Public Broadcasting Service News Hour* (online), 2 May 2005, available at www.pbs.org/newshour/indepth_coverage/military/proliferation/countries/romania.html

Mosgovaya, Natasha, 'Netanyahu to AIPAC: Israel cannot return to "indefensible" 1967 lines', *Haaretz* (online), 24 May 2011, available at www.haaretz.com/news/diplomacy-defense/netanyahu-to-aipac-israel-cannot-return-to-indefensible-1967-lines-1.363705

Osman, Nurfika, 'Talks with Malaysia on Ambalat border dispute to resume in July', *Jakarta Globe*, 16 June 2009, available at www.thejakartaglobe.com/national/talks-with-malaysia-on-ambalat-border-dispute-to-resume-in-july/312607

Pedatzur, Reuven, 'What is a defendable border' (in Hebrew), *Haaretz* (online), 6 June 2011, available at www.haaretz.co.il/hasite/spages/1230373.html

Pitsuwan, Fuadi, 'Time for ASEAN peacekeeping force', *The Diplomat* (online), 2 May 2011, available at http://thediplomat.com/2011/05/02/time-for-asean-peacekeeping-force

Reilly, William M., 'UN Security Council hears Cambodia, Thailand on border dispute', *Xinhua Net* (online), 15 February 2011, available at http://news. xinhuanet.com/english2010/world/2011–02/15/c_13732477.htm

Rubin, Alissa J., 'Afghan policewoman is killed, fourth in last six months', *New York Times*, 5 December 2013, available at www.nytimes.com/2013/12/06/ world/asia/gunmen-kill-afghan-policewoman.html

Sen, Ashish Kumar, 'IAEA seeks permission from Myanmar for Nuke Inspectors to visit', *Washington Times* (online), 13 January 2011, available at www.washingtontimes.com/news/2011/jan/13/iaea-seeks-permission-from-myanmar-for-nuke-inspec

Shavit, Ari, '1967', *Haaretz* (online), 12 May 2011, available at www.haaretz.com/ print-edition/opinion/1967–1.361194

Sherwood, Harriet, 'Dmitry Medvedev restates Russian support for Palestinian State', *Guardian* (online), 18 January 2011, available at www.guardian.co.uk/ world/2011/jan/18/dmitry-medvedev-russia-palestinian-state

Stoil, Rebecca Anna, '"Special Situation" declared for Sderot', *Jerusalem Post* (online), 14 December 2007, available at www.jpost.com/servlet/Satellite? cid=1196847330565&pagename=JPost%2FJPArticle%2FShowFull

Toameh, Khaled Abu, 'Spain will recognize Palestinian State on 1967 borders', *Jerusalem Post* (online), 30 May 2011, available at www.jpost.com/Middle East/Article.aspx?id=222873

Weizman, Steve, 'Israeli soldiers: "no clear red lines" in Gaza War', *Yahoo News* (online), 16 July 2009, available at http://news.yahoo.com/s/ap/20090715/ ap_on_re_mi_ea/ml_israel_palestinians

Williams, Dan, 'Israel approves more Egyptian troops in Sinai', *Reuters* (online), 16 February 2011, available at http://in.reuters.com/article/2011/02/16/idIN India-54932520110216

Wolf, Pinchas, 'Rivlin: deployment of troops in Sinai? Only after Knesset approval' (in Hebrew), *Walla News Network* (online), 26 August 2011, available at http://news.walla.co.il/?w=/9/1854429

Wren, Christopher, 'Making it easier to uncover nuclear arms', *New York Times* (online), 16 June 1995, available at www.nytimes.com/1995/06/16/world/ making-it-easier-to-uncover-nuclear-arms.html

'Barak: we'll allow helicopters, more troops in Sinai', *Yediot Aharonot* (online), 26 August 2011, available at www.ynetnews.com/articles/0,7340,L-4114141,00. html

'Erekat: if '67 lines are an illusion, peace is an illusion', *Jerusalem Post* (online), 23 May 2011, available at www.jpost.com/DiplomacyAndPolitics/Article.aspx? id=221788

'G-8 leaders expected to back Obama on 1967 borders', *Haaretz* (online), 27 May 2011, available at www.haaretz.com/news/diplomacy-defense/g8-leaders-expected-to-back-obama-on-1967-borders-1.364450

'G-8 leaders omit mention of 1967 borders in Middle East statement', *Haaretz* (online), 27 May 2011, available at www.haaretz.com/news/diplomacy-defense/g8-leaders-omit-mention-of-1967-borders-in-middle-east-statement-1.364459

'Iran uranium haul enough to make a bomb', *Weekend Australian* (Sydney), 21 February 2009, 12

'Israel agrees to some Egyptian troops in Sinai', *Yediot Aharonot* (online), 31 January 2011, available at www.ynetnews.com/articles/0,7340,L-4021 890,00.html

'Israel ire as Argentina and Brazil recognize Palestine', *BBC News* (online), 7 December 2010, available at www.bbc.co.uk/news/world-middle-east-11941172

'Israel may amend Military Appendix of Egypt Peace Treaty', *Jerusalem Post* (online), 1 September 2011, available at www.jpost.com/Defense/Article. aspx?id=236235

'Israel OKs Egypt attack helicopters in Sinai', *Jerusalem Post* (online), 9 August 2012, available at www.jpost.com/MiddleEast/Article.aspx?id=280732

'Israel rejects UN Council flotilla investigation', *Voice of America News* (online), 24 August 2010, available at www.voanews.com/english/news/Israel-Rejects-UN-Council-Flotilla-Investigation-101379189.html

'Israel says no to more Egyptian troops in Sinai', *Jerusalem Post* (online), 7 February 2011, available at www.jpost.com/Defense/Article.aspx?id=207115

'Knesset Speaker Rivlin instructed to explore whether permission for the deployment of Egyptian troops in Sinai is subject to Knesset approval' (in Hebrew), *Haaretz* (online), 31 January 2011, available at www.haaretz.co. il/news/politics/1.1470101

'Mubarak plays last card, the Army; police vanish', *World Tribune* (online), 31 January 2011, available at www.worldtribune.com/worldtribune/WTARC/ 2011/me_egypt0078_01_31.asp

'Pak CJ takes notice of Swat girl flogging', *Free Library*, available at www.thefreeli brary.com/Pak+CJ+takes+notice+of+Swat+girl+flogging.-a0199262393

'Pakistani soldiers storm mosque', *BBC News*, 10 July 2007, available at http://news. bbc.co.uk/2/hi/6286500.stm

'Quartet may support Palestinian State along 1967 borders', *Jerusalem Post* (online), 19 April 2011, available at www.jpost.com/DiplomacyAndPolitics/ Article.aspx?ID=217136&R=R1

'Radio address by Mrs. Bush', *American Presidency Project*, 17 November 2001, available at www.presidency.ucsb.edu/ws/?pid=24992

'RI welcomes int'l court's decision on Thai-Cambodian conflict', *AntaraNews.com* (online), 19 July 2011, available at www.antaranews.com/en/news/73914/ri-welcomes-intl-courts-decision-on-thai-cambodian-conflict

'Shahbaz Bhatti assasinated', *Express Tribune*, 2 March 2011, available at Tribune.
com.pk/story/126287/shabaz-bhatti-attacked-in-islamabad
'Singapore asks China to clarify claims on S. China Sea', *Reuters*, 20 June 2011,
available at www.reuters.com/article/2011/06/20/idUSL3E7HK1H520110620
'The future of food: crisis prevention: what is causing food prices to soar and what
can be done about it?', *The Economist*, 24 February 2011, available at www.
economist.com/node/18229412
'Threats/violence against musicians and attacks on music shops 2000–2011',
*Pakistan Press Foundation*, 28 November 2011, available at www.pakistan
pressfoundation.org/publications-reports/12780
'TNI moves to secure Ambalat', *Jakarta Post*, 31 May 2009, available at www.thej
akartapost.com/news/2009/05/31/tni-moves-secure-ambalat.html
'Today's borders are the "indefensible" ones', *Haaretz* (online), 22 May 2011,
available at www.haaretz.com/print-edition/opinion/today-s-borders-are-
the-indefensible-ones-1.363224
'Turkey FM: we can't stop upcoming aid flotilla to Gaza', *Haaretz* (online), 30
May 2011, available at www.haaretz.com/news/diplomacy-defense/turkey-
fm-we-can-t-stop-upcoming-aid-flotilla-to-gaza-1.364980
'US privately backs Pakistan's "Sharia Law for Peace" deal with Taliban', *Daily
Telegraph*, available at www.telegraph.co.uk/news/worldnews/asia/paki
stan/4681480/US-privately-backs-Pakistans-Sharia-law-for-peace-deal-
with-Taliban.html

# INDEX

CPSIA information can be obtained
at www.ICGtesting.com
Printed in the USA
LVHW012119070119
603029LV00020B/244